Susan Gretsinger

JOHN CASSIAN: THE CONFERENCES

Ancient Christian Writers

THE WORKS OF THE FATHERS IN TRANSLATION

EDITED BY

WALTER J. BURGHARDT
JOHN DILLON
DENNIS D. McMANUS

No. 57

JOHN CASSIAN: THE CONFERENCES

TRANSLATED AND ANNOTATED

BY

BONIFACE RAMSEY, O.P.

PAULIST PRESS
New York, N.Y. / Mahwah, N.J.

Jacket art entitled *Saint Jerome in his Study* from the Bible of Borso d'Este (Biblioteca Estense, Modena, Italy) courtesy of Scala/Art Resource, NY.

COPYRIGHT © 1997
BY
BONIFACE RAMSEY, O.P.

Library of Congress Cataloging-in-Publication Data

Cassian, John, ca. 360-ca. 435.
[Collationes patrum XXIV. English]
John Cassian : the conferences / translated and annotated by Boniface Ramsey.
pm. cm. – (Ancient Christian writers ; no. 57)
Includes bibliographical references and indexes.
ISBN 0-8091-0484-9 (cloth)
1. Monastic and religious life–Early works to 1800. 2. Spiritual life–Christianity–Early works to 1800. 3. Asceticism–Early works to 1800. I. Ramsey, Boniface. II. Title. III. Series.
BR65.C33C65 1997
255–dc21 97-6523
CIP

Published by Paulist Press
997 Macarthur Boulevard
Mahwah, New Jersey 07430

PRINTED AND BOUND IN THE UNITED STATES OF AMERICA

FOR

LAWRENCE J. DONOHOO, O.P.

CONTENTS

The Third Part of The Conferences of John Cassian (XVIII–XXIV)

Indexes

ABBREVIATIONS

ACW	Ancient Christian Writers. Westminster, MD. et alibi 1946ff.
CCSA	Corpus Christianorum, Series Apocryphorum. Tournhout 1983ff.
CCSL	Corpus Christianorum, Series Latina. Tournhout 1953ff.
Chadwick	Owen Chadwick. *John Cassian: A Study in Primitive Monasticism.* 2nd ed., Cambridge, Eng. 1968.
Colish	Marcia L. Colish. *The Stoic Tradition from Antiquity to the Early Middle Ages. II. Stoicism in Christian Latin Thought through the Sixth Century*—Studies in the History of Christian Thought 35. Leiden 1985.
CS	Cistercian Studies. Spencer, Mass. et alibi 1969ff.
CSCO	Corpus Scriptorum Christianorum Orientalium. Louvain 1903ff.
DACL	*Dictionnaire d'archéologie chrétienne et de liturgie.* Paris 1907–1953.
DHGE	*Dictionnaire d'histoire et de géographie ecclésiastiques.* Paris 1912ff.
DS	*Dictionnaire de spiritualité.* Paris 1932-1994.

DTC	*Dictionnaire de théologie catholique.* Paris 1903–1950.
Gazet	Gazet, Alardus. *Prefatio et Commentarium* in PL 49, col. 30ff.
GCS	Die griechischen christlichen Schriftsteller der ersten drei Jahrhunderte. Leipzig 1897ff.
Gibson	Gibson, Edgar,. C.S. "John Cassian" in Nicene and Post-Nicene Fathers, series 2, vol. ii, Grand Rapids, 1982.
Grillmeier	Grillmeier, Alroys. *Das Konzil von Chalkedon.* Würzburg 1951.
JAC	*Jahrbuch für Antike und Christentum.* Münster 1958ff.
JECS	*Journal of Early Christian Studies.* Baltimore 1993ff.
LXX	Septuagint.
Pauly-Wissowa	G. Wissowa et al., eds. *Paulys Realencyclopädie der klassischen Altertumswissenschaft.* Stuttgart 1893ff.
PG	J.-P. Migne, ed. Patrologia Graeca. Paris 1857–1866.
Pichery	Pichery, E. *Les Conférences* in Sources chrétiennes, vols 42, 52, and 64. Paris 1955–59.
PL	J.-P. Migne, ed. Patrologia Latina. Paris 1844–1855, with supplementary vols.
RAC	*Reallexikon für Antike und Christentum.* Stuttgart 1950ff.
RAM	*Revue d'ascétique et de mystique.* Toulouse 1920ff.

Ramsey, "Almsgiving"	Boniface Ramsey, "Almsgiving in the Latin Church: The Late Fourth and Early Fifth Centuries," in *Theological Studies* 43 (1982) 226–259.
Regnault	*Les sentences des Pères du Désert. Nouveau receuil.* Apophthegmes inédits ou peu connus rassemblés et présentés par Dom Lucien Regnault, traduits par les moines de Solesmes. Solesmes 1970.
Rousseau	Philip Rousseau. *Ascetics, Authority, and the Church in the Age of Jerome and John Cassian.* Oxford 1978.
SA	Studia Anselmiana. Rome 1933ff.
SC	Sources chrétiennes. Paris 1942ff.
SCA	Studies in Christian Antiquity. Washington 1941ff.
Weber	Hans-Oskar Weber. *Die Stellung des Johannes Cassianus zur ausserpachomianischen Mönchstradition: Eine Quellenuntersuchung* (Beiträge zur Geschichte des alten Mönchtums und des Benediktinerordens 24.) Münster 1960.

A LIST AND EXPLANATION OF SOME TERMS USED THROUGHOUT *THE CONFERENCES*

Abba: The Aramaic word for "father," adopted in Egyptian monasticism. As a title of respect and sometimes, as in 20.1.2, having reference to the superior of a group of monks.

Abstinence: A translation of *continentia* (which Cassian uses to refer to the restraint of the pleasures of eating as well as of those of sex) and also of *abstinentia.*

Anchorite: Defined in 18.6.2, this is the term for a monk who lives by himself in the desert.

Apostle, the: A common title for Paul in Christian antiquity.

Cenobium: Defined in 18.10, this connotes a group of monks living together with a common rule.

Chosen orientation: The usual translation of *propositum,* which refers to the monk's decision and determination to lead the monastic life. It was early used in the context of virginity. Cf. Hippolytus, *Trad. apost.* 12; Cyprian, *De hab. virg.* 18; Jerome, *Ep.* 22.14f.

Desert: A translation of three different words—*deserta, heremus,* and *solitudo.*

Ecstasy: A translation of *excessus.*

Hospitality:	A translation of *humanitas,* which frequently connotes hospitality in later Latin. Cf. Maximus of Turin, *Serm.* 21.1 (CCSL 23.79); Benedict, *Reg.* 53.9.
Lawgiver, the:	A translation of *legislator,* referring to Moses.
Lent:	A translation of *quadragesima.*
Monastery:	Defined in 18.10, this refers merely to a dwelling, whether for one monk or for several.
Pentecost:	A translation of *quinquagesima,* this refers to the Easter season rather than to a particular day.
Skete:	Part of the Nitrian Desert in the ancient Aegyptus Prima, about fifty miles south of Alexandria and located to the west of the Nile.
Synaxis:	A transliteration of the Greek word for assembly. It applies to a gathering for prayer, which might or might not include the eucharist. In *Inst.* 2.10.1 Cassian uses the term for the nighttime prayer services which he is describing in that section of his work. In Pachomian monasticism some light work might accompany the prayer. Cf. Pachomius, *Praecepta* 4ff.
Thebaid, the:	A vast area in upper (or southern) Egypt, occupying approximately one-half of the ancient diocese of Egypt and divided into two parts–Thebais Prima and Thebais Secunda. The region was mostly desert.
Theoria:	A transliteration of the Greek word for viewing or contemplation. Cassian uses it exclu-

sively with respect to divine contemplation, and in this regard it is more precise than the Latin *contemplatio,* which is sometimes employed in other senses by him. Cf. 10.10.1, where *contemplatio* and *theoria* appear in the same sentence, the former understood as attentiveness.

Way of life: The usual translation of *conversatio.*

PREFACE

The present volumes contain the first complete translation of *The Conferences* of John Cassian to appear in English, as well as the first extended commentary on an annotation of that work to have been published since that of the learned Benedictine Alard Gazet (known in Latin as Gazaeus) in 1617. Gazet (on whom more can be found in DTC 6.1.1174–1175 and DHGE 20.186) wrote his commentary to accompany his edition of Cassian's works, and it is reprinted with *The Conferences* themselves in PL 49.477–1328. This massive study is characterized by an immense erudition and by the fact that its author did not hesitate to address virtually every question that the text posed him and that would have interested his contemporaries. Although often polemical, it is still worthwhile to consult, and it has been referred to several times in the pages that follow. But for those who do not read Latin, the language in which it was written, the great learning that it demonstrates is valueless. Moreover, even impressive scholarship such as Gazet's must occasionally be reverently supplemented by subsequent efforts. The commentary and notes at hand, much shorter than Gazet's, intend to serve that role.

The reader will notice that the text of Cassian's work itself is divisible into three parts–the conferences themselves, the chapters of the conferences, and subdivisions within the chapters. When a particular place in *The Conferences* is referred to in the course of the commentary and annotations, this reference ordinarily occurs in numerical form alone, following the division just mentioned–as, for example, 14.9.3. But when there might be some doubt that the reference is in fact to *The Conferences* rather than to some other work, it occurs as, for example, *Conlat.* 14.9.3. (*Conlat.* is the abbreviation used here for *Conlationes,* which is the Latin title of the treatise.) References to patristic and other ancient writings are usually not accompanied by any indication of the relevant editions and page numbers unless a writing is obscure or unless such an indication would help to locate a given passage more precisely.

As far as the translation is concerned, I have made every effort to be as faithful as possible to Cassian's own intentions. In particular I have attempted to render certain key words consistently throughout. In translating biblical quotations I have been absolutely consistent. When a discrepancy occasionally occurs in the English of a scriptural verse–cited one way in one place and slightly differently in another–it is because Cassian's own Latin contains a corresponding discrepancy, which may be due to his having quoted from memory, or from a variant text.

In referring to scriptural quotations in the notes and index I have generally used the numbering for chapters and verses that is found in The New Jerusalem Bible and that sometimes differs from other editions. I have not done so, however, when making reference to citations from the Septuagint version. In the very few instances when a verse not from the Septuagint is not currently accepted as authentic, it is marked in the notes and in the index with an asterisk.

My translation is made from Michael Petschenig's critical edition, a century old and still unsurpassed, in the Corpus Scriptorum Ecclesiasticorum Latinorum. E. Pichery's edition in Sources chrétiennes is an almost verbatim reproduction of Petschenig's, and in fact it was not intended to be a totally new work. Mention should also be made of H. Hurter's edition, published about a year after Petschenig's, in the series Sanctorum Patrum Opuscula Selecta; this, too, differs very little from Petschenig. In the course of my translating I have occasionally consulted not only the French of Pichery but also the English renderings of Edgar C. S. Gibson in the Nicene and Post-Nicene Fathers (containing all but the two conferences that touch somewhat explicitly on sexual issues), of Owen Chadwick in The Library of Christian Classics (containing only seven conferences), and of Colm Luibheid in The Classics of Western Spirituality (containing nine conferences).

For having helped bring my translation and commentary into the light of day I owe a particular debt of gratitude to Dennis

McManus, the editor of Ancient Christian Writers at Paulist Press, who followed my work with the kindest interest and offered valuable criticism. I also thank Sr. Mary Ann, O.P., of Our Lady of Grace Monastery in North Guilford, Connecticut, who, out of sheer love for Cassian, volunteered to take upon herself the immense burden of committing the manuscript of the translation to a word processor. I cannot omit mentioning here Dr. Rozanne Elder and two anonymous readers who went through the manuscript in its early stages and provided criticism. For offering me assistance on specific questions on the text I am grateful to Fathers William Conlan, O.P., G. M. de Durand, O.P., and Lawrence Frizzell. But in addition to these I must also thank the brothers of the Dominican priories in Jersey City and Ottawa where, in the midst of numerous other activities, the vast bulk of this work was accomplished. Whether actively interested in this project or merely bemused by it, they added something to it.

It is not out of place, incidentally, that a Dominican friar, rather than someone more immediately in the monastic tradition, should have translated and commented on these *Conferences*. For Saint Dominic himself is known to have loved this work and to have carried it with him wherever he went, along with the Gospel of Matthew and the Epistles of Paul.

Finally, it remains to say that these volumes are a humble offering to a dear friend.

Boniface Ramsey, O.P.
Saint Vincent Ferrer Priory
New York City
Easter, 1997

INTRODUCTION

JOHN CASSIAN

John Cassian was probably born in Dacia, roughly equivalent to present-day Romania, about the year 360. In one somewhat rare personal passage (cf. *Conlat.* 14.12) he alludes to the education that he had as a child; if we are to credit his words as being factually accurate, it appears that he had the training in the classics that was typical both of the era and of a genteel upbringing. While he was in his twenties or thirties he left his native land and the large family property that he describes in *Conlat.* 24.1.3 and, in the company of a friend named Germanus (who is said in *Conlat.* 14.9.4 to be slightly older than Cassian himself), joined a monastery in Bethlehem. From Palestine he and Germanus visited Egypt twice, spending perhaps as long as ten years there and making the acquaintance of some of the most famous ascetics of that region.

Toward the beginning of the fifth century he departed from Egypt for Constantinople, still with Germanus; the two of them were most likely fleeing the upheavals that were rocking Egyptian monasticism just then and that were associated with the theology of the long-dead but still controversial Origen. One scholar thinks, however, that Cassian and Germanus either may simply have wanted to go home (cf. *Conlat.* 24.1.2ff.) and stopped in Constantinople en route or were specifically drawn there by the reputation of John Chrysostom, who was then the bishop of the city (cf. Rousseau 171–172). After a few years Cassian left Constantinople, where he had met Chrysostom and been ordained to the diaconate by him. His destination this time was Rome, where with Germanus, now a priest, he brought letters from the Constantinopolitan clergy to Pope Innocent that denounced the expulsion of Chrysostom from his see (cf. Palladius, *Dial.* 3). At Rome he was himself ordained to the priesthood. It has been suggested that after this ordination he left Rome for Antioch, where he exercised the priesthood for a number of years (cf. E. Griffe, "Cassien a-t-il été prêtre d'Antioche?" *Bulletin de littérature ecclésiastique* 55 [1954]: 240–244). Finally, in any event, he went to Marseilles, where he founded two monasteries, composed three treatises (*The Institutes of the Cenobia and the Remedies for the Eight Principal Vices, The Conferences,* and *On the Incarnation of Christ against Nestorius*) and ended his days sometime in the early 430s. (For general studies of Cassian, with fuller accounts of his life, cf. DTC 2.2. 1823–1829; Léon Christiani, *Jean Cassien: La spiritualité du désert* [S. Wandrille, 1946], 2 vols.; DHGE 11.1319–1348; DS 2.1.214–276; Jean-Claude Guy, *Jean Cassien: Vie et doctrine spirituelle* [Paris, 1961]; Rousseau 167–234.)

An exact dating and a relatively detailed account of Cassian's life have never been established and almost certainly never will be. His own writings are themselves not helpful in this regard. As far as the inner man is concerned, however, we can postulate some things. The major themes that emerge in his two great monastic works—discretion, moderation, single-mindedness, love, prayer, among others—were obviously his chief preoccupations. These two treatises, *The Institutes* and *The Conferences,* as well as the third, also bear witness to his zeal for the tradition and to his eagerness to hand it on. Finally, Cassian's monastic works reveal a remarkably ordered and synthetic mind and one that was endowed with considerable psychological acumen. Yet when he refers to himself, as he occasionally does in *The Conferences,* he does not appear as a distinct and developed personality in any modern sense but rather as one whose whole being hangs tautly on the words his mentors speak, and whose joy or sorrow at almost any given moment is a direct consequence of what they have said to him. So self-effacing is Cassian, in fact, that Germanus, his companion throughout the work, is the usual interlocutor. With rare exception we look in vain here for a fuller and less stylized self-disclosure. But self-disclosure was not a priority among the Church's earliest writers, and there is reason for delighted astonishment when it sometimes occurs in a few of them, notably of course in Augustine.

Cassian's influence, however, or rather the influence of his monastic writings, might be said to be in inverse proportion to the obscurity of his life. Already in the fifth century two abridgments of *The Institutes* were made in Gaul and Africa, the former of which, by Eucherius of Lyons and entitled *Epitomes operum Cassiani*, has survived and appears in PL 50.867–894. In the sixth century Benedict prescribed the reading of *The Conferences* (in *Reg.* 42.3) and of both *The Institutes* and *The Conferences* (in *Reg.* 73.5), while Cassiodorus recommended *The Institutes* to his monks at Vivarium in his work *De inst. div. litt.* 29 (PL 70.1144). Cassian inspired, sometimes without even being mentioned by name, such major Western thinkers as Gregory the Great (d. 604), Alcuin (d. 804), Rhabanus Maurus (d. 856), Rupert of Deutz (d. 1129), and Thomas Aquinas (d. 1274), who cites him more than a dozen times in the section on moral theology of his *Summa Theologiae*. It would not be an exaggeration to refer to the author of *The Conferences* as one of the great, albeit less well known, preceptors of the West—even in the face of the occasional problems that this work poses and that will be discussed as they arise.

The Conferences

By far the longest of Cassian's three works, *The Conferences* are in fact among the longest works of Christian antiquity, running to more than seven hundred pages in Petschenig's edition. This vast treatise, composed of twenty-four separate conferences, is divided into three major parts, the first containing ten and the remaining two containing seven conferences each. These three parts purport to record conversations that were had in different locations, and at different times, in the Egyptian desert. Thus, the first ten conferences are placed in Skete, the following set of seven is placed in the vicinity of the town of Thennesus, and the final seven near the town of Diolcos. None of these locations was very far from the great metropolis of Alexandria. Although Cassian speaks in 11.1 of having wanted to penetrate the Thebaid, which was hundreds of miles south of Alexandria and which was much favored by many monks because of its remoteness, he seems never to have done so; at least he does not mention it.

Somewhat strangely, the three major parts of *The Conferences* are not arranged in chronological order. Passages in 1.1, 11.1, and 17.30.3 indicate that the second and third parts are based on events that occurred during Cassian's first trip to the Egyptian desert, whereas the first part of the work refers to events of the second trip. The reason for this seems to be that Cassian had not originally intended to write the second and third parts and that he included in the first part everything that he felt would be pertinent to his readers, which by either happenstance or design was derived from his second sojourn, only to discover later that others did not share his view and desired him to expand his ideas. This solution is suggested by Cassian's own words in 2 praef. 2f. (Cf. pp. 399–400.)

Each of the three parts of *The Conferences* is provided with its own preface, and the information that is given in the prefaces is useful in helping to establish the dating of the composition of the respective parts. We know that the Castor whose death is mentioned in 1 praef.1f. died in 426, and consequently the preface and probably all the conferences of the first part must have been completed by that year. The Honoratus and Eucherius of the second preface are spoken of as *fratres,* or brothers. Since Honoratus, however, became bishop of Arles in 426, and since as a bishop he would not have been called *frater* by Cassian, who was a priest, but rather *episcopus,* as he is in the third preface, the second preface and probably all the conferences in the second part must also have been completed by 426. The same Honoratus is referred to as still living in the third preface; hence this preface and probably all the conferences of the third part were completed no later than the very beginning of 429, inasmuch as Honoratus died in January of that year. In summary, then, *The Conferences* appear to have been composed between sometime in 426 and the beginning of 429. Assuming that Cassian was born in the 360s, he was in his sixties when he wrote his great work. *The Institutes* already lay behind him, and the treatise *On the Incarnation of Christ against Nestorius* was to be composed not far in the future, shortly before his death in the early 430s.

While the period within which *The Conferences* were written can be fixed with accuracy, the probably less important problem of determining when the conversations that form the basis for the twenty-four conferences supposedly occurred cannot so easily be solved. We know only that they would have taken place while Cassian and Germanus were in Egypt, that the two friends sojourned twice in that land sometime during the last two decades of the fourth century, and that their second sojourn seems to have extended a year or two into the fifth, when the Anthropomorphite movement became violent. The tenth conference can be dated to 399, when the letter written by Theophilus and mentioned in 10.2.2 was sent throughout Egypt. Perhaps this means that the ninth conference, led by the same Abba Isaac who leads the tenth, can be placed in that year also or in late 398. The only other historical event that might have provided a handle for dating is the Saracen massacre that is alluded to in 6.1.1, but in fact it is not known precisely when that occurred.

The abbas to whom the different conferences are attributed number fifteen, some of them being responsible for two or even three conferences. There is no good reason to doubt that any of the fifteen actually existed. A few of them—like Paphnutius, Isaac, and Piamun—appear to have attestation from other sources. Although most of the others are no more than names to us now, they were probably all well-known figures in their day, which is why Cassian and Germanus are said either to have sought them out themselves or to have been taken to them by others.

At this point the question may be raised as to what extent the twenty-four conferences reproduce actual conversations and to what extent Cassian himself exercised a creative role in writing them. It seems somewhat unlikely that they are mere fabrications. The quite sober portraits of the abbas who participated in the conferences contribute to a sense of the genuine. Despite the larger-than-life qualities of a number of them, they are on the whole men of saintly moderation rather than flamboyant wonder-workers, although, as a passage like 15.3ff. makes plain, they are not necessarily averse to wonder-working. The conferences, moreover, are placed in a fairly realistic context. There are descriptions of places (as in 11.1 and 11.3.1f.) and of relatively insignificant customs (as in 1.23.4f.), which give us an indication of Cassian's firsthand knowledge of monastic Egypt. But the events at the center of that context—namely, the conferences themselves—would have occurred at least a quarter of a century previous to the actual composition of the work.

Our knowledge of the ancient dialogical form strongly suggests that *The Conferences* as a whole are elaborated versions of past conversations—occasionally, and perhaps often, elaborated beyond immediate recognition. The process of elaboration would include the influence of persons and philosophies to which Cassian does not directly advert but apart from which his treatise would be inconceivable. His sources have been studied especially in Salvatore Marsili, *Giovanni Cassiano ed Evagrio Pontico. Dottrina sulla carità e contemplazione* (SA 5) (1936); Weber; and Colish 114–122. To the roles played by Evagrius, the non-Pachomian tradition, and Stoicism, with which these works deal, must be added still others. Among them Augustine occupies a large place, both as a positive and as a negative influence. Not only is the famous thirteenth conference a negative response to Augustine's teaching on grace, but there is reason to believe that the seventeenth is a negative response to his teaching on lying. The notes to the present translation seek to indicate still more of Augustine's influence, in smaller ways, and suggest that Cassian was fairly familiar with his great contemporary. (Cf. Boniface Ramsey, "John Cassian: Student of Augustine," *Cistercian Studies Quarterly* 28 [1993]: 5–15; idem, "Addendum to Boniface Ramsey, 'John Cassian: Student of Augustine,'" ibid. 199–200). It is also possible that Augustine was somewhat familiar with Cassian, at least according to one scholar (cf. Ulrich Duchrow, "Zum Prolog von Augustinus De doctrina christiana," *Vigiliae Christianae* 17 [1963]: 165–172).

Cassian's treatment of the unnamed Augustine's view of grace in the thirteenth conference, in fact, offers an excellent example of the problem of his own elaboration of material at hand and of the influences (in this case negative) at work on him. The actual conference supposedly took place before the beginning of the fifth century, but Augustine's position was a product of the 420s. There is no doubt, nonetheless, that this conference is an intentional reply to Augustine rather than simply a fortuitous composition. Is Abba Chaeremon's teaching on the relationship between grace and free will, which is so opposed to Augustine's, really his own? To what extent might it have been his own? He expresses views that are not, after all, foreign to Eastern ascetical thought, and Cassian might simply have trundled them out at this opportune moment. Or is this really Cassian's teaching, and is this conference one of perhaps a few that have either very little or no basis at all in a real conversation?

Where precisely Chaeremon, Piamun, Nesteros, and the others leave off and Cassian begins we shall surely never know with exactitude. At the very least, however, the synthesis of the whole and the emphasis on certain themes rather than on others are Cassian's. It would be absurd to think that, in all the time the author spent in Egypt, he would have spoken with only fifteen abbas and would have had only twenty-four memorable and worthwhile conversations. He must have met many more abbas and entered into many more discussions. The very opening of the twenty-fourth conference, 24.1.1, refers to the mystical quality of the number twenty-four, and from this we may reasonably conclude that we are dealing here with a well-planned arrangement—with, in other words, a calculated choice of conversations/conferences and themes (and of abbas), all corresponding, of course, to Cassian's own view of what was most important. Having had to go beyond the ten of his original scheme, ten being itself a perfect number, he opted for twenty-four because of that number's connection with the elders of Revelation 4:4. On the other hand, it is quite possible that Cassian wrote twenty-four conferences simply because he had neither more nor less to say than could be accommodated by that number, and then sought to justify his choice by recourse to a mystical explanation. From what we know of patristic numerology, after all, virtually any number could be made to yield mystical meanings.

Within these twenty-four conferences, particularly when they are taken in tandem with their sister work, *The Institutes*, there are rather few significant aspects of ancient monastic practice and spirituality that do not surface. We would hardly know how comprehensive the treatise really is from reading the titles of the different conferences, which do not give a true insight into their scope. (Both these titles, incidentally, and the headings of the chapters of each conference are by a later hand than Cassian's.) The sixth conference, for example, entitled "On the Slaughter of Some Holy Persons," deals among other matters with the good, the bad, and the indifferent; various sorts of temptations; the value of the monk's remaining in his cell; and the impossibility of a sudden moral collapse. This spread of topics is typical not only of Cassian in particular but of the fathers in general, in whose sermons and treatises ideas tumble over one another in what seems to the modern reader to be an utterly haphazard way. While it is true that themes are in fact sometimes introduced in an apparently unconnected fashion, often in the form of questions posed by Germanus, a close examination of almost any conference will reveal a notable coherence. The twenty-first conference is a good case in point. It begins with a long narrative about a personal conversion that looks like it has nothing to do with the declared topic—the Pentecost relaxation. But, as the introduction to that conference seeks to demonstrate, the themes suggested in the narrative (firstfruits, tithing, the Gospel's surpassing of the law) are elaborated in the pages that follow.

In his article entitled "Understanding Cassian: A Survey of the Conferences" (*Cistercian Studies Quarterly* 19 [1984]: 101–121), Adalbert de Vogüé has indicated that there appears to exist a complex and refined interrelationship among almost all the different conferences. Not only do they follow one another in logical order, picking up previously introduced themes and elaborating on them. In addition, in his view, both the odd-numbered and the even-numbered conferences develop certain common ideas and constitute two parallel series. The odd-numbered conferences are occupied in some form or other with the goal of the monk, purity of heart, whereas the even-numbered ones deal with discretion and with making one's way carefully between opposing vices. "First comes the march towards the ideal, in which Cassian notes the role of divine help," de Vogüé writes (p. 108) of the two sets of conferences respectively, "and then succeeds the combat against the symmetrical temptations of too much and too little; at first, the gaze is forward, then it looks to right and left; first is proposed the fullness of good, and then one guards oneself against evil under its two opposed forms." Finally (as noted pp. 117–118), there are even some parallels between tenth conferences—between the eleventh and the twenty-first, the twelfth and the twenty-second, and the third, the thirteenth, and the twenty-third.

Thus, beneath the occasional seeming hodgepodge of *The Conferences* there often lies a careful scheme that can be laid bare.

Like many writings of antiquity (and of later eras, for that matter), *The Conferences* are cast as dialogues—although, to be sure, they are not dialogues between equals nor between persons assuming the role of equals but very clearly between masters and disciples. One purpose of the dialogical form is the passing on of truth or wisdom in conversational fashion, and this is certainly the case with *The Conferences*. This purpose determines how both Cassian and Germanus and the old men whom they interview are portrayed. The two friends are in many respects the ideal recipients of wisdom. They have traveled a long distance and presumably subjected themselves to considerable inconvenience in pursuit of it. For wisdom's sake they have even, as we learn from the seventeenth conference, broken a solemn oath made in one of Christianity's most sacred places and put themselves in jeopardy with their religious superiors. Finally, when they are actually engaged in dialogue with the old men, they prove themselves models of docility, listening to the elders with the most tense interest and eagerness.

Alas, however, Cassian's and Germanus's model behavior is purchased at the price of a certain pallid characterization. In the presence of the old men they are generally self-effacing, little more than mere listeners, asking only the questions and making only remarks that will serve to draw out the speakers still further. If doubt is sometimes expressed—as when Germanus boldly says to Abba Nesteros: "This statement does not at all seem to us to be based on truth or to be supported by credible reasoning" (14.15)—it is only so that a particular abba may clarify his point. And, in any event, doubt is not equivalent to resistance in such instances. Furthermore, the periods of time preceding and following the conferences are given over entirely, on the part of the two friends, to anticipatory emotions and to feelings of wonder, gratitude, sadness, or compunction, based on whatever they may have heard.

Cassian and Germanus hardly give the impression of existing apart from *The Conferences*. It is the old men who are more forcefully delineated; their personalities, activities, and even physical appearances are described in a way that the two friends' are not. Abba Chaeremon, for example, is more than a hundred years old but intellectually alert; only "his back was so bent with age and with constant prayer that he went about with his hands down and touching the ground, as if he had returned to his earliest infancy" (11.4.1). Abba Paphnutius, again, is more than ninety years old, but once a week he carries back to his cell a week's supply of water, transporting it on his shoulders over nearly five miles; for his love of the desert and because he is so rarely seen even by the other anchorites he is popularly called "the Buffalo" (cf. 3.1.3, 18.15.1). From the spiritual point of view the abbas in question are endowed with an experience and a wisdom that are equal to their years, and their charisms, ascetic practices, and discourse attest to their unusual holiness. Men like these have rich lives of their own, and in comparison with them Cassian and Germanus seem far less compelling and attractive. Nor are the elders afraid to speak, for what they say ranges on for pages at a time, in contrast to the far briefer questions and interjections of the two younger monks.

However artificial or inadequate this depiction of both masters and disciples may seem to the contemporary reader, it corresponds with Cassian's own intentions. The elders were to be accepted without question as the repositories of authority and the keepers of tradition, and their words had a quasi-absolute value. You must "follow with great humility whatever you see our elders do or teach," Abba Piamun tells Cassian and Germanus. "Nor should you be moved or diverted or held back from imitating them even if the reason or the cause for a particular thing or deed is not clear to you at the time, because," he continues, "the knowledge of everything is attained to by those who think well and with simplicity about all matters and who strive to imitate faithfully rather than to discuss everything that they see being taught and done by the elders" (18.3.1). Cassian and Germanus are paradigms of attentiveness to their teachers and their words, and their self-effacing personalities bespeak this attentiveness. So attentive and ardent are they, in fact, that those who address them are rendered more capable and eloquent (cf. 1.23.1f.).

This attitude of attentiveness to the truth, to wisdom, and to the word that speaks them, as well as that possibility of being transformed by the word which Cassian and Germanus so clearly manifest, is found throughout the Scriptures. But it enjoys a powerful resurgence in the literature of the desert. It marks the very beginning of the monastic movement—namely, when the adolescent Antony hears Christ's words proclaimed during the reading of the Gospel in church and is immediately inspired to leave everything and follow his Master (cf. Athanasius, *V. S. Antonii* 2ff.). From that point on monastic literature is full of younger monks listening to older monks as to a kind of supreme authority, even if not necessarily with the same dramatic effects as Antony experienced. For the elders are now, because of their holiness, the authentic interpreters of Scripture. Abba Poemen even goes so far as to suggest that the elders are a more reliable guide to Christian conduct than is Scripture itself, which is often subject to misinterpretation (cf. *Apophthegmata patrum,* de abbate Ammun 2).

The kind of teaching that *The Conferences* describe—namely, oral instruction by persons who very clearly hold positions of authority—is typical of the oral-aural culture of ancient society and can be found, for instance in Proverbs 1:8ff. and Didache 3f. "An oral-aural economy of knowledge is necessarily authoritarian to an extent intolerable in a more visualist culture," writes Walter Ong in an important monograph, contrasting knowledge mediated by the spoken word with that mediated by the written word. "This is not simply because someone at the top is peremptorily imposing his views on those below. Such will be the later caricature of authority when it is under attack. The actuality is more complex. A personality structure built up in an oral society, feeling knowledge as essentially something communicated [by word of mouth], will be relatively more concerned that this knowledge tie in with what others say and relatively less concerned with its relationship to observation. In such a society, knowledge is a tribal possession, not a matter of individual speculation." (*The Presence of the Word: Some Prolegomena for Cultural and Religious History,* repr. Minneapolis, 1981, 231). The only qualification that need be added to this statement for it to apply more precisely to *The Conferences* and to most other desert literature is that this literature, for all its emphasis on unyielding adherence to the teachings of the elders, does in fact lay stress not only on words but also on deeds: The words of the elders are valid only because their deeds are valid—and observably so. Not for Cassian the paradoxical advice of the great Byzantine master Symeon the New Theologian (949–1022), that a spiritual director must continue to be revered and trusted even if he should be seen to commit fornication before the eyes of his spiritual charge (cf. *Cat.* 26, in SC 113.94).

As far as their form is concerned, then, *The Conferences* may be reduced to the passing on of Christian ascetic wisdom from masters to disciples, and both masters and disciples are intended by Cassian to appear as models of their types. The work's focus on teaching in this context is only rarely diverted. Apart from the descriptions of the various abbas, which must not be considered extraneous, a few words are also expended on activities other than teaching and on sketching the environment, but they are not many. These other activities consist to a large degree in going to bed at night, and the recounting of this serves in a number of instances as a transition from one conference to another, since the conferences are frequently said to have concluded at night. As for the environment, it is the desert, and Cassian introduces it at the very beginning of his work, asking his readers to reflect on where the great abbas lived and what influence the *solitudo vastissima* might have had on them (cf. 1 praef. 7).

This *solitudo vastissima*—vast and uncharted more in psychological and spiritual terms than geographically—serves as a backdrop for the conferences and contributes to placing in relief the dialogue between master and disciple, even though descriptions of it are only sparsely scattered through the text. Here in the harsh wilderness, where no one was tempted by any natural fertility of the land to cultivate a garden or to seek distraction outside his cell (cf. 24.3.1), the sole alternative to the word of wisdom and truth was the word of sin and delusion, and the sole alternative to the elders was the demons.

Demons were rife everywhere, according to the thought of Egyptian theologians and monks, and they were especially present in desert places. Jesus himself had encountered the devil in the desert (cf. Mt 4:1–11; it is interesting to note that this experience of his is the most oft alluded to in *The Conferences*—in 5.4, 5.6, 22.10, and 24.17). If Antony, who really discovered the desert for monasticism (cf. Athanasius, *V. S. Antonii* 3), went out into it, it was at least partly for the purpose of engaging in battle with these spirits of the air. Not only would they do physical violence to a monk and appear to him in lascivious guise to break down his psychological and spiritual defenses, but they would even seek, as Pachomius experienced, to make him laugh in order to win domination over him (cf. *V. prima gr. Pachomii* 19). Nothing was too simple for them to try, no possibility of entry into the human heart and mind was so negligible that it could be dismissed. An extra biscuit eaten clandestinely in the evening (surely understandable in view of a young man's hunger and the fact that he was officially limited to one rather paltry meal a day!) nearly brought about the downfall of Abba Moses when he was a boy. When compunction finally overcame him, however, and in the presence of several other monks he produced a biscuit that had been hidden on his person and sobbingly confessed his theft, a sulphurous lamp also emerged from the place where the biscuit had been concealed, and it filled the cell with its stink, thereby giving indisputable witness to the demonic presence (cf. 2.11.1ff.). A mere biscuit could be, in its own way, as full of satanic suggestion as a cache of gold coins or the village prostitute.

The remedy against deception by the demons—which Cassian frequently calls by the word "illusion" (or *inlusio* in Latin, with its resonances of mockery and jeering)—was precisely to unburden oneself to the elders and to obtain from them a word of wisdom. "Not only all actions but even all thoughts [should be] offered to the inspection of the elders, so that, not trusting in one's own judgment, one may submit in every respect to their decisions and may know how to judge what is good and bad according to what they have handed down" (2.10.1). No matter how otherwise gifted a monk was, if he did not seek guidance from without but trusted in himself he was susceptible to *inlusio* and *deceptio*. Thus, for example, the monk Heron, whose solitude and abstinence over the course of fifty years were a source of wonder to his contemporaries.

Despite all this he fell disastrously, deceived by a demon who appeared to him in the guise of an angel of light. Was not the reason for his fall the fact that "he possessed little of the virtue of discretion and wanted to be governed by his own prescriptions rather than to obey the counsels and conferences of the brothers and the teachings of our forebears" (2.5.2)?

Discretion was the virtue that distinguished between good and bad, or more often between good and the mere appearance of good, and it was ordinarily practiced by submitting oneself humbly to the judgment and the insight of others. This submission to others was the surest possible guarantee in a fallible existence that subjectivity would not becloud one's judgment, thereby confusing the good with the spontaneous object of one's desires. Discretion is the ruling virtue of *The Conferences,* and Cassian introduces it already toward the end of the first conference, as soon as he can after having set out in preliminary fashion the goal *(scopos/destinatio)* and the end *(telos/finis)* of the monastic life. (As is typical of Cassian, the use of the terms is essentially arbitrary and could hence contribute to confusion. The goal is in effect the next-to-last objective of the Christian life and the end its final objective.) The second conference is devoted exclusively to discretion, and from then on its presence is either explicit or implicit throughout the work. Indeed, *The Conferences* as a whole are nothing else than an extended exercise in discretion by Cassian and Germanus; the two friends are, precisely, submitting themselves completely to the judgment of fifteen elders over the course of twenty-four conferences.

If discretion is the ruling virtue of *The Conferences,* even being modeled for the reader in the two friends' interviews with the abbas, the goal that the work proposes is purity of heart, and the end is the kingdom of heaven. The first conference, as has been noted, is largely given over to a discussion of these two things. They may be defined and their relationship to discretion may be expressed as follows.

The kingdom of heaven, alternatively referred to as the kingdom of God and as eternal life, is the monk's ultimate object of attainment. It is extra-temporal, although it may also truly be said to reside within a person who lives in the temporal world and is practicing holiness. Cassian makes an unmistakable allusion to this temporal possession of the kingdom of heaven in some memorable and near-ecstatic lines in the tenth conference. Then, he writes, without explicitly mentioning the kingdom, "every love, every desire, every effort, every undertaking, every thought of ours, everything that we live, that we speak, that we breathe, will be God...and that unity which the Father now has with the Son and which the Son has with the Father will be carried over into our minds and our senses" (10.7.2).

Purity of heart is that practice of holiness, at different times described as love or perfection or contemplation or tranquillity, "without [which] the aforesaid end will not be able to be seized" (1.5.2). Purity of heart has also been said to be interchangeable with *apatheia*–a word that Cassian would have avoided because of its associations with Evagrius, whose use of it was criticized, along with Evagrius himself, in some striking lines in Jerome (*Ep.* 133.3): "Evagrius Ponticus...put out a book and maxims on *apatheia*, which we would call impassibility or imperturbability–when the mind is never disturbed by the vice of perturbation and, to put it simply, is either a stone or God." The same section in the letter links Evagrius and the term *apatheia* with the Pelagianism that Jerome in particular hated. (Cf. Antoine Guillaumont, *Les "Kephalaia Gnostica" d'Evagre le Pontique et l'histoire de l'origénisme chez les Grecs et chez les Syriens* [Patristica Sorboniensia 5] [Paris, 1962], 79–80.) The state of purity of heart, in any event, is the last condition to be arrived at by the monk in the world of time. It is, moreover, the sole condition necessary for the attainment of the kingdom of heaven: It both presupposes all possible good observances, to the degree that they are necessary for a given individual, and imposes meaning and direction on all such observances, which must be considered secondary in respect to it. "It behooves us," Cassian declares in 1.7.2, "...to carry out the things that are secondary–namely, fasts, vigils, the solitary life and meditation on Scripture–for the sake of the principal goal, which is purity of heart or love, rather than for their sake to neglect this principal virtue."

Finally, discretion lies at the service of purity of heart: It is the virtue that enables the pursuit of purity of heart by clarifying the means that the monk must employ in that pursuit. Or perhaps it could be characterized as the very atmosphere in which purity of heart is achieved.

After the first conference the kingdom of heaven–the end of the monk–is not much spoken of again. *The Conferences* are really, it must be said, under the double aegis of discretion and purity of heart, even though these two themes are themselves often implicit. It has already been noted that the practice of discretion even finds a vehicle in the dialogical form of the work. The actual substance of the dialogues, however, is taken up with the concern to acquire purity of heart, and each of the conferences represents part of an overall strategy for its acquisition. This purpose undergirds even the conferences that we might consider more informational and hence as pertaining more properly to discretion, which requires a certain minimum of data. In *The Conferences,* though, nothing is merely informational, not even the discussions, for example, on principalities and on making promises. Everything is directed, like discretion itself, to purity of heart.

This vast work, then, is about obtaining purity of heart through the exercise of discretion, all for the sake of preparing oneself for the kingdom of heaven. If we know this, then we have grasped the fundamental scheme of *The Conferences,*.

The systematizing genius of Cassian, evident at the very beginning of *The Conferences,*, where he introduces the great themes that will dominate and guide the treatise, continues to manifest itself throughout the work. Thus, in the third conference he speaks of the three different kinds of calling or conversion to the monastic life, of the three different kinds of renunciation that the monastic life implies, and then of the three different kinds of possessions that should or should not be renounced. This conference follows the two initial ones in a quite natural progression, inasmuch as conversion and renunciation stand at the beginning of that life whose theoretical basis has already been sketched in the first two conferences. More to the point, however, as far as systematization is concerned, is the remarkable analysis of both conversion and renunciation that at least comes close to exhausting the various alternatives in these two areas. The breakdown into genus and species that occurs here is very typical of Cassian and demonstrates his extremely organized approach to reality. It is an organization that may be sought in vain in many other early Christian writers.

The three callings, three renunciations, and three sorts of possessions that are evoked in the third conference find parallels everywhere in *The Conferences*. To return to the first conference: In addition to the goal and the end that were discussed shortly before, three ways of understanding the idea of the kingdom of heaven are offered, three sources of human thoughts are exposed, and a four-part method of discretion is explained. The fourth conference treats of the two reasons for the divine plan and trial, three distinctions relative to the constitution of the human person as found in a passage from the Apostle, four meanings of the term "flesh" and three conditions of the soul. The fifth conference, which is one of the most complex in terms of analysis and categorization of subject matter, is taken up with the eight principal vices and their interrelationships; these vices are compared with eight nations that are mentioned in the Old Testament. The sixth conference makes a threefold division of created reality, discourses on the spiritual significance of ambidexterity (with its symbolism of right and left) as it appears in some lines from the Book of Judges, and speaks of the three kinds of trials. The remaining eighteen conferences are no less rich in this kind of analysis.

Along with this rather highly organized presentation of material, *The Conferences* betray an admirable insight into the workings of the human mind and an understanding of human needs. (Indeed, the orderly arrangement of the work itself suggests a certain recognition on Cassian's part of the mind's need for clarity.) Typical of this insight and understanding is, for example, the fifth conference's treatment of the interconnection of the eight principal vices, which manifests an almost breathtaking finesse; the various discussions of mental wandering, perhaps especially in the seventh conference; the analysis of anger in the second half of the sixteenth conference, which is all the more striking inasmuch as the conference as a whole is devoted to friendship; the careful advice offered in 20.7ff. with respect to the recollection of past misdeeds; and the counsel not to disdain relaxation in 24.20f. Because Cassian is more a psychologist than a theologian (in the rather narrow sense in which that term is used today), his approach in the famous thirteenth conference to the vexed problem of the interaction of human freedom and divine grace is a common-sense one that seems to fit neatly into the structure of human behavior and responsibility.

Part of Cassian's psychological acuity certainly consists in the characteristic moderation of the positions that he espouses in *The Conferences*. To appreciate this fully, his work need only be compared with some other products of the Egyptian desert—with Palladius's *Lausiac History,* the *Historia monachorum in Aegypto,* the *Apophthegmata patrum,* or even Athanasius's *Life of Saint Antony*. There are, it is true, "things in these books that [will appear] impossible or hard," as Cassian says in 1 praef. 6 with regard to what he has recorded. The mere living in the *solitudo vastissima* itself qualifies as such, quite apart from whatever rigorous exercises might be added to that. But *The Conferences* do not recommend any ascetical practices that could be called absurd or life-threatening for a person who was reasonably well trained. Quite the contrary, practices of this sort are depicted as crazy rather than heroic. More precisely, they are lacking in discretion, as were the two monks who, Cassian relates in 2.6, decided to walk through the desert without bringing any food with them, foolishly trusting instead that God himself would provide for their needs. Discretion appears thus as the begetter and guardian of moderation. And if it is necessary to lay down rules, as Cassian does at the end of the second conference with respect to a daily portion of bread, it is so that moderation may be preserved.

Of a piece with this moderation is Cassian's refusal to absolutize canonized monastic practices, such as "the solitary life, vigils, the reading of and meditation on the sacred books, and fasting" (21.14.2). The goodness of these things is dependent on the disposition of their practitioner and the moment when they are done. Cassian's comparative reticence about miracles falls in with this moderate tone; although it would have been virtually impossible at the beginning of the fifth century to have written a treatise of this sort without some mention of them, they are kept to a minimum. Even his stand on lying and breaking promises in the seventeenth conference—so surprising to the Western reader—is nothing else on one level than another aspect of this moderation, in contrast to Augustine's stark rigorism on the subject.

Perhaps it also makes sense, finally, to place the noteworthy development in Cassian's thought from exaltation of the solitary life at the beginning of *The Conferences* to acceptance and approval of cenobitism by the end of them at least partly within the context of moderation. Rousseau 182 describes this development succinctly: "In the early stages, [Cassian] appears to have had in mind two distinct groups of people [i.e., cenobites and solitaries], pursuing their ideals side by side. Subsequently, he suggested that the two modes of life might be more accurately considered as possible stages in the lives of individuals. Finally, he surrendered to the historical development of asceticism, and agreed that the solitary life might not be practical, nor even desirable, in spite of its theoretical excellence." The last conference, where cenobitism is set on an at least equal footing with anchoritism, is also the one where the relaxational advantages of the presence of the brothers are expatiated upon. A moderate life, secure from the dangers of the extremes that preoccupied Cassian in the second conference, on discretion, seems to have demanded a greater exposure to human society on the part of the monk.

As good an organizer as he showed himself to be, and as keen an observer of the workings of the human mind as he surely was, Cassian was nonetheless—as has already been suggested—not a great speculative theologian. This fact is embarrassingly evident in his last work, against Nestorius. As Gibson writes in the preface to his translation of that text: "Taken as a whole, the treatise is of distinctly less value than Cassian's earlier writings, and betrays the haste in which it was composed by the occasional use of inaccurate language on the subject of the Incarnation, and of terms and phrases which the mature judgment of the Church has rejected" (Gibson 190). But theological inexpertise can be found in the pages of *The Conferences* as well. Here too Cassian's christological language has the potential for confusion: He uses the inexact expression *homo assumptus* with reference to Christ in 7.22.2, 9.34.10, and 16.6.4. His perhaps laudable attempt in the famous thirteenth conference to offer a counterbalance to Augustine's relentless doctrine of grace has a disappointing quality to it, being notable from the theological point of view less for its profundity than for its mustering of scriptural proof texts. Cassian's positive position with respect to occasional lying in the sixteenth conference suffers when compared with Augustine's rigorously argued stance to the contrary in the *De mendacio* and the *Contra mendacium;* although his view is indisputably more humane than Augustine's, it is also susceptible of being interpreted in a morally opportunistic fashion.

But we would be foolish to read Cassian as a speculative theologian; his talents were not in speculative theology, nor is his reputation there. He was, rather, a master of the inner life, and it is with that realization that we must now approach him.

THE FIRST PART OF THE CONFERENCES OF JOHN CASSIAN

◆

CONFERENCES I–X

TRANSLATOR'S NOTE TO THE FIRST PART

In this first of three prefaces Cassian compares *The Institutes* and the first ten books of *The Conferences* (if we are to credit 2 praef. 2 it would appear that he had not yet planned on writing the remaining fourteen; but cf. p. 397), speaking of the former as touching on "the external and visible life of the monks" and of the latter as dealing with "the invisible character of the inner man" (1 praef. 5). The two works in question are analogous, respectively, to two kinds of prayer–namely, the canonical, meticulously regulated prayer described in the second and third books of *The Institutes* and the perpetual, apostolically mandated, and even occasionally ecstatic prayer that is discussed at the conclusion of this first part of *The Conferences,* in 10.10f. Indeed, from references in *Inst.* 2.1 and 2.9.1 to a subsequent treatment of perpetual prayer "in the conference of the elders," it appears that *The Institutes* and this first part of *The Conferences,* both written at the request of Pope Castor, were simultaneously planned and were intended to be complementary from the start.

It is clear from what is said in 1 praef. 5 and from one or two other observations made here by Cassian that the original ten books of *The Conferences* are destined to deal with sublimer realities than are *The Institutes.* These sublimer realities may be summed up simply as the solitary or anchorite life, on which this first part of the treatise focuses. The heroes of the first part, the seven abbas whose conversations these are said to be, are themselves solitaries; moreover, Helladius, one of the two persons to whom this section is dedicated, "has set out to pursue the sublime institutes of the anchorites" (1 praef. 3). This being the case, the ten conferences that follow apply not to monks in general but to anchorites in particular, even if these latter are not specifically indicated (cf. Julien Leroy, "Les préfaces des écrits monastiques de Jean Cassien," RAM 42 [1966]: 167–170). It is noteworthy that the word *instituta* appears five times in this preface (compared with three times in the preface to *The Institutes*), and because of this it has been suggested that the first part of *The Conferences* might well be called *The Institutes of the Anchorite Life,* thus paralleling the title of Cassian's earlier work, *The Institutes of the Cenobia* (cf. ibid. 169).

One of the great themes of *The Conferences* as a whole, albeit especially of the first part, presents itself for the first time in 1 praef. 3 in the form of a very brief allusion. Here the priest Helladius is said to be desirous of instruction "not in things of his own design but in [the] traditions" of the anchorites. The same theme recurs in 1 praef. 6, where Cassian expresses his concern to have "a complete recollection of those same traditions" so as to be able to pass them on in their integrity. This attentiveness to tradition, coupled with a mistrust of one's own judgments, will be revealed in the second conference as characteristic of that virtue of discretion whose understanding and practice are central to the treatise.

CASSIAN'S PREFACE TO THE FIRST PART

1. The obligation that was incurred with respect to the blessed Pope Castor in the preface of those volumes that summarized in twelve books the institutes of the cenobia and the remedies for the eight principal vices has, with the Lord's help, been more or less fulfilled; our feeble nature was just capable of it. I would certainly have liked to see what his or your judgment was on this, after a careful examination had been made—whether, in matters at once so deep and so lofty, which so far as I know have never before been written about, we have said something worthy of your recognition and of the desire of all the holy brothers. 2. Now, however, since in the meantime the aforesaid bishop has left us and gone to Christ, I thought that there should be dedicated to you above all, O most blessed Pope Leontius and holy brother Helladius, the ten conferences of the greatest fathers—anchorites who dwelled in the desert of Skete—which he, inflamed with an incomparable zeal for holiness, had ordered to be written in like words, not thinking in the breadth of his charity what a heavy weight he was laying on weak shoulders. 3. One of you, united to the aforementioned man by family affection and priestly dignity and still more by the fervor of holy zeal, claims his due as a brother by hereditary right. The other, not as one who has set out to pursue the sublime institutes of the anchorites through his own presumption but taking the right road of teaching almost before he began to learn, thanks to the guidance of the Holy Spirit, has desired to be instructed not in things of his own design but in their traditions. In this respect, now that I have settled in a harbor of silence, a vast sea lies before me, inasmuch as I am daring to commit to writing something on the institutes and teaching of such men. 4. As the solitary life is greater and more sublime than that of the cenobia, and the contemplation of God—upon which

those inestimable men were ever intent—than the active life that is led in communities, so must the bark of a limited understanding be tossed about amidst the dangers of deeper waters. Your part, then, is to help our efforts with your devout prayers, lest the holy material that is to be presented be imperiled by us because of inexpert, albeit faithful, words, or again lest our simplicity be overwhelmed in the depths of this same material.

5. Consequently, let us proceed from the external and visible life of the monks, which we have summarized in the previous books, to the invisible character of the inner man, and from the practice of the canonical prayers let our discourse arise to the unceasing nature of that perpetual prayer which the Apostle commands.[1] Thus the person who has read the previous work and is worthy of the name of that spiritual Jacob because of the supplanting of the carnal vices[2] may now—taking up not so much my own institutes as those of the fathers and passing over to the deserts and as it were the dignity of Israel,[3] thanks to an insight into the divine purity—be also similarly taught what must be observed at this summit of perfection. 6. And so let your prayers obtain from him who has judged us worthy to see them and to be their disciples and friends the bestowal of a complete recollection of those same traditions and a pleasing mode of expression. Thus, while explaining those things as holily and as completely as we received them, we may be able to put before you those very same men, embodied somehow in their own institutes and (what is more) speaking in the Latin tongue.

Before anything else, we want the reader of these conferences as well as of the previous volumes to be advised that if perhaps he thinks, by reason of his status and chosen orientation or from the point of view of ordinary custom and way of life, that there are things in these books that are impossible or hard, he should not judge them by the standard of his own ability but according to the dignity of the speakers, whose zeal and chosen orientation he should first mentally grasp, since those who have truly died to this world's life are bound by no love for kinsfolk nor by any ties of worldly deeds. 7. Finally, let him also consider the kinds of places in which they are living. Thanks to them, they who have established themselves in the vastest solitude and are separated from the companionship of all mortal beings, thereby possessing spiritual enlightenment, contemplate and proclaim things that will perhaps seem impossible to those who are unpracticed and ignorant by reason of their condition and their mediocre behavior. In this regard, however, if anyone wishes to give a true opinion and desires to see whether these things can be fulfilled, let him first hasten to seize upon their chosen orientation with similar zeal and by a similar way of life. Only then will he realize that what seemed beyond human capacity is not only possible but even most sweet.

But now let us get on to their conferences and institutes.

Textual References

1. Cf. 1 Thes 5:17.
2. Cf. Gn 27:36.
3. Cf. Gn 32:29.

NOTES TO THE TEXT

1 praef. 1 Pope Castor: The title of pope was not uncommon for a bishop at this period. Castor held the see of Apta Iulia in Narbonensis Secunda, now Apt in the Vaucluse in France, not far north of Marseilles. At his request *The Institutes* was written, as we know from *Inst.*, praef. 2ff., in order to assist him in the establishment of a monastery in his diocese. Cf. DHGE 11.1455–1456.

1 praef. 2 Pope Leontius was possibly bishop of Forum Iulii in Narbonensis Secunda, now Fréjus in the department of Var in France. He is said in 1 praef. 3 to have been related to Castor.

Holy brother Helladius: A priest when this preface was written, Helladius is said to be a bishop in 2 praef. 2, but we are not told of what town. "Holy brother" suggests Helladius's equality of rank with Cassian, who was also a priest.

1 praef. 4 The image of the sea and of a marine voyage appears also in 7.34.1, 8.25.5, 10.8.5, 10.10.13, 18.1.2, 22.14, 22.16, and 24.26.19. Employed as it is at the very beginning as well as at the very end of *The Conferences,* and occasionally elsewhere, it helps to lend cohesion to the work. The image of life as a sea voyage is an ancient and oft-used one. Cf. Hugo Rahner, *Greek Myths and Christian Mystery,* trans. by Brian Battershaw (New York, 1963), 341–353.

The disclaimer of writing ability, which appears here and in 1 praef. 4, is frequently used by ancient (and later) authors. It is both a conventional form of modesty and a subtle ploy to draw the reader's attention to a given work's good points. The first Christian use of this artifice seems to be in Irenaeus, *Adv. haer.*, 1 praef. 3. Cassian himself employs it elsewhere in 10.1, 2 praef. 2, 17.30.3, 24.26.18; *Inst.*, praef. 2ff.; *De incarn.*, praef. In 3 praef. 2, however, he praises the composition of his work, speaking of it as carefully constructed and well-balanced. For other such disclaimers in desert literature cf. Palladius, *Hist. laus.*, prol. 4; *Hist. monach. in Aegypto,* prol. 2.

1 praef. 5 "That spiritual Jacob...dignity of Israel": Jacob/ Israel is a model or image of contemplation because of the visions and experiences recorded in Gn 28:12–15 and frequently thereafter. Cf. 5.23.1, 12.11.2; *De incarn.* 7.9.2ff.; Origen, *Hom. in Gen.* 15.3; idem, *Hom. in Num.* 11.4; idem, *Comm. in Cant. Cant.*, prol. (GCS 33.78–79).

1 praef. 6 On being "bound by no love for kinsfolk" cf. 24.1.2ff. and the relevant note.

FIRST CONFERENCE
THE FIRST CONFERENCE OF ABBA MOSES: ON THE GOAL AND THE END OF THE MONK

TRANSLATOR'S INTRODUCTION

The initial conference introduces the reader to Cassian and Germanus, speaks of the closeness of their friendship, and establishes the setting as the desert of Skete. From Cassian's words in 17.30.2, where he says that he and Germanus went to Skete on their second voyage to Egypt, it is evident that this first part of *The Conferences* is in fact the last from the point of view of the chronology of their travels.

Moses, the first of the fifteen abbas who figure largely in *The Conferences*, makes his appearance at once. Although we cannot be absolutely certain who he was, he may very possibly be identified with the Moses who is mentioned in *Inst.* 10.25, whom Cassian says that he met. He is, in any event, not the most famous of this name—Moses the Ethiopian, who was a reformed robber and murderer (cf. 3.5.2; Palladius, *Hist. laus.* 19; Sozomen, *Hist. eccl.* 6.29). In 2.11.1 the present Moses indicates that he had entered monasticism as a youth, whereas the reformed criminal had come in as an adult. Had he been a criminal, moreover, Cassian would probably have made at least some reference to his notoriety in this or the succeeding conference, where he is also featured.

The discussion starts with Moses' distinction between (intermediate) goals and (final) ends; it eventually centers on the monk's pursuit of his goal and from there it quite naturally slips into the concluding topic, which is discretion.

Moses explains that the monk's goal is purity of heart and

that his end is the kingdom of God. The former is the most proximate and ultimately the sole preparation for the latter, and to it all human activities must be subordinated. The old man very emphatically relegates even the most canonized monastic practices, several times mentioning them specifically by name (as in 1.7.1, when he speaks of solitude, "fasts, vigils, labors, nakedness of body, readings and other virtuous things"), to a secondary position with respect to purity of heart. That purity of heart is not to be narrowly understood is evident from the fact that the goal is also referred to as holiness and divine contemplation. Contemplation, on which several chapters focus and whose model is the Mary of Luke 10:38–42, means the fixing of the mind on God and Christ in a constant and habitual fashion rather than merely sporadically. But it can take place, as is clear from 1.15, in a variety of ways. At one point Moses indicates that there is some identity between the goal and the end inasmuch as the kingdom of God is said, like purity of heart itself, to be within us. Indeed, the reader will see that the scriptural passages that refer to the kingdom can just as easily be understood of that interior purity.

When the two friends seem astonished at the fact that the works of mercy that gain one entrance into the kingdom of heaven will not endure in heaven, Moses counters by observing that the reward must be distinguished from the deeds that obtain the reward. These good deeds are necessary in the present world because of its injustice, but in the world to come there will be no injustice and hence no need of acts to redress injustice. As Paul says, even the charisms of the Spirit will pass away in heaven and only love will remain. Moses' explanation here serves to relativize still further the activities that he has denoted as secondary.

Germanus then asks how one who is preoccupied with good works and with the necessary care of his body can devote himself unceasingly to God. Moses begins by remarking that the unceasing contemplation of God is impossible in any event but that it should constantly be striven for. Much of the rest of his answer consists in making clear to his listeners that there are only two alternatives for the Christian–namely, the kingdom of God or the kingdom of the devil–and that, as a result of one's conduct, one belongs to either the former or the latter. Even the dead, although temporarily without their bodies, rejoice in the former or suffer in the latter.

It is after this that Germanus raises the issue of the mental distractions that make it difficult to keep one's attention fixed on divine realities. The old man addresses the matter by noting that certain practices, such as meditating on Scripture, fasting, and the like, keep the mind relatively free of earthly musings, even though one can never be completely free of them. Then he takes up the topic of discretion, which in this context applies to the task of discerning which thoughts come from God, which from the devil, and which from within the given individual. The bulk of the discussion of discretion is occupied with the fourfold manner in which it is practiced: First, a person should scrutinize his thoughts to discover whether they are of the Spirit or merely have a spiritual appearance. Second, he should see that he is not being led astray by a misuse of Scripture or, indeed, in the third place, by a misuse of any otherwise good thing, such as fasting or keeping vigil. Fourth, he should verify both the content of whatever action he plans on pursuing and his motivation in pursuing it.

The conference concludes with some complimentary words directed to Cassian and Germanus for their eager attentiveness; the recommendation that they exercise discretion by retiring for the night; and an unexpectedly detailed account of some monastic sleeping habits.

I. The First Conference of Abba Moses: on the Goal and the End of the Monk

Chapters

I. On our stay in Skete, and on the chosen orientation of Abba Moses.
II. Abba Moses' question about what should be the scopos and what should be the end of the monk.
III. Our reply.
IV. Abba Moses' question concerning the aforesaid suggestion.
V. A comparison with someone who is trying to hit a target.
VI. On those who renounce the world and strive for perfection without love.
VII. On seeking tranquillity of heart.
VIII. On the principal effort made to attain the contemplation of divine realities, and a comparison with Mary and Martha.
IX. A question about why the practice of the virtues does not remain with a person.
X. The reply, that it is not their reward but their doing that will cease.
XI. On the perpetual nature of love.
XII. A question about the duration of spiritual contemplation.
XIII. The reply, about the heart's way to God and about the kingdom of God and the kingdom of the devil.
XIV. On the perpetual nature of the soul.
XV. On contemplating God.
XVI. A question about the constant movement of our thoughts.
XVII. The reply: What the mind can do about the state of thoughts and what it cannot do.
XVIII. A comparison between a millstone and the soul.
XIX. The three sources of our thoughts.
XX. On discerning thoughts, according to the example of an approved money-changer.
XXI. The deception of Abba John.
XXII. The four-part method of discretion.
XXIII. On how the words of the teacher are proportionate to the worthiness of the hearers.

I. When I, along with the holy Abba Germanus (with whom I was so closely befriended from the very time of our basic training and the beginnings of our spiritual soldiery, both in the cenobium and in the desert, that everyone used to say, by way of pointing out the identity of our companionship and our chosen orientation, that we were one mind and soul inhabiting two bodies), was looking in the desert of Skete, where the most experienced fathers of the monks and every perfection dwelled, for Abba Moses, who in the midst of those splendid flowers gave off a particularly sweet odor because of both his practical and his contemplative virtue, and, as together we were tearfully begging for an edifying word from that abba, since we were eager to be thoroughly instructed by him, he finally began to speak, worn out by our pleading. (In fact we had been quite aware of his inflexible attitude, such that he would never consent to open the portal of perfection except to those who faithfully desired it and who sought it in utter contrition of heart. Otherwise, if he disclosed it without further ado to those who were unwilling or to those whose desire was not a consuming one, he would seem to be committing either the vice of boasting or the crime of betrayal by pandering important things, which should only be known to those seeking perfection, to the unworthy and to those who would receive them disdainfully.)

II.1. "All the arts and disciplines," he said, "have a certain scopos or goal, and a telos, which is the end that is proper to them, on which the lover of any art sets his gaze and for which he calmly and gladly endures every labor and danger and expense. For the farmer, avoiding neither the torrid rays of the sun one time nor the frost and ice another, tirelessly tills the soil and subdues the unyielding clumps of earth with his frequent plowing, and all the while he keeps his scopos in mind: that, once it has been cleared of all the briers and every weed has been uprooted, by his hard work he may break the soil into something as fine as sand. In no other way does he believe that he will achieve his end, which is to have a rich harvest and an abundant crop, with which he may thenceforth both live his life in security and increase his substance. 2. Laboring in dedicated fashion, he even willingly removes produce from his well-stocked barns and puts it in crumbling ditches, not thinking of present diminution when he reflects on the future harvest. Likewise, those who are accustomed to engage in commerce do not fear the uncertain behavior of the sea, nor are they afraid of any risks, since they are spurred on by winged hope to the end of profit. Neither are those who are inflamed by worldly military ambition, seeking as they do the end of honors and power, conscious of calamities and the dangers of their long treks, nor are they crushed by present fatigue and wars, since they wish to attain the end of high rank that they have set for themselves.

3. "Our profession also has a scopos proper to itself and its own end, on behalf of which we tirelessly and even gladly expend all our efforts. For its sake the hunger of fasting does not weary us, the exhaustion of keeping vigil delights us, and the continual reading of and meditating on Scripture does not sate us. Even the unceasing labor, the being stripped and deprived of everything and, too, the horror of this vast solitude do not deter us. Without doubt it is for its sake that you yourselves have spurned the affection of relatives, despised your homeland and the delights of the world and have journeyed through so many foreign parts in order to come to us, men rude and unlearned, living harshly in the desert. Tell me, therefore," he asked, "what is your goal and what is your end, which drives you to endure all these things so willingly?"

III. And when he insisted on having our answer to this question, we replied that we bore all these things for the sake of the kingdom of heaven.

IV.1. On hearing this he said: "Good! You have spoken well about your end. But before anything else you should know what ought to be our scopos or our goal, by constantly clinging to which we may be able to attain our end." And when we had in all simplicity confessed our ignorance, he added: "As I have said, in every art and discipline a certain scopos takes precedence. This is the soul's goal and the mind's constant intention, which cannot be maintained nor the final end of the longed-for fruit arrived at except by an encompassing diligence and perseverance. 2. For, as I have said, the farmer who has as his end a secure and comfortable life, thanks to his fruitful lands, pursues his scopos or goal by clearing his field of all the briers and emptying it of every unfruitful weed, and he does not believe that he will achieve his end of peaceful affluence in any other way than as it were by first possessing by toil and hope what he desires to have the actual use of. Neither does the businessman lay aside his desire of procuring merchandise, by which he may more easily get rich, since he would long for money in vain if he did not choose the means that would get him to it. And those who want to be honored with any of this world's honors first decide on what office or position they should devote themselves to, so that within the normal course of events they may also be able to attain the final end of the sought-after dignity. 3. Hence, too, the end of our course is the kingdom of God. But we should inquire carefully into the nature of our goal. If we have not in similar fashion grasped this we shall be wearied fruitlessly by our toil, because if the road is uncharted, then those who undertake the hardships of the journey will have nothing to show for it."

As we listened to this in amazement, the old man continued: "The end of our profession, as we have said, is the kingdom of God or the kingdom of heaven; but the goal or scopos is purity of heart, without which it is impossible for anyone to reach that end. 4. Fixing our gaze on this goal, then, as on a definite mark, we shall take the most direct route. If our attention should wander somewhat from it we shall at once return to its contemplation, accurately correcting ourselves as if by a kind of rule that will always measure all our efforts and recall them to this one mark, if our mind should have deviated ever so slightly from the proposed direction.

V.1. "It is like those who are accustomed to handling weapons of war: When they want to show off their expertise in this art before a king of this world, they strive to aim their javelins or arrows at some very small targets that have the prizes pictured on them. They are certain that other than by the targeted mark they cannot arrive at the end, the sought-after prize, which they will possess as soon as they have been able to hit the goal that was set. If perchance it has been removed from their sight, however off-course the vain thrust of the unskilled might be, still they will not think that they have departed from the direction that was set because they have no sure gauge that would show either how accurate the aim was or how bad it was. And, therefore, when they have poured their missiles ineffectually into the airy void, they are unable to judge where they have gone wrong and where they have been led astray, for there is no indication to show them how far they wandered from the direction, nor can an uncertain eye teach them how they must correct or change their aim.

2. "Thus, indeed, the end of our chosen orientation is eternal life, according to the very words of the Apostle: 'Having your reward, indeed, in holiness, but your end in eternal life.'[1] But the scopos is purity of heart, which has not undeservedly been called holiness. Without this the aforesaid end will not be able to be seized. It is as if he had said in other words: Having your scopos, indeed, in purity of heart, but your end in eternal life. When he was teaching us about our immediate goal the same blessed Apostle significantly used the very term 'scopos' when he said: 'Forgetting what is behind, but reaching out to what is ahead, I press on to the goal, to the prize of the heavenly calling of the Lord.'[2] 3. This appears more clearly in Greek: κατα σκπον διωκω, which means: I press on to the goal. It is just as if he had said: By way of this goal I forget what is behind–namely, the vices of my earlier life–and I strive to attain to the end, which is the heavenly prize. Whatever therefore can direct us to this scopos, which is purity of heart, is to be pursued with all our strength, but whatever deters us from this is to be avoided as dangerous and harmful. For it is for its sake that we do and endure everything, for its sake that family, homeland, honors, wealth, the pleasures of this world, and every enjoyment are disdained–so that perpetual purity of heart may be kept. 4. With this goal always set before us, therefore, our actions and thoughts are ordered to attaining it in the most direct way. If it is not constantly fixed before our eyes, not only will all our labors be rendered equally useless and shaky and be made vain and profitless, but all sorts of confusing thoughts will be aroused as well. It is inevitable that the mind which does not have a place to turn to or any stable base will undergo change from hour to hour and from minute to minute due to the variety of its distractions, and by the things that come to it from outside it will be continually transformed into whatever occurs to it at any given moment.

VI.1. "This is why we see some people who disdain very great riches in this world–and not only large sums of gold and silver but also magnificent properties–being disturbed over a penknife, a stylus, a needle, or a pen. If they paid close attention to their purity of heart they would never allow this to happen with respect to small things, since lest this happen to them with respect to great and precious things they chose to give those up completely. 2. And often some people hold on to a book so tightly that in fact they do not easily permit another person to read or touch it, and hence they bring upon themselves occasions of impatience and death precisely when they are being urged to acquire the rewards of patience and love. And when they have given away all their wealth for the sake of Christ's love, but still retain the heart's old affection for the littlest things and are always quickly irritated because of them, they become in every respect fruitless and barren, like those who do not have the love of which the Apostle speaks. Foreseeing this in the Spirit, the blessed Apostle said: 'If I gave all my goods to feed the poor and handed my body over to be burned, but I did not have love, it would profit me nothing.'[3] 3. Hence it is clearly proved that perfection is not immediately arrived at by being stripped and deprived of all one's wealth or by giving up one's honors, unless there is that love whose elements the Apostle describes, which consists in purity of heart alone. For what else does it mean not to be envious, not to be boastful, not to be angry, not to do evil, not to seek the things that are one's own, not to rejoice over iniquity, not to think evil and all the rest,[4] if not always to offer God a perfect and utterly clean heart and to keep it unsullied by any passion?

VII.1. "For the sake of this, then, everything is to be done and desired. For its sake solitude is to be pursued; for its sake we know that we must undertake fasts, vigils, labors, bodily deprivation, readings, and other virtuous things, so that by them we may be able to acquire and keep a heart untouched by any harmful passion, and so that by taking these steps we may be able to ascend to the perfection of love.

"These observances do not exist for themselves. If perchance we are unable to carry out some strict obligation of ours because we are prevented by some good and necessary business, we should not fall into sadness or anger or indignation, which we would have intended to drive out by doing what we omitted. 2. For what is gained by fasting is less than what is spent on anger, and the fruit that is obtained from reading is not so great as the loss that is incurred by contempt for one's brother. It behooves us, then, to carry out the things that are secondary–namely, fasts, vigils, the solitary life, and meditation on Scripture–for the sake of the principal scopos, which is purity of heart or love, rather than for their sake to neglect this principal virtue which, as long as it remains integral and intact, will prevent anything bad from happening to us whenever one of the things that are secondary has to be omitted out of necessity. For it will be of no use to have fulfilled everything if this primary object, for the sake of attaining which all things are to be pursued, has been lost. 3. It is for this reason that a person hastens to acquire for himself and to assemble the implements of a given art–not so that he may possess them without using them, nor so that he may consider the enjoyment that he hopes for from them to consist in the mere possession of those tools, but so that by making use of them he may effectively master and lay hold of the end of that discipline, for which these are helps. Thus fasts, vigils, meditating on Scripture, and the being stripped and deprived of every possession are not perfection, but they are the tools of perfection. For the end of that discipline does not consist in these things; rather, it is by them that one arrives at the end. 4. In vain, therefore, will a person undertake these exercises who is satisfied with them as if they were the highest good and who fixes his heart's attention only on them and not on attaining the end, on account of which these other things are to be sought, and who makes every effort for the sake of virtue but, while indeed possessing the tools of the discipline, is ignorant of the end, in which all that is profitable is to be found. Whatever may disturb the purity and tranquillity of our mind, then, however useful and necessary it may appear, must be avoided as harmful. For in following this rule we shall be able both to avoid the byways of errors and distractions and, thanks to a clear direction, to arrive at the desired end.

VIII.1. "This should be our principal effort, then; this should be constantly pursued as the fixed goal of our heart, so that our mind may always be attached to divine things and to God. Whatever is different from this, however great it may be, is nevertheless to be judged as secondary or even as base, and indeed as harmful.

"Martha and Mary are very beautifully portrayed in the Gospel as examples of this attitude and manner of behavior. For although Martha was indeed devoting herself to a holy service, ministering as she was to the Lord himself and to his disciples, while Mary was intent only on spiritual teaching and was clinging to Jesus' feet, which she was kissing and anointing with the ointment of a good confession, yet it was she whom the Lord preferred, because she chose the better part, and one which could not be taken from her. 2. For as Martha was toiling with devout concern and was distracted with her work, she saw that she could not accomplish so large a task by herself, and she asked the Lord for her sister's help: 'Does it not concern you that my sister has left me to serve by myself? Tell her to help me, then.'[5] She was calling her not to a disreputable task, to be sure, but to a praiseworthy service. Yet what did she hear from the Lord? 'Martha, Martha, you are concerned and troubled about many things, but few things are necessary, or even one. Mary has chosen the good part, which shall not be taken away from her.'[6]

"You see, then, that the Lord considered the chief good to reside in theoria alone–that is, in divine contemplation. 3. Hence we take the view that the other virtues, although we consider them necessary and useful and good, are to be accounted secondary because they are all practiced for the purpose of obtaining this one thing. For when the Lord said: 'You are concerned and troubled about many things, but few things are necessary, or even one,' he placed the highest good not in carrying out some work, however praiseworthy, but in the truly simple and unified contemplation of him, declaring that 'few things' are necessary for perfect blessedness–namely, that theoria which is first established by reflecting on a few holy persons. Ascending from the contemplation of these persons, someone who is still advancing will arrive with his help at that which is also called 'one'–namely, the vision of God alone, so that, when he has gone beyond even the acts of holy persons and their wonderful works, he may be fed on the beauty and knowledge of God alone. 4. So it is that 'Mary has chosen the good part, which shall not be taken from her.' This too should be looked at more closely. For when he says: 'Mary has chosen the good part,' although he says nothing about Martha and certainly does not seem to reprimand her, nonetheless in praising the former he asserts that the latter occupies a lower position. Again, when he says: 'Which shall not be taken from her,' he indicates that the latter's position could be taken from her (for a person cannot uninterruptedly practice a ministry in the body), but he teaches that the zeal of the former can surely not come to an end in any age."

IX. At this we were greatly stirred. "What then?" we said. "Will the burden of fasting, diligence in reading, and the works of mercy, righteousness, piety, and hospitality be taken from us and not remain with their practitioners, especially since the Lord himself promises the reward of the kingdom of heaven for those works when he says: 'Come, blessed of my Father, take possession of the kingdom prepared for you from the foundation of the world. For I was hungry and you gave me to eat, I was thirsty and you gave me to drink,'[7] and so forth? How is it, then, that these things, which lead their doers into the kingdom of heaven, will be taken away?"

X.1. MOSES: "I did not say that the reward of the good work would be taken away. As the Lord himself says: 'Whoever has given to one of these least only a cup of cold water to drink in the name of a disciple, amen I say to you, he shall not lose his reward.'[8] But I am saying that the action, which either bodily necessity or a requirement of the flesh or the inequity of this world calls for, will be taken away. For diligence in reading and the affliction of fasting are exercised for the sake of cleansing the heart and chastising the flesh only in the present, as long as 'the desire of the flesh is against the spirit.'[9] We see that sometimes even now these things are taken away from those who are worn out by great labors or sickness or old age, and we see that a person cannot constantly exercise them. 2. All the more so, then, will these things cease in the future, when 'this which is corruptible will put on incorruptibility'[10] and this body, which is now animal, will rise spiritual,[11] and the flesh will begin no longer to desire against the spirit. The blessed Apostle speaks clearly about this too when he says: 'Bodily discipline is beneficial for a few things, but piety'—which is undoubtedly to be understood as love—'is beneficial in all respects, since it holds the promise of the life that now is and of the one that is to come.'[12] That this is said to be beneficial for a few things is a clear indication that it can neither be continually exercised nor of itself confer the highest perfection on our efforts. 3. The term 'a few things' can in fact refer to either thing. It can refer to the shortness of the time, because bodily discipline cannot coexist with a person both in the present and in the future, and certainly also to the small benefit that is gained by bodily discipline, for bodily affliction produces some initial progress but not the perfection of love itself, which holds the promise of the present life and of the one that is to come. And therefore we consider the exercise of the aforesaid works to be necessary, because without them the heights of love could not be scaled.

4. "The things that you refer to as works of piety and mercy are necessary in this age, as long as inequity continues to dominate. Their practice would not be called for even here were there not an overwhelming number of poor, needy, and sick people, which is the result of the wickedness of men who have seized for their own use—but not used—those things that were bestowed upon all by the Creator of all. 5. As long as such inequity is rampant in this world, then, this behavior will be necessary and beneficial to the one who practices it, crowning a good disposition and a pious will with the reward of an eternal legacy. But this will cease in the world to come, where equity will rule and when there will no longer exist the inequity that made these things obligatory. Then everyone will pass over from this multiform or practical activity to the contemplation of divine things in perpetual purity of heart. Those whose concern it is to press on to knowledge and to the purification of their minds have chosen, even while living in the present world, to give themselves to this objective with all their power and strength. While they are still dwelling in corruptible flesh they set themselves this charge, in which they will abide once corruption has been laid aside, when they come to that promise of the Lord, the Savior, which says: 'Blessed are the pure of heart, for they shall see God.'[13]

XI.1. "And why should you be surprised if those duties that were previously mentioned will pass away, when the holy Apostle can describe the still more sublime charisms of the Holy Spirit as transitory but indicates that love alone will abide without end? 'Whether there are prophecies,' he says, 'they shall come to naught; or tongues, they shall cease; or knowledge, it shall be destroyed.'[14] But of this he says: 'Love never disappears.'[15] 2. For all the gifts that are given for use and necessity are temporal and they will certainly pass on as soon as the present age has been consummated, but love will never be taken away. For not only in the present world does it operate effectively in us but also in the one to come it will, once the burden of fleshly necessity has been laid down, abide and be still more effective and excellent; it will never be corrupted by any defect but will cling to God more ardently and intently because of its perpetual incorruption."

XII. GERMANUS: "Who then, enclosed in perishable flesh, can be so fixed upon this theoria that he never thinks of the arrival of a brother, or of visiting the sick, of the work of his hands or at least of showing hospitality to travellers and visitors? And who, finally, is not troubled by care and concern for the body itself? We also want to learn to what degree the mind is able to cling to the invisible and incomprehensible God."

XIII.1. MOSES: "To cling to God unceasingly and to remain inseparably united to him in contemplation is indeed, as you say, impossible for the person who is enclosed in perishable flesh. But we ought to know where we should fix our mind's attention and to what goal we should always recall our soul's gaze. And when our mind has been able to seize it, it should rejoice, and when it is distracted from it, it should mourn and sigh, realizing that it has fallen away from the highest good when it notices that it is separated from that gaze, and it should judge as fornication even a moment's separation from the contemplation of Christ. 2. When we have lost sight of him even briefly, let us turn our mind's regard back to him, directing the eyes of our heart as by a very straight line. For everything lies in the soul's inner sanctuary. There, after the devil has been expelled and the vices no longer reign at all, the kingdom of God can be established in us, as the evangelist says: 'The kingdom of God will not come with observation, nor will they say: Here it is, or there it is. For amen I say to you that the kingdom of God is within you.'[16] But within us there can be nothing else than knowledge or ignorance of the truth, and the love of either the vices or the virtues, by which we make ready a kingdom in our hearts either for the devil or for Christ. 3. The Apostle also describes the characteristics of this kingdom when he says: 'For the kingdom of God is not food and drink, but righteousness and peace and joy in the Holy Spirit.'[17] Thus, if the kingdom of God is within us, and the kingdom of God is itself righteousness and peace and joy, then whoever abides in these things is undoubtedly in the kingdom of God. And on the contrary, those who are involved in unrighteousness and discord and the sadness that produces death are dwelling in the kingdom of the devil and in hell and death. These are the signs that distinguish the kingdom of God and that of the devil. And in fact, if we look with the elevated gaze of our mind at the condition wherein the heavenly and supernal virtues that are truly in the kingdom of God make their home, what else should it be thought to be than perpetual and continual joy? 4. For what belongs so much to true blessedness and so befits it as continual tranquillity and everlasting joy?

"And that you may be more certain that what we are saying here is really the case and not based on my own opinion but on the authority of the Lord himself, listen to him describing in the clearest fashion the characteristics and condition of that world: 'Behold,' he says, 'I am creating new heavens and a new earth, and there shall be no remembrance of the former things, nor shall they come to mind. But you shall rejoice and be glad forever in the things that I am creating.'[18] And again: 'Joy and gladness shall be found in it, thanksgiving and the sound of praise. And there shall be month upon month and sabbath upon sabbath.'[19] And again: 'They shall receive joy and gladness; sorrow and groaning shall flee away.'[20] 5. And if you want to have a still clearer idea of that life and of the city of the holy ones, listen to the words that are directed to Jerusalem itself by the voice of the Lord: 'I will make,' he says, 'your visitation peace and your overseers righteousness. Iniquity shall no longer be heard in your land, nor desolation and destruction in your borders. And salvation shall possess your walls and praise your gates. No longer shall there be a sun to enlighten the day for you, nor shall the brightness of the moon shed its light upon you, but the Lord shall be an everlasting light for you, and your God shall be your glory. Your sun shall no longer set, and your moon shall no longer be diminished, but the Lord shall be an everlasting light, and the days of your mourning shall be ended.'[21] 6. And hence the blessed Apostle does not declare in a general or vague way that any joy whatsoever is the kingdom of God, but pointedly and precisely that only what is in the Holy Spirit is such. For he knew that there was another joy which is reprehensible, about which it is said: 'The world will rejoice.'[22] And: 'Woe to you who laugh, because you will weep.'[23] For the kingdom of heaven is to be understood in a threefold manner–either as the heavens that are to reign, that is, as the holy ones with respect to others who have been placed under them, according to the words: 'You be over five cities, and you be over ten,'[24] and according to what is said to the disciples: 'You shall sit upon twelve thrones, judging the twelve tribes of Israel';[25] or as the heavens that will begin to be reigned over by Christ, when God, once all things have been subjected to him, will have begun to be 'all in all';[26] or as the holy ones who are to reign in heaven with the Lord.

XIV.1. "For this reason everyone who lives in this body knows that he must be committed to that special task or ministry to which he has given himself in this life as a participant and a laborer, and he ought not to doubt that in that everlasting age he will also be the partner of him whose servant and companion he now wishes to be, according to what the Lord says: 'If anyone serves me, let him follow me, and where I am, there also will my servant be.'[27] For just as the kingdom of the devil is gained by conniving at the vices, so the kingdom of God is possessed in purity of heart and spiritual knowledge by practicing the virtues. 2. And where the kingdom of God is, there without a doubt is eternal life, and where the kingdom of the devil is, there–it is not to be doubted–are death and hell. Whoever is there cannot praise the Lord, as the prophet says: 'The dead will not praise you, Lord, neither will all who go down into hell' (this is doubtless the hell of sin). 'But we,' he says, 'who live'–not to vices or to this world, namely, but to God–'shall praise the Lord, from this time forth and forever. For in death there is no one who is mindful of God. But in hell'—the hell of sin—'who will confess' to the Lord?[28] 3. There is no one. For no one, even if he professed a thousand times that he was a Christian and a monk, confesses God when he sins. No one who does the things that the Lord condemns is mindful of God, nor does he profess in a truthful way that he is the servant of one whose commandments he disdains with reckless obstinacy. The blessed Apostle declares that the widow who gives herself to pleasure is in that death when he says: 'The widow who gives herself to pleasure is dead while she lives.'[29] But there are many who, while living in this body, are dead and are unable to praise God as they lie in hell, and on the other hand there are those who, although dead in the body, bless and praise God in the spirit, in the words of the text: 'Spirits and souls of the righteous, bless the Lord.'[30] And: 'Let every spirit praise the Lord.'[31] 4. "And in the Apocalypse the souls of the slain are said not only to praise God but also to speak directly to him.[32] In the Gospel, too, the Lord speaks quite clearly to the Sadducees: 'Have you not read,' he says, 'what was said by God when he spoke to you: I am the God of Abraham and the God of Isaac and the God of Jacob? He is not the God of the dead but of the living. For all are living to him.'[33] Of them the Apostle also says: 'Therefore God is not ashamed to be called their God, for he has prepared a city for them.'[34]

"Now, that they are not idle and incapable of feeling anything after being separated from this body is demonstrated by the gospel parable which tells of the poor Lazarus and the rich man clothed in purple. One of these is brought to a most blessed place, the repose of Abraham's bosom, while the other is burned up by the unbearable heat of an eternal fire.[35] 5. And if we wish to understand what is said to the thief—'Today you shall be with me in paradise'[36]—what else does this obviously signify than that not only do their former intellectual capacities abide in their souls but also that, even in their changed condition, they enjoy a state of existence which is appropriate to their deserts and actions? For the Lord would never have promised this to him if he knew that his soul, after being separated from his flesh, was going to be deprived of feeling and would be dissolved into nothing. For it was not his flesh but his soul that was to enter paradise with Christ.

6. "To be shunned, and indeed to be detested as utterly horrible, is that most wicked distinction of the heretics who do not believe that Christ could also be in paradise on the very same day that he descended into hell and who separate the words 'Amen I say to you today'[37] from 'you shall be with me in paradise.' Thus this promise is understood not as having been fulfilled immediately after his passage from this life but as to be fulfilled after the event of the resurrection. They do not realize that before the day of his resurrection he said to the Jews, who believed that he, like them, was subject to human limitations and to fleshly weakness: 'No one has gone up into heaven except him who has come down from heaven, the Son of Man who is in heaven.'[38] 7. By this it is clearly demonstrated that the souls of the dead are not only not deprived of their feelings but do not even lack the dispositions of hope, sadness, joy, and fear, and that they have already begun to taste something of what is reserved for them at the general judgment. Nor are they, according to the opinion of some infidels, turned back into nothing after their departure from this place of sojourn, but they live more fully and cling more intently to the praise of God.

8. "But let us leave aside for a little while the testimony of Scripture so that we may say something about the nature of the soul to the extent that our mediocre understanding permits. Is it not the height, should I say, not of foolishness but of insanity, to hold heedlessly to the opinion that that more precious part of the human being–in which, according to the blessed Apostle,[39] the very image and likeness of God consists–loses its feeling once the bodily burden by which it is oppressed in the present world has been laid down? This element, which contains in itself the whole power of reasoning, gives feeling to the dumb and unfeeling matter of the flesh through a participation in itself. For, indeed, the structure of that reasoning power logically implies that the mind, once it is free of the fleshly heaviness that now weights it down, will recover its intellectual faculties for the better and, rather than lose them, will receive them back purer and finer. 9. So much does the blessed Apostle recognize that what we say is true that he even desires to part from this flesh so that by this separation of his he may be the more intimately joined to the Lord. As he says: 'I

desire to be dissolved and to be with Christ, for that is far better, since while we are in the body we are absent from the Lord.'[40] And therefore 'we are bold and have the good wish rather to be absent from the body and to be present to the Lord. For this reason we also strive to please him, whether absent or present.'[41] Thus he declares that the soul's sojourn in this flesh is a removal from the Lord and an absence from Christ, and he believes with absolute confidence that its separation and departure from this flesh is a being present to Christ. 10. The same Apostle speaks still more clearly about this most alive state of these souls when he says: 'You have come to Mount Zion and to the city of the living God, the heavenly Jerusalem, and to the multitude of many thousands of angels, and the church of the firstborn who are inscribed in heaven, and the spirits of the righteous made perfect.'[42] About these spirits he says somewhere else: 'We have had the fathers of our flesh as our instructors, and we reverenced them. Shall we not all the more subject ourselves to the Father of spirits and live?'[43]

XV.1. "But the contemplation of God is arrived at in numerous ways. For God is not known only through wondering at his incomprehensible substance, because that is still concealed in the hope of the promise, but he is also clearly perceived in the grandeur of the things that he has created, in reflecting upon his justice and in the assistance provided by his daily providence—namely, when we consider with most pure minds the things that he has accomplished with his holy ones over the course of generations; when with trembling heart we admire that power of his by which he governs, directs, and rules all things, as well as the vastness of his knowledge and the eye from which the secrets of hearts cannot be hidden; when we think that he knows the sands of the sea and that he has measured the number of the waves; when we contemplate with amazement the raindrops, the days and hours of the ages, how all things past and future are present to his knowledge; 2. when we look with a kind of overwhelming wonder at his ineffable gentleness, by which he tolerates with unwearying patience the numberless crimes committed in his sight at each and every moment, and at the call through which he has received us, thanks to his mercy and not to our own already existing deserts, and finally at the many occasions of salvation that he has bestowed on those who are to be adopted–because he commanded that we should be born in such a way that grace and the knowledge of his law might be given us from our very cradles, and because he himself, conquering the adversary in us, bestows on us eternal blessedness and everlasting rewards for the sole pleasure of his good will; and when, lastly, he accepted the dispensation of his incarnation for our salvation and extended the marvels of his mysteries to all peoples. 3. There are also other innumerable things of this sort to contemplate, which come to our minds (where God is seen and grasped by a pure vision) in accordance with the character of our life and the purity of our heart. Certainly no one in whom there still dwells something of carnal desire will lay hold of these things eternally, because, as the Lord says: 'You shall not be able to see my face, for no one shall see me and live'[44]–namely, to this world and to earthly desires."

XVI. GERMANUS: "Why is it, then, that superfluous thoughts insinuate themselves into us so subtly and hiddenly when we do not even want them, and indeed do not even know of them, that it is very difficult not only to cast them out but even to understand them and to catch hold of them? Can the mind, then, sometimes be found free of these, and is it ever able to avoid being invaded by illusions of this sort?"

XVII.1. MOSES: "It is, indeed, impossible for the mind not to be troubled by thoughts, but accepting them or rejecting them is possible for everyone who makes an effort. It is true that their origin does not in every respect depend on us, but it is equally true that their refusal or acceptance does depend on us. By saying that it is impossible for the mind not to be attacked by thoughts, however, we do not mean that all of this must be attributed to an invasion and to those spirits which try to impose them on us. Otherwise there would be no free will in a person, nor would the effort expended in our own correction be of any help to us. 2. But it is, I say, largely up to us whether the character of our thoughts improves and whether either holy and spiritual thoughts or earthly and carnal ones increase in our hearts. Therefore we practice the frequent reading of and constant meditation on Scripture, so that we may be open to a spiritual point of view. For this reason we frequently chant the psalms, so that we may continually grow in compunction. For this reason we are diligent in vigils, fasting, and praying, so that the mind which has been stretched to its limits may not taste earthly things but contemplate heavenly ones. When these things cease because negligence has crept in again, then, it is inevitable that the mind, by the accumulated filth of the vices, will soon turn in a carnal direction and fall.

XVIII.1. "This activity of the heart is not inappropriately compared to millstones, which the swift rush of the waters turns with a violent revolving motion. As long as the waters' force keeps them spinning they are utterly incapable of stopping their work, but it is in the power of the one who supervises to decide whether to grind wheat or barley or darnel. Indeed, only that will be ground which has been accepted by the person entrusted with the responsibility for the work.

2. "In the same way the mind cannot be free from agitating thoughts during the trials of the present life, since it is spinning around in the torrents of the trials that overwhelm it from all sides. But whether these will be either refused or admitted into itself will be the result of its own zeal and diligence. For if, as we have said, we constantly return to meditating on Holy Scripture and raise our awareness to the recollection of spiritual realities and to the desire for perfection and the hope of future blessedness, it is inevitable that the spiritual thoughts which have arisen from this will cause the mind to dwell on the things that we have been meditating on. 3. But if we are overcome by laziness and negligence and let ourselves be taken up with wicked behavior and silly conversations, or if we get involved in worldly concerns and unnecessary preoccupations, the result will be as if a kind of weed had sprung up, which will impose harmful labor on our heart. And, according to the words of the Lord, the Savior, wherever the treasure of our works and intentions is, there also will necessarily abide our heart.[45]

XIX.1. "Above all we should know what the three sources of our thoughts are: They come from God, from the devil, and from ourselves. They are from God when he deigns to visit us by the illumination of the Holy Spirit, which raises us up to a higher level of progress; and when we have made little gain or have acted lazily and been overcome and he chastens us with a most salutary compunction; and when he opens to us the heavenly sacraments and changes our chosen orientation to better acts and to a better will. This was the case when King Ahasuerus was chastised by the Lord and was moved to examine the annals, whereupon he remembered the good deeds of Mordechai, exalted him to the highest degree of honor, and immediately recalled his exceedingly cruel sentence concerning the killing of the Jewish people.[46] 2. Or when the prophet mentions: 'I will hear what the Lord God has to say in me.'[47] There is another one, too, who says: 'An angel said, who was speaking in me.'[48] Or when the Son of God promises that he will come, together with the Father, and that they will make their dwelling in us.[49] And: 'It is not you who speak but the Spirit of your Father who speaks in you.'[50] And the vessel of election[51] says: 'You seek a proof of Christ, of him who speaks in me.'[52]

3. "And from the devil a whole series of thoughts is born, when he attempts to subvert us both by delight in wickedness and by hidden snares, fraudulently passing off evil things for good with the most subtle finesse and transforming himself for us into an angel of light.[53] Or when the evangelist says: 'When supper was finished and the devil had already put it in the heart of Judas Iscariot, son of Simon, to betray the Lord.'[54] And again he says: 'After the morsel Satan entered into him.'[55] Peter also says to Ananias: 'Why has Satan tempted your heart, to lie to the Holy Spirit?'[56] And what we read in the Gospel that was predicted long before in Ecclesiastes: 'If the spirit of a ruler should rise up against you, do not leave your place.'[57] 4. Also what is said to God against Ahab in the Third Book of Kings in the person of an unclean spirit: 'I will go out and I will be a lying spirit in the mouth of all his prophets.'[58]

"They also come from us, however, when we spontaneously remember things that we are doing or have done or have heard. Concerning such things the blessed David says: 'I thought of ancient days, and I kept the eternal years in mind, and I meditated. At night I was exercised in my heart, and I examined my spirit.'[59] And again: 'The Lord knows that the thoughts of men are vain.'[60] And: 'The thoughts of the righteous are judgments.'[61] Also in the Gospel the Lord says to the Pharisees: 'Why do you think evil in your hearts?'[62]

XX.1. "We should, then, be continually aware of this threefold distinction and with a wise discretion examine all the thoughts that emerge in our heart, first tracing their origins and causes and their authors, so that, in accordance with the status of whoever is suggesting them, we may be able to consider how we should approach them. Then we shall become, in keeping with the precept of the Lord, approved money-changers.[63] The very high skill and training of such persons exists for the sake of determining whether something is gold of the purest sort—what is popularly called *obrizum*—or whether it has been less purified by fire. It also exists for the sake of not being deceived by a common brass denarius if it is being passed off as a precious coin under the guise of shining gold; this is assured by a very careful examination. These people not only shrewdly recognize coins displaying the heads of usurpers but also discern with a still finer skill those which are stamped with the image of the true king but are counterfeits. Finally, they submit them to careful weighing in case they are lighter than they should be.

2. "All of these things we ourselves have to carry out in a spiritual manner, as this gospel saying demonstrates. First, we should carefully scrutinize whatever enters our hearts, especially if it is a doctrine to which we have been exposed, to see if it has been purified by the divine and heavenly fire of the Holy Spirit or if it is a part of Jewish superstition or if, coming from the pridefulness of worldly philosophy, it has the mere look of piety to it. We shall be able to accomplish this if we fulfill what the Apostle says: 'Do not believe every spirit, but test the spirits to see if they are from God.'[64] 3. This is how some have been deceived who, after their monastic profession, have been seduced by elegant words and by certain teachings of the philosophers which, at first hearing, attracted them superficially at a given moment. These teachings fooled the hearers, much like shining gold, because of a few pious sentiments not inconsistent with religion. But since they were, so to say, counterfeit brass coins, they impoverished those who had been taken in and made them miserable forever, either by reintroducing them into the tumult of the world or by drag-

ging them into heretical errors and bloated presumptions. We read in the Book of Joshua son of Nun that this also happened to Achan: He coveted a gold bar from the camp of the Philistines and stole it, and thus he deserved to be placed under sentence and condemned to eternal death.[65]

4. "Secondly, we should look closely to see that no wicked interpretation fastened on to the pure gold of Scripture deceives us by the precious appearance of its metal. This was how the crafty devil attempted to deceive even the Lord, the Savior, as if he were a mere man: He tried to make an adaptation, corrupting with a wicked interpretation things that should generally be understood as applying only to the righteous and particularly to him who did not need the protection of angels, when he said: 'For he will command his angels concerning you, that they may guard you in all your ways, and in their hands they will carry you, lest perchance you strike your foot against a stone.'[66] Thus he changed the precious words of Scripture by his clever use of them and gave them a contrary and harmful meaning, like someone who presents us with the image of a usurper's face under the guise of deceptive gold. He also tries to lead us astray with counterfeits by exhorting us to pursue a certain pious work which, since it is not the legitimate coinage of the elders, leads to vice under the appearance of virtue and brings us to a bad end by deceiving us either with immoderate and inappropriate fasting or severe vigils or inordinate praying or excessive reading. 5. He also persuades us to give ourselves to acts of meditation and to pious visitations, by which he would pry us away from the spiritual ramparts of the monastery and from our retreat of cherished calm, even suggesting that we worry and be concerned about nuns and destitute women, by snares of this sort inextricably entangling the entrapped monk with baleful preoccupations. And, indeed, he inveigles us into desiring the holy clerical office under the pretext of edifying many and for the love of spiritual gain, thus tearing us away from the humility and severity of our present chosen orientation.

6. "Although all these things are contrary to our salvation and to our profession, they nonetheless easily deceive the unskilled and the unwary since they are covered by a kind of veil of mercy and religion. For they imitate the coins of the true king

because they appear very pious at first sight, but they have not been stamped by lawful minters—that is to say, by the approved and Catholic fathers—nor do they come from the central and public workshop of their conferences, but they are clandestinely fabricated by the fraud of demons and, to their detriment, are offered to the unskilled and the ignorant. Although they might seem good and necessary at first sight, yet if afterwards they begin to have a negative effect on the solidity of our profession and in some way weaken the whole body of our chosen orientation, they are rightly cut off and cast away from us just like anything that is necessary and seems to perform the office of a right hand or a foot but that causes scandal. 7. For it is preferable to be without the member of one commandment—that is, without one work and its fruit—and to be healthy and solid in the other members and to enter the kingdom of heaven crippled, than with all the commandments to trip against some stumbling block that through pernicious habit would separate us from our habitual rigor and from the discipline of the orientation that we have chosen and embraced. This would bring such a great loss upon us that we would never be able to compensate for future setbacks, and all our past achievements and the whole body of our activity would be burned up in the fires of Gehenna.[67] 8. Proverbs also speaks well about these kinds of deceptions: 'There are paths that seem to be right to a man, but they arrive finally at the depths of hell.'[68] And again: 'An evil person does harm when he involves himself with a righteous one.'[69] That is to say, the devil is deceptive when he veils himself in the appearance of holiness. 'But he hates the sound of the watchman'[70]—namely, the power of discretion that comes from the words and the advice of the elders.

XXI.1. "We have heard how even the Abba John, who used to live at Lycon, was recently deceived in this way. For when he had put off eating because of a two-day fast and his body was worn out and enfeebled, the devil approached him in the form of a black Ethiopian on the following day, just as he was about to eat. Embracing his knees he said: 'Pardon me, for it was I who inflicted this labor on you.' Then that man, so great and perfect in the ordering of his discretion, understood that in having exercised an exaggerated abstinence he had been duped by the devil's cleverness and been so preoccupied with his fasting that he had considered unnecessary weariness, which would in fact be spiritually harmful, more important than his exhausted body. He was deceived by a counterfeit coin, and while he was venerating the image of the true king on it he was too little aware of whether it was lawfully minted.

2. "The final thing to be observed by this approved moneychanger, which we said had to do with examining and weighing, will be accomplished if we reflect meticulously on whatever our thoughts suggest that we should do. This we must place in the scale of our heart and weigh with the most delicate balance to see whether it has the proper weight of common goodness, and whether it is sufficiently heavy with the fear of God and integral in meaning, or whether it is too light because of human ostentation or some novel presumption, or whether the pride of empty vainglory has diminished or eroded the weight of its worth. Hence, let us bring it out immediately in public to weigh by having recourse to the deeds and testimonies of the prophets and apostles, and let us hold on to the things that balance with them as being integral and perfect and very cautiously and carefully reject, as being imperfect and condemnable, whatever does not weigh conformably with them.

XXII.1. "This discretion, then, will be necessary for us in the fourfold manner of which I have spoken—that is, in the first place, so that the material itself, whether real gold or false, may not be concealed from us; secondly, so that we may reject thoughts that lie about works of piety as being adulterated and counterfeit coins since they are not lawfully minted and have a false image of the king; then, so that with similar discernment we may be able to turn down those which, because of an evil and heretical interpretation, portray in the precious gold of Scripture the face not of the true king but of a usurper; and finally, so that we may refuse as too light and condemnable and insufficiently heavy those coins whose weight and value have been eaten away by the rust of vanity, which does not let them balance out in the scale of the elders. Otherwise we shall stumble into what we are warned by the Lord's commandment to be on the watch for with all our strength, and we shall be defrauded of all the deserts and rewards of our labors:

'Do not store up for yourselves treasures on earth, where rust and moth destroy and where thieves break in and steal.'[71] 2. For whatever we have done with a view to human glory we know that we have stored up for ourselves as a treasure on earth, according to the Lord's words, and that consequently, having been as it were hidden in the soil and buried in the earth, it will be ravaged by different demons and consumed by the devouring rust of vainglory and so eaten up by the moths of pride that it will be of no use or profit to the person who hid it.

"All the secret places of our heart, therefore, must be constantly scrutinized and the prints of whatever enters them must be investigated in the most careful way, lest perchance some spiritual beast, a lion or a dragon, pass through and secretly leave its dangerous traces; then, once our thoughts were neglected, access to the sanctuary of our heart would be offered to still others. Thus at every moment we should cultivate the earth of our heart with the gospel plow—that is, with the continual remembering of the Lord's cross—and we shall be able to root out from ourselves the nests of harmful animals and the hiding places of venomous serpents."

XXIII.1. As we listened in stupefaction to these things and were inflamed with an insatiable love by what he was saying, the old man looked at us and, having stopped speaking for a short while out of amazement at our desire, finally added: "My sons, your zeal has provoked us to a long discourse and, in proportion to your desire, a kind of fire is producing a warmer reception of our conference. From this very fact I can see that you are truly thirsty for the teaching of perfection, and I want to tell you a little more about the sublimity and grace of discretion, which among all the virtues holds the supreme and first place, and to demonstrate its excellence and usefulness not only from daily examples but also from the ancient reflections and sayings of the fathers. 2. For I often recall that, when people would ask me with groaning and tears for a word of this sort, I was desirous of giving them some teaching myself but was completely unable to. Not only my mind but even my tongue failed so utterly that I did not see how I could give them even the smallest word of consolation to take home with them. From such signs it is evident that it is the Lord's grace that inspires a word in the speakers proportionate to the worthiness and desire of the hearers.

"Because the brief period of night that remains is insufficient to expound this word, let us instead give it up to bodily repose and save the narrative in its integrity for some future day or night, since the whole night would be needed if we were not to leave some of it out. 3. For it is fitting that the best counselors on discretion should demonstrate primarily in this respect the seriousness of their own intention and prove whether they are or can be capable of it by the gauge of patience, so that when they treat of that virtue which is the begetter of moderation, they will never incur the vice of excess, which is its contrary, and so violate by deed and action its characteristics and its nature, to which they are paying honor by their words. In this regard, then, may the good of discretion, which we have decided to explore further with the Lord's assistance, be of service to us from the start and not let us exceed the measure of speech and of time when we are discussing its excellence and moderation, which are recognized to be part of it, as the first of the virtues."

4. Putting an end to our conference with these words, then, the blessed Moses encouraged us, as eager as we were and still hanging on to his speech, to try to sleep for a while. He advised us to lie down on the same mats that we were sitting on, and, instead of a pillow, to put under our heads little bundles which are gathered into long slender packets and tied together with heavier papyrus stalks at foot-and-a-half intervals. These sometimes provide the brothers, when they are sitting together at a synaxis, with a very low seat in place of a footstool, and sometimes they are put under the sleepers' necks, where they give a support to the head that is not too hard but yielding and pleasant. For such monastic uses these things are considered very advantageous and convenient, because they are not only somewhat soft and may be put together with little effort and at small expense, but also because they are naturally flexible and light and easy to carry around whenever that is necessary. And thus, following the instructions of the old man, we at last composed ourselves for sleep in the solemn stillness, at once burning with joy as a result of the conference that had been given and excited by the prospect of the discussion that had been promised.

Textual References

1. Rom 6:22.
2. Phil 3:13–14.
3. 1 Cor 13:3.
4. Cf. 1 Cor 13:4–7.
5. Lk 10:40.
6. Lk 10:41–42.
7. Mt 25:34–35.
8. Mt 10:42.
9. Gal 5:17.
10. 1 Cor 15:53.
11. Cf. 1 Cor 15:44.
12. 1 Tm 4:8.
13. Mt 5:8.
14. 1 Cor 13:8b.
15. 1 Cor 13:8a.
16. Lk 17:20–21.
17. Rom 14:17.
18. Is 65:17–18.
19. Is 51:3; 66:23.
20. Is 35:10.
21. Is 60:17–20.
22. Jn 16:20.
23. Lk 6:25.
24. Lk 19:19, 17.
25. Mt 19:28.
26. 1 Cor 15:28.
27. Jn 12:26.
28. Ps 115:17–18; 6:5.
29. 1 Tm 5:6.
30. Dn 3:86.
31. Ps 150:6.
32. Cf. Rv 6:9–10.
33. Mt 22:31–32.
34. Heb 11:16.
35. Cf. Lk 16:19–31.
36. Lk 23:43b.
37. Lk 23:43a.
38. Jn 3:13.

39. Cf. 1 Cor 11:7; Col 3:10.
40. Phil 1:23; 2 Cor 5:6.
41. 2 Cor 5:8–9.
42. Heb 12:22–23.
43. Heb 12:9.
44. Ex 33:20.
45. Cf. Mt 6:21.
46. Cf. Est 6:1–10:3.
47. Ps 85:8.
48. Zec 1:14.
49. Cf. Jn 14:23.
50. Mt 10:20.
51. Cf. Acts 9:15.
52. 2 Cor 13:3.
53. Cf. 2 Cor 11:14.
54. Jn 13:2.
55. Jn 13:27.
56. Acts 5:3.
57. Eccl 10:4.
58. 3 Kgs 22:22.
59. Ps 76:6–7 LXX.
60. Ps 94:11.
61. Prv 12:5.
62. Mt 9:4.
63. Cf. Logion 43, in A. Resch, *Agrapha: Ausserkanonische Evangelienfragmente* (Leipzig, 1889), 116–127.
64. 1 Jn 4:1.
65. Cf. Jos 7.
66. Ps 91:11–12.
67. Cf. Mt 18:8.
68. Prv 16:25 LXX.
69. Prv 11:15a LXX.
70. Prv 11:15b LXX.
71. Mt 6:19.

Notes to the Text

1. The first lines of the present paragraph are full of military imagery—"basic training" *(tirocinium),* "spiritual soldiery" *(militia spiritalis),* and "companionship" (*contubernium,* a word with military connotations). The idea of the spiritual life as a form of soldiery is already suggested in Rom 13:12, 2 Cor 6:7, and esp. Eph 6:11–17. On the use of military imagery in the early Church cf. Adolf Harnack, *Militia Christi: The Christian Religion and the Military in the First Three Centuries,* trans. by David McI. Gracie (Philadelphia, 1981), 27–64; and for the background to such imagery in pagan thought, esp. that of the Stoa, cf. Hilarius Emonds, "Geistlicher Kriegsdienst: Der Topos der militia spiritualis in der antiken Philosophie," in *Heilige Überlieferung: Festgabe Ildefons Herwegen* (Münster, 1938), 21–50. Particularly in the seventh and eighth conferences the demons are seen in terms of military adversaries—as armies engaged in attacks and battles. Cf. also 3.6.4, 4.12.5, 16.1; *Inst.* 1.1.1, 1.11.1, 2.1, 2.3.2, 4.5, 5.19.1, 5.21.1, 7.21, 10.3, 11.3, 11.7. For monks the desert was a chosen battlefield, the place where they were certain to meet the demons and to engage them directly. Secular life, however, could also be referred to in military terms, as appears in 4.21.1—"this world's soldiery" *(militia saeculi).* Cassian unintentionally underrates baptism here by speaking of his monastic novitiate as the beginning of his spiritual soldiery, for baptism was also viewed in military terms in Christian antiquity. Cf. Jerome, *Ep.* 14.2; Chrysostom, *Hom. bapt.* Stav. 1.1, Montfaucon 2.30ff. For explicit references to baptism in *The Conferences* cf. 5.22, 20.8.1, 22.1.30 ("the baptized"), 21.34.1, 21.34.2 (? "the grace of adoption"), 23.15.1f. Cf. also the note at *Inst.* 1.3.

We were one mind and soul: This common way of speaking about friendship has its roots in Aristotle, *Eth. nicomach.* 9.6. Cf. Gregory Nazianzen, *Or.* 43.20; Cyril of Scythopolis, *V. S. Euthymii* 7; idem, *V. S. Sabae* 29; Augustine, *Conf.* 4.6.11. Cassian's and Germanus's friendship is described again in 16.1.

Those splendid flowers: On the desert as a place of luxuriant blossoms cf. *Inst.* 5.4.1f. (where the monk is compared to a bee); Jerome, *Ep.* 14.10; Eucherius, *De laude heremi* 40; John Moschus, *Pratum spirituale,* praef. Cf. also 3 praef. 2. The image almost certainly alludes to the fulfilling of the eschatological promise in Is 35:1–2. Cf. G. J. M. Bartelink, "Les oxymores Desertum civitas et Desertum floribus vernans," in *Studia Monastica* 15 (1973): 13–15.

Moses' sweet odor is consonant with his sanctity. On the fragrance of virtue cf. 9.19, 10.10.9, 17.19.2, 20.19.1, 20.12.14, 24.25.6. On spiritual knowledge as fragrant cf. 14.16.7. For pleasing odors as accompanying a divine visitation cf. 4.5. In general cf. Waldemar Deonna, 'Ευωδια: Croyances antiques et modernes. L'odeur suave des dieux et des élus," in *Genava* 17 (1939): 167–262; Bernhard Kötting, "Wohlgeruch der Heiligkeit," in *Jenseitsvorstellungen in Antike und Christentum: Gedenkschrift für Alfred Stuiber* (JAC, Ergänzungsband 9) (1982): 168–175. On the evil odor of sin cf. the note at 2.11.5.

Moses' fear of disclosing spiritual things to the unworthy lest he be accused of either vanity or betrayal represents a theme that recurs in 14.14 (cf. the note at 14.14.1) and 14.17 (where the spiritual basis for this belief is given). Cf. also 10.9.3 where "betrayal or lightmindedness" is spoken of. The idea is important in both Clement of Alexandria and Origen. For the former cf. *Strom.* 1.1.6, and for the latter cf. Henri Crouzel, *Origène et la connaissance mystique* (Tournai, 1961), 155–166. Evagrius, *Gnost.* 25 (SC 356.129), observes that not everyone is worthy to hear deep truths or even to touch the books in which they are written. Cf. also *Inst* 7.13.

1.2 On the ordering of the different arts and disciplines serving as a model for the ordering of the spiritual life cf. also 14.1.2f.

A comparison between secular pursuits (such as the farming, commerce, and soldiering mentioned here and in 1.4.2) and spiritual ones can be found in the New

Testament in the gospel parables and also in 1 Cor 9:24–27 and Jas 5:7–8. For more farming imagery in particular cf. 13.3.1ff. For farming and commercial imagery in a context identical with Cassian's here cf. Macarius, *Hom. spir.* 14.1.

1.2.1 The terminology for the "scopos or goal" *(scopos* and *destinatio)* and the "telos, which is the end" *(telos* and *finis)* is fairly consistent throughout the present conference, although there is a discrepancy in 1.7.3f., where Cassian apparently refers to purity of heart, which is a goal of the monastic life, as a *finis*. Cf. the notes at 9.2.1 and 19.4.3. Scopos and telos are simply Latin transliterations of Greek words whose history can be traced at least to Plato. Cf. Edouard des Places, *Lexique de la langue philosophique et religieuse de Platon* (Paris, 1964), s.vv. σκοπος and τελος. The distinction between them, as between *destinatio* and *finis*, is somewhat arbitrary. For a study of the term scopos in particular and of its three most important possible meanings in early Christian literature—namely, goal, watchman, and model—cf. Marguerite Harl, "Le guetteur et la cible: Les deux sens de scopos dans la langue religieuse des chrétiens," in *Revue des études grècques* 74 (1961): 450–468.

1.2.3 On spurning the affection of relatives and despising one's homeland here and in 1.5.3 cf. 24.1.2ff. and the relevant note.

1.5.1 The complexity of this passage on shooting at a target is pointed out in Terrence Kardong, "Aiming at the Mark: Cassian's Metaphor for the Monastic Quest," in *Cistercian Studies Quarterly* 22 (1987): 213–220. The author suggests that Cassian may be using the image of clout shooting, in which a circular target (symbolizing the "end" or *finis*) is drawn on the ground, while an upright marker (symbolizing the "goal" or *scopos*) is placed near the center of the target in order to direct the shooter's aim. Clout shooting customarily involves a great distance between the contestant and the target, sometimes as much as 200 yards. For a similar image cf. *Inst.* 5.15.

1.5.4 On the instability of the human mind and the ease with which it is distracted from God cf. also 1.16ff., 4.2ff., 6.13ff., 7.3.3ff., 7.4.2ff., 9.7.1f., 10.8.4ff., 10.13f., 14.11.5ff., 23.5.7ff. On this theme in patristic literature and particularly in Evagrius and Cassian cf. DS 3.1348–1351. The mobility of the mind does not go unnoticed in pagan literature either. Cf. Apuleius, *De deo Socratis* 12.

1.6.1f The ability to give up "everything" by entering monastic life while at the same time maintaining a very possessive attitude toward some small and relatively insignificant object is also remarked in 4.21, 9.6.4, 16.6.1, 16.6.4; *Inst.* 4.15.1. Cf. Jerome, *Tract. de Ps. 119* (CCSL 78.259): "We have abandoned mothers, relatives, brothers, sisters, wives, children, our homelands, our homes, the places where we were born and brought up, and we have entered the monastery. And we have left behind all these things so that on account of something insignificant and frivolous we might get into an argument with our brothers in the monastery! We have abandoned property, our homeland, the world, and we start a fight in the monastery over a pen!" A monk's reluctance to part with a book, however, as mentioned in 1.6.2, is fairly understandable, given the value of books in antiquity.

1.6.3. The identification of the state described in 1 Cor 13:4–5 (not being envious, boastful, etc.) with that of a pure heart, unsullied by passions, is also made in Ps.-Macarius, Coll. 3, *Hom.* 7.4.3 (SC 275.126–128), ibid. 28.3.1ff. (ibid. 336–338).

1.8 The use of Mary as an image of the contemplative and of Martha as an image of the active life originates with Origen, *Frag. in Luc.* 171 (GCS 49.298); idem, *Frag. in Ioann.* 80 (GCS 10.547–548). Cf. also 23.3.1; Augustine, *Serm.* 103f.; Bede, *Exp. in Luc.* 3, *ad* 10:38. For a study of the understanding of "the good part" here and in 23.3.1, which sees Cassian as opposing contemplation and the works of mercy in an unevangelical fashion, cf. D. A. Csányi, "Optima pars: Die Auslegungsgeschichte von Lk

10, 38–42 bei den Kirchenvätern der ersten vier Jahrhunderte," in *Studia Monastica* 2 (1960): 59–64.

1.8.3 Simple and unified contemplation: *Contemplatione...simplex et una*. The one thing necessary *(unum)* is more clearly identified with contemplation by these qualifiers.

1.9f On the disappearance of the works of mercy in the life to come cf. Augustine, *Serm.* 236.3.

1.10.4 Cassian seems to imply here an original state in which material equity among all persons existed but that was later destroyed by the wickedness of some. This view is already suggested in Christian literature toward the end of the second century in Irenaeus, *Adv. haer.* 4.30.1. Almsgiving, referred to here as "works of piety and mercy," was the usual way of redressing the inequity. Cf. Ramsey, "Almsgiving," 255–259.

1.13.1 On mental distractions qualified as fornication cf. also 14.11.5. The image probably derives ultimately from the Old Testament custom of referring to Israel's defections from the Lord in the same way. Cf. esp. Ez 16; Hos 1–2. For similar figurative uses of fornication cf. Augustine, *Conf.* 1.13.21, 2.6.14.

1.13.6 The kingdom of heaven offered numerous possibilities of interpretation in patristic literature, of which Cassian gives three. It is understood as Christ himself in Cyprian, *De orat. dom.* 13; as the Holy Spirit in Gregory of Nyssa, *De orat. dom.* 3; as faithful Christians (which is similar to Cassian's third interpretation) in Augustine, *Serm.* 57.5.5; as contemplation in Evagrius (Ps.-Basil), *Ep.* 8.12; as a life of virtue in Origen, *De orat.* 25.1; and as the end of the present age in Tertullian, *De orat.* 5.

1.14.6 Origen, *Comm. in Ioann.* 32.32.395, and Epiphanius, *Panarion* 42.11, mention the difficulties occasioned by Lk 23:43 (as does, in the eleventh century, Theophylact, *Enarr. in Luc., ad loc.*, PG 123.1104–1105). In *Comm. in Ioann.* 32.32.395 Origen proposes a solution by observing that "today" can refer to the whole present age, and ibid. 10.37.245 he suggests that the resurrection began on the cross, when the promise was made, and was not completed until the third day. On punctuation variations in Scripture, used to support heretical ideas, cf. Augustine, *De doct. christ.* 3.2.3.

1.15 This enumeration of the different forms of contemplation is reminiscent of Basil, *Reg. fus. tract.* 2, in which similar reasons for gratitude to God are listed.

1.15.2 The marvels of his mysteries: *Mirabilia mysteriorum suorum*. The mysteries frequently refer to the sacraments of baptism and the eucharist in early Christian literature, and they may be understood as such here.

1.17 The difference between being troubled by thoughts and accepting them or consenting to them is also drawn in Origen, *De princ.* 3.1.3. Cf. 7.8.2.

1.19 These three sources of thoughts may be found in Origen, *De princ.* 3.2.4. Origen is at pains to point out, esp. ibid. 3.2.1f., that the demons are not the sole instigators of our evil thoughts. Cf. also Basil, *Reg. brev. tract.* 75.

1.20.1 This "precept of the Lord" ("Be approved money-changers"), which is called a "gospel saying" in 1.20.2, is an agraphon very often cited by the fathers. Its history is given in A. Resch, *Agrapha: Ausserkanonische Evangelienfragmente* (Leipzig, 1889), 116–127.

On the term *obrizum* cf. Pauly-Wissowa 17.2.1741–1743.

On the value of the denarius in Cassian's time cf. ibid. 5.212.

1.20.2 "Jewish superstition" may refer to the exclusively literal interpretation of Scripture that the Jews were almost universally accused of practicing (cf., e.g., Jerome, *Tract. de Ps.* 95.2) and that could be misleading if it were not accompanied by a spiritual interpretation.

1.20.3 On the elegant words and teachings of philosophers cf. the note at 15.3.1f.

1.20.5 The remark here about pious visitations and overweening concern for nuns and other devout women recalls the famous description of acedia in *Inst.* 10.2.4.

Desiring the holy clerical office: This temptation is mentioned in *Inst.* 11.14ff.; Evagrius, *Prac.* 13; *V. prima gr. Pachomii* 27; *Hist. monach. in Aegypto* 1 (PL 21.397: an addition of Rufinus), 1.25; Cyril of Scythopolis, *V. S. Sabae* 18 (ed. by Schwartz, Leipzig, 1939, 102, where it is noted that "the source and root of the love of power is the desire to become a cleric"). The clerical office posed a danger to those who wished to pursue a monastic life, and there are numerous stories of monks mutilating themselves in one way or another, or threatening to do so, in order to avoid the diaconate, the priesthood, or the episcopate. Cf. *Hist. monach. in Aegypto* 20.14; Palladius, *Hist. laus.* 11.1ff.; Callinicus, *V. Hypatii* 11.9 (SC 117.114). Cf. also the pertinent note in SC 171.529–531. Nonetheless, some monks whom Cassian praises are said to have accepted ordination, which suggests that it was possible to fulfill the clerical functions in humble fashion. Cf. 4.1 and 11.2.1 (with the relevant notes). Athanasius, *Ep.* 49.7ff., urges the monk Dracontius to accept the episcopate, citing several monks as examples in this regard. And in 4.20.3 Cassian observes that it is possible to disdain the clerical office out of pride.

1.21.1 John of Lycon (or Lycopolis) is presented as a celebrated personality in *Inst.* 4.23ff. He is described at considerable length in *Hist. monach. in Aegypto* 1 and Palladius, *Hist. laus.* 35, and he is mentioned as a paragon of orthodoxy in Jerome, *Ep.* 133.3. Cf. also 24.26.16f. and the relevant note.

The devil or a demon frequently appears in monastic literature as a black man or boy, and sometimes as a black girl, often characterized as an Ethiopian. Cf. 2.13.7, 9.6.1; Athanasius, *V. S. Antonii* 6; Palladius, *Hist. laus.* 23.5; *Verba seniorum* 5.23, 20.14; *Hist. monach. in Aegypto* 8.4; Regnault 58, N426; ibid. 183–185, PE iii 16, 1–7; ibid. 202–204, R43; ibid. 271, Arm. II 430 (79) A; ibid. 319–320, Eth. Coll. 14,27; Theodoret of Cyrus, *Hist. relig.* 21.23; Gregory the Great, *Dial.* 2.4; John Moschus, *Pratum spirituale* 30 (an Ethiopian who appears to a monk and confesses to having struck Christ during his passion). For background in pagan and nonmonastic literature cf. Franz Joseph Dölger, *Die Sonne der Gerechtigkeit und der Schwarze: Eine religionsgeschichtliche Studie zum Taufgelobnis* (Liturgiewissenschaftliche Quellen und Forschungen 14) (2nd ed., Münster, 1971), esp. 49–83. For the suggestion that an antipathy to blackness in Egypt in particular can be traced to Psamtik II, an Ethiopian who was pharaoh from 595 to 589 B.C., cf. Pierre du Bourguet, "La couleur noire de la peau du démon dans l'iconographie chrétienne a-t-elle une origine précise?" in *Actas del VIII Congreso Internacional de Arqueologia Cristiana* (Vatican-Barcelona, 1972), 271–272. For a general study of this issue, which cites heavily from monastic literature and which compares early Christian attitudes to blacks favorably with modern ones, cf. Peter Frost, "Attitudes toward Blacks in the Early Christian Era," in *The Second Century* 8 (1991): 1–11.

1.22.1 The four methods of discretion as presented in 1.20f. appear here with the second and third transposed.

1.22.2 Lions, dragons, and other spiritual beasts are spoken of and their names partially explained in 7.32.4f. The lion in particular may also be a beneficent symbol. Cf. *Physiologus* 1, trans. by Michael J. Curley (Austin, 1979), 68–69; Augustine, *De doct. christ.* 3.25.36; and in general L. Charbonneau-Lassay, *Le bestiare du Christ* (Paris, 1940; repr. Milan, 1980), 35–53. The dragon, except in East Asia, is less susceptible of a benign interpretation. Cf. ibid. 391–401.

The image of the human heart or soul as a field or garden to be cultivated, which also appears in 4.3, 4.19.7, 21.8.1, and 23.15.7, probably owes its popularity in Christian literature at least in part to Mt 13:3–23 par. But it can be found as well in Philo, *De agric.* 8ff. For specifically monastic uses of the image cf. Ps.-Macarius, *Hom. spir.* 28.3; idem, Coll.3, *Hom.* 20.2.2f. (SC 275.240–242); Regnault 89–90, N520 (where confusion arises between two monks because one understands "garden" literally and another spiritually); Dorotheus of Gaza, *Instruc.* 12.130ff. (SC 92.390–392).

The plow often stands for the cross in patristic literature, although here it stands for the remembering of the cross. Cf. Jean Daniélou, *Primitive Christian Symbols,* trans. by Donald Attwater (Baltimore, 1964), 89–101.

1.23.4 On the details concerning bedding in this paragraph cf. Gazet's note in PL 49.521–522. The mats *(psiathia)* used for sitting (as well as for sleeping) are mentioned again in 15.1.1 and in *Inst.* 4.13. Cf. also *Apophthegmata patrum,* de abbate Ioseph in Panepho 1.

SECOND CONFERENCE
THE SECOND CONFERENCE OF ABBA MOSES: ON DISCRETION

Translator's Introduction

The second conference takes up the theme of discretion that had already been introduced toward the end of the first, and once again it is Abba Moses who leads the discussion. The topic had been treated in a rather abstract manner in the previous conference, in terms of the triple origin of thoughts and the fourfold way of judging them. Here, however, after discretion has been firmly established as a gift of grace and Antony's definition of the virtue has been offered, the treatment of the subject in question turns toward the practical—namely, toward teaching by example and, finally, toward setting down certain guidelines for eating.

It has already been noted (cf. p. 18) that *The Conferences* as a whole provides a model for the exercise of discretion. The possibilities of that model are particularly elaborated in the present conference, in which Moses, who is himself an elder of high repute, has recourse to and quotes from Antony, the greatest of all the elders, and from a number of others. The passing on of wisdom from generation to generation, which is so central to Cassian's understanding of the practice of discretion, is thus exemplified for the reader. Indeed, it is Antony, from the first generation of abbas, and not Moses, the leader of the discussion, who actually defines discretion. And Antony in turn, in the course of his definition, quotes liberally from Scripture, thus implying that his view is not his own but comes from the source of all wisdom.

This definition is described as being the outcome of a discussion not utterly unlike those twenty-four that constitute *The*

Conferences. We are told that some elders approach Antony to ask him about perfection; they give their differing thoughts on the matter, adducing as the indispensable means to attaining perfection the same monastic practices that Moses had characterized as secondary in the first conference; finally Antony himself speaks and introduces the notion of discretion as the regulatory principle in the pursuit of perfection; and then the others concur. We are perhaps being shown here, in an idealized fashion, the process by which the teachings of the elders came to be formulated.

Antony's definition is in fact a rather sprawling affair, but it can be summarized by saying that discretion is the judgment whereby a person discerns what is correct and, in particular, avoids excess of any kind, even of the apparent good. Already in classical thought, under the name of φρονησις or *prudentia,* discretion was seen as the governing virtue, distinguishing good from bad, and Cassian in one respect does no more than repeat that insight (cf. Aristotle, *Eth. nicomach.* 6.5; Cicero, *De inventione* 2.53). His repetition, however, is an insistent one, and the reason for this is certainly the tendency of desert monasticism toward extremes, epitomized in the person of the unfortunate Heron of 2.5. On the other hand, Cassian does not merely repeat his pagan sources, with which he did not necessarily have direct contact anyhow, for he places discretion squarely in the context of the practice of humility.

The difficulty that Cassian's understanding of discretion presents does not arise from his emphasis on the primacy of this virtue but rather from the method that he proposes for its acquisition—namely, the constant and humble submission of all one's thoughts to the judgment of the elders. This idea is not original with Cassian, since it had already appeared briefly in Basil (*Reg. fus. tract.* 26), but it is he who develops it. It is true that an important qualification is made to the effect that not all the elders can be trusted with others' thoughts, but a twofold problem remains. In the first place, the counsel of the elders is endowed with a well-nigh infallible authority that, on principle alone, does not seem warranted. Second and correspondingly, the responsibility of the younger monks appears unjustifiably restricted by their obligation to submit in all respects to the older ones.

Despite these criticisms, however, one does not sense a spirit of authoritarianism in *The Conferences*. The story of Abba Apollos and the downcast monk, which is related in the thirteenth chapter and which is intended to show that an elder cannot be judged solely by his grey hairs, also demonstrates in passing the type of interchange that could occur between a holy and insightful old man and the younger man who had come to him with troubling thoughts. This kind of interchange would be marked by the greatest gentleness and even, if deemed necessary, by the elder's admission of his own temptations and failings. The practice of submission to the elders, in other words, might be far less an abject experience than the theory of it would seem to imply. Moreover, the act of submission, however highly recommended it may have been, still presupposed the exercise of free choice on the part of those seeking counsel: One could, of course, always reject the advice that one received, or one could seek further advice. The seventeenth conference, which justifies lies and the breaking of promises if that would be conducive to one's spiritual good, pits the less experienced elders of Palestine against the more experienced ones of Egypt, and in so doing it also serves to justify the rejection of what is perceived to be inferior counsel in favor of seeking better counsel elsewhere. Finally, it should be noted that Cassian is not preoccupied here with what might be referred to as "merely human" considerations; he is looking beyond issues like the most enlightened exercise of authority and responsibility, as important as they are, to the prospect of attaining purity of heart and, ultimately, the kingdom of heaven. In view of this prospect it was possible for a monk to give himself completely to another's direction without, it would seem, overly regretting whatever personal discomforts this might entail. This attitude is suggested in a series of stories in *Inst.* 4.24ff., which tell of monks who promptly and uncomplainingly perform demeaning and even irrational tasks at their elders' behest, ranging from John of Lycon's watering dry sticks to Patermutus's throwing his own son into the river. The words written of one in 4.29 apply to these monks and to others like them: "He was not at all shaken by the strangeness of such a mean and unheard-of task, and he paid no heed to its indignity...for through the grace of obedience he wished to acquire the humility of Christ, which is true nobility." In the end, in fact, there is no real alternative to some sort of submission to the insights of others, because God has chosen in the ordinary course of events to speak to us not directly but through others. The very existence of *The Conferences* themselves–in which some human beings, who have received their wisdom at least in part from having spoken to other human beings, mediate it to others again–is a testimony to this process.

That Cassian should devote as many pages as he does toward the end of the present conference to "the proper measure for fasting"–two biscuits a day–and precisely when it is best to eat may initially seem inordinate. But this rule for fasting has been handed down from previous generations and, moreover, provides a useful example of discretion's genius in treading the narrow path between too much and too little. Additionally, we shall be helped to understand its place here by the realization that food posed a most serious temptation to the monks of the desert and that, according to Cassian's scheme, gluttony ranked first among the vices (cf. 5.3; *Inst.* 5). The proper attitude toward food was one of discretion's most constant preoccupations.

The conference concludes with a brief recapitulation of both it and its predecessor. The use of banquet imagery in the final paragraph charmingly complements the long discussion on fasting.

On the topic of discretion in particular cf. Regis Appel, "Cassian's *Discretio:* A Timeless Virtue," in *American Benedictine Review* 17 (1966): 20–29; Joseph T. Lienhard, "On 'Discernment of Spirits' in the Early Church," in *Theological Studies* 41 (1980): 505–529, esp. 525–526.

II. The Second Conference of Abba Moses: On Discretion

Chapters

I.1. After we had taken our morning sleep and were rejoicing in the first light of dawn as it shone upon us, and when we had begun to ask for the discourse that had been promised to us, the blessed MOSES started in this way:

"Seeing you inflamed with such a burning desire, I have the impression that the very short time of rest which I wanted to take away from our spiritual conference and devote to the refreshment of the flesh did not help your bodily repose. When I consider this fervor of yours, my own concern also increases. For I too am obliged to exercise a care all the more devout in paying my debt when I see just how seriously you are claiming it. As it reads: 'If you should sit down to eat at the table of a ruler, consider carefully the things that are placed before you, and put out your hand in the knowledge that you will have to prepare such things.'[1] 2. Therefore, as we are about to speak of the good of discretion and its power, which we were beginning to talk about at last night's conference when our discourse ended, we believe that it is appropriate first of all to demonstrate its excellence from the sayings of our fathers. Thus, when it has been made clear what our forebears thought and said about this matter, and we have mentioned some long past and more recent declines and falls of different persons who collapsed wretchedly because they paid little attention to this, we shall be in a good position to extract what is useful and helpful from it. Once these things have been discussed we shall be better informed as to how we ought to seek after and cultivate it, given its lofty dignity and its grace.

3. "For this is no small virtue, nor is it one that can be gotten hold of by human effort in some way or other and without the assistance of the divine generosity. For we read that, among the noblest gifts of the Holy Spirit, it too is numbered by the Apostle as follows: 'To one is given a word of wisdom by the Spirit, to another a word of knowledge by the same Spirit, to another faith in the same Spirit, to another the grace of healing in the one Spirit.'[2] And shortly thereafter: 'To another the discerning of spirits.'[3] Finally,

once the whole catalogue of spiritual charisms has been completed, he adds: 'But one and the same Spirit accomplishes all these things, distributing to each person as he wishes.'[4]

4. "You see, then, that the gift of discretion is no earthly or paltry matter but a very great bestowal of the divine grace. Unless a monk has sought this grace with utter attentiveness and, with sure judgment, possesses discretion concerning the spirits that enter into him, it is inevitable that, like a person wandering in the dark of night and in deep shadows, he will not only fall into dangerous ditches and down steep slopes but will even frequently go astray on level and straight ways.

II.1. "I remember that once, when I was still a boy and living in the region of the Thebaid, where the blessed Antony used to dwell, some elders came to him to ask about perfection. And although the conference was drawn out from dusk until dawn, this was the question that took up most of the night. What was discussed at great length was what virtue or observance could keep a monk permanently unharmed by the snares and deceptions of the devil and bring him up on the right path and with sure steps to the summit of perfection. 2. Each one gave an opinion in keeping with the depth of his insight. Some said that this consisted in pursuing fasts and vigils, because a mind stretched to its limits by these things and having achieved purity of heart and body could more easily be united with God. Others held that it was to be found in contempt for all things; if the mind were stripped of everything within it, it would attain more quickly to God, for from then on there would be no snares as it were to keep it back. Still others deemed that solitude–namely, distance and the remote parts of the desert–was necessary, and that someone living there could address God more familiarly and cling to him more closely. Some defined it by saying that the duties of love or hospitality were to be performed, because the Lord promised quite particularly in the Gospel that he would give the kingdom of heaven to people who acted in this way when he said: 'Come, blessed of my Father, take possession of the kingdom prepared for you from the foundation of the world. For I was hungry and you gave me to eat, I was thirsty and you gave me to drink,'[5] and so forth.

"And when they had thus determined that more certain

access to God could be obtained by different virtues and the greater part of the night had been taken up with this question, blessed Antony finally spoke: 3. 'All the things that you have mentioned are indeed necessary and useful for those who thirst for God and who desire to come to him. But the innumerable falls and experiences of many people do not at all permit us to attribute the highest grace to these things. For we often see that those who keep fasts and vigils most rigorously and who live far off in the solitude in wondrous fashion, who also deprive themselves of any belongings to such an extent that they do not so much as allow a single day's food or one denarius to be left over, and who even fulfill the demands of hospitality with the utmost devotion, are so suddenly deceived that they are unable to bring to a satisfactory conclusion the work that they have begun, and they cap off the highest fervor and a praiseworthy way of life with a disreputable end. Therefore we would be able to know clearly what was the best way to come to God if we carefully sought out the reason for the ruin and deception of these people. 4. For although the works of the aforesaid virtues abounded in them, the lack of discretion by itself did not permit those works to endure to the end. Nor can another reason be found for their fall, except that they were less well instructed by the elders and were utterly unable to grasp the meaning of discretion, which avoids excess of any kind and teaches the monk always to proceed along the royal road and does not let him be inflated by virtues on the right hand—that is, in an excess of fervor to exceed the measure of a justifiable moderation by a foolish presumption—nor let him wander off to the vices on the left hand because of a weakness for pleasure—that is, under the pretext of controlling the body, to grow soft because of a contrary lukewarmness of spirit.

5. "'This, then, is discretion. According to the words of the Savior, it is called the eye and the light of the body in the Gospel: "Your eye is the light of your body. If your eye is single, your whole body will be light. But if your eye is evil, your whole body will be darkness."[6] The reason for this is that it sees and casts light on all a person's thoughts and actions and discerns everything that must be done. 6. But if this is evil in a person—that is, if it has not been fortified by true judgment and knowledge or has been

deceived by some error and presumption—it makes our whole body darkness—that is, it obscures all the clarity of our mind and also our actions, wrapping them in the blindness of vice and the darkness of confusion. For he says: "If the light that is in you is darkness, how great will the darkness be!"[7] No one doubts that, when the judgment of our heart goes astray and is seized by the night of ignorance, our thoughts and our deeds, which proceed from the deliberation of discretion, are involved in the greater darkness of sin.

III.1. "'Finally, because he never had this eye of discretion, he who by God's judgment first deserved to rule over the people of Israel was cast out of his kingdom like something dark out of a healthy body. Having been deceived by the darkness and error of this light, he decided that his own sacrifices were more acceptable to God than obedience to Samuel's command, and in the very act by which he had hoped that he would propitiate the divine majesty he committed sin instead.[8] 2. Ignorance of this discretion, I say, constrained Ahab the king of Israel, after the triumph of the glorious victory that had been conceded to him by God's favor, to believe that his own mercy was better than the very severe execution of the divine command, which seemed to him to be a cruel decree. Enfeebled by this thought, he wished to temper a bloody victory with clemency and, having been made dark throughout his body because of his imprudent mercy, he was condemned to a death from which there was no recourse.[9]

IV.1. "'This is the discretion which is not only the light of the body but which is also referred to as the sun by the Apostle, as it is written: "The sun should not go down on your anger."[10] It is also said to be the guidance of our life, as it is written: "Those who have no guidance fall like leaves."[11] It is very correctly called counsel, without which the authority of Scripture permits nothing at all to be done. We are not even permitted to take the spiritual wine "that rejoices the heart of man"[12] apart from its governance, as it is written: "Do everything with counsel; drink wine with counsel."[13] And again: "Like a city with its walls broken down and without ramparts, such is the man who does not act with counsel."[14] 2. The example and image used in this text, which compares a person to a city that is broken down and without walls, demonstrates how dangerous it is for a monk to be deprived of this. Herein is wisdom, herein is knowledge and understanding. Without them can neither our interior dwelling be built nor spiritual riches be gathered, as it is written: "With wisdom a dwelling is built, and with knowledge it is set up again; with understanding its cellars are filled with all precious riches and good things."[15] 3. This, I say, is the solid food that can only be taken by the fully grown and the strong, as it is written: "Solid food is for the fully grown, for those who through practice have their senses exercised to discern good and evil."[16] So useful and necessary is it shown to be to us that it is even compared to the word of God and to its powers, as it is written: "The word of God is alive and active and sharper than any two-edged sword, piercing to the division of soul and spirit, of joints and marrow, and discerning the thoughts and intentions of the heart."[17] 4. These words clearly indicate that no virtue can either be perfectly attained or endure without the grace of discretion.'

"And so, according to the opinion both of blessed Antony and of all the others, discretion was understood as that which would lead the fearless monk on a steady ascent to God and would always preserve the aforesaid virtues undamaged; as that with which the heights of perfection could be scaled with little weariness; and as that without which many of those who labor even with a good will would be unable to arrive at the summit. For discretion is the begetter, guardian, and moderator of all virtues.

V.1. "And in order that a recent example, as we have promised, may also confirm this understanding voiced of old by the holy Antony and by the other fathers, recall what you lately saw happen with your own eyes—namely, that a very few days ago the old man Heron was cast down from the heights to the depths by an illusion of the devil. We remember that he lived fifty years in this desert, that he maintained a rigorous abstinence with extraordinary strictness, and that with a marvelous zeal he went more deeply into the desert than anyone else living here. 2. After so many labors, then, how and why was he deluded by the tempter and did he fall very seriously, thereby striking all who were living in this desert with mournful sorrow? Was it not because he possessed little of the virtue of discretion and preferred to be governed by his own understanding of things rather than to obey the counsels and conferences of the brothers and the institutes of our forebears? For with such rigor did he always exercise an inflexible abstinence in his fasting and so constantly did he seek the recesses of the desert and of his cell that even the celebration of the day of Easter would never move him to share a meal with the brothers. 3. On this day, when all the brothers had gathered in the church for the yearly solemnity, he alone would not join them lest he seem to deviate somewhat from his chosen orientation by eating a little pulse. Deceived by this presumption, he welcomed with the highest veneration the angel of Satan as an angel of light.[18] Like an obedient and willing slave to his commands, he threw himself into a well so deep that its bottom was invisible. He did not doubt the promise of the angel, who had assured him that, thanks to his virtues and labors, he could not possibly endanger himself. 4. So as to prove his faith in the most obvious way by making trial of his own safety, the deluded man hurled himself into the aforesaid well in the middle of the night, with the intention of demonstrating how deserving his virtue was upon emerging unharmed from there. When, after a great deal of effort on the part of the brothers, he was pulled out of it nearly dead, he expired three days later. But what is worse than this, he went along so stubbornly with his own deception that he could not be persuaded, even when faced with death, that he had been deluded by the cleverness of demons. 5. Therefore, despite his many and deserving labors and the length of years that he endured in the desert, those who mourned his death could barely obtain from the priest, Abba Paphnutius, as an act of the highest mercy and kindness, that he should not be considered a suicide and also judged unworthy of the memorial and offering for the dead.

VI.1. "What shall I say of those two brothers who, when they were living beyond that desert of the Thebaid where the blessed Antony had once dwelt, were not sufficiently motivated by prudent discretion and, while traveling across the immense vastness of the desert, decided to eat no food at all except what the Lord himself would offer them? 2. When the Mazices (a people more inhuman and cruel than almost any other barbarian nation, for they are driven to bloodshed by a ferocious temperament alone rather than by a desire for booty, as other nations are) sighted them from afar wandering in the desert and nearly dead from hunger, they approached them with bread, contrary to their own savage nature. One of them, with the aid of discretion, received with joy and thanksgiving what was offered to him as if it came from the Lord. He considered that the food was divinely ministered to him and that it was God's doing that these men, who always delighted in human blood, should have given life-saving sustenance to persons who were on the point of expiring and perishing. But the other, refusing the food as having been offered him by a human being, was carried off by starvation. 3. Although the two men started out with a blameworthy idea, nonetheless one of them, with the aid of discretion, corrected what he had thoughtlessly and foolishly begun. The other, however, held out in his foolish presumption and was totally ignorant of discretion. Thus he brought upon himself the death which the Lord desired to keep from him by not believing that it was by divine inspiration that cruel barbarians, forgetting their own savagery, had offered them bread instead of the sword.

VII. "And what should I say about the man who, while welcoming a demon in the guise of angelic brightness[19] over a long period of time, was often deceived by his innumerable revelations and believed that he was a messenger of righteousness? (I do not want to mention his name because he is still alive.) When these revelations were being received, his light took the place of a lamp in the man's cell every night. At last he was ordered by the demon to offer to God his own son, who was living with him in the monastery, so that by this sacrifice he might equal the dignity of the patriarch Abraham.[20] So taken in was he by this idea that he would have committed the murder except that his son, seeing him sharpening his knife with unaccustomed care and looking for the bonds with which he was going to tie him up for the sacrifice when he made an oblation of him, fled away terrified, having a premonition of the coming crime.

VIII.1. "It would take a long time, too, to tell the story of the deception of the monk from Mesopotamia who maintained an abstinence that few in that province could imitate. Hidden alone in his cell, he had practiced this for many years, and in the end he was deceived by diabolical revelations and dreams that, after so many labors and virtues, in which he had exceeded all the monks living in that place, he fell wretchedly into Judaism and the circumcision of the flesh. 2. For after the devil, wishing to draw him by frequent visions to believe in future deceptions, had, like a messenger of truth, revealed things that were perfectly true, he finally showed the Christian people along with the leaders of our religion and faith, the apostles and martyrs, as dark and repulsive and all evil-looking and deformed. And on the other hand there were the Jewish people with Moses, the patriarchs and the prophets, bounding with the greatest joy and shining with a splendid light—all to persuade him that if he wished to share in their dignity and blessedness he should hasten to be circumcised.

"Surely none of these men would have been so tragically deluded if they had made an effort to follow the rule of discretion. Thus the falls and experiences of many show how dangerous it is not to have the grace of discretion."

IX.1. To this GERMANUS said: "From these recent examples and from the understanding of the ancients it is abundantly clear that discretion is in some way the source and root of all the virtues. We want to learn, then, how it should be acquired, and how it can be known whether it is true and from God or false and diabolical. Thus, according to the gospel parable which you discussed previously, where we are commanded to become approved money-changers,[21] when we see the image of the true king stamped on the coin we shall be able to discern what does not appear on legal coinage and reject it (as you said in yesterday's conference in plain language) as counterfeit, having been instructed in the skill which you treated fully and in detail and which you said must be possessed by the spiritual and gospel money-changer. For what profit will it be to have known the dignity of its virtue and grace if we do not know how it is to be sought for and acquired?"

X.1. Then MOSES said: "True discretion is not obtained except by true humility. The first proof of this humility will be if not only everything that is to be done but also everything that is thought of is offered to the inspection of the elders, so that, not trusting in one's own judgment, one may submit in every respect to their understanding and may know how to judge what is good and bad according to what they have handed down. 2. This instruction will not only teach a young man how to walk on the right paths by the true way of discretion but will also preserve him unhurt from all the snares and traps of the enemy. Whoever lives not by his own judgment but by the example of our forebears shall never be deceived, nor shall the crafty foe be able to take advantage of the ignorance of a person who does not know how to hide all the thoughts coming to birth in his heart because of a dangerous embarrassment but either rejects them or accepts them according to the considered opinion of the elders. 3. For as soon as a wicked thought has been revealed it loses its power, and even before the judgment of discretion is exercised the loathsome serpent–drawn out as it were into the light from its dark and subterranean cave by the power of the confession–departs as a kind of laughingstock and object of dishonor. For his harmful counsels hold sway in us as long as they lie concealed in our heart. And that you may reflect with more profit on the power of this idea, I shall tell you what Abba Serapion did, which he would very frequently tell the younger men for the sake of their instruction.

XI. 1. "'When I was still a boy,' he would say, 'and was living with Abba Theonas, I got into this habit, due to the attacks of the enemy: after I had eaten with the old man at the ninth hour, every day I would secretly hide one biscuit in my bosom, which I ate clandestinely at night without his knowledge. Even though I committed this theft on a regular basis, with the consent of my will and the recklessness of deeply rooted desire, yet each time that I came back to myself after the lawless desire had been satisfied, the crime of theft that I had fallen into was more tortuous to me than the eating of the stolen thing had been pleasant. 2. And when I was compelled every day, not without sorrow of heart, to carry out this wicked work prescribed for me as it were by Pharaoh's overseers instead of brickmaking,[22] and I was unable to get myself out from under their cruel tyranny and was ashamed to disclose the covert theft to the old man, by God's providence it happened that, in order to snatch me from this yoke of willing captivity, some brothers sought out the old man's cell for the sake of edification.

3. "'When the meal was finished the spiritual conference began. The old man, responding to the questions that they had

asked about the vice of gluttony and the despotism of hidden thoughts, was discussing their nature and explaining the frightful dominion that they exercise as long as they are concealed. Meanwhile, struck with compunction by the power of the conference and terrified by my guilty conscience (for I believed that these things had been spoken of because the Lord had revealed my inmost thoughts to the old man), I was first shaken by secret sighs. Then as my heart's compunction grew I broke into open sobbing and tears, and from my bosom, the knowing accomplice of my theft, I produced the biscuit that by wicked habit I used to take out to eat clandestinely, and I put it in the center. I threw myself on the ground with a plea for pardon, confessing how every day I would eat secretly, and with an outpouring of tears I begged them to ask the Lord to free me from my horrible captivity.

4. "'Then the old man said: "Take heart, my boy. Your confession freed you from this captivity even before I spoke. Today you have triumphed over your conqueror and adversary, defeating him by your confession more decisively than you yourself had been overthrown by him because of your silence. Up until now, when you never gainsaid him either by your own or by anybody else's response, you gave him leave to have the mastery in you, as Solomon says: 'Because those who do evil are not quickly opposed, therefore the heart of the children of men is full within them, so that they may do evil.'[23] And therefore, after he has been disclosed, this most wicked spirit will no longer be able to disturb you, nor shall the filthy serpent ever again seize a place to make his lair in you, now that by a salutary confession he has been drawn out from the darkness of your heart into the light." 5. The old man had not even finished these words when lo, a burning lamp coming from my breast so filled the cell with the odor of sulphur that the overwhelming stench nearly made it impossible for us to remain there. Resuming his admonition, the old man said: "See, the Lord has visibly demonstrated to you the truth of my words, so that you might see with your own eyes the instigator of this passion driven from your heart by your salutary confession, and so that you might recognize from his open expulsion that, once the wicked foe has been revealed, he will never again have a place in you."

"'And so,' he said, 'it has been in accordance with the old man's words. To such an extent has the domination of that diabolical tyranny in me been destroyed by the power of this confession and been rendered forever ineffective that the enemy has never again tried to stir up the thought of this desire in me, nor after this have I ever again felt myself shaken by the temptation to pursue that furtive desire. 6. This is what we read in Ecclesiastes as well, expressed beautifully in a figurative way. "If a snake bites without hissing," it says, "there is no abundance for the charmer,"[24] indicating that the bite of a silent snake is dangerous. This means that if a diabolical suggestion or thought has not been disclosed by confessing it to a charmer (namely, to a spiritual man, who by the songs of Scripture can heal a wound immediately and draw the snake's harmful venom out of a person's heart), he will not be able to help the one who is in danger and about to perish.

"'In this way, therefore, we shall very easily be able to attain to the knowledge of true discretion. Thus, following in the footsteps of the elders, we shall presume neither to do anything new nor to come to any decisions based on our own judgment, but we shall proceed in all things just as their tradition and upright life inform us. 7. Whoever has been thoroughly instructed in this manner will not only attain to the perfect ordering of discretion but will also remain absolutely safe from all the snares of the enemy. For by no other vice does the devil draw and lead a monk to so sudden a death as when he persuades him to neglect the counsels of the elders and to trust in his own judgment and his own understanding. For since all the arts and disciplines that come from human genius and that do nothing more than make pleasant this short life cannot be properly grasped by someone who has not been taught by an instructor, even though they are palpable and visible, how foolish it is to believe that this alone does not require a teacher–this which is invisible and hidden and is not seen except by the purest heart, in which error does not bring with it a temporal and easy punishment but incurs the soul's perdition and everlasting death! 8. For day and night he is in conflict not with visible but with invisible and savage enemies, nor is the spiritual contest with one or two but with innumerable hordes, and a defeat is the more dangerous to everyone inasmuch as the enemy is more aggressive and the combat more concealed. Therefore the traces of the elders should always be followed with the greatest care, and everything that arises in our hearts should be brought to them without embarrassment.'"

XII. GERMANUS: "The principal cause of our dangerous shame, on account of which we try to hide our evil thoughts, arose in the following way: We knew a superior of the elders in the region of Syria, it was believed, who, after a certain brother had made a simple confession of his thoughts, was shaken with anger and harshly reproached him on account of them. This is why, since we conceal the things that disturb us within ourselves and are ashamed to make them known to the elders, we are unable to obtain a remedy for them."

XIII.1. MOSES: "Just as all young men are not similarly fervent in spirit and instructed in discipline and the best habits, so neither in fact can all the elders be found to be similarly perfect and upright. For the riches of the elders are not to be measured by their grey hairs but by the hard work of their youth and the deserts of their past labors. For it is said: 'How will you find in your old age what you have not gathered in your youth? For old age is honorable not because of long duration, nor is it computed in terms of a number of years, for a man's understanding is grey hair, and a spotless life is old age.'[25] 2. Therefore we should not follow in the footprints of all the elders whose heads are covered with grey hair and whose long life is the only thing that recommends them, nor should we accept their traditions and counsel. Instead we should follow those who we recognize have shaped their lives in a praiseworthy and upright manner as young men, and who have been instructed not in their own presumptions but in the traditions of their forebears. For there are some—and, more's the pity, they are the majority—who have grown old in the lukewarmness and idleness that they learned in their youth and who claim authority for themselves based not on their mature behavior but on their many years. 3. It is with respect to them that the Lord's reproach is rightly made through the prophet: 'Strangers devoured his strength, and he himself did not know it; and grey hairs were spread about on him, and he was unaware of it.'[26]

"It is not an upright life, I say, or the praiseworthy and imitable rigor of their chosen orientation that has put forward these men as examples for the younger men, but only old age. The clever enemy offers their grey hairs as a specious authority for the deception of young men. With fraudulent subtlety, using them as examples, he hastens to subvert and deceive even those who–thanks to their own and others' insight–could have been motivated to take the path of perfection, and by their teachings and institutes he leads them into either a harmful lukewarmness or a deadly hopelessness.

4. "Since I want to give you examples of this, I shall tell of just one thing that happened which could provide you with necessary instruction. (I shall leave out the name of the person in question lest we ourselves act like the man who made public the sins of the brother who had revealed them to him.) This person, then, who was a diligent young man, had for the sake of his progress and well-being come to a certain old man whom we know very well and had confessed in simplicity that he was disturbed by carnal impulses and by the spirit of fornication. He believed that in the words of the old man he would find encouragement for his efforts and healing for the wounds that he had suffered. Instead the old man reprimanded him in the harshest language and declared that anyone who could be titillated by this kind of sin and desire was a wretched person and unworthy of bearing the name of monk, and he so wounded him with his reproaches that he dismissed him from his cell in a state of terrible hopelessness, disconsolate to the point of deadly sadness.

5. "Now the Abba Apollos, the most upright of the elders, came upon him as he was sunk in a deep depression and preoccupied no longer with remedying his passion but with gratifying the desire that he had conceived. And from the look of dejection on his face he guessed the consuming and violent struggle that was going on wordlessly in his heart, and he asked him what the cause of such consternation might be. When he was unable to make any response to the old man's gentle urgings, the old man gradually understood that it was not without reason that he wanted to conceal in silence the cause of a sadness so great that he could not keep it from his face, and he began to ask him still more insistently

about the cause of his hidden sorrow. 6. At this he was caught up short, and he confessed that he was going to the village in order to take a wife and return to the world after having left the monastery, since, in the opinion of the first old man, he could not be a monk and was no longer able to resist the urges of the flesh and to find remedies against their onslaught. The old man consoled him with gentle words and asserted that he himself was disturbed every day by the same impulsive urges and seething emotions and that therefore he should certainly not fall into despair or be astonished at the violence of the attack, which would be overcome not so much by intense effort as by the mercy and grace of the Lord. Then he begged from him a single day's delay and, having beseeched him to return to his cell, rushed off to the monastery of the aforesaid old man.

7. "When he got near it he stretched out his hands and poured out this prayer with weeping: 'O Lord,' he said, 'you who alone are the gracious arbiter of hidden strength and human infirmity and its secret physician, turn the attack on the young man against that old man, so that he may learn to be considerate with regard to the infirmities of those who struggle and even in his old age to be compassionate toward the frailty of the young.' And when he had concluded this prayer with a groan, he saw a black Ethiopian standing by the old man's cell and aiming fiery darts at him. At once he was wounded by them, and he left his cell and began to run around hither and thither as if he were crazed and drunk, and with his comings and goings he could no longer stay in it. Moved to distraction, he started off on the same road that the young man had left. 8. When Abba Apollos noticed that he had been turned into something like a madman driven by the furies, he realized that the devil's fiery missile, which he had seen, had been fixed in his heart and that his mental unbalance and intellectual confusion had been caused by unbearable seething emotions. Coming up to him, then, he said: 'Where are you rushing to and what is so childishly disturbing you that you have forgotten the gravity of old age? What is making you run around so frantically?' 9. And when, ashamed because of his guilty conscience and his obscene excitement, he realized that his visceral passion had been

discovered and that the secrets of his heart had been laid bare to the old man, he did not dare to give an answer to his questioner.

"'Return,' he said, 'to your cell and realize at last that up until now you have either been ignored by the devil or disdained by him, and that you have not been counted among those against whose progress and zeal he daily struggles and fights—you who were unable to defer (never mind withstand!) for a single day the one dart that he aimed at you after all the years that you have spent in this way of life. The Lord let you be wounded by this so that at least in your old age you might learn to be compassionate toward others' infirmities and might be taught by your own example and experience to be considerate with respect to the frailty of the young. For, when you received a young man who was suffering from a diabolical attack, you not only did not encourage him but even, cast down as he was in dangerous hopelessness, handed him over to the enemy to be, as far as you were concerned, gruesomely devoured by him. 10. Without a doubt the enemy would never have laid siege to him with so terrible an attack—with which he has disdained to assail you until now—if he had not begrudged him his future progress and hastened to anticipate and head off with his fiery darts that virtue which he saw was present in his will. He certainly knew that the one whom he judged it worth his effort to attack with such vehemence was the stronger. From your own example, therefore, learn to be compassionate toward those who struggle, and never frighten with bleak despair those who are in trouble or unsettle them with harsh words. Instead, encourage them mildly and gently and, according to the precept of that most wise Solomon: "Spare not to save those who are being led to death and to redeem those who are being slain."[27] Following the example of our Savior, learn not to break the bruised reed or to extinguish the smoking flax,[28] and ask the Lord for that grace by which you yourself may also be able to sing with assurance in deed and in power: "The Lord has given me a learned tongue so that I might know how to sustain by a word the one who is weary."[29] 11. For no one could endure the snares of the enemy or the seething emotions of the flesh that burn as if they were real fires, nor could anyone extinguish and smother them, unless the grace of God came to the help of our frailty and protected and defended it.

And therefore, since a conclusion has been reached in this salutary turn of events, by which the Lord desired to free that young man from his dangerous and seething emotions and to teach you about vehement attacks and a compassionate disposition, let us together pray to him that he might command the removal of this scourge, which the Lord deigned to bring upon you for your profit, and that he might put out with the overflowing dew of his Spirit the devil's fiery darts, which he permitted you to be inflicted with at my instance. "For he makes sorrowful, and he heals again, he strikes and his hands heal. He humbles and he exalts, he kills and he restores to life, he brings down to hell and leads back."'[30]

12. "Although at the old man's one prayer the Lord removed this trial as quickly as he had permitted it to be introduced, still he taught by firsthand evidence that not only are someone's openly confessed sins not to be reproached, but also that the pain of a suffering person is not to be despised in belittling fashion. And therefore by no means let the ignorance or shallowness of one old man or of a few deter you and cut you off from that salutary path about which we have spoken and from the traditions of our forebears. The clever enemy misuses their grey hairs to deceive the young. But everything should be revealed to the elders without any obfuscating embarrassment, and from them one may confidently receive both healing for one's wounds and examples for one's way of life. Thanks to them we shall experience the same assistance and a like result if we strive to aim at nothing whatsoever by our own judgment and presumption.

XIV. "Finally, it is evident that this understanding is greatly pleasing to God, for not without reason do we find this same instruction even in Holy Scripture. Thus, the Lord did not desire of himself to teach the boy Samuel through divine speech, once he had been chosen by his own decision, but he was obliged to return twice to the old man.[31] He willed that one whom he was calling to intimate converse with himself should even be instructed by a person who had offended God, because he was an old man. And he desired that one whom he judged most worthy to be selected by himself should be reared by an old man so that the humility of him who was called to a divine ministry might be tested and so that the pattern of this subjection might be offered as an example to young men.

XV.1. "Also, when Christ himself called and spoke to Paul, even though he could have revealed to him the way of perfection then and there, he willed to send him to Ananias and he ordered him to learn the way of truth from him when he said: 'Rise and enter the city, and there you will be told what you must do.'[32] Him too he sent to an old man, then, and determined that he must be instructed by his teaching rather than by his own. Otherwise what might have been rightly done with regard to Paul would have given a bad example of presumption to those who came after him, since each individual would conclude that he too should be trained in similar fashion under the guidance and by the teaching of God alone rather than by the instruction of his elders. 2. The Apostle himself teaches not only in his writings but also by deed and example that this presumption is to be utterly detested. He says that he went up to Jerusalem for this reason alone–so that in a kind of private and familial session he might communicate with his fellow apostles and predecessors the Gospel which he was preaching to the Gentiles, aided by the grace of the Holy Spirit and in the power of signs and wonders. 'I communicated with them,' he says, 'the Gospel that I am preaching among the Gentiles, lest perhaps I might be running or might have run in vain.'[33] 3. Who, then, would be so presumptuous and blind as to dare to trust in his own judgment and discretion when the vessel of election[34] testifies that he needed to confer with his fellow apostles? From this it is clearly proven that the Lord shows the way of perfection to no one who has the means of being educated but who disdains the teaching and the instruction of the elders and who considers as insignificant that saying which ought to be diligently observed: 'Ask your father and he will declare it to you, your elders, and they will tell you.'[35]

XVI.1. "With every effort, then, the good of discretion must be acquired by the virtue of humility, which can keep both extremes from hurting us. It is an old saying that extremes meet: ακροτητες ισοτητες. For the extreme of fasting comes to the same end as overeating does, and the excessive prolongation of a vigil is as detrimental to a monk as the torpor of a heavy sleep is. For it is inevitable that a person who has been weakened by an excess of abstinence will return to that state in which a negligent person is caught because of his heedlessness. Thus we frequently see that people who could not be deceived by gluttony have been overcome by immoderate fasting and, on account of their weakness, have fallen into the very passion which they had conquered. 2. Unreasonable vigils and night watches, too, have overcome people whom sleep was unable to get the better of. Therefore, according to the Apostle, 'by the arms of righteousness on the right hand and on the left'[36] we must make our way temperately and tread between either extreme under the guidance of discretion in such fashion that we shall neither let ourselves be snatched from the path of abstinence which is in keeping with the tradition nor, on the other hand, by harmful carelessness, fall into the desires of gormandizing and of the stomach.

XVII.1. "I remember that frequently I so completely resisted the desire for food that, when I had put off eating for two or three days, the very thought of food never entered my mind. Likewise, sleep was so removed from my eyes because of the devil's assaults that many nights and days I would pray that the Lord would give a little bit of sleep to my eyes, and I was well aware that I was more seriously endangered by repugnance for sleep and food than I was by the struggle against lethargy and gluttony. 2. Therefore, just as we should be on guard lest, out of a desire to coddle our bodies, we slip into a harmful waywardness and presume to indulge in food before the prescribed time and to exceed the measure thereof, so also we should accept the refreshment of food and sleep at the proper time, even if it is unpleasant. For both struggles are the adversary's doing, and excessive abstinence trips up a person more disastrously than does thoughtless satiety. For from the latter one can mount to the proper measure of strictness with the help of a salutary compunction, but in the case of the former no such thing is possible."

XVIII. GERMANUS: "What is the proper measure for abstinence, then, by holding on to which with temperate balance we can make our way unharmed by both extremes?"

XIX. MOSES: "We know that among our forebears this was a matter of frequent discussion. In speaking about the abstinence of different persons, who lived only on beans or just on vegetables or fruit, they proposed to all of them a meal of bread alone, whose proper measure they fixed at two biscuits–small loaves which certainly hardly weigh a pound."

XX. This we gladly accepted, responding that we did not consider this to be a measure of abstinence, since we would never be able to eat all of it.

XXI.1. MOSES: "If you want to test the force of this rule, always keep to this measure, and never add any cooked food to it on Sunday or Saturday or when the brothers happen to pay a visit. The body that has been fed with these things–namely, that has been supported by extra food–will not only be able to be sustained by a small amount on the other days but will even be able to put off a whole meal without any trouble. 2. Whoever is always satisfied with the aforesaid amount will never be strong enough to do this or to put off eating his bread until the next day. For I remember that our elders (and I recall that it was often the same with us) went through this, enduring this meager fare with such hardship and difficulty and holding to the aforesaid amount with such strain and hunger that they imposed this limit on their eating with near reluctance and with groaning and sorrow.

XXII.1. "But this is the general norm for abstinence–that each person concede himself as much as his strength, the state of his body, and his age require for sustaining the body and not for satisfying the desire to fill himself up. For whoever acts inconsistently, at one time tightening his stomach with the dryness of fasting and at another bloating it with an excess of food, will in either case do considerable damage. 2. For as the mind that is worn out by a dearth of food loses the vigor of prayer, being obliged to nod when it is weighed down with too great a weariness of the flesh, so likewise, on the other hand, one that is oppressed by an excess of eating will be unable to pray purely and alertly to God. Nor indeed will it be able to hold uninterruptedly to the purity of its chastity, for even on those days when it seems to discipline the flesh with a more severe abstinence, the remains of past meals ignite a fire of fleshly desire in it.

XXIII.1. "For whenever a large amount of food has collected inside us, it has to be removed and gotten rid of in accordance with the very law of nature which does not permit an excess of any superfluous fluid that might be harmful or have an adverse effect to remain where it is. Therefore our body should always be disciplined by a reasonable and consistent abstemiousness, so that even if we who dwell in the flesh are unable to be completely free of this natural necessity, at least it will come upon us rarely, and this pollution will not wet us more than three times a year. Yet a peaceful slumber should allow this discharge to happen without any sexual excitement, and no perverse image, which is the sign of a hidden concupiscence, should provoke it.

2. "Hence this is the moderate and consistent measure of abstinence that we have spoken about, which is also approved by the judgment of the fathers—that daily hunger should have its daily ration of bread, keeping both soul and body in one and the same condition and not letting the mind either waste away from weariness with fasting or grow heavy with repletion. For it results in such frugality that after dusk a person sometimes does not know or remember if he has eaten.

XXIV.1. "And so hard is this to achieve that those who are ignorant of perfect discretion would prefer to prolong their fasting even for two days and to keep what they would have eaten today for the next day, provided that when it is time to eat they may take as much as they want. You know from recent events that Benjamin, your fellow citizen, held obstinately to this. Every day he took two biscuits and, not observing a constant abstemiousness with consistent discipline, preferred always to prolong his fast for two days, provided that when it was time to eat he could fill his greedy belly with twice as much. That is to say, by eating four biscuits he enjoyed as much as he wanted, and his two-day fast served as a kind of preparation for filling his stomach to excess. 2. With his obstinacy and stubbornness of mind, with his following his own understandings rather than the traditions of the elders, you doubtless remember to what sort of an end his chosen orientation came. Abandoning the desert, he fell back into the empty philosophy of this world and earthly vanity, setting the seal on the aforesaid opinion of the elders by the example of his own case. By his downfall he taught everyone that no one who trusts in his own understanding and his own judgment can ever mount to the summit of perfection, but that he will in fact be deceived by the dangerous illusion of the devil."

XXV. GERMANUS: "How, then, can we keep to this measure uninterruptedly? For sometimes at the ninth hour, when the stational fasting has ended and some brothers come by, it is necessary to add something to the prescribed and accustomed amount for their sakes; otherwise the hospitality that we are commanded to show everyone will be completely neglected."

XXVI.1. MOSES: "Both duties should be observed at the same time and with equal care. For we ought both to keep very carefully to the proper amount of food for the sake of abstinence and purity and likewise, out of love, to show hospitality and encouragement to the brothers who come by, because it is patently absurd that in setting your table for a brother–in fact for Christ himself–you should not eat together with him or should absent yourself while he is eating. 2. Therefore we shall find ourselves guilty in neither way if we maintain this custom–that at the ninth hour, after having eaten one of the two biscuits that are ours by right according to the established measure, we hold on to the other one until dusk in case of visitors. If a brother comes we should eat it together with him, adding nothing to the customary measure. If we follow this arrangement, a brother's visit, which ought to be a great joy for us, will not disturb us in the least, provided that we render him the duties of hospitality in such a way as to subtract nothing from the rigor of our abstinence. But if no one comes, we may freely eat the second one also, which is as it were ours by right according to the established measure. 3. Since at the ninth hour one biscuit will already have been eaten, this meager fare will not weigh down the stomach at dusk, which often happens with those who believe that they are keeping to a stricter abstinence and who put off all their eating until dusk. For a recent meal does not permit the mind to function clearly and alertly during either the evening or the night prayers. Therefore the ninth hour, a convenient and useful time for eating, has been authorized. With this the monk who is eating will not only be alert and at ease during the nightly vigils but will even be perfectly ready for the evening prayers themselves, since he will already have digested his food."

4. At just such a banquet, with two courses of instruction, did the holy Moses fill us. He demonstrated not only the grace and virtue of discretion in words of manifest learning but also, in the discussion that took place previously, the reasoning behind renunciation and the goal and end of our chosen orientation. Thus he greatly clarified what we had been pursuing before merely with an enthusiastic spirit and zeal for God, but with eyes closed as it were, and he made us realize how far we had strayed until then from purity of heart and from the right direction, since even the discipline of all this world's visible arts cannot exist without being ordered to a goal and cannot possibly be attained without having an end in view.

TEXTUAL REFERENCES

1. Prv 23:1–2 LXX.
2. 1 Cor 12:8–9.
3. 1 Cor 12:10.
4. 1 Cor 12:11.
5. Mt 25:34–35.
6. Mt 6:22–23a.
7. Mt 6:23b.
8. Cf. 1 Sm 15.
9. Cf. 1 Kgs 20.
10. Eph 4:26.
11. Prv 11:14 LXX.
12. Ps 104:15.
13. Prv 31:3 LXX.
14. Prv 25:28 LXX.
15. Prv 24:3–4.
16. Heb 5:14.
17. Heb 4:12.
18. Cf. 2 Cor 11:14.
19. Cf. ibid.
20. Cf. Gn 22:1–18.
21. Cf. Logion 43, in A. Resch, *Agrapha: Ausserkanonische Evangelienfragmente* (Leipzig, 1889), 116–127.
22. Cf. Ex 5.
23. Eccl 8:11 LXX.
24. Eccl 10:11 LXX.
25. Sir 25:3; Wis 4:8–9.
26. Hos 7:9.
27. Prv 24:11 LXX.
28. Cf. Mt 12:20.
29. Is 50:4.
30. Jb 5:18 LXX; 1 Sm 2:6–7.
31. Cf. 1 Sm 3.
32. Acts 9:6.
33. Gal 2:2.
34. Cf. Acts 9:15.
35. Dt 32:7.
36. 2 Col 6:7.

2.1.3f. The emphasis here and in 2.13.6 and 2.13.11 on the necessity of grace is repeated frequently in *The Conferences*. The doctrine found in the thirteenth conference should be viewed in the light of other utterances of Cassian's made elsewhere. Cf. 3.12ff., 4.4.1, 4.5, 4.15.2, 5.14.2, 5.15.2ff., 7.2.1f., 7.8.2, 10.10.5, 10.11.2, 11.9.2, 12.4.1ff., 12.8.6, 12.12, 12.15.2ff., 22.6.3.

2.2.3 On the value of the denarius cf. the note at 1.20.1.

2.5 A certain Heron of Alexandria is spoken of in Palladius, *Hist. laus.* 26 and 47.4. This Heron was, like the one mentioned here, also extremely ascetical, as we learn ibid. 26; later he fell into dissolution, but he finally died reconciled. In the second of the two references Heron is mentioned only in passing. A few lines earlier in this second reference, however, we are told that an unnamed brother died when a well caved in on him. It is interesting to speculate that the story of Heron in 2.5 may be a conflation of some aspects of the Heron whom Palladius had heard of and a vague recollection of a monk dying in a well, whom Palladius brings up almost in tandem with his Heron. Otherwise Cassian's Heron and Palladius's are not identical. Cf. Weber, 89–90.

The demonically inspired suicide that is recounted in this chapter was not the only one of its kind to have happened in the desert. There are two others of the same sort in *V. prima gr. Pachomii* 96.

2.5.1 "Heron was cast down from the heights to the depths" both figuratively and literally, inasmuch as he died after jumping into a deep well.

2.5.2 Heron's fasting on the very day of Easter, which is strongly implied although not directly stated here, is a sure indication that something is wrong. 21.11ff. and *Inst.* 2.18 relate that the fast was broken during Eastertide, and Tertullian, *De corona* 3, shows that at least by the beginning of the third century fasting was considered unlawful during that season. Cf. also Gregory the Great, *Dial.* 2.1. Nonetheless we are told with at least implicit approval that some monks fasted during the Easter season. Cf. Athanasius, *V. S. Antonii* 12ff. (where an unbroken twenty-year fast is spoken of); Regnault 176–177, PE II 19.5.

2.5.3 Delusion by the devil or a demon appearing as an angel of light, following the words of 2 Cor 11:14, was not an uncommon occurrence in the desert. Cf. 2.7, 16.11.1; *Verba seniorum* 15.68; *Hist. monach. in Aegypto* 2.9; Regnault 271, Arm. II 430 (77) A.

2.5.5 The Paphnutius who appears here is undoubtedly the same as the one who figures in 3.1.1 and 10.2.3. In all three cases the person in question is referred to as a priest.

The memorial and offering for the dead: This certainly refers to the eucharist, which seems to have been celebrated for the dead as early as the second half of the second century. Cf. *Acta Ioannis* 85f. (CCSA 1.291–293). But whether "memorial" may also be understood here as an anniversary commemoration is uncertain. Such commemorations, however, were known at the beginning of the third century, as appears in Tertullian, *De corona* 3, and one is mentioned in 19.1.1.

2.6 There is an almost parallel story to this in *Inst.* 5.40, where we read of two boys who were sent to bring some figs to an elder far off in the desert; they got lost on their journey and died from hunger and thirst, never having touched the figs. Cassian praises their obedience, but in another context he might well have condemned what appears to have been an act of great indiscretion.

2.6.2 On the Mazices, or Mazaci, a widely spread people of Libyan origin, cf. Pauly-Wissowa 15.1.5–6. On their ravages among the monks of Egypt cf. also John Moschus, *Pratum spirituale* 112.

2.8 The attractiveness of Judaism to Christians in this period is borne out in Chrysostom's eight homilies *C. Iudaeos*. For a brief commentary on this passage cf. Bernhard Blumenkranz, *Les auteurs chrétiens latins du moyen âge sur les juifs et le Judaïsme* (Paris, 1963), 16 and n. 9.

2.8.1 Mesopotamia was the region roughly to the northeast of Syria and between the Tigris and the Euphrates Rivers. The monk in question was from Mesopotamia but lived in Egypt.

2.10.3 The Serapion mentioned here is probably the one around whom the fifth conference is built. Cf. p. 177.

2.11.1ff. Although there are many dissimilarities, this story nonetheless bears comparison with the famous incident of the fig tree in Augustine, *Conf.* 2.4.9ff. Both accounts have in common a sensitive adolescent, food, and an act that in itself is only slightly immoral but that has potent symbolic effect and grave repercussions subsequently for the doer of the act.

2.11.1 This Theonas is perhaps the same as the one who appears in the twenty-first to twenty-third conferences. Cf. p. 711.

2.11.2 An implicit likeness is drawn here between Pharaoh and Satan. The comparison is an ancient one and appears in Christian literature already in the second half of the second century. Cf. Melito of Sardis, *Hom. pasch.* 67 and SC 123.172–173, n. 475.

2.11.3 The brief scene recorded here is a model of the process of conversion, moving from an effective awareness of guilt to a plea for pardon. On the guilty conscience in particular cf. the note at 20.5.3.

2.11.5 The odor of sulphur produced by the lamp is a sure sign of a diabolical presence. Sulphur, or brimstone, in particular is associated with the divine wrath and hence with hell, the dwelling of the demons. Cf. Gn 19:24; Ps 11:6; Is 34:9; Rv 9:17–18, 14:10, 19:20, 20:10.

A foul smell of some sort not uncommonly accompanies contact with demons. Cf. Athanasius, *V. S. Antonii* 63; Evagrius, *Prac.* 39; Palladius, *Hist. laus.* 23.5; *Verba seniorum* 5.23; Cyril of Scythopolis, *V. S. Euthemii* 24 (ed. by Schwartz, Leipzig, 1939, 36); *V. Danielis Styl.* 17.33 (ed. by Delehaye, Brussels, 1923, 32). On the stench of sin, metaphorically understood, cf. 9.19, 14.14.3, 20.9.1, 20.10, 20.12.4, 24.25.6; Origen, *Hom. in Cant. Cant.* 1.2; Ps.-Macarius, Coll. 3, *Hom.* 25.5.1f. (SC 275.282); *Verba seniorum* 5.16; Regnault 304–305, Eth. Coll. 13,70; Chrysostom, *Hom. bapt.* Stav. 6.22. On the stench of sin, literally understood, cf. *Verba seniorum* 20.18; Besa, *The Life of Shenoute* 40 (trans. by Bell, CS 73, 1983, 54). On the fragrance of virtue cf. the note at 1.1.

2.11.6 Jerome, *Comm. in Eccl.* 10.11, gives two possible interpretations of the verse in question, one of which parallels Cassian's. Jerome has translated the verse from the Greek himself, however, and hence his version is different from Cassian's.

2.13 That age does not necessarily imply wisdom, which is the burden of this chapter, is also observed in Jerome, *Ep.* 58.1.

2.13.4 If Moses is referring to 2.12, he is mistaken in saying that someone's sins had been publicized. We are told only that the elders' superior was angered at a monk's disclosure of his thoughts to him.

2.13.4ff. On the present account cf. Weber 32–35. A narrative that recalls this one in several respects occurs in *Verba seniorum* 10.85. Stories of persons who end up suffering from the very same thing that makes them contemptuous of others are common in desert (and other) literature. Cf. Regnault 18, N20. Cf. also 11.10.

2.13.5 This Apollos is almost certainly identical with the one who appears in 24.9.1ff. He is the subject of *Hist. monach. in Aegypto* 8.

2.13.6 It was not uncommon for the brother to whom one had confessed one's sins and evil inclinations, particularly in the area of sexuality, to say that he was troubled in the very same way. Cf. *Verba seniorum* 5.13. Sometimes, however, this might be a lie intended for the sake of encouragement. Cf. ibid. 5.27.

On the use of the term "monastery" for the dwelling of a single monk, as seems to be the case here, cf. 18.10 and the relevant note.

2.13.7 Arbiter: The image appears also in 4.6.3 and 7.20.2. Cf. the note to the latter.

Secret physician: Cf. Gervais Dumeige, "Le Christ médicin dans la littérature chrétienne des premiers siècles," in *Rivista di Archeologia Cristiana* 48 (1972): 115–141; DS 10.891–901; Gerhard Fichtner, "Christus als Arzt: Ursprünge und Wirkungen eines Motivs," in *Frühmittelalterliche Studien* 16 (1982): 1–18. Cf. also 6.11.8, 7.28, 13.7.4, 13.18.2, 19.12.1; *Inst.* 8.14.

Apollos's groan here is less a sigh of heaviness of heart than an indication of seriousness of purpose, and as such it recalls Mk 7:34. Cf. also *Mart. Polycarpi* 9.2; *Conlat.* 24.1.4; *Inst.* 5.

A black Ethiopian: Cf. the note at 1.21.1.

2.13.7ff. Eph 6:16 equips Satan with fiery darts, and fiery darts or arrows are a usual part of the demonic armament. They are ordinarily understood as evil (and more particularly as impure) thoughts that intrude themselves on the mind. Cf. 2.13.11, 7.5.5, 12.6.3, 12.11.3; Macarius, *Hom. spir.* 25.2; Evagrius, *Schol. in Prov.* 78 (SC 340.178), 195 (ibid. 290); idem, *Ep.* 27 (ed. by Frankenberg, Berlin, 1912, 584); Diadochus of Photice, *Cap. gnost.* 82 (SC 5 bis, 141).

2.13.9f. On the idea that it is better to be engaged in struggle than to be free of temptation or trial cf. 9.23, 18.13.1, 18.13.4f., 22.3.3, 24.25.1; Athanasius, *V. S. Antonii* 10.

2.14f. Cassian's argument here that God ordinarily teaches by means of other human beings rather than directly by himself is found also in Augustine, *De doct. christ.* praef. 4ff.; John Moschus, *Pratum spirituale* 199 (where angels are said to refuse to correct a priest who is unwittingly using a heretical eucharistic formula because "God has disposed matters in such a way that human beings are to be corrected by human beings").

2.15.1 Although Ananias is referred to here as an old man, in fact Acts 9:10–19, which tells of him, says nothing of his age. This perhaps suggests that anyone in a position to offer sound teaching to someone else may enjoy the title of old man or elder, and the tenor of the present conference does not gainsay this possibility.

2.16.1 Extremes meet: The origin of the saying as it stands is unknown, but the teaching found here and in the following chapters has its source in Aristotle, *Eth. nicomach.* 2.6ff. In patristic literature the doctrine of virtue as the just mean is especially well put in Gregory of Nyssa, *De virg.* 7.1f. Cf. SC 119.352, n.2, and to the references there add Evagrius, *Schol. in Prov.* 53 (SC 340.144–146). On avoiding extremes cf. also 6.10; *Inst.* 11.4.

2.22.1 That fasting must be adapted to the circumstances of the individual is noted in *Inst.* 5.5. The idea is a commonplace in monastic literature. Cf. Basil, *Reg. fus. Tract.* 19.

2.23.1 Here, as in 22.3.2 and 22.6.4f., fasting is said to do what controlling one's intake of water is said to do in 12.11.4f. Cf. the relevant note.

2.24 This Benjamin is otherwise unknown. Gazet's note in PL 49.555 reads: "It would be inquisitive and beside the point to ask who this Benjamin might be." He then goes on to suggest who he might be.

2.25 Stational fasting (the phrase reads *soluta iam statione ieiunii*) seems to refer here to the set period of fasting on any given day. As such it appears for the first time in Hermas, *Pastor,* sim. 5.1.1f., and so Cassian seems to understand it when he uses the term *statio* in 21.29.2

and in *Inst.* 5.20 and 24. Thus, according to the present passage, stational fasting is a daily event and concludes about the ninth hour, which is mid-afternoon. But the term can also apply to the observance of fasting on the particular days of Wednesday and Friday, which are first mentioned as fast days for Christians in *Didache* 8.1 and first referred to as stational days in Tertullian, *De orat.* 19; idem, *De ieiun.* 10. The word *statio* is most likely of military derivation, meaning guard duty. Cf. Christine Mohrmann, "Statio," in *Vigiliae Christianae* 7 (1953): 221–245.

2.26.1 The identification of one's brother monk and Christ himself ultimately depends on Mt 25:31–46.

THIRD CONFERENCE
THE CONFERENCE OF ABBA PAPHNUTIUS: ON THE THREE RENUNCIATIONS

TRANSLATOR'S INTRODUCTION

With the third conference the reader is introduced to Abba Paphnutius, who is described at length in the first chapter and who, we learn, is nicknamed "the Buffalo." It is probable that this is the same Paphnutius mentioned by Palladius in *Hist. laus.* 47.3ff., especially inasmuch as Palladius's Paphnutius makes a distinction in 47.5 that Cassian's makes as well in 3.20.1—namely, between the divine will or approval and the divine permission. He is also said by both authors to have been very old. In addition, we learn from 4.1.1 that he was a priest, which seems to make him the same Paphnutius as appears in *Apophthegmata patrum,* de abbate Eudaemone. Cassian's description of Paphnutius, in any event, takes up the theme of discretion from the previous conference by stressing his submission to monastic discipline and to the teachings of the elders.

After having dealt with the aims of monasticism and its most fundamental virtue in the first and second conferences, it seems not unnatural that Cassian should treat here, as he does, of both the different callings to the monastic life and the renunciations that life entails. There are three such callings—namely, from God himself, from human example, and from some sort of need. The idea for this division is not original with Cassian; Antony had already spoken of three different callings at the beginning of the first of the seven letters that are attributed to him (cf. PG 40.977-978). Antony's first calling is from God, and he, like

Cassian, cites Abraham as an example. His second and third callings, respectively, are from fear of punishment and from weariness of affliction, both of which together correspond roughly to Cassian's third. But there is no equivalent in Antony to Cassian's second calling, from human example. Certainly the explicit recognition, such as is found in Antony and Cassian, that a call to monasticism (or conversion) could include an element of reluctance or involuntariness is a piece of genial psychological insight. Although the first calling may be the noblest and the third the most self-interested, it is the outcome of the calling that determines its ultimate value. Thus Judas's calling, albeit from God himself, ended in betrayal; but Paul's, which began in apparent reluctance, was crowned with triumph.

A discussion of the three kinds of renunciation follows immediately. These three renunciations are progressively more spiritually oriented, moving from contempt of worldly wealth to the rejection of vicious activities and dispositions to, lastly, the turning away from everything present and visible. The first two may be translated as bodily renunciation and renunciation of heart, or as the renunciation of what belongs to others and the renunciation of what belongs to oneself. The third is an internalization of the first two. Moses points out that these renunciations must be achieved in order and, likewise, that they are valueless unless all three are attained, for the first two are only a preparation for the third. Upon arriving at the third, the mind is opened to such an ecstasy that it will not be disturbed by anything external to itself. But the attainment of this third renunciation, as well as the entrance into the promised land that follows on it and that may be characterized as "purity of heart in this body, [when] all the passions have been driven out" (3.10.5), is a gift of the Lord, just as, indeed, the first and second renunciations are his gift. And this, then, becomes the topic of the remainder of the conference.

The second half of the conference, more or less, is taken up with an exposition of the interaction between divine aid, or grace, and human activity, for Germanus, disturbed by what the old man has just said about the giftedness of the renunciations, asks whether human behavior can be characterized as praiseworthy "if God begins and ends in us everything that pertains to our perfection" (3.11). Paphnutius's response to the question must be read while taking into account the thirteenth conference, which deals with the same issue. The present long passage seeks to balance both components of the equation–grace and human activity. If the balance at times seems unsatisfactory, it is because Cassian occasionally appears to relegate grace to the initiation and to the perfection of good will, while leaving the ordinary implementation of that good will to the human agent. "We are very clearly taught," Paphnutius declares, for example, in 3.19.1, "that the beginning of a good will is bestowed upon us at the Lord's inspiration, when either by himself or by the encouragement of some human being or through need he draws us to the path of salvation, and also that the perfection of the virtues is granted by him in the same way, but that it is up to us to pursue God's encouragement and help in either a haphazard or a serious manner." Yet, in another passage, some pages later, Paphnutius expresses concern that he might even be misperceived as downplaying free will when his real intention is simply "to prove that God's help and grace are necessary...at every day and moment" (3.22.3). The Cassian of the third conference is not completely identical with the Cassian of the controversial thirteenth conference, one difference being that there is no polemical urgency in the former. But both are similar in their methodology of simply citing strings of proof texts from Scripture and in a certain failure to be more rigorous in their argumentation.

The final few sentences of the present conference return to the topic of the three renunciations and sum up Paphnutius's teaching in that area, but they make no mention whatsoever of the immediately preceding chapters on grace and human activity.

III. The Conference of Abba Paphnutius: On the Three Renunciations

Chapters

I.1. In that choir of holy men, who shone like bright stars in the night of this world, we saw the holy Paphnutius resplendent with brilliant knowledge as if he were a large celestial body. He was the priest of our community—that is to say, of the one which dwelled in the desert of Skete, where he lived to a great old age. He was never far from the cell that he had inhabited as a young man, which was five miles away from the church. He had, however, moved a little closer so that when he was burdened with age he would not be troubled by such a long distance when he went to church on Saturday and Sunday. Indeed, not content to return empty-handed from there, he used to bring a jug of water—enough for a whole week—back to his cell on his shoulders, and although he was more than ninety years old he never permitted the young men to carry it for him.

2. From his youth he gave himself over with such zeal to the training of the cenobia that in the short time he lived in them he was equally enriched with both the good of submission and the knowledge of all the virtues. Mortifying each aspect of his will with the discipline of humility and obedience, he thereby extinguished all his vices and achieved perfection in every virtue that the institutes of the monasteries and the teaching of the earliest fathers had laid down. Having gone on to higher things and burning with zeal, he strove to penetrate the remote parts of the desert. Thus, no longer held back by any human companionship, he would more easily be united with the Lord to whom, while surrounded by a large number of brothers, he longed to be inseparably joined. 3. When with great fervor he had surpassed even the virtues of the anchorites themselves in his desire and yearning for that ceaseless and divine theoria and was keeping away from everyone, he penetrated still vaster and more inaccessible solitudes and hid himself in them for a long time, such that even the anchorites themselves would stumble upon him only rarely and with difficulty. There he was believed to delight in and to enjoy

the daily companionship of angels, and because of this characteristic they called him "the Buffalo."

II.1. Desiring to be instructed by his teaching, then, and stirred by our thoughts, we arrived at his cell just as dusk was falling. After a period of silence he began to praise our chosen orientation, because we had abandoned our homeland and were wandering through so many different provinces for the love of the Lord, striving with great effort to endure the barrenness and the vastness of the desert and to imitate their rigorous way of life, which even those who have been born and raised in the same want and poverty can hardly bear. 2. Then we responded that we had come for his teaching and his tutelage in order that we might be somewhat instructed in such a great man's learning and perfection, which innumerable signs had made us aware that he possessed, and not so that we might be credited with any praiseworthy deeds that we had not yet accomplished or have our feelings puffed up by his words. With suggestions of this sort the enemy sometimes titillated us when we were in our cells. Therefore we begged to hear things that would strike us with compunction and humble us rather than things that would flatter us or exalt us.

III.1. Then the blessed PAPHNUTIUS said: "There are three kinds of callings, and we also understand that there are three renunciations necessary for the monk who has answered any of these callings. We should investigate carefully the reason why there are what we have said are three kinds of callings, so that if we see that we have been drawn to the service of God by the first kind of calling we may adapt our manner of life to suit its lofty nature. For it will be useless to have begun in sublime fashion if from such beginnings we do not finish in a corresponding manner. 2. But if we see that we have been removed from a worldly way of life by the last kind, then we should take care to push ourselves with spiritual fervor all the more eagerly to a better end since we seem to have started out from a rather shaky beginning.

"Secondly, we should also certainly know the reason why there is a threefold renunciation, because we shall never be able to attain to perfection if we are unaware of it or if, knowing of it, we do not strive to act upon it fully.

IV.1. "By way of distinguishing these three kinds of callings, then, the first is from God, the second is by human agency, and the third is out of need. As often as some inspiration comes into our heart, even sometimes when we are sleeping, which spurs us on to desire eternal life and salvation and which encourages us to follow God and to adhere to his commands with a salutary compunction, it is from God. Thus we read in Holy Scripture that it was by the Lord's voice that Abraham was called out of his homeland and away from all those who were dear to him and from his father's house when the Lord said: 'Leave your country and your kinsfolk and your father's house.'[1]

2. "And we know how the blessed Antony was called, whose conversion was instigated by God alone. He went into a church and there he heard the Lord proclaiming in the Gospel: 'Whoever does not hate father and mother and children and wife and fields, and his own soul besides, cannot be my disciple.'[2] And: 'If you wish to be perfect, go, sell all that you have and give to the poor, and you will have treasure in heaven, and come, follow me.'[3] Swayed neither by human exhortation nor by human teaching, he received this commandment of the Lord with the greatest compunction of heart, as if it were directed right to him, and at once he renounced everything and followed Christ.

3. "What we have designated the second kind of calling is that which comes about through human agency, when, moved by the example or teachings of certain holy persons, we are inflamed with a desire for salvation. We who have been stirred up by the teachings and virtues of the aforesaid man and have given ourselves over to this pursuit and profession remember that this was how we ourselves were drawn by the grace of the Lord. We read in Holy Scripture, too, that this was how the children of Israel were liberated by Moses from the affliction of Egypt.

4. "But the third kind of calling is that which proceeds from need, when we are compelled at least involuntarily to hasten to the God whom we had disdained to follow in time of prosperity, after we have enjoyed the wealth and pleasures of this world but then are unexpectedly subjected to trials which threaten us with the dangers of death or strike us with the loss and confiscation of our property or fill us with compunction over the death of our

loved ones. 5. We frequently find this calling from need in Scripture as well, when we read that, on account of their sins, the children of Israel were delivered over by the Lord to their enemies and that, having changed their course because of their domination and savage cruelty, they cried out to the Lord. 'And the Lord sent them,' it says, 'a deliverer named Ehud, the son of Gera, the son of Jemini, who used either hand as if it were his right hand.'[4] And again it says: 'They cried out to the Lord, who raised up a deliverer for them, Othniel, the son of Kenaz, the younger brother of Caleb, and he freed them.'[5] 6. And it is said of them in a psalm: 'When he slew them, then they sought him, and they turned and at dawn they came to God, and they remembered that God was their helper.'[6] And again: 'They cried out to the Lord when they were troubled, and he freed them from their distress.'[7]

V.1. "Of these three kinds, then, although the first two seem to be supported by better beginnings, nonetheless we find that even on the third level, which seems inferior and lukewarm, there have been people who are perfect and very fervent in spirit, similar to those who have made an excellent beginning in the Lord's service and have passed the rest of their lives in praiseworthy intensity of spirit. Likewise there are many who have become tepid and have fallen from a higher level and very frequently ended up in tragedy. Hence, just as it was no drawback to the former that they seem to have been converted not by their own will but by force of necessity, inasmuch as the Lord's kindness furnished the occasion whereby they might feel compunction, likewise their having been converted in some sublime fashion profited the latter nothing whatsoever, because they did not strive to live out the rest of their days accordingly.

2. "Now with regard to Abba Moses, who lived in the part of this desert which is called Calamus, nothing was lacking for him to be rewarded with perfect blessedness. Impelled by the fear of death which hung over him because of the crime of murder, he betook himself to a monastery. He so seized upon his need to be converted that with a virtuously ready spirit he turned it into a voluntary act and arrived at the highest summit of perfection. Similarly, in opposite fashion, it was of no value to many persons whose names I ought not to mention that they attached themselves to the Lord's

service from a better beginning, when from then on, due to subsequent laziness and hardness of heart, they slipped away into a harmful lukewarmness and into the deep abyss of death.

3. "We see that this is also clearly brought out in the call of the apostles. For what did it profit Judas to have willingly accepted the most sublime honor, that of the apostleship, in the same way that Peter and the other apostles were received into it, when he brought the splendid beginnings of his calling to the terrible end of covetousness and avarice and even went so far as to hand over the Lord like a cruel parricide? 4. Or what drawback was it to Paul that, having been suddenly blinded, he seems to have been drawn as it were unwillingly to the path of salvation, when afterward he followed the Lord with all the fervor of his soul, crowning with willing devotion what had begun in necessity and concluding with a matchless end a life that was glorious because of so many virtues?

"Everything, therefore, has to do with the end. From its perspective, whoever has been consecrated by the beginnings of even the best conversion can find himself in an inferior position because of negligence, and whoever has been drawn by necessity to profess the title of monk can become perfect through fear of God and diligence.

VI.1. "Now something must be said about the renunciations which the tradition of the fathers and the authority of Holy Scripture show to be three and which each one of us ought to pursue with all our zeal. The first is that by which in bodily fashion we despise all the wealth and resources of the world. The second is that by which we reject the erstwhile behavior, vices, and affections of soul and body. The third is that by which we call our mind away from everything that is present and visible and contemplate only what is to come and desire those things that are invisible.

2. "We read that the Lord commanded Abraham to do these three things all at once when he said to him, 'Leave your country and your kinsfolk and your father's house.' First he spoke of 'your country'—namely, of the resources of this world and of earthly wealth; secondly, of 'your kinsfolk'—namely, of the former way of life and behavior and vices that have been related to us from our birth by a connection as it were of a certain affinity or consanguinity; thirdly, of 'your father's house'—namely, of every vestige of this

world which the eyes gaze upon. 3. For there are two fathers that are sung of by David, speaking for God—namely, the one who must be forsaken and the one who must be longed for. Thus: 'Listen, O daughter, and see, and bend your ear; forget your own people and your father's house.'[8] The person who says: 'Listen, O daughter' is certainly a father, and yet he testifies that the one whose house and people he insists must be forgotten is also the father of his daughter. This is the case when we have died with Christ to the elements of this world and, in the words of the Apostle, we contemplate 'not those things that are seen but those that are unseen, for the things that are seen are temporal, but those that are unseen are eternal,'[9] and, departing in heart from this temporal and visible house, we direct our eyes and our mind to the one in which we shall abide forever. 4. We shall accomplish this when, walking in the flesh but not according to the flesh, we have begun to soldier for the Lord and are crying out in deed and virtue that phrase of the blessed Apostle: 'Our citizenship is in the heavens.'[10]

"The three books of Solomon refer to these three renunciations. For Proverbs is related to the first renunciation; by it the desire for fleshly things and the earthly vices are cut off. Ecclesiastes, wherein all that is accomplished under the sun is declared vain, is related to the second renunciation. The Canticle of Canticles, in which the mind transcends everything that is visible and is already joined to the Word of God by the contemplation of heavenly things, is related to the third.

VII.1. "Therefore it will not be of much value for us to have embraced the first renunciation with a very devout faith if we do not seize upon the second with the same zeal and the same fervor. When we have attained this, we shall also be able to reach the third. Here, having left the house of our former parent, who we remember has been our father from the time of our birth according to the old man, when 'we were by nature children of wrath like the rest,'[11] we shall turn our mind's gaze completely to heavenly things. 2. Of this father it is said to Jerusalem, who had disdained God, her true father: 'Your father was an Amorite, and your mother a Hittite.'[12] And in the Gospel: 'You are of your father the devil, and you wish to fulfill your father's desires.'[13]

"When you have left him and have gone from visible to invisible realities you will be able to say with the Apostle: 'We know that if our earthly dwelling place is destroyed we shall have a dwelling from God, an eternal home in heaven, not made by hand.'[14] And what we mentioned a little bit before: 'Our citizenship is in the heavens, whence we also await a Savior, the Lord Jesus, who will change our lowly body in conformity to his glorious body.'[15] And the words of blessed David: 'I am a sojourner on the earth, and a pilgrim like all my fathers.'[16] Thus we shall become, according to the word of the Lord, like those about whom the Lord was speaking to his Father in the Gospel: 'They are not of this world, just as I am not of this world.'[17] And again, in speaking to the apostles themselves: 'If you were of this world, the world would indeed love what was its own, but because you are not of this world, but I have chosen you from this world, therefore the world hates you.'[18]

3. "We shall deserve to attain to the true perfection of the third renunciation, therefore, when our mind is not dulled by any contact with fleshly coarseness. Once it has been planed by a careful filing, it will have passed over so far from every earthly affection and characteristic to those things which are invisible, thanks to ceaseless meditation on divine realities and to spiritual theoria, that, intent on supernal and incorporeal things, it will not feel that it is bowed down by the fragility of the flesh and by bodily location. Also, it will be seized by such an ecstasy that it will not only not hear any voices corporeally or be busied with seeing the images of present things but will not even notice with the eyes of the flesh bulky items and looming objects that happen to be nearby.

4. "No one can understand the truth and power of this except the person who has perceived the things that are being spoken about with experience as his teacher—that is to say, if the Lord has turned the eyes of his heart away from all present things, so that he considers them not as about to take place but as already over and done with, and sees them dissolved into nothing like empty smoke. Like Enoch, who walked with God and who was carried off from a human way of life and its affairs, he must not be found in the vanity of the present world. That this happened to him in his very body is mentioned in a passage from Genesis, as follows: 'Enoch walked with God, and he was not found, for God

took him.'[19] The Apostle also says: 'By faith Enoch was carried off, that he might not see death.'[20] About this death the Lord says in the Gospel: 'Whoever lives and believes in me shall never die.'[21]

5. "Therefore, if we desire to achieve true perfection we ought to strive so that, just as with our body we have disdained parents, homeland, wealth, and the pleasures of the world, we may also in our heart abandon all these things and not turn back again in our desires to what we have left behind, like those who were led out by Moses. Although, to be sure, they did not return in body, nonetheless they are said to have turned back to Egypt in their heart, for they abandoned the God who had led them out with such powerful signs and they venerated the idols of Egypt that they had once disdained. Scripture recalls it thus: 'In their hearts they turned back to Egypt, saying to Aaron: Make for us gods who will go before us.'[22] We would be censured along with those who dwelled in the desert and who desired the disgusting food of vice and filthiness after having eaten the heavenly manna, and we would seem to complain like them: 'It was well with us in Egypt, when we sat over pots of flesh and ate onions and garlic and cucumbers and melons.'[23] 6. Although this manner of speaking first referred to that people, nonetheless we see it now daily fulfilled in our life and profession. For everyone who has first renounced this world and then returns to his former pursuits and his erstwhile desires proclaims that in deed and in intention he is the same as they were, and he says: It was well with me in Egypt.

"I fear that there will be found as many such people as we read there were multitudes of sinners in the time of Moses. For although six hundred and three thousand armed men were said to have left Egypt,[24] no more than two of these entered the promised land.[25] 7. Hence we must strive to take our models of virtue from the few and far between, since, according to that figure of speech in the Gospel, many are said to be called but few are said to the chosen.[26] Bodily renunciation and removal from Egypt, as it were, will be of no value to us, therefore, if we have been unable to obtain at the same time the renunciation of heart which is more sublime and more beneficial.

"The Apostle declares in regard to the bodily renunciation that we have been talking about: 'If I gave all my goods to feed the poor and handed my body over to be burned, but did not have love, it would profit me nothing.'[27] 8. The blessed Apostle would never have said this had he not in spirit foreseen the future—that some people who had given all their property to feed the poor would not be able to arrive at gospel perfection and at the lofty summit of love because they were dominated by pride and impatience and clung in their hearts to their former vices and wicked behavior; they would be utterly unconcerned to purify themselves of these things, and for this reason they would not attain to the love of God which never fails. 9. These people, who are unable to reach the second level of renunciation, are even less capable of arriving at the third, which is without doubt more sublime.

"Yet, consider carefully the fact that he did not simply say: If I give my property. He seems to have spoken of one who is not yet fulfilling the gospel commandment and who, like those who are lukewarm, has kept something back for himself. Instead he says: 'If I gave all my property as food for the poor'—that is, even if I completely renounced earthly riches. 10. To this renunciation he added something greater: 'And handed over my body to be burned, but did not have love, I would be nothing.' It is as if he had said in other words: Suppose I gave all my property as food for the poor according to that gospel commandment which says: 'If you wish to be perfect, go, sell all that you have and give to the poor, and you will have treasure in heaven,' making such a renunciation that of these things I keep nothing at all for myself. And suppose to this distribution I added martyrdom in the form of burning my flesh, such that I hand over my body for the sake of Christ. Yet if I am impatient or angry or envious or proud or inflamed by others' insults, or if I seek what is my own or think what is evil or do not bear patiently and willingly all the things that could be inflicted upon me, 11. the renunciation and the burning up of the outer man will be of no value to me interiorly if I am still involved in my former vices. For, while in the fervor of my first conversion I disdained the mere substance of this world (which is defined as neither good nor bad but indifferent), I was unconcerned about getting rid of the harmful characteristics of a vicious heart and about attaining to the Lord's love, which is patient, kind, not envious, not puffed up, not easily angered, does not act falsely, does not seek what is its own, thinks no evil, bears all things, endures all things,[28] and, lastly, never permits the one who pursues it to fall because of sin's deceitfulness.

VIII.1. "We should make every effort, then, so that our inner man too may reject and dispose of all the wealth of the vices that he has accumulated in his former way of life. These are our own, always clinging to body and soul, and unless they have been rejected and cut off while we are still in this body they will remain with us after our death. For just as the virtues—and love itself, which is their source—that have been pursued in this world make the one who loves them beautiful and splendid even after the end of this life, so also the vices bring to their eternal dwelling the mind which has somehow been clouded and infected by their dark shades. 2. For the beauty or the ugliness of the soul increases in proportion to the condition of its virtues or vices. The color that it has picked up from these makes it either so splendid that it deserves to hear from the prophet: 'The king will desire your beauty,'[29] or so black, foul, and ugly that it acknowledges its own foul wickedness itself and says: 'My wounds stink and are festering because of my foolishness,'[30] and the Lord himself says to it: 'Why is the wound of the daughter of my people not covered over?'[31]

3. "These, then, are our own riches, which always stay with the soul and which neither king nor enemy can either bestow or remove. These are our own riches, which not even death itself will be able to separate from our soul. We shall either be able to attain perfection by renouncing them or be punished with eternal death by being fettered to them.

IX.1. "Riches are understood in a threefold way in Holy Scripture—that is, as bad, good, and indifferent. The bad are those of which it is said: 'The rich have been needy and hungry.'[32] And: 'Woe to you, rich, for you have received your consolation.'[33] To have cast off these riches is the highest perfection. By way of distinguishing, they are poor who are praised by the Lord's word in the Gospel: 'Blessed are the poor in spirit, for theirs is the kingdom of heaven.'[34] And in the psalm: 'This poor man cried out, and the Lord heard him.'[35] And again: 'The poor and the needy will praise your name.'[36]

2. "And the good are those which it is a matter of great

virtue and nobility to have acquired and which the righteous man is praised for possessing when David says: 'The generation of the upright shall be blessed. Glory and riches shall be in his house, and his righteousness shall abide forever.'[37] And again: 'The redemption of a person's soul is his riches.'[38] In the Apocalypse these riches are spoken of to the one who does not have them and who is blameworthily poor and naked. 'I shall begin to vomit you out of my mouth, because you say: I am rich and wealthy and need nothing, and you do not know that you are wretched and miserable and poor and blind and naked. I advise you to buy fire-tried gold for yourself from me so that you may become wealthy, and so that you may put on white garments and not let the shame of your nakedness appear.'[39]

3. "And the indifferent are those which can be either good or bad, since they can tend either way depending on the desire and the character of those who use them. The blessed Apostle says with regard to these: 'Charge the rich of this world not to be haughty or to hope in uncertain riches but in God, who gives us everything abundantly to enjoy; to do good, to give freely, to share, to store up for themselves a good foundation in the future, so that they may seize the true life.'[40] Again, when that rich man in the Gospel, with whose crumbs the poor Lazarus outside his doors wanted to fill himself, held on to these riches and never cared for the poor, he was condemned to the unbearable fires of Gehenna and to eternal flames.[41]

X.1. "When we abandon the visible riches of this world, then, we reject not our own but others' wealth, even though we boast either of having acquired it by our own labor or of having inherited it from our ancestors. For, as I have said, nothing is ours except this one thing, which is possessed by the heart, which clings to the soul, and which can never be taken away by anyone. Christ speaks accusingly about visible riches to those who hold on to them as if they were their own and who do not want to share them with the needy: 'If you have not been faithful in what is another's, who will give you what is yours?'[42] It is not only daily experience, therefore, which clearly teaches that these riches are another's; even the very word of the Lord has called them such.

2. "Concerning invisible and wicked riches, though, Peter

says to the Lord: 'Behold, we have left everything and followed you. What then shall we have?'[43] But the fact is that they got rid of nothing more than their worthless torn nets. Unless this 'everything' had been understood in terms of that renunciation of vice which is truly great and important, we would find that the apostles had not left anything precious and that the Lord had no reason to bestow on them such glorious blessedness that they deserved to hear him say: 'In the regeneration, when the Son of Man sits on the throne of his majesty, you also shall sit upon twelve thrones, judging the twelve tribes of Israel.'[44]

3. "If, then, those who utterly renounce earthly and visible property are for incontestable reasons unable to attain to apostolic love and cannot easily mount to the still more sublime third level of renunciation, which is accessible to very few, what must they think of themselves who do not succeed in getting to the first level, which is the easiest, who hold on to the money of their old uncleanness along with their former faithlessness, and who assert that the mere title of monk is boastworthy? 4. Therefore, what we have called the first renunciation, which concerns what belongs to others, is insufficient of itself to confer perfection on the renunciant unless he has attained to the second, which is in fact the renunciation of what belongs to us. Once we have arrived there, after having driven out all our vices, we shall also mount to the heights of the third renunciation. At that stage we transcend in spirit and mind not only everything that occurs in this world and particularly human possessions, but we also despise the entire universe, which is believed to be magnificent, as subject to vanity and soon to pass away.

"In this regard, in the words of the Apostle, we consider 'not those things that are seen but those that are unseen, for the things that are seen are temporal, but those that are unseen are eternal,' so that then we may deserve to hear the sublime words addressed to Abraham: 'Come to the land which I shall show you.'[45] 5. With this it is clearly shown that a person must observe these three previously mentioned renunciations with all the ardor of his mind. Otherwise he cannot attain to this fourth thing, which is bestowed upon the perfect renunciant by way of remuneration and reward—that he should deserve to enter the promised land, where the thorns and troubles of the vices do not grow. This will be possessed in purity of heart in this body, after all the passions have been driven out. This does not depend on the virtue or effort of the one who toils; it is the Lord himself who promises that he will show this when he says: 'Come to the land which I shall show you.' 6. From this it is obvious that the beginning of our salvation is by the Lord's call, when he says: 'Leave your country,' and that the consummation of perfection and purity is likewise bestowed by the same Lord, when he says: 'Come to the land which I shall show you'—that is, not to the one which you can know of yourself or find through your own effort, but to the one which I shall show you not only when you are unaware of it but even when you are not looking for it. Thus it is plain that we hasten to the way of salvation as a result of the Lord's inspiration, such that once we have been led by his teaching and illumination we arrive at the perfection of the highest blessedness."

XI. GERMANUS: "In what does free will consist, then, and how may our efforts be considered praiseworthy if God begins and ends in us everything that pertains to our perfection?"

XII.1. PAPHNUTIUS: "It would be odd indeed if in every work and practice of discipline there were only a beginning and an end, and not also something in the middle. Accordingly, just as we know that God offers opportunities for salvation in different ways, so also it is up to us to be either more or less attentive to the opportunities that have been granted to us by God. For just as 'leave your country' was a matter of God's beckoning, so the leaving was a matter of Abraham's obedience; and just as there was need of an obedient person so that the words 'come to the land' would be fulfilled, so the words that are added—'which I shall show you'—are due to the grace of the God who commands and promises.

2. "Yet we should be certain that, even if we practice every virtue with unflagging effort, it is by no means thanks to our own diligence and application that we are able to attain perfection. Nor would human zeal suffice to attain by its own labors to such sublime rewards of blessedness unless the Lord were cooperating with us and we had begun while he was guiding our heart in the right direction. Therefore, praying together with David, we ought to say at every moment: 'Make my steps perfect in your paths so

that my footsteps may not slip.'[46] And: 'He has established my feet upon a rock, and he has directed my steps.'[47] Thus the unseen guide of the human mind may deign to redirect to virtuous concerns that will of ours which inclines to vice through its ignorance of the good and through passionate desire. 3. This is clearly declared in a verse of the prophet, where we read: 'I was pushed and overturned so that I might fall,'[48] which refers to the weakness of free will. And: 'The Lord sustained me.'[49] Here too the Lord's assistance is shown to be always present, so that with its help we may not be utterly destroyed by our free will, for when he sees that we have stumbled he sustains and strengthens us by stretching out his hands, as it were. And again: 'If I said: My foot has slipped'—namely, because of the will's slippery nature—'your mercy, Lord, helped me.'[50] Once more he joins the help of God to his own instability when he confesses that the foot of his faith was not moved due to his own effort but to the mercy of the Lord. 4. And again: 'According to the multitude of the sorrows in my heart'—which arose in me through free will—'your consolations have rejoiced my soul.'[51] This means: By your inspiration they came into my heart and opened up the prospect of future good things, which you have prepared for those who labor for your name's sake, and they not only removed all the anxiety of my heart but even conferred the highest joy. And again: 'Unless the Lord had helped me, my soul would soon have dwelt in hell.'[52] He testifies that due to the wickedness of free will he was going to live in hell except that he was saved by the help and protection of the Lord. 5. For 'a person's steps are directed by the Lord'[53] and not by free will, and 'although one who is righteous should fall'—as far as free will is concerned—'he shall not be bruised.'[54] Why? 'Because the Lord supports him with his hand.'[55] This is very much the same as saying that no righteous person is able of himself to obtain righteousness unless the divine mercy offers the support of its hand to him every time that he stumbles and trips, lest he be overthrown and be completely lost when he has fallen down because of the weakness of his free will.

XIII.1. "Nor indeed have holy men ever testified that they attained by their own effort the right path to travel on as they made their way to the increase and perfection of virtue, but this they would beseech of the Lord and say: 'Direct me in your truth.'[56] And: 'Direct my way in your sight.'[57] Another one declares that it is not by faith alone but also by experience and as it were in the very nature of things that he has seized upon this: 'I have known, O Lord, that a person's way is not in him, nor is it in a man to walk and to direct his own steps.'[58] And the Lord himself says to Israel: 'I will direct him like a green fir tree; from me your fruit has been found.'[59]

XIV. "They also long every day to arrive at knowledge of the law itself not through the effort of reading but with God as their teacher and enlightener, as they say to him: 'Show me, O Lord, your ways, and teach me your paths.'[60] And: 'Open my eyes and I shall consider the wonders of your law.'[61] And: 'Teach me to do your will, for you are my God.'[62] And again: 'You who teach man knowledge.'[63]

XV.1. "This very understanding, whereby he may recognize God's commands which he knew were prescribed in the book of the law, is what blessed David asks to acquire from the Lord when he says: 'I am your servant; give me understanding so that I may learn your commands.'[64] Indeed, he possessed an understanding that had already been given him by nature, and also a knowledge of God's commands, which were discussed in the law; it was at his fingertips, in fact. And yet he begged the Lord that he might receive it more fully, knowing that what nature had given would never suffice for him if his intelligence were not enlightened by the Lord and by his daily illumination, so that he might understand the law spiritually and acknowledge its commandments more clearly. The vessel of election[65] proclaims quite plainly what we are speaking about: 'For it is God who works in you both to will and to accomplish, for the sake of his good pleasure.'[66] 2. What could be more clearly said than his declaring that both our good will and the completed work are accomplished in us by the Lord? And again: 'It is granted to you for Christ's sake not only to believe in him but also to suffer for him.'[67] Here too he has declared that the beginning of our conversion and faith and the endurance of sufferings are all granted us by the Lord. David understood this in similar fashion, and he prays that this very thing may be bestowed on him by the Lord's mercy when he says:

'Confirm, O God, what you have worked in us.'[68] Thus he shows that the beginnings of salvation and the grace conferred by God's gift are not enough for him unless they have been perfected by his mercy and daily assistance.

3. "For it is not free will but the Lord who 'looses those who are bound.'[69] It is not our power but the Lord who 'raises up the fallen.'[70] It is not the effort of our reading but the Lord who 'enlightens the blind,'[71] since in Greek it is said: κυριος σοφοι τυφλους, which means that the Lord makes blind the wise. It is not our concern but the Lord who 'cares for the stranger.'[72] It is not our strength but the Lord who 'lifts up'—or 'supports'—'all those who are falling.'[73] We say these things not so as to nullify our zeal and labor and efforts, as if they were expended foolishly and to no avail, but so that we might know that we cannot strive without God's help, nor can we successfully attempt to lay hold of the immeasurable reward of purity unless it has been bestowed upon us through the Lord's help and mercy. For 'the horse is ready for the day of battle, but help is from the Lord, for no man is powerful in strength.'[74] 4. We should always sing with the blessed David, then: 'My strength and my praise is the Lord'—not free will—'and he has become my salvation.'[75] The teacher of the Gentiles, aware of the fact that he was made capable of the ministry of the New Testament not by his own worthiness or toil but by the mercy of God, proclaims: 'Not that we are capable of thinking of anything of ours as if it were from ourselves, but our sufficiency is from God.'[76] This can be rendered in inferior Latin, but more expressively: Our capability is from God. Then it follows: 'who has also made us capable ministers of the new covenant.'[77]

XVI.1. "So much did the apostles realize that everything which pertains to salvation was bestowed on them by the Lord that they asked for faith itself to be given them by the Lord when they said: 'Increase our faith,'[78] for they did not presume that its fullness would come from free will but believed that it would be conferred on them by a gift of God. The Author of human salvation teaches us how even our faith is unstable and weak and by no means sufficient unto itself, unless it has been strengthened by the Lord's help, when he says to Peter: 'Simon, Simon, behold Satan has sought to sift you like wheat, but I have asked my Father that your faith might not fail.'[79] 2. Someone else, finding that this was happening in himself, and seeing that his faith was being driven onto the rocks of a disastrous shipwreck by the waves of unbelief, asked the same Lord for help with his faith when he said: 'Lord, help my unbelief.'[80]

"So much did the evangelical and apostolic men realize that every good thing is accomplished by the Lord's help, and so certain were they that they could not by their own power and free will preserve their faith itself unharmed, that they besought this as a help and a gift to them from the Lord. 3. If there was need of the Lord's help in Peter so that he would not fail, who would be so presumptuous and blind as to believe that he would not need the Lord's daily assistance to preserve this? This is especially the case inasmuch as the Lord himself expressed this very thing clearly in the Gospel when he said: 'Just as the branch cannot bear fruit of itself unless it abides on the vine, neither can you unless you abide in me.'[81] And again: 'Apart from me you can do nothing.'[82] 4. How foolish and sacrilegious it is, then, to assign any of our good acts to our own effort and not to the grace and help of God is clearly proved by the Lord's testimony to the effect that no one can bring forth spiritual fruit without his inspiration and cooperation. For 'every good gift and every perfect benefit is from above, coming down from the Father of lights.'[83] Zechariah also says: 'Whatever is good is his, and whatever is excellent is from him.'[84] And therefore the blessed Apostle says continually: 'What do you have that you have not received? And if you have received it, why do you boast as if you had not received it?'[85]

XVII.1. "The blessed Apostle declares thus that all the endurance by which we are able to put up with the trials that afflict us comes not from our own strength but from the mercy and guidance of God: 'No trial has seized you except what is common to humanity. But God is faithful, who will not permit you to be tried beyond your capacity. But with the trial he will also provide a way out, so that you may be able to endure.'[86] The same Apostle also teaches that God fits and strengthens our souls for every good work and brings about in us those things that are pleasing to him: 'May the God of peace, who has brought out of darkness the great shepherd of the sheep in the blood of the eternal testament, Jesus Christ, fit you in all goodness, doing in you what is pleasing in his sight.'[87] He also prays that this may occur in the case of the Thessalonians when he says: 'May the Lord Jesus Christ and God our Father, who has loved us and given us eternal consolation and a good hope in grace, encourage your hearts and confirm you in every good work and word.'[88]

XVIII.1. "Finally the prophet Jeremiah, speaking for God, clearly testifies that the fear of God, by which we may hold fast to him, is poured into us by the Lord when he says: 'And I will give them one heart and one way so that they may fear me all their days, and it shall be well with them and with their children after them. And I will make an everlasting covenant with them, and I will not cease to do good to them. And I will put my fear in their heart so that they may not depart from me.'[89] Ezekiel also says: 'I will give them one heart, and I will place a new spirit in their bowels, and I will remove the stony heart from their flesh, and I will give them a heart of flesh so that they may walk in my precepts and keep my laws and do them; and they shall be my people, and I will be their God.'[90]

XIX.1. "By these words we are very clearly taught that the beginning of a good will is bestowed upon us at the Lord's inspiration, when either by himself or by the encouragement of some human being or through need he draws us to the path of salvation, and also that the perfection of the virtues is granted by him in the same way, but that it is up to us to pursue God's encouragement and help in either a haphazard or a serious manner. Depending on the outcome, we have been very fittingly promised either a reward or punishment to the extent that we have either neglected or been zealous to conform with devout obedience to that design and providence of his which has been most graciously directed toward us.

2. "This is described clearly and plainly in Deuteronomy: 'When,' it says, 'the Lord your God has brought you into the land that you will enter into in order to possess it, and he has destroyed many nations in your presence, the Hittite and the Girgashite and the Amorite, the Canaanite and the Perizzite, the Hivite and the Jebusite, seven nations much more numerous and much stronger than you, and the Lord has handed them over to you, you shall

utterly destroy them. You shall make no treaty with them, neither shall you enter into marriage with them.'[91] Scripture declares, therefore, that it is by the grace of God that they are led into the promised land, that many nations are destroyed in their presence, and that nations more numerous and stronger than the people of Israel are delivered into their hands. 3. But it testifies that it is up to Israel to destroy them utterly or to spare them and have mercy on them, to make a treaty with them or not, and to enter into marriage with them or not. It is obvious from this testimony what we ought to ascribe to free will and what to the plan and daily help of the Lord, and that it belongs to divine grace to offer us opportunities of salvation and favorable moments and victory, but that it is up to us to pursue either intently or lazily the benefits that God bestows.

"We see this approach quite clearly expressed also in the healing of the blind men. For the fact that Jesus passed before them was a grace of divine providence and condescension, while the fact that they cried out and said: 'Have mercy on us, Lord, Son of David'[92] was a work of their faith and willingness to believe. 4. That they received their eyesight was a gift of divine compassion. But the example of the ten lepers who were healed together indicates that, even after receiving a gift, both the grace of God and the use of free will remain.[93] When one of them gave thanks, due to the goodness of his will, the Lord, asking for the other nine and praising the one, showed that he exercises an unceasing concern even with regard to those who are unmindful of his kind deeds. For this very thing is the benefit of his visitation—that it both receives and approves the grateful and seeks out and reproves the ungrateful.

XX.1. "We ought to believe with a firm faith that nothing at all can be done in this world without God. For it must be admitted that everything occurs either by his will or by his permission. We should believe that good things are accomplished by the will of God and by his help, while unfavorable things are accomplished by his permission, when on account of our wickedness and hardness of heart the divine protection abandons us and allows the devil or the shameful passions of the body to master us. 2. We are taught this very plainly by the words of the Apostle when he says: 'Therefore God gave them up to shameful passions.'[94] And again: 'Because they did not acknowledge God, God gave them up to a reprobate mind, so that they would do what was not right.'[95] And the Lord himself says through the prophet: 'And my people did not hear my voice, and Israel did not obey me. Therefore,' he says, 'I let them go after their hearts' devices. They shall walk in their own devices.' "[96]

XXI. GERMANUS: "This is a testimony which very clearly shows that the will is free: 'If my people had heard me.'[97] And elsewhere: 'And my people did not hear my voice.' For when it says: 'If they had heard,' it shows that it was in its power to make or not to make a choice. How, then, is our salvation not located in us, when he himself has bestowed on us the ability to hear or not to hear?"

XXII.1. PAPHNUTIUS: "You have indeed carefully reflected on the phrase 'If they had heard me,' but you have not paid any attention to who it is that is speaking to whoever is listening or not listening, nor to what follows: 'I would soon have put down their enemies, and upon those troubling them I would have laid my hand.'[98] Let no one try to take what we have put forward in showing that nothing is accomplished without the Lord and twist it by a wicked interpretation in defense of free will in such a way that he attempts to remove from man the grace of God and his daily assistance, using these words to do so: 'And my people did not hear my voice.' And again: 'If my people had heard me, if Israel had walked in my ways,'[99] and so forth. But let him notice that just as the faculty of free will is demonstrated by the people's disobedience, so likewise God's daily concern for them in crying out, so to say, and admonishing them is also manifest. 2. For when he says: 'If my people had heard me,' he clearly indicates that he spoke to them first. That the Lord is accustomed to do this not only through the written law but also through daily admonitions is explained in Isaiah: 'All day long I have stretched out my hands to a people that do not believe me and that contradict me.'[100] Both, then, can be proved by this testimony, which says: 'If my people had heard me, if Israel had walked in my ways, I would soon have put down their enemies, and upon those troubling them I would have laid my hand.' 3. Just as free will is demonstrated by the people's disobedience, so likewise the design of God and his help is stated at the beginning and the end of that verse, where it indicates that he spoke first and that he would have put down their enemies thereafter if he had been listened to by them. By what we have brought forward we do not want to remove the free will of the human being but to prove that God's help and grace is necessary for him at every day and moment."

4. Instructed by these words and not so much cheerful as moved with compunction in our hearts, we were dismissed by Abba Paphnutius from his cell before midnight. The principal lesson that we gleaned from his conference was this–that although we believed that we had to attain to the heights of perfection by achieving the first renunciation, which we were striving to pursue with all our strength, we just realized that we had not yet even begun to dream of the summit of monasticism when, after having learned very little in the cenobia about the second renunciation, we discovered that we had not heard anything about the third, in which all perfection is contained and which is vastly superior to the other two.

Textual References

1. Gn 12:1a.
2. Lk 14:26.
3. Mt 19:21.
4. Jgs 3:15.
5. Jgs 3:9
6. Ps 78:34–35.
7. Ps 107:19.
8. Ps 45:10.
9. 2 Cor 4:18.
10. Phil 3:20.
11. Eph 2:3.
12. Ez 16:3.
13. Jn 8:44.
14. 2 Cor 5:1.
15. Phil 3:20–21.
16. Ps 119:19, 39:12.
17. Jn 17:16.
18. Jn 15:19.
19. Gn 5:24 LXX.
20. Heb 11:5.
21. Jn 11:26.
22. Acts 7:39–40.
23. Nm 11:18; Ex 16:3; Nm 11:5.
24. Cf. Ex 38:26.
25. Cf. Nm 14:38.
26. Cf. Mt 22:14.
27. 1 Cor 13:3.
28. Cf. 1 Cor 13:4–7.
29. Ps 45:11.
30. Ps 38:5.
31. Jer 8:22.
32. Ps 34:10.
33. Lk 6:24.
34. Mt 5:3.
35. Ps 34:6.
36. Ps 74:21.
37. Ps 112:2–3.
38. Prv 13:8 LXX.

39. Rv 3:16–18.
40. 1 Tm 6:17–19.
41. Cf. Lk 16:19–31.
42. Lk 16:12.
43. Mt 19:27.
44. Mt 19:28.
45. Gn 12:1b.
46. Ps 17:5.
47. Ps 40:2.
48. Ps 118:13a.
49. Ps 118:13b.
50. Ps 94:18.
51. Ps 94:19.
52. Ps 94:17.
53. Ps 37:23.
54. Ps 37:24a.
55. Ps 37:24b.
56. Ps 25:5.
57. Ps 5:8.
58. Jer 10:23.
59. Hos 14:9.
60. Ps 25:4.
61. Ps 119:18.
62. Ps 143:10.
63. Ps 94:10.
64. Ps 119:125.
65. Cf. Acts 9:15.
66. Phil 2:13.
67. Phil 1:29.
68. Ps 68:28.
69. Ps 146:7.
70. Ps 146:8b.
71. Ps 146:8a.
72. Ps 146:9.
73. Ps 145:14.
74. Prv 21:31 LXX; 1 Sm 2:9 LXX.
75. Ps 118:14.
76. 2 Cor 3:5.

77. 2 Cor 3:6.
78. Lk 17:5.
79. Lk 22:31–32.
80. Mk 9:24.
81. Jn 15:4.
82. Jn 15:5.
83. Jas 1:17.
84. Zec 9:17 LXX.
85. 1 Cor 4:7.
86. 1 Cor 10:13.
87. Heb 13:20–21.
88. 2 Thes 2:16–17.
89. Jer 32:39–40.
90. Ez 11:18–20.
91. Dt 7:1–3.
92. Mt 20:31.
93. Cf. Lk 17:11–19.
94. Rom 1:26.
95. Rom 1:28.
96. Ps 81:11–12.
97. Ps 81:13a.
98. Ps 81:14.
99. Ps 81:13.
100. Is 65:2 LXX.

3.1.1 The impressive image with which the conference opens is perhaps inspired by Mt 13:43 and 1 Cor 5:41.

Saturday and Sunday: A reference to churchgoing on Saturday and Sunday in Skete occurs in 18.15.6. On going to church on Saturday and Sunday in Nitria cf. Palladius, *Hist. laus.* 7.5; *Hist. monach. in Aegypto* 20.7. *Inst* 3.2, like 18.15.6, is explicit that Holy Communion was received in Egyptian monasteries on Saturday and Sunday morning. Cf. Armand Veilleux, *La liturgie dans le cénobitisme pachômien en quatrième siècle* (SA 57) (1968): 228–229, 234–235. On the antiquity of the custom of Christians' meeting for worship on Saturday cf. Paul F. Bradshaw, *Daily Prayer in the Ancient Church* (London, 1981), 68.

Living far from a source of water and consequently being obliged to carry one's supply of it over a long distance was a calculated ascetical practice. Cf. 24.2.3, 24.10; *Inst.* 4.24.3, 5.36.2; *Verba seniorum* 7.31, 19.17; Palladius, *Hist. laus.* 19.8.

3.1.3 That the person who prays enjoys the companionship of angels is suggested in Clement of Alexandria, *Strom.* 7.7.49; Origen, *De orat.* 11.

Because of this characteristic: The characteristic in question is Paphnutius's solitude, and he is called "the Buffalo" on account of that animal's presumed love of solitude. There are stories of monks who lived with buffaloes for ascetical reasons, although Paphnutius is not one such. Cf. *Verba seniorum* 20.11; Regnault 88. N516.

3.4.2 The reference here is to Athanasius, *V. S. Antonii* 2, although Athanasius does not cite the first scriptural passage, Lk 14:26. That Antony should be placed in tandem with Abraham, who is mentioned in the previous paragraph, is some indication of the great esteem in which he was held. As Abraham's calling leads to his becoming "the father of a multitude of nations" (Gn 17:4), so Antony's leads to his becoming the father of monks.

3.5.2 This Moses was the famous Ethiopian. Cf. p. 35.

The desert of Calamus is also called Porphyrion. Cf. 24.4.1. Porphyrion seems to be identical with Porphyrites on Mount Porphyrites, between the Nile and the Red Sea. Cf. Palladius, *Hist. laus.* 34.3; idem, *Dial.* 17.

3.5.3 The idea that the end rather than the beginning counts in a course of action, illustrated by the examples of Judas and Paul, also occurs in Jerome, *Ep.* 54.6.

3.6.4 On soldiering for the Lord cf. the note at 1.1.

A similar comparison using these three "books of Solomon" appears in Origen, *Comm. in Cant. Cant.*, prol. (GCS 33.75–79). There they are related respectively to three branches of knowledge—namely, the moral or ethical, the natural, and the introspective or contemplative. The third book, the Canticle of Canticles, thus has contemplative significance in both Origen and Cassian. That the Canticle of Canticles should yield a deep mystical meaning is a commonplace in patristic literature from at least the time of Origen. Cf. Marvin H. Pope, *Song of Songs* (Anchor Bible 7C) (Garden City, N.Y., 1977), 114–122. The idea of an ascent within Scripture itself, from books offering a lower meaning to others offering a higher one, may also be found in Gregory of Nyssa, *In psalm. inscrip.*, where the psalter is divided into five parts that correspond to five stages of the spiritual life, each part or stage representing an advance over the previous one. Cf. also 5.21.3 and the note at 14.9.5.

3.7.3 These words on ecstasy look forward to 9.31 (which is a better known and more succinct expression of the same state) and 19.4.1f. They are paralleled in Ps.-Macarius, Coll. 3, *Hom.* 15.5 (SC 275.176); Diadochus of Photice, *Cap. gnost.* 14 (SC 5 bis, 91). Cf. also 4.5.

3.7.4 That experience is an indispensable teacher in the learning of spiritual truths is an oft-repeated theme in *The Conferences*. Cf. 4.15.2, 7.4.1, 8.16.1, 12.4.1, 12.5.4, 12.8.1ff., 12.12.1f., 12.13.1, 12.16.1, 13.18.1f., 14.17.1, 14.18, 3 praef. 3, 19.7, 21.32.1, 21.34.4, 21.36.3f., 23.21.3. For a study of the use of the language of experience (which is sometimes contrasted with other kinds of learning) in Cassian cf. Pierre Miquel, "Un homme d'expérience: Cassien," *Collectanea Cisterciensia* 30 (1968): 131–146.

3.7.5 On disdaining parents and homeland cf. 24.1.2ff. and the relevant note.

Egypt is occasionally a negative symbol in early Christian literature because of its rampant idolatry and not only because of its persecution of the Chosen People. Cf. 5.22; Ps.-Hippolytus, *Hom. pasch.* 12 (SC 27.139–141: "Egypt is the vast and black image of a dark and profound error, because out of it there arose the first floods of deceit—cattle, fish, birds, wild animals and all living creatures of that sort, deified and honored as gods"); Origen, *Hom. in Jesu Nave* 5.6 *ad fin.; Hist. monach. in Aegypto* 8.21ff. (which gives a fanciful account of the origins of Egyptian idolatry); Cyril of Alexandria, *Comm. in Isaiam* 1.2 (PG 70.77); Louis Bouyer, *The Paschal Mystery,* trans. by Sr. Mary Benoit (Chicago, 1950), 58. The monastic Egyptian preoccupation with demons, evident everywhere in the literature that it produced in its first few centuries, is very likely related to this view of Egypt: The pagan gods have simply been transformed into demons. Cf. the note at 7.32.

3.9.1ff. Cassian's willingness to speak of riches as being indifferent *(media)* or even good places him among those Fathers who take a moderate view of wealth, as opposed to those who are grudging or even hostile to it and to the wealthy, at least in some of their writings. For a study that emphasizes this hostility, citing Clement of Alexandria, Basil, Ambrose, Chrysostom, and Augustine, cf. Charles Avila, *Ownership: Early Christian Teaching* (Maryknoll, N.Y., 1983). A fuller collection of texts, with commentary, may be found in Peter C. Phan, *Social Thought* (Message of the Fathers of the Church 20) (Wilmington, 1984). The terminology of good, bad, and indifferent, which had already been employed in passing in 3.7.11, reappears in 6.3ff. (in the same context as here) and 21.12.4ff. Indifference is mentioned by itself in 8.5, although cf. the relevant note. The categories of good, bad, and indifferent are themselves of Stoic origin. Cf. Johannes von Arnim, ed., *Stoicorum veterum fragmenta* 1 (Leipzig-Berlin, 1921), 47–48; ibid. 3 (1923), 17–39. On Cassian's use of these categories to establish the rudiments of a theory of relative values cf. Jean-Claude Guy, "La place du *contemptus mundi* dans le monachisme ancien," RAM 41 (1965): 245–248.

3.10.2 That Peter gave up only a ripped net and some inconsequential fishing gear is noted also in Chrysostom, *Serm. in Ep. ad Rom.* 7 (PG 60.452). Cf. as well as Augustine, *Enarr. in Ps.* 103, serm. 3.16.

3.10.5 That the object of the monastic life is entrance into the promised land is suggested also in Lucien Regnault, ed. and trans., *Les sentences des Pères du Désert. Série des Anonymes* (Solesmes, 1985), 56, N142; ibid. 263, N617. This is a variation on the more popular theme of the monastic life as a return to paradise, for which cf. Boniface Ramsey, *Beginning to Read the Fathers* (New York, 1985), 152–153; and to the references there add Chrysostom, *Serm. in Matth.* 68.3.

3.12ff. For other references to grace cf. the note at 2.1.3f.

3.15.4 The "inferior Latin" reads: *Idonitas nostra ex Deo est. Idonitas* is a late Latin neologism.

3.16.2 Shipwreck is already an image for the loss of faith in 1 Tm 1:19. For a study of the image cf. Hugo Rahner, *Symbole der Kirche: Die Ekklesiologie der Väter* (Salzburg, 1964), 433–450. Cf. also 15.3.1.

3.20.1 On the distinction between the divine will and the divine permission cf. Origen, *De princ.* 3.2.7; idem, *Hom. in Gen.* 3.2 ("Many things occur without [God's] willing them, but nothing apart from his providence"); John of Gaza, *Lettre à un laïc* 466 (trans. by L. Regnault et al., *Barsanuphe et Jean de Gaza: Correspondence* [Solesmes, 1972], 315); Dorotheus of Gaza, *Instruc.* 15.155 (SC 92.434–436).

3.22.4 The cenobium (referred to here in the plural) in which Cassian and Germanus learned very little about the second renunciation and nothing at all about the third was their own in Bethlehem. On the inferior instruction that the two friends received there cf. 5.12.3, 17.3ff., 18.2.2ff., 19.1.3ff., 21.11.

FOURTH CONFERENCE
THE CONFERENCE OF ABBA DANIEL: ON THE DESIRE OF THE FLESH AND OF THE SPIRIT

TRANSLATOR'S INTRODUCTION

The Daniel of the present conference is an otherwise unknown figure, not to be identified with the Daniel of the *Apophthegmata patrum*. The story of his ordination first to the diaconate and then to the priesthood, with which the conference is introduced, serves to establish his high credentials. But the fact that he continued to act as Paphnutius's deacon even after his priestly ordination is perhaps intended to show that even the assumption of ecclesiastical office does not change one's relationship to an elder. At the price of unliturgical behavior, the spiritual hierarchy transcends the official hierarchy of the Church.

The substance of the conference begins when the two friends ask Daniel a question on the origin of wandering thoughts. He responds by saying that such wandering comes from any one of three sources–a person's own negligence, an attack of the devil, or the design *(dispensatio)* of God. These three sources correspond fairly closely to the three sources of human thoughts in general that are enumerated toward the end of the first conference–namely, the person himself, the devil, and God. Daniel speaks of the first two sources of mental wandering with dispatch and then turns to the third and to an explanation of what he means by the divine design. This design permits wandering thoughts, otherwise characterized here as barrenness and abandonment by God, lest a person grow proud of his good thoughts and come to believe that they lie within his own control, and also in order that a person's steadfastness may be tested, as was Job's and Israel's.

The conflict in a person's mind between wandering thoughts and the desire to adhere to God is beneficial inasmuch as it demonstrates how dependent one is on the divine assistance. It is paralleled, moreover, by the conflict between the spirit and the flesh that is spoken of in Galatians 5:17; indeed, the two conflicts—between an unstable mind and the yearning to cling to God, and between the spirit and the flesh—are ultimately the same. On hearing of the adversary relationship of spirit and flesh, Germanus asks for a clearer explanation. It seems to him, he says, that there are three things at issue in the Apostle's words—namely, the conflict of the flesh against the spirit, the desire of the spirit against the flesh, and the will. In his response Daniel adds a fourth element, which is the fact of doing what one does not want to do. He then discusses the different possible meanings of the terms "flesh" and "spirit," and finally he addresses himself to the nature of the conflict itself.

This conflict, he declares, is beneficial because it obliges a person to maintain an equilibrium between overweening spiritual ideals on the one hand and excessive bodily yearnings on the other: "The desire of the spirit [does not] let the mind be dragged into unrestrained wickedness, nor, on the other hand, does the frailty of the flesh permit the spirit to be inflated with unreasonable desires for virtue" (4.12.5). In other words, the conflict between spirit and flesh compels a person to the practice of discretion. Thus we have resumed here the central theme of the second conference.

It is important to note that the possibility for this conflict consists in the fact that the will is balanced between the spirit and the flesh. It "occupies a somewhat blameworthy middle position and neither delights in the disgrace of vice nor agrees to the hardships of virtue" (4.12.1). The will, which only seeks a culpable peace due to its lukewarmness, is ultimately forced by the inordinate demands of both flesh and spirit to opt for discretion. The position of the will here is reminiscent of that of the human being in general in some early writers, who place the individual squarely between good and evil, not inclining utterly to either the one or the other (cf. Melito of Sardis, *Hom. pasch.* 48; Methodius, *Symposium* 3.7). Finally, the doing of what one does not want to do, which is the fourth element that Daniel had spoken of, is an inevitable accompaniment of the conflict in question. The beneficial aspect of this is that it drives a person to ascetical exercises and hence to perfection itself.

The conflict between the spirit and the flesh is played out particularly in the realm of sexuality. Here the alternatives are spiritual pride on the one hand and sexual heedlessness on the other, but the price that is paid for an equilibrium between the two is a "simple" genital pollution. Many eunuchs, according to Daniel, cannot experience this sexual aspect of the struggle between spirit and flesh, and their lukewarmness is worse than a capitulation to either excess. There is an implicit warning here, it seems, against equating discretion with tepidity.

As a result of another question from Germanus there follows a discussion of the three possible conditions of the human soul—namely, carnal, animal, and spiritual. These conditions correspond roughly to the three renunciations mentioned in the previous conference; indeed, Daniel himself suggests a connection by speaking several times of renunciation from this point on. Most of the remainder of the conference, however, after the three conditions have once been set out, is devoted to the first—carnality—and does not really touch on the animal or the spiritual. Hence the first of the renunciations, that of worldly wealth, receives considerable attention. The conference concludes with a few words, though, about the second renunciation, which deals with the attitudes of the renunciant.

IV. The Conference of Abba Daniel: On the Desire of the Flesh and of the Spirit

Chapters

I.1. Among the other men devoted to the Christian philosophy we also saw Abba Daniel, who was indeed equal in every kind of virtue to those who were dwelling in the desert of Skete, although he was more particularly adorned with the grace of humility. By reason of his purity and gentleness he was chosen for the office of the diaconate by the blessed Paphnutius, the priest in that desert, even though he was younger than many others. To such an extent did this same blessed Paphnutius rejoice in his virtues that he even hastened to put on a par with himself in the priestly order one whom he knew to be his equal in the attainments of his life and in grace. For, finding it intolerable that he should remain any longer in a lower ministry and desiring to provide a most worthy successor to himself while he was still alive, he promoted him to the honor of the priesthood. 2. Yet he relinquished nothing of his former humble manner and never made anything of his higher order in the other's presence, but whenever Abba Paphnutius was making the spiritual offerings he carried out his previous ministry as a deacon. The blessed Paphnutius was frustrated in his hope and choice of a successor, however, even though he was such a great man that he also possessed the grace of foreknowledge on many occasions. For shortly afterward he sent on ahead to God the man whom he had prepared as his own successor.

II. We asked this blessed Daniel, then, why when we were sitting in our cell we would be so filled with gladness of heart and a kind of unspeakable joy and abundance of holy sentiments that no words or even feelings could approach it. Pure and ready prayer would also be uttered, and a mind that was full of spiritual fruit would make supplication and would sense that its effectual and swift prayers were attaining to God even during sleep.

On the other hand, why, with no apparent cause, would we so suddenly be filled with anguish and oppressed with a certain irrational sadness that we would sense that we ourselves were not only withering up from such feelings but that our cell too was dreadful, our reading was worthless, and our very prayer was uttered in an unstable, tottering, and somehow drunken manner? Even with groaning and straining our mind could not be recalled to its former direction, and the more intently it would be brought back to the vision of God the more vehemently it would be taken off on some slippery digression to wandering distractions. So bereft of every spiritual fruit would it be that it could be roused from this deadly sleep, as it were, neither by a desire for the kingdom of heaven nor by the fear of Gehenna that would be held out to it.

To this he replied:

III. "Three reasons have been handed down by our forebears for this mental barrenness of which you speak. It comes either from our own negligence or from an attack of the devil or as the Lord's design and trial. It is a question of negligence when, by our fault and due to lukewarmness, we show that we are careless and lax and, having through laziness cultivated the soil of our heart with wicked thoughts, we let germinate thorns and thistles. As these spring up in it, we consequently become barren of every spiritual fruit and devoid of contemplation. It comes from an attack of the devil, however, when the adversary penetrates our mind with his subtle wiles, even sometimes when we are involved in good activities, and either unaware or unwilling we are drawn away from the highest attentiveness.

IV.1. "But there is a twofold reason for the design and trial. First, so that, by being forsaken by the Lord for a short while and humbly seeing the frailty of our spirit, we may not become proud because of any previous purity of heart which has been granted us by his visitation; and so that, by proving to us that when we are forsaken by him we cannot regain that condition of joy and purity by any groans and effort of our own, we may understand that even our previous joy of heart was conferred on us not by our own doing but by his condescension, and that present joy must be sought anew from his grace and illumination. 2. The second reason for this trial is to put to the proof our perseverance and steadfastness of mind and our desire, and also to manifest in us with what yearning of heart and earnestness of prayer we must look for the visitation of the Holy Spirit when he has left us. Thus, when we realize how much effort it takes to seek out that spiritual joy and gladness of heart once it has departed, we may strive to guard it more carefully and to hold on to it more attentively once it has been found. For it seems to be the case that whatever is in the habit of being poorly guarded is believed to be able to be easily retrieved.

V. "From this it is clearly proven that it is the grace and mercy of God which always work good things in us, that when they are missing the laborer's zeal is worthless, that without his help—once again—no eagerly pursued effort is able to bring us back to a previous state, and that these words are continually being fulfilled in us: 'It is not of the one who wills or of the one who runs, but of God who is merciful.'[1] This grace, however, sometimes does not refuse to visit the negligent and the lax with the holy inspiration of which you speak and with an abundance of spiritual thoughts. It inspires the unworthy, arouses the sleeping, and enlightens those who are held in the blindness of ignorance. Mercifully it reproves and chastises us and pours itself into our hearts, so that thus stirred up by its compunction we might be moved to rise up out of the sleep of inertia. Finally, too, we are often suddenly filled in these visitations with odors that go beyond the sweetness of human making, such that a mind which has been relaxed by this delightful sensation is seized with a certain spiritual ecstasy and forgets that it is dwelling in the flesh.

VI.1. "To such a degree did the blessed David recognize as beneficial what we have referred to as a departure and, so to speak, abandonment by God that he preferred never to pray that he would not be utterly deserted by God, for he knew that this would be helpful neither for himself nor for human nature in its pursuit of perfection. But he prayed instead that this might be tempered when he said: 'Do not forsake me forever,'[2] as if he were saying in other words: I know that you are accustomed to forsake your holy ones for a beneficial purpose, in order to put them to the proof, 2. for they could not be tried by the adversary unless they were forsaken by you for a little while. Therefore I do not ask that you never forsake me, because it would not profit me not to be aware of my weakness and to say: 'It is good for me that you have humbled me'[3] and not to have training in combat. Certainly I could not have this if the divine protection were always and uninterruptedly with me. When I am defended by you the devil does not dare to try me. He objects and rebukes both me and you with what he is accustomed to saying against your champions with slanderous words: 'Does Job worship God for nothing? Have you not hedged him and his household and all his property round about?'[4] Instead I ask that you not forsake me 'forever,' which in the Greek is εως σφοδρα—that is, to an excessive degree. 3. As useful as it is to me that you should leave me for a little while in order to test the steadfastness of my desire, so it is harmful if you let me be abandoned for too long because of my deserts and my sins. For no human strength will be able to endure by its own steadfastness if it is too long abandoned by your help in time of trial. Nor will it be able to give way instantly before the power and wherewithal of the adversary if you yourself, who are aware of human strengths and are the arbiter of our struggles, 'do not permit us to be tried beyond our capacity, but with the trial also provide a way out, so that we may be able to endure.'[5]

4. "We read something like this as it appears in mystical fashion in the Book of Judges with respect to the extermination of the spiritual nations that are opposed to Israel: 'These are the nations that the Lord forsook, so that by them he might instruct Israel, so that they might grow accustomed to fighting with their enemies.'[6] And again, a little further on: 'The Lord left them so that he might test Israel with them, whether or not they would hear the commandments of the Lord that he had laid down for their forefathers by the hand of Moses.'[7] 5. God did not begrudge Israel their peace nor look with malice upon them, but he planned this conflict in the knowledge that it would be beneficial. Thus, constantly oppressed by the onslaught of the nations, they would never feel that they did not need the Lord's help. Hence they would always meditate on him and cry out to him, and they would neither lapse into sluggish inactivity nor lose their ability to fight and their training in virtue. For frequently security and prosperity have brought low those whom adversities cannot overcome.

VII.1. "We also read in the Apostle that this conflict has been set in our members too for our advantage: 'For the desire of the flesh is against the spirit, and that of the spirit against the flesh. But these are opposed to one another, so that you may not do what you want to do.'[8] Here you have conflict deeply rooted in our body, so to say, according to the design of the Lord. For how can whatever is true in each case and admits of no exceptions be considered other than attributable by nature to the very stuff of humanity after the fall of the first man? And why should it not be believed that what is seen to be innate and ingrown in all has been put there by the decision of a Lord who seeks not our hurt but our well-being? 2. He declares that this is the reason for the struggle between flesh and spirit when he says: 'So that you may not do what you want to do.' Therefore, if we could accomplish what God has determined we cannot accomplish, namely doing what we want to do, can this be believed to be anything other than harmful? This conflict, which is beneficial in some way, has been put in us by the Creator's design, provoking and compelling us to a better condition. If it were removed there is little doubt that a dangerous repose would take its place."

VIII. GERMANUS: "Although we are beginning to understand this, nonetheless, since we cannot completely grasp the Apostle's words, we want this to be explained to us more clearly. For three things seem to be indicated here–first, the conflict of the flesh against the spirit; second, the desire of the spirit opposed to the flesh; and third, our will, which is placed as it were in the middle and about which it is said: 'So that you may not do what you want to do.' In this regard, although, as I have said, we have gleaned some hints from the things that have been exposed to our understanding, still we want this to be set out somewhat more plainly to us, since this conference has offered the opportunity to do so."

IX.1. DANIEL: "It falls to the intellect to discern the divisions and the outlines of questions, and understanding's highest function is to know that you do not know. Hence it is said: 'Wisdom will be credited to the fool who asks questions,'[9] for although the questioner does not know the answer to his question, nonetheless, because he inquires prudently and comes to understand what he does not understand, this very thing–his having prudently acknowledged what he does not know–is credited to him as wisdom.

2. "According to your division, therefore, three things seem to be named by the Apostle here–the flesh's desire against the

spirit and that of the spirit against the flesh; and this conflict seems to have for its cause and reason the fact that we cannot do, as it says, what we want to do. There remains, then, a fourth fact which you have not seen at all–namely, that we do what we do not want to do. Therefore we need, first of all, to recognize the force of the two desires of the flesh and of the spirit; then we shall be able to discuss what our free will is, which is poised between the two; and finally we shall in similar fashion discover what cannot belong to our will.

X.1. "We see that the word 'flesh' is used in numerous ways in Holy Scripture. Sometimes it signifies the human being in his entirety, namely as composed of body and soul, as in this case: 'The Word was made flesh.'[10] And: 'All flesh shall see the salvation of our God.'[11] Sometimes it means sinful and carnal human beings, as in this case: 'My spirit shall not remain in those men, because they are flesh.'[12] 2. Occasionally it refers to sins themselves, as in this case: 'You are not in the flesh but in the spirit.'[13] And again: 'Flesh and blood shall not possess the kingdom of God.' And there follows: 'Neither shall corruption possess what is incorruptible.'[14] Sometimes it refers to consanguinity and affinity, as in this case: 'Behold, we are your bone and your flesh.'[15] And in the Apostle: 'If somehow I might make my flesh jealous and save some of them.'[16]

3. "We should ask, then, which of these four meanings we ought to understand as applying to 'flesh' here. It is clear that it has nothing at all to do with one of the suggestions: 'The Word was made flesh,' or: 'All flesh shall see the salvation of God.' But neither does it have anything to do with another suggestion–'My spirit shall not remain in these men, because they are flesh'–since 'flesh' as a simple term for sinful man is not thus understood in the phrase: 'The desire of the flesh is against the spirit, and that of the spirit against the flesh.' Neither does it speak of two substances but of two realities which, in one and the same human being, struggle both together and individually according to the alternations and changes imposed by time.

XI.1. "Therefore we should understand 'flesh' as referring here not to man–that is, to the substance of man–but to the will of the flesh and to its worst desires, just as 'spirit' does not designate something substantial but the good and spiritual desires of the soul. The same blessed Apostle expressed this meaning a little before when he began: 'But I say, walk by the spirit and you will not fulfill the desires of the flesh. For the desire of the flesh is against the spirit, and that of the spirit against the flesh. But these are opposed to one another, so that you may not do what you want to do.'[17] 2. Since both of these–namely, the desires of the flesh and those of the spirit–exist in one and the same human being, an interior battle is daily waged within us as long as the desire of the flesh, which swiftly descends into vice, rejoices in those delights which pertain to present repose. On the contrary, the desire of the spirit, which is opposed to this, so yearns to be entirely absorbed in spiritual pursuits that it is even willing to exclude the necessities of the flesh, and so much does it long to be constantly taken up with these pursuits that it does not want to pay any attention at all to the frailty of the flesh.

"The flesh delights in luxuries and pleasure, but the spirit does not give in even to natural desires. 3. The former wants to be sated with sleep and to be filled with food, but the latter is so replete with vigils and fasts that it does not want to take even the sleep and food that are necessary to life. The former desires to abound in all kinds of plenty, but the latter is even content not to have the paltriest bit of bread each day. The former longs to be sleek with bathing and daily to be crowded around with troops of flatterers, but the latter rejoices in squalid filth and the vastness of the inaccessible desert, and it is horrified at the presence of any mortal. The former cherishes the honors and praise of human beings, but the latter glories in the affronts and persecutions that come upon it.

XII.1. "Between these two desires, then, the free will of the soul occupies a somewhat blameworthy middle position and neither delights in the disgrace of vice nor agrees to the hardships of virtue. It seeks to refrain from fleshly passions in such a way that it would by no means wish to endure those necessary sorrows without which the desires of the spirit cannot be laid hold of–hoping to obtain bodily chastity without disciplining the flesh, to acquire purity of heart without the exertion of vigils, to abound in the spiritual virtues while enjoying fleshly repose, to possess the grace of patience without the aggravation of any contrariness, to practice the humility of Christ without jettisoning worldly honors, to pursue religious simplicity along with secular ambition, to serve Christ to the accompaniment of human praise and acclamation, to be strictly truthful without the least offense to anyone. Finally, it prefers to pursue future goods in such a way as not to lose present ones.

2. "This will would never bring us to true perfection but would place us in a very lukewarm state and make us like those who are rebuked by the Lord's reproach in the Apocalypse–'I know your works, that you are neither cold nor hot. Would that you were cold or hot. But now you are lukewarm, and I will begin to vomit you out of my mouth'[18]–if these warring insurrections from both sides did not destroy this very lukewarm condition.

"For when we are subservient to this will of ours and want to let down our guard a little, all at once stings of the flesh make their appearance, wound us with their vices and passions, and do not permit us to abide in the state of purity that we delight in; they drag us to that chilling path of pleasures which horrifies us and which is full of briers. 3. On the other hand, if we have been inflamed with spiritual fervor and, wishing to extinguish the works of the flesh regardless of human frailty, have tried with swelling heart to make ourselves practice virtue to an exaggerated degree, the weakness of the flesh intervenes and gives us pause in our blameworthy spiritual excess. And so it is that, during this struggle in which both desires fight against one another, the soul's free will, which wishes neither to submit completely to fleshly desires nor to expend its energy for the sake of virtue, is somehow guided aright. As long as this contest goes on between the two it cuts off a more dangerous willing on the part of the soul by establishing a kind of equilibrium in the scales of our body. This marks out precise boundaries for spirit and flesh, and it does not permit the predominance of either a mind inflamed with spiritual ardor on the right hand or a flesh stung with sinfulness on the left.

4. "While this conflict is stirred up within us every day to our benefit, we are salutarily driven to that fourth condition, which we do not want, in order to acquire purity of heart not at leisure or at ease but with constant toil and a contrite spirit; to seize hold of

chastity of the flesh with severe fasting, hunger, thirst, and watchfulness; to set a direction for the heart by means of reading, vigils, unceasing prayer, and the squalor of the desert; to seize hold of patience through training in tribulation; to serve our Creator in the midst of blasphemy and numerous taunts; and to pursue truth, if necessary, in the face of this world's hatred and enmity. Thus—with such a struggle going on in our body and while we ourselves are far from sluggish ease and pushed to the toil and zeal for virtue that we do not want—our equilibrium is best maintained. 5. On the one side a fervent spirit tempers the lukewarm inclination of our will, while on the other an even warmth pervades the unyielding frigidity of the flesh. Neither does the desire of the spirit let the mind be dragged into unrestrained wickedness, nor, on the other hand, does the frailty of the flesh permit the spirit to be inflated with unreasonable desires for virtue. Otherwise, in the first case the shoots of every kind of vice may blossom forth, or in the second haughtiness, the origin of our illbeing, may make its appearance and pierce us quite seriously with the dagger of pride. But the proper equilibrium which results from the struggle of these two opens up the healthy and temperate path of virtue between the both of them and teaches the soldier of Christ always to proceed along the royal road.

6. "And so it will happen that when, on account of the lukewarmness of this indolent free will that we have spoken about, the mind has turned too readily toward the desires of the flesh, it will be restrained by the desire of the spirit, which is not in the least inclined to earthly vice. On the other hand, if through an immoderate fervor resulting from an overflowing heart our spirit has been snatched up to things that are impossible and ill-advised, it will return to its proper equilibrium thanks to the weakness of the flesh. Then, transcending the very lukewarm condition of our free will, it will proceed with all due moderation and with toilsome effort along the level path of perfection.

7. "We read in the Book of Genesis that something similar was ordained by the Lord with regard to the construction of that famous tower, when a confusion of tongues suddenly occurred and repressed the sacrilegious and wicked attempts of men.[19] For a disharmony would have remained there in opposition to God, and

indeed in opposition to those who had begun to tempt his divine majesty, unless by God's design a diversity of languages had created division among them and had, by their dissonance, forced them to advance to a better state, and unless a good and beneficial discord had recalled to salvation those who had been persuaded to destroy themselves by their wicked agreement. Thus when division occurred they began to feel the human frailty that previously, elated by their evil conspiracy, they had been unaware of.

XIII.1. "From the diversity in this conflict there arises a delay and from this strife there comes a pause which is so beneficial to us that when, due to the body's resistance, we cannot immediately pursue to the end what we have wickedly conceived, we are sometimes changed for the better because of the subsequent remorse or the reconsideration that usually follows upon postponing a work and thinking about it in the interval. 2. And those who we know are restrained by no fleshly hindrance from fulfilling the desires of their wills–namely, the demons and evil spirits–we hold to be more detestable than human beings, although in fact they have fallen from a higher order of angels, because as soon as they have conceived of something wicked they at once pursue it to its evil end. In them possibility is immediate to desire, for as swift as their mind is to think of something, equally swift is their pernicious and unrestricted substance to carry it out, and since the ability to do whatever they want lies near at hand, no salutary hesitation intervenes for them to change what they have wickedly conceived.

XIV. "For a spiritual substance which is free of the flesh's resistance has no excuse for an evil choice arising in itself, and thus there is no pardon for its wickedness, because it has not been provoked to sin from without, as we are, by any assault of the flesh, but is inflamed by the viciousness of an evil will alone. Therefore its sin is unpardonable and its disease irremediable. Just as it succumbs without the involvement of any earthly matter, so it cannot obtain forgiveness or a place of repentance. It is clear from these facts that this struggle of flesh and spirit against one another which rages in us is not only not bad but is even of great benefit to us.

XV.1. "In the first place this is so because it immediately

reproves our laziness and negligence and, like a most careful instructor, never lets us wander from the straight line of strictness and discipline. If our heedlessness exceeds the measure of due seriousness by just a little bit it at once goads and rebukes us with stings that spur us to return to an appropriate restraint.

"Secondly, there is the matter of perfect chastity and purity when, thanks to the grace of God, we see that we have been free for a long time from genital pollution. Lest we believe that we shall no longer be troubled by this simple disturbance of the flesh and thereby grow proud deep within ourselves, as if we did not carry about the corruptibility of the flesh, it humiliates us and catches us up short once again with an ejaculation that is very unobtrusive and simple and that reminds us by its sting that we are but human beings. 2. For, to a certain degree, although we are accustomed to fall indiscriminately into other kinds of sins and, indeed, ones that are more serious and wicked, and to commit them without being struck by compunction, in this one our conscience is more especially humiliated. Through this illusion it is also bitten by the memory of forgotten passions, and it understands clearly that it has made itself unclean out of natural impulses, which it used to be unaware of when it was still more unclean due to spiritual sins. As it turns at once to the task of correcting its former carelessness, it is warned at the same time that it must not place its confidence in past accomplishments of purity which it sees that it has lost by falling away from the Lord ever so little. Nor can the gift of this purification be possessed except by the grace of God alone, as our experience of the matter teaches us in a certain way, so that if we delight in always pursuing integrity of heart we must constantly strive to acquire the virtue of humility.

XVI. "That the pride attached to this purity is more pernicious than any other crime and shameful deed and that on its account we would acquire no reward for our chastity, however integral, those powers that we mentioned before are the witnesses. Since they are believed to have no fleshly tinglings of this kind, they were cast down into perpetual ruin from that sublime and heavenly position on account of a prideful heart alone. We would be utterly lukewarm and beyond remedy, then, because we would have nothing in our body or in our conscience to point out our negligence, nor would we ever strive to attain to a fervent perfection but would let go of our strict moderation and abstinence unless this fleshly tingling within us humiliated and checked us and made us careful and attentive about purifying ourselves of spiritual vices also.

XVII. "Finally, we notice that this lukewarmness exists very frequently in those who are eunuchs in body because they are, as it were, freed from this fleshly constraint and consider themselves to stand in no need of either the effort of bodily abstinence or a contrite heart. Weakened by this sense of security, they never really struggle to seek for and possess perfection of heart or even purification from spiritual sins. This condition, which comes from their fleshly state, becomes animal, which is certainly a worse situation. For the person who passes from cold to lukewarm is, in the Lord's words, said to be more detestable."

XVIII. GERMANUS: "The value of the struggle that occurs between flesh and spirit seems to us to have been so clearly expressed that we believe that we can almost touch it with our hands. Consequently we also want to have explained to us what the difference is between the carnal and the animal man and how the animal can be worse than the carnal."

XIX.1. DANIEL: "According to the scriptural definition, there are three conditions for the soul: The first is carnal, the second animal, and the third spiritual. We read in the Apostle that they are thus designated. Of carnal persons it is said: 'I gave you milk to drink, not solid food, for you were not yet able. But indeed you are still not able, for you are still carnal.'[20] And again: 'Since there is envy and strife among you, are you not carnal?'[21] The animal is spoken of in this way: 'The animal man does not perceive the things that are of the spirit of God, for that is foolishness to him.'[22] But of the spiritual it is said: 'The spiritual man judges all things, but he himself is judged by no one.'[23] And again: 'You who are spiritual instruct such persons in a spirit of mildness.'[24]

2. "Therefore, once having made our renunciation, we should strive to stop being carnal. That is to say, once we have begun to cut ourselves off from the way of life of worldly people and to withdraw from that obvious uncleanness of the flesh, we should strive immediately to lay hold of the spiritual condition

with all our strength. Otherwise we may flatter ourselves that, according to the outer man, we seem to have renounced this world and to have withdrawn from the contagion of carnal fornications, as if we had thereby attained to the height of perfection. We would thereupon become increasingly more lax and careless with regard to correcting our other passions and, held fast between the two, we would be unable to arrive at the condition of spiritual advancement, thinking that it was utterly sufficient for our perfection that we seem to be separated from the way of life of this world and its pleasures in the outer man and that we are exempt from corruption and from carnal intercourse. Having thus been found in that lukewarm condition which is considered worst of all, we would realize that we would be vomited out of the mouth of the Lord, according to those words of his which say: 'Would that you were hot or cold. But now you are lukewarm, and I shall begin to vomit you out of my mouth.'

3. "Not undeservedly does the Lord declare that those whom he had already received in the bowels of his love but who had become wickedly lukewarm would be vomited out with a kind of visceral convulsion. Although they could have provided nourishing food for him, they preferred to be torn out of his bowels, having become worse than those who never entered the Lord's mouth as food, just as we detest as more loathsome what nausea makes us cough up. For even when our mouth takes in something cold, it is warmed and swallowed with a healthful result. But whatever has once been spat out because of the evil of its pernicious lukewarmness we are unable even to look at from afar without great disgust, never mind put near our lips.

4. "Very justifiably, then, is this declared to be worse, for a carnal person—that is, a worldling or a pagan—will attain more easily to a salutary conversion and to the height of perfection than one who has professed himself a monk but has not seized upon the path of perfection as it appears in the rule of discipline and who no longer burns with spiritual fervor. At least the former has been humiliated by sins of the body and, realizing that he is unclean through fleshly contact, is sometimes struck with compunction and hastens to the source of true purification and to the summit of perfection. He is horrified at the frigid state of faithlessness in

which he finds himself, and with an ardent spirit he flies the more easily to perfection. 5. But the person who, as we have said, has started out in lukewarm fashion and has begun to misuse the name of monk has not yet set out on the path of this profession with the requisite humility and fervor. Whoever has once been infected with this wretched disease and has somehow been weakened by it will no longer be able to taste what is perfect, nor will he be able to be instructed by anyone else's admonitions. For, according to the Lord's words, he says in his heart: 'I am rich and wealthy and need nothing.'[25] 6. What follows will therefore also be appropriate to this person: 'But you are wretched and miserable and poor and blind and naked.'[26] He has become even worse than a worldling because he does not realize that he is wretched and blind and naked and wanting correction and in need of someone's admonition and instruction. For this reason, indeed, he does not let himself be exhorted by any saving word, since he does not see that the title of monk is too heavy a burden for him and that he is weighed down by everyone's opinion. While all believe that he is holy and venerate him as a friend of God, he will certainly be subjected in the future to a judgment and punishment which are that much more severe.

7. "Why should we dwell any longer on matters that are well known to us and that we have sufficiently verified by experience? We frequently see cold and carnal persons–that is, worldlings and pagans–attain to spiritual warmth, but never anyone who is lukewarm or animal. We also read in the prophet that the Lord detests these persons so much that he has commanded spiritual and learned men to stop admonishing and teaching them and not to waste the seed of the saving word on them as if on barren and fruitless soil that is overgrown with harmful briers. Instead, disdaining this, they should cultivate new soil. That is, they should transfer all the care of their teaching and the vigor of the saving word to pagans and worldlings, for so it reads: 'The Lord says this to the men of Judah and to the inhabitants of Jerusalem: Cultivate your fallow ground, and do not sow among thorns.'[27]

XX.1. "Finally, it is embarrassing to say, we notice that many people have made their renunciation in such a way that it is obvious that they have altered nothing of their former sins and behavior with the sole exception of their rank and their worldly attire. For they love to acquire money which they did not have before, and in fact they do not get rid of what they had or—what is sadder still—they even want to get more with the excuse that, as they insist, it is right that they should always support their family or the brothers with it. Or else they hoard it under the pretext of establishing a community, which they presume that they would be able to found as if they were abbas. 2. If ever they sought truthfully for the way of perfection, they would strive to achieve this with all their strength—namely, having stripped themselves not only of money but also of their former likes and every distraction, to place themselves, alone and naked, under the guidance of the elders, so as not only not to be concerned about others but even about themselves. What happens on the contrary, however, is that in striving to attain a high place among the brothers they never submit to the elders. Starting out in pride and desirous of instructing others, they neither deserve to learn themselves nor to do things that are worth being taught. Since, in the Savior's words, they have become blind leaders of the blind, they will surely both fall into a ditch.[28]

3. "Although there is one genus of this pride, there are two species—one that constantly mimics seriousness and gravity, and another that with unrestrained license dissolves into foolish guffaws and laughter. The former, to be sure, enjoys the quiet, but the latter scorns being constrained by silence and is not even ashamed now and again to say things that are inappropriate and silly, while at the same time blushing to be considered inferior to others or less learned than they. The one is ambitious for the clerical office because of pride, but the other disdains it, considering it inappropriate to or unworthy of its former position or life or high birth.

"Yet a close examination of each of these determines and decides which one ought to be declared worse. 4. To be sure, it is one and the same kind of disobedience to go against an elder's command either because of zealous activity or because of laziness, and it is just as harmful to break the monastic rule for the sake of sleep as for the sake of keeping vigil. It is as great a thing to transgress the abba's precept in order that you may read as it is to disdain it in order that you may sleep, nor is it another sort of pride to neglect a brother for the sake of fasting than for the sake of eating, except that the faults which give the impression of being virtuous and spiritual are more pernicious and irremediable than those which arise openly from carnal pleasure. The former are at once rebuked and healed like diseases that have been openly exposed and made manifest, but the latter, hidden under the guise of virtue, remain incurable and make more desperately sick those whom they have so dangerously deceived.

XXI.1. "Something ridiculous should be mentioned. We notice how some people, after the fervor of their initial renunciation, in which they have forsaken private property or abundant resources and this world's soldiery and betaken themselves to monasteries, are so zealously attached to things that cannot be completely renounced and that are necessary in this life, although they are small and insignificant, that their concern for these things overarches their passion for all their previous possessions. To have despised extensive goods and property will certainly be of little profit to these people, because they have transferred their feelings for those things (on account of which feelings these things should be despised) to small and insignificant items. 2. For, in holding on to the vice of covetousness and avarice—which they cannot exercise with respect to precious things—in regard to trifles, they prove that they have not cut off but only exchanged their former passion. Since they are excessively attached to mats, baskets, blankets, books, and other things of the sort, however trifling they may be, they are still held bound by the same yearnings as before. They even guard and defend these things so jealously that they are not ashamed to be upset with a brother because of them nor even—what is worse—to quarrel with him. 3. Still laboring under the disease of their former covetousness, they are not content to have in the established quantity and measure what bodily use and necessity oblige a monk to possess. They point to the avarice in their hearts, too, when they strive to have those necessities in a more attractive manner than others, or when they are overly diligent and prevent other people from touching things that should be the common property of all the brothers, carefully and attentively guarding them as if they were their own property.

4. It is as if a mere difference of metals and not the very passion of covetousness were harmful; as if, since it is not permitted to get angry about great matters, one would be guiltless in becoming so with regard to trifling ones; and as if we had not forsaken valuable things in order the more easily to learn how to disdain trifling ones. For what difference is there whether someone is covetous with respect to vast and splendid possessions or with respect to trifling ones, except that he is to be considered more blameworthy who, in having spurned the greatest things, is entangled in the least ones? Therefore this renunciation does not achieve perfection of heart because, although it has a poor man's property, it has not laid aside a rich man's will."

Textual References

1. Rom 9:16.
2. Ps 119:8.
3. Ps 119:71.
4. Jb 1:9–10 LXX.
5. 1 Cor 10:13.
6. Jgs 3:1–2.
7. Jgs 3:4.
8. Gal 5:17.
9. Prv 17:28 LXX.
10. Jn 1:14.
11. Lk 3:6.
12. Gn 6:3 LXX.
13. Rom 8:9.
14. 1 Cor 15:50.
15. 2 Sm 5:1 LXX.
16. Rom 11:14.
17. Gal 5:16–17.
18. Rv 3:15–16.
19. Cf. Gn 11:1–9.
20. 1 Cor 3:2.
21. 1 Cor 3:3.
22. 1 Cor 2:14.
23. 1 Cor 2:15.
24. Gal 6:1.
25. Rv 3:17a.
26. Rv 3:17b.
27. Jer 4:3.
28. Cf. Mt 15:14.

4.1.1 Christian philosophy: On the use of the term "philosophy" in connection with Christianity, which dates from the middle of the second century, cf. Gustave Bardy, "'Philosophie' et 'philosophe' dans le vocabulaire chrétien des premiers siècles," *RAM* 25 (1949): 97–108; and specifically with regard to monasticism cf. Gregorio Penco, "La vita ascetica come 'filosofia' nell' antica tradizione monastica," in *Studia Monastica* 2 (1960): 79–93.

On Paphnutius, the leader of the discussion in the third conference, cf. p. 113.

It should be noted that Daniel himself has no say in his ordination to the diaconate and the priesthood; everything is arranged by the elder. Even the bishop who performed the ordination goes unmentioned and is presumably a secondary figure. On Daniel's ordination cf. also the note at 1.20.5.

4.2ff. On wandering thoughts cf. the note at 1.5.4.

4.3 On the image of the heart as arable here and in 4.19.7 cf. the note at 1.22.2.

4.4ff. The words about being forsaken by the Lord, particularly for the sake of increasing one's yearning for him, recall Origen, *Comm. in Cant. Cant.* 3 (GCS 33.202–203); idem, *Hom. in Cant. Cant.* 1.7.

4.4.1 For other references to grace, mentioned also in 4.5 and 4.15.2, cf. the note at 2.1.3f.

4.5 Odors that go beyond the sweetness of human making: Cf. the note at 1.1.

On the ecstasy spoken of here cf. 3.7.3 and the relevant note.

4.6.2 Champions: *Athletas.* Cf. the note at 7.20.

4.6.3 Arbiter: For other uses of the term cf. the note at 2.13.7, and for a similar context to the present use cf. 7.20.2.

4.9.1 Understanding's highest function is to know that you do not know: Daniel's words here are suggestive of those of the Delphic oracle in Plato, *Apol.* 23b: "O humans, the wisest among you is the one who knows, as Socrates does, that ultimately he knows nothing." Cf. also ibid. 21d. A somewhat similar sentiment is expressed in 10.9.3.

4.10.1f. For a similar analysis of the term "flesh," based on scriptural data, cf. Augustine, *De civ. Dei* 14.2; Gregory the Great, *Moralia in Iob* 14.72.

4.11.3 Rejoicing in squalid filth was a perhaps unfortunate aspect of some early monasticism. In this the chief exemplar was Antony of Egypt. Cf. Athanasius, *V. S. Antonii* 47, 93 and ACW 10.119–120, n. 171 for further examples and explanation. Pagans occasionally reproached the monks for their unkempt ways. Cf. Rutilius Namatianus, *De reditu suo* 523f.

4.12.4 The fourth condition spoken of here refers back to 4.9.2.

4.12.5 On the image of the soldier of Christ cf. the note at 1.1.

The image of the royal road has its scriptural basis in Nm 20:17, 21:22. In antiquity royal roads were generally the straightest and most secure routes between two major places. Cf. Jean Leclercq, "La voie royale," in *Supplément de la Vie Spirituelle,* Nov. 1948, 338–352; idem, *The Love of Learning and the Desire for God,* trans. by Catherine Misrahi (New York, 1961), 130–135. Cf. also 6.9.3, 24.24.5f., 24.25.2, *Inst.* 11.4.

4.13.2 The demons' swiftness is attributable to their highly refined corporeality, for which cf. the note at 7.13. This swiftness is understood in terms of physical motion, as in Tertullian, *Apol.* 22; Athanasius, *V. S. Antonii* 31; Augustine, *De divinatione daemonum* 3.7. They are also said to possess a spiritual swiftness, as in Evagrius, *Prac.* 51 (where it is noted that the demons of impurity and blasphemy are almost quicker than the human mind).

4.15ff. The temptation to pride arising from sexual purity is remarked already in the earliest noncanonical Christian literature and frequently thereafter. Cf. 1 *Clem.* 38.2; Ignatius, *Poly.* 5.2. Cf. also the reference to "proud purity" in 6.11.2. Augustine, *De s. virg.* 32.32ff., counsels humility to virgins at great length. Given the fact that virginity often generates pride, it is not surprising that such pride is often punished by a fall into some kind of illicit sexual activity. Cf. 22.6.2; *Inst.* 12.20ff.; *V. prima gr. Pachomii* 8; Evagrius, *Prac.* 13; Palladius, *Hist. laus.* 28, 47.9; Gregory the Great, *Moralia in Iob* 11.13.21, 26.16.28, 32.14.21. The justification for a fall of this sort is hinted at in 4.16. Cf. also Augustine, *De civ. Dei* 14.13: "I dare say that it is beneficial to the proud to fall into open and manifest sinfulness, so that those who have already fallen by pleasing themselves may be displeasing to themselves." Less drastically, however, pride might simply result in a nocturnal emission when one had thought that such could no longer happen. Cf. 12.6.7f.

4.15.1 The arbitrary and uncontrollable character of genital movement, dealt with at some length in the twelfth conference, is an occasional theme in Augustine, for whom cf. *De civ. Dei* 13.13, 14.16; *De nupt. et concup.* 1.6.7. On the same in infants and small children cf. 7.2.1; *Inst.* 7.3.1.

Simple disturbance...Ejaculation that is very unobtrusive and simple: Cf. the note at 22.3.5.

4.15.2 On experience as teacher cf. the note at 3.7.4.

4.17 Lukewarmness is customarily associated with eunuchs. Cf. 12.5.1f. This view is somewhat qualified, however, in 12.10.3f. On the ancient opinion of the character of eunuchs cf. Pauly-Wissowa, Supplementband 3.453–454.

Which comes from their fleshly state: I have read *descendens*(comes) rather than *discedens* here.

4.19.3 On the Lord's nourishing food as the salvation of others cf. Hilary, *Comm. in Matth.* 3.2; Ambrose, *Exp. evang. sec. Luc.* 4.16; Jerome, *Tract. in Marci evang.* 11.11–14 (CCSL 78.488); Maximus of Turin, *Serm.* 66.4 (CCSL 23.278).

4.20.1 On the excuses used for hoarding money in a monastery cf. *Inst.* 7.7.

4.20.2 Alone and naked: This image of the monk, stripped of everything, is paralleled in Jerome, *Ep.* 120.1: "Sell everything that you have, give to the poor and follow the Savior and, naked and alone, you shall follow the cross that stands naked and alone."

4.20.3 Laughing was usually looked at askance in early monastic literature as it suggested frivolity, impeded compunction, and permitted access to the influence of demons. Cf. 7.19.3, 9.3.3. For studies cf. Basilius Steidle, "Das Lachen im alten Mönchtum," in *Benediktinische Monatschrift* 20 (1938): 271–280; Irénée Hausherr, *Penthos: The Doctrine of Compunction in the Christian East*, trans. by Anselm Hufstader (CS 53) (1982): 95–105.

On ambition for the clerical office cf. the note at 1.20.5.

4.21 On coveting trifles cf. 1.6.1f. and the relevant note.

This world's soldiery: *Militiam saeculi.* This stands in contrast to soldiery for Christ, for which cf. the note at 1.1.

FIFTH CONFERENCE
THE CONFERENCE OF ABBA SERAPION: ON THE EIGHT PRINCIPAL VICES

Translator's Introduction

Abba Serapion, who leads such dialogue as there is in this fifth conference (his long discourse is interrupted only once), is most likely to be identified with the figure of the same name in 2.11. Whether, however, he is the same as some of the Serapions who appear elsewhere in early Christian literature is uncertain, given the brevity of his description here. (Cf. Jerome, *Ep.* 108.14; Palladius, *Hist. laus.* 7.3, 46.2 [where one is referred to as "the Great"]; *Hist. monach. in Aegypto* 18.1; Sozomen, *Hist. eccl.* 6.28.)

Cassian was not the first to write of the eight vices that are treated in this conference. Evagrius had already done so in *Prac.* 6ff., where he speaks of them as λογισμοι, or "thoughts," and at greater length in his *Tract. de octo spiritibus malitiae* (PL 79.1145–1164, under the name of Nilus). He in turn was preceded by others who laid the groundwork, but who spoke in terms of only seven vices. (Cf. Otto Zöckler, *Das Lehrstück von den sieben Hauptsünden: Ein Beitrag zur Dogmen- und Sittengeschichte* [Munich, 1893]; L. Wrzol, "Die Hauptsündenlehre des Johannes Cassianus und ihre historischen Quellen: 1. Der historische Ursprung der Hauptsündenlehre," *Divus Thomas: Jahrbuch für Philosophie und spekulative Theologie,* 3. Serie, 1 [1923]: 385–404; Irénée Hausherr, "L'origine de la théorie orientale des huit péchés capitaux," *Orientalia Christiana* 30 [1933]: 164–175; Morton W. Bloomfield, "The Origin and Concept of the Seven Cardinal Sins," *Harvard Theological Review* 34 [1941]: 121–128; A. Vögtle, "Woher stammt das Schema der Hauptsünden?" *Theologische Quartalschrift* 22 [1941]: 217–237; Morton W. Bloomfield, *The Seven Deadly Sins*

[East Lansing, Mich., 1952]; Weber 23–25; SC 170.63–84; RAC 13.734–770.) Cassian himself had in fact anticipated the doctrine of the fifth conference in the eight books (5–12) that he had devoted to these vices in *The Institutes.* The fifth conference, however, is not merely a summary of those eight books, which are somewhat sprawling in their discussion of the subject matter; it also represents a refinement, since it analyzes the interrelationship of the vices in a way that *The Institutes* does not, as well as offering other nuances.

The present conference lists the vices in the same order as appears in *The Institutes,* and, like that work, it divides them into the categories of natural and unnatural (cf. *Inst.* 7.1ff.). A further distinction touching on the vices' four kinds of operation—with or without bodily activity, from without or from within—does not, however, appear in *The Institutes;* neither, finally, does that between carnal vices and spiritual vices. Shortly after the introduction of these distinctions Serapion digresses at some length on Christ's temptations, observing that he, as the perfect image of God, could only be tempted as Adam was when he was in the Garden and was himself still an unsullied image of the divine—namely, by gluttony, vainglory, and pride. This section (5.5f.) is one of the two longest christological passages in *The Conferences.* It is interesting to note that the other, in 22.9ff., is also concerned with Christ's relationship to sin and that it too raises the issue of his temptations.

The tenth chapter demonstrates how the first six vices are linked together, such that the first begets the second, the second the third, and so forth. Therefore, in order to conquer the sixth, the fifth must be overcome, and so on. The idea of this sort of concatenation is not unique to Cassian. It had already appeared in germ in Aristotle and the Stoics and, in more developed fashion, in Evagrius (cf. SC 170.91–93, and to the sources listed there, add Gregory of Nyssa, *De virg.*4.5, 15.2). But it is Cassian who first treats the connection between the vices in a recognizably systematic manner. The last two vices, though, namely vainglory and pride, are not linked to the first six in this way; they do, however, have a connection between themselves (as do the first and second, the third and fourth, and the fifth and sixth). These last two are particularly dangerous, among other reasons, because they are begotten precisely when the first six have been vanquished.

There follows a breakdown of the eight vices into their species, beginning with gluttony: "There are three kinds of gluttony" (5.11.1). The classification seems virtually exhaustive.

Then Serapion notes that different people suffer in different ways from these vices, although everyone suffers to a certain degree from all of them. Thus, there are those who are troubled primarily by fornication, while others are tormented mostly by wrath, and so forth. The old man suggests a strategy to deal with the ensemble of them. The strategy in question, which effectively takes up the rest of the conference, may be reduced to three points–namely, the discovery and uprooting of one's principal vice and then gradually of the others; the refusal to succumb to pride upon having achieved this; and the attribution of one's victory to the divine assistance. When the eight major vices have been destroyed, then their numerous offspring–of which Cassian typically names two dozen, not counting the "many others that it would take too long to mention" (5.16.3)–will be destroyed as well.

But gluttony, the first of the vices, stands in a special category and must be dealt with in a somewhat qualified fashion. If the other seven vices may be compared to the seven nations that the Israelites drove out of the promised land, gluttony may be likened to Egypt: "That nation, in which the children of Israel were born, is not ordered to be completely destroyed but only to have its land forsaken, while the other seven are commanded to be utterly destroyed" (5.19.1). The reason for this distinction is that there is always need of food. Hence "we obviously do not destroy the Egyptian nation. Instead we withdraw from it through a certain discretion, by not thinking of superfluous or elegant fare but by being content, as the Apostle says, with ordinary food and clothing" (5.19.2).

A few chapters later, after having discussed gluttony at some length, Serapion rather unexpectedly adds two more vices to his list of eight in order to establish a correspondence with the ten nations whose territory is promised to Abraham's descendants. These new vices are idolatry and blasphemy. Blasphemy, for one, is certainly an important vice in desert literature (cf. Evagrius,

Prac. 43, 46, 51; idem, *Antirrheticus* 8.41 [ed. by Frankenberg, Berlin, 1912, 543]; Palladius, *Hist. laus.* 23.5, 38.11). But Cassian seems to include these two vices here principally because he must somehow account symbolically for the ten nations in question.

The conference concludes with some words on gluttony and fasting, followed by a brief recapitulation of the strategy necessary to overcome the vices.

V. The Conference of Abba Serapion: On the Eight Principal Vices

Chapters

I. In that community of very old men there was a man by the name of Serapion who was particularly adorned with the grace of discretion and whose conference I think is worth the effort to put down in writing. When we had begged him to say something about the assault of the vices that would cast light on their origins and causes, he began in this way:

II. "There are eight principal vices that attack humankind. The first is gluttony, which means the voraciousness of the belly; the second is fornication; the third is filargyria, which is avarice or love of money; the fourth is anger; the fifth is sadness; the sixth is acedia, which is anxiety or weariness of heart; the seventh is cenodoxia, which is boastfulness or vainglory; and the eighth is pride.

III. "Of these vices there are two kinds. They are either natural like gluttony or unnatural like avarice. But they have four kinds of operation. Certain ones cannot be consummated without bodily action, such as gluttony and fornication. Certain others, however, can be completed without any bodily action whatsoever, such as pride and vainglory. Some take their motivating causes from without, such as avarice and anger. Others, however, are aroused from within, such as acedia and sorrow.

IV.1. "Let us make this still clearer not only by a short discussion as well as we are able, but also by scriptural texts.

"Gluttony and fornication, although they are in us naturally (for sometimes they also arise without any provocation from the mind but solely due to the instigation and itching of the flesh), nonetheless require external matter in order to be consummated, and thus they operate through bodily action. For 'everyone is tempted by his own lust. When lust has been conceived it gives birth to sin, but when sin has been consummated it brings forth death.'[1] 2. The first Adam would not have been able to be deceived by gluttony had he not had something to eat and immediately and lawlessly misused it, nor was the second tempted without the enticement of some substance, when it was said to him: 'If you are the Son of God, tell these stones to become loaves of bread.'[2] It is clear to everyone that fornication also is not committed except by means of the body, as God says to the blessed Job with reference to this spirit: 'Its strength is in the loins, and its power in the navel of the belly.'[3] 3. Therefore these two in particular, which are exercised by means of the flesh, more especially require not only the spiritual concern of the soul but also bodily abstinence, since the mind's attentiveness is not enough of itself to check their urgings (as it sometimes does in the case of anger or sadness and other passions, which it can expel by mental effort alone and without chastising the flesh). Bodily discipline must come to its assistance, and this is accomplished by fasting, vigils, and works of penance, and to these is added living in a remote place, because just as they are generated through the fault of both soul and body, so they cannot be overcome except by the toil of both.

4. "Although the blessed Apostle has declared that all the vices in general are carnal, since he has numbered enmity and anger and heresies among the other works of the flesh,[4] nonetheless we make a distinction based on a twofold division for the sake of a more refined understanding of their remedies and their natures. For we say that some of them are carnal, while some others are spiritual. The carnal ones pertain especially to the enjoyment and feelings of the flesh; by them it is so delighted and gratified that it sometimes even arouses peaceful minds and drags them reluctantly to acquiesce in its will. 5. About these the Apostle says: 'In which all of us at one time walked in the desires of the flesh, doing the will of our flesh and of our thoughts, and we were by nature children of wrath like the rest.'[5]

"But we call spiritual those that, having arisen at the prompting of the soul alone, not only give no pleasure to the flesh but even inflict it with serious sufferings and merely provide the sick soul with the food of a miserable enjoyment. Therefore these have need of the medicine of a simple heart, whereas those that are carnal are only remedied by a twofold cure, as we have said. Hence it is important to those who strive for purity first of all to remove from themselves the very stuff of these carnal passions, by which either an occasion for or the memory of those same passions can be aroused in the soul that is still sick. 6. For a twofold sickness necessarily requires a twofold cure. Seductive images and matter need to be removed from the body, lest lust attempt to break out into deeds, and by the same token a more careful meditation on Scripture, constant watchfulness, and solitude must be applied to the soul, lest it so much as conceive this in thought. In the case of the other vices, however, human companionship is of no harm, and indeed it is even of great help to those who really want to be rid of them, since they are frequently rebuked by the presence of other people, and although aggravations more readily appear, they are quickly remedied.

V. "Therefore our Lord Jesus Christ, although he was declared by the Apostle to have been tempted 'in every respect as we are,' is nonetheless said to have been 'without sin.'[6] That is, he was without the contagion of this passion, having had no experience whatsoever of the pricks of fleshly lust by which we are inevitably stung, even unwittingly and unwillingly, for in his regard there was nothing like our own insemination and conception, as the archangel said in announcing how his conception would take place: 'The Holy Spirit shall come upon you, and the power of the Most High shall overshadow you. Therefore the holy one that is to be born of you shall be called the Son of God.'[7]

VI.1. "The one who possessed the incorruptible image and likeness of God had to be tempted himself by the same passions by which Adam also was tempted when he still enjoyed the inviolate image of God—that is, by gluttony, vainglory, and pride—and not by those in which he entangled himself after having broken the commandment, when the image and likeness of God was violated and he had already fallen through his own fault. For it was by gluttony that he took the food from the forbidden tree; by vainglory that it was said: 'Your eyes shall be opened';[8] and by pride that it was said: 'You shall be as gods, knowing good and evil.'[9] 2. By these three vices, then, we read that the Lord, the Savior, was also tempted: by gluttony when the devil said to him: 'Tell these stones to become loaves of bread'; by vainglory when he said: 'If you are the Son of God, cast yourself down';[10] and by pride when he showed him all the kingdoms of the world and their glory, and he said: 'All these things I will give you if you fall down and adore me.'[11] Thus, having been attacked by these very same temptations, he taught us also by his own example how we should conquer the tempter.

"Therefore both the one and the other are called Adam, the former having been the first to go to ruin and death and the latter having been the first to go to resurrection and life. 3. Through the former the whole human race is condemned, but through the latter the whole human race is freed. The former was fashioned of untilled and untouched earth, the latter was born of the Virgin Mary. It behooved him, then, to suffer temptations, but it was not necessary that they be excessive. For one who had conquered gluttony could not be tempted by fornication, which proceeds from the former's repletion and from its root. Even the first Adam would not have been struck by this if he had not been deceived by the enticements of the devil and contracted the passion which generates it.

"For this reason the Son of God is not said to have come, without qualification, in sinful flesh but rather 'in the likeness of sinful flesh.'[12] Although he had real flesh, which is to say that he ate and drank and slept and was also really fastened by nails, he did not have real sin contracted through wrongdoing but only what seemed to be such. 4. For he did not experience the burning pricks of carnal desire that even arise when we do not want them, due to nature's action, but he experienced a certain similarity through participating in our nature. When he was truly accomplishing all the things that pertain to our condition and was bearing every human weakness, he was consequently thought to be subject to this passion as well, so that in these weaknesses he even seemed to carry about in his flesh the stuff of this vice and sin. 5. The devil tempted him, then, only with the vices by which he had also deceived that first man, conjecturing that, as a man, he could be mocked in other ways too if he saw that he was seduced by the things with which he had overthrown the first man. But he was unable to inflict him with a second disease, sprouting from the root of the principal vice that served as a source, since he was defeated in the first battle. He saw that he had not been touched at all by the first stages of this sickness and that it was too much to expect the fruit of sin from him, since he discerned that he had never possessed its seeds and roots.

6. "Although Luke gives the last temptation as: 'If you are the Son of God, cast yourself down,'[13] this can be understood as

the passion of pride. The one mentioned previously, which Matthew places as third and in which, according to the aforesaid evangelist Luke, the devil promised him all the kingdoms of the world, showing them to him in an instant, can then be taken to be the passion of avarice. For once gluttony was conquered he was unable to prevail over him with fornication, and so he passed on to avarice, which he knew was the root of all evils.[14] Here again he was overcome, and he did not dare to afflict him with any of the vices that followed and that he knew sprouted from its root and stock. So he passed on to the last passion, that of pride, by which he knew that even the perfect and those who have conquered all the vices could be struck. He remembered that on its account he himself had been thrown down from the heavenly places when he was Lucifer, along with many others, without having been incited by any preceding passion. 7. According to the order that we have spoken of, then, which is described by the evangelist Luke, the seductions and forms of temptations with which the clever enemy attacked the first and the second Adam concur very neatly. For to the former he says: 'Your eyes shall be opened,' and to the latter: 'He showed him all the kingdoms of the world and their glory.'[15] In one place he says: 'You shall be as gods,' and in the other: 'If you are the Son of God.'

VII.1. "Let us say something in the same order that we had proposed about the effects of the other passions too, the explanation of which we were obliged to interrupt because of our exposition on gluttony and on the Lord's temptations. Vainglory and pride are also consummated without any action on the body's part. For why do these things, which cause the ruin of the captive soul for the exclusive purpose of winning praise and pursuing human glory, need bodily action? 2. Or what bodily activity was there in the aforesaid Lucifer's ancient pride, which he conceived solely in mind and thought? As the prophet mentions: 'You who said in your heart: I will go up to heaven, I will set my throne above the stars of God, I will ascend above the height of the clouds, I will be like the Most High.'[16] He had no one to provoke him to this pride. It was in thought alone that his crime and his eternal ruin were perfectly achieved, especially inasmuch as there followed no works of the tyranny that he was striving for.

VIII.1. "Although avarice and anger do not have the same nature (for the first is unnatural, but the second seems to have its origins within us), nonetheless they arise in similar fashion, since the causes that engender them usually come from without. Frequently those who are still rather weak complain that they fall into these vices through being irritated or incited by others and that they are driven to anger or to avarice through others' provocation.

"That avarice is unnatural, however, is plainly evident from the fact that its origins demonstrably do not have their source in us and that it does not arise from what pertains to the possession of soul and flesh and to the stuff of living. 2. For it is certain that nothing has to do with the utility and needs of our common nature apart from daily food and drink. But everything else, with whatever eagerness and love it may be looked upon, is nonetheless clearly unrelated to human need and even to the utility of human life itself. Therefore this, which exists as it were outside of nature, only disturbs monks who are lukewarm and wavering, whereas the things that are natural constantly try even the most proven monks and, indeed, those who dwell in the desert. 3. So true has this been shown to be that we even know of some pagan nations which are completely free of the passion of avarice, for they have never suffered, either by use or custom, from the disease of this vice. We also believe that that first world, which existed for a long period of time before the Flood, was ignorant of the frenzy of this desire.

"It is proved beyond a doubt that this is extinguished in one of us who has rightly exercised renunciation when he has abandoned all his property and so yearns for monastic discipline that he does not hold back a single denarius of it for himself. 4. We can find many thousands of people as witnesses to this. Nonetheless, when, after having dispersed all their wealth in one brief moment, they have eradicated this passion to such a degree that they are no longer even slightly disturbed by it, they continue to fight against gluttony, and unless they struggle with great attentiveness of heart and abstinence of body they cannot be safe.

IX.1. "Sadness and acedia are not usually engendered by some external provocation, like the others that we have spoken about previously. For they are known to distress frequently and very bitterly even the solitaries and those who live in the desert and have no human contact. Whoever has lived in the desert and experienced the struggles of the inner man will easily testify from these same experiences how very true this is.

X.1. "Although these eight vices, then, have different origins and varying operations, yet the first six–namely, gluttony, fornication, avarice, anger, sadness, and acedia–are connected among themselves by a certain affinity and, so to speak, interlinking, such that the overflow of the previous one serves as the start of the next one. For from an excess of gluttony there inevitably springs fornication; from fornication, avarice; from avarice, anger; from anger, sadness; and from sadness, acedia. Therefore these must be fought against in a similar way and by the same method, and we must always attack the ones that follow by beginning with those that come before. 2. For a tree whose width and height are harmful will more easily wither up if the roots which support it are exposed and cut beforehand, and pestilential waters will dry up when their rising source and rushing streams have been stopped up with skillful labor.

"In order to conquer acedia, sadness must first be overcome; in order to drive out sadness, anger must be cast out beforehand; in order to extinguish anger, avarice must be trampled on; in order to eradicate avarice, fornication must be repressed; in order to overthrow fornication, the vice of gluttony must be disciplined.

3. "But the two remaining ones, vainglory and pride, are linked in similar fashion, like the vices that we have spoken of, such that growth in the first becomes the start of the second, for an overflow of vainglory begets the beginnings of pride. But these differ wholly from those first six vices and are not leagued with them since they are not only not generated by them but even arise in a contrary manner and order. For when the former have been rooted out these sprout forth all the more, and at the death of the former these spring up and grow more vigorously. 4. Hence we are also attacked by these two vices in a different way. We fall into one of those six vices when we have been seduced by the one that comes before it, but we are in danger of falling into these two when we are victorious and, indeed, particularly after triumphs.

Each vice, then, since it is begotten by an increase in the one that comes before it, is purged away when the one before it is diminished. Therefore vainglory must be suffocated in order for pride to be driven out. Thus, whenever the preceding ones have been overcome, those that follow fall idle, and, with the extinction of the ones that go before, the remaining passions wither away without any effort. 5. And although the eight vices that we have spoken about are connected and joined among themselves according to the scheme that we have mentioned, yet they are divided more particularly into four couplets. Fornication is allied by a special relationship to gluttony, anger is closely yoked to avarice, acedia to sadness, and pride to vainglory.

XI.1. "Now let us discuss individually the different kinds of each vice. There are three kinds of gluttony. The first impels a monk to hasten to eat before the fixed and lawful hour. The second is pleased with a full stomach and with devouring any edibles whatsoever. And the third desires more refined and delicate foods. These three entail no small loss for a monk unless he struggles to extricate himself from all of them with equal diligence and care. For just as breaking the fast before the canonical hour is never to be dared, so likewise filling one's stomach and the preparation of costly and choice dishes must be avoided. From these three causes different and very bad states of health of the soul are produced. 2. From the first is born hatred for the monastery; with that there grows a dread of the same dwelling place and an inability to endure it; and this is always soon followed by departure and swift flight. From the second the burning pricks of lasciviousness and wanton desire are aroused. The third also fastens the inextricable bonds of avarice on the necks of its captives and never permits the monk to be rooted in Christ's utter deprivation.

"We notice that the traces of this passion are in us when perchance, having been invited to eat by one of the brothers, we are not content to eat the food with the condiment with which it was seasoned by our host but demand with importunate and unbridled boldness that something be poured on it or added to it. 3. There are three reasons why this must never happen. In the first place, because the mind of the monk must be practiced in the discipline of endurance and moderation and must, according to the Apostle, learn what a sufficiency consists in.[17] For whoever takes offense at a slightly unpleasant taste and is unable to restrain the pleasure of the palate even for a moment will be completely incapable of controlling the hidden and greater desires of the body. Secondly, because it sometimes happens that the particular thing that we are asking for at a given moment is lacking and we would shame our host in his need and frugality by making known this poverty, which he would prefer to be known to God alone. Thirdly, because occasionally the condiment that we ask to have added is unpleasant to others, and we discover that we are annoying many people in trying to cater to our own gormandizing and desire. Therefore this boldness in us is to be disciplined in every respect.

4. "There are three kinds of fornication. The first takes place in the union of the sexes. The second occurs without touching a woman, and for it we read that Onan, the son of the patriarch Judah, was struck down by the Lord.[18] This is called impurity in Holy Scripture. About this the Apostle says: 'I say to the unmarried and to widows that it is good for them to stay just as I am. But if they cannot exercise self-control, let them marry; for it is better to marry than to burn.'[19] The third is that which is conceived in the soul and in the mind, and about which the Lord says in the Gospel: 'Whoever looks at a woman with lust has already committed adultery with her in his heart.'[20]

5. "The blessed Apostle declares that these three kinds must all be extinguished in the same way when he says: 'Put to death your members that are on earth: fornication, impurity, wantonness,'[21] and so forth. And again he speaks of two of these to the Ephesians: 'Fornication and impurity should not be mentioned among you.'[22] And again: 'Know this, that no fornicator or impure or avaricious person (which is slavery to idols) has an inheritance in the kingdom of Christ and God.'[23] 6. Just as we should guard against these three with equal care, so one is enough to keep us out of the kingdom of Christ.

"There are three kinds of avarice. The first does not permit renunciants to be deprived of their wealth and property. The second persuades us by a still greater covetousness to take back what we have dispersed and distributed to the poor. The third demands that we long for and acquire what in fact we did not possess before.

7. "There are three kinds of anger. One blazes up interiorly, and it is called θυμος in Greek. Another breaks out in word and deed and effect, and it is denominated οργη. About these the Apostle says: 'Now, put all these things away—anger, indignation.'[24] The third, unlike that which flares up, is not finished in a short space of time but is held over for days and seasons, and it is called μηνις. 8. All of these must be condemned by us with an equal horror.

"There are two kinds of sadness. The first is begotten once anger has ceased, or from some hurt that has been suffered or from a desire that has been thwarted and brought to naught. The other comes from unreasonable mental anguish or from despair. There are two kinds of acedia. One makes those who are seething with emotion fall asleep. The other encourages a person to abandon his cell and to flee.

"Although vainglory is multiform and multifarious and exists in many subdivisions, nonetheless it is of two kinds. The first is that by which we are uplifted because of carnal and external things. The second is that by which we are inflamed with the desire for empty praise because of spiritual and hidden things.

XII.1. "Yet in one way vainglory is beneficial for beginners, for those who are still stirred up by carnal vices. If, thanks to a word spoken at the time when they happen to be harassed by the spirit of fornication, they should think of the dignity of the priestly office or of the opinion of people who might believe that they are holy and blameless, and if only because of this consideration they should reject the impure urges of desire, judging them as base and unworthy either of their own good name or of that rank, they are restraining the greater evil with a lesser one. For it is better for a person to be troubled by the vice of vainglory than for him to fall into the fire of fornication, from which he could not or could barely be saved once he had been ruined. 2. One of the prophets expresses this sense very well when he speaks in the person of God: 'On my own account I will remove my wrath afar off, and with my praise I will bridle you lest you perish.'[25] That is to say: As long as you are shackled by the praises of vainglory, you will never rush into the depths of hell and sink irretrievably by the commission of deadly sins.

"It is not surprising that this passion is so strong that it can hold back someone who is hastening to the destruction of fornication, since the frequent experience of many people shows that once someone has been poisoned by this disease he becomes so tireless that he does not even feel fasts of two or three days. 3. Even in this desert we have often seen some people admit that when they were living in the cenobia of Syria they were easily able to go without eating for five days, whereas now they are so hungry at the third hour that they can hardly keep the daily fast until the ninth hour. When someone asked why, after having lived in a cenobium where he felt no hunger and often disdained to eat for whole weeks, he should now be hungry at the third hour, Macarius replied pointedly: 'Because here there is no one to see you fasting and to support and sustain you with his praises. But there the attention of others and the food of vainglory filled you to repletion.'

4. "There is an illustration of this–namely, of the fact that when vainglory makes its appearance the vice of fornication is expelled, as we have said–which is put in beautiful and clear language in the Book of Kings. It occurs when Nebuchadnezzar, king of the Assyrians, has come up from Egypt and taken the captive people of Israel away from Neco, king of Egypt, to his own country, not in order to restore to them their former freedom and their birthplace but to lead those who would be transported to his own land, which was still further away than where they had been held captive in the land of Egypt.[26] This illustration can be well understood in the following way. Although it is more tolerable to be subject to the vice of vainglory than to that of fornication, yet it is more difficult to escape from the domination of vainglory. 5. For, so to say, one who has been held captive for a relatively long time will return less easily to his native soil and to his old-established freedom, and rightly is that prophetic rebuke directed to him: 'Why have you grown old in a foreign land?'[27] Whoever is not removed from earthly vices is appropriately said to have grown old in a foreign land.

"There are two kinds of pride. The first is carnal. The second is spiritual, which is still more pernicious, for it more particularly attacks those who it finds have made progress in some virtues.

XIII. "Although these eight vices, then, disturb the whole human race, nonetheless they do not assail everyone in the same way. In one person the spirit of fornication is dominant, in another wrath rides roughshod, in a third vainglory tyrannizes, and in still another pride holds sway. And although it is evident that we are all attacked by all of these, yet we each suffer in different ways and manners.

XIV.1. "Therefore we must so join battle against them that everyone spies out the vice by which he is particularly besieged and struggles chiefly against it, fixing all the care and attention of his mind on fighting it and keeping watch on it, brandishing the sighs of his heart and the many darts of his groans against it at every moment, employing the effort of his vigils and the meditations of his heart against it, pouring out the unceasing tears of his prayers to God, and insistently and continually demanding an end to the assault on him. 2. For it is impossible for a person to deserve to triumph over a passion before he has understood that he is not able to obtain victory in the struggle by his own diligence and his own effort, even though in order to be cleansed he must always be careful and attentive, day and night.

"When he finds himself freed from it, he should once again and with similar intensity shine light on the hidden places of his heart, locate for himself whatever is still more horrible that he notices remaining, and move against it in particular with all the arms of the Spirit. Thus, when he has consistently overcome more powerful foes, he will have a quick and easy victory over the ones that remain, because the mind too becomes stronger through a succession of triumphs, and subsequent struggles with weaker foes make for readier successes in the battle. So it is with those who are accustomed to fight for prizes against all sorts of beasts in the presence of the kings of this world. (This kind of spectacle is commonly called a *pancarpum.*) 3. These persons, I say, make their first attack against the beasts that they have noticed are stronger and fiercer, and when these have been killed they more easily destroy the ones that are left, which are less terrible and less aggressive. Likewise, it is always the case that when the more powerful vices have been overthrown and are succeeded by weaker ones we shall obtain a perfect victory without any hardship.

"Yet it must not be thought that whoever struggles chiefly against one vice and seemingly does not pay much heed to the darts of others can be more easily wounded at an unexpected moment. 4. This will never happen. It is impossible for one who is concerned about the purification of his heart and has armed the attention of his mind for fighting any given vice not to have a certain fear of all the other vices and a similar watchfulness with respect to them as well. How indeed will a person deserve to obtain victory over the passion from which he yearns to be freed if he makes himself unworthy of the prize of cleansing by being contaminated with other vices? But when our heart's chief concern has been directed to fighting against one passion in particular, so to speak, we shall pray more intently about it and be especially careful and assiduous in our supplication, so that we may be worthy to watch out for it more diligently and thus obtain a swift victory. 5. The Lawgiver himself teaches us that we must keep to this plan of battle and not trust in our own strength in these words: 'You shall not fear them, because the Lord your God is in your midst, a God great and terrible. He himself will consume these nations in your sight, little by little and by degrees. You will not be able to destroy them all at once, lest perhaps the beasts of the earth multiply against you. And the Lord your God will deliver them over in your sight, and he will slay them until they are completely destroyed.'[28]

XV.1. "But he likewise warns that we must not be proud of our victory over them: 'Lest after you have eaten and are filled,' he says, 'have built beautiful houses and lived in them, have acquired cattle and flocks of sheep, an abundance of everything, of silver and gold, your heart be lifted up and you not remember the Lord your God, who led you out of the land of Egypt, out of the house of slavery, and was your leader in the great and terrible desert.'[29] Solomon also says in Proverbs: 'If your enemy has fallen, do not be glad. Do not be lifted up when he is ruined, lest the Lord see and be displeased and turn away his wrath from him'[30]—that is, lest seeing your proud heart he cease to assail him and you be forsaken by him and begin to be troubled once again by the passion that you had previously vanquished by the grace of God. 2. For the prophet would not have prayed and said: 'O Lord, do not deliver over to the beasts the soul that confesses to you,'[31] unless he had known that, because of their pride of heart, some would be delivered over again to vices that they had overcome, so that they would be humbled.

"Therefore we should be certain from experience and have learned from innumerable scriptural texts that we cannot conquer such great enemies by our own strength but only with the support of God's help, and that every day we must attribute to him the sum of our victory. This is recalled thus by the Lord speaking through Moses: 'Do not say in your heart, when the Lord your God has destroyed them in your sight: Because of my righteousness the Lord has led me in to possess this land, while those nations were wiped out because of their sins. 3. For it was not because of your righteous deeds and the uprightness of your heart that you were led in to possess their land, but because they acted wickedly they were destroyed as you entered in.'[32] I ask, what could be said more clearly against that pernicious opinion and presumption of ours, by which we want to attribute everything that we do to our free will and to our own effort? 'Do not say in your heart, when the Lord your God has destroyed them in your sight: Because of my righteousness the Lord has led me in to possess this land.' 4. Did he not express himself clearly to those whose souls' eyes are open and whose ears hear? Namely, when you have enjoyed a notable success in warring against the carnal vices and you see that you have been freed from their filthiness and from this world's way of life, you should not be puffed up with the success of the struggle and the victory and ascribe this to your own strength and wisdom, believing that you were able to obtain victory over evil spirits and carnal vices through your own efforts and application and free will. There is no doubt that you would never have been able to prevail over these if the Lord's help had not fortified and protected you.

XVI.1. "These are the seven nations whose lands the Lord promised to give to the children of Israel when they left Egypt. We must accept the fact that, according to the Apostle, all the things that happened to them in a figure were written for our instruction.[33] Thus it is said: 'When the Lord your God has brought you into the land that you will enter into in order to possess it, and he has destroyed many nations in your presence, the Hittite and the Girgashite and the Amorite, the Canaanite and the Perizzite and the Hivite and the Jebusite, seven nations much more numerous than you are, and stronger than you, and the Lord has handed them over to you, you shall utterly destroy them.'[34] 2. The reason that they are said to be much more numerous is that there are more vices than virtues. Therefore in the list they are counted as seven nations, to be sure, but when it is a question of destroying them they are said to be innumerable. Thus it is said: 'And he has destroyed many nations in your presence.' For more numerous than Israel is the people of carnal passions, which proceeds from this sevenfold stock and root of the vices. 3. From it sprout murder, wranglings, heresies, thefts, false witness, blasphemies, overeating, drunkenness, slander, silliness, immodest speech, lies, perjuries, foolish talk, buffoonery, restlessness, greediness, bitterness, uproar, indignation, contempt, murmuring, temptation, despair, and many others that it would take too long to mention.

"Although we may consider these things insignificant, we should listen to what the Apostle thought about them and how he passed judgment on them. 'Do not murmur,' he says, 'as some of them murmured and were destroyed by the destroyer.'[35] And about temptation: 'Let us not tempt Christ, as some of them tempted and were destroyed by serpents.'[36] About slander: 'Do not love slander, lest you be destroyed.'[37] And about despair: 'In despair they handed themselves over to lasciviousness in the working of every error, unto uncleanness.'[38] 4. That uproar is condemned, along with anger and indignation and blasphemy, we are taught very clearly by the words of the Apostle when he commands: 'All bitterness and anger and indignation and uproar and blasphemy should be removed from you, as well as all malice,'[39] and many other things similar to these.

"Although these are much more numerous than the virtues, nonetheless when the eight principal vices have been conquered (which clearly give birth to each of the others) all of them are completely laid to rest and are utterly destroyed forever along with the eight. 5. For from gluttony are born overeating and drunkenness; from fornication—immodest speech, buffoonery, silliness, and foolish talk; from avarice–lying, fraud, robberies, perjuries, the desire for filthy lucre, false witness, violence, inhospitality, and greediness; from anger–murder, uproar, and indignation; from sadness–rancor, faintheartedness, bitterness, and despair; from acedia–laziness, sleepiness, rudeness, restlessness, roving about, instability of mind and body, talkativeness, and curiosity; from vainglory–wranglings, heresies, bragging, and putting one's trust in novelties; from pride–contempt, envy, disobedience, blasphemy, murmuring, and slander.

"We are very aware of the fact that these plagues are quite strong from the way that they assault us. 6. For the delight in carnal passions that rages in our members is stronger than zeal for virtue, which is only acquired by the highest discipline of heart and body. But if you contemplate with the eyes of the spirit those innumerable troops of enemies that the blessed Apostle enumerates when he says: 'Our struggle is not against flesh and blood but against principalities, against powers, against the world rulers of this darkness, against spirits of evil in heavenly places,'[40] as well as what is said of the righteous man in the ninetieth psalm: 'A thousand shall fall at your side, and ten thousand at your right hand,'[41] you will see with eminent clarity that they are much more numerous and powerful than we who are carnal and earthly, since they are endowed with a spiritual and ethereal substance."

XVII. GERMANUS: "Why, then, are there eight vices that attack us, when Moses enumerates seven nations that are opposed to the people of Israel, and what advantage is there for us in possessing the territories of the vices?"

XVIII.1. SERAPION: "That there are eight principal vices which attack the monk is everyone's firm opinion. Not all that are figuratively called nations are named in one place because in Deuteronomy Moses, or rather the Lord through him, was speaking to those who had already left Egypt and been freed from a very strong people–namely, the Egyptians. This figure also rightly pertains to us, who have been liberated from the worldly snares of gluttony and recognize that we are set free from the vice of the stomach and of gormandizing. 2. And for a similar reason we have a conflict with the seven remaining nations, not at all taking into account the first, which has already been overcome. Its territory is not given into Israel's possession, but it is ordained by the precept of the Lord that Israel should abandon it forever and leave it. Therefore fasts should be moderate so that it is not necessary, because of an excessive abstinence which has been taken on through fleshly weakness or infirmity, to return to the land of Egypt—that is, to the former fleshly desire of gormandizing, which we rejected when we renounced this world. Those who had gone out into the desert of the virtues but longed for the fleshpots that they used to sit over in Egypt went through this in a figurative way.

XIX.1. "That nation, in which the children of Israel were born, is not ordered to be completely destroyed but only to have its land forsaken, while the other seven are commanded to be utterly destroyed. The reason why this is so is that with whatever spiritual ardor we may be inflamed and have entered the desert of the virtues, we can never rid ourselves of the proximity and the service of gluttony and of a certain daily contact with it. For the desire for food and for things to eat will always live in us as an inborn and natural quality, although we should make an effort to cut off its superfluous appetites and desires. Since these cannot be destroyed altogether, they should be avoided by a certain turning away. 2. About this it is said: 'Do not make provision for the flesh in its desires.'[42] As long, then, as we are occupied with this care, which we are commanded not to do away with altogether but to maintain without its desires, we obviously do not destroy the Egyptian nation. Instead we withdraw from it through a certain discretion, by not thinking of superfluous or elegant fare but by being content, as the Apostle says, with ordinary food and clothing.[43]

3. "This is also commanded in figurative fashion in the law: 'You shall not abhor the Egyptian, because you were a sojourner in his land.'[44] For food that is necessary for the body is not refused without hurting it and involving the soul in sin.

"But the movements of those seven perturbations, which are harmful in every respect, must be completely uprooted from the recesses of our soul. Concerning them it is said: 'All bitterness and anger and indignation and uproar and blasphemy should be removed from you, as well as all malice.' And again: 'Fornication and every impurity and avarice should not be mentioned among you, nor filthiness nor foolishness nor buffoonery.'[45] 4. We can cut out the roots of these vices which have been added to our nature, then, but we shall never be able to cut off the practice of gluttony. For we cannot, however much progress we make, cease to be what we were born to be. That this is the case is shown as much by the life and behavior of us insignificant persons as by that of all the perfect. Although they have cut away the urges of the other passions and go to the desert utterly fervent of mind and impoverished of body, nonetheless they cannot be freed from concern for their daily fare and from the baking of their yearly supply of bread.

XX. "The image of this passion, by which even a spiritual and very good monk is inevitably hounded, is quite properly said to be an eagle. Although it soars ever so high, beyond the lofty clouds, and in its flight is hidden from every mortal eye and from the surface of the whole earth, the needs of the belly force it to drop again to the lowest valleys, to descend to earth and to entangle itself in carrion. From this it is most evident that the spirit of gluttony, unlike that of the other vices, cannot be altogether cut off or completely destroyed, but its pricks and its superfluous desires can only be restrained and moderated through a virtuous mind.

XXI.1. "When one of the elders was discussing the nature of this vice with some philosophers, who believed that they could treat him like a rustic because of his Christian simplicity, he expressed himself very well by posing a riddle: 'My father left me,' he said, 'indebted to numerous creditors. Although I have fulfilled my obligations to the others and am quit of their vexatious dunnings, there is one whom I am unable to satisfy even with a daily payment.' 2. And when they, unaware of what he was getting at, earnestly asked him what he meant, he replied: 'Due to my nature I have been hemmed in by many vices. Thanks to the Lord, however, who inspired me with a desire for freedom, I have satisfied all these as it were troublesome creditors by renouncing this world and forsaking all the property that fell to me at my father's death, and so I am completely rid of them. But in no way have I succeeded in getting rid of the urges of gluttony. 3. For although I have reduced it to a small portion and a very little amount, I cannot escape the force of its daily pressure, but I must be pursued by its constant dunning and with continual outlays await a freedom that never comes, while I pay its insatiable toll at the appointed moments.'

"Then they declared that he whom beforehand they had disdained as an illiterate rustic had an excellent understanding of the first part of philosophy—namely, ethics—and they were greatly astonished that he was able to attain by nature to that which no worldly education had conferred on him, while they themselves had been unable to achieve this even with much effort and lengthy study.

"It is enough to have said these particular things about gluttony. Now let us return to the discussion where we had begun to speak about the general relationship of the vices.

XXII. "When the Lord was speaking to Abraham about the future (which you were not asking about at all), we do not read that seven nations are numbered but rather ten, whose territory is promised to be given to his seed.[46] This number is clearly obtained once idolatry and blasphemy have been added. The multitude of impious pagans and blasphemous Jews have been subjected to these things until they come to the knowledge of God and the grace of baptism, as long as they are dwelling in the spiritual Egypt. But if someone has accepted renunciation, left that place, conquered gluttony by the grace of God, and come to the spiritual desert, he has been freed from the attack of three nations and will only wage war against the seven that are enumerated by Moses.

XXIII.1. "We understand that we are commanded to possess the lands of those wicked nations for our well-being in this way. Each vice has its own place in our heart. Claiming this for itself, it destroys the Israel that is in the depths of our soul—namely, the contemplation of the highest holy realities, which it never ceases to resist. For virtues cannot live together with vices. 'For what do righteousness and wickedness have in common? Or what fellowship is there between light and darkness?'[47] 2. But once the vices have been overcome by the people of Israel—that is, by the virtues struggling against them—chastity will thenceforth seize for itself the place in our heart which the spirit of lust and fornication used to have; patience will lay claim to what wrath had laid hold of; a beneficial sadness and one that is full of joy will take over from what death-dealing sadness had occupied; fortitude will begin to cultivate what acedia was laying waste; humility will honor what pride used to despise. And so, when all these vices have been expelled, their places in the dispositions will be occupied by the opposing virtues. These are deservedly called children of Israel—namely, of the soul that sees God. When they have expelled all the passions of the heart, they must be believed not so much to have taken over others' property as to have regained their own.

XXIV.1. "For, as an old tradition teaches, when the world was divided the children of Shem were allotted the very lands of the Canaanites into which the children of Israel were led, which afterward the posterity of Ham laid hold of by violence and force, through a wicked invasion. In this it was most righteously judged by God, who expelled the ones from the foreign places that they had wickedly seized and restored to the others the ancient property of their fathers, which had been assigned to their stock at the division of the world.

2. "This event is also understood to have a bearing upon us for a very clear reason. For the will of the Lord did not assign by nature the possession of our heart to the vices but to the virtues. After the fall of Adam they were thrust out of their own region by the vices that had grown insolent—that is, by the Canaanite peoples; and when they have been restored to it by the grace of God and by our diligence and effort, they must be believed not so much to have occupied foreign territory as to have received back their own.

XXV.1. "These eight vices are alluded to in the Gospel in this way: 'When an unclean spirit has gone out of a person, he passes through dry places seeking rest, and he does not find it. Then he says: I will return to the house of mine that I left. And when he comes he finds it empty, swept, and put in order. Then he goes and takes seven spirits worse than himself, and they go in and dwell there. And the last state of that person is worse than the first.'[48] Notice that in one instance we read of seven nations, apart from that of the Egyptians, from which the children of Israel had gone out, and likewise in the other instance seven spirits are said to return, apart from the one who is said to have left the person first.

2. "In the Book of Proverbs Solomon also speaks of this sev-

enfold source of vice in this way: 'If your enemy asks you in a loud voice, do not give in to him, for there are seven evils in his soul.'[49] That is to say, if the spirit of gluttony which has been overcome starts to coax you in humble fashion, asking as it were that you relax some of the intensity with which you began and that you permit it to exceed the limits of abstinence and the measure of a proper strictness, do not become irresolute because of its subjection or return to your former laxity and the old desires to gormandize because of its smilingly peaceable attitude, by which you seem to have been temporarily rendered immune to fleshly impulses. For through this the spirit that you had conquered is saying: 'I will return to the house of mine that I left,' and the seven spirits of the vices that proceed from it without delay will be more bitter to you than the passion which had been overcome in the beginning, and they will soon drag you down to worse kinds of sins.

XXVI.1. "Therefore, while we are burdened with fasting and abstinence we must strive, once the passion of gormandizing has been overcome, from that moment on not to let our soul be void of the necessary virtues. But we should the more carefully fill all the recesses of our heart with them lest the spirit of desire return and find us bereft of them and, not content to gain admittance for itself alone, introduce into the soul along with itself this sevenfold source of vices and make our last state worse than the first. 2. For after this happens, the soul which boasts of having renounced this world will be more vile and more impure, and it will be struck by more serious torment due to the domination of the eight vices in it, than had been the case when it was living in the world and had professed neither the discipline nor the name of monk. For these seven spirits are said to be more wicked than the first one, which had left, because the desire to gormandize—commonly known as gluttony—would not be harmful of itself if it did not introduce other more serious passions—namely, those of fornication, avarice, anger, sadness, and pride. Without a doubt these are in themselves harmful and deadly to the soul. 3. Therefore, whoever hopes to acquire the purity of perfection by abstinence alone, that is, by bodily fasting, will never be able to obtain it unless he realizes that he must exercise himself in order to be more capable—

with his flesh beaten down by fasting and not uplifted by overeating—of fighting against the other vices.

XXVII.1. "Yet it ought to be known that the same battle plan is not observed in each one of us since, as we have mentioned, we are not all attacked in the same way. Each one of us must throw himself into the fray with an eye to the particular manner in which he is being assaulted, such that one has to fight first against the vice that is placed third, and another against that which is placed fourth or fifth. And to the degree that these vices gain the ascendancy in us and demand different strategies, we ourselves must draw up battle plans according to which the progress which follows each victory and triumph will bring us to purity of heart and to the fullness of perfection."

2. Thus far did the Abba Serapion make clear to us the nature of the eight principal vices, discussing the kinds of passions lying concealed in our heart, their causes and their relationships, since we were daily being destroyed by them and were theretofore unable either to understand them completely or to discern them. So lucidly did he do this that we seemed to see them before our eyes as if in a mirror.

Textual References

1. Jas 1:14–15.
2. Mt 4:3.
3. Jb 40:11 LXX.
4. Cf. Gal 5:19–21.
5. Eph 2:3.
6. Heb 4:15.
7. Lk 1:35.
8. Gn 3:5a.
9. Gn 3:5b.
10. Mt 4:6.
11. Mt 4:9.
12. Rom 8:3.
13. Lk 4:9.
14. Cf. 1 Tm 6:10.
15. Mt 4:8.
16. Is 14:13–14.
17. Cf. Phil 4:11.
18. Cf. Gn 38:9–10.
19. 1 Cor 7:8–9.
20. Mt 5:28.
21. Col 3:5.
22. Eph 5:3.
23. Eph 5:5.
24. Col 3:8.
25. Is 48:9.
26. Cf. 2 Kgs 23–24.
27. Bar 3:10.
28. Dt 7:21–23.
29. Dt 8:12–15.
30. Prv 24:17–18 LXX.
31. Ps 74:19.
32. Dt 9:4–5.
33. Cf. 1 Cor 10:6.
34. Dt 7:1–2.
35. 1 Cor 10:10.
36. 1 Cor 10:9.
37. Prv 20:13 LXX.
38. Eph 4:19.

39. Eph 4:31.
40. Eph 6:12.
41. Ps 91:7.
42. Rom 13:14.
43. Cf. 1 Tm 6:8.
44. Dt 23:7 LXX.
45. Eph 5:3–4.
46. Cf. Gn 15:18–21.
47. 2 Cor 6:14.
48. Mt 12:43–45.
49. Prv 26:25 LXX.

5.3 On Cassian's dependence on Evagrius in distinguishing between natural and unnatural vices cf. Weber 24.

5.4.2 Lawlessly...enticement: *Inlicite...inlicitatione.*

5.6.1f. The link between Adam's eating the forbidden fruit and Christ's refusing to turn stones into bread is a commonplace in patristic literature. Cf. Irenaeus, *Adv. haer.* 5.21.1f.; Origen, *Frag. in Luc.* 96 (GCS 49.265); Ambrose, *Exp. evang. sec. Luc.* 4.17 (Lk 4:3); Maximus of Turin, *Serm.* 5.1 (CCSL 23.206).

5.6.3f. For a fuller exegesis of Rom 8:3 cf. 22.11 with the relevant note.

5.6.3 Real sin contracted through wrongdoing: *Peccatum eius quod praevaricatione contraxit verum.* This is translated by Gibson as "no true sin inherited from the fall," and by Pichery more ambiguously as "le péché que la chair contracta dans la prévarication." There is no compelling reason to suggest that, given both the ordinary usage of the word and its present context, *praevaricatione* need be translated here as "Fall" rather than simply as "wrongdoing."

5.8 The unnaturalness of avarice is also referred to in Chrysostom, *Serm. in Matth.* 80.3; idem, *Serm. in Ioann.* 65.3, 74.3; idem, *De virg.* 75.1.

5.8.3 A willingness to praise pagans for their lack of avarice may also be found in Augustine, *De civ. Dei* 5.12 and 18; idem, *De op. monach.* 25.32; idem, *Ep.* 104.6. Augustine, however, is not speaking of pagans contemporary with himself, but of those of the past.

On the value of the denarius cf. the note at 1.20.1.

5.11.1 On the three kinds of gluttony cf. also *Inst.* 5.23.1.

The accustomed and lawful hour...The canonical hour: Cf. the note at 2.25.

5.11.4 It is clear from this passage that Cassian understands fornication in a very broad sense and not merely as sexual intercourse between unmarried persons. Cf. Michel Foucault, "The Battle for Chastity," in Philippe Ariès and

André Béjin, eds., *Western Sexuality: Practice and Precept in Past and Present Times,* trans. by Anthony Forster (Oxford, 1985), 17–18. The second kind of fornication, referred to as "impurity" (*immunditia*), seems to be masturbation, given the allusion to Onan (cf. Gn 38:9–10).

5.11.6 On the three kinds of avarice cf. also *Inst.* 7.14 and 12.26.

5.12 Evagrius, *Prac.* 58, asserts that the demon of vainglory stands in opposition to that of impurity. Augustine, *De civ. Dei* 5.13, observes that vainglory cannot coexist with the baser vices.

5.12.1 The dignity of the priestly office: Cf. the note at 1.20.5.

5.12.3 The Macarius mentioned here may be one of many of that name who are known to us from other sources. At least five appear in Palladius's *Hist. laus.* alone. Cf. Cuthbert Butler, *The Lausiac History of Palladius* 2 (Texts and Studies 6.2) (Cambridge, 1904), 193–194. The story that is told here is somewhat demeaning of Syrian monasticism, which represented the monastic background of Cassian and Germanus. Cf. the note at 3.22.4.

5.14.2 For other references to grace, which is also spoken of in 5.15.2ff., cf. the note at 2.1.3f.

On the term *pancarpum* cf. Gazet's commentary in PL 49.629–630.

5.16ff. On the struggles between the Jews and the seven nations understood in spiritual terms cf. Origen, *Hom. in Iesu Nave,* passim. The vices are also referred to as nations that must be destroyed in Ps.-Macarius, Coll. 3, *Hom.* 28.3.6 (SC 275.340).

5.16.2 For the notion that the number of the vices exceeds that of the virtues cf. also *Inst.* 7.15.3.

5.17 According to Chadwick 95, Germanus's question here indicates that eight vices were not universally accepted and that the more usual number was seven (which seems to have been largely the case before Evagrius), despite Serapion's assertion to the contrary at the beginning of 5.18.1.

5.19ff. Cassian's insight that "we can never rid ourselves of the proximity and the service of gluttony and of a certain daily contact with it" and that the desire to eat must be restrained rather than uprooted is paralleled in Augustine, *Conf.* 10.31.43ff., esp. 47.

5.20 The image of the eagle is probably inspired by Mt 24:28 par. ("Where the corpse is, there the vultures will gather"). The fathers often placed the eagle and the vulture together in their commentaries on this passage, and in fact most Greek and Latin texts of the passage read "eagles" in place of "vultures." Cf. RAC 1.93.

5.21 The encounter recorded here between an "illiterate rustic" elder and some philosophers has parallels elsewhere in desert literature. Cf. 8.17f.; Athanasius, *V. S. Antonii* 72ff.; *V. prima gr. Pachomii* 82; *Verba seniorum* 16.16. The philosophers are always bested by the monks. The theme of the country bumpkin who has more real wisdom and practical knowledge than his book-educated adversary is a commonplace in literature in general.

5.21.3 On ethics as the first part of philosophy cf. the notes at 3.6.4 and 14.9.5.

5.22 For other references to baptism cf. the note at 1.1.
Spiritual Egypt: Cf. the note at 3.7.5.

5.23.1 On Israel as a symbol of contemplation cf. the note at 1. praef. 5.

5.24.1 The old tradition referred to here is recorded in Ps.-Clement, *Recog.* 1.30ff.

SIXTH CONFERENCE
THE CONFERENCE OF ABBA THEODORE: ON THE SLAUGHTER OF SOME HOLY PERSONS

TRANSLATOR'S INTRODUCTION

A rare reference to an actual historical event opens the sixth conference and serves as the occasion for the discussion that follows. The slaughter of some monks in Palestine by Saracen bandits was, we are told, a scandal to many, and Cassian and Germanus ask Abba Theodore how God could have permitted this to happen to his holy ones. As to the identity of this Theodore, it is possible that he is the same as the one who is spoken of in *Inst.* 5.33ff. The Theodore of *The Institutes,* however, is said not to have known Greek very well, and that would have been the language used by the two friends; we are also told that he would reflect on difficult questions for seven days and nights, whereas the Theodore of the present conference responds at once to the question that is asked of him. Might not Cassian have alluded somehow to these characteristics if the two Theodores were the same? In any event, nothing is said of this Theodore apart from the fact that he lived in Cellae, and that does not leave much room for establishing his identity.

The response to the question about the sufferings of the holy comes initially in the form of an appeal to belief in the fact that God does not abandon the righteous, despite whatever may happen to them in this world. It continues with Theodore's distinction between the good, the bad, and the indifferent, which had already appeared in 3.9. The indifferent, defined as that which can be either good or bad, depending on circumstances, includes even violence and death itself. But the good is nothing "other than virtue alone, which comes from the fear and love of God, and...the bad is nothing other than sin alone and separation from God" (6.4.1). With this established, it is easy to show that God does not bring bad upon the righteous, even though what is actually indifferent is referred to as bad by the masses and sometimes even by Scripture itself, as Germanus points out. What is indifferent for the one who suffers from something inflicted by another, however, is bad for the one who inflicts the suffering, unless this be inflicted with some good intention, as when God administers discipline or a physician performs a painful operation.

The next few pages are devoted to guiding Theodore's interlocutors safely between the Scylla and the Charybdis of the apparent good and the apparent bad, which are in reality only two forms of the indifferent and which may be referred to as prosperity and adversity. We are thus once again in the realm of discretion, whose task is to keep to the middle path. But this is not precisely the discretion that picks its way between the self-induced and sinful extremes of excessive fasting and gluttony or excessive wakefulness and oversleeping, for example, as in previous conferences. It is a discretion, rather, that is usually exercised with regard to the things that happen to a person from without and that have the tendency to induce extreme reactions, whether of elation or depression. The symbol of the successful avoidance of such an elation or depression is the ambidextrous man. As he uses both hands with equal facility, so the person whom he symbolizes makes equal good use of both the good and the bad that befall him and so maintains an interior equilibrium.

Although trials, then, are of two kinds (namely, with respect to the apparent good and the apparent bad), people are nonetheless tried in three different ways—to be proven, to be cleansed, and to be punished. Theodore eventually adds a fourth way as well—to manifest the glory of God. This section concludes with the remark that, in whatever trial he may undergo, the mind of the perfect person is steadfast.

With this is introduced the final section, which deals with the mutability of the mind. Elsewhere in *The Conferences* this is considered to be a drawback and the cause of the wandering thoughts that so plague the monk, but here it is presented as an occasion not only for regression but also for progress. The mind cannot stand still; it must go either forward or backward. This ability to change is even characteristic of the blessed spirits, as is evident from the fact that some of them fell; and if the others did not change for the worse and fall, this was only due to divine grace. Indeed, God alone never changes by nature. The conference ends with the observation that, when a change for the worse occurs, it is not a sudden event but must have been prepared for over a long period of time.

VI. The Conference of Abba Theodore On the Slaughter of Some Holy Persons

Chapters

I.1. In the area of Palestine near the village of Tekoa, which had the honor of giving birth to the prophet Amos,[1] there is a vast desert that stretches to Arabia and the Dead Sea, into which the flowing waters of the Jordan empty, and, by a very large extension, to the ashes of Sodom. The monks who had lived there for a very long time—men of outstanding life and holiness—were suddenly killed by roving Saracen bandits. 2. We heard that their bodies were carried off by the bishops of that region and by the whole population of Arabia with great veneration and were placed among the relics of the martyrs, with the result that countless people from two towns got into a very serious conflict and that, as the situation grew aggravated, the holy plunder even occasioned a clash of weapons. They fought among themselves with pious devotion to see which of them had the greater claim to their burial place and their relics, the ones boasting of their proximity to where they had lived, the others of their nearness to their place of origin.

We, however, were considerably disturbed both on our own account and for the sake of the brothers who were scandalized, and we wondered why men of such great worthiness and of so many virtues would be slain by bandits and why the Lord had permitted such a crime to be perpetrated on his servants, that he would give men who were remarkable in every respect over into the hands of the impious. In a melancholy mood, then, we went to the holy man Theodore, who was exceptional by reason of his practical way of life. 3. He was living in Cellae, which is located between Nitria and Skete and in fact is five miles from the monasteries of Nitria and separated by eighty miles of wilderness from the desert of Skete, where we were living. We poured out our concern to him about the slaughter of the aforesaid men, marveling at such patience in God that he would permit men of this worth to be slain in such a way that those who should have freed others from a trial of this sort by the weight of their own holiness would not tear themselves from out of the hands of the impious, and that God would have let such an evil deed happen to his servants. Then the blessed Theodore replied:

II.1. "This question usually disturbs the souls of those who have little faith and knowledge and who think that the deserts and rewards of holy persons, which are not bestowed in the present but reserved for the future, are given in the short space of this life. 2. But we must not take up their erroneous opinions, for we do not hope in Christ in this life only. Otherwise, according to the Apostle, 'we would be more miserable than all other men,'[2] because in this world we would receive none of the promises and in the one to come we would also lose them on account of our lack of faith. Unaware of the facts of the matter, we would be perplexed and anxious and fall into temptation if we saw ourselves given up to these same people, or if we ascribed (the mere saying of which is wicked) unrighteousness or unconcern for human affairs to God because he does not spare holy men and those who live rightly from trials or here and now requite the good with good things and the bad with bad things. 3. Then we would deserve to be condemned with those whom the prophet Zephaniah reproaches when he says: 'Who say in their hearts: The Lord will not do good, but neither will he do evil.'[3] Or else we would certainly be found with those who are said to blaspheme God with this sort of complaint: 'Everyone who does evil is good in the sight of the Lord, and such people please him. But where indeed is the God of righteousness?'[4] A little later they add the blasphemy which says: 'Whoever serves the Lord does so in vain. What gain is there in our having kept his precepts and in our having walked sad before the Lord? Therefore we now call the arrogant happy, for those who do iniquity are enriched, and they have tempted God and have been saved.'[5]

4. "In order to escape this ignorance, then, which is the root and cause of this most wicked error, we must first of all know what is really good and what is bad. Then, holding on to the true understanding of Scripture and not to the false one of the crowd, we shall never be deceived by the error of faithless persons.

III.1. "There are three things in this world—namely, the good, the bad, and the indifferent. We ought to know what, properly speaking, is good, what is bad, and what is indifferent, so that our faith, strengthened by real knowledge, might remain undamaged by any temptation.

"As far as human affairs are concerned, then, nothing should be believed to be the chief good other than the virtue of the soul alone, which leads us by a sincere faith to divine realities and makes us cling unceasingly to the unchangeable good. On the other hand, nothing should be called bad other than sin alone, which separates us from a good God and joins us to the wicked devil.

2. "Indifferent things are those which can go in either direction depending on the desire and will of the user, such as wealth, power, honor, bodily strength, health, beauty, life itself and death, poverty, bodily sickness, insults, and other things similar to these which can have good or bad consequences according to the character and desire of the user.

"For even wealth frequently has good consequences, in the words of the Apostle who charges 'the rich of this world to give freely, to share with the poor, to store up for themselves a good foundation in the future, so that' in this way 'they may seize the true life.'[6] In the words of the Gospel, it is good for those who 'make friends for themselves from wicked mammon.'[7] 3. It can be turned to bad, again, when it is accumulated only for hoarding or for the sake of luxury and is not distributed for the needs of the poor.

"Likewise, that power and honor and bodily strength and health are indifferent and can veer to either side is clearly proven from the fact that many holy persons in the Old Testament possessed all these things, having been very rich and highly honored and strong in body, and they are also known to have been most acceptable to God. 4. On the other hand, those who misused these things in bad fashion and turned them to serve their own wickedness were not inappropriately either punished or destroyed, as is frequently indicated in the Book of Kings.

"That life and death themselves are indifferent is shown by the birth of Saint John and of Judas. So advantageous was the life of the one to himself that his birth is also said to have brought joy to others, as it is written: 'Many rejoiced at his birth.'[8] Of the other's life, however, it is said: 'It would have been good for him if that man had not been born.'[9] 5. It is said of the death of John, as of the death of all the holy ones: 'Precious in the sight of the Lord is the death of his holy ones.'[10] But of that of Judas and of those like him: 'The death of sinners is very bad.'[11]

"The blessedness of the poor Lazarus, full of sores, shows how useful even bodily sickness can sometimes be. Scripture mentions nothing virtuous about him apart from the mere fact that he very patiently bore deprivation and bodily sickness, and for this he deserved to possess Abraham's bosom as his blessed destiny.[12] 6. Deprivation and persecutions and insults, which are considered to be bad in the opinion of the crowd, are also clearly shown to be beneficial and necessary from the fact that holy men have not only never desired to avoid them but have even, once having become the friends of God, sought them with all their strength, steadfastly endured them, and pursued them as the price of eternal life. The blessed Apostle says in agreement with this: 'Therefore I am happy in sickness, in reproaches, in necessities, in persecutions, in distress, for Christ's sake. For when I am weak, then I am strong, for power is made perfect in weakness.'[13]

7. "Therefore, those who are exalted by the greatest wealth and honor and power in this world must not be believed to have thereby obtained the chief good, which is understood in terms of virtue alone, but rather something indifferent. For just as these resources are seen to be beneficial and good to the righteous who use them correctly and unavoidably, since they offer the possibility of a good work and of fruit in eternal life, so likewise they are valueless and bad and offer an occasion of death and sin to those who misuse them in bad fashion.

IV.1. "Maintaining these distinctions as fixed and unchanging, therefore, and knowing that nothing is good other than virtue alone, which comes from the fear and love of God, and that the bad is nothing other than sin alone and separation from God, let us now discuss whether God has ever permitted evil to be brought upon his holy ones, either by himself or by someone else. You will certainly find that this has never happened at all, for no one has ever been able to bring the evil of sin upon someone who was unwilling and resistant, but only upon one who accepted it in himself due to a slothful heart and a corrupt will. 2. Even though the devil wished to bring the evil of sin upon the blessed Job by employing each of his wicked devices, and even though he not only despoiled him of all his property but also—after the horrible and unexpected sorrow occasioned by the loss of his seven children—overwhelmed him with a terrible disease from the top of his head to the soles of his feet and with unendurable sufferings, he was utterly unable to taint him with sin because he remained unyielding through it all and did not give way to blasphemy."

V. GERMANUS: "We frequently read in Holy Scripture that God created evil or that he has brought it upon human beings, as for example: 'Apart from me there is no one. I the Lord, and no one else, form the light and create the darkness, make peace and create evil.'[14] And again: 'Is there evil in the city that the Lord has not done?'"[15]

VI.1. THEODORE: "Sometimes Holy Scripture is accustomed to speaking loosely of evils rather than of afflictions, not because they are properly evils by nature but because they are thought to be evil by those upon whom they fall to their advantage. For it is necessary that the divine judgment, in communicating with human beings, express itself by way of human words and sentiments. Now an amputation or a cauterization for a healthful purpose, which a doctor carefully imposes on those who have suffered contact with some disease, is considered evil by those who endure it. Neither is a spur agreeable to a horse nor correction to a delinquent. 2. All forms of discipline are felt as bitter at the time to those who are being instructed, as the Apostle says: 'At the time no discipline seems to be reason for gladness but for grieving. Afterward, however, it produces the peaceful fruit of righteousness for those who have been exercised by it.'[16] And: 'The Lord chastises the one whom he loves, and he scourges every son whom he receives. For what son is not corrected by his father?'[17]

"Hence things are sometimes spoken of as evils rather than as afflictions, as in the words: 'God repented of the evil that he said he would do to them, and he did not do it.'[18] And again: 'You, Lord, are gracious and merciful, patient and very gracious and repenting of evils'[19]—that is, of the tribulations and hardships which you are obliged to bring upon us on account of our sins. 3. Another prophet, knowing that these things are beneficial for some people and not indeed begrudging them their salvation but looking out for their interests, prays: 'Add evils to them, Lord, add evils to the haughty of the earth.'[20] And the Lord himself says: 'Behold, I will inflict evils upon them'[21]—that is, sorrows and desolation, by means of which, once they have been wholesomely chastised, they may at last turn and hasten to me, whom they despised in time of prosperity.

"Therefore we cannot understand these things as the chief evils, for they are of value to many people and are the cause of their eternal joy. Consequently (to return to the question that was asked) it should not be believed that all the evils that are thought to be brought upon us by our enemies or by other persons are evil; rather they are indifferent. For they will not be found to be such as he thinks they are who has inflicted them upon a raging soul, but such as he thinks who endures them. 4. Therefore when death befalls a holy man it is not to be believed that an evil has befallen him but rather something indifferent. Although this is an evil for the sinner, for the righteous it is repose and a liberation from evils. 'For death is repose to a man whose way is hidden.'[22] Hence the righteous man does not undergo any loss from this because he has not suffered anything new. Instead, as the result of an enemy's wickedness he has endured what nature demanded of him—not without the reward of eternal life—and with the abundant profit derived from suffering and the recompense of a great reward he has paid the debt of death that is owed by human beings and that is exacted by an inflexible law."

VII. GERMANUS: "Therefore, if the righteous person who has been slain not only endures nothing evil but even receives a reward for his suffering, how can his murderer be called a criminal when he has not performed a disservice but rather a service?"

VIII.1. THEODORE: "We are discussing the nature of the good, the bad, and what we have referred to as the indifferent, not the disposition of those who do these things. For an impious and wicked person will not go unpunished because his wickedness was unable to harm a righteous person. The long-suffering and virtue of the righteous earn a reward not for the one who has inflicted death and torture but for the one who has patiently endured what was inflicted upon him. Hence the latter will be deservedly punished for his fierce cruelty because he desired to inflict evil, while the former has endured nothing evil because, patiently sustaining trials and sorrows in his strength of soul, he caused the things that were inflicted upon him with bad intent to bring him to a better state and to the blessedness of eternal life.

IX.1. "For Job's patience earned no reward for the devil, who made him more illustrious by his trials, but for him who bore them courageously. Nor will Judas be compensated with immunity from everlasting punishment because his betrayal profited the salvation of the human race. It is not the result of the deed that must be considered but rather the disposition of the doer. Therefore we should hold firmly to this understanding—that no one can bring evil upon another person if he has not already brought it upon himself due to the slothfulness and weakness of his heart. The blessed Apostle confirms this very opinion in a brief passage: 'We know that for those who love God everything works together for the good.'[23] 2. When he says that 'everything works together for the good' he includes not only all the things that are fortunate but also all the things that are thought to be unfortunate.

"In another place the same Apostle describes himself as having passed through this when he says: 'By the arms of righteousness on the right hand and on the left'—that is, 'by glory and dishonor, by bad reputation and good reputation, as deceivers and truthful, as sad yet always rejoicing, as needy yet as enriching many,'[24] and so forth. 3. Everything, then, which is considered fortunate and which is said to be on the right side, which the holy Apostle refers to in terms of glory and a good reputation, and also everything which is thought to be unfortunate, which he clearly speaks of as dishonor and a bad reputation and which he puts at the left side, becomes the weaponry of righteousness for the perfect man if he sustains in great-hearted fashion whatever befalls him. For, struggling with these and using as weapons the very adversities by which he feels himself being attacked, and fortified by them as by a bow or a sword or a sturdy shield, against those who bear them, he will gain ground in patience and virtue, triumphing gloriously in the very face of the enemies' lethal spears, neither elated by prosperity nor dejected by adversity but always proceeding along on an even course and on the royal road, never moved away from that state of calm at the appearance of joy, as it were toward the right, nor as it were pushed to the left by an onrush of adversity or when sadness predominates. For 'there is much peace for those who love your name, and for them there is no stumbling block.'[25]

4. "But of those who change according to the nature and variety of circumstances it is said: 'A fool will change like the moon.'[26] Just as it is said of the perfect and the wise: 'For those who love God everything works together for the good,' so also it is declared of the weak and the foolish: 'Everything is against a foolish man.'[27] He is neither improved by prosperity nor corrected by adversity. For it belongs to the same virtue to endure calamity bravely and to moderate prosperity, and it is quite certain that he who is overcome in one of these can tolerate neither. Yet a person can be broken more easily by prosperity than by adversity. For sometimes the latter restrains and humbles the hesitant, causes them to commit fewer sins and corrects them with a beneficial compunction. But the former puffs up the mind with its flattering and dangerous seductions and ruinously casts down those who are secure in their happiness.

X.1. "These are the persons, then, who are referred to in Holy Scripture as αμφοτεροδεξιοι—that is, as ambidextrous. Ehud, 'who used either hand as if it were his right hand,'[28] is described as such in the Book of Judges. We shall also be able to possess this quality in a spiritual way if by a good and correct use we put the things which are considered fortunate and right-handed and the things which are called unfortunate and left-handed on the right side, so that whatever befalls may become for us, in the words of the Apostle, 'the arms of righteousness.' For we see that our inner man consists in two parts or, as I might say, two hands. No holy person can be without what we call the left hand, but perfect virtue is discerned in the fact that by proper use he turns both into a right hand.

2. "Let us make what we are saying more understandable: The holy person has a right hand—namely, his spiritual achievements. He has this when, fervent in spirit, he masters all his desires and lusts; when, safe from every diabolical attack, he rejects and cuts off the vices of the flesh without any effort or difficulty; when, raised up from the earth, he contemplates all present and earthly realities as mere smoke and an empty shadow

and disdains them as soon to disappear; when, with ecstatic mind, he not only ardently desires future realities but even sees them with clarity; when he is effectively fed by spiritual theoria; when he sees unlocked to himself the heavenly sacraments in all their brightness; when he sends prayers purely and swiftly to God; and when, inflamed with spiritual ardor, he passes over to invisible and eternal realities with such utter eagerness of soul that he cannot bring himself to believe that he is in the flesh.

3. "He also has a left hand when he is involved in the turmoil of trials; when the desires of his flesh are inflamed by seething emotions and impulses; when the fire of aggravations enkindles the fury of his wrath; when he is struck by the arrogance of pride or vainglory; when he is depressed by a death-dealing sadness; when he is disturbed by the ploys and the attack of acedia; and when, in the absence of any spiritual warmth, he is dulled by a kind of tepidity and irrational mournfulness, so that not only is he deserted by good and warm thoughts but psalmody, prayer, reading, and the solitude of his cell terrify him, and every virtuous practice takes on a certain unbearable and darkly loathsome quality. When a monk is struck by these things he realizes that he is being assailed from the left.

4. "Whoever, then, is on what we have referred to as the right side is not elated at the approach of vainglory and, courageously struggling with the things that are on the left side, is not disheartened by any despair. Rather he seizes the arms of patience from adversity for the sake of exercising his virtue, uses both hands as right hands, and, having triumphed in both respects, snatches the palm of victory from the left as much as from the right.

5. "This is what we read that the blessed Job deserved to obtain. He was crowned on the right, to be sure, when, going about as the wealthy and rich father of seven children, he offered daily sacrifices to the Lord for their purification,[29] not wishing to make them acceptable and pleasing to himself so much as to God; when he opened his doors to every stranger; when he was the foot of the lame and the eye of the blind;[30] when the shoulders of the sick were warmed by the wool of his sheep;[31] when he was the

father of orphans and the protector of widows; and when he did not rejoice in his heart over his enemy's downfall.

6. "Thanks to a still more sublime virtue, though, the same man triumphed on the left side over his adversities when, bereaved of his seven children at one fell swoop, he did not, like a father, give way to bitter grief but, like a true servant of God, rejoiced in the will of his Creator; when, having gone from wealth to extreme poverty, from riches to nakedness, from health to sickness, from fame and renown to ignominy and contempt, he retained his strength of soul uncorrupted; when, bereft of all his property and wealth, he made a dunghill his home and, his own most severe tormentor, scraped his running sores with a potsherd and, plunging his fingers into his deepest ulcers, took out from every part of his body the masses of worms.

7. "In all these things he never despairingly fell into blasphemy or murmured against his Creator on any account. Quite to the contrary, so unshaken was he by the heavy burden and the harshness of his trials that his very cloak, which he had retained from his original possessions to cover his body and which alone was able to be saved from the devil's rampage because he was wearing it, he took off and laid aside, adding a voluntary deprivation to the terrible rapine that he had suffered.[32] 8. He also cut off the hair of his head,[33] which alone had remained intact of his former glory, and cast it to his tormentor. Ridding himself of what his fierce enemy had left him, he exulted over him and reviled him with those heavenly words: 'If we have received good things from the hand of the Lord, shall we not accept evil? Naked I came from my mother's womb, naked shall I return there. The Lord has given, the Lord has taken away. As it has pleased the Lord, so it has been done. May the name of the Lord be blessed.'[34]

"I would also with good reason refer to Joseph as ambidextrous. In prosperity he was more thankful than his father, more devout than his brothers, and more acceptable to God. In adversity he was chaste, faithful to the Lord, most gentle to those who were imprisoned, heedless of insults, kind to his enemies, and not only respectful of his jealous and very nearly murderous brothers but even munificent in their regard.[35]

9. "These men, therefore, and others like them are rightly

called αμφοτεροδεξιοι—that is, ambidextrous. For they used either hand as if it were their right hand and, passing through those things which the Apostle enumerates, they could all say alike: 'By the arms of righteousness on the right hand and on the left, by glory and dishonor, by bad reputation and good reputation,'[36] and so forth.

"Solomon also speaks of the right hand and the left hand in the Song of Songs in the person of the bride: 'His left hand is under my head, and his right hand will embrace me.'[37] Although she indicates that both are beneficial, yet she puts the former under her head because adversities should be subject to the guidance of the heart. They are only beneficial to the extent that they discipline us for a time, instruct us for salvation, and make us perfectly patient. But for being fondled and forever protected she desires the bridegroom's right hand to cling to her and to hold her fast in a saving embrace.

10. "We shall be ambidextrous ourselves, therefore, when neither an abundance nor a lack of present things changes us—when the former does not push us into harmfully lax pleasures and the latter does not draw us into despair and complaining, but when in either case we are thankful to God and draw similar fruit from both successes and failures. That the truly ambidextrous teacher of the Gentiles was this way himself he testifies when he says: 'I have learned to be satisfied in whatever I find myself. I know how to be humbled and I know how to abound. Everywhere and in everything I have been instructed how to be full and how to be hungry and how to abound and how to endure want. I can do everything in him who strengthens me.'[38]

XI.1. "Now although we have said that trials are of two kinds, namely in reference to prosperity and adversity, nonetheless it should be realized that everyone is tried in a threefold way—frequently in order to be proven, sometimes in order to be cleansed, and occasionally on account of sins.

"We read that the blessed Abraham, like Job and many other holy persons, endured numberless tribulations in order to be proven. Consider also what is said by Moses to the people in Deuteronomy: 'You shall remember that entire way by which the Lord your God led you through the desert for forty years in order to afflict and try you and so that what you were meditating in your soul would be made known, whether you were keeping his commandments or not.'[39] And what is said in the psalm: 'I tested you at the water of contradiction.'[40] And also to Job: 'Do you think that I have spoken to you for any other reason than that you might appear righteous?'[41]

2. "This occurs for the sake of cleansing, however, when he humbles his righteous ones for their small and as it were insignificant sins or because of their proud purity, giving them over to various trials in order to purge away now all the unclean thoughts and—as I might say in the words of the prophet—dross[42] which he sees have collected in their inmost being, and in order to submit them like pure gold to the judgment to come, permitting nothing to remain in them that the searching fire of judgment might afterwards find to purge with penal torment. As it is written: 'Many are the tribulations of the righteous.'[43] And: 'My son, do not neglect the discipline of the Lord, and do not be wearied when you are rebuked by him, for the Lord chastises the one whom he loves, and he scourges every son whom he receives. For what son is not corrected by his father? But if you are without discipline, in which all partake, then you are bastards and not sons.'[44] And in the Apocalypse: 'Those whom I love I reprove and chastise.'[45] 3. Jeremiah also, in the person of God, speaks to these people under the image of Jerusalem: 'I will consume all the nations in which I scattered you, but you I will not consume. But I will chastise you in judgment, so that you may not appear innocent to yourself.'[46] David prays for this salutary cleansing when he says: 'Examine me, Lord, and try me; stir up my reins and my heart.'[47] Isaiah, too, understands the value of this trial when he says: 'Correct us, Lord, but in judgment, and not in your wrath.'[48] And again: 'I shall confess to you, Lord, for you were angry with me. Your wrath has turned away, and you have consoled me.'[49]

4. "The affliction of trials is brought to bear because of sin, however, as when the Lord warns that he will send afflictions upon the people of Israel, saying: 'I will set the teeth of wild animals upon them, with the fury of things that creep upon the earth.'[50] And: 'In vain have I struck your children; you have not accepted chastisement.'[51] In the psalms also: 'Many are the

scourges of sinners.'[52] And in the Gospel: 'See, you have been made whole. Sin no more lest something worse befall you.'[53]

"We have also, in fact, come upon a fourth reason. Following the authority of Scripture we see that some sufferings are inflicted upon people simply in order to show forth the glory and the works of God, according to the Gospel text: 'Neither this man nor his parents sinned, but that the works of God might be shown forth in him.'[54] And again: 'This sickness is not unto death but for the glory of God, so that the Son of God might be glorified through it.'[55]

5. "But there are also other kinds of vengeance by which some people who have gone beyond the limits of wickedness are struck at the time. Thus we read that Dathan and Abiram and Korah were condemned,[56] and particularly those of whom the Apostle speaks: 'Therefore God gave them up to shameful passions and to a reprobate mind.'[57] This is to be considered more serious than other punishments. Of these the psalmist says: 'They are not in the labors of men, and they shall not be scourged with men.'[58] 6. For they do not deserve to be saved by the Lord's visitation or to be healed by temporal afflictions–they 'who in despair have handed themselves over to lasciviousness in the working of every error, unto uncleanness,'[59] and who in their hardness of heart and with their frequent habit of sinning are beyond the purgation of this very brief age and the punishment of the present life. The divine word reproves them too through the prophet: 'I have destroyed you as God destroyed Sodom and Gomorrah, and you have become like a firebrand snatched from the fire, and not even thus have you returned to me, says the Lord.'[60] And Jeremiah: 'I have slain and destroyed my people, and still they have not turned back from their ways.'[61] And again: 'You struck them and they did not grieve; you bruised them and they refused to accept correction; they have hardened their faces more than rock, they have refused to return.'[62]

7. "The prophet, seeing how no temporal medicine is able to cure them and already as it were despairing of their salvation, declares: 'The bellows have given way in the fire, the lead has melted in vain, for your iniquities have not been consumed. Call them reprobate silver, for the Lord has cast them away.'[63] The

Lord complains that he has applied this salutary purgative fire without effect to those who have grown hardened in their misdeeds, and he speaks to them as to a Jerusalem that is encrusted with a heavy rust of sinfulness: 'Set it empty upon live coals so that it may get hot and its brass may melt, and let its pollution melt in its midst. Much labor was expended and none of its rust has left it, not even with fire. Your uncleanness is disgraceful, for I have desired to cleanse you, and you were not cleansed from your filthiness.'[64] 8. Therefore, like a very skillful physician who has tried every treatment and sees that no remedy is left that could have an effect on their illness, the Lord is as it were overcome by the magnitude of their wickedness. He is forced to give up that merciful chastisement of his, and so he denounces them and says: 'I will no longer be angry with you, and my jealousy has departed from you.'[65]

"With respect to others, however, whose hearts have not hardened because of frequent sinning and who have no need of that very severe and—as I might call it—caustic and fiery medicine, but for whom instruction in the saving word is enough for salvation, it is said: 'I will correct them by hearing of their tribulation.'[66]

9. "We are not unaware of other causes for the censure and punishment that are brought upon those who have sinned very gravely, not in order to expiate their crimes or to abolish what their sinfulness deserves but in order to correct the living and inspire fear in them. We see clearly that this happened in the case of Jeroboam the son of Nebat, Baasha the son of Ahijah, and Ahab and Jezebel, as the divine judgment declares: 'Behold, I will bring evil upon you, and I will cut down your posterity, and of Ahab I will slay every male, and whoever is shut up and the last in Israel. And I will make your house like the house of Jeroboam the son of Nebat and like the house of Baasha the son of Ahijah because of what you did to provoke me to anger, and because you made Israel sin. The dogs shall eat Jezebel in the field of Jezreel. If Ahab dies in the city the dogs shall eat him, but if he dies in the country the birds of the air shall eat him.'[67] And there is what is proclaimed as a great threat: 'Your corpse shall not be interred in the burial place of your ancestors.'[68]

10. "This short and momentary penalty would not suffice to

purge away the impious lies of the one who first invented golden calves to lead a people astray forever and who contributed to their wicked separation from the Lord,[69] or their countless and evil crimes of sacrilege. But the terror of these punishments might serve as an example to others who feared them and who, either neglectful of the future or not wholly believing, would only be moved by the consideration of present realities. Thus they might realize, thanks to the warning provided by this severity, that with that highest divine majesty there was no lack of concern for human affairs and for daily activity, and that, by way of things which they greatly feared, they might clearly see that God was the requiter of every act.

11. "We have in fact noticed that even for less serious faults some people have suffered the very sentence of death by which those who we said were the authors of sacrilegious prevarication were also punished. This happened in the case of the man who had been collecting wood on the sabbath,[70] as well as in that of Ananias and Sapphira, who by their misguided faithlessness kept back a little bit of their property.[71] It is not that these sins were equally grave but that, when these persons had been found committing a new offense, they had to furnish a kind of example to others of the penalty and terror of sinfulness. Thus, from then on, whoever was tempted to do the same thing would know that at the future judgment he would receive the same condemnation as the others, even if in this life his punishment was deferred.

12. "Seeing that, since we wanted to run through the different kinds of trials and punishments, we have digressed from our narrative of how, as we were saying, the perfect man is always steadfast in either trial, let us now return to where we were.

XII. "The mind of the righteous man, then, must not be like wax or some other soft material, which always gets its form and shape from the mark that is stamped on it and that remains there until it receives the impression of another mark. Thus it never keeps its own character and always takes on the form of whatever is stamped on it. On the contrary, our mind must be like a kind of adamant seal, so that it always retains its own character inviolable and shapes and transforms whatever happens to it into its own likeness, without, however, being stamped itself by the things that happen to it."

XIII. GERMANUS: "Is our mind able to hold on to one state constantly and to remain always in the same condition?"

XIV.1. THEODORE: "As the Apostle says, it is necessary for 'one who is renewed in the spirit of his mind'[72] to make progress every day, 'always reaching out to what is ahead.'[73] The alternative is that the neglectful person reverses himself and falls back into a worse state. Therefore the mind will never be able to remain in one and the same condition. As in the case of a person who is trying hard to push forward a boat that is held back by the river's current, he will certainly either go upstream by cutting off the torrent with the strength of his arms or, letting his hands drop, be thrown headlong by the rushing water.

2. "It will be a clear sign of our setback, then, if we know that we have acquired nothing more, and we should not doubt that we have fallen back completely on the day when we do not notice that we have progressed to higher things. For, as I have said, the mind of man cannot remain constantly in the same state, nor will any holy persons, while living in this flesh, possess the height of the virtues in such a way that they will abide unchangingly. For something must always be either added to them or taken away from them, and no perfection will exist in any creature that is not subject to the passion of change. As it says in the book of the blessed Job: 'What is a human being that he should be spotless, and one who is born of woman that he should appear righteous? Behold, among his holy ones no one is changeless, and the heavens are not pure in his sight.'[74]

3. "We confess that God alone is unchanging. Him alone does the prayer of the holy prophet address in this way: 'You yourself are the same.'[75] And he says of himself: 'I am God, and I do not change.'[76] For only he to whom nothing can ever be added and from whom nothing can ever be taken away is by nature always good, always complete, and always perfect. Therefore we must always push ourselves with unceasing care and concern to attain the virtues, and we must constantly occupy ourselves in their exercise, lest our progress suddenly cease and regression occur. For, as we have said, the mind cannot remain in one and

the same condition—that is, so that it does not either increase or decrease in virtue. Not to have gained is to have lost, because when the desire of making progress ceases, the danger of falling back will appear.

XV. "Therefore one must abide constantly in one's cell. For as often as a person has wandered out of it and has returned to it like a novice who is only starting to live there, he will waver and be disturbed. The person who stays in his cell has acquired an intensity of mind that, once let go slack, he will not be able to recover again without effort and pain. And when he has thus returned he will not think about the progress that he missed, which he would have been able to add if he had not left his cell, but he will be glad if he could think that he has gained back the condition from which he had fallen. Just as time that has passed and slipped away cannot be summoned up again, so neither can gains be won back once they have been lost. For however much this intensity of mind may be cultivated afterward, this will be the progress of that particular day and of that particular moment and not the recouping of a lost profit.

XVI.1. "But that even the heavenly powers, as we have said, are subject to change is proclaimed by those of their number who fell because of the sinfulness of their corrupt will. Therefore neither must those who have persevered in the blessedness in which they were created be thought of as possessing an unchanging nature because they, having acted differently, did not likewise behave wickedly. For it is one thing to possess an unchanging nature and another not to be changed because of zeal for virtue and perseverance in the good, which is due to the grace of an immutable God. 2. Whatever is acquired and maintained through diligence can also be lost through negligence. Consequently it is said: 'You should not call a person blessed before his death,'[77] because whoever is still involved in this struggle and—as I might say—wrestling match, even though he usually overcomes and obtains the palm of victory, still cannot be free of fear and of concern about an uncertain result.

3. "God alone, then, is said to be unchangeable and good—he who possesses goodness not because of laborious effort but by nature, and who cannot be anything other than good. Therefore

no virtue can be possessed unwaveringly by a human being, but for it to be firmly maintained once it has been acquired it must always be preserved with the same concern and effort with which it was obtained.

XVII.1. "But we must not believe that a slip is the cause of a person's sudden ruin. Rather, having been misled by wicked instruction at the beginning, or because of a longstanding spiritual unconcern, the virtue of the mind gradually decreases and thus, as sinfulness slowly increases, a person falls into a wretched condition. For 'injury precedes destruction, and an evil thought precedes ruin.'[78] In the same way a house never suddenly collapses except because of some old weakness in the foundation or because of extended disregard by its tenants. Thus the structure of the roof is eventually destroyed by what had begun as a tiny leak, but into which, through long neglect, a stormy tempest of rain pours like a river, once a large breach has been made. For 'by slothfulness a dwelling will be brought low, and through lazy hands a house will leak.'[79]

2. "Solomon remarks that the same thing happens to the soul in a spiritual way when he says in other words: 'Leaks drive a person out of his house on a stormy day.'[80] Neatly, then, does he compare spiritual carelessness to a neglected roof, through which as it were certain tiny leaks of passion penetrate to the soul. If these little and insignificant leaks are let go unattended they weaken the structure of the virtues, and afterward they pour in in a heavy shower of sinfulness. As a consequence, on a stormy day—that is, in time of trial—the mind is expelled by the onrushing assault of the devil from the dwelling place of virtue, in which it had once reposed as if it were its own house when it maintained a careful watchfulness."

3. When this was over we took such boundless delight in our spiritual repast that we were filled with more joy of soul from this conference than we had been touched with sadness before because of the death of the holy ones. For not only were we instructed in matters where we were in doubt but, having posed that question, we even came to comprehend things that we did not know enough to ask about because of the poverty of our intelligence.

Textual References

1. Cf. Am 1:1.
2. 1 Cor 15:19.
3. Zep 1:12.
4. Mal 2:17.
5. Mal 3:14–15.
6. 1 Tm 6:18–19.
7. Lk 16:9.
8. Lk 1:14.
9. Mt 26:24.
10. Ps 116:15.
11. Ps 34:21.
12. Cf. Lk 16:20–22.
13. 2 Cor 12:10, 9.
14. Is 45:6–7.
15. Am 3:6 LXX.
16. Heb 12:11.
17. Heb 12:6–7.
18. Jon 3:10 LXX.
19. Jl 2:13 LXX.
20. Is 26:15 LXX.
21. Jer 11:11.
22. Jb 3:23 LXX.
23. Rom 8:28.
24. 2 Cor 6:7–10.
25. Ps 119:165.
26. Sir 27:11.
27. Prv 14:7 LXX.
28. Jgs 3:15.
29. Cf. Jb 1:5.
30. Cf. Jb 29:15.
31. Cf. Jb 31:20.
32. Cf. Jb 1:20a.
33. Cf. Jb 1:20b.
34. Jb 2:10; 1:21.
35. Cf. Gn 37:2–47:12.
36. 2 Cor 6:7.
37. Sg 2:6.
38. Phil 4:11–13.

39. Dt 8:2.
40. Ps 81:7.
41. Jb 40:3 LXX.
42. Cf. Is 1:25.
43. Ps 34:19.
44. Heb 12:5–8.
45. Rv 3:19.
46. Jer 30:11.
47. Ps 26:2.
48. Jer 10:22.
49. Is 12:1.
50. Dt 32:24.
51. Jer 2:30.
52. Ps 32:10.
53. Jn 5:14.
54. Jn 9:3.
55. Jn 11:4.
56. Cf. Nm 16.
57. Rom 1:26, 28.
58. Ps 73:5.
59. Eph 4:19.
60. Am 4:11.
61. Jer 15:7.
62. Jer 5:3.
63. Jer 6:29–30.
64. Ez 24:11–13.
65. Ez 16:42.
66. Hos 7:12 LXX.
67. 1 Kgs 21:21–24.
68. 1 Kgs 13:22.
69. Cf. Ex 32.
70. Cf. Nm 15:32–36.
71. Cf. Acts 5:1–11.
72. Eph 4:23.
73. Phil 3:13.
74. Jb 15:14–15.
75. Ps 102:27.
76. Mal 3:6.

77. Sir 11:28.
78. Prv 16:18 LXX.
79. Eccl 10:18 LXX.
80. Prv 27:15 LXX.

6.1.1 Tekoa, now known as Tequ, is some few miles south of Bethlehem in present-day Israel.

The ashes of Sodom are referred to as still extant in *Itinerarium Egeriae* 12. The ashes, however, are probably to be understood as the ruins of the city that was destroyed by a rain of brimstone and fire, as recorded in Gn 19:24.

On the monks who were massacred cf. the brief notice in *Acta Sanctorum,* Maii 6.746, where it is sadly remarked that, as the power of the Saracens in Palestine gradually waned, so also did the cult of those whom they had killed.

The Saracens were nomadic Arabs of the Syro-Arabian desert who had a reputation for attacking the frontiers of the Empire. Cf. Pauly-Wissowa, 2e Reihe, 1.2388–2390.

6.1.2 Arabia refers to the area immediately to the east of Palestine, roughly equivalent to the western section of present-day Jordan.

Disputes over the possession of the bodies of holy persons were not uncommon in this period. Cf. Jerome, *V. S. Hilarionis* 46; Theodoret of Cyrus, *Hist. relig.* 10.8, 15.5, 16.4, 19.3 (the seizure of a living monk, who submitted to the act in silence), 21.9 (a similar incident).

6.1.3 Cellae, or Cellia or Kellia, received its name from the number of monks' cells there. Cf. *Hist. monach. in Aegypto* 22 (PL 21.444–445: an addition of Rufinus); Sozomen, *Hist. eccl.* 6.31. It was to the north of Skete. For which cf. the note at 1 praef. 2. For an exhaustive archeological account of the area cf. Rodolphe Kasser et al., *Kellia: Topographie* (Recherches Suisses d'Archéologie Copte 2) (Geneva, 1972).

Nitria was to the north of Cellae and took its name from a nearby village that produced nitre. Cf. Sozomen, *Hist. eccl.* 6.31.

6.3ff. On the language of good, bad, and indifferent cf. the note at 3.9.1ff., and on the indifference of misfortune in particular (which is discussed in 6.6.3f.) cf. Origen, *De princ.* 3.2.7.

6.9.1 On intention as determinative of the value of an act, with an appeal to the example of Judas's betrayal, cf. 17.12 and the relevant note.

6.9.3 To be swayed neither by prosperity nor by adversity and to maintain one's calm *(tranquillitas)* is a monastic ideal found in 19.1.3; *Inst* 9.13; Athanasius, *V. S. Antonii* 14; Sulpicius Severus, *V. S. Martini* 27; Jerome, *Ep.* 24.5; Theodoret of Cyrus, *Hist. relig.* 4.10.

On the image of the royal road cf. the note at 4.12.5.

6.10 The division of the human being into two parts, as here, is an important theme in Origen, who, basing himself on the double creation account of Gn 1–2 and on 2 Cor 4:16, speaks of an inner and an outer man. Cf. Origen, *Comm. in Cant. Cant.*, prol. (GCS 33.63ff); idem, *Dial. c. Heracl.* 11f. For an interpretation of Jgs 3:15, which speaks of Ehud's ambidexterity, cf. Origen, *Hom. in Iudic.* 3.5, where it is stated that the holy all have two right hands, inasmuch as lefthandedness has a bad connotation. Cf. also 12.5.5 and 16.22.2 (with the relevant note); *Inst.* 11.4. Evagrius, *De orat.* 72, speaks of demons attacking differently from the right and from the left, with somewhat the same effects as mentioned here by Cassian.

6.11.2 Proud purity: Cf. the note at 4.15ff.

The searching fire of judgment: *Scrutans...iudicii ignis.* For a study of the fire that purges rather than destroys cf. W. C. van Unnik, "The 'Wise Fire' in a Gnostic Eschatological Vision," in Patrick Granfield and Josef A. Jungmann, eds., *Kyriakon: Festschrift Johannes Quasten* (Münster, 1970), 1.277–288.

6.11.8 On the image of the Lord as physician cf. the note at 2.13.7.

6.11.10 "The one who first invented golden calves" is Satan.

6.12 That the mind must be like adamant rather than like wax is a Stoic image. Cf. Colish 118 (where unfortunately no references are given). Cf. also Plato, *Leg.* 633d; Origen, *C. Celsum* 4.26. On the other hand, sometimes it is good to be "like wax before a fire," which symbolizes a beneficial flexibility, as in 17.26. In this latter regard cf. also Basil, *Reg. Fus. tract.* 15.

6.13ff. On the mutability of the human mind cf. the note at 1.5.4.

6.14.3 On the divine immutability cf. also 23.3.4.

6.15 There are frequent references in desert literature to the necessity of remaining in one's cell. Among the most noteworthy are *Verba seniorum* 7.24 (where an inclination to leave one's cell in order to receive communion is viewed as a diabolical temptation); *Apophthegmata patrum*, de abbate Antonio 10; ibid., de abbate Evagrio 1; ibid., de abbate Macario 41; Palladius, *Hist. laus.* 16. Cf. also 7.23.3 and 24.3ff. The famous words of Pascal, *Pensées* 139, bear repeating here: "Quand je m'y suis mis quelquefois à considérer les diverses agitations des hommes, et les périls et les peines où ils s'exposent, dans la cour, dans la guerre, d'où naissent tant de querelles, de passions, d'entreprises hardies et souvent mauvaises, etc., j'ai découvert que tout le malheur des hommes vient d'une seule chose, qui est de ne savoir pas demeurer au repos dans une chambre." The idea that mobility is unconducive to the development of the contemplative spirit is a Stoic one. Cf. Seneca, *Epp. moral.* 2.1, 28.1, 69.1. That remaining in one's cell in and of itself does not bring virtue, however, is asserted in 18.13ff., esp. 16.

6.16.2 On the image of life as a wrestling match (*scamma*) cf. 7.20 and the relevant note.

SEVENTH CONFERENCE THE FIRST CONFERENCE OF ABBA SERENUS: ON THE CHANGEABLENESS OF THE SOUL AND ON EVIL SPIRITS

Translator's Introduction

Abba Serenus, around whom the seventh and eighth conferences center, is an otherwise unknown figure, although he may be the same person who receives brief mention in the *Apophthegmata patrum* under that name. To him is confided the long discussion on demons, which is crucial from two points of view. In the first place, instruction on demonic activity is practically necessary, given the desert dwellers' strong awareness of the ubiquitous influence of evil spirits. Second, Serenus's two conferences deal with the classic objects of that virtue of discretion which is one of the leitmotivs of *The Conferences*. In other words, discretion is classically understood to be about spirits (as in 1 Cor 12:10 and Athanasius, *V. S. Antonii* 16–43; this latter is the archetype of all monastic conferences, and at least three-fourths of it is devoted to distinguishing the characteristics of spirits and particularly of demons). It seems appropriate that Cassian's own *ex professo* treatment of the evil spirits should be handled by an abba whose most noteworthy gift is perfect purity of spirit and body. Sexual temptation in all its variety was, as desert and other monastic literature abundantly testifies, one of the demon's strong points.

The topic is introduced with Cassian's and Germanus's complaint about mental distractions, that familiar theme in *The Conferences*. The two lay the blame for this condition on nature, but Serenus replies by saying that, although the mind is indeed inclined to constant change, it can learn to be still. The scriptural image of this acquired inner calm is the centurion of Matthew 8:9, who exercises perfect control over those subject to him and whose weapons are designed to prevent incursions of any kind. In order to attain to this mental control a person must practice unceasing self-denial and yearn for God to be all in all in him. It seems clear from the military imagery used here, if for no other reason, that the control of which Cassian speaks is not one of blissful repose but rather one that successfully sustains repeated attacks.

Germanus's assertion—that mental distractions could perhaps be somewhat restrained were it not for the vast army of demons inciting the mind to do what it does not want to do—brings us to the main issue of the conference. Serenus's response to Germanus is that the demons may indeed incite but that they cannot force the mind. It is true that the demons, being spiritual, have an affinity with the human soul or mind, which is also spiritual, yet they are unable to penetrate into the very substance of the soul. They can mingle with human flesh, thus weighing it down and thereby oppressing the soul, as is the case with demoniacs, but only God can actually unite with the soul. The reason for this is that the demons, like all spiritual beings apart from God himself, are characterized by a subtle materiality that makes the human soul inaccessible to them. And so the demons' knowledge of the secrets of the mind is not infallible; it is instead a clever deduction from the observable behavior of a given human being.

With this Serenus proceeds to discuss the differences among the demons. They specialize in particular vices; nor do all have the same aggressiveness. Toward the end of the conference Serenus will return to these differences and will note that evil spirits range from relatively harmless jokers to murderous fiends. Their names, of which there are many, correspond to their natures. It is certain, however, that the struggle to dominate a human being is often as difficult for the demon as it is for the man or woman whom the demon is tormenting, and sometimes it is even more difficult.

The demons afflict human beings exclusively within the ambit of divine permission, and this is clear from the story of Job, whom Satan tried only to the extent that God allowed. The trials that Job suffered and that other holy persons suffer are not necessarily punishments for grave sins; they are often intended to have, rather, a purgative effect. Hence demoniacs should not be denied Holy Communion, as if the horrible afflictions to which they are subject somehow indicate a proportionate blameworthiness. Far more wretched than demoniacs, however repulsive they may be, are those persons who give no indication of diabolical possession but who commit all sorts of sins.

The conference ends before dawn on a Sunday, and the participants retire, only to awaken soon afterward in time for the synaxis.

Cassian's demonology, in this as in the following conference, is influenced by Evagrius and ultimately by Origen. On the former cf. DS 3.196–205, and on the latter cf. in particular *De princ.* 3.2; Stephanus Bettencourt, *Doctrina ascetica Origenis seu quid docuerit de ratione animae humanae cum daemonibus* (SA 16) (1945); DS 3.182–189. On Cassian's demonology cf. DS 3.208–210.

VII. The First Conference of Abba Serenus: On the Changeableness of the Soul and on Evil Spirits

Chapters

I. The chastity of Abba Serenus.
II. The question asked by the aforesaid elder about the state of our thoughts.
III. Our reply, on the changeableness of the soul.
IV. The discussion of the old man on the state of the soul and its power.
V. The perfection of the soul, taken from the comparison of the centurion in the Gospel.
VI. On persevering in being watchful of our thoughts.
VII. A question about the changeableness of the soul and about the attacks of evil beings from heavenly places.
VIII. The reply, on the help of God and on the power of free will.
IX. A question about the relationship between the soul and demons.
X. The reply, about how unclean spirits are united to human minds.
XI. An objection concerning whether unclean spirits can be admitted into or united with the souls of those whom they have filled.
XII. The reply, on how unclean spirits exercise dominion in demoniacs.
XIII. That one spirit cannot be penetrated by another spirit, and that God alone is incorporeal.
XIV. An objection: To what degree demons should be believed to see into the thoughts of human beings.
XV. The reply: What demons can and cannot do with regard to the thoughts of human beings.
XVI. A comparison: To what degree unclean spirits may be taught to understand the thoughts of human beings.
XVII. Concerning the fact that each demon does not introduce every passion into human beings.
XVIII. A question as to whether among the demons an order of attack and a system of alternation is observable.

I. Desiring to introduce to zealous minds the abba Serenus, a man of the greatest holiness and abstinence and one who reflected his own name, whom we admired with a unique veneration more than we did the others, we feel that we cannot carry out our wish unless we seek to insert his conferences into our little books. Beyond every other virtue, which by the grace of God shone forth not only in his activity and his comportment but even in his face itself, the gift of chastity so filled him with its special quality that he no longer felt disturbed by natural impulses even when asleep. I think that first it is necessary to explain how, with the help of the grace of God, he came to such great purity of the flesh, since it seems beyond the possibilities of human nature.

II.1. With prayers day and night, then, and with fasting and vigils, he pleaded tirelessly for internal chastity of heart and soul. When he saw that he had obtained the answer to his prayers and that all the seething emotions of fleshly lust were extinguished in his heart, inflamed as it were by the very sweet taste of purity, he was the more athirst with zeal for chastity and began to pursue fasting and supplication still more intently. Thus the mortification of this passion, which had been bestowed on his inner man by a gift of God, might achieve such external purity as well that in fact he would no longer be disturbed by that simple and natural movement which is aroused even in children and infants. Thanks to the experience of the gift that he had received, which he realized was not due to his own efforts but had come by the grace of God, he was yet more ablaze to obtain this one as well, believing that God could far more easily uproot the urges of the flesh that human skill is unable to draw out either by potions or medicines or surgical instruments, since by his gift he had conferred that purity of spirit which is so lofty and which cannot be acquired by human effort or toil.

2. As he was untiringly devoting himself with constant supplication and tears to the request that he had made, there came to him an angel in a vision of the night. He seemed to open his belly, pull out a kind of fiery tumor from his bowels, cast it away, and

restore all his entrails to their original place. "Behold," he said, "the impulses of your flesh have been cut out, and you should know that today you have obtained that perpetual purity of body which you have faithfully sought." Let it suffice to say briefly that this came from the grace of God, which was bestowed on the man in question in a remarkable way.

3. For the rest, I think that it is unnecessary to say anything about those virtues which he possessed in common with other great men, lest the narrative which is devoted to this man seem to suggest that others did not have what is attributed to him in particular.

Afire with great longing for a conference with him and for instruction from him, therefore, we took care to see him during the days of Lent. When he had asked us in the most gentle way about the nature of our thoughts and the condition of our inner man and what our stay in the desert for such a long time had contributed to its purity, we addressed these concerns to him:

III.1. "The passing of time and the dwelling in the desert that you assume, upon reflection, ought to have brought us to the perfection of the inner man has conferred this alone on us: We have learned what we are unable to be, yet it has not made us be what we are striving to be. For we realize that with this knowledge we have acquired neither a fixed stability in the purity that we have sought after nor any strength to endure but only an increase of confusion and shame. 2. It is true that each day we zealously practice meditation in every discipline and make progress, going from uncertain beginnings to a sure and solid skill and coming to know what at first we had known obscurely or been completely unaware of, proceeding by what I would call firm steps in the practice of that discipline and becoming perfectly and easily versed in it. Nonetheless I find that, as I strive laboriously in this purity, I have progressed in this alone: I know what I cannot be. Hence I think that nothing but hard work will be my lot as a result of such contrition of heart, so that there may always be reason for weeping. Yet I do not cease to be what I must not be.

3. "Therefore, what use is it to have learned what is best if the thing that we know about cannot be laid hold of? For when we think that our heart is stretching out toward its goal, our mind,

insensibly turned away from that to its former wanderings by a powerful impetus, slips away and, preoccupied with commonplace distractions, is so frequently captivated by so many things that we almost despair of the correction that we long for, and this discipline seems superfluous.

4. "When the mind that has gotten involved in silly distractions for a few moments returns to the fear of God and to spiritual contemplation, before it becomes fixed there it disappears again still more quickly. When we have been as it were aroused and realize that it has wandered away from its proposed intent, and we are brought back to the theoria that it had abandoned, we want to bind it by the most tenacious attentiveness of heart, as if by chains, but even as we are attempting this it slips away again, speedier than an eel, from the recesses of our mind.

5. "Hence, inflamed by daily practices of this kind, yet seeing that our heart has not received any firm strength from them, we are broken by despair and are drawn to this opinion: We believe that these wanderings of the soul which exist in the human race are not our own fault but nature's."

IV.1. SERENUS: "It is a dangerous presumption to claim to understand the nature of anything hastily, before the matter has been thoroughly discussed and its characteristics have been analyzed, and to make a guess founded on one's own inexpertise rather than to offer an opinion based on the condition and qualities of the practice itself or on the experience of other people. Suppose someone who could not swim and knew that the water could not bear the weight of his body wished, from the experience of his own inability, to assert that no one encased in solid flesh could ever be upheld by the watery element. This opinion of his, which he seemed to bring forth out of his experience, should not therefore be judged as true, since by very clear proof and by eyewitness this is clearly not only not impossible but even most easily accomplishable by others.

2. "The νους, therefore, which is the mind, is understood as αεικινη τος και πολυκινητος—that is, as always changeable and as manifoldly changeable. This is also spoken of in other words in the Wisdom of Solomon as follows: και γεωδες σκηνος βριθει νουν πολυφροντιδα—that is: 'The earthly tent weighs down the mind

that considers many things.'[1] Because of its nature, then, it can never stand idle but, unless it has some foresight into where it will move and what will preoccupy it, it will inevitably run about and fly everywhere due to its own changeableness until, having become accustomed by lengthy practice and constant habituation (in which you say that you are making an effort in vain), it gains experience and learns with what things to equip its memory, to what purpose it should direct its unceasing flights, and why it should acquire the power to remain fixed in one place. Thus it will be able to drive out the opposing suggestions of the enemy by which it is distracted and to remain in the state and condition that it desires.

3. "We should not, then, attribute this wandering of our heart either to human nature or to God who created it. The scriptural judgment is a true one: 'God made man righteous, but they themselves have sought out many thoughts.'[2] Their quality, therefore, depends on us because 'a good thought,' it says, 'comes near to those who know it, but a prudent man will find it.'[3] For if the finding of something has been made subject to our own prudence and effort, then the not finding of it is certainly to be ascribed to our own idleness and imprudence and not to the fault of nature. The psalmist also agrees with this opinion when he says: 'Blessed is the man whose help is from you, O Lord. He has set up ascents in his heart.'[4]

"You see, then, that it is in our power to set up in our hearts either ascents, which are thoughts that touch God, or descents, which sink down to earthly and carnal things. 4. If these had not been in our power, the Lord would not have rebuked the Pharisees: 'Why do you think evil in your hearts?'[5] Nor would he have commanded through the prophet and said: 'Remove the evil of your thoughts from my sight.'[6] And: 'How long will wicked thoughts remain in you?'[7] Nor would he have said that on the day of judgment their character, like that of our deeds, would be demanded of us, as the Lord warns through Isaiah: 'Behold,' he says, 'I am coming to gather their works and thoughts together with all nations and tongues.'[8] Nor would we deserve to be condemned or defended by their testimony in that terrible and fearful judgment, according to the words of the blessed Apostle when he says: 'Their thoughts within them accusing or defending them, on the day when God will judge the secrets of men according to my gospel.'[9]

V.1. "The image of this perfect mind is very beautifully designated by the centurion in the Gospel. His virtue and steadfastness did not let him be led astray by the thoughts that assailed him but, in accordance with his judgment, he admitted the good ones and drove away the opposing ones without any difficulty. This is set out tropically as follows: 'I also am a man under authority, having soldiers under me, and I say to one: Go, and he goes; and to another: Come, and he comes; and to my slave: Do this, and he does it.'[10]

2. "If we also, struggling manfully against disturbances and vices, are able to subject them to our authority and discretion and, warring in our flesh, can extinguish our passions, subjugate the unstable cohort of our thoughts to the rule of reason, and by the saving standard of the Lord's cross drive out the fearful troops of the opposing powers from the territory of our heart, as a reward for such triumphs we shall be promoted to the rank of this spiritual centurion, who we read was mystically designated by Moses in Exodus: 'Establish for yourself χιλιαργας, and centurions, and rulers of fifties and tens.'[11] 3. Thus, raised to the height of this dignity, we also shall have this power and strength of command, so that we may not be led astray by thoughts that we do not want but may be able to remain in and cling to those by which we are spiritually delighted, commanding evil suggestions to go, and they will go, but telling the good to come, and they will come. We shall also enjoin upon our slave—that is, our body—the things that pertain to chastity and abstinence, and it will carry them out without any objection, no longer raising against us the opposing urges of lust but showing itself completely subservient to the spirit.

4. "Listen to what the blessed Apostle says about what kind of weapons this centurion has and for what military exercises they are used: 'The weapons of our warfare,' he says, 'are not carnal but powerful to God.'[12] He said what kind they were—that is, not carnal and weak but spiritual and powerful to God. Then he indicates for what conflicts they will be used: 'For the destruction of fortifications, for purging thoughts and every height that lifts itself up against the knowledge of God, for leading captive every intellect in

obedience to Christ, and being prepared to revenge every disobedience, when first your obedience has been fulfilled.'[13]

5. "Since it will be necessary to go through these things one by one at another time, I only want to show you now the different kinds and properties of the weapons with which, if we want to fight the Lord's battles and serve among the gospel centurions, we too must always be armed when we march out. 'Take up,' he says, 'the shield of faith with which you will be able to extinguish all the fiery darts of the evil one.'[14] It is faith, then, which intercepts the burning darts of wanton desires and extinguishes them through fear of the future judgment and belief in the heavenly kingdom. 6. 'And,' he says, 'the breastplate of love.'[15] This is the thing which, covering the vital organs in our breast and protecting the exposed parts from the deadly wounds of disturbances, blunts the enemies' thrusts and does not permit the devil's missiles to penetrate to our inner man, for it 'suffers all things, puts up with all things, endures all things.'[16] 'And for a helmet, the hope of salvation.'[17] The helmet is the head's defense. Since our head is Christ,[18] we must always protect it in every trial and persecution with the hope of future good things as with an impregnable helmet and especially maintain our faith in him unhurt and whole. 7. For it is possible for someone to survive, although barely, if he has been deprived of his other members, but without a head a person cannot live even for a short space of time. 'And the sword of the Spirit, which is the word of God.'[19] For it is 'sharper than any two-edged sword, piercing to the divisions of soul and spirit, of joints and marrow, and discerning the thoughts and intentions of the heart,'[20] dividing and cutting off whatever it finds in us is carnal and earthly.

8. "Whoever is protected by these weapons is always defended from the enemy's spears and devastation and will not be led as a captive and a slave, bound in the chains of the ravagers, to the territory of hostile thoughts, nor will he hear through the prophet: 'Why have you grown old in a foreign land?'[21] But he will live triumphant and victorious in that region of thoughts where he wanted to be.

"Do you also want to understand the strength and fortitude of this centurion, by which he bears these weapons that we have spoken about and that are not carnal but powerful to God? 9.

Listen to the king himself and how he recruits the strong men that he gathers for his spiritual army, marking them and proving them: 'Let the weak say,' he says, 'that I am strong.'[22] And: 'The one who suffers shall be a fighter.'[23] You see, then, that the Lord's battles can only be fought by the suffering and the weak. Indeed, certainly fixed in this weakness, our gospel centurion said with confidence: 'When I am weak, then I am strong.'[24] And again: 'Strength is perfected in weakness.'[25] One of the prophets says about this weakness: 'The one who is weak among them shall be as the house of David.'[26] The patient sufferer shall also fight these battles with that patience of which it is said: 'Patience is necessary for you so that you may do the will of God and receive a reward.'[27]

VI.1. "Yet we shall discover by our own experience that we must and can cling to the Lord if we have mortified our wills and cut off the desires of this world, and we shall be taught by the authority of those who, speaking to the Lord, confidently say: 'My soul has clung to you.'[28] And: 'I have clung to your testimonies, Lord.'[29] And: 'It is good for me to cling to God.'[30] And: 'Whoever clings to the Lord is one spirit.'[31]

2. "We must not, therefore, slacken our grip out of weariness with these wanderings of the soul. For 'whoever cultivates his land shall be filled with bread, but the one who pursues idleness shall be filled with poverty.'[32] Nor should we fall away from this attentive observance on account of pernicious despair, because 'in everyone who is careful there is an abundance, for one who is carefree and without sorrow shall be in need.'[33] And again: 'A man in sorrow labors for himself and forcibly prevents his own ruin.'[34] And also: 'The kingdom of heaven suffers force, and the violent bear it away.'[35]

3. "For no virtue is perfected without effort, nor is it possible for anyone to mount to the stability of mind that he desires without great contrition of heart. For 'man is born in trouble.'[36] In order that he might 'attain to the perfect man, the measure of the stature of the fullness of Christ,'[37] he must always be watchful with still greater attentiveness and labor with constant care.

4. "But no one will arrive at the fullness of this measure in the world to come except the person who has reflected on it and been initiated into it in the present and who has tasted it while still living

in this world; who, having been designated a most precious member of Christ, possesses in this flesh the pledge of that union through which he is able to be joined to Christ's body; who desires only one thing, thirsts for one thing, and always directs not only every deed but even every thought to this one thing, so that he may already possess in the present what has been pledged him and what is spoken of with regard to the blessed way of life of the holy in the future—that is, that 'God may be all in all'[38] to him."

VII. GERMANUS: "This fickleness of the mind could perhaps be somewhat restrained if so great a number of adversaries were not surrounding it and constantly pushing it to what it does not want—to what, indeed, the changeableness of its own nature is ceaselessly impelling it. Since such a numerous, powerful, and frightful host encompasses it, we would believe that it would be impossible especially for this frail flesh to resist them if we were not encouraged in this regard by your words, as if by heavenly oracles."

VIII.1. SERENUS: "Those who have experienced the struggles of the inner man cannot doubt that our adversaries are constantly lying in wait for us. But we declare that they are so offset by our progress that we believe that they only incite us to wickedness but do not force us. Moreover, no one could completely avoid a sin that they wanted to burn into our hearts if they had a powerful means of forcing us, as they have of suggesting to us. 2. Therefore, just as to them there has been given the ability to instigate, so to us there has been given the power to reject as well as the freedom to accept. Yet, if we greatly fear their power and attacks, let us also take into account, on the other side, the protection and help of God, about which it is said: 'Greater is the one who is in us than the one who is in this world.'[39] His help fights with far greater strength on our behalf than the multitude of them struggles against us. For God is not only the one who suggests good things but also their patron and promoter, such that he sometimes draws us to salvation even involuntarily and unbeknownst to ourselves.

3. "It is clear, then, that no one can be deceived by the devil except the person who has chosen to offer him the assent of his will. Ecclesiastes has expressed this plainly in these words: 'Because those who do evil are not quickly opposed, therefore the

heart of the children of men is full within them, so that they may do evil.'[40] Hence it is evident that a person transgresses because, when wicked thoughts attack him, he does not at once resist and oppose them. For it says: 'Resist him and he will flee from you.'[41]

IX. GERMANUS: "What, I ask, is that vague and confused connection between the soul and those wicked spirits, by which they are able I would not say to be joined with so much as to be united to it, so that they can imperceptibly speak to it, enter into it, and suggest to it whatever they wish, and so that they are able to impel it to whatever they please and to see and examine its thoughts and movements, so that there is so close a union between them and the mind that, apart from the grace of God, one can hardly determine what comes from their instigation and what from our own will?"

X. SERENUS: "It is not surprising that a spirit can be imperceptibly joined to a spirit and that it can exercise a hidden persuasive influence where it has been permitted to. For among them, as among human beings, there is a certain substantial similarity and relationship, since the understanding of the nature of the soul may likewise be applied to their substance. But, on the other hand, it is completely impossible for them to enter into and be united with one another in such a way that one can contain the other. This is rightly attributed only to the Godhead, which alone is an incorporeal and simple nature."

XI. GERMANUS: "We think that what we see happening in the case of the possessed is quite contrary to this position, when under the influence of unclean spirits they say and do things that they are unaware of. Why, then, should we not believe that there are united to those spirits the souls of those whom we see have become as it were their instruments and, having left their natural state, have taken on their movements and emotions, such that they no longer produce their own voice and gestures and desires but those others'?"

XII.1. SERENUS: "What you say happens in the case of demoniacs—when those who are possessed by unclean spirits say and do what they do not want and are forced to do things of which they are unaware—is not contrary to the aforementioned understanding of ours. For it is quite certain that they do not endure this incursion of spirits in only one way. Some are possessed in such a manner that they have no idea what they are doing and saying, while others know and remember afterward. It should not be thought that, in the incursion of an unclean spirit, it penetrates into the substance of the soul itself and that consequently the former, as if it were united to it and somehow clothed in it, utters phrases and words by the mouth of the victim. In no way should it be believed that they can do this. It is very clearly understood that this takes place not through some kind of diminution of the soul but through a weakening of the body, when an unclean spirit makes its way into those organs in which the soul's vigor is contained, imposes an unbearable and immeasurable weight on them, and overwhelms the intellectual faculties and deeply darkens their understanding. 2. We see that this sometimes happens also through the fault of wine or fever or excessive cold or other unfavorable conditions that are externally caused. The devil, who had received power over the blessed Job's flesh, did not succeed in bringing this upon him, having been forbidden by the command of the Lord, who said: 'Behold, I hand him over to you; only spare his soul.'[42] That is to say, only do not drive him mad by weakening his soul's abode, and do not obscure the understanding and wisdom of the one who withstands you by suffocating the governance of his heart with your weight.

XIII.1. "Nor even if a spirit is mingled with this dense and solid matter (that is, with flesh), which can very easily be done, is it therefore to be believed that it can be so united to a soul, which is also a spirit, that it can also make it the bearer of its own nature. This is possible to the Trinity alone, which so penetrates every intellectual nature that it is able not only to embrace and encompass it but even to flow into it and, being itself incorporeal, to be poured into a body.

"For although we declare that some natures are spiritual, as are the angels, the archangels and the other powers, our soul itself and of course the subtle air, yet these are by no means to be considered incorporeal. 2. They have a body appropriate to themselves by which they subsist, although it is far more refined than our own bodies. In the words of the Apostle: 'There are heavenly bodies and earthly bodies.'[43] And again: 'It is sown an animal body, and it rises a spiritual body.'[44]

"From this it is clear that nothing is incorporeal but God alone, and therefore only to him can every spiritual and intellectual substance be penetrable because he alone is whole and everywhere and in all things, such that he may examine and survey the thoughts and internal dispositions of human beings and all the inmost recesses of the mind. 3. It was of him alone that the blessed Apostle spoke when he said: 'The word of God is alive and active and keener than any two-edged sword, piercing to the divisions of soul and spirit, of joints and marrow, and discerning the thoughts and intentions of the heart. No creature is invisible in his sight, but all are exposed and open to his eyes.'[45] And blessed David says: 'Who forms their hearts individually.'[46] And again: 'He himself knows the secrets of the heart.'[47] And Job also: 'You alone know the hearts of human beings.'[48]

XIV. GERMANUS: "You say that for this reason these spirits cannot ever look into our thoughts. We think that it is utterly absurd to hold this opinion when Scripture says: 'If the spirit of a ruler should rise up against you.'[49] And again: 'When the devil had put it in the heart of Simon Iscariot to betray the Lord.'[50] How, then, can we believe that our thoughts do not lie open to them, when we see that for the most part the seeds for them spring up at their suggestion and instigation?"

XV.1. SERENUS: "No one doubts that unclean spirits can understand the characteristics of our thoughts, but they pick these up from external and perceptible indications–that is, either from our gestures or from our words, and from the desires to which they see that we are inclining. Otherwise they are completely unable to examine those which have not yet emerged from the inmost parts of the soul. 2. Likewise, they come up with the thoughts that they insinuate, whether they are accepted or however they are accepted, not from the nature of the soul itself–that is, from its inner workings, which are, as I would say, concealed deep within us–but from movements and indications of the outer man.

"Take, for example, the case of their suggesting gluttony. If they see a monk raising his eyes curiously to the window or to the sun or asking anxiously about the time of day, then they know that he has been seized by the desire of gormandizing. If, while insinuating fornication, they notice that he has let himself be struck by the shaft of wanton desire, or if they see that his flesh has been stirred or even that he has not sighed as he should have over the lewdness of an impure suggestion, then they understand that the dart of wanton desire has been fixed in the depths of his soul. 3. If they have incited him to sadness or anger or rage, they discern from bodily gestures and from perceptible movements whether these things have taken hold of his heart when they see him groaning, for example, when he had been silent, or sighing with a certain indignation, or his face pale or blush, and thus they have subtle knowledge of who is given to what vice. They understand clearly that each one of us takes pleasure in the particular one to whose pursuit they soon discover he has given his consent and agreement by a nod or a movement of the body.

4. "It is not surprising that these things can be grasped by those airy powers, since we see that this is also very often the case with insightful men—namely, they recognize the state of the inner man from one's bearing and expression and from external characteristics. There is no doubt that these things can be grasped still more easily, then, by these beings who, since they are of a spiritual nature, are indeed far more subtle and wise than human beings.

XVI. "This is reminiscent of those thieves who are accustomed to examine the hidden stores of the people in the homes that they stealthily want to break into. In the darkness of the night they carefully sprinkle tiny grains of sand and so discover, thanks to a slight ringing that occurs when they fall, the secret treasures that they are unable to catch a glimpse of. Thus they get an exact knowledge of the thing and of its metal, since it has been betrayed as it were by the sound that was produced. Likewise, so that these others might explore the treasury of our heart, they sprinkle certain harmful suggestions in us like grains of sand, and when they see a fleshly disposition emerge in accordance with the character of their suggestions they recognize what is concealed in the inmost recesses of the inner man, as if by a kind of ringing that comes forth from hidden chambers.

XVII. "Yet we should know that not every demon imprints every passion in human beings, but that particular spirits brood over particular vices. Some, in fact, take delight in impurity and in the filth of wanton desire, others in blasphemy, while others are more especially intent on anger and rage. Others, again, feed on sadness, and still others are pleased with vainglory and pride. Each one insinuates that vice into human hearts in which he himself rejoices, but all do not equally inflict their wickedness; instead, they take turns, provoked by the susceptibility of the time, the place, and the person."

XVIII. GERMANUS: "Must it be believed, then, that among them wickedness is ordered and—as I would say—disciplined, so that a certain alternation is observed by them and a rational scheme of attack is carried out, when it is well known that neither measure nor reason exists except among the good and the upright? As Scripture has it: 'You shall seek wisdom among the wicked and you shall not find it.'[51] And: 'Our enemies are senseless.'[52] And again: 'There is no wisdom, nor is there courage or counsel among the impious.'"[53]

XIX.1. SERENUS: "Among the wicked it is certain that there is no enduring agreement in all of them, nor can perfect harmony exist even with respect to the very vices in which they take common delight. For, as you said, discipline and measure can never be observed in undisciplined things. Yet in some instances, when a joint endeavor or necessity demands it or partnership in some gain encourages it, they have to come together in a temporary accord.

2. "We see very clearly that in the army of evil spirits they not only maintain times and alternations among themselves but are even known to haunt particular spots and to occupy them constantly. For since it is necessary for them to carry out their attacks by means of set trials, through particular vices and at particular times, it is very evident to us that no one can simultaneously be led astray by the emptiness of vainglory and be inflamed by the lust of fornication, nor can he at the same time be puffed up by the swelling haughtiness of spiritual pride and fall into the humiliation of carnal gluttony. 3. Neither can a person both break into foolish cackling and laughter and be provoked by the urges of anger, and even less can he be preoccupied by the bitterness of consuming sadness. Rather, a spirit must set out by itself to attack the mind in such a way that if it departs vanquished it gives it over

to another spirit to be attacked more vehemently, but even if it is victorious it still hands it over to another to be similarly deceived.

XX.1. "We should also by no means be unaware of the fact that not all have the same ferocity and desire, nor indeed the same courage and wickedness. With beginners and the weak only the weaker spirits are paired off in battle, and once these evil spirits have been overcome ever more robust contenders take up the fight against the athlete of Christ. For the difficulty of the struggle increases in direct proportion to a person's strength and progress. 2. Indeed, a holy person would never be able to bear the wickedness of such great enemies and to face their onslaughts but would succumb to their cruelty and savagery were it not for the fact that Christ, the most merciful arbiter and the overseer who presides over our struggle, balances out the strength of the contestants, repels and restrains their fierce attacks, and with the trial provides a way out, so that we are able to endure.[54]

XXI.1. "We do not believe, however, that they engage in this struggle without any effort of their own. For they themselves also have a certain anxiety and sadness in the conflict, especially when they meet with stronger rivals—that is, with holy and perfect men. Otherwise no conflict or struggle but only a simple and, as I might say, safe deception of human beings would fall to their lot. How, then, would the Apostle say: 'Our struggle is not against flesh and blood but against principalities, against powers, against the world rulers of this darkness, against spirits of evil in heavenly places'?[55] And also: 'I do not fight as one beating against the air'?[56] And again: 'I have fought the good fight'?[57] 2. For when a fight and a contest and a battle are spoken of, there is inevitably toil and effort and anxiety on both sides, and grief and distress awaits one of them after defeat, while joy follows upon victory. But when one leisurely and safely fights another who is struggling laboriously, and the former uses his will as his only weapon to defeat his opponent, this should not be called a battle or a struggle or a contest but a kind of unfair and unreasonable travesty of a match.

3. "But clearly, in attacking the race of human beings, they labor and toil as much as we do in order to be able to seize the victory that they desire over someone, and the distress which was awaiting us if we had been overcome by them will be turned back

on them, according to the words: 'The head of their encircling, the labor of their own lips shall cover them over.'[58] And: 'His sorrow shall be turned upon his own head.'[59] And again: 'The snare that he does not know of shall come to him, and let the net that he hid seize him, and let him fall into that very snare'[60]—namely, the one who pursues the deception of human beings. They themselves grieve, then, no less than we, and, in the manner that they overcome us, they themselves are similarly overcome and, once defeated, depart in disgrace.

4. "He who possessed the healthy eyes of the inner man, daily observing their destruction and their conflicts, seeing them rejoice over each destruction and downfall and fearing lest they eventually rejoice over him as well, beseeched the Lord and said: 'Enlighten my eyes that I may never fall asleep in death, that my enemy may never say: I have prevailed against him. Those who trouble me will exult if I have been moved.'[61] And: 'My God, do not let them rejoice over me. Do not let them say in their hearts: Aha, aha, just as we wished. Neither let them say: We have devoured him.'[62] And: 'They gnashed their teeth over me. Lord, how long will you look at this?'[63] For 'he lies in wait like a lion in his lair. He lies in wait to seize the poor man.'[64] And: 'He seeks his food from God.'[65]

5. "Again, when they have made every attempt and have not succeeded in deceiving us, it is inevitable that, having labored in vain, 'those who seek our souls should be confounded and be ashamed, so that they may leave them alone. Let those who think evil in our regard be covered with shame and distress.'[66] Jeremiah also says: 'Let them be confounded, and let me not be confounded. Let them be in dread, and let me not be in dread. Bring down upon them the fury of your wrath, and destroy them with a double destruction.'[67] For no one doubts that when we have overcome them they must be destroyed by a double destruction—first because, while human beings seek after holiness, they who once possessed it have lost it and have become the cause of man's damnation; and then because spiritual beings have been conquered by fleshly and earthly ones.

6. "Seeing the destruction of the enemy, then, and his own victory, one of the holy proclaims with exultation: 'I will pursue my

enemies and I will overtake them, and I will not turn back until they are defeated. I will destroy them, and they shall not be able to stand. They shall fall beneath my feet.'[68] Praying against them again, the same prophet says: 'Judge, Lord, those who harm me, fight those who fight me. Take up weapons and shield and rise up to help me. Unsheathe the sword and close off those who pursue me. Say to my soul: I am your salvation.'[69] 7. And when all our passions are subdued and destroyed and we have conquered, we shall then deserve to hear that word of blessing: 'Your hand shall be raised above your enemies, and all your enemies shall perish.'[70]

"When we read or sing all these things, therefore, and others like them that have been included in the Sacred Books, if we do not take them as having been written against those evil spirits that lie in wait for us day and night we shall not only not derive from them any increase of gentleness and patience but we shall even conceive a kind of cruel feeling that is contrary to gospel perfection.[71] 8. For we shall not only be taught not to pray for our enemies and not to love them, but we shall even be incited to detest them with an implacable hatred, to curse them, and unceasingly to pour out prayer against them. To understand that holy men and friends of God would have uttered these things in such a spirit is exceedingly wicked and impious. Before the coming of Christ the law was not imposed upon them precisely because they, transcending its commands and anticipating the divine plan, chose rather to be obedient to the gospel precepts and to pursue apostolic perfection.

XXII.1. "That they do not have the power to hurt any human being, however, is clearly demonstrated by the example of the blessed Job, when the enemy did not dare to try him more than he was permitted by the divine dispensation.[72] And the confession of the same spirits who speak in the gospel writings attests: 'If you cast us out, send us into the herd of swine.'[73] If they have no power to go into unclean and mute animals without the permission of God, all the more should we believe that they are unable of their own will to enter into human beings who have been created in the image of God. 2. Otherwise no one—neither the young men whom we see dwelling very steadfastly in this desert nor even the perfect—would be able to live alone in the desert besieged by so many multitudes of such enemies if they had in their power the ability and the freedom to do harm and to attack. The words of our Lord and Savior, which he spoke to Pilate in the humility of his assumed manhood, clearly confirm this: 'You would have no power over me unless it had been given you from above.'[74]

XXIII.1. "But we have sufficiently learned both from our own experience and from the accounts of the elders that the demons do not have the same power now that they had at an earlier time, at the beginnings of anchorite life, when still only a few monks lived in the desert. For so great was their savagery that only a few who were very stable and advanced in age were able to endure dwelling in the desert. In the cenobia themselves, where eight or ten used to live, their brutality would rage to such an extent and their assaults were felt with such frequency and were so visible that everyone did not dare to go to sleep at the same time during the night. Instead, while some took turns sleeping others would keep vigil and be intent on psalms and prayers and readings. 2. And when the necessity of nature had made them sleepy and the others had woken up, the guards were given the care in like manner of those who were about to go to sleep.

"Hence it cannot be doubted that one of two things has conferred this security and confidence now not only on us who seem somewhat strengthened because of the experiences of age but also on those who are younger: Either the power of the cross has also penetrated the desert and by its gleaming grace has blunted the wickedness of the demons everywhere, or our negligence has made them milder than when they first began to attack, since they disdain to fight against us with the same intensity with which they once raged against those accomplished soldiers of Christ, destroying us more ominously with deceitfulness now that visible trials have ceased.

3. "We see some people fall into such lukewarmness that they even have to be coaxed by more lenient warnings lest they desert their cells and wander all around, thus getting into more trouble and involving themselves in what I might call still grosser vices. One would believe that great fruit could be drawn from them if they were only able to remain in the desert, even if they were somewhat

lazy. The elders are in the habit of telling them of this powerful remedy: Stay in your cells, and eat and drink and sleep as much as you want, so long as you remain in them constantly.

XXIV.1. "It is certain, then, that unclean spirits cannot penetrate those whose bodies they will lay hold of unless they have first possessed their minds and thoughts. And when they have stripped them of the fear and recollection of God and of spiritual meditation, they boldly attack those who are easily overcome and who are as it were bereft of all divine protection and aid, and from then on they make their home in them as if in property that has been handed over to them.

XXV.1. "But it is clear that those who do not seem to be filled with them in bodily fashion but are possessed more perniciously in soul—that is, those who are involved in vice and pleasure—are more seriously and violently disturbed. For according to the words of the apostle: 'A person is the slave of the one by whom he is overcome.'[75] In this respect, however, they are more desperately sick: Although they are their slaves they know neither that they are assailed by them nor that they are under their domination.

2. "Moreover, we know that even holy men have been given over bodily to Satan or to great sufferings on account of some slight sins. For the divine clemency does not permit the least blemish or stain to be found in them on the day of judgment. According to the words of the prophet, which are in fact God's, he purges away all the dross of their uncleanness in the present so that he may bring them to eternity like fire-tried gold or silver, in need of no penal cleansing. 3. 'And I will,' he says, 'utterly purge away your dross, and I will remove all your alloy. And after this you shall be called the city of the righteous, the faithful city.'[76] And again: 'Just as silver and gold are tried in a furnace, so the Lord chooses hearts.'[77] And again: 'Fire tries gold and silver, but a man is tried in the furnace of humiliation.'[78] And this also: 'The Lord chastises the one whom he loves, and he scourges every son whom he receives.'[79]

XXVI.1. "In the Third Book of Kings we see this clearly exemplified in the case of that prophet and man of God who was immediately destroyed by a lion because of a single sin of disobedience that he contracted not even out of the workings or the viciousness of his own will but through another's deceptive behavior. Scripture says of him: 'That is the man of God who was disobedient to the word of the Lord, and the Lord delivered him over to a lion, and it destroyed him, according to the word of the Lord which he spoke.'[80] When this happened, the very sparingness and abstinence of the predator (for the voracious beast did not dare to eat anything at all of the corpse that had fallen to him) appeared as not only the punishment for his present offense and heedless error but also as the deserts of his righteousness, on account of which the Lord delivered over his prophet for a time to the tormenter.

2. "In our own day, too, there was a clear and open demonstration of this in the cases of Abba Paul and Abba Moses, who lived in the place in this desert that is known as Calamus. For the former dwelled in the desert which is right near the city of Panephysis, and this desert we know had been created not long before by a flood of very salty water. This covers the whole surface of that region every time that the north wind blows, surging out of the swamps and so overflowing the nearby land that it makes the old villages there, which for a long time have been utterly deserted for this very reason, look like islands.

3. "Here, then, Abba Paul had made such progress in purity of heart in the stillness and silence of the desert that he did not even permit himself to look at a woman's clothing, much less on a woman's face. For when a woman from nearby chanced to meet him on his way to the cell of a certain elder, along with Abba Archebius who was from the same desert, he, distressed at encountering her, ran back to his own monastery in greater haste than a person would use to flee from a lion or an immense dragon, forgoing the duty of the pious visit that he had set out upon. The situation was such that he was not even prevailed upon by the shouts and pleas of the aforesaid Abba Archebius, who was calling him back so that they might stay on the road that they had started out on in order to ask the elder what they had planned.

4. "Although this was done with zeal for chastity and ardor for purity, nonetheless because it was not done according to knowledge[81] and because the observance of discipline and the measure of appropriate strictness were excessive (for he believed

that not merely familiarity with women, which really is harmful, but even the very form of that sex was to be abominated) he immediately suffered such a seizure that his whole body was paralyzed and none of its members could perform any of their functions. For not only his feet and hands but even the mechanism of his tongue, by which speech is formed, were affected, and his very ears lost their sense of hearing. The result was that nothing remained of his humanity apart from an immobile and senseless shape. 5. To such a state was he reduced that men's care was in no way sufficient to minister to his sickness, and only womanly attention was of use to him. For when he was brought to a cenobium of holy virgins, food and drink, which he was unable even to beckon for, was produced for him with feminine graciousness, all his needs of nature were satisfied, and this same care was at his disposal for nearly four years—that is, until the end of his life. 6. Although all his members were so paralyzed by this malady that each one of his joints was lifelessly immobile and insensible, nonetheless the grace of his virtuousness flowed forth from him to such an extent that when sick persons were anointed with oil that had touched what was more his corpse than his body they were at once cured of all their infirmities. Thus, through this malady of his it became abundantly clear even to unbelievers that the sickness of all his members was ordained according to the design and love of the Lord and that the grace of health was bestowed upon him by the power of the Holy Spirit as a testimony to his purity and as a proof of his goodness.

XXVII. "But the second, who we said lived in this desert, was delivered over to such a dreadful demon that, once possessed by him, he would stuff his mouth with human excrement. This occurred, despite the fact that he too was a unique and incomparable man, in swift punishment for a single word that he spoke a little roughly when he was arguing with Abba Macarius and was anticipated in a particular opinion. By the rapidity of his cure and through the author of the remedy the Lord showed that he had applied this purifying scourge as a grace—namely, so that the blemish of a momentary offense might not remain in him. For at once, thanks to the aforesaid Abba Macarius's humble prayer, the wicked spirit quickly took to flight and left him.

XXVIII. "It clearly follows from this that those whom we see delivered over to different trials or to these spirits of wickedness must not be abominated or despised, for we ought to hold unwaveringly to two things. The first is that not one of these persons is ever tried without the permission of God. The second is that everything which is brought upon us by God, whether it appears sad or joyful at the time, is ordained as by a most tender father and a most merciful physician for our benefit. Therefore they are handed over as it were to pedagogues in order to be humiliated. Thus, when they leave this world, those who according to the Apostle have been delivered over for the present 'to Satan for the destruction of the flesh so that the spirit may be saved in the day of our Lord Jesus Christ'[82] may either be brought to the other life in a more purified condition or be struck with a lighter punishment."

XXIX. GERMANUS: "And why do we always see them not only despised and held in horror by all but even made to abstain from the Lord's communion in our provinces, based on the words of the Gospel: 'Do not give what is holy to dogs, and do not cast your pearls before swine,'[83] when, as you say about them, it should be believed that this humiliating trial is being laid upon them for the sake of their purification and well-being?"

XXX.1. SERENUS: "If we have this knowledge–indeed, what I have understood earlier as faith–so that we believe that all things are accomplished and ordained by God for the well-being of souls, we shall not only never despise them but we shall even pray ceaselessly for them as for our own members and suffer along with them from the depths of our being and with all our hearts (for when 'one member suffers, all members suffer'[84]), knowing that we cannot possibly attain perfection without these members of ours, just as we read that our forebears were unable to arrive at the fullness of the promise without us. As the Apostle says concerning them: 'All these who were approved by the testimony of faith did not receive the promises, since God had provided something better for us so that they would not be perfected without us.'[85]

2. "But we do not recall that Holy Communion was ever forbidden them. Rather, it was thought that, if possible, they should

be given it every day. For the words of the Gospel ('Do not give what is holy to dogs'), which you understand in an odd fashion, do not support the belief that Holy Communion becomes food for demons rather than purification and protection for body and soul. When it is received by a person it burns out as it were by a kind of fire the spirit that occupies his members and that is trying to hide in them, and it flees. 3. It was thus that we recently saw Abba Andronicus cured, as well as many others. For the enemy will revile the one whom he is besieging all the more when he sees him cut off from the heavenly medicine, and the more he thinks he is removed from the spiritual remedy the more fearfully and frequently he will make trial of him.

XXXI.1. "Moreover, they are to be considered really pitiable and wretched who, although they defile themselves with every crime and shameful deed, not only show no visible sign of diabolical possession but do not even experience a trial proportionate to their deeds or any corrective punishment. For those whose 'hardness and impenitent heart' exceeds the punishment of the present life and 'stores up for itself wrath and indignation on the day of wrath and of the revelation of the just judgment of God, when their worm shall not die and their fire shall not be extinguished,'[86] do not deserve the quick and expeditious medicine of the present life.

2. "The prophet, concerned at the sufferings of the holy ones and seeing that they are subject to various tribulations and trials while sinners not only pass through this world without any humiliating scourge but even enjoy abundant riches and great prosperity in all their affairs, speaks out against them, inflamed with a zeal that cannot be repressed and with an ardent spirit: 'My feet almost moved, my steps nearly slipped. For I was jealous at the wicked, seeing the peace of sinners. For there is no regard in their death, nor strength in their misfortune. Theirs is not the travail of men, nor are they scourged with men.'[87] This means that those who have not deserved to be scourged with men in the present, as not sharing in the lot and discipline of sons, must be punished in the future with the demons.

3. "Jeremiah too, when he disputes with God over the prosperity of the impious and even though he confesses that he doubts the justice of the Lord, says: 'You are just indeed, Lord,

when I dispute with you.'[88] Nonetheless, asking about the reasons for such great inequality, he adds: 'But I will speak what is just to you: Why does the way of the wicked prosper? Why does it go well with all who do evil and act wickedly? You have planted them, and they have taken root. They prosper and bring forth fruit. You are near to their mouth and far from their reins.'[89]

4. "The Lord, speaking through the prophet, laments their ruin, anxiously directs physicians and teachers to heal them, provokes them in a certain way to a similar lamentation, and says: 'Babylon has suddenly fallen; she is destroyed. Wail over her, bring balm for her pain, if perhaps she can be cured.'[90] But the angels to whom the responsibility for human salvation has been entrusted reply in desperation, or at least the prophet does, speaking on behalf of the apostles and spiritual men and teachers who see the inflexibility of their mind and their impenitent heart: 5. 'We have cared for Babylon, and she has not been healed. Let us leave her and let each one of us return to his own land, for her judgment has reached as far as the heavens and it has been raised as high as the clouds.'[91] In the person of God Isaiah speaks to Jerusalem of their desperate sickness: 'From the sole of the foot even to the top of the head there is no health in her. Wound and bruise and swelling sore are not bandaged or dressed or anointed with oil.'[92]

XXXII.1. "But it is proved beyond a doubt that there are as many occupations among the unclean spirits as there are among human beings. For it is clear that some of them, which ordinary people refer to as *plani,* are such tricksters and jokers that they constantly infest certain places and roads where they do not take delight in tormenting passers-by whom they can deceive but are content simply with derision and illusions, and they strive to weary them rather than to harm them. Certain ones do nothing but pass the night in harmlessly possessing human beings. Others are given over to such fury and savagery that they are not content with troubling those whom they possess by violently lacerating their bodies but even seek to assail passers-by from a distance and to murder them brutally. They are like the ones described in the Gospel, for fear of whom no one would dare to take that road.[93]

There is no doubt that these and their like take pleasure with insatiable ferocity in wars and bloodshed.

2. "We see that others, which ordinary people also refer to as *bacucci,* so corrupt the hearts of those whom they have seized with a kind of empty pride that they sometimes raise themselves up beyond their normal height and posture arrogantly and pompously, while at other times, as if they were inclined to be placid and friendly, they accommodate themselves in a manner that is democratic and engaging. Likewise, considering themselves famous and estimable in the eyes of all, they sometimes show by bodily inclinations that they are adoring higher powers, while at other times they believe that they are being adored by other people, and they go through all the motions of real ceremonies, whether proudly or humbly.

3. "We find that others not only engage in lying but even inspire people to blaspheme. We who have heard a demon openly confess that he spread abroad an impious and sacrilegious teaching through Arius and Eunomius are ourselves witnesses of this. We also read in the Fourth Book of Kings that one of this kind clearly declared: 'I will go out and I will be a lying spirit in the mouth of all his prophets.'[94] The Apostle speaks about these in the following way when he reproaches those who are deceived by such: 'Paying attention to seducing spirits and to the teachings of demons that tell lies in hypocrisy.'[95]

4. "The Gospels testify that there are also other kinds of demons—that is, of mutes and of the deaf.[96] The prophet remarks that some spirits, too, incite to wanton desire and lasciviousness when he says: 'The spirit of fornication deceived them, and they went fornicating away from their God.'[97] Scriptural authority likewise teaches that there are demons of the night, of the day, and of noonday.[98]

"Their diversity is such that it would take a long time if we wanted to search all the Scriptures and to go through them individually, seeing which ones are designated by the prophet as onocentaurs, which as satyrs, which as sirens, which as enchantresses, which as screechers, which as ostriches, and which as urchins;[99] which is the asp and which the basilisk in the psalm;[100] which is called a lion, which a dragon, and which a scorpion in the Gospel;[101] which is 'the prince of this world,'[102] and which are referred to by the Apostle as 'the rulers of this darkness' and which as 'the spirits of evil.'[103] 5. We must not think these names have been given to them by chance or haphazardly. Rather, by using the names of these wild animals, which are either less harmful or more dangerous in our regard, the ferocity and rage of those other beings is denoted. Moreover, from a comparison with the virulent wickedness and domination that a kind of preeminence in evil confers upon certain wild animals and serpents, those others are also called by the names of these. Thus one is denominated a lion because of his wild fury and raging ferocity, another a basilisk because of that death-dealing poison which kills before it is noticed, and still another an onocentaur or an urchin or an ostrich because of the mildness of his malice."

XXXIII. GERMANUS: "We certainly do not doubt that the ranks which the Apostle enumerates also refer to them, because 'our struggle is not against flesh and blood but against principalities, against powers, against the world rulers of this darkness, against spirits of evil in heavenly places.'[104] Yet we wish to know where such a great diversity among them comes from and how so many kinds of wickedness exist. Were they created in order to cooperate with these ranks of evil and in some way to struggle on behalf of this wickedness?"

XXXIV.1. SERENUS: "Although your questions would steal from our eyes a whole night's repose, such that we would never be aware of the nearness of the approaching dawn and would be drawn insatiably to join the words of this conference to the rising of the sun, nonetheless because the search for the answer to the question that was posed will lead us into a kind of vast and very deep sea of questions, which the shortness of the present moment does not permit us to traverse, I think that it would be more convenient for us to save it for a future night's investigation. In that way spiritual joy and more abundant fruit may be bestowed on me from a serious conversation with you when this question has been raised, and with the Holy Spirit providing prosperous breezes for us we shall be able to enter more easily into the heart of the questions that have been asked. 2. Therefore, let us get a little sleep and drive away the heaviness that is creeping into our eyes as the day already begins to dawn. Then let us go together to the church, for the solemnity of Sunday beckons us to this. When we have returned after the synaxis we shall discuss with redoubled joy the things that the Lord will have given for our common instruction in accordance with your desire."

Textual References

1. Wis 9:15 LXX.
2. Eccl 7:29 LXX.
3. Prv 19:7 LXX.
4. Ps 83:6 LXX.
5. Mt 9:4.
6. Is 1:16.
7. Jer 4:14b.
8. Is 66:18.
9. Rom 2:15–16.
10. Mt 8:9.
11. Ex 18:21.
12. 2 Cor 10:4a.
13. 2 Cor 10:4b–6.
14. Eph 6:16.
15. 1 Thes 5:8a.
16. 1 Cor 13:7.
17. 1 Thes 5:8b.
18. Cf. Eph 1:22; Col 1:18.
19. Eph 6:17.
20. Heb 4:12.
21. Bar 3:10.
22. Jl 3:10 LXX.
23. Jl 3:11 LXX.
24. 2 Cor 12:10.
25. 2 Cor 12:9.
26. Zec 12:8 LXX.
27. Heb 10:36.
28. Ps 63:8.
29. Ps 119:31.
30. Ps 73:28.
31. 1 Cor 6:17.
32. Prv 28:19.
33. Prv 14:23 LXX.
34. Prv 16:26 LXX.
35. Mt 11:12.
36. Jb 5:7.
37. Eph 4:13.
38. 1 Cor 15:28.

39. 1 Jn 4:4.
40. Eccl 8:11 LXX.
41. Jas 4:7.
42. Jb 2:6 LXX.
43. 1 Cor 15:40.
44. 1 Cor 15:44.
45. Heb 4:12–13.
46. Ps 33:15.
47. Ps 44:21.
48. 2 Chr 6:30.
49. Eccl 10:4.
50. Jn 13:2.
51. Prv 14:6 LXX.
52. Dt 32:31 LXX.
53. Prv 21:30 LXX.
54. Cf. 1 Cor 10:13.
55. Eph 6:12.
56. 1 Cor 9:26.
57. 2 Tm 4:7.
58. Ps 140:9.
59. Ps 7:17.
60. Ps 35:8.
61. Ps 13:3–4.
62. Ps 35:24–25.
63. Ps 35:16–17.
64. Ps 10:9.
65. Ps 104:21.
66. Pss 40:15, 35:26.
67. Jer 17:18.
68. Ps 18:37–38.
69. Ps 35:1–3.
70. Mi 5:8.
71. Cf. Mt 5:44.
72. Cf. Jb 1:12.
73. Mt 8:31.
74. Jn 19:11.
75. 2 Pt 2:19.
76. Is 1:25–26.

77. Prv 17:3 LXX.
78. Sir 2:5.
79. Heb 12:6.
80. 1 Kgs 13:26.
81. Cf. Rom 10:2.
82. 1 Cor 5:5.
83. Mt 7:6.
84. 1 Cor 12:26.
85. Heb 11:39–40.
86. Rom 2:5; Is 66:24.
87. Ps 72:2–5 LXX.
88. Jer 12:1a.
89. Jer 12:1b–2.
90. Jer 51:8.
91. Jer 51:9.
92. Is 1:6.
93. Cf. Mt 8:28.
94. 1 Kgs 22:22.
95. 1 Tm 4:1–2.
96. Cf. Lk 11:14; Mk 9:17.
97. Hos 4:12.
98. Cf. Ps 91:5–6.
99. Cf. Is 13:21–22, 34:12–14.
100. Cf. Ps 91:13.
101. Cf. Lk 10:19.
102. Jn 14:30.
103. Eph 6:12.
104. Eph 6:12.

7.1 Who reflected his own name: Serenus means "serene." The name is appropriate inasmuch as the subject of the present conference is the cultivation of inner serenity in the face of demonic onslaughts.

The grace of God shone forth...even in his face itself: On the radiant faces of holy persons and ascetics, which is a common theme, cf. 11.2.2, 11.4.2, 22.1.1; Pachomius, *Catechesis* 1 (CSCO 160.13); Athanasius, *V. S. Antonii* 67; *Hist. monach. in Aegypto* 2.1, 6.1; *Verba seniorum* 18.36; John Moschus, *Pratum spirituale* 69. For antecedents in pagan literature cf. the passages gathered in Johannes von Arnim, ed., *Stoicorum veterum fragmenta* 3 (Leipzig-Berlin, 1923), 154–156; to these add Porphyry, *V. Plotini* 13. The radiant, attractive face is also frequently the attribute of the martyr in Christian literature. Cf. Acts 6:15; *Mart. Pol.* 12.1; *Pass. Perp. et Felic.* 6.1. On the face as expressive of the soul in general cf. Origen, *Comm. in Cant. Cant.* 3(4) (GCS 33.232–233); Didymus, *Comm. in Gen.* 122f. (SC 233.286–288).

7.2.1 Simple and natural movement...even in children and infants: Cf. the notes at 4.15.1 and 22.3.5.

7.2.1f. For other references to grace, mentioned here and in 7.8.2, cf. the note at 2.1.3f.

7.2.2 A similar story of chastity granted by way of an operation performed in a dream is recounted of Abba Elijah in Palladius, *Hist. laus.* 29.3f. Cf. Weber 89; John Moschus, *Patrum spirituale* 3. An operation on a monk's liver in like circumstances is recorded in *Verba seniorum* 20.11. This kind of dream was not unknown in pagan antiquity. Cf. Artemidorus, *Oneirocritica* 5.95 (ed. by Pack, Leipzig, 1963, 324).

7.3.3ff. On distractions, mentioned here and in 7.4.2ff., cf. the note at 1.5.4.

7.4.1 On experience as teacher cf. the note at 3.7.4. The experience spoken of here is of course not real but only seeming. For similar examples of unwillingness to believe what one is not familiar with cf. 12.8.4 and 12.13.1.

7.4.2 The source of the Greek phrase is unknown.

7.5 On the military imagery here in particular cf. the note at 1.1.

7.5.1 Tropically: *Tropica significatione*. On the tropical or tropological interpretation of Scripture cf. 14.8.

7.5.2. The saving standard of the Lord's cross: *Dominicae crucis salutari vexillo*. The Roman victory standard—τροπαιον in Greek and *vexillum* in Latin—was associated with the cross from at least the middle of the second century. Cf. Justin, 1 *Apol.* 55; Tertullian, *Apol.* 16.

7.5.5 On burning darts cf. the note at 2.13.7f.

7.6.4 The conclusion of this section anticipates 10.6.4ff. (beginning with "God will be 'all in all' for us").

7.8.2 On the demonic power to instigate thoughts and the human power to reject them cf. 1.17 and the relevant note.

7.9 Whatever they please: I have read *placuerint* rather than *placuerit* here.

7.12f. That demons are relegated to occupying the bodies of their victims because they cannot affect their souls directly is also observed by John of Apamaea, *Dial.* 6 (SC 311.117–118).

7.12.2 This section is mistakenly marked §3 in Petschenig's edition.

7.13 A certain refined but nonetheless real corporeality was attributed to angels by a number of fathers. Cf. DTC 1.1.1195–1200. The attribution of such corporeality to demons was almost universal. Cf. DTC 4.1.339–376. The materiality of the soul, however, was a rare belief; its most famous exponent is Tertullian in his *De anima* 22.2. Cassian's insistence on the absolute incorporeality of God recurs in 10.3ff.

7.13.3 The citation of Job is an error.

7.15f. That the demons know human thoughts from observing human behavior is an idea found in Evagrius, *Prac.* 47. Cf. the relevant note in SC 171.606–609, and to the references there add Evagrius, *Schol. in Prov.* 76 (SC 340.174). Ps.-Macarius, *Hom. spir.* 26.9, also treats of Satan's knowlege of human thoughts, but he explains that this is possible because of the devil's great age (he is said to be six thousand years old!), which presumably has given him corresponding insight. He does not know all thoughts, however. Cf. Weber 53–54; Augustine, *De divinatione daemonum* 5.9.

7.15.2 The signs of preoccupation with eating are similar to those that characterize acedia as given in *Inst.* 10.2.

7.19.3 On "foolish cackling and laughter" cf. the note at 4.20.3.

7.20 The image of the monk as an athlete (or more specifically as a wrestler) and of the monastic life as an athletic contest (or more specifically as a wrestling match) is extremely common in monastic literature, and references would be too numerous to list. The image is encountered in Cassian in 4.6.2, 6.16.2, 13.14.1 (where Job is called an athlete), 18.11.1, 18.14.5, 19.14.3; *Inst.* 5.12ff., 8.22, 10.5, 12.32.1. A particularly elaborate text appears in Regnault 52–53, N406: "In the games the athlete strips himself of his clothing. Likewise, in the midst of his evil thoughts the monk must lift his hands to heaven in the form of a cross and call on God to help him. The athlete is naked in the arena, naked and unencumbererd, rubbed down with oil and instructed by a trainer as to how to fight. The athlete advances thus to meet his adversary, and he throws sand–that is, earth–in order thereby to stop him easily. Observe this in yourself, O monk. The trainer is God, who gains us the victory; we are the combatants and the enemy is our adversary; the sand is the concerns of the world. Do you see the enemy's strategy? Stay unencumbered, then, and you will carry off the victory. Indeed, when the mind is weighed down by a carnal spirit, it does not lay hold of the spiritual word."

7.20.2 The image of Christ as arbiter and overseer, which is taken from the public games and athletic contests, appears also in *Inst.* 6.9. Cf. Victor Codina, *El aspecto christologico en la espiritualidad de Juan Casiano* (Orientalia Christiana Analecta 175) (Rome, 1966), 30–31. For uses of the image of arbiter alone cf. 2.13.7 and the relevant note, and for a similar context cf. 4.6.3.

7.21.8 Cassian's words about the "holy men and friends of God" obeying the gospel precepts and pursuing apostolic perfection represent a particularly striking way of referring to the Old Testament as anticipating the New, which is a universal theme of patristic theology. Cf. Augustine, *C. duas epp. Pelag.* 3.4.6ff.

7.22.2 Assumed manhood: *Hominis adsumpti. Homo assumptus* is not an unheard-of term in reference to Christ in patristic literature. Cf. also 9.34.10, 16.6.4 (where a similar but not identical expression occurs); *Inst.* 12.17.1; *De incarn.* 1.5.4. Cf. A. Gaudel, "La théologie de l'Assumptus Homo': Histoire et valeur doctrinale," *Revue des sciences religieuses* 17 (1937): 64–90, 214–234; ibid. 18 (1938): 45–71, 201–217; Herman Diepen, "L'Assumptus Homo à Chalcédoine," *Revue Thomiste* 51 (1951): 573–608; Alois Grillmeier, *Christ in Christian Tradition* 1, trans. by John Bowden (2nd ed., Atlanta, 1975), 144, 350, 385–388, 399, 406, 432. The term is susceptible of an orthodox understanding, although it poses the problem raised succinctly in Diepen 574: "Si le Christ est un seul et le même, un Fils, un quelqu'un, comme la foi nous enseigne, *unus masculinus* comme diront les scolastiques; n'est-il pas étrange qu'un nom de sujet, le nom d'un tout, un prénom masculin, ou le terme d'homme, soient appliqués à une partie de son être?" The expression becomes particularly problematic in the two other places cited in *The Conferences*—9.34.10 and 16.6.4—where it is used in connection with *persona,* which could easily give the impression that the "assumed man" was himself a person. Cassian's intent is certainly orthodox, and he was, in any event, writing before the christological formulations of the Councils of

Ephesus (431) and Chalcedon (451). But his language, particularly in places in the *De incarn.,* is still careless. Cf. the critique in Grillmeier 468–471.

7.23 The allusion to the beginnings of monasticism and to the possibility that Cassian's contemporaries have grown increasingly negligent sounds the theme of decline from an earlier ideal. Cf. the note at 18.5.

7.23.3 On remaining in one's cell cf. the note at 6.15. The same advice given here–namely, that so long as one remains in one's cell one may eat, drink, and sleep as much as one wants–appears almost verbatim in *Apophthegmata patrum,* de abbate Arsenio 11. This counsel is almost surely an exaggeration for the sake of emphasizing the importance of physical stability.

7.26.2 The Paul and the Moses spoken of here are perhaps identical with the two abbas of the same name who are mentioned in *Inst.* 10.24f. Both appear there together, and they are said to have lived in the Porphyrian desert, also known as the desert of Calamus. But further identification of the two is not possible.

On Calamus cf. the note at 3.5.2.

Panephysis, at the site of the present-day Aschmoun er-Ruman, is described again in 11.3. It was located in Augustamnica Secunda in the ancient diocese of Egypt, on the southern shore of Lake Thennesus, between two mouths of the Nile.

7.26.3 Flight from women is spoken of in *Inst.* 11.18, where the famous advice is offered: "A monk must always flee from women and bishops." Such a sentiment is a commonplace in ascetical literature. Cf. Ps.-Clement, *Ep. 2 de virg.*, passim; Evagrius, *Prac.* 96; *Apophthegmata patrum,* de abbate Marco 3; ibid., de abbate Poemene 76; ibid., de abbate Sisoe 3; *Hist. monach. in Aegypto* 1.4ff., 1.36; Regnault 71, N459; John Moschus, *Pratum spirituale* 88 (the story of a monk's grave that rejects a female corpse), 217. 7.26.4ff. represents a criticism of the exaggerations that often accompanied this flight, as does *Verba seniorum* 4.62: "A monk met some handmaidens of God on a certain road. Upon seeing them he left the path. But their superior said: 'If you were a perfect monk, you would not have looked at us in such a way as to know that we were women.' " For a study that seeks to show a more accepting attitude toward women in ancient monasticism cf. Louis Leloir, "La femme et les Pères du désert," *Collectanea Cisterciensia* 39 (1977): 149–159. On the possibility of heterosexual friendships within the context of monasticism cf. Rosemary Rader, *Breaking Boundaries: Male/Female Friendship in Early Christian Communities* (New York, 1983), 72–85.

Archebius is mentioned at length in *Inst.* 5.37f., and in *Conlat.* 11.2 we read that he became bishop of Panephysis.

7.26.4 Paul's deed is described in terms of a classic act of indiscretion—namely as a veering toward an excessive austerity.

7.27 "The second" is the Moses who appears in 7.26.2.

On Macarius cf. the note at 5.12.3.

7.28 A most merciful physician: Cf. the note at 2.13.7.

The comparison between demons and pedagogues in this context seems a justifiable one, given the severity with which children were treated in school in antiquity. Cf. Stanley F. Bonner, *Education in Ancient Rome* (Berkeley/Los Angeles, 1977), 143–145.

7.30.2 The fourteenth canon of the First Council of Orange (441), possibly under Cassian's influence, also decreed that Holy Communion was not to be denied to demoniacs. But the admission of demoniacs to communion had not been the general practice previous to the beginning of the fifth century. Cf. Franz Joseph Dölger, "Der Ausschluss der Besessenen (Epileptiker) von Oblation und Kommunion nach der Synode von Elvira," *Antike und Christentum* 4 (1934): 110–129.

For references in desert literature to the daily reception of communion cf. 9.21.1 (?), 14.8.5; *Inst.* 6.8; *Hist. monach. in Aegypto* 2.7f., 8.50, 8.56. Daily communion, however, does not imply a daily eucharistic liturgy. Cf. Chadwick 69–70.

The Andronicus mentioned here in passing is otherwise unidentifiable.

Heavenly medicine...spiritual remedy: For other such medicinal imagery with regard to the eucharist cf. 22.5.2; 22.6.3; 23.21.1f.; Ignatius, *Eph.* 20.2; Ephrem, *Hymni de nativ.* 4.99, 19; Ambrose, *De sacr.* 5.4.25.

7.31.1 The quick and expeditious medicine of the present life: The meaning of this phrase depends on whether or not the genitive "of the present life" *(temporis istius)* is to be understood as in apposition with "medicine." If so, it would suggest that the trials of the present life are themselves the medicine and antidote for one's sinfulness. If not, the likelihood is that Cassian is referring to his immediately previous use of "medicine" in terms of "Holy Communion." In the former case, then, the impenitent would be seen as undeserving of the sufferings that could correct them; in the latter they would be declared unworthy of receiving the eucharist. The former understanding appears to be supported by the succeeding paragraph.

7.32 That there should be such a large variety of demons as appears here is partly the legacy of Jewish literature, both canonical and noncanonical. Cf. *Encyclopaedia Judaica* 5.1521–1526. Demons are also in constant evidence in the New Testament, but they are less objects of fascinated attention. The creatures that Serenus lists in 7.32.4 were almost certainly not understood as demons by the canonical authors in whose writings they are mentioned, but they may be figuratively taken as such. Some of the diversity of the demonic world arises from the fact that both Jews (cf. Dt 32:17) and Christians (cf. Justin, *1 Apol.* 5; Clement of Alexandria, *Protrep.* 2.41.2; Minucius Felix, *Oct.* 27; Tertullian, *Apol.* 23) identify at least some of the demons with the pagan gods, who are themselves extremely diverse. The astonishing spectrum of Egyptian gods—"serpents and cattle and wild beasts and birds and fish from the river, not to mention foot-baths and embarrassing noises" (Theophilus, *Ad Autolycum* 1.10)–may help to explain the spectrum of demons in the Egyptian desert. Cf. the note at 3.7.5. Hermann Hesse's short story "The Field Devil" is a charming and somewhat melancholy tale based on the understanding that wide differences exist among demons. Cf. *Stories of Five Decades,* trans. by Ralph Manheim and Denver Lindley (New York, 1974), 138–144.

7.32.3 Arius (d. c. 336) was the most famous heresiarch of antiquity and the champion of the doctrine of the subordination of the Son to the Father. His teaching is said to have been inspired by demons in Athanasius, *V. S. Antonii* 82.

Eunomius (d. c. 395) held a doctrine similar to that of Arius. To it he added the notion of the complete intelligibility of the Father. Cf. also 15.3.1.

7.34.1 On the marine imagery here cf. the note at 1 praef. 3f.

EIGHTH CONFERENCE
THE SECOND CONFERENCE OF ABBA SERENUS: ON THE PRINCIPALITIES

TRANSLATOR'S INTRODUCTION

The seventh conference studies the demons more particularly in their relationship with human beings; the eighth, also led by Abba Serenus, tends rather to treat the demons in themselves, although not without a view to their human contacts. Germanus, citing Ephesians 6:12 and Romans 8:38–39, passages that list some kinds of spirits, starts the discussion by inquiring about the origin of the demons. Were they created by God, in all their variety, specifically to wage war against humankind?

Instead of answering this question immediately, Serenus begins with some lengthy preliminaries about the interpretation of Scripture and about the possibility of understanding it both historically and allegorically. Having alluded to the obscurity of the scriptural teaching on the subject of demons, but nonetheless determined to be guided by that teaching, Serenus proceeds to affirm the goodness of everything that God created and hence of those angelic beings that were created before the foundation of the visible world and that eventually fell and came to be called demons. As far as their variety is concerned, the demons either maintained in hell the hierarchy that they originally had in heaven or imitated those ranks after their fall, for there is a variety of angels as well.

Germanus then observes that he had believed that envy of the first parents was the cause of the devil's fall. Serenus replies, however, that he had already sinned before he deceived Adam and Eve through envy, because Scripture refers to him as a serpent even before he is said to have come in contact with them. "He fell a first time by pride, for which he deserved to be called a serpent, and a second fall followed as a result of envy" (8.10.3). After this, in turn, God cast him into the depths. The old man's reflections on Adam's deception give him the opportunity to warn the two friends against letting themselves be deceived by bad counsel, as this implies a certain degree of blameworthiness in the persons deceived.

Here Serenus turns to the characteristics of the demons—the fact that they occupy the airy void between heaven and earth, their hideous appearance, their mutual adversity (which is the result of their having befriended mutually opposed nations on earth), their titles, functions, and hierarchy, and their assignment to individual human beings, such that each human being has a personal demon as well as a personal angel. It is fortunate that human beings cannot ordinarily see them, for otherwise they would either be horrified by their aspect or seek to imitate them in their wickedness. Finally, as aggressive as demons may be against humans, they may also obey them in one of two instances, either when rendered submissive by human holiness or when soothed by the sacrifices and incantations of the wicked.

The last part of the conference constitutes a response to two questions posed by Germanus—namely, whether the demons could have had intercourse with the daughters of men, as suggested in Gn 6:2, and whether the devil had a father, given the words of Jn 8:44 ("he is a liar and the father of it"). Serenus replies to the first by asserting that a spiritual being could not have had carnal relations with a corporeal being; hence the demons did not have intercourse with women. He explains the account in Gn 6:2, instead, in terms of the reprehensible intermarriages between the offspring of Seth and that of Cain. When they mingled with the wicked daughters of Cain, Seth's sons "abandoned that true discipline of natural philosophy which was handed down to them by their forebears and which that first man, who was at once immersed in the study of all natural things, was able to grasp clearly and to pass on in unambiguous fashion to his descendants" (8.21.4). The tragic story, which concludes with an account of how magic and superstition were introduced into the world in place of the study of reality, is a subtle piece of propaganda on behalf of the wisdom of the elders, the value of tradition, and hence discretion. There follows a brief digression on how the law forbidding intermarriages such as these would have applied, since it was promulgated after the event, and this then permits the old man to point out that the holy ones of the Old Testament had a natural and spontaneous knowledge of the law.

Finally, in response to the second of Germanus's questions, Serenus says that God himself was the devil's father, for God created him. This issue, it may be noted, could claim some actuality in Cassian's time: It had already been raised by certain heretics, who asserted that the devil was the offspring of a being other than God (cf. Epiphanius, *Panarion* 1.3.38.4, 1.3.40.5).

And so, after a few parting words on maintaining the fear and the love of God as a protection against the devil's attacks, the old man brings the conference to an end.

VIII. The Second Conference of Abba Serenus: On the Principalities

Chapters

I.1. When everything was accomplished that the solemnity of the day demanded and the congregation in church had been dismissed, we returned to the old man's cell and there we were first splendidly refreshed. For in place of the brine which, along with a little bit of oil added to it, was his customary daily meal, he mixed in some sauce and poured over it more oil than usual. For when anyone is about to take his daily meal he puts in a few drops of oil—not so that he may enjoy some kind of pleasant flavor from the taste of it (indeed, the amount is so small that it is hardly enough to smear the passages of the throat, never mind to pass through it), but so that by doing this he may weaken the boastfulness of heart that usually creeps in flatteringly and surreptitiously with a stricter abstinence, and so that he may blunt the urges of pride, since when abstinence is exercised secretly and carried out in the absence of witnesses it does not cease to tempt in subtle fashion the one who hides it. 2. Then he put out some salt and three olives each. Finally, in addition to these other things, he produced a basket containing ground chick peas, which they call *trogalia,* from which we took only five morsels each, two prunes, and a fig apiece. For whoever has exceeded this amount in that desert is blameworthy.

When the meal was finished and we had begun to ask for the promised answer to the question, the old man said: "Pose your question, which we have put off answering until now."

II. Then GERMANUS said: "Where, we want to know, have such a variety and diversity of powers opposed to man come from, which the blessed Apostle enumerates as follows? 'Our struggle is not against flesh and blood but against principalities, against powers, against the world rulers of this darkness, against spirits of evil in heavenly places.'[1] And again: 'Neither angels nor principalities nor powers nor any other creature will be able to separate us from the love of God that is in Christ Jesus our Lord.'[2] Where, then, has so malicious an adversary, who is opposed to us, come from? Should it be believed that these powers were created by the Lord for the purpose of warring against human beings in grades and ranks?"

III.1. SERENUS: "The authority of Holy Scripture has said some things so lucidly and clearly for our instruction, even to those of limited intelligence, that not only are they not veiled in the obscurity of a hidden meaning but they do not even need to be explained, and they offer intelligibility and meaning at first glance.

"Some others, however, are so covered over and obscured by mystery that in examining and understanding them there lies open before us an immense field of toil and concern. 2. It is clear that God has arranged matters thus for several reasons: first, lest if the divine sacraments had no veil of spiritual understanding covering them, they would be equally intelligible and comprehensible to everyone, to both the faithful and the profane, and thus there would be no distinction between the lazy and the zealous as regards virtue and prudence; then, so that even among those of the household of the faith the slothfulness of the lazy might be reproached and the ardor and effort of the zealous might be proved, inasmuch as vast areas to be understood lie before them.

3. "Therefore, Holy Scripture is very aptly compared to an abundant and fertile field which, although it brings forth and produces many things that do not need to be cooked in order to serve as food for human beings, brings forth other things that would be unsuited or harmful for human use if their raw bitterness were not gotten rid of and if they did not become tender and digestible through cooking. But some are naturally so good either way that their uncooked rawness is not unpleasant or offensive, although cooking makes them more healthful. Many, also, are only useful as food for irrational beasts of burden and animals and wild beasts and birds but are of no benefit as food for human beings; even if they remain in their raw state without ever being cooked they are healthful for animals.

4. "This arrangement, we see, is found clearly in the most fertile paradise of the spiritual Scriptures, in which certain things shine forth so clearly and luminously on the literal level that, since they do not need a more sublime interpretation, they feed and nourish the listeners abundantly by the mere sound of the letter,

as in this example: 'Hear, O Israel: The Lord your God is one Lord.'[3] And: 'You shall love the Lord your God from your whole heart, and from your whole soul, and from your whole strength.'[4]

"But if certain other things were not made digestible through an allegorical interpretation and made tender by a probing spiritual fire they would in no way become healthful food for the inner man without a degree of corruption, and in eating them there would be more harm than good, as in this example: 'Let your loins be girt and your lamps burning.'[5] And: 'Whoever does not have a sword should sell his tunic and buy himself a sword.'[6] And: 'Whoever does not take up his cross and follow me is not worthy of me.'[7] 5. Some of the strictest monks, having indeed 'a zeal for God, but not according to knowledge,'[8] understood this literally. They made themselves wooden crosses and carried them constantly on their shoulders, evoking not edification but rather derision in all who saw them.

"But some things are so suitably and properly taken either way—that is, both historically and allegorically—that either interpretation provides vital support to the soul, as in this example: 'If anyone strikes you on the right check, offer him your other as well.'[9] And: 'When they persecute you in one city, flee to another.'[10] And: 'If you wish to be perfect, go, sell all that you have and give to the poor, and you will have treasure in heaven, and come, follow me.'[11]

6. "It also produces 'grass for the cattle,'[12] and with this fodder all the fields of Scripture are filled. That is to say, it produces a simple and unadorned historical narrative, by which simpler folk and those who are less capable of perfect and integral reasoning—about whom it is said: 'Lord, you will save both man and beast'[13]—are made more vigorous and strong, according to their position and capacity, just for the labor and effort of their daily life.

IV.1. "Concerning these last things, then, for which a clear interpretation has been offered, we too can confidently pursue our own understanding and boldly give our opinion. But those things which the divine Spirit has reserved for our meditation and exercise and which he has concealed in Holy Scripture, wishing them to be understood by signs and conjectures, must be gone over so slowly and carefully that any assertion or confirmation in their regard is up to the person who disputes them or accepts them. 2. For sometimes, when differing opinions are put forth about the same matter, both can be judged as reasonable and can be accepted either absolutely or qualifiedly without detriment to the faith—that is, so that neither is completely believed or utterly rejected, and so that the second opinion does not necessarily derogate from the first when neither of them is found to oppose the faith.

"Such is the case with Elijah's coming in the person of John, and that he is to be the precursor of the Lord's coming again;[14] and with the abomination of desolation which stood in the holy place and which was that likeness of Jupiter which we read was placed in the Temple at Jerusalem, and that it is to stand again in the Church with the coming of the Antichrist, and all those other things that follow in the Gospel and that are understood to have been fulfilled before the captivity of Jerusalem and as going to be fulfilled before the end of this world.[15] Of these, neither statement is opposed to the other, nor does the first understanding annul the second.

V. "Therefore, although the question that you asked does not really seem to have been raised frequently by people and is not clear to most, and although what we suggest might consequently seem obscure to some, we should temper our point of view (since it is not injurious to belief in the Trinity) in such a way that it may be held among those which are accounted indifferent. Nonetheless this should not be based on opinion, like mere suspicion and conjecture, but everything should be proven by plain texts from Scripture.

VI. "Far be it from us, then, to confess that God has created anything that is substantially bad. As Scripture says: 'Everything that God made was very good.'[16] For if we said that these beings had been created such by God and had been made so that they would occupy these grades of wickedness and always be ready to deceive and destroy human beings, we would, contrary to the teaching of the aforementioned Scripture, be faulting God by calling him the creator and author of evil. That is, we would be saying that he himself brought evil wills and natures into being, creating them such that they would always persevere in wickedness and never be able to pass over to the disposition of a good will. We have found the reason for this diversity, then, in the tradition of the fathers, which derives from Holy Scripture.

VII.1. "None of the faithful doubt that before the founding of this visible creation God made the spiritual and heavenly powers. For the very reason that they knew that they came into existence out of nothing for the sake of such blissful glory, thanks to the kindness of the Creator, they offered him extended and perpetual thanks and ceaselessly clung to the praise of him. 2. For we must not think that God first began his creation and his work with the establishment of this world, as if he did not exercise his providence and divine superintendence during those innumerable previous ages, and as if it should be believed that he had no one upon whom to confer the benefits of his kindness, being alone and a stranger to bountifulness. This is too mean and inappropriate a thought to have of that measureless and eternal and incomprehensible majesty. As the Lord himself says of those powers: 'When the stars were made together, all my angels praised me in a loud voice.'[17] 3. Those who were present at the creation of the stars, then, are most clearly proven to have been created before that beginning in which it is said that heaven and earth were made, for they are reported to have praised the Creator with a loud voice and with wonder for all those visible creatures that they saw proceed forth out of nothing.

"Before that temporal beginning, then, which is spoken of by Moses, when time took its start according to the historical and indeed the Jewish understanding (that is, leaving aside our own understanding, by which we say that Christ is the beginning of all things and that he is the one in whom the Father created everything, according to the words: 'Through him all things were made, and without him nothing was made'[18])—before, I say, that temporal beginning of Genesis there is no doubt that God created all those heavenly powers and forces. 4. The Apostle enumerates them according to rank and sets them out thus: 'In Christ were created all things in heaven and on earth, visible and invisible, whether angels or archangels or thrones or dominations or principalities or powers. All things were created through him and in him.'[19]

VIII.1. "The lamentation of Ezekiel and that of Isaiah teach very clearly that several princes from among their number fell.

Among them we recognize the prince of Tyre, otherwise known as Lucifer, who rose in the morning, being lamented with a doleful plaint. 2. The Lord speaks thus to Ezekiel about him: 'Son of man, raise a plaint over the prince of Tyre, and say to him: Thus says the Lord God: You were the signet of perfection, full of wisdom, perfect in beauty, in the delights of the paradise of God. Every precious stone was your covering–sardius, topaz and jasper, chrysolite and onyx and beryl, sapphire and carbuncle and emerald. Gold was the work of your beauty, and your borings were prepared on the day that you were created. You were a cherub stretched out and protecting, and I placed you on the holy mountain of God; you walked in the midst of stones of fire. You were perfect in your ways from the day of your creation, until iniquity was found in you. In the multitude of your doings your inner parts were filled with iniquity, and you sinned. And I cast you down from the mountain of God, and I destroyed you in the midst of the stones of fire, O protecting cherub. In your beauty your heart was lifted up; in your beauty you lost your wisdom. I cast you down upon the earth, I set you before the face of kings so that they might behold you. In the multitude of your iniquities and in the iniquity of your doings you polluted your holiness.'[20]

3. "Isaiah also says of the other: 'How did you fall from heaven, Lucifer, you who rose in the morning? How did you fall to the ground, you who wounded nations? You who said in your heart: I will go up to heaven, I will set my throne above the stars of God, I will sit on the mountain of the covenant, in the sides of the north. I will ascend above the height of the clouds, I will be like the Most High.'[21]

"Yet Scripture does not recall only those who fell from that pinnacle of blessedness; it speaks of the dragon that pulled down a third of the stars along with him.[22] One of the apostles says more clearly: 'The angels who did not submit to his rule but who left their dwelling he has kept in eternal chains, in darkness, until the judgment of the great day.'[23] 4. This too is said to us: 'You shall die like men, and you shall fall like one of the princes.'[24] What else does this mean but that many princes fell?

"From these indications the reason for this diversity can be understood. The differences of rank, which the adversary powers are said to possess on the model of the holy and heavenly virtues, they either continue to hold now from the station in which each one of them was originally created, or else those who plunged from the heavens laid claim among themselves, in a perverse imitation of the forces that remained there and to the degree that each had fallen into evil, to the formers' grades and titles of rank."

IX. GERMANUS: "Up till now we believed that the particular cause and beginning of the devil's ruinous transgression, for which he was cast out of his angelic station, was envy, when he deceived Adam and Eve with spiteful cleverness."

X.1. SERENUS: "The reading from Genesis shows that this was not the origin of his transgression and downfall. It holds that before their deception he was branded with the name of a serpent when it says: 'The serpent was wiser'—or, as the Hebrew books express it—'more clever than all the beasts of the earth that the Lord God made.'[25] You see, then, that he had forsaken his angelic holiness before he tricked the first man, such that he not only deserved to be marked with the ignominy of this name but was even placed ahead of the other beasts of the earth by reason of his subtle wickedness. For Scripture would not have designated a good angel by such a term, nor would it say of the ones who remain in that blessedness: 'The serpent was wiser than all the beasts of the earth.' 2. This name could not only never be applied to Gabriel or Michael, but it would not even be appropriate for a good human being. Clearly, therefore, both the term 'serpent' and the comparison with the other beasts bespeak not the dignity of an angel but the disgrace of a sinner.

"Finally, the envy and deception by which he was instigated to deceive the man was the cause of his ruin beforehand, for he saw that he who had only recently been formed from the slime of the earth was destined for that glory from which he remembered that he had fallen when he was one of the princes.

3. "Consequently he had already fallen a first time by pride, for which he deserved to be called a serpent, and a second fall followed as a result of envy. When this found him still in possession of a certain uprightness, so that he was even able somehow to converse with the man and to counsel him, he was beneficially cast down into the depths at the Lord's decision. Thus he would never

again, as he had before, look up and go about erect, but he would cling to the ground and creep along; flat on his stomach, he would feed upon the earthly food and works of the vices. From then on he would disclose his hidden hostility and place between himself and man a beneficial enmity and a salutary discord, so that in being feared as a dangerous enemy he would be unable to harm man any more through specious friendships.[26]

XI.1. "This should teach us in particular that we ought to reject bad counsel, for although the author of a deception may be struck with an appropriate penalty and condemnation, yet the one who is led astray does not lack for punishment either, even if it is somewhat lighter than his who is the author of the deception. We see this very clearly expressed here. For Adam, who was deceived (or rather, as I would say in the words of the Apostle, who 'was not deceived'[27] but who yielded to the woman who was deceived and seems to have concurred in her fateful consent), was only sentenced to the sweat of his brow and to toil, and this was meted out to him by way of the curse and sterility that were laid not upon him but upon the earth.[28] 2. The woman who persuaded him to do this thing was deserving of much groaning and sorrow and sadness, and she was also condemned to bear a perpetual yoke of subjection.[29] But the serpent, who was the first instigator of this offense, was penalized with an everlasting curse.[30] Therefore we must be on the watch with the greatest care and concern for evil counsels, because just as they bring punishment on their author, so neither are they without both sinfulness and punishment for the one who has been deceived.

XII.1. "But this air which is spread out between heaven and earth is so thick with spirits, which do not fly about in it quietly and aimlessly, that divine providence has quite beneficially withdrawn them from human sight. For human beings, utterly unable to gaze upon these things with fleshly eyes, would be overwhelmed by an unbearable dread and faint away because of their frightening confluence and the horrible expressions that they can take upon themselves and assume at will. Or else they would daily grow worse because of their constant example and would be ruined by imitating them, and thus between human beings and the unclean powers of the air there would develop a kind of harmful familiarity and a dangerous relationship, whereas the shameful things that are done now among human beings are concealed by enclosing walls and distance and a certain embarrassment. 2. If they saw them openly and continually they would be driven to a more insane rage, there being not a single moment when they would not see them engaged in crime. For no fleshly weariness or domestic activity or concern for daily bread ever makes them cease, even unwillingly, from what they have begun, unlike in our case.

XIII.1. "It is very clear that they desire the onslaughts by which they attack human beings, even when these set them against one another. For, in similar fashion, they do not cease to incite discord and conflict with unwearied struggle on behalf of some peoples that they have befriended because of a kind of mutual wickedness. We see this very plainly depicted in the vision of the prophet Daniel, when the angel Gabriel speaks as follows: 'Do not fear, Daniel, for from the first day when you set your heart to understand that you should afflict yourself in the sight of your God your words have been heard, and I have come because of your words. But the prince of the kingdom of the Persians resisted me for twenty-one days. And behold, Michael, one of the chief princes, came to my help, and I remained there next to the king of the Persians. But I have come to teach you what will befall your people in the last days.'[31]

2. "There is no doubt whatsoever that the prince of the kingdom of the Persians was the adversary power that befriended the Persian nation, which was hostile to the people of God. And he stood in the way of the benefit that he saw the archangel was going to procure in response to the request that the prophet had made of the Lord, being envious lest the angel's salutary consolation come to Daniel too quickly and lest he comfort the people of God over which the archangel Gabriel had been set. The latter said that he would have been unable to come to him even then because of the vehemence of his onslaught were it not that the archangel Michael helped him and, resisting the prince of the kingdom of the Persians and interjecting himself into the conflict and opposing him, protected him from his attack and let him come to instruct the prophet after the twenty-first day.

3. "And shortly afterward it says: 'The angel said: Do you

know why I came to you? And now I will return to fight against the prince of the Persians. For when I went out, the prince of the Greeks appeared coming. But I shall tell you what is set down in the writings of truth, and no one is my helper in all these things but Michael, your prince.'[32] And again: 'At that time Michael, the great prince, who stands for the children of your people, shall arise.'[33] 4. We read, then, that there is another who is called the prince of the Greeks, and he favored the people subject to him while seeming to be opposed both to the people of Israel and to the nation of the Persians.

"Hence it is quite clear that the discords and conflicts and animosity of peoples, which the adversary powers promote among themselves by these provocations, are also carried on against themselves. They either rejoice in their clients' victory or are tormented by their defeat, and therefore they cannot be at peace among themselves as long as one of them is constantly struggling with aggressive rivalry against the leader of another people on behalf of those over whom he himself is set.

XIV.1. "In addition to those that we have just given, therefore, we can see clearly other reasons why these beings are called principalities and powers. Namely, they dominate and rule over different peoples, and they at least lord it over lesser spirits and demons, about whom the Gospels testify that—by their own say-so—there are legions.[34] For they cannot be called dominations unless there are those over whom they can exercise the sway of their domination, nor can they be named powers or principalities unless there are those over whom they might claim to be princes. 2. We find this spoken of very openly in the Gospel by the blaspheming Pharisees: 'By Beelzebub, the prince of demons, he casts out demons.'[35] We also read that they are called 'the rulers of darkness'[36] and that one has the title of 'the prince of this world.'[37] Yet the blessed Apostle asserts that these grades will be eliminated in the world to come, when all things have been subjected to Christ, when, as he says, 'he has handed over the kingdom to God the Father, when he has destroyed every principality and power and domination.'[38] This would certainly never happen unless they were removed from the sway of those over whom powers and dominations and principalities are known to exercise authority in this world.

XV. "There is no doubt that the same titles are not assigned without reason to the good ones, and that they are the names of duties or merit or dignity. For it is evident that some are called angels—that is, messengers—from the duty of bearing messages, and the nature of the name itself teaches that the archangels are those who are set over these others. The dominations are such inasmuch as they exercise dominion over some, the principalities because they have those over whom they are princes, and the thrones because they cling to God and are his intimate servants to such a degree that the divine majesty reposes in them in a special way as on a kind of throne, and he as it were rests securely in them.

XVI.1. "But that the unclean spirits are ruled by worse powers and are subject to them we read elsewhere than in those scriptural texts where, in the Gospels, the Lord responds to the calumniating Pharisees: 'If I cast out demons by Beelzebub, the prince of demons.'[39] The clear visions and the experiences of holy persons also have much to teach us.

"For when one of our brothers was traveling through this desert and the day was drawing to a close, he found a certain cave and made a stop there, wishing to celebrate the evening synaxis in it. As he was singing the psalms there in his customary manner it drew past midnight. 2. When he had finished his observance he lingered a while in order to rest his weary body, and all at once he began to see on every side innumerable troops of demons coming together. Passing by in a vast throng and in a lengthy procession, some went before their leader while others followed him. Then he himself arrived—much taller and more frightening to look at than all the others—and, when a throne had been placed and he had seated himself in a kind of lofty tribunal, he began to submit each one's deeds to a minute examination. Those who said that they had not yet been able to get the best of those with whom they were struggling he commanded to be expelled from his presence harshly and in disgrace, as being sluggish and lazy, berating their vain efforts at great length with raging anger. But the ones who announced that they had led astray those who had been assigned to them he let go in the presence of everyone with the highest praise and with universal rejoicing and approval, as being brave and glorious warriors and an example to all.

3. "In the midst of this, one particularly wicked spirit came up in especially good humor because he was going to relate a spectacular triumph. He mentioned the name of a well-known monk, and he asserted that after having besieged him continually for fifteen years he had finally overcome him, destroying him that very night by the sin of fornication. For not only had he led him to debauch a consecrated girl but he had even persuaded him to marry her. When this had been told and all were rejoicing exceedingly, he departed, extolled with the highest praises from the prince of darkness and crowned with great glory.

4. "Once the dawn broke and the whole multitude of demons had vanished from before his eyes, the brother doubted what the unclean spirit had said. Instead he thought that he had wished to deceive him with an old trick and to brand an innocent brother with the sin of unchastity, and he remembered the gospel saying: 'He did not stay in the truth, he speaks of what is his own, for he is a liar and the father of it.'[40] So he went to Pelusium, where he knew there lived the man who the unclean spirit had said was cast down, for he was a brother who was very well known to him. When he asked for him he found out that, on the very night that the foul demon had announced his ruin to the throng and to the prince, he had abandoned his monastery, gone to the town, and fallen into a wretched sin with the girl in question.

XVII.1. "Now Scripture testifies that two angels, one good and one bad, are attached to each one of us. And of those that are good the Savior says: 'Do not despise one of these little ones. For I tell you that their angels in heaven always see the face of my Father who is in heaven.'[41] Likewise: 'The angel of the Lord shall encamp around those who fear him, and he shall save them.'[42] There is also what is said in the Acts of the Apostles with reference to Peter, that 'it is his angel.'[43] The book of *The Shepherd* teaches very explicitly about both.[44] 2. But if we consider the one who tried the blessed Job we see very clearly that he who was always plotting against him was never able to incite him to sin, and therefore he begged for power from the Lord, since he was bested not by Job's strength but by the defense of the Lord, who was always protecting him. And of Judas it is also said: 'Let the devil stand at his right hand.'[45]

XVIII.1. "With respect to the differences among the demons, we have learned a great deal from those two philosophers who had formerly had experience through magic both of their laziness and of their courage and savage wickedness. For they, who had despised the blessed Antony as an ignorant and illiterate man and who had at least wanted to drive him out of his cell by magic feats and demonic trickery if they could not harm him in any other way, sent some very wicked spirits upon him. They were driven to this attack by the sting of envy, because great crowds of people would come to him every day as to a friend of God. 2. These same savage demons did not even dare to approach him when at one time he signed himself with the cross on his breast and on his forehead and at another gave himself humbly to deep prayer, and they turned back to those who had sent them without having accomplished their purpose. So they sent others upon him who were more ferociously wicked, and they too expended their efforts in vain and returned unsuccessfully. Even so, others who were yet more powerful were set upon the victorious soldier of Christ, and they could not prevail at all. Their snares, so formidable and laid with every magical skill, only served to demonstrate the great power inherent in the Christian profession. These cruel and powerful shadows, which they thought could cover over the sun and the moon if they were directed toward them, were not only unable to hurt this man but could not even drive him out of his monastery for an instant.

XIX.1. "Then in astonishment they immediately came to Abba Antony and disclosed the magnitude of their assaults and the reasons for and the stratagems of their hidden envy, and they begged to become Christians at once. But when he asked them when the assault had occurred, he declared that at that time he had been struck by the very bitter impulses of thoughts.

2. "From this experience the blessed Antony proved and established that opinion of ours which we offered in yesterday's conference, that demons are utterly unable to get into a person's mind or body and do not have any ability to force their way into someone's soul unless they have first deprived it of every holy

thought and of spiritual contemplation and have left it empty and bare.

"It should be known, however, that the unclean spirits obey human beings in two ways. Either they are rendered submissive to the holiness of the faithful through divine grace and power or, having been soothed by sacrifices and by certain songs of the impious, they fawn over them as over friends. 3. The Pharisees, who had themselves been deceived by this opinion, thought that the Lord, the Savior, had commanded the demons in this way when they said: 'By Beelzebub, the prince of demons, he casts out demons.'[46] This was in keeping with that custom according to which they knew that their own magicians and sorcerers, invoking his name and performing sacrifices which they realized would delight and please him, had power even over the demons subject to him, since they are his servants."

XX. GERMANUS: "Since by God's design a reading from Genesis was produced a little while ago which made such a significant impression on us that now we can pursue properly what we have always wanted to learn, we also wish to know what should be thought about those apostate angels that are said to have had intercourse with the daughters of men.[47] Understood literally, would this be possible for a spiritual nature? Likewise, in regard to the gospel testimony concerning the devil that you spoke of a little while ago—'he is a liar and the father of it'—we want to hear who his father is supposed to be."

XXI.1. SERENUS: "You have posed two good questions, which I shall answer as far as possible in the order in which you asked them.

"By no means should it be believed that spiritual natures can have carnal relations with women. But if this could ever have happened in a literal sense, why does it not occur now, at least occasionally, and why do we not see some people born of women without sexual intercourse, having been conceived by demons? Since it is particularly clear that they take great delight in filthy wantonness, they would doubtless prefer to engage in this directly rather than through human beings if it were at all possible. As Ecclesiastes says: 'What is it that has been? The same that is. And what is it that has been done? The same that will be. And there is nothing new under the sun that would say and declare: Behold, this is new. It already existed in the ages that came before us.'[48]

2. "But here is the answer to the question that was asked: After the death of the righteous Abel, Seth was born in the place of his deceased brother, so that the whole human race would not have its origin in a fratricidal and wicked man. He succeeded not only to his brother's line but to his righteousness and goodness as well. His offspring, following their father's righteousness, always remained cut off from any association or relationship with their kin who descended from the sacrilegious Cain, as the division in the genealogy very clearly shows when it says: 'Adam begot Seth, Seth begot Enosh, Enosh begot Kenan, Kenan begot Mahalalel, Mahalalel begot Jared, Jared begot Enoch, Enoch begot Methuselah, Methuselah begot Lamech, Lamech begot Noah.'[49] Likewise, the genealogy of Cain is set down separately as follows: 'Cain begot Enoch, Enoch begot Kenan, Kenan begot Mehalalel, Mehalalel begot Methuselah, Methuselah begot Lamech, Lamech begot Jabal and Jubal.'[50]

3. "And so the generation that descended from the stock of the righteous Seth always married in its own line and to its own kin, and it long maintained the holiness of its ancestors and forefathers. It was not at all infected by the sacrileges and malice of the wicked progeny that retained in itself the seed of impiousness as if by an ancestral tradition. As long as that separation was maintained between those of their generation, then, the seed of Seth, proceeding from the best root, were called angels of God or (as some texts have it) sons of God on account of their holiness. On the contrary, the others are referred to as sons of men because of their own or their ancestors' wickedness and because of their worldly deeds.

4. "Although this beneficial and holy division between them existed up until that time, when afterward the sons of Seth—who were the sons of God—saw the daughters of those who were born of the offspring of Cain, they were inflamed by desire for their beauty and took wives from them for themselves. They imparted their parents' wickedness to their husbands and from the very first turned them away from their inborn holiness and ancestral simplicity. Very fittingly was this word directed to them: 'I have

said: You are gods, and you are all sons of the Most High. But you shall die like human beings, and you shall fall like one of the princes.'[51] These are the ones who abandoned that true discipline of natural philosophy which was handed down to them by their forebears and which that first man, who was at once immersed in the study of all natural things, was able to grasp clearly and to pass on in unambiguous fashion to his descendants.

5. "For he had gazed upon the infancy of this world while it was as it were still tender and trembling and unformed, and by a divine inbreathing he was filled not only with a plenitude of wisdom but also with the grace of prophecy. Thus, as the tenant of this as yet inchoate world, he could name every animal and not only discern the rage and poison of every sort of beast and serpent but also distinguish the qualities of herbs and trees and the natures of stones and the changes of seasons that he had not yet experienced. He could realistically say: 'The Lord has given me a true knowledge of the things that exist, so that I might know the arrangement of the earth and the powers of the elements, the beginning and the end and the middle of the seasons, the changes of their alternations and the divisions of their times, the courses of the years and the arrangement of the stars, the natures of animals and the rages of beasts, the power of spirits and the thoughts of human beings, the differences between trees and the qualities of roots. Whatever is hidden and open I have learned.'[52]

6. "The seed of Seth, then, enjoyed this universal knowledge from generation to generation, thanks to its ancestral tradition, as long as it remained separate from the sacrilegious breed, and what it had received in holy fashion it also exercised thus for the worship of God and for the general good. But when it intermingled with the wicked generation it fell into profane and harmful deeds that it had dutifully learned at the instigation of demons, and thereupon it boldly instituted the strange arts of wizards, sleights and magic tricks, teaching its descendants that they should abandon the sacred cult of the Divinity and worship and adore the elements and fire and the demons of the air.

7. "How this familiarity with strange things, which we have spoken of, did not perish with the Flood but became known to subsequent ages should be briefly told, I think, since this explanation

gives us the chance to do so, even though the answer to the question that was asked does not at all require it. And so, as the ancient traditions testify, Ham, the son of Noah, who was instructed in these superstitions and sacrilegious and profane arts, knowing that he would be utterly unable to take a book about them into the ark, which he was going to enter with his righteous father and his holy brothers, engraved these wicked arts and profane commentaries on plates of various kinds of metal which could not be ruined by exposure to water, and on very hard stone. 8. When the Flood was over he sought for them with the same curiosity with which he had concealed them and handed them on—a seedbed of sacrilege and unending wickedness—to his descendants.

"Hence the popular opinion, according to which it is believed that angels handed on wizardry and other arts to men, has an element of truth. From the sons of Seth and the daughters of Cain, then, as we have said, still more wicked sons were begotten who were powerful hunters, very violent and savage men. On account of their huge bodies and their great cruelty and maliciousness they were called giants.[53] 9. These were the first to plunder their neighbors and to prey on other men, earning their living by pillaging rather than being content with the effort of their own toil and labor, and so greatly did their crimes increase that the world could not be cleansed except by a flood. Therefore, inasmuch as the sons of Seth, spurred on by wanton desire, had transgressed the commandment which had been kept by a natural instinct ever since the foundation of this world, it needed to be reestablished thereafter by the letter of the law: 'You shall not give your daughter to his son as a wife, nor shall you take from their daughters for your son, because they will lead your hearts astray, so that you will depart from your God and follow their gods and serve them.'"[54]

XXII. GERMANUS: "They could rightly be blamed for sinful conduct because of this boldness in marrying if that precept had been given them. But since the observance of this separation had not yet been established by any regulation, how could the mixing of races be held against them, inasmuch as no commandment had forbidden it? For law does not usually condemn past crimes but future ones."

XXIII.1. SERENUS: "When God created each human being he placed in him, as something natural, a knowledge of the law. If this had been observed by every individual according to the Lord's plan, as was the case in the beginning, it would certainly not have been necessary for that other law to be given which he promulgated thereafter in writing. For it was superfluous to offer an external means of health when the one that had been placed within continued to be effective. But since, as we have said, this latter one had already been utterly corrupted by the freedom to sin and by the practice of sinning, the severe stringency of the Mosaic law was imposed as its administrator and avenger and, to use the very words of Scripture, as its helper. Thereby, through fear of punishment in the present life, human beings would not completely extinguish the good of natural knowledge. As the prophet says: 'He gave the law as a help.'[55] 2. It is also described by the Apostle as having been given as an instructor to little children,[56] teaching them and protecting them, lest by a kind of forgetfulness they slip away from that discipline in which they had been instructed by nature.

"For that a complete knowledge of the law has been poured into every human being since the beginning of creation is clearly proved by the fact that before the law, and even before the Flood, we know that all the holy ones observed the commandments of the law without having read the letter. For how could Abel know, when the law did not yet command it, that he was supposed to offer a sacrifice to God of the first-born of his sheep and of their fat, if he had not been taught by a law that had been placed in him by nature?[57] How did Noah distinguish, when there was not yet a commandment of the law to distinguish them, between clean and unclean animals, if he had not been instructed by a natural knowledge?[58] 3. How is it that Enoch learned to walk with God when he had never received the law's illumination from anyone?[59] Where had Shem and Japheth read: 'You shall not uncover your father's nakedness,'[60] so that they went in backwards and covered over their father's shame?[61] How is it that Abraham was warned and that he rejected the spoils of his enemies which were offered him, so that he would not receive recompense for his effort,[62] and why did he pay tithes to the priest Melchizedek, as the Mosaic law prescribed?[63] How is it that this very same Abraham, as well as Lot, humbly offered travelers and strangers the duties of hospitality and the washing of feet[64] when the gospel command had not yet shone forth?[65] 4. How is it that Job achieved as much devout faith, as much pure chastity, and as much knowledge of humility, gentleness, mercy, and hospitality as we see are not even attained now by those who have memorized the Gospels?

"Which of the holy ones do we read did not observe any of the law before the law? Which of them did not keep: 'Hear, O Israel: The Lord your God is one Lord'? Which of them did not fulfill: 'You shall not make for yourself a graven image or any likeness of what is in heaven or on earth or in the waters under the earth'?[66] 5. Which of them did not observe: 'Honor your father and your mother,'[67] or what follows in the Decalogue: 'You shall not kill, you shall not commit adultery, you shall not steal, you shall not give false testimony, you shall not covet your neighbor's wife,'[68] and other things still greater than these, which anticipated not only the commands of the law but even those of the Gospel?

XXIV.1. "We understand, then, that God created everything perfect from the beginning and that it would have been unnecessary for anything to be added to his original plan, as if it were improvident and imperfect, if everything had remained in the state and condition in which it was created by him. Therefore we agree with God's just judgment of those who sinned before the law and even before the Flood, because those who transgressed the natural law without any excuse deserved to be punished.

"And we will not fall into the blasphemous calumny of those who, ignorant of this arrangement, disparage the God of the Old Testament, detract from our faith, and say in mockery: Why did your God want to set down a law after so many thousands of years, after having let so many centuries go by without a law? 2. But if he devised something better afterward it would seem that at the beginning of the world he knew things less well and that, after having learned as it were from experience, he began to have a more correct view of the situation and to ameliorate what he had planned for at first. This does not at all accord with the limitless foreknowledge of God, nor are such things suggested about him by heretical madness without terrible blasphemy. As Ecclesiastes says: 'I have learned that all the things which God made in the beginning will exist forever. Nothing shall be added to them, and nothing shall be taken away from them.'[69]

"And therefore: 'The law was not imposed on the righteous, but on the unrighteous and the disobedient, on the wicked and on sinners, on criminals and on the defiled.'[70] 3. For those who had a healthy and complete understanding of the natural and ingrafted law were never in need of a law to be added from without, set down in writing and given as a help to that natural law. Hence it is very clear that this written law did not have to be given from the beginning, for it was superfluous as long as the natural law was still standing and had not been completely violated, and that gospel perfection could not be bestowed before the law had acted as a restraint. For they were unable to hear: 4. 'Whoever strikes you on your right cheek, offer him the other as well,' who were not satisfied with avenging the misdeeds done to them by an equal retaliation but who would requite the slightest blow with deadly kicks and spear wounds, and who for a single tooth would demand the lives of those who struck them. Nor could 'love your enemies'[71] be said to those in whom it was considered a great advantage and a good thing that they loved their friends, but who turned away from their enemies, differing from them merely by hatred and not trying to oppress and kill them.

XXV.1. "But the thing that had concerned you about the devil, that 'he is a liar and the father of it,' namely, that the Lord seems to call both him and his father liars, is too absurd even to be briefly imagined. For, as we said a short while ago, spirit does not generate spirit, just as soul cannot beget soul. Yet we should not doubt that solid flesh coalesces from human seed, as the Apostle clearly notes with regard to both substances, flesh and soul, saying what should be ascribed to what begettor: 'We have had the fathers of our flesh as instructors, and we reverenced them. Shall we not all the more subject ourselves to the father of spirits and live?'[72] 2. What could be a clearer distinction than that he should call human beings 'the fathers of our flesh' but speak firmly of God alone as the father of our souls?

"Although in the very putting together of this body the labor alone is to be ascribed to human beings, yet the highest part of the making is God's, the Creator of all things, as David says: 'Your hands have made me and shaped me.'[73] And blessed Job: 'Have you not milked me like milk,' he says, 'and curdled me like cheese? You have put me together with bones and nerves.'[74] And the Lord says to Jeremiah: 'Before I formed you in the womb I knew you.'[75]

3. "But Ecclesiastes very clearly and correctly understands the nature and origin of both substances from an examination of the source and beginning from which each proceeds and from a consideration of the end toward which each strives, and he also pronounces on the distinction between body and soul when he says: 'Before the dust returns to the earth as it was, and the spirit returns to God, who gave it.'[76] What could be said more clearly than his having declared that the stuff of the flesh, which he has called dust because it originated from the seed of man and seems to be sown by his doing, will return to the earth once more just as it was taken from the earth, whereas he has indicated that the spirit, which is not begotten from the mingling of the sexes but is bestowed particularly by God alone, will return to its Creator? 4. This is clearly expressed, too, by that inbreathing of God by which Adam was first ensouled.[77]

"From these texts, then, we understand clearly that no one can be called 'the father of spirits' but God alone, who makes them out of nothing whenever he wishes, whereas human beings can only be referred to as 'the fathers of our flesh.' According to this, therefore, the same is true of the devil: Because he was created as a spirit and an angel and as good, he had no one as his father but God his Creator. When he was lifted up in pride and said in his heart: 'I will ascend above the height of the clouds, I will be like the Most High,'[78] he became a liar 'and did not stay in the truth.'[79] Rather, bringing forth a lie from his own storehouse of wickedness, he became not only a liar but even the father of that very lie by which, promising divinity to the man and saying: 'You shall be as gods,'[80] 'he did not stay in the truth.' From the beginning, instead, he became a murderer, inducing Adam into a state of mortality and slaying Abel at his own instigation by his brother's hand.[81]

5. "But now the approaching dawn is bringing to a close our discussion held by lamplight over the course of nearly two nights,

and our rough brevity has drawn the bark of this conference out from a fathomless sea of questions to the safe harbor of silence. As far in it as the breath of the divine Spirit may have brought us, yet the vastness that opens out before our eyes is ever more immeasurable. In the words of Solomon: 'It will become much farther from us than it was, and a great depth. Who shall find it out?'[82] 6. Therefore let us beseech the Lord that the fear of him and the love which cannot fail[83] may remain fixed in us, making us wise in all things and keeping us ever unharmed from the devil's missiles. For with these protections it is impossible for anyone to fall into the snares of death. But between the perfect and the imperfect there is this difference: In the former, love is stable and, so to speak, more mature; it abides more tenaciously and makes them persevere more firmly and more easily in holiness. In the latter, however, since it is more feeble and easily grows cold, it quickly and frequently drives them to get caught in the snares of sin."

When we had heard this, the words of the conference so inflamed us that, leaving the old man's cell with greater spiritual ardor than when we arrived, we thirsted for the accomplishment of his teaching.

TEXTUAL REFERENCES

1. Eph 6:12.
2. Rom 8:38–39.
3. Dt 6:4.
4. Dt 6:5.
5. Lk 12:35.
6. Lk 22:36.
7. Mt 10:38.
8. Rom 10:2.
9. Mt 5:39.
10. Mt 10:23.
11. Mt 19:21.
12. Ps 104:14.
13. Ps 36:6.
14. Cf. Mt 11:14.
15. Cf. Dn 9:27; 2 Mc 6:2; Mt 24:15–4.
16. Gn 1:31.
17. Jb 38:7 LXX.
18. Jn 1:3.
19. Col 1:16.
20. Ez 28:11–18.
21. Is 14:12–14.
22. Cf. Rv 12:4.
23. Jude 6.
24. Ps 82:7.
25. Gn 3:1 LXX.
26. Cf. Gn 3:14–15.
27. 1 Tm 2:14.
28. Cf. Gn 3:17–19.
29. Cf. Gn 3:16.
30. Cf. Gn 3:14–15.
31. Dn 10:12–14.
32. Dn 10:20–21.
33. Dn 12:1.
34. Cf. Lk 8:30.
35. Lk 11:15.
36. Eph 6:12.
37. Jn 14:30.
38. 1 Cor 15:24.

39. Lk 11:19.
40. Jn 8:44.
41. Mt 18:10.
42. Ps 34:7.
43. Acts 12:15.
44. Cf. Hermas, *Pastor,* mand. 6.2
45. Ps 109:6.
46. Cf. Mt 12:24; Lk 11:15.
47. Cf. Gn 6:2.
48. Eccl 1:9–10 LXX.
49. Gn 5:3–29.
50. Gn 4:17–21.
51. Ps 82:6–7.
52. Wis 7:17–21 LXX.
53. Cf. Gn 6:4.
54. Dt 7:3l; Ex 34:16; 1 Kgs 11:2.
55. Is 8:20 LXX.
56. Cf. Gal 3:24.
57. Cf. Gn 4:4.
58. Cf. Gn 7:2.
59. Cf. Gn 5:22.
60. Lv 18:7.
61. Cf. Gn 9:23.
62. Cf. Gn 14:22–24.
63. Cf. Gn 14:20.
64. Cf. Gn 18–19.
65. Cf. Jn 13:34.
66. Ex 20:4.
67. Ex 20:12.
68. Ex 20:13–17.
69. Eccl 3:14 LXX.
70. 1 Tm 1:9.
71. Mt 5:44.
72. Heb 12:9.
73. Ps 119:73.
74. Jb 10:10–11 LXX.
75. Jer 1:5.
76. Eccl 12:7 LXX.

77. Cf. Gn 2:7.
78. Is 14:14.
79. Jn 8:44a.
80. Gn 3:5.
81. Cf. Gn 4:8.
82. Eccl 7:24 LXX.
83. Cf. 1 Cor 13:8.

8.1 This is the longest passage in *The Conferences* to describe monastic fare. Concerning the monastic diet, we know that bread was a staple. Cf. 2.19ff. Palladius, *Hist. laus.* 52, tells us, however, that there were some who abstained from it. There are references to the use of lettuce and other green vegetables, fruit, herbs, porridge, oil, and fish. Cf. ibid. 38.12f., 57.2. Palladius says that even wine and meat could be had, so long as they were taken in reasonable amounts and at the appropriate time. Cf. ibid., prol. 10ff. It is clear from *Inst.* 5.5 that, in general, almost anything in reasonable quantity could be eaten and drunk, although ibid. 4.22 we are told that there was a preference for dry and uncooked food. There were variations, of course, depending on the particular day or season when the food was taken; in Lent it was common to eat uncooked food, for example, whereas on feast days a dish might be seasoned with oil or some other condiment. Even festal meals, though, were austere in comparison with present-day standards. Cf. Maria Dembińska, "Diet: A Comparison of Food Consumption between Some Eastern and Western Monasteries in the 4th–12th Centuries," *Byzantion* 55 (1985): 434–445.

8.1.1 On the use of a few drops of oil in order to stave off boastfulness cf. also 19.6.2f.

8.3f. Cassian distinguishes here between the two most fundamental senses of Scripture, the historical and the spiritual, the latter being referred to in terms of allegory. The spiritual sense is further divided in 14.8 into tropology, allegory (understood more restrictedly than in the present section), and anagogy. The spiritual sense is said to exist for the sake of differentiating between the zealous and the lazy; a spiritual interpretation also provides the key to otherwise unintelligible passages. The historical or literal parts of Scripture provide nourishment for "simpler folk," although they state truths for the educated as well. Cassian seems less anti-intellectual here than he does in *Inst.* 5.34, where he declares that a monk ought not to bother with commentators but should set out to pursue virtue as the sole prerequisite for acquiring a knowledge of Scripture. In 8.3.5 he implies that mere virtuous zeal is an inadequate exegetical tool. Likewise, while decrying the different interpretations of commentators in *Inst.* 5.34 as the result of their failure to achieve inner purity, in 8.4.2 Cassian shows that he is open to varying interpretations. On the senses of Scripture in the patristic era cf. Henri DeLubac, *Exégèse médiévale: Les quatre sens de l'Ecriture* 1.1–1.2 (Paris, 1959), and on Cassian in particular cf. 1.1.190–193.

8.3.3ff. The comparison of Scripture with a field is also made in Origen, *De princ.* 4.3.11; Athanasius, *Ep. fest.* 13.5; Gregory the Great, *Moralia in Iob* 16.48.62.

8.3.4f. Cassian's view of Scripture as susceptible of literal, allegorical, and both literal and allegorical understandings recalls a similar view in Augustine, *Serm.* 89.4ff. Augustine's division, however, is sixfold, since it takes into account both words and deeds in Scripture, each of which could be understood in one of the three aforesaid ways.

8.3.5 The incident in which monks made wooden crosses and carried them provides a typical example of monastic literalism, paralleled (with more disastrous results) in the Anthropomorphite crisis recorded in 10.2.2ff.

8.4.2 On the same passage of Scripture as able to offer numerous possibilities of interpretation cf. Augustine, *Conf.* 12.17.24ff.

8.5 By saying that his point of view is indifferent, Serenus means that it is but one of several positions that may be held. This is not exactly the same usage of the term "indifferent" as appears in 3.9.1ff., 6.3, or 21.12.4ff., where it indicates something that may be either good or bad. Serenus's interpretation of the scriptural data concerning the origins of the demons is indifferent because it is one of several that may be held.

8.6 In Augustine, *De Gen. ad litt.* 11.20.27ff., we read that some Christians believed that God had, in his goodness, created the devil evil and that this primordial evil contributed to the harmony of the universe. Cassian is perhaps directing himself against these persons here rather than against the Manicheans, who believed that an evil god had created evil beings.

8.7 Fixing the moment of the angels' creation was a preoccupation of some of the early theologians, and there were basically two opinions in the matter. The first held that the angels were created before the creation recorded in Gn 1. Cassian represents this view when he declares that "none of the faithful doubt that before the founding of this visible creation God himself made the spiritual and heavenly powers." The second opinion was to the effect that the angels were somehow included in the creation account of Gn 1. This position is perhaps most notably represented in Augustine, *Conf.* 13.3.4; idem, *De civ. Dei* 11.9. On this issue in general cf. DTC 1.1.1193–1195. A creation of the angels that would have occurred before the creation that is spoken of in Gn 1 could have been a creation from eternity; thus it is that the angelic creation is closely related to the question of whether God has always been Lord and whether an eternal divine lordship implies that there has always existed something over which God has exercised that lordship. That God has always been Lord and that hence there must always have been (spiritual) creatures is suggested by Cassian in the present passage, and in this he follows Origen, *De princ.* 1.2.10, 1.4.3ff., 3.5.3. That God has always been Lord without the implication that there have always been (spiritual) creatures cf. Augustine, *De civ. Dei* 12.15. That God was not Lord until there was a creation cf. Tertullian, *Adv. Hermogenem* 3; Augustine, *De Trin.* 5.16.17.

8.7.3 The historical and indeed the Jewish understanding: The Jews are frequently if erroneously blamed for promoting a literal or historical understanding of Scripture while denying its spiritual meaning, since a spiritual understanding would have been consonant with the truth of Christianity. The accusation is as old as the New Testament. Cf. Mt 13:10–17; Jn 3:10, 5:39–47. The patristic position is succinctly given in Jerome, *Tract. de Ps.* 95.2.

8.9f. Lucifer's downfall is attributed sometimes to envy and sometimes to pride. Envy as the cause is already suggested in Justin, *Dial. c. Tryph.* 124. In Augustine, *De Gen. ad litt.* 11.16.21, the view is taken that pride must necessarily have preceded the envy, and this is Cassian's position as well.

8.12.1 On the demonic inhabitation of the air cf. Jean Daniélou, "Les démons dans l'air dans la 'Vie d'Antoine,'" in Basilius Steidle, ed., *Antonius Magnus Eremita 356–1956: Studia ad Antiquum Monachismum Spectantia* (SA 38) (1956): 136–147.

The demons' ability to transform themselves into frightening shapes is a commonplace in ancient literature. Cf. *Acta Thomae* 44 (ed. by Lipsius-Bonnet 2.161: "O hideous one....O many-formed one: He appears as he wishes, but his essence cannot be changed"); Athanasius, *V. S. Antonii* 28.

8.15 Angels—that is, messengers: The term "angel" comes from the Greek word for messenger.

8.16 This story of a monk who overhears demons telling (whether or not unbeknownst to them is not really clear) of another monk's fall into impurity as a result of demonic instigation is paralleled in *Verba seniorum* 5.24, 5.39 (for which cf. Weber 91–93), 15.89.

8.16.1 On experience as teacher cf. the note at 3.7.4.

The evening synaxis: This is a strange use of the term "synaxis," since it implies only one person and not a group.

8.16.4 Pelusium was located in Augustamnica Prima in Egypt at the easternmost mouth of the Nile. The site is currently known as Tell Farama.

8.17 The teaching on the two angels, which comes from Hermas, *Pastor,* mand. 6.2, is also cited in 13.12.7. In addition to an agraphon that appears in 1.20.1 and 2.9, which Cassian undoubtedly took to be canonical, *The Shepherd* is the only other noncanonical writing that is cited in *The Conferences.* It is mentioned in the Muratorian Fragment, dating from the end of the second century, and is there recommended to be read privately by the faithful; it itself is dated to the middle of that century. Both here and in 13.12.7 Cassian introduces *The Shepherd* in the context of quoting Scripture, without suggesting any significant difference between it and Scripture.

8.18f. The Antony mentioned here is almost certainly the subject of Athanasius's *V. S. Antonii.* Cf. ibid. 4, where Antony is referred to as "the friend of God," as this Antony is in 8.18.1.

8.18.2 On the use of the sign of the cross against demons cf. Wilhelm Schneemelcher, "Das Kreuz Christi und die Dämonen: Bermerkungen zur Vita Antonii des Athanasius," in Ernst Dassmann and K. Suso Frank, eds., *Pietas: Festschrift für Bernhard Kötting* (JAC, Ergänzungsband 8) (1980): 381–392. The signing of the forehead, as mentioned here, was the earliest form of the sign of the cross; the forehead both represented the rest of the body and itself stood in particular need of protection. Cf. RAC 8.1232–1234. That Antony should also have signed himself on the breast is simply an extension of the gesture to another highly important part of the body.

Soldier of Christ: Cf. the note at 1.1.

On the use of the term "monastery" for the dwelling of a single monk, as here, cf. 18.10 and the relevant note.

8.19.2 What was "offered in yesterday's conference" is most clearly stated in 7.24.

8.19.3 Although Cassian's accusation here is certainly false in its particulars, the Jews in fact practiced magic and were well known for doing so. Cf. Ludwig Blau, *Das altjüdische*

Zauberwesen (Budapest, 1898; repr. Graz, 1974), passim, esp. 23–37 (on persons who practiced magic) and 61–86 (on invocations); Judah Golden, "The Magic of Magic and Superstition," in Elisabeth Schüssler Fiorenza, ed., *Aspects of Religious Propaganda in Judaism and Early Christianity* (Notre Dame, Ind., 1976), 115–147; Philip S. Alexander, "Incantation and Books of Magic," in Emil Schürer, *The History of the Jewish People in the Age of Jesus Christ,* new Eng. version rev. and ed. by Geza Vermes et al. (Edinburgh, 1986), 3.1.342–379.

8.20f. The apocryphal First Book of Enoch 6ff. is the source of the interpretation of Gn 6:2 to the effect that some of the angels fell because they were seduced by feminine beauty. A number of fathers espoused this position, notably Clement of Alexandria, *Paed.* 3.2.14; Tertullian, *De cult. fem.* 1.2.1ff.; Cyprian, *De hab. virg.* 14. For Jewish exegesis of the passage, which is also along this line, cf. Philip S. Alexander, "The Targumim and Early Exegesis of 'Sons of God' in Genesis 6," in *The Journal of Jewish Studies* 23 (1972): 60–71. Cassian, however, like Augustine in *De civ. Dei* 15.23, rejects this interpretation as not being consonant with the demons' spiritual nature. For the view that it refers instead to the union of the sons of Seth and the daughters of Cain, which Cassian favors, cf. Charles Robert, "Les fils de Dieu et les filles des hommes," *Revue biblique* 4 (1895): 340–373, 525–552.

8.21.5 Adam's intellectual and prophetic gifts are a commonplace of both Jewish and early Christian thought, and the naming of the animals in Gn 2:19–20 seems to constitute the source of their attribution to him. Cf. Louis Ginzberg, *The Legends of the Jews,* trans. by Henrietta Szold (Philadelphia, 1947), 1.60–61; 5.83–84, nn. 29–32.

8.23.4 On memorizing the Gospels cf. 14.10.4 and the relevant note.

8.24.1f. The question as to why God would impose a law "after so many thousands of years" is similar in some of its implications to the question as to why God decided to create the human race at one moment rather than another, which seems to have exercised some persons in Christian antiquity. Cf. Augustine, *De civ. Dei* 12.14.

8.25.5 On the marine imagery cf. the note at 1 praef. 3f.

NINTH CONFERENCE
THE FIRST CONFERENCE OF ABBA ISAAC: ON PRAYER

TRANSLATOR'S INTRODUCTION

The ninth and tenth conferences represent the conclusion of a work that was, as has previously been noted (cf. p. 8), probably originally planned for only ten conferences. As such they are the point to which the eight previous conferences are directed. Prayer is the subject of these two final conferences, and its importance is underlined at the very beginning of the ninth: "The end of every monk and the perfection of his heart incline him to constant and uninterrupted perseverance in prayer" (9.2.1). But this constant prayer demands, in turn, perfection of heart and the virtues that go with it. An extended discussion on constant prayer, however, does not take place until the tenth conference; the ninth serves as a sort of preliminary, among other things establishing the conditions for prayer and the different possible characteristics of prayer.

Both conferences record the teaching of a certain Abba Isaac. His personal acquaintance with the great Antony, mentioned in 9.31, suggests that he is probably to be identified with the first of two Isaacs who are spoken of in Palladius (*Dial.* 17). The careers of these two, in any case, were very similar: Both were priests, had numerous disciples, and were persecuted by Bishop Theophilus of Alexandria subsequent to the events recounted in *The Conferences*.

After he has declared the centrality of prayer and the necessity of the practice of virtue in order to abide in prayer, Isaac soon passes from external virtue to its internal counterpart. The sins of the outer person are in fact easy to avoid in comparison with those of the inner person, and against these latter the greatest material deprivation and the deepest solitude are not necessarily guarantees of protection. Once the vices of the inner person have been conquered and the mind has been established in tranquillity it will be possible to enjoy unceasing prayer. "For...when the thoughts of the mind have been seized by this purity and have been refashioned from earthly dullness to the likeness of the spiritual and the angelic, whatever they take in, whatever they reflect upon, and whatever they do will be most pure and sincere prayer" (9.6.5).

With this Isaac would seem to have said his piece, but Germanus makes an observation about wandering thoughts and then goes on to inquire about the character of prayer. The old man replies by noting that there are as many different kinds of prayer as there are conditions of soul and that these conditions determine the character of one's prayer. In addition to this quasi-infinity of highly subjective prayers, however, there are also the four kinds of which Paul writes in 1 Timothy 2:1—namely, supplication, prayer, intercession, and thanksgiving. Although modern scholarship tends to regard these four terms as liturgically repetitive and as "not to be rigorously distinguished" (A. J. B. Higgins in *Peake's Commentary on the Bible,* London, 1962, 1002), the ancient commentators, beginning with Origen (*De orat.* 14.2ff.), were usually not thus inclined. Cassian himself specifically rejects the idea that they are without intrinsic significance in 9.10, which may or may not imply that others did not hold his opinion. These four kinds of prayer, in any event, all bear the possibility of great fervor and ardor, and a single individual may use each of them at one time or another, depending on the circumstances, as Christ himself did. And, indeed, they can all be put together to form a more comprehensive prayer. Still, the four kinds of prayer are not equal to one another, and there is an upward progression from supplication, which "seems to pertain more especially to beginners who are still being harassed by the stings and by the memory of their vices" (9.15.1), to thanksgiving, which sometimes attains to wordless ecstasy.

Following this discussion of the different kinds of prayer, Isaac continues with an exposition of the Lord's Prayer. Hardly any ancient treatment of prayer in general, beginning with Tertullian's late second-century *De oratione,* failed to include an exegesis of the Matthean version of the Our Father in particular. As exalted as this prayer may be, though, it opens up to one that is still higher—namely, the wordless ecstasy that has already been alluded to.

With this Isaac suddenly turns to the topic of compunction. The transition to this theme is not very clear, but perhaps compunction is being viewed here as an immediate antecedent to the ecstatic prayer that was being spoken of before. Whatever the case, the various causes of compunction receive attention first, and then some of its forms are described. Germanus thereupon observes with regret that the tears that often accompany compunction cannot be produced at will. Isaac replies by listing many of the different situations that occasion spontaneous weeping. While forced weeping is not altogether harmful, since it at least implies a good intention, it is nonetheless better to avoid it: Tears that do not well up spontaneously tend to dilute the soul's fervor.

The old man adds to this teaching on compunction some words of Antony on perfect prayer, and then he remarks that confidence in having been heard is a sure sign that one's prayers have in fact been heard. Germanus asks in response how a sinful person can possess such confidence. Isaac replies that even a sinner may be sure that his prayers have been heard if, for example, he gives alms or prays with someone else; but persistence is the most infallible indicator in this regard. Prayer will surely be answered, in any event, if it is in conformity with the divine will, as Christ's was answered, for his will was perfectly at one with that of his Father.

The conference ends with a few remarks on prayer in secret, on the value of frequent and brief prayer, and on prayer as the true sacrifice.

IX. The First Conference of Abba Isaac: On Prayer

Chapters

XXVIII. A question about the fact that an outpouring of tears is not in our power.

XXIX. The reply, on the different kinds of compunction that are accompanied by tears.

XXX. Concerning the fact that tears should not be forced when they do not come spontaneously.

XXXI. The opinion of Abba Antony on the state of prayer.

XXXII. On the indication that one has been heard.

XXXIII. An objection, that the assurance of having been heard, which was previously spoken about, is only suitable for holy persons.

XXXIV. The reply, on the different causes of being heard.

XXXV. That prayer should be offered in one's room with the door shut.

XXXVI. On the value of short and silent prayer.

I. With the Lord's help the conferences of the old man—namely, Abba Isaac—which we now present will fulfill the promise made in the second book of *The Institutes* about the perpetual and unceasing continuity of prayer. Once they have been set forth I believe that I shall have satisfied both the commands of Pope Castor, of blessed memory, and your own desire, O blessed Pope Leontius and holy brother Helladius. Excuse the length of the book thus far. It is longer than we had intended, even with our efforts not only to compress what must be told into a few words but also to pass over numerous things in silence. For, after he had said a great deal about different institutes, which we have chosen to omit in our concern for brevity, the blessed ISAAC finally spoke these words:

II.1. "The end of every monk and the perfection of his heart incline him to constant and uninterrupted perseverance in prayer; and, as much as human frailty allows, it strives after an unchanging and continual tranquillity of mind and perpetual purity. On its account we tirelessly pursue and ceaselessly apply ourselves to every bodily labor as well as to contrition of spirit. Between the two there is a kind of reciprocal and inseparable link. For, as the structure of all the virtues tends to the perfection of prayer, so, unless all things have been joined together and cemented under this capstone, in no way will they be able to remain firm and stable. 2. For just as the perpetual and constant tranquillity of prayer about which we are speaking cannot be acquired and perfected without those virtues, neither can these latter, which lay the foundation for it, achieve completion unless it be persevered in.

"Therefore we shall be unable to deal properly with the effect of prayer or by an abrupt discourse to arrive at its principal end, which is achieved as a result of the work of all the virtues, if everything that should be either rejected or acquired in order to obtain it has not first been set out and discussed in an orderly way, and unless the things that pertain to the construction of that spiritual and sublime tower, following the directives of the gospel parable, have been carefully reckoned and prepared beforehand.[1] 3. Yet the things that have been prepared will be of no benefit nor will they let the highest capstones of perfection be placed properly upon them unless a complete purging of vice has been carried out first. And once the tottering and dead rubbish of the passions has been dug out, the firm foundations of simplicity and humility can be placed in what may be called the living and solid ground of our heart, on the gospel rock.[2] When they have been constructed, this tower of spiritual virtues which is to be built can be immovably fixed and can be raised to the utmost heights of the heavens in full assurance of its solidity. 4. For if it rests upon such foundations, even though the heaviest rains of the passions should come down and violent torrents of persecutions should beat against it like a battering ram and a savage tempest of adversary spirits should rush upon it and press upon it, not only will it not fall into ruin but no force of any kind will ever disturb it.

III.1. "Therefore, so that prayer may be made with the fervor and purity that it deserves, the following things should be observed in every respect. First, anxiety about fleshly matters should be completely cut off. Then, not only the concern for but in fact even the memory of affairs and business should be refused all entry whatsoever; detraction, idle speech, talkativeness, and buffoonery should also be done away with; the disturbance of anger, in particular, and of sadness should be entirely torn out; and the harmful shoot of fleshly lust and of avarice should be uprooted. 2. And thus, when these and similar vices that could also make their appearance among men have been completely thrust out and cut off and there has taken place a cleansing purgation such as we have spoken of, which is perfected in the purity of simplicity and innocence, the unshakable foundations of deep humility should be laid, which can support a tower that will penetrate the heavens. Then the spiritual structure of the virtues must be raised above it, and the mind must be restrained from all dangerous wandering and straying, so that thus it might gradually begin to be elevated to the contemplation of God and to spiritual vision.

3. "For whatever our soul was thinking about before the time of prayer inevitably occurs to us when we pray as a result of the operation of the memory. Hence we must prepare ourselves

before the time of prayer to be the prayerful persons that we wish to be. For the mind in prayer is shaped by the state that it was previously in, and, when we sink into prayer, the image of the same deeds, words, and thoughts plays itself out before our eyes. This makes us angry or sad, depending on our previous condition, or it recalls past lusts or business, or it strikes us with foolish laughter—I am ashamed even to say it—at the suggestion of something ludicrous that was said or done, or it makes us fly back to previous conversations. 4. Therefore, before we pray we should make an effort to cast out from the innermost parts of our heart whatever we do not wish to steal upon us as we pray, so that in this way we can fulfill the apostolic words: 'Pray without ceasing.'[3] And: 'In every place lifting up pure hands without anger and dissension.'[4] For we shall be unable to accomplish this command unless our mind, purified of every contagion of vice and given over to virtue alone as to a natural good, is fed upon the continual contemplation of almighty God.

IV.1. "For the character of the soul is not inappropriately compared to a very light feather or plume. If it has not been harmed or spoiled by some liquid coming from outside, thanks to its inherent lightness it is naturally borne to the heavenly heights by the slightest breath. But if it has been weighed down by a sprinkling or an outpouring of some liquid, not only will it not be borne off by its natural lightness and snatched up into the air, but it will even be pressed down to the lowest places on the earth by the weight of the liquid that it has taken on.

2. "Likewise, if our mind has not been burdened by the worldly vices and concerns that assail it and been spoiled by the liquid of a harmful wantonness, it will be lightened by the natural goodness of its purity and be lifted up to the heights by the subtlest breath of spiritual meditation. Leaving behind low and earthly places, it will be carried away to heavenly and invisible ones. Hence we are rightly warned by the precepts of the Lord: 'See that your hearts not be weighed down by surfeiting and drunkenness and worldly concerns.'[5]

3. "Therefore, if we wish our prayers to penetrate not only the heavens but even what is above the heavens, we should make an effort to draw our mind, purged of every earthly vice and

cleansed of all the dregs of the passions, back to its natural lightness, so that thus its prayer might ascend to God, unburdened by the weight of any vice.

V.1. "Yet it should be known why the Lord indicated that the mind was weighed down. For he did not mention adultery or fornication or murder or blasphemy or pillage, which everyone acknowledges are deadly and damnable, but surfeiting and drunkenness and worldly concerns or anxieties. To such an extent does no worldly person fear these or judge them damnable that some people—I am ashamed to say—even while calling themselves monks engage in these very distractions as if they were harmless and beneficial. 2. Although when they have been perpetrated in a literal sense these three things weigh down the soul, separate it from God, and press it to the earth, yet avoiding them is easy, particularly for us who are cut off by such a great distance from all of this world's way of life and who have no reason whatsoever to be taken up with visible concerns and drunkenness and surfeiting.

"But there is another surfeiting that is no less dangerous and a spiritual drunkenness that is harder to avoid, as well as a concern and a worldly anxiety that frequently seize hold of us even after we have perfectly renounced all our property and are abstaining completely from wine and rich foods and, in fact, are living in the desert. About these things the prophet says: 'Purge yourselves, you who are drunk, and not with wine.'[6] 3. And another one says: 'Be astonished and wonder, waver and reel: be drunk, and not with wine; be moved, and not with drunkenness.'[7] Consequently the wine of this drunkenness must be, according to the prophet, 'the fury of dragons.'[8] Listen to what root this wine proceeds from: 'From the vineyard of Sodom,' he says, 'is their vine, and from Gomorrha their shoots.'[9] 4. Do you also want to know the fruit of this vine and the seed of that shoot? 'Their grape is a grape of gall, a cluster of bitterness for them.'[10]

"Unless we have been completely purged of every vice and unless we have abstained from a surfeit of all the passions, our heart will be weighed down—not with a drunkenness from wine or any abundance of every kind of food but with a drunkenness and a surfeiting that is far worse. For that worldly cares can sometimes beset even us who are involved in none of this world's activity is clearly demonstrated from the rule of the elders. They understood that whatever exceeds the minimum of daily food and the unavoidable requirements of the flesh contributes to worldly concern and anxiety. 5. Here are some examples: if working for one solidus were able to provide for the needs of our body, but we wished to exhaust ourselves by more effort and labor for the sake of earning two or three solidi; and if two tunics were enough clothing for day and night, but we succeeded in becoming the owners of three or four; and if a dwelling of one or two rooms were enough, but we were moved by worldly ambition and a desire for spaciousness to build four or five rooms, exquisitely furnished and larger than required by utility. In these instances we would be displaying the passion of worldly lust wherever we could.

VI.1. "Absolutely irrefutable experience has taught us that this occurs at the instigation of demons. For one of the most proven elders happened to pass by the cell of a certain brother who was laboring under this sickness of mind that we have spoken of, and this man was restlessly constructing and repairing unnecessary things and exerting himself in mundane distractions. From a distance he noticed that he was pounding a very hard rock with a sledgehammer, and he saw a certain Ethiopian standing by him and striking hammer blows along with him, their hands joined together, and he was urging him on in this work with fiery brands. He stayed there for quite a long while, astonished at the sight of the cruel demon and at the deceptive power of such an illusion. 2. For when the brother was completely worn out and wanted to rest and to put an end to his work, he was encouraged at this spirit's instigation and was pressed to take up the hammer again and not to cease from applying himself to the work that he had started, such that he was unweariedly sustained by his urgings and did not feel how burdensome all his effort was.

"At last the old man, greatly upset by the demon's cruel mockery, went up to the brother's cell, greeted him, and said: 'What are you working at, brother?' And he said: 'We are toiling away at this very hard rock, and we have hardly been able to break it up at all.' 3. To this the old man said: 'Well did you say "we," for you were not alone when you were striking it, but there was another with you whom you did not see. He stood by you during this work, not so much to help you as to press you on with all his force.'

"Therefore, merely abstaining from affairs which we are unable to accomplish or complete even if we wanted to certainly does not prove that the disease of worldly ambition does not dwell in our minds. The same is true of despising those things which, if we affected them, would make us look important among both spiritual and worldly persons. It is rather a matter of our also rejecting with unwavering strictness of mind those things which cater to our power and which have the appearance of a kind of goodness. 4. And in fact the things that seem small and insignificant and that we see are considered with indifference by persons of our profession are no less burdensome to the mind because of their characteristics than those greater things that usually intoxicate the minds of worldly people in keeping with their status. They do not permit a monk, for whom even a brief separation from that highest good must be believed to be immediate death and utter ruin, to lay aside earthly impurity and to long for God, upon whom his attention should ever be fixed.

5. "And when the mind has been established in tranquillity and has been freed from the bonds of every fleshly passion, and the heart's attention is unwaveringly fastened upon the one and highest good, it will fulfill the apostolic words: 'Pray without ceasing.' And: 'In every place lifting up pure hands without anger and dissension.' For, if we may speak in this way, when the thoughts of the mind have been seized by this purity and have been refashioned from earthly dullness to the likeness of the spiritual and the angelic, whatever they take in, whatever they reflect upon, and whatever they do will be most pure and sincere prayer."

VII.1. GERMANUS: "If only we were able to enjoy uninterruptedly these spiritual thoughts in the same way and with the same ease that we usually conceive their beginnings. For when they have been conceived in our heart through the recollection of Scripture or through recalling some spiritual deeds or, even more, through a glimpse of the heavenly mysteries, they immediately vanish, having as it were imperceptibly taken flight. 2. And when our mind finds further occasions for spiritual thoughts, others creep back in and those that had been laid hold of slip rapidly away. Thus the mind has no constancy of its own, nor does it possess of its own power any immutability with regard to holy thoughts even when it seems somehow or other to hold on to them, and it can be believed that it has conceived them by chance and not by its own effort. For how can anyone think that their origin is to be ascribed to our own doing when persevering in them is beyond us?

3. "But let us not, while pursuing this issue, digress any further from the discourse that we began and put off any longer the proposed explanation regarding the nature of prayer. We shall keep this other matter for its own time. Right now we want to be informed about the character of prayer, especially since the Apostle tells us never to cease from it when he says: 'Pray without ceasing.' 4. Therefore we want to learn about its character first—that is, about what sort of prayer should always be said—and then about how we can possess this very thing, whatever it is, and practice it without ceasing. For daily experience and the words of your holiness, according to which you declared that the end of the monk and the summit of all perfection consisted in perfect prayer, demonstrate that this can be achieved with no small effort of the heart."

VIII.1. ISAAC: "I do not think that all the different kinds of prayer can be grasped without great purity of heart and soul and the enlightenment of the Holy Spirit. For as many characteristics can be produced as there are conditions in one soul and, indeed, in all souls. 2. Therefore, although we know that we cannot ascertain all the different kinds of prayer because of our dullness of heart, nonetheless we shall try to analyze them somehow to the extent that our limited experience permits us to do so. According to the degree of purity to which each mind has attained, and according to the nature of the condition either to which it has declined because of what has happened to it or to which it has renewed itself by its own efforts, these change at every moment. Therefore it is absolutely certain that no one's prayers can be uniform. 3. For a person prays one way when he is happy and another way when he is burdened by a weight of sadness or despair; one way when he is enjoying spiritual successes and another way when he is oppressed by numerous attacks; one way when he is begging pardon for sins and another way when he is asking for grace or some virtue or, of course, for the annihilation of some vice; one way when he is struck with compunction by reflecting on Gehenna and by fear of future judgment and another way when he is inflamed by the hope and desire for future goods; one way when he is needy and in danger and another way when he is safe and at peace; one way when he is enlightened by revelations of heavenly mysteries and another way when he is fettered by sterility of virtue and dryness of thought.

IX. "Therefore, once these aspects of the character of prayer have been analyzed—although not as much as the breadth of the material demands but as much as a brief space of time permits and our feeble intelligence and dull heart can grasp hold of—there remains to us a still greater difficulty: We must explain one by one the different kinds of prayer that the Apostle divided in fourfold fashion when he said: 'I urge first of all that supplications, prayers, intercessions, and thanksgivings be made.'[11] There is not the least doubt that the Apostle established these distinctions in this way for a good reason.

2. "First we must find out what is meant by supplication, what is meant by prayer, what is meant by intercession, and what is meant by thanksgiving. Then we must investigate whether these four kinds are to be used simultaneously by the person praying—that is, whether they should all be joined together in a single act of prayer—or whether they should be offered one after the other and individually, so that, for example, at one time supplications should be made, at another prayers, at another intercessions or thanksgivings; and whether one person should offer God supplications, another prayers, another intercessions, and another thanksgivings, depending on the maturity to which each mind is progressing according to the intensity of its effort.

X.1. "First, therefore, the very properties of the names and words should be dealt with and the difference between prayer, supplication, and intercession analyzed. Then, in similar fashion, an investigation must be made as to whether they are to be offered separately or together. Third, we must look into whether the very order that was laid down on the authority of the Apostle has deeper implications for the hearer or whether these distinctions should simply be accepted and be considered to have been drawn up by him in an inconsequential manner.

"This last suggestion seems quite absurd to me. For it ought not to be believed that the Holy Spirit would have said something through the Apostle in passing and for no reason. And therefore let us treat of them again individually in the same order in which we began, as the Lord permits.

XI.1. "'I urge first of all that supplications be made.' A supplication is an imploring or a petition concerning sins, by which a person who has been struck by compunction begs for pardon for his present or past misdeeds.

XII.1. "Prayers are those acts by which we offer or vow something to God, which is called ευχη in Greek—that is, a vow. For where the Greek says: τας ευχας μου τω κυριω αποδωσω, the Latin has it: 'I will pay my vows to the Lord.'[12] According to the nature of the word this can be expressed as follows: I will make my prayers to the Lord. And what we read in Ecclesiastes: 'If you vow a vow to God, do not delay to pay it,'[13] is written similarly in the Greek: εαν ευξη ευχην τω κυριω—that is: If you make a prayer to the Lord, do not delay to pay it.

2. "This will be fulfilled by each one of us in this way. We pray when we renounce this world and pledge that, dead to every earthly deed and to an earthly way of life, we will serve the Lord with utter earnestness of heart. We pray when we promise that, disdaining worldly honor and spurning earthly riches, we will cling to the Lord in complete contrition of heart and poverty of spirit. We pray when we promise that we will always keep the most pure chastity of body and unwavering patience, and when we vow that we will utterly eliminate from our heart the roots of death-dealing anger and sadness. When we have been weakened by sloth and are returning to our former vices and are not doing these things, we shall bear guilt for our prayers and vows and it will be said of us: 'It is better not to vow than to vow and not to pay.'[14] According to the Greek this can be said: It is better for you not to pray than to pray and not to pay.

XIII. "In the third place there are intercessions, which we are also accustomed to make for others when our spirits are fervent, beseeching on behalf of our dear ones and for the peace of the whole world, praying (as I would say in the words of the Apostle himself) 'for kings and for all who are in authority.'[15]

XIV. "Finally, in the fourth place there are thanksgivings, which the mind, whether recalling God's past benefits, contemplating his present ones, or foreseeing what great things God has prepared for those who love him, offers to the Lord in unspeakable ecstasies. And with this intensity, too, more copious prayers are sometimes made, when our spirit gazes with most pure eyes upon the rewards of the holy ones that are stored up for the future and is moved to pour out wordless thanks to God with a boundless joy.

XV.1. "These four kinds sometimes offer opportunities for richer prayers, for from the class of supplication which is born of compunction for sin, and from the state of prayer which flows from faithfulness in our offerings and the keeping of our vows because of a pure conscience, and from intercession which proceeds from fervent charity, and from thanksgiving which is begotten from considering God's benefits and his greatness and lovingkindness, we know that frequently very fervent and fiery prayers arise. Thus it is clear that all these kinds which we have spoken about appear helpful and necessary to everyone, so that in one and the same man a changing disposition will send forth pure and fervent prayers of supplication at one time, prayer at another, and intercession at another.

"Nonetheless the first kind seems to pertain more especially to beginners who are still being harassed by the stings and by the memory of their vices; the second to those who already occupy a certain elevated position of mind with regard to spiritual progress and virtuous disposition; the third to those who, fulfilling their vows completely by their deeds, are moved to intercede for others also in consideration of their frailty and out of zeal for charity; the fourth to those who, having already torn from their hearts the penal thorn of conscience, now, free from care, consider with a most pure mind the kindnesses and mercies of the Lord that he has bestowed in the past, gives in the present, and prepares for the future, and are rapt by their fervent heart to that fiery prayer which can be neither seized nor expressed by the mouth of man.

2. "Yet sometimes the mind which advances to that true disposition of purity and has already begun to be rooted in it, conceiving all of these at one and the same time and rushing through them all like a kind of ungraspable and devouring flame, pours out to God wordless prayers of the purest vigor. These the Spirit itself makes to God as it intervenes with unutterable groans, unbeknownst to us, conceiving at that moment and pouring forth in wordless prayer such great things that they not only—I would say—cannot pass through the mouth but are unable even to be remembered by the mind later on.

3. "Hence, in whatever state a person is, he sometimes finds himself making pure and intense prayers. For even from that first and lowest sort, which has to do with recalling the future judgment, the one who is still subject to the punishment of terror and the fear of judgment is occasionally so struck with compunction that he is filled with no less joy of spirit from the richness of his supplication than the one who, examining the kindnesses of God and going over them in the purity of his heart, dissolves into unspeakable gladness and delight. For, according to the words of the Lord, the one who realizes that more has been forgiven him begins to love more.[16]

XVI. "Yet, as we advance in life and grow perfect in virtue, we should by preference pursue the kinds of prayer that are poured out as a result of contemplating future goods or from an ardent charity, or at least—to speak in lowly fashion and in conformity with a beginner's standard—that are produced for the sake of acquiring some virtue or destroying some vice. For we shall be utterly unable to attain to the more sublime types of prayer about which we have spoken if our mind has not been slowly and gradually brought forward through the series of those intercessions.

XVII.1. "By his own example the Lord himself deigned to initiate us into these four kinds of prayer, so that in this way too he would fulfill what was said of him: 'Which Jesus began to do and teach.'[17] For he used the form of supplication when he said: 'Father, if it be possible, let this cup pass from me.'[18] Or what is sung in the psalm in his person: 'My God, my God, look upon me. Why have you forsaken me?'[19] There are other things similar to these, too.

2. "It is prayer when he says: 'I have glorified you on earth, I have finished the work that you gave me to do.'[20] Or: 'I sanctify myself for their sake, that they themselves may also be sanctified in the truth.'[21]

"It is intercession when he says: 'Father, I wish that those whom you have given me may also be with me where I am, so that they may see my glory, which you have given me.'[22] And of course when he says: 'Father, forgive them, for they do not know what they are doing.'[23]

3. "It is thanksgiving when he says: 'I confess to you, Father, Lord of heaven and earth, because you have hidden these things from the wise and the prudent and have revealed them to little ones. Thus, Father, for so it seemed good to you.'[24] And of course when he says: 'Father, I give you thanks because you have heard me. But I knew that you always hear me.'[25]

"But although our Lord distinguished the four kinds of prayers to be offered, individually and at different times, as we understand, nonetheless he shows as well by his own example that they can also be included together in a perfect prayer. This he does in that prayer which we read that he poured out at great length toward the end of the Gospel according to John.[26] 4. From this text (because it is too long to go through all of it) the careful inquirer will be able to see that this is so from the course of the reading itself. The Apostle clearly expresses the same meaning in the Letter to the Philippians when he sets down these four kinds of prayer in a somewhat different order, showing that they must sometimes be offered all at once with the fervor of a single prayer. As he says: 'Let your petitions be made known to God in every prayer and supplication, with thanksgiving.'[27] Thereby he wished us to learn particularly that thanksgiving should be mingled with intercession in prayer and in supplication.

XVIII.1. "And so a still more sublime and exalted condition follows upon these kinds of prayer. It is fashioned by the contemplation of God alone and by fervent charity, by which the mind, having been dissolved and flung into love of him, speaks most familiarly and with particular devotion to God as to its own father.

2. "The schema of the Lord's prayer has taught us that we must tirelessly seek this condition when it says: 'Our Father.'[28]

When, therefore, we confess with our own voice that the God and Lord of the universe is our Father, we profess that we have in fact been admitted from our servile condition into an adopted sonship.

"Then we add: 'Who art in heaven,'[29] so that, avoiding with utter horror the dwelling place of the present life, wherein we sojourn on this earth as on a journey and are kept at a far distance from our Father, we may instead hasten with great desire to that region in which we say that our Father dwells and do nothing that would make us unworthy of this profession of ours and of the nobility of so great an adoption, or that would deprive us as degenerate of our paternal inheritance and cause us to incur the wrath of his justice and severity.

3. "Having advanced to the rank and status of sons, we shall from then on burn constantly with that devotion which is found in good sons, so that we may no longer expend all our energies for our own benefit but for the sake of our Father's glory, saying to him: 'Hallowed be thy name.'[30] Thus we testify that our desire and our joy is the glory of our Father, since we have become imitators of him who said: 'The one who speaks of himself seeks his own glory. But the one who seeks the glory of him who sent him is true, and there is no unrighteousness in him.'[31]

"Finally, the vessel of election,[32] filled with this disposition, wished to become anathema from Christ if only a household many times larger would be gained for him and the salvation of the entire Israelite people would increase the glory of his Father.[33] 4. For he who knew that no one can die for the sake of life could safely choose to perish for the sake of Christ. And again he says: 'We rejoice when we are weak but you are strong.'[34]

"But what is there so astonishing if the vessel of election chooses to become anathema for the sake of Christ's glory and for the sake of his brothers' conversion and the well-being of the pagans, when the prophet Micah also wished to become a liar and to be removed from the inspiration of the Holy Spirit if only the people of the Jewish nation might avoid the plagues and the ruinous captivity that he had predicted by his prophecy? As he says: 'Would that I were not a man who had the Spirit, and I told a lie instead!'[35] And let us pass over the sentiment of the Lawgiver, who did not refuse to die with his brothers, who were themselves going to die, when he said: 'I beseech you, O Lord; this people has committed a great sin. Either forgive them this evil or, if you do not, wipe me out from the book that you have written.'[36]

5. "The words 'Hallowed be thy name' can also be quite satisfactorily understood in this way–namely, that the hallowing of God is our perfection. And so when we say to him: 'Hallowed be thy name,' we are saying in other words: Make us such, Father, that we may deserve to understand and grasp how great your hallowing is and, of course, that you may appear as hallowed in our spiritual way of life. This is effectively fulfilled in us when 'people see our good works and glorify our Father who is in heaven.'[37]

XIX. "The second petition of a most pure mind eagerly desires the kingdom of its Father to come immediately. This means that in which Christ reigns daily in holy persons, which happens when the rule of the devil has been cast out of our hearts by the annihilation of the foul vices and God has begun to hold sway in us through the good fragrance of the virtues; when chastity, peace, and humility reign in our minds, and fornication has been conquered, rage overcome, and pride trampled upon. And of course it means that which was promised universally to all the perfect and to all the sons of God at the appointed time, when it will be said to them by Christ: 'Come, blessed of my Father, take possession of the kingdom prepared for you from the foundation of the world.'[38] Desiring and hoping for this with intent and unwavering gaze, we tell him: 'Thy kingdom come.'[39] For we know by the witness of our own conscience that when he appears we shall soon be his companions. No sinner dares to say this or to wish for it, since a person who knows that at his coming he will at once be paid back for his deserts not with a palm or rewards but with punishment has no desire to see the Judge's tribunal.

XX.1. "The third petition is of sons: 'Thy will be done on earth as it is in heaven.'[40] There cannot be a greater prayer than to desire that earthly things should deserve to equal heavenly ones. For what does it mean to say: 'Thy will be done on earth as it is in heaven,' if not that human beings should be like angels and that, just as God's will is fulfilled by them in heaven, so also all those who are on earth should do not their own but his will? No one will really be able to say this but him who believes that God regulates all things that are seen, whether fortunate or unfortunate, for the sake of our well-being, and that he is more provident and careful with regard to the salvation and interests of those who are his own than we are for ourselves.

2. "And of course it is to be understood in this way—namely, that the will of God is the salvation of all, according to the text of blessed Paul: 'Who desires all to be saved and to come to the knowledge of the truth.'[41] Of this will the prophet Isaiah, speaking in the person of God the Father, also says: 'All my will shall be done.'[42] When we tell him, then: 'Thy will be done on earth as it is in heaven,' we are praying in other words: Father, just as those who are in heaven are saved by the knowledge of you, so also are those who are on earth.

XXI.1. "Then: 'Give us this day our επιουσιον—that is, supersubstantial—'bread,'[43] which another evangelist has referred to as 'daily.'[44] The former indicates the noble quality of this substance, which places it above all other substances and which, in the sublimity of its magnificence and power to sanctify, surpasses every creature, whereas the latter expresses the nature of its use and its goodness. For when it says 'daily' it shows that we are unable to attain the spiritual life on a day without it.

2. When it says 'this day' it shows that it must be taken daily and that yesterday's supply of it is not enough if we have not been given of it today as well. Our daily need for it warns us that we should pour out this prayer constantly, because there is no day on which it is not necessary for us to strengthen the heart of our inner man by eating and receiving this. But the expression 'this day' can also be understood with reference to the present life—namely: Give us this bread as long as we dwell in this world. For we know that it will also be given in the world to come to those who have deserved it from you, but we beg you to give it to us this day, because unless a person deserves to receive it in this life he will be unable to partake of it in that life.

XXII.1. "'And forgive us our trespasses as we forgive those who trespass against us.'[45] Oh, the unspeakable mercy of God! It has not merely given us a form of prayer and taught us how to act in a manner acceptable to him, uprooting both anger and sadness through the requirements of the formula that he gave, by which he ordered that we should always pray it. It has also conferred on those who pray an opportunity by disclosing to them the way that they may bring upon themselves the merciful and kind judgment of God, and it has conferred a certain power by which we can moderate the sentence of our Judge, persuading him to pardon our sins by the example of our own forgiveness, when we tell him: 'Forgive us as we forgive.'

2. "And so, securely confident in this prayer, a person who has been forgiving to his own debtors and not to his Lord's will ask pardon for his offenses. For some of us—which is bad—are accustomed to show ourselves mild and very merciful with respect to things that are committed to God's disadvantage, although they may be great crimes, but to be very harsh and inexorable exactors with respect to the debts of even the slightest offenses committed against ourselves. 3. Whoever, then, does not from his heart forgive the brother who has offended him will, by this entreaty, be asking not for pardon but for condemnation for himself, and by his own say-so he will be requesting a harsher judgment for himself when he says: Forgive me as I also have forgiven. And when he has been dealt with according to his own petition, what else will the consequence be than that, following his own example, he will be punished with an implacable anger and an irremissible condemnation? Therefore, if we wish to be judged mercifully, we must ourselves be merciful toward those who have offended us. For we shall be forgiven to the degree that we have forgiven those who have injured us by any wrongdoing whatsoever.

4. "Some people fear this, and when this prayer is recited together in church by the whole congregation they pass over this line in silence, lest by their own words they obligate rather than excuse themselves. They do not understand that it is in vain that they contrive to quibble in this way with the Judge of all, who wished to show beforehand how he would judge his suppliants. For since he does not wish to be harsh and inexorable toward them, he indicated the form that his judgment would take. Thus, just as we want to be judged by him, so also we should judge our brothers if they have offended us in anything, 'because there is judgment without mercy for the one who has not acted mercifully.'[46]

XXIII.1. "Next there follows: 'And subject us not to the

trial.'[47] In this regard there arises a question of no small importance. For if we pray not to be allowed to be tried, how will the strength of our steadfastness be tested, according to the words: 'Whoever has not been tried has not been proven'?[48] And again: 'Blessed is the man who undergoes trial'?[49] Therefore, the words 'Subject us not to the trial' do not mean: Do not allow us ever to be tried, but rather: Do not allow us to be overcome when we are tried. 2. For Job was tried, but he was not subjected to the trial. For he did not ascribe folly to God, nor did he as a blasphemer, with wicked tongue, accede to the will of the one trying him, to which he was being drawn. Abraham was tried[50] and Joseph was tried,[51] but neither of them was subjected to the trial, for neither of them consented to the one trying them.

"Then there follows: 'But deliver us from evil.'[52] This means: Do not allow us to be tried by the devil 'beyond our capacity, but with the trial also provide a way out, so that we may be able to endure.'[53]

XXIV.1. "You see, then, what sort of measure and form for prayer have been proposed to us by the Judge who is to be prayed to by it. In it there is contained no request for riches, no allusion to honors, no demand for power and strength, no mention of bodily health or of temporal existence. For the Creator of eternal things wishes nothing transitory, nothing base, nothing temporal to be asked for from himself. And so, whoever neglects these sempiternal petitions and chooses to ask for something transitory and passing from him does very great injury to his grandeur and largesse, and he offends rather than propitiates his Judge with the paltriness of his prayer.

XXV.1. "This prayer, then, although it seems to contain the utter fullness of perfection inasmuch as it was instituted and established on the authority of the Lord himself, nonetheless raises his familiars to that condition which we characterized previously as more sublime. It leads them by a higher stage to that fiery and, indeed, more properly speaking, wordless prayer which is known and experienced by very few. This transcends all human understanding and is distinguished not, I would say, by a sound of the voice or a movement of the tongue or a pronunciation of words. Rather, the mind is aware of it when it is illuminated by an infusion of heavenly light from it, and not by narrow human words, and once the understanding has been suspended it gushes forth as from a most abundant fountain and speaks ineffably to God, producing more in that very brief moment than the self-conscious mind is able to articulate easily or to reflect upon. Our Lord himself represented this condition in similar fashion in the form of those prayers that he is described as having poured out alone on the mountain[54] and silently, and when he prayed in his agony he even shed drops of blood as an inimitable example of his intense purpose.[55]

XXVI.1. "But who, endowed with whatever experience, could satisfactorily explain the very different types of compunction, with their origins and causes, by which the mind, ardent and enkindled, is moved to pure and fervent prayers? By way of example we shall propose a few of these to the extent that, with the Lord's illumination, we are able to recall them at present. Sometimes, while we have been singing, the verse of some psalm has offered the occasion for fiery prayer. Now and then the melodious modulation of a brother's voice has excited insensible minds to intense prayer. 2. We know as well that the clarity and seriousness of the cantor have contributed a great deal to the fervor of those in attendance. Likewise, the exhortation of a perfect man and a spiritual conference have frequently aroused the disposition of those present to very abundant prayers. We know, too, that we have been no less seized by utter compunction due to the downfall of a brother or some dear friend. The recollection of our own lukewarmness and negligence has also sometimes introduced a salutary ardor of spirit into us. And in this fashion there is no doubt that innumerable occasions exist when, by the grace of God, the lukewarmness and sluggishness of our minds can be aroused.

XXVII. "But to investigate how and in what ways these different kinds of compunction are brought out from the deepest recesses of the soul is a matter of no little difficulty. For frequently the fruit of a very beneficial compunction emerges from an ineffable joy and gladness of spirit, such that it even breaks forth into shouts because of a joy that is too vast to be repressed, and the heart's delight and the great exultation reach the cell of one's neighbor. But sometimes the mind is hidden by such silence within the bounds of a profound speechlessness that the stupor brought on by a sudden illumination completely prevents the forming of words, and the stunned spirit either keeps every expression within or releases and pours out its desires to God in unutterable groans. Sometimes, however, it is filled with such an abundance of compunction and with such sorrow that it cannot deal with it except by an outpouring of tears."

XXVIII.1. GERMANUS: "Even I for my part, for all my insignificance, am not unaware of this feeling of compunction. For frequently, when tears well up at the memory of my past offenses, I am so shaken by an unspeakable joy at the Lord's visitation–as you have said–that the greatness of this happiness dictates that I should not despair of their being pardoned. I think that nothing is more sublime than this condition, if only returning to it were in our own power! 2. For sometimes, when I wish to excite myself with all my strength to a similar tearful compunction and I place before my eyes all my errors and sins, I am unable to achieve again such an abundance of tears, and my eyes become as hard as the hardest flint, so that not even a single drop of moisture falls from them. Therefore, as much as I rejoice in that outpouring of tears, I regret that I am unable to regain it whenever I wish."

XXIX.1. ISAAC: "Not every outpouring of tears is prompted by a single sentiment or a single virtue. For the weeping that is produced when the thorn of sinfulness pricks our heart with compunction appears in one way. About that it is said: 'I have labored in my groaning. Every night I will wash my bed, I will water my couch with tears.'[56] And again: 'Let tears run down like a torrent day and night, and do not give yourself rest nor let the apple of your eye be silent.'[57]

2. "It arises in another way from the contemplation of eternal goods and the desire for that future glory, for the sake of which, too, abundant fountains of tears erupt out of irrepressible joy and overwhelming happiness. All the while our soul is thirsting for the strong and living God, saying: 'When shall I come and appear before the face of God? My tears have been my bread by day and by night.'[58] Daily, with mourning and lamentation, it declares: 'Woe is me that my sojourning has been prolonged.'[59] And: 'Too long has my soul been a sojourner.'[60]

3. "There is another way that tears flow, proceeding not, indeed, from any consciousness of deadly crimes but nonetheless from a fear of Gehenna and from an awareness of that terrible judgment. The prophet, smitten with this terror, prays to God and says: 'Do not enter into judgment with your servant, for in your sight no one living shall be justified.'[61]

"There is still another kind of tears, which is begotten not from one's own conscience but from another's hardness and sinfulness. Samuel is described as having wept over Saul with this kind,[62] the Lord in the Gospel,[63] and Jeremiah before that over the city of Jerusalem when he says: 'Who will give water for my head and a fount of tears for my eyes? And day and night I shall weep for the slain of the daughter of my people.'[64] 4. This is certainly the sort of tears of which it is sung in the one hundred and first psalm: 'I have eaten ashes for my bread, and I mixed my cup with tears.'[65] These are not at all prompted by the sentiment that provokes them in the sixth psalm, in the person of a penitent, but by the distress of this life and by the cares and hardships with which the righteous in this world are weighed down. Not only the text of the psalm but even its title shows this clearly. It is set down as follows: 'The prayer of a poor man when he was distressed and poured out his prayer to God.'[66] This is the poor man who is spoken of in the Gospel: 'Blessed are the poor in spirit, for theirs is the kingdom of heaven.'[67]

XXX.1. "There is a considerable difference between these tears, then, and those which are squeezed by a hardened heart from dry eyes. Although we believe that the latter are not utterly fruitless (for the attempt to shed them is done with a good will, particularly by persons who have not yet succeeded either in attaining to perfect knowledge or in being completely cleansed of the stains of past or present vices), nonetheless an outpouring of tears should never be forced in this way by those who have already acquired a virtuous disposition. Nor should the tears of the outer man be laboriously striven for; even if they have somehow been produced, they will never arrive at the abundance of spontaneous tears. 2. For attempts at them will tend to drag down the mind of the person praying, to lower it, submerge it in human concerns, and displace it from that heavenly height whereon the awed mind of the one praying should be irremovably stationed, and they will compel it, once it has slackened the intensity of its prayers, to weaken in the face of sterile and forced tears.

XXXI. "And so that you might see the disposition that is associated with true prayer, I shall offer you not my own but blessed Antony's opinion. We know that he sometimes prayed at such length that frequently, when he was in an ecstasy of mind while praying and the rising sun was beginning to shine forth, we would hear him declaring in his fervor of spirit: 'Why are you hindering me, O sun, you who are rising now in order to keep me from the brilliance of this true light?' From him also come these heavenly and more than human words on the end of prayer: 'That is not a perfect prayer,' he said, 'wherein the monk understands himself or what he is praying.' And if we ourselves, according to the measure of our littleness, may dare to add something to this admirable opinion, we shall indicate, from our own experience, the signs of a prayer that is heard by the Lord.

XXXII. "When no hesitation distracts us as we pray and, by a kind of hopelessness, makes us lose confidence in our petition, but we think that we have obtained what we are looking for, thanks to our outpouring of prayer, we should not doubt that our prayers have made their way efficaciously to God. For a person will deserve to be heard and to receive to the extent that he believes that he can be seen by God and that God can act on his behalf. For these words of our Lord are irrevocable: 'Whatever you ask for when you pray, believe that you will receive and it shall come to you.'"[68]

XXXIII. GERMANUS: "We believe that this confidence of being heard certainly proceeds from a pure conscience. But how can we, whose heart is still being pricked with compunction by the thorn of sinfulness, possess it when we are without the accompanying qualities by which we may confidently presume that our prayers will be heard?"

XXXIV.1. ISAAC: "The words of the Gospels and those of the prophets testify that prayers are heard for different reasons, which are based on the different and varied conditions of souls. For in the agreement of two persons, you see indicated in the Lord's own words the fruit of a hearing, according to the text: 'If two of you agree on earth about asking for anything whatsoever, it shall be done for them by my Father who is in heaven.'[69] You have another such in the fullness of faith that is compared to a mustard seed: 'If,' he says, 'you have faith like a mustard seed, you shall say to this mountain: Go from here, and it will go, and nothing shall be impossible for you.'[70] 2. You have it in the constant repetition of prayer, which the Lord called persistence because of its unwearied perseverance in petitioning: 'Amen, I say to you, that he will get up and give him as much as he needs on account of his persistence, if not on account of friendship.'[71] You have it in the fruits of almsgiving: 'Shut up an alms,' it says, 'in the heart of the poor person, and it will pray for you in time of tribulation.'[72] You have it in an emended life and in the works of mercy, according to the words: 'Loose the bonds of wickedness, undo the oppressive bundles.'[73] 3. And after a few words in which the sterility of fruitless fasting is castigated, it says: 'Then you shall call and the Lord shall hear you. You shall cry out and he shall say: Behold, here I am.'[74] Sometimes, indeed, the very magnitude of one's distress assures an answer, according to the text: 'I cried out to the Lord when I was distressed, and he heard me.'[75] And again: 'Do not afflict the stranger, because if he cries out to me I will hear him, for I am merciful.'[76]

"You see, then, in how many ways the grace of being heard is obtained, so that no one should be discouraged by a sense of his own hopelessness in asking for things that are beneficial and eternal. 4. For if, in contemplating our misery, I should admit that we are completely bereft of all the virtues that we mentioned previously and have neither that praiseworthy agreement of two people nor that faith which is compared to a mustard seed nor those works of kindness which the prophet describes, can we not at least have the persistence which he provides to everyone who wishes it, for the sake of which alone he promises that he will give whatever he, as Lord, has been asked for? And therefore our prayers should be insistent and without the hesitation born of lack of confidence, and there should be no doubt that by continuing in them we shall obtain everything that we have asked for and that is agreeable to God.

5. "For the Lord, who wants to bestow what is eternal and heavenly, encourages us as it were to coerce him by our persis-

tence. He not only neither disdains nor refuses the persistent but he even welcomes and praises them, and he very graciously promises that he will give them whatever they have perseveringly hoped for when he says: 'Ask and you shall receive, seek and you shall find, knock and it shall be opened to you. For everyone who asks receives, and everyone who seeks finds, and to everyone who knocks it shall be opened.'[77] And again: 'Everything whatever that you ask for in prayer you shall receive if you believe, and nothing shall be impossible for you.'[78]

6. "Therefore, if all the other causes for being heard that we have spoken of fail us completely, at least the urgency of persistence should quicken us: It is within the power of whoever wills it and does not depend on worthiness or effort. But certainly let no supplicant doubt that he will not be heard even if he may have doubted that he was heard. That this should unweariedly be asked of the Lord, however, we are also taught by the example of the blessed Daniel. Although he was heard from the first day that he began to pray, he received the answer to his petition after the twenty-first day.[79] 7. Hence neither must we ourselves cease from pursuing a prayer once we have begun, even if we think that we are not being heard soon enough, for perchance either the grace of being heard has been postponed for some good reason by the Lord's design or the angel who has gone out from the face of the Almighty to bring us a divine gift has met delay and resistance from the devil; certainly he could not press the desire for the gift that he bore if he discovered that we were no longer intent upon the petition that we had made. No doubt this would also have happened to the aforementioned prophet if he had not with incomparable virtue persevered in his prayers until the twenty-first day.

8. "Let hopelessness, then, not completely discourage us from a confident trust. When we think that we have not obtained what we have prayed for, let us not doubt the solemn promise of the Lord, who said: 'Everything whatever that you ask for in prayer you shall receive if you believe.' We should recall the words of the blessed evangelist John, by which the uncertainty of this matter is clearly resolved: 'This is,' he says, 'the confidence that we have in him, that, whatever we ask for according to his will, he hears us.'[80]

9. "Therefore he commands us to have the full and sure confidence of being heard only with regard to the things that are in conformity not with our convenience and comfort but with the Lord's will. In the Lord's Prayer itself we are instructed to take this into account and to say: 'Thy will be done'—that is, thine not ours. For if we recall the text of the Apostle, that 'we do not know what to pray for as we ought,'[81] we realize that we sometimes ask for things which are contrary to our salvation and that what we ask for is quite properly denied us by him who sees our well-being more clearly and truly than we do. 10. This was certainly the case, too, with the teacher of the Gentiles, when he prayed that there be removed from him the angel of Satan who had been given him by the Lord's decision, in order to buffet him for his own good: 'Therefore I asked the Lord three times that this might leave me. And he said to me: My grace is sufficient for you, for strength is perfected in weakness.'[82]

"Our Lord himself, praying in the person of the man that he had assumed, expressed this understanding when he prayed, in order to offer us by his own example—as he did with other things—a form of prayer as well. Thus: 'Father, if it be possible, let this cup pass from me, yet not as I will but as you do,'[83] although certainly his will did not differ from his Father's will. 11. 'For he had come to save what was lost, and to give his life as a ransom for many.'[84] About this he says: 'No one takes my life from me, but I lay it down of myself. I have power to lay it down, and I have power to take it up again.'[85] With respect to the unity of will which he always had with his Father, this is sung in his person by the blessed David in the thirty-ninth psalm: 'My God, I have desired to do your will.'[86] For if we read of the Father: 'For God so loved the world that he gave his only begotten Son,'[87] we nevertheless find as well with regard to the Son: 'Who gave himself for our sins.'[88] 12. And just as it is said of the former: 'Who did not spare his own Son, but handed him over for us all,'[89] it is likewise recounted of the latter: 'He was offered because he himself willed it.'[90] The will of the Father and that of the Son are understood to be so completely united that their operation even in the mystery of the Lord's very resurrection, so we are taught, was harmonious. For just as the blessed Apostle declares that the Father accomplished the resurrection of his body when he says: 'God the Father, who raised him from the dead,'[91] so also the Son bears witness that he will raise the temple of his body when he says: 'Destroy this temple, and in three days I will raise it up.'[92] 13. And therefore, instructed by these examples of the Lord that we have spoken of, we should ourselves conclude all our entreaties with a similar prayer and always add these words to every petition of ours: 'Yet not as I will but as you do.' But it is quite obvious that one who prays with an attentive mind cannot observe that threefold inclination which the communities of the brothers are accustomed to practice as a conclusion to their synaxis.

XXXV.1. "Before anything else, we must carefully observe the gospel command which says that we should go into our room and pray to our Father with the door shut.[93] We shall fulfill this in the following way. We pray in our room when we withdraw our hearts completely from the clatter of every thought and concern and disclose our prayers to the Lord in secret and, as it were, intimately. 2. We pray with the door shut when, with closed lips and in total silence, we pray to the searcher not of voices but of hearts. We pray in secret when, intent in heart and mind alone, we offer our petitions to God alone, so that even the adversary powers cannot discover the nature of our petition. 3. We must pray with the greatest silence, therefore, not only so that we may not disturb our brothers standing nearby with our murmurings and outcries and distract the minds of those who are praying, but also so that what we are petitioning for may be hidden from our enemies, who plot against us greatly as we pray. Thus we shall fulfill the command: 'Keep the door of your mouth from her who sleeps in your bosom.'[94]

XXXVI.1. "For this reason prayer should be made frequently, to be sure, but briefly, lest if we take our time the lurking enemy be able to put something in our heart.

"This is the true sacrifice, for 'a contrite spirit is a sacrifice to God.'[95] This is the saving oblation, these the pure libations, this 'the sacrifice of righteousness,'[96] this 'the sacrifice of praise,'[97] these the true and fatted offerings, these 'the holocausts full of marrow,'[98] which are offered by contrite and humble hearts and which, thanks to this disciplined and attentive spirit that we have spoken of, we shall be able to sing when we have grown strong in virtue: 'Let my prayer come like incense in your presence, the raising of my hands like an evening sacrifice.'[99]

2. "The approach of that very hour and of the night, in fact, warns us to attend to this with appropriate devotion. Although, according to the measure of our insignificance, much seems to have been brought forth on this subject and the conference has lasted a long time, yet we believe that, given the sublime and difficult nature of the matter, very little indeed has been said."

3. Amazed by these words of the holy Isaac rather than satisfied by them, we rested our limbs in sleep for a short while after the evening synaxis had been celebrated. Intending to return again early in the morning in the expectation of a fuller discussion, we went back home, rejoicing as much in the possession of these teachings as in the assurance of what was promised. For we understood the excellence of prayer as it had just then been presented to us, but we saw that we had not yet fully grasped from the discussion the order and virtue by which to acquire and maintain it permanently.

Texual References

1. Cf. Lk 14:28.
2. Cf. Mt 7:24–25.
3. 1 Thes 5:17.
4. 1 Tm 2:8.
5. Lk 21:34.
6. Jl 1:5 LXX.
7. Is 29:9.
8. Dt 32:33 LXX.
9. Dt 32:32a LXX.
10. Dt 32:32b LXX.
11. 1 Tm 2:1.
12. Ps 116:14.
13. Eccl 5:3 LXX.
14. Eccl 5:4 LXX.
15. 1 Tm 2:2.
16. Cf. Lk 7:47.
17. Acts 1:1.
18. Mt 26:39a.
19. Ps 22:1.
20. Jn 17:4.
21. Jn 17:19.
22. Jn 17:24.
23. Lk 23:34.
24. Mt 11:25–26.
25. Jn 11:41–42.
26. Cf. Jn 17.
27. Phil 4:6.
28. Mt 6:9a.
29. Mt 6:9b.
30. Mt 6:9c.
31. Jn 7:18.
32. Cf. Acts 9:15.
33. Cf. Rom 9:3.
34. 2 Cor 13:9.
35. Mi 2:11.
36. Ex 32:31–32.
37. Mt 5:16.
38. Mt 25:34.

39. Mt 6:10a.
40. Mt 6:10b.
41. 1 Tm 2:4.
42. Is 46:10.
43. Mt 6:11.
44. Lk 11:3.
45 6. Mt 6:12.
46. Jas 2:13.
47. Mt 6:13a.
48. Sir 34:10.
49. Jas 1:12.
50. Cf. Gn 22:1–18.
51. Cf. Gn 39:7–13.
52. Mt 6:13b.
53. 1 Cor 10:13.
54. Cf. Lk 5:16.
55. Cf. Lk 22:44.
56. Ps 6:6.
57. Lam 2:18.
58. Ps 42:2–3.
59. Ps 120:5.
60. Ps 120:6.
61. Ps 143:2.
62. Cf. 1 Sm 15:35.
63. Cf. Lk 19:41.
64. Jer 8:23.
65. Ps 102:9.
66. Ps 102, title.
67. Mt 5:3.
68. Mk 11:24.
69. Mt 18:19.
70. Mt 17:20.
71. Lk 11:8.
72. Sir 29:12.
73. Is 58:6.
74. Is 58:9.
75. Ps 120:1.
76. Ex 22:20, 26.

77. Lk 11:9–10.
78. Mt 21:22, 17:20b.
79. Cf. Dn 10:2–4.
80. 1 Jn 5:14.
81. Rom 8:26.
82. 2 Cor 12:8–9.
83. Mt 26:39.
84. Mt 18:11, 20:28.
85. Jn 10:18.
86. Ps 40:8.
87. Jn 3:16.
88. Gal 1:4.
89. Rom 8:32.
90. Is 53:7.
91. Gal 1:2.
92. Jn 2:19.
93. Cf. Mt 6:6.
94. Mi 7:5.
95. Ps 51:17.
96. Ps 51:19.
97. Ps 50:23.
98. Ps 66:15.
99. Ps 141:2.

9.1 The promise referred to is made in *Inst.* 2.9.

On Castor, Leontius, and Helladius cf. the note at 1. praef. 1f.

9.3.1ff. The mental disposition for prayer is first discussed in patristic literature in Tertullian, *De orat.* 11f., and it receives a more extended treatment in Origen, *De orat.* 8.2ff., 31.2. According to Origen, the very preparation to pray is itself highly beneficial, inasmuch as it removes the person making the preparation from external concerns and places him in the presence of God.

9.3.3 On "foolish laughter" cf. the note at 4.20.3.

9.4 The comparison between the soul and a feather is made in Evagrius, *Gnost.* 2.6 (Patrologia Orientalis 28.62). Cf. Weber 29. On the natural upward movement of the soul cf. Gregory of Nyssa, *De vita Moysis* 2.224ff. and the sources noted in Gregory of Nyssa, *The Life of Moses*, trans. by Abraham J. Malherbe and Everett Ferguson (New York, 1978), 184–185, n. 304.

9.5.5 The solidus was a gold coin established by Constantine and current for several centuries; there were seventy-two to a pound of gold. Cf. Pauly-Wissowa, 2e Reihe, 3.1.920–926.

9.6.1 On a demon appearing as an Ethiopian cf. the note at 1.21.1.

9.6.4 On the burdensomeness of small and insignificant things cf. 1.6.1 and the relevant note.

9.6.5 To the likeness of the spiritual and angelic: *Ad spiritalem atque angelicam similitudinem.* The use of *similitudo,* which is translated rather weakly as "exemplaire" by Pichery, hearkens back to the terminology of "image" and "likeness" *(imago and similitudo)* in Gn 1:26. "Likeness" sometimes has dynamic connotations in patristic literature (cf. DS 6.819–820, 7.2.1406–1425), and so it appears here in Cassian, in the context of refashioning. The term is slightly ambiguous, however, inasmuch as it is not precisely the likeness of God that is being referred to. Cf. also 11.6.3 (with the relevant note), 11.7.3f., 11.9.2f., 11.14.

9.7.1 On wandering thoughts cf. the note at 1.5.4

9.11ff. Cassian differs here from Origen's view of the four kinds of prayer in *De orat.* 14.2. Supplication, for Origen, is made out of need, but it has no necessary reference to sin; prayer is a request for higher things, and it is accompanied by praise; intercession is made by one who has greater confidence (hence the Spirit is said to intercede rather than to pray: cf. ibid. 14.5); and thanksgiving is taken in its most obvious sense. Cassian's understanding of the second kind–namely, prayer–perhaps derives from what Origen says ibid. 3, where he identifies a certain type of prayer with making a vow. Cf. also Gregory of Nyssa, *De orat. dom.* 2. His understanding of supplication seems to be derived from Evagrius. Cf. Weber 74.

9.18.2ff. Our Father: Cassian speaks of our adoption as offspring of God, which is implied in his commentary. On adoption in this context cf. Origen, *De orat.* 22.2; Cyprian, *De orat. dom.* 9; Chromatius, *Praef. orat. dom.* (CCSL 9.446); Augustine, *De serm. Dom. in monte* 2.4.15f.; Theodore of Mopsuestia, *On the Lord's Prayer* (*Woodbrooke Studies* 6 [1933]: 6–7).

Who art in heaven: This phrase suggests to Cassian a disdain for earth and a desire for heaven on the part of the adopted offspring. Cf. Origen, *De orat.* 22.5; Gregory of Nyssa, *De orat. dom.* 2; Chrysostom, *Serm. in Matth.* 19.6; Theodore of Mopsuestia, *On the Lord's Prayer* (loc. cit. 8).

Hallowed be thy name: The first petition of the Lord's Prayer is presented here as having two meanings. It signifies that human energy should be spent for the sake of the divine glory. Cf. "Evagrius," in RAM 15 (1934): 88–89; Gregory of Nyssa, *De orat. dom.* 3; Chrysostom, *Serm. in Matth.* 19.7; Theodore of

Mopsuestia, *On the Lord's Prayer* (loc. cit. 8). But it also means that God is to be hallowed in us. Cf. Tertullian, *De orat.* 3; Cyprian, *De orat. dom.* 12; Cyril of Jerusalem, *Cat. myst.* 5.12; Gregory of Nyssa, *De orat. dom.* 3; Ambrose, *De sacr.* 5.4.21; Chromatius, *Praef. orat. dom.* (loc. cit.); Jerome, *Comm. in Matth.* 1, *ad loc.*

Thy kingdom come: According to Cassian, this petition also has two possible meanings. It alludes to an interior event, characterized primarily by the triumph of virtue. Cf. Origen, *De orat.* 25.1 and 3; Gregory of Nyssa, *De orat. dom.* 3; Theodore of Mopsuestia, *On the Lord's Prayer* (loc. cit. 8f.). And it has an eschatological intent. Cf. Tertullian, *De orat.* 5; Origen, *De orat.* 25.2; Cyprian *De orat. dom.* 13; Chrysostom, *Serm. in Matth.* 19.7.

Thy will be done on earth as it is in heaven: This petition as well may be understood in two ways. It recommends an angelic or heavenly life for Christians. Cf. Origen, *De orat.* 26.6; Cyril of Jerusalem, *Cat. myst.* 5.14; Gregory of Nyssa, *De orat. dom.* 4; Chrysostom, *Serm. in Matth.* 19.7; Jerome, *Comm. in Matth.* 1, ad loc.; Augustine, *Ep.* 130.11.21; Theodore of Mopsuestia, *On the Lord's Prayer* (loc. cit. 10f.). And it implies that God's will is universal salvation. Cf. Cyprian, *De orat. dom.* 18; Evagrius, loc. cit. 89; Chrysostom, *Serm. in Matth.* 19.7. In 9.34.9ff. Cassian suggests further ramifications of the clause when he distinguishes strongly between the will of God and that of the person praying.

Give us this day our daily bread: There are discussions of επιουσιος in Origen, *De orat.* 27.7ff.; Ambrose, *De sacr.* 5.4.24; Jerome, *Comm. in Matth.* 1, ad loc. On the controverted meaning of the term cf. Gerhard Kittel, *Theological Dictionary of the New Testament,* ed. and trans. by Geoffrey Bromiley (Grand Rapids, 1964), 2.590–599. "This day" may be understood as applying to each day. Cf. Cyril of Jerusalem, *Cat. myst.* 5.15. It can, on the other hand, signify the present age, as opposed to the age to come. Cf. Origen, *De orat.* 27.13;

Gregory of Nyssa, *De orat. dom.* 4; Augustine, *De serm. Dom. in monte* 2.7.27; idem, *Ep.* 130.11.21. Cassian is somewhat vague concerning the meaning of the petition as a whole, although it clearly has a spiritual rather than a material thrust for him. The usual spiritual meaning of "daily bread" was either the eucharist or Christ himself. These are mentioned together in Tertullian, *De orat.* 5; Augustine, *De serm. Dom. in monte* 2.7.25. Cassian's words in 9.21.2 about receiving this bread in the life to come make it highly unlikely that he sees it as the eucharist. Several passages in his works, however, indicate that Cassian was familiar with the practice of the daily reception of Holy Communion. Cf. 7.30.2 (and the relevant note), 14.8.5; *Inst.* 6.8.

And forgive us our trespasses as we forgive those who trespass against us: Cassian's interpretation of this clause is the classic one, and it agrees with that of the other commentators cited above.

And subject us not to the trial: These words mean not that we should not be tried but that we should not succumb to the trial. Cf. Origen, *De orat.* 29.9; Cyril of Jerusalem, *Cat. myst.* 5.17; Augustine, *De serm. Dom. in monte* 2; John Moschus, *Pratum spirituale* 209. Cf. also the note at 2.13.9f.

But deliver us from evil: This last petition has substantially the same meaning as the one preceding it.

9.19 Foul vices...good fragrance of the virtues: Cf. the notes at 1.1 and 2.11.5.

Desiring and hoping...his companions: The Latin verbs of these two sentences are in the singular and their subject is unnamed. Gibson understands the subject as "the heart," and Pichery as "l'âme."

9.24 Cassian's words about the nature of the petitions in the Lord's Prayer are very similar to Augustine's comments in *Ep.* 130.12.22f.

9.26.1 Cassian's comment here about the specifically musical aspect of singing, as opposed to the words that are being sung, bears comparison with Augustine, *Conf.* 10.33.49f.

9.26.2 Cantor: This term translates *psallens*. It is preferable to "singer" inasmuch as it takes into consideration the liturgical implications of the passage.

9.28ff. On the phenomenon of tears, frequently mentioned in monastic literature, cf. DS 9.287–303.

9.31 The Antony who appears here is certainly the subject of Athanasius's *V. S. Antonii.*

Antony's words about not understanding self or prayer in the act of praying have an ecstatic aspect to them that recalls 3.7.3. Cf. the relevant note. Cf. also Evagrius (Ps.-Origen), *Selecta in Ps.* 126 (PL 12.1644): "Just as we do not know that we are sleeping when we sleep, neither do we know that we are contemplating when we contemplate."

9.34.10 In the person of the man that he had assumed: *Ex persona hominis adsumpti.* The phrase is an ambiguous one. Cf. the note at 7.22.2.

9.34.13 Gazet in PL 49.815 suggests that the threefold inclination spoken of here is related to Christ's threefold request in Mt 26:39ff. to be released from drinking the cup of suffering, but he does not offer anything to support his contention. The origin and meaning of the practice remains obscure. Chadwick 50 is of the opinion that the phrase in question is a scribal interpolation because it so notably interrupts the flow of thought, although he believes that it was inserted very early. In any event, the phrase is hard to understand. One manuscript reads "who does not pray" instead of "who prays," which may make more sense.

9.35 The admonition to pray in the secret of one's room is interpreted both spiritually, as here, and literally. For other such spiritual interpretations cf. Origen, *De orat.* 20.2; Hilary, *Comm. in Matth.* 5.1; Ambrose, *De sacr.* 6.3.12ff.; Chrysostom, *Serm. in Matth.* 19.3f. The admonition is understood literally in Cyprian, *De orat. dom.* 4.

9.35.3 The enemies from whom one must keep one's prayers hidden are the demons, who cannot know a person's thoughts unless they are somehow expressed. Cf. 7.13ff. and the note at 7.15f.

9.36.1 Frequent but brief prayers are mentioned as typical of the Egyptian monks in Augustine, *Ep.* 130.10.20. Brief prayers are encouraged in Benedict, *Reg.* 20.3ff. Cf. Irénée Hausherr, *The Name of Jesus,* trans. by Charles Cummings (CS 44) (1978): 203–214.

The identification of prayer as the true spiritual sacrifice is very similarly drawn in Tertullian, *De orat.* 28.

TENTH CONFERENCE
THE SECOND CONFERENCE
OF ABBA ISAAC:
ON PRAYER

TRANSLATOR'S INTRODUCTION

The opening lines of the tenth conference indicate that the relatively long account of Egyptian monastic anthropomorphism, which occupies the second and third chapters of the conference, is directly related to understanding the teaching with which the succeeding chapters are concerned. The story of the monk Serapion's naive conception of God, concluding on a note of high pathos, serves as a warning against the intrusion of the material world into the world of the spirit. Serapion's mind, cluttered with the erroneous and deadly image of a God with human contours, stands in contrast to the mind that is bereft not only of any representation of God but even of "the memory of any word whatsoever [and] the likeness of any deed [and] a shape of any kind" (10.5.3). The mind that pursues this latter state is the one that can ascend to God in prayer. Cassian's doctrine of imageless prayer certainly has a precedent in Evagrius (*De orat.* 66ff.; cf. Weber 59). The account of Serapion's anthropomorphism is probably intended less to point out the folly of that crude understanding of God than to put the notion of imageless prayer in the highest relief possible. Cassian also treats of anthropomorphism in *Inst.* 8.2ff. (For the background to and the history and ramifications of the anthropomorphite controversy in Egypt at this time cf. Elizabeth A. Clark, *The Origenist Controversy: The Cultural Construction of an Early Christian Debate* [Princeton, 1992], 43–84.

On this problem in the early Church in general cf. DTC 1.2.1370–1372; DHGE 3.535–537).

Yet Abba Isaac, who utters the uncompromising words just cited from 10.5.3 and who is the chief speaker of this conference, as he had been of the previous one, seems not to exclude certain mental images. At least he declares in the sixth chapter that the purified mind may entertain the possibility of seeing Christ in his humility or his glory. His meaning appears to be, though, that such an image will not be an aid to prayer but rather its reward.

Pure prayer, in any event, is for the one who, on the model of Christ himself, has withdrawn from the turbulent throng. Such a person is eminently in a position to maintain an unbroken communion with God, so that everything he does *is* God. And this, which is the end of all perfection, is equivalent to transforming one's whole life into a single and continuous prayer.

With his soaring words on ceaseless prayer—encompassing "every love, every desire, every effort, every undertaking, every thought of ours, everything that we live, that we speak, that we breathe" (10.7.2)—Isaac would appear, as in the ninth conference, to have reached the apogee and the conclusion of his reflections fairly early on. But once again it is Germanus who raises a practical consideration, thus prolonging the discussion. How, namely, may the awareness of God be conceived in the mind and kept there? He suggests that there must be some preliminary steps to take before one can arrive at the lofty goal that has been proposed. In response to Germanus's appeal Isaac offers the repetitive saying of Psalm 70:1 ("O God, incline unto my aid; O Lord, make haste to help me") as the means to attain this end. He explains that this verse is appropriate in all circumstances. (It is worth noting that the situations Cassian chooses as examples of when to use the verse in question are expressed in the form of antitheses: gluttony—distaste for food; sleepiness—inability to sleep; sexual temptation—sexual tepidity; pride—humility; mental barrenness—mental ecstasy; fear of demons—courage in the face of demons; adversity—prosperity. Psalm 70:1 obviously serves as a kind of stabilizing element vis-à-vis the dangers posed by the two extremes of a given antithesis, and the practice of repeating it is in keeping with the discretion described in the second conference. Thus the end of the present series of ten conferences recapitulates, under the heading of prayer, the series' most important theme–discretion.) If this verse is said constantly, one will not only achieve the continual recollection of God but will also succeed in emptying one's mind of the whole panoply of intruding thoughts.

The repetition of Psalm 70:1 prepares the way for further spiritual progress. In particular, Isaac links it with a deepening and connatural knowledge of Scripture, such that when one prays the psalms, especially, they are appropriated completely as one's own. Germanus then asks, as his final question, how one may keep to this verse without distraction. Isaac responds by recommending vigils, meditation, and prayer as the three elements that will stabilize a wandering mind. But they in turn must be protected by the faithful observance of cenobitic practices.

Cassian is not the first to recommend that a particular phrase be repeated over and over again in prayer. (For some of the background to his recommendation cf. Irénée Hausherr, *The Name of Jesus,* trans. by Charles Cummings [CS 44] [1978]: 203–214.) Almost certainly inspired by Cassian, Benedict (*Reg.* 18.1) places Ps 70:1 at the beginning of the monastic office, where it remains to this day.

The conference concludes with what is probably an oblique glance back at Serapion, as Cassian declares that even simple and illiterate persons can attain to perfection of heart by meditating on the verse in question, thus keeping their minds fixed on God.

X. The Second Conference of Abba Isaac: On Prayer

Chapters

I. In the midst of these lofty institutes of the anchorites that have been recorded, albeit inexpertly, by the gift of God, the requirements of the narrative itself oblige us to insert and weave in something that might seem like adding a blemish to a beautiful body. Yet I do not doubt that even here no little instruction may be gained by some rather simple persons with respect to the image of Almighty God which is read about in Genesis, especially when the basis for such an important dogma is considered. For there can be no ignorance of this without great blasphemy and detriment to the Catholic faith.

II.1. In the region of Egypt the following custom is observed according to an ancient tradition: When the day of Epiphany has been celebrated–which the priests of that province understand to be both the day of the Lord's baptism and that of his birth according to the flesh, meaning that they celebrate the solemnity of each sacrament on this one feast day and not separately as in the Western provinces–a letter from the bishop of Alexandria is sent to all the churches of Egypt. In it both the beginning of the Lenten season and the day of Easter are designated not only for each town but also for all the monasteries.

2. In accordance with this custom, then, a very few days after the previously mentioned conference with Abba Isaac had taken place, there arrived the solemn letter of Theophilus, bishop of the aforesaid city. Along with the Easter announcement he also argued extensively against the foolish heresy of the anthropomorphites and demolished it at great length. Because of their errant naiveté, however, this was received with such great bitterness by nearly all the various sorts of monks who were living throughout the province of Egypt that the vast majority of the elders decided that the aforementioned bishop should be abominated by the entire body of the brothers as a person who had been tainted by a very serious heresy. For this seemed to go contrary to the words of Holy Scripture by denying that Almighty God had a human form, although Scripture very clearly testified to the fact that

Adam had been created in his image. 3. To such an extent was this letter repudiated by those who dwelt in the desert of Skete and who, in perfection and knowledge, surpassed all who lived in the monasteries of Egypt that, apart from Abba Paphnutius, the priest of our community, none of the other priests who presided over the other three churches in that desert would allow it to be read at all, either privately or publicly, in their communities.

III.1. Among those who were ensnared in this error was a man of long-standing strictness, fully accomplished in practical discipline, whose name was Serapion. His ignorance with regard to the aforesaid dogma was prejudicial to everyone who held the true faith for the very reason that he surpassed nearly all the monks both by his commendable life and by his advanced age. 2. When this man could not be brought to the path of correct faith by the numerous exhortations of the holy priest Paphnutius, because this opinion seemed to him to be new and never to have been taught by the ancients and been handed down by them, a certain deacon named Photinus, a man of very great knowledge, happened to come along from the region of Cappadocia with the desire of seeing the brothers who resided in that desert. The blessed Paphnutius welcomed him with great rejoicing, intending to confirm the faith contained in the letter of the aforesaid bishop. Placing him in the midst of all the brothers, he inquired as to how the Catholic churches throughout the East interpreted what is said in Genesis: "Let us make man according to our image and likeness."[1] 3. Then he explained that the image and likeness of God was treated by all the heads of the churches not according to the lowly sound of the letter but in a spiritual way, and he proved this with a long discourse and many examples from Scripture, showing that nothing of this sort could be the case with that immeasurable and incomprehensible and invisible majesty—that it could be circumscribed in a human form and likeness, that indeed a nature which was incorporeal and uncomposed and simple could be apprehended by the eye or seized by the mind. Thereupon the old man, moved by the many very powerful statements of that most learned man, was finally drawn to the faith of the Catholic tradition.

4. When he gave his unconditional assent in this regard,

Abba Paphnutius and the rest of us were filled with joy that the Lord had not permitted a man so old and accomplished in so many virtues, who had gone astray merely on account of ignorance and rustic naiveté, to wander from the path of right faith up to the end. We arose, and all of us together poured out prayers of thanksgiving to the Lord. But the old man got so confused in his mind during the prayers, when he realized that the anthropomorphic image of the Godhead which he had always pictured to himself while praying had been banished from his heart, that he suddenly broke into the bitterest tears and heavy sobbing and, throwing himself to the ground with a loud groan, cried out: "Woe is me, wretch that I am! 5. They have taken my God from me, and I have no one to lay hold of, nor do I know whom I should adore or address." Greatly shaken by this, and with the effects of the previous conference still fresh in our hearts, we returned to Abba Isaac and went up to him, speaking to him in these words:

IV.1. "Although the newness of what has just recently occurred—namely, the desire aroused by the previous conference, which had for its subject the state of prayer—was drawing us to leave everything else behind and hasten to your blessedness, yet this serious error of Abba Serapion (conceived as it is, we think, by the cunning of the wickedest demons) added to our longing. For we are struck with no little sense of despair when we think that by the flaw of this ignorance he has not only brought utterly to naught the great labors which he accomplished so laudably over the course of fifty years in this desert but has also run the risk of everlasting death. 2. Therefore we want to know, first of all, why such a serious error crept in upon him. Then we ask to be taught how we may attain to the level of prayer that you were discussing at great length and so magnificently. For that wonderful conference only had the effect of stirring up our dull minds, but it did not show us how we could accomplish it or grasp it."

V.1. ISAAC: "Small wonder that a very simple man and one who was never thoroughly instructed about the substance and nature of the Godhead could have been held back and deceived until now, and that, to be more truthful, he could have remained in his early error by reason of his simplicity and his habituation to ancient error. He was not, as you think, led on by some new delusion of the demons but by the ignorance that characterized the earliest pagans. For, as is the way of that error, according to which they used to worship demons in human form, now also they hold that the incomprehensible and ineffable majesty of the true Deity should be adored under the limitations of some image, and they do not believe that anything can be grasped and understood if no image of it is set up, which they can always approach with their petitions, circumscribe in their minds, and keep constantly before their eyes. 2. It is against the errors of these people that the text is well directed: 'They changed the glory of the incorruptible God into the likeness of an image of a corruptible man.'[2] And Jeremiah says: 'My people have changed their glory for an idol.'[3]

"Although it was from these beginnings that this error rooted itself in the thoughts of some people, as we have mentioned, nonetheless because of ignorance and naiveté it has also infected the minds of those who have never been polluted by pagan superstition and has been made plausible by the passage where it is said: 'Let us make man according to our image and likeness.' It was thus that, as a result of this detestable interpretation, the so-called anthropomorphite heresy arose, which insists with obstinate perversity that the immeasurable and simple substance of the Godhead possesses our contours and a human shape. 3. Yet, if someone has been instructed in Catholic teaching, he will detest this as pagan blasphemy and will thereby attain to that purest form of prayer which will not only mix no representation of the Godhead or bodily contour into its supplication (the mere mention of which is wicked) but will indeed permit itself neither the memory of any word whatsoever nor the likeness of any deed nor a shape of any kind.

VI.1. "For, as I said in the preceding conference, every mind is upbuilt and formed in its prayer according to the degree of its purity. To the extent that it withdraws from the contemplation of earthly and material things, its state of purity lets it progress and causes Jesus to be seen by the soul's inward gaze—either as still humble and in the flesh or as glorified and coming in the glory of his majesty. 2. For they will not be able to see Jesus coming in his royal power who, still as it were held fast in Jewish frailty, cannot say with the Apostle: 'If we have known Christ according to the flesh, yet now we no longer do.'[4] But they alone see his Godhead with purest eyes who, mounting from humble and earthly tasks and thoughts, go off with him to the lofty mountain of the desert which, free from the uproar of every earthly thought and disturbance, removed from every taint of vice, and exalted with the purest faith and with soaring virtue, reveals the glory of his face and the image of his brightness to those who deserve to look upon him with the clean gaze of the soul. 3. For the rest, Jesus is also seen by those who dwell in cities and towns and villages—that is, by those who have an active way of life and its obligations—but not with that brightness with which he appears to those who are able to climb with him the aforesaid mount of the virtues—namely, to Peter, James, and John.[5] For it was in the desert that he appeared to Moses and spoke to Elijah.[6]

4. "Wishing to confirm this and to leave us examples of perfect purity, our Lord, although he did not himself need the support of withdrawal or the benefit of the desert in order to attain it, since these are external things and he is the source of inviolable holiness (for the fullness of purity could not be soiled by any filth of the crowds, nor could he who cleanses and sanctifies all polluted things be contaminated by human contact), nonetheless went off alone to the mountain to pray.[7] Thus he taught us by the example of his withdrawal that, if we too wish to address God with purity and integrity of heart, we should likewise draw apart from all the turbulence and confusion of the crowd. Thus, while sojourning in this body, we shall in some fashion be able to prepare ourselves for the likeness as it were of that blessedness which is promised to the holy ones in the future, and God will be 'all in all'[8] for us.

VII.1. "For then will be brought to fruition in us that prayer of our Savior which he prayed to his Father on his disciples' behalf when he said: 'That the love with which you have loved me may be in them, and they in us.'[9] And again: 'That all may be one, as you Father in me and I in you, that they also may be one in us.'[10] Then that perfect love of God, by which 'he loved us first,'[11] will have also passed into our heart's disposition upon the fulfillment of this prayer of the Lord, which we believe can in no way be rendered void. 2. This will be the case when every love, every desire, every effort, every undertaking, every thought of ours, everything that we live, that we speak, that we breathe, will be God, and when that unity which the Father now has with the Son and which the Son has with the Father will be carried over into our understanding and our mind, so that, just as he loves us with a sincere and pure and indissoluble love, we too may be joined to him with a perpetual and inseparable love and so united with him that whatever we breathe, whatever we understand, whatever we speak, may be God. In him we shall attain, I say, to that end of which we spoke before, which the Lord longed to be fulfilled in us when he prayed: 'That all may be one as we are one, I in them and you in me, that they themselves may also be made perfect in unity.'[12] And again: 'Father, I wish that those whom you have given me may also be with me where I am.'[13]

3. "This, then, is the goal of the solitary, and this must be his whole intention—to deserve to possess the image of future blessedness in this body and as it were to begin to taste the pledge of that heavenly way of life and glory in this vessel. This, I say, is the end of all perfection—that the mind purged of every carnal desire may daily be elevated to spiritual things, until one's whole way of life and all the yearnings of one's heart become a single and continuous prayer."

VIII.1. GERMANUS: "Our amazement at the previous conference, because of which we hurried back here, is considerably increased. For we fall into greater despair the more our desire for perfect blessedness is inflamed by the stimulus of this teaching, since we do not know how we can strive for and acquire the discipline regarding something so sublime. Therefore, we beg you to listen patiently to our explanation of what we had begun to meditate on at great length when we were in our cell, since perhaps what we say will have to be drawn out, although we know that your blessedness is not usually offended by the follies of the weak. Indeed, these should be brought out into the open so that what is absurd in them may be corrected.

2. "Accordingly, we are of the opinion that the perfection of any art or discipline necessarily takes this course: Beginning with certain light rudiments, it starts off easily and gently so that, having been nursed as it were with rational milk and been brought along little by little, it may mature and thus slowly and gradually mount

from the depths to the heights. When it has, so to say, entered thereby upon more level principles and into the gates of the profession that is being approached, it will arrive directly and effortlessly at the inmost recesses and loftiest heights of perfection. 3. For how can a boy pronounce simple aggregations of syllables if he has not first carefully learned the letters of the alphabet? Or how can someone who is not yet capable of connecting short and simple phrases acquire the skill of reading rapidly? And in what way can someone who is poorly instructed in grammar acquire competence in rhetoric and philosophy? Therefore I do not doubt that there are also certain fundamental elements of instruction belonging to this most sublime discipline, which teaches us to cling constantly to God. Once these have been firmly fixed, then the loftiest heights of perfection may be set in place and raised up.

4. "We have some idea that the principles in question are these—first of all, that we should know by what sort of meditation God may be grasped and reflected upon; and then that we should be able to maintain this matter unchangeably, whatever it is, for we have no doubt that it is the summit of all perfection. Consequently, we want to have explained to us how this awareness of God may be conceived in the mind and perpetually maintained there. Thus, when we notice that we have slipped from it, we shall have this before our eyes, and when we come to our senses again we shall have the wherewithal to return there, and we shall be able to take it up again without any delays and difficult searching en route.

5. "For it happens that when we have strayed from spiritual theoria and then come back to ourselves, as if we were awakened from out of a deadly sleep, and seek that by which we may be able to revive the spiritual awareness that had disappeared, we are held back by the delay of searching. Before we find it we lose sight of our goal once again, and before any spiritual vision is brought forth, our heart's attentiveness, already conceived, vanishes. This confusion certainly besets us because we do not keep something special fixed before our eyes as a kind of formula to which the errant mind can be recalled after numerous detours and divagations and into which it can enter, as into a safe harbor, after repeated shipwrecks. 6. And so it happens that the mind is con-

stantly shackled by this ignorance and neediness and is ever wandering to and fro, tossed about by different things as if it were drunk. It does not even hold on firmly and perseveringly to anything spiritual that has come to it by chance rather than by its own effort, for, constantly moving from one thing to another, it is as unaware of their arrivals and their beginnings as it is of their endings and their departures."

IX.1. ISAAC: "Your search, so meticulous and careful, foreshadows that purity is near at hand. For a person will not be able even to ask about these things, never mind examine and discern them, unless a diligent and thorough effort of the mind and a vigilant concern have drawn him to scrutinize the depths of those questions, and unless the constant striving for and actual experience of a disciplined life have made him seek out the threshold of this purity and knock at its portals. 2. Therefore, since I see that you have not, I would say, been standing at the doors of that true prayer about which we have been speaking, but rather with the very hands of your experience are as it were touching its inmost recesses and already seizing some parts of it, I do not think that I shall have any trouble in bringing you—with the Lord as my guide—into its inner chambers as well, inasmuch as you are already as it were walking about in the vestibule, nor do I think that you will be hindered by any obstacle or difficulty from grasping the things that will be explained. 3. For the one who recognizes with prudence what ought to be investigated is very near to learning, and the one who begins to understand what he is unaware of is not far from knowledge. Therefore I do not fear to risk the reproach of betrayal or lightmindedness if I divulge the things that I kept back when I was speaking about the perfection of prayer in the previous discussion. I think that the power of those things would have been disclosed to you, who practice them eagerly, by the grace of God, even without the help of our words.

X.1. "Hence, in keeping with that teaching which you very wisely likened to the instruction of children (who are unable to learn the letters of the alphabet and who can neither recognize their outlines nor trace out their forms with a steady hand unless with unceasing attentiveness and daily imitation they make copies, using models and patterns impressed in wax), the formula for this spiritual theoria should also be transmitted to you. Always fixing your gaze very steadfastly upon it, you should learn to reflect on it uninterruptedly to your own benefit and become capable of mounting to still higher insights by using it and meditating on it.

2. "The formula for this discipline and prayer that you are seeking, then, shall be presented to you. Every monk who longs for the continual awareness of God should be in the habit of meditating on it ceaselessly in his heart, after having driven out every kind of thought, because he will be unable to hold fast to it in any other way than by being freed from all bodily cares and concerns. Just as this was handed down to us by a few of the oldest fathers who were left, so also we pass it on to none but the most exceptional, who truly desire it. This, then, is the devotional formula proposed to you as absolutely necessary for possessing the perpetual awareness of God: 'O God, incline unto my aid; O Lord, make haste to help me.'[14]

3. "Not without reason has this verse been selected from out of the whole body of Scripture. For it takes up all the emotions that can be applied to human nature and with great correctness and accuracy it adjusts itself to every condition and every attack. It contains an invocation of God in the face of any crisis, the humility of a devout confession, the watchfulness of concern and of constant fear, a consciousness of one's own frailty, the assurance of being heard, and confidence in a protection that is always present and at hand, 4. for whoever calls unceasingly on his protector is sure that he is always present. It contains a burning love and charity, an awareness of traps, and a fear of enemies. Seeing oneself surrounded by these day and night, one confesses that one cannot be set free without the help of one's defender. This verse is an unassailable wall, an impenetrable breastplate, and a very strong shield for all those who labor under the attack of demons. It does not permit those troubled by acedia and anxiety of mind or those depressed by sadness or different kinds of thoughts to despair of a saving remedy, showing that he whom it invokes is always looking upon our struggles and is not detached from his suppliants. 5. It warns those of us who are enjoying spiritual successes and are glad of heart that we must never be exalted or puffed up because of our good fortune, which it testifies cannot

be maintained without the protection of God, for it begs him to come to our aid not only at all times but also quickly.

"This verse, I say, is necessary and useful for each one of us in whatever condition we may live. For whoever desires to be helped always and in all things shows that he needs God as a helper not only in hard and sad affairs but also and equally as much in favorable and joyful ones, so that just as he may be snatched from the former he may abide in the latter, knowing that in neither instance can human frailty endure without his assistance.

6. "If I am seized by the passion of gluttony, look for food that is unheard-of in the desert, and feel myself, in the midst of the stark desert, drawn unwillingly to the desire for sumptuous repasts by the aromas of such things coming in upon me, then I should say: 'O God, incline unto my aid; O Lord, make haste to help me.' If I am tempted to anticipate the established hour for eating or am struggling with great sadness in my heart to maintain the proper and accepted degree of abstemiousness, then I should cry out with groaning: 'O God, incline unto my aid; O Lord, make haste to help me.' 7. If, because of an attack of the flesh, weakness of stomach puts me off when I am in need of more severe fasting, or if dry bowels and constipation alarm me, then, in order that my desire may be fulfilled or at least that the seething emotions of fleshly lust may be laid to rest without my resorting to more severe fasting, I should pray: 'O God, incline unto my aid; O Lord, make haste to help me.' If I go to eat at the proper hour but dread taking my meal and am repelled by every kind of food that nature demands, then I should cry out with lamentation: 'O God, incline unto my aid; O Lord, make haste to help me.'

8. "If a headache disturbs and hinders me when I want to attend to my reading for the sake of stability of heart, and if at the third hour sleep causes my face to fall upon the sacred page, and if I am compelled to prolong or to anticipate the established time of rest, and, finally, if the overwhelming pressure of sleep is forcing me to absent myself from the canonical singing of the psalms at the synaxis, then too I should cry out: 'O God, incline unto my aid; O Lord, make haste to help me.' If sleep is kept from my eyes and I see that for many nights I am worn out by a sleeplessness of diabolical origin, and if a quiet night's rest is completely cut off

from my eyes, then I should pray with sighs: 'O God, incline unto my aid; O Lord, make haste to help me.'

9. "If carnal titillation suddenly pricks me while I am still struggling against the vices, and if it tries, with its caressing pleasurableness, to get me to consent as I lie sleeping, then, lest an alien fire blaze up and burn the sweetly scented blossoms of chastity, I should cry: 'O God, incline unto my aid; O Lord, make haste to help me.' If I think that the impulses of wanton desire have died down and that the genital heat in my members has grown cool, then, in order that this virtue, once begotten, may indeed by the grace of God abide longer and remain in me, I should say intently: 'O God, incline unto my aid; O Lord, make haste to help me.'

10. "If I am disquieted by the urges of anger, avarice, or sadness, and if I am being pressed to cut off the gentleness that I have proposed to myself and that is dear to me, then, lest the disturbance of rage carry me off into a poisonous bitterness, let me cry out with loud groaning: 'O God, incline unto my aid; O Lord, make haste to help me.' If I am severely tried by transports of acedia, vainglory, or pride, and if my mind is subtly fancying that others are negligent or lukewarm, then, lest this wicked suggestion of the enemy overcome me, I should pray with an utterly contrite heart: 'O God, incline unto my aid; O Lord, make haste to help me.' 11. If with unceasing compunction of spirit I have laid aside the swelling of pride and have acquired the grace of humility and simplicity, then, lest 'the foot of pride come upon me' again 'and the hand of the sinner disturb me'[15] and I be pierced through more gravely by rejoicing at my victory, I should cry out with all my strength: 'O God, incline unto my aid; O Lord, make haste to help me.'

"If I am boiling over with a multitude of different distractions of soul and with a fickle heart and am unable to control my wandering thoughts, and if I cannot even pour out my prayer without interruption and without imagining foolish phantasies and recalling words and deeds, and if I feel myself constricted by such dry barrenness that I feel I am not begetting any spiritual thoughts at all, then, in order that I may deserve to be freed from this foulness of mind, from which I am unable to extricate myself with many groans and sighs, I will cry out in my need: 'O God, incline unto my aid; O Lord, make haste to help me.' 12. If, on the other hand, I feel that, thanks to the Holy Spirit's visitation, I have attained direction of soul, steadfastness of thought, and joy of heart, along with an unspeakable gladness and ecstasy of mind, and if with an abundance of spiritual thoughts I have, due to a sudden illumination from the Lord, perceived an overflow of very holy ideas which had been completely hidden from me before, then, in order that I might deserve to abide longer in these, I should frequently and anxiously cry: 'O God, incline unto my aid; O Lord, make haste to help me.'

13. "If I am encompassed by the nocturnal terrors of the demons and aroused by them, if I am disquieted by visions of unclean spirits, and if the very hope of salvation and life is being withdrawn from me by my agitated horror, then, taking refuge in the safe harbor of this verse, I will exclaim with all my strength: 'O God, incline unto my aid; O Lord, make haste to help me.' If, on the other hand, I have been refreshed by the Lord's consolation and encouraged by his presence and I feel myself surrounded as if by countless thousands of angels, such that I suddenly long for contact and dare to provoke conflict with those whom before I used to fear more than death and at whose touch–indeed, at whose very nearness–I used to experience horror of mind and body, then, in order that by the grace of God the vigor of this steadfastness might abide longer in me, I should cry out with all my strength: 'O God, incline unto my aid; O Lord, make haste to help me.'

14. "This verse should be poured out in unceasing prayer so that we may be delivered in adversity and preserved and not puffed up in prosperity. You should, I say, meditate constantly on this verse in your heart. You should not stop repeating it when you are doing any kind of work or performing some service or are on a journey. Meditate on it while sleeping and eating and attending to the least needs of nature. This heart's reflection, having become a saving formula for you, will not only preserve you unharmed from every attack of the demons but will also purge you of every vice and earthly taint, lead you to the theoria of invisible and heavenly realities, and raise you to that ineffably ardent prayer which is experienced by very few. 15. Let sleep overtake you as you meditate upon this verse until you are formed by hav-

ing used it ceaselessly and are in the habit of repeating it even while asleep. Let this be the first thing that comes to you when you awake, let it anticipate every other thought as you get up, let it send you to your knees as you arise from your bed, let it bring you from there to every work and activity, and let it accompany you at all times. You should meditate on this, according to the command of the Lawgiver, when 'sitting at home and going out on a journey,'[16] when sleeping and rising. You should write this on the threshold and doors of your mouth, you should place it on the walls of your house and in the recesses of your heart, so that when you prostrate yourself in prayer this may be your chant as you bow down, and when you rise from there and go about all the necessary affairs of life it may be your upraised and constant prayer.

XI.1. "Let the mind hold ceaselessly to this formula above all until it has been strengthened by constantly using and continually meditating upon it, and until it renounces and rejects the whole wealth and abundance of thoughts. Thus straitened by the poverty of this verse, it will very easily attain to that gospel beatitude which holds the first place among the other beatitudes. For, it says, 'Blessed are the poor in spirit, for theirs is the kingdom of heaven.'[17] And thus whoever is admirably poor with poverty of this sort will fulfill those prophetic words: 'The poor and the needy will praise the name of the Lord.'[18] 2. And in fact what poverty can be greater or holier than that of one who realizes that he has no protection and no strength and who seeks daily help from another's bounty, who understands that his life and property are sustained at each and every moment by divine assistance, and who rightly professes that he is the Lord's true beggar, daily crying out humbly to him: 'I am needy and poor; God helps me'?[19]

"Ascending thus to the manifold knowledge of God, thanks to his illumination, from then on he begins to be filled with more sublime and more sacred mysteries, according to the words of the prophet: 'The mountains are for stags, the rocks are a refuge for hedgehogs.'[20] 3. This very aptly fits the sense that we have spoken of, because whoever abides in simplicity and innocence is harmful and troublesome to no one. Content with his simplicity alone, he desires merely to defend himself from being the prey of those who lie in ambush for him. Having become as it were a spiritual hedgehog, he is protected by the constant shelter of that gospel rock which is the recollection of the Lord's passion, and, fortified by continual meditation on the aforesaid verse, he resists the snares of the attacking enemy. Concerning these spiritual hedgehogs it is also said in Proverbs: 'A feeble race are the hedgehogs, who have made their homes in the rocks.'[21]

4. "And what, indeed, is feebler than the Christian, what is weaker than the monk, who not only does not revenge himself for wrongs but who does not even permit a mild and silent annoyance to arise inwardly? Whoever makes progress in this state not only possesses the simplicity of innocence but is also armed with the virtue of discretion and has become the destroyer of poisonous serpents, having crushed Satan underfoot. With eager mind he conforms to the type of the rational stag, and he grazes on the prophetic and apostolic mountains—that is, on their highest and most sublime mysteries. Thriving on the pasturage that they always offer and taking into himself all the dispositions of the psalms, he will begin to repeat them and to treat them in his profound compunction of heart not as if they were composed by the prophet but as if they were his own utterances and his own prayer. Certainly he will consider that they are directed to his own person, and he will recognize that their words were not only achieved by and in the prophet in times past but that they are daily borne out and fulfilled in him.

5. "For divine Scripture is clearer and its inmost organs, so to speak, are revealed to us when our experience not only perceives but even anticipates its thought, and the meanings of the words are disclosed to us not by exegesis but by proof. When we have the same disposition in our heart with which each psalm was sung or written down, then we shall become like its author, grasping its significance beforehand rather than afterward. That is, we first take in the power of what is said, rather than the knowledge of it, recalling what has taken place or what does take place in us in daily assaults whenever we reflect on them. When we repeat them we call to mind what our negligence has begotten in us or our diligence has obtained for us or divine providence has bestowed upon us or the enemy's suggestion has deprived us of or slippery and subtle forgetfulness has taken away from us or

human weakness has brought upon us or heedless ignorance has concealed from us. 6. For we find all of these dispositions expressed in the psalms, so that we may see whatever occurs as in a very clear mirror and recognize it more effectively. Having been instructed in this way, with our dispositions for our teachers, we shall grasp this as something seen rather than heard, and from the inner disposition of the heart we shall bring forth not what has been committed to memory but what is inborn in the very nature of things. Thus we shall penetrate its meaning not through the written text but with experience leading the way. So it is that our mind will arrive at that incorruptible prayer to which, in the previous discussion, as far as the Lord deigned to grant it, the conference was ordered and directed. This is not only not laid hold of by the sight of some image, but it cannot even be grasped by any word or phrase. Rather, once the mind's attentiveness has been set ablaze, it is called forth in an unspeakable ecstasy of heart and with an insatiable gladness of spirit, and the mind, having transcended all feelings and visible matter, pours it out to God with unutterable groans and sighs."

XII. GERMANUS: "We think that you have set out not only the teaching of this spiritual discipline, which we were asking for, but also, quite clearly and lucidly, perfection itself. For what could be more perfect and what more sublime than to cling to the awareness of God by such a short meditation, to leave behind all the limits of the visible by reflecting on a single verse, and as it were to embrace the dispositions of every prayer in a brief phrase? Therefore we ask that the one thing which still remains be explained to us–namely, how we can hold fast to this verse which you have given us as a formula, so that just as by the grace of God we have been freed from the foolishness of worldly thoughts we may likewise firmly grasp spiritual ones.

XIII.1. "For when our mind has understood a passage from any psalm, imperceptibly it slips away, and thoughtlessly and stupidly it wanders off to another text of Scripture. And when it has begun to reflect on this passage within itself, the recollection of another text shuts out reflection on the previous material, although it had not yet been completely aired. From here, with the introduction of another reflection, it moves elsewhere, and thus the mind is constantly whirling from psalm to psalm, leaping from a gospel text to a reading from the Apostle, wandering from this to the prophesies and thence being carried away to certain spiritual histories, tossed about fickle and aimless through the whole body of Scripture. It is unable to reject or retain anything by its own doing, nor can it come to a conclusion about anything by fully judging or examining it, having become a mere toucher and taster of spiritual meanings and not a begettor and possessor of them.

2. "And so the mind, always aimlessly on the move, is distracted by different things even at the time of the synaxis, as if it were drunk, and it never accomplishes any function proficiently. For instance, when it is praying it is recalling a psalm or some reading. When it is chanting it is meditating on something else than what the text of the psalm itself contains. When it is doing a reading it is thinking of what it wished to do and what it wished it had done. Thus it receives and rejects nothing in a disciplined and proper manner, and it seems to react to chance incursions, not having the ability to hold fast to the things that please it nor to remain in them. 3. Consequently the first thing that we must know is how we can adequately carry out these spiritual functions and especially how we can cling tightly to this verse, which you have given us as a formula, so that the beginnings and endings of all our thoughts may not toss freely about but may be under our control."

XIV.1. ISAAC: "Although I think that enough was said on this topic when we were speaking some time ago about the state of prayer, nonetheless, since you ask that these same things be repeated to you, I shall talk briefly about steadfastness of heart. There are three things that stabilize a wandering mind–namely, vigils, meditation, and prayer. Being faithful and constantly attentive to them produces a solid firmness of soul. 2. Yet this cannot be laid hold of unless, by tireless constancy in work dedicated not to avarice but to the holy practices of the cenobium, we have first completely renounced every care and anxiety of the present life. Thus we shall be able to fulfill the apostolic command: 'Pray without ceasing.'[22] For whoever is in the habit of praying only at the hour when the knees are bent prays very little. But whoever is distracted by any sort of wandering of heart, even on bended knee, never prays. And therefore we have to be outside the hour of prayer what we want to be when we are praying. For the mind at the time of its prayer is necessarily formed by what went on previously, and when it is praying it is either raised to the heavens or brought low to the earth by the thoughts on which it was dwelling before it prayed."

3. Thus far did Abba Isaac speak to us, in our wonderment, about the character of prayer. His teaching on meditating on the aforesaid verse, which he gave as a format to be maintained by beginners, we greatly admired and firmly desired to practice, since we believed that it was short and easy. But we have experienced that it is considerably more difficult to observe than that practice of ours by which we used to run through the whole body of Scripture, meditating here and there, without being bound by any persevering application. It is clear, then, that no one is ever excluded from perfection of heart because of illiteracy, nor is simplicity an obstacle to attaining purity of heart and soul, which is very near to all, if only they would, by continually meditating on this verse, keep the mind's whole and entire attention fixed on God.

Textual References

1. Gn 1:26.
2. Rom 1:23.
3. Jer 2:11.
4. 2 Cor 5:16.
5. Cf. Mt 17:1.
6. Cf. Ex 3:2; 1 Kgs 19:9–18.
7. Cf. Mt 14:23.
8. 1 Cor 15:28.
9. Jn 17:26.
10. Jn 17:21.
11. 1 Jn 4:10.
12. Jn 17:22–23.
13. Jn 17:24.
14. Ps 70:1.
15. Ps 36:11.
16. Dt 6:7.
17. Mt 5:3.
18. Ps 74:21.
19. Ps 39:18 LXX.
20. Ps 104:18.
21. Prv 30:26 LXX.
22. 1 Thes 5:17.

10.1 On Cassian's disclaimer of writing ability here cf. the note at 1 praef. 3f.

10.2.1 The feast of the Epiphany, January 6, could accommodate several different commemorations, often simultaneously as in Egypt, at this period in both East and West. In addition to Christ's birth and baptism, different Western churches celebrated the adoration of the Magi and the wedding at Cana on this day. Hence Cassian is not precisely correct when he says that the Western provinces separated the observance of Christ's birth and his baptism; in some places they did in fact separate them but in others they did not. Cf. Bernard Botte, *Les origines de la Noël et de l'Epiphanie* (Louvain, 1932; repr. 1961).

The custom according to which the bishop of Alexandria sent what came to be called "festal letters" around to announce the date of Easter and to address other issues relative to that feast is first attested of Dionysius of Alexandria (d. c. 264) in Eusebius, *Hist. eccl.* 7.20ff. The practice was canonized at the Council of Nicea (325). Cf. Leo the Great, *Ep.* 121.1. It is Cassian who tells us that these letters were usually sent on the day of Epiphany.

10.2.2ff. Cuthbert Butler, *The Lausiac History of Palladius* 1 (Texts and Studies 6.1) (Cambridge, 1898), 208, cites this whole passage as clearly indicating Cassian's presence at the event involving Serapion. "It is impossible to read this impressive passage without the conviction that Cassian must have witnessed the scene he so graphically describes. By its circumstantiality, its realism, its pathos, its bare humanism as contrasted with anything like 'tendenziös' idealizing, it is stamped with the stamp of truth: it is separated by an impassible gulf from the fiction written in the fourth and fifth centuries."

10.2.2 Theophilus, bishop of Alexandria from 385 to 412, was a powerful and highly ambiguous figure. The event recorded here, when he lost the support of a vast number of monks, occurred in 399 and marks his turn from sympathy with Origen's thought (which strongly rejected anthropomorphism: cf. Origen, *De orat.* 23.3) to a virulent anti-Origenism. Thanks to this conversion of convenience he was able to regain his standing with the monks, but his volte-face brought with it several unhappy consequences. Cf. Socrates, *Hist. eccl.* 6.7ff.; Sozomen, *Hist. eccl.* 8.11ff.; Chadwick 28–29.

The anthropomorphism spoken of here was certainly the result of ignorance rather than of calculation, and it well deserves the adjective "foolish" (*inepta*). That heroic asceticism and sanctity could exist side by side with a pitiable want of instruction regarding the most essential elements of the faith is strikingly illustrated in *Apophthegmata patrum,* de abbate Daniele 7f. The question of monastic anti-intellectualism, which is closely related to that of monastic ignorance of the teachings of the faith, is discussed in André-Jean Festugière, *Les moines d'Orient 1: Culture ou sainteté: Introduction au monachisme oriental* (Paris, 1961).

The use of Gn 1:26, alluded to here and cited in 10.3.2, to substantiate the anthropomorphite position goes back at least to the end of the second century and Melito of Sardis, according to Origen, *Frag. in Gen.* ad 1:26 (PG 12.93).

10.2.3 On Paphnutius cf. the note at 2.5.5.

10.3.1 Of this Serapion nothing else is known.

10.3.2 Of this Photinus nothing else is known. Rousseau 190–191 sees him as representing the authority of the Church in confrontation with the delusion of the charismatic and aged (but unwise) Serapion.

Cappadocia is a region in present-day east-central Turkey.

The Catholic churches throughout the East: "The East" *(Oriens)* may perhaps mean the civil diocese of Oriens, comprising Syria and some neighboring regions, as distinguished from Egypt (where anthropomorphism was a problem), rather than the East in general. Cf. *Inst.* 2.8 (?), 3.3.1, 3.4.3, 3.9.1f., 4.19.1, 4.22.

10.6.1 The reference to the preceding conference is to 9.8.1f.

10.6.1ff. The idea that Christ appears to different people in different forms, according to their capacity to receive him, occurs in Origen, *C. Celsum* 2.64, 4.16, 6.77. All three of these references mention the Transfiguration, as does Cassian. Cf. Henri Crouzel, *Origène et la connaissance mystique* (Tournai, 1961), 470–474; and for the probable source of Origen's notion in Gnostic thought cf. Jacques E. Ménard, "Transfiguration et polymorphie chez Origène," in Jacques Fontaine and Charles Kannengiesser, eds., *Epektasis: Mélanges patristiques offerts au Cardinal Jean Daniélou* (Paris, 1972), 367–372. The notion is also found in monastic literature in Ps.-Macarius, *Hom. spir.* 4.12f.

10.6.4ff. These words (beginning with "God will be 'all in all' for us" and concluding with 10.7.2) recall the conclusion of 7.6.4.

10.7.2 The present passage bears a remarkable resemblance to Origen, *De princ.* 3.6.3.

10.8.2 Rational milk: Cf. Clement of Alexandria, *Paed.* 3, Hymnus 42–53 (SC 158.198–200).

10.8.4ff. On mental wandering here and in 10.13f. cf. the note at 1.5.4.

10.8.5 On the marine imagery here and in 10.10.13 cf. the note at 1 praef. 3f.

10.9.3 On the importance of realizing what one does not know cf. 4.9.1 and the relevant note.

On risking the reproach of betrayal for divulging spiritual teachings cf. the note at 1.1. The teaching on the repetition of Ps 70:1, as is observed in 10.10.2, is passed on "to none but the must exceptional, who truly desire it."

10.10.3 Body of Scripture: *Scripturarum...instrumento.* Cf. the note at 14.10.2.

10.10.5 On the necessity of divine protection, or grace, here and in 10.11.2 cf. the note at 2.1.3f.

10.10.8 Sacred page: A synonymous expression for Scripture as a whole. Cf. Jerome, *Ep.* 22.17.

10.10.9 The sweetly scented blossoms of chastity: Cf. 17.19.2 and the note at 1.1. On garden imagery with respect to virginity and chastity cf. Methodius of Olympus, *Symposium,* passim.

10.11.1 This formula above all: *Istam, istam...formulam.* The emphasis is worth noting.

10.11.2ff. Roughly the same meaning for both animals as is given here may be found in Jerome, *Tract. de Ps.* 103.18 (CCSL 78.185–186); Augustine, *Enarr. in Ps.* 103, serm. 3.18. In *Physiologus* 16 and 45 the hedgehog is a symbol of the devil, whereas the stag is a slayer of dragons, which symbolize demons. The hedgehog is also an image of wickedness in Gregory the Great, *Moralia in Iob* 33.29.53.

10.11.4ff. The idea that the person praying the psalms can experience them as his or her own (rather than as someone else's composition) is to be found in Athanasius, *Ep. ad Marcellinum* 11 (PG 27.24), which is in turn cited in Cassiodorus, *Expositio psalmorum*, praef. 16. The related idea that the psalms express all the emotions occurs in Ambrose, *Exp. in Ps.* 1.7ff.

10.14.2 After having spoken exclusively in terms of the solitary life (cf. 10.6.4 and 10.7.3), Cassian now makes mention of "the holy practices of the cenobium." Is this an inconsistency, or does he presuppose that the solitary has already lived a cenobitic life for a period of time?

The distinction between constant prayer and prayer at fixed hours first appears in Clement of Alexandria, *Strom.* 7.7.40. The first explicit reference to the notion that a person's whole life may be a carrying out of the apostolic exhortation to ceaseless prayer is made in Origen, *De orat.* 12.2.

THE SECOND PART OF THE CONFERENCES OF JOHN CASSIAN

◆

CONFERENCES XI–XVII

TRANSLATOR'S NOTE TO THE SECOND PART

This brief preface not only introduces the seven conferences of the second part but also alludes to the seven of the third part. At this point, then, at the latest, the scheme of a work comprising twenty-four conferences had at least been conceived, and it is possible that in fact all twenty-four had already been written before the preface was. The present seven, dedicated to two persons hitherto unmentioned, are meant to make up for "those things concerning perfection which were perhaps treated rather obscurely or passed over in our previous works" (2 praef. 2). By saying that the first ten conferences were insufficient for their audience and that he was obliged to add to them, Cassian suggests that he had not originally planned to produce more than ten. Yet this runs up against a statement which appears in *Inst.* 2.18 to the effect that some things would be explained in *The Conferences*–namely, certain rules for kneeling and fasting–which are not actually explained until 21.11ff. This in turn gives the impression that what Cassian says in the present preface is merely a literary device and that he had envisioned *The Conferences* more or less as they now stand even when he was composing the preceding work. The possibility that this may be the case, however, faces difficulties of its own. These difficulties are, first, the fact that no mention is made of subsequent conferences in the preface to the initial ten conferences; second, the comprehensiveness of the first set of ten conferences, covering the basics of monastic life and concluding on a very high note with prayer, as if this were all that Cassian had meant to say; third, the admission that the first part may have been obscure and incomplete; and, fourth, the fact that the first set of conferences purports to be from the second sojourn in Egypt, whereas the remaining fourteen are, rather awkwardly perhaps, placed during the first sojourn (cf. p. 8). Given these difficulties, we have a right to ask whether Cassian forgot to make good on his promise in *Inst.* 2.18 until he wrote the third part of *The Conferences,* or whether the promise was inserted subsequently, after *The Conferences* were completed. It must be admitted, in any event, that the problem is not easily soluble. If it is true, however, that the present seven conferences—and indeed all of the fourteen that remain—were not part of the original plan, then we may infer that they were seen by Cassian as supplementary to the first group of ten rather than as adding material of the same degree of importance as had previously been published. They are, in other words, somewhat in the nature of appendices, regardless of the significance of the themes they deal with.

CASSIAN'S PREFACE TO THE SECOND PART

1. Many of the holy persons who are instructed by your example, it is true, can hardly rival the degree of your perfection, by which you shine forth in this world with marvelous brightness like great lights. Yet you, O holy brothers Honoratus and Eucherius, are so on fire with the praise of those sublime men from whom we received the first institutes of the anchorite life that in fact one of you, who presides over a large cenobium of brothers, desires his community, which is taught by daily gazing upon your holy way of life, to be instructed as well in the precepts of these fathers. The other wished to come to Egypt in order to be edified by the bodily presence of those same men, thus quitting this province that is as it were sluggish with the numbness of a Gallic frost in order, like the most chaste turtledove, to fly over those lands upon which the sun of righteousness[1] looks so closely and which are overflowing with the ripe fruit of virtue. 2. The virtue of love could not help but wring this out of me, so that in considering the desire of the one and the effort of the other I would not escape the difficult danger of writing, as long as to the first there might be added authority among his sons and from the second there might be removed the obligation of a dangerous voyage. Accordingly, since neither *The Institutes of the Cenobia,* which we wrote down in twelve books as best we could and dedicated to the blessed memory of Bishop Castor, nor the ten conferences of the fathers living in the desert of Skete, which we put together haphazardly at the command of the holy Bishops Helladius and Leontius, were able to satisfy your ardent faith, now, in order that the purpose of our journey might also be known, I think that seven conferences of three fathers (whom we saw first and who lived in another desert) which come from the

same pen should be dedicated to you. Thereby those things concerning perfection which were perhaps treated rather obscurely or passed over in our previous works may be compensated for. 3. But if even these are unable to satisfy your holy and zealous longing, there are seven other conferences that are to be sent to the brothers who live on the Stoechadian Islands, and I think that they will meet your ardent desire.

Textual References

1. Cf. Mal 3:30.

2 praef. 1 Honoratus was a priest at the time of the writing of this preface, and hence Cassian refers to him as "brother." Cf. the note on Helladius at 1 praef. 2. He had founded the famous monastery at Lérins c. 410, to which his presiding "over a large cenobium of brothers" is an allusion. In either 426 or 427, after the preface was composed, Honoratus became bishop of Arles, and he died in 429. Hilary, his successor in Arles, produced the *Sermo de vita S. Honorati,* which is the chief source for his life.

Eucherius, a person of some prominence in the secular world, married and the father of two sons, nonetheless withdrew to Lérins c. 410. He was a staunch upholder of monastic and especially anchorite ideals, as is evident from two of his writings—*De laude heremi* and *De contemptu mundi et saecularis philosophiae.* In 434 he became bishop of Lyon, and he died between 450 and 455. Eucherius, also addressed as "brother," must have been a priest when Cassian wrote this preface. Cf. DHGE 15.1315–1317.

2 praef. 2 On Cassian's disclaimer of writing ability cf. the note at 1 praef. 3.

On Castor cf. the note at 1 praef. 1.

On Helladius cf. the note ibid.

On Leontius cf. the note ibid.

2 praef. 3 The three Stoechadian Islands, now known as the Îles d'Hyères, are southwest of Lérins.

ELEVENTH CONFERENCE THE FIRST CONFERENCE OF ABBA CHAEREMON: ON PERFECTION

Translator's Introduction

As has previously been mentioned (cf. p. 8), it is evident from the very opening lines of the eleventh conference that the second part of Cassian's work is, from the point of view of the events narrated, chronologically the first. Here Cassian speaks of his and Germanus's original yearning for Egypt and their initial setting out for the monastic sites of that land. Their earliest sojourn in that fabled country, however, introduces them not to the deep desert (to which in fact they never attain) but rather to a marshy area not very far from the Mediterranean, and this area is described in some detail at the beginning of the conference. First received by a local bishop, Archebius, the two friends are brought by him to Abba Chaeremon, and it is the teaching of this latter that is featured in the eleventh, twelfth, and thirteenth conferences. Cassian's Chaeremon may be the same as the one whose death is very briefly alluded to in Palladius (*Hist. laus.* 47.4), but there is no way of knowing for sure whether the two are identical. Indeed, referring to Chaeremon's role in the thirteenth conference, Prosper of Aquitaine (*C. collatorem* 2.1) speaks of him as an invention of Cassian; this opinion, though, is probably to be explained by Prosper's pique at Cassian's divergent view of grace in that conference.

After a few preliminary words have been exchanged between Chaeremon and his interlocutors, the old man settles down to speak of the three things that forestall vicious behavior—

namely, fear of punishment, hope of reward, and love. To these three checks on evil there correspond three virtues–faith, hope, and love. The virtues in question are all directed toward a good end, to be sure, but they are not all equally excellent, for they correspond in turn to three significantly different states: Fear belongs to the condition of a slave, hope to that of a hireling, and love to that of a son. Only those who have attained to the image and likeness of God may be numbered in the third state, which is the noblest. Much of Cassian's teaching here suggests a familiarity with Basil, *Reg. fus. tract.*, proem. (PG 31.896). Cf. Weber 78–79; Dorotheus of Gaza, *Instruc.* 4 (SC 92.220–248).

Persons who avoid vice out of fear are far less stable in virtue than are those who do so out of love. The former act as if coerced, and when the coercive element is no longer present they cease to be attracted to the good. The latter, however, are drawn to the good for its own sake. They will generally act virtuously, yet even they cannot avoid "those small sins that are committed by word, by thought, by ignorance, by forgetfulness, by necessity, by will, and by surprise" (11.9.6). Persons who are moved by love will have in particular the gift of compassion for others in their weakness, realizing that they themselves are utterly dependent on the divine mercy.

Germanus then raises the question of how acting out of fear or for the sake of a reward could be considered imperfect, inasmuch as Scripture seems to speak well of these motivations. Chaeremon's response is that Scripture takes into account the different levels and capabilities of people, but that less lofty motivations lead to less lofty rewards; love is always the best reason for doing anything, and its recompense is the highest. There exists, however, an attitude of loving fear, which may be defined as a reluctance to hurt a person whom one loves, and this is not to be confused with fear of punishment; it is identical with the "fear of the Lord" that appears in Isaiah 11:2 and that is referred to as a "treasure" and linked with wisdom and knowledge in Isaiah 33:6.

The conference concludes with Germanus's request that Chaeremon speak of chastity, since perfect love requires perfect chastity, and the old man promises to do so. The final chapter charmingly connects the image of the heavenly food of divine meditation with the bodily necessity of eating.

On the influence not only of Basil but also of Irenaeus on the present conference cf. M. Olphe-Galliard, "Vie contemplative et vie active d'après Cassien," RAM 16 (1935): 274–278; idem, "Les sources de la Conférence XI de Cassien," ibid. 289–298.

XI. The First Conference of Abba Chaeremon: On Perfection

Chapters

I. When we were living in a cenobium in Syria and, after an initial training in the faith, had gradually and increasingly begun to desire a greater grace of perfection, we at once decided to go to Egypt and, after having penetrated the remote desert of the Thebaid, to visit many of the holy ones, whose reputation had made them glorious everywhere, if not for the sake of imitating them, then at least for the sake of becoming acquainted with them. Therefore, having completed our voyage, we came to an Egyptian town named Thennesus. Its inhabitants are so surrounded by the sea and by salt swamps that, because there is no land, they have devoted themselves to commerce alone and get their wealth and substance from sea trade. Indeed, when they want to build houses there is no land, unless it is brought from far away in boats.

II.1. When we arrived there God looked with favor on our desires and arranged a meeting with the most blessed and excellent man Bishop Archebius, who had been snatched from a community of anchorites and given as bishop to the town of Panephysis. So strictly did he maintain his chosen orientation toward solitude his whole life through that he relaxed nothing of his former humble bearing, nor was he flattered by the honor that had accrued to him. He used to declare that he had been admitted to this office as one who was unfit for it, and he would complain that he had been expelled from the anchorite life as unworthy, because he had remained in it for thirty-seven years and was utterly unable to achieve the purity demanded by such a profession.

When he was in the aforesaid Thennesus, then, where the process of electing a bishop had brought him, he received us kindly and very hospitably, being aware of our desire to search out the holy fathers even in the furthest reaches of Egypt. 2. "Come," he said, "and visit for a while the elders who dwell not far from our monastery, whose old age and holiness, in bodies now bent over, shines so brightly in their faces that the mere sight of them is able to teach a great deal to those who gaze upon them.

From them you shall learn, not so much by words as by the very example of a holy life, what I regret that I have let slip and am unable to teach because I have already lost it. But I believe that my lack will be somewhat compensated for by my zeal if, as you look for that gospel pearl[1] which I myself do not have, I at least point out to you where you can more easily acquire it."

III.1. Taking his staff and satchel, then, as is the custom there with all monks who set out on a journey, he himself, acting as our guide, brought us to his city–that is, to Panephysis. Its lands, and indeed the greater part of the neighboring region, which was once very rich (since, as the report goes, everything was furnished for the royal table from it), had been overrun by the sea when it was shaken by a sudden earthquake. The villages were all destroyed, and the once fertile lands were so covered with salt marshes that one would think that what is sung spiritually in the psalm was a literal prophecy about that region: "He turned rivers into a desert and springs of water into thirsty ground, a fruitful land into a salty waste for the wickedness of those who dwell in it."[2] 2. In these places and in this way, then, the inundation made islands as it were of many towns located on high outcroppings that their inhabitants had fled from. These offer a longed-for retreat for holy solitaries, and on them lived three old men who were very old anchorites–namely, Chaeremon, Nesteros, and Joseph.

IV.1. The blessed Archebius wanted to take us first to Chaeremon, both because he was nearer to his monastery and because he was older than the other two. For since he was more than a hundred years old, active only in spirit, his back was so bent with age and with constant prayer that he went about with his hands down and touching the ground, as if he had returned to his earliest infancy. 2. As we gazed upon his remarkable face and bearing (for although all his members were already weak and dying he had never laid aside the severity of his past strictness) and humbly asked for a word and a teaching, declaring that our desire for spiritual instruction had been the only reason for our coming, he sighed deeply and said: "How can I give you any teaching when the feebleness of old age has slackened my former severity and likewise destroyed my confidence in speaking? 3. For how could I presume to teach what I myself do not do? Or should I instruct another person in what I know that I do less of or more lukewarmly? Hence I have allowed none of the younger men to live with me at this point in my life, lest someone else's strictness be slackened by my example. For the authority of the instructor will be valueless unless he has fastened it in his hearer's heart by what he has himself achieved."

V. Considerably surprised, we responded thus to these words: "It is true that the roughness of this place and the solitary life which even a robust young man could barely tolerate should be enough for all our instruction, and they do instruct us quite abundantly and strike us with compunction, even when you say nothing. Yet we ask that you break your silence a little and instead deign to fill us with those things by which we may be able to embrace—more by admiration than by imitation—the virtue that we see in you. For even if that lukewarmness of ours which has been revealed to you does not deserve to obtain what we are looking for, at least the effort of such a long journey should obtain it. It was for this that we hastened here from our initial training in the cenobium at Bethlehem, desiring your instruction and seeking our own progress."

VI.1. Then the blessed CHAEREMON said: "There are three things that restrain people from vice—namely, the fear of Gehenna or of present laws; or hope and desire for the kingdom of heaven; or a disposition for the good itself and a love of virtue. For we read that fear detests the contagion of evil: 'The fear of the Lord hates wickedness.'[3] Hope, too, prevents the incursion of any vice, for 'all who hope in him shall not fail.'[4] Love also dreads the destruction of sin, because 'love never fails.'[5] And again: 'Love covers a multitude of sins.'[6]

2. "Therefore the blessed Apostle includes the entire sum of salvation in the perfection of these three virtues, saying: 'Now there abide faith, hope, love, these three.'[7] For it is faith that, through dread of future judgment and punishment, makes us refrain from the contagion of vice; hope that, calling our minds away from things present, despises all the pleasures of the body and waits for heavenly rewards; love that, inflaming us mentally with the love of Christ and with the fruit of spiritual virtue, makes us utterly despise whatever is contrary to those things.

"Although these three seem to tend to one end, inasmuch as they move us to abstain from what is unlawful, nonetheless they differ from one another by considerable degrees of excellence. 3. For the first two belong properly to those who are tending toward perfection and have not yet acquired a love of virtue, but the third belongs particularly to God and to those who have received in themselves the image and likeness of God. For only he does what is good who is moved not by fear or by the hope of reward but by a disposition for the good alone. As Solomon says: 'The Lord has done all things for himself.'[8] For the sake of his own goodness he bestows an abundance of every good thing on the worthy and the unworthy, because he can neither be wearied by wrongdoing nor disturbed by human wickedness; he always abides perfectly good and by nature unchangeable.

VII.1. "If a person is tending to perfection, then, he will mount from that first degree of fear—which we have properly designated as servile and about which it is said: 'When you have done everything, say: We are useless slaves'[9]—to the higher level of hope, progressing by a degree. Here the comparison is not with a slave but with a hireling, because now the person looks forward to the payment of a wage and is as it were untroubled by the absolution of his sins and the fear of punishment and is conscious of his own good works. Although he seems to strive for a reward for what is pleasing, still he is unable to attain to the disposition of a son who trusts in the generosity of his father's indulgence and who has no doubt that everything which belongs to his father is his.

2. "To this even the prodigal, who had abandoned even the name of son along with his father's property, did not dare to aspire when he said: 'I am no longer worthy to be called your son.'[10] For after he was denied taking his fill of the husks of the swine—that is, of the filthy food of vice—he reflected upon himself and was struck with compunction by a salutary fear, and he began to loathe the uncleanness of the swine and to dread the pains of dire hunger. Having become like a slave, he thought now of a wage and desired the status of a hireling, saying: 'How many of my father's hirelings have an abundance of bread, and here I am perishing of hunger! I will return, therefore, to my father and I will say to him: Father, I have sinned against heaven and before

you. I am no longer worthy to be called your son. Make me as one of your hirelings.'[11] 3. But his father, hurrying to meet him, accepted these words of humble repentance with a love greater than that with which they had been spoken. Not content to grant him less, he passed over the other two degrees without delay and restored him to his former dignity of sonship.

"Hence we also, mounting by the indissoluble grace of love to the third degree of sons, who believe that everything which belongs to their father is theirs, must strive to be worthy of receiving the image and likeness of the heavenly Father and of being able to proclaim in imitation of the true Son: 'All that the Father has is mine.'[12] 4. The blessed Apostle also declares this about us when he says: 'All things are yours, whether Paul or Apollos or Cephas, or the world or life or death, or things present or things to come: all things are yours.'[13] The commands of the Savior call us to this likeness as well: 'Be perfect, as your heavenly Father is perfect.'[14] For a disposition for the good is sometimes cut off in people when the mind's vigor has been slackened by lukewarmness or joy or pleasure, which removes either the fear of Gehenna in the present or the desire for things to come. 5. There is in those things, to be sure, a certain measure of progress that draws us on, so that in beginning to resist vice through the fear of punishment or the hope of reward we may come to the degree of love. As it is said: 'There is no fear in love, but perfect love casts out fear. Since fear has punishment, the one who fears is not perfect in love. Therefore let us love, because God has first loved us.'[15]

6. "We shall, then, be unable to mount to that true perfection unless, just as he first loved us for no other reason than our salvation, we also love him for no other reason than sheer love of him. Hence we must strive to mount, in perfect ardor of mind, from this fear to hope and from hope to the love of God and the love of virtue itself, so that we may attain to a disposition for the good itself and, to the extent possible to human nature, hold firmly to what is good.

VIII.1. "There is a great difference between the person who puts out the fire of vice in himself through the fear of Gehenna or through the hope of a future reward and the person who dreads wickedness and impurity because he is disposed toward the divine love and who holds to the good solely out of a love of purity and a desire for chastity, not looking to a promised future reward but delighting in his awareness of the present good and doing everything out of a pleasure in virtue rather than with an eye toward punishment. 2. This condition can neither misuse an opportunity to sin when no human witnesses are present nor be defiled by hidden thoughts of pleasure since, inasmuch as it holds inwardly to a disposition for the virtuous itself, it not only does not accept in its heart whatever is contrary to this but even looks upon it with the greatest abhorrence.

"For it is one thing for a person who is delighted by a present good to hate the contagions of vice and of the flesh and another thing for him to refrain from unlawful desires through an awareness of future reward, one thing for him to fear present loss and another thing for him to dread the punishment to come. Finally, it is far greater not to wish to depart from the good because of goodness itself than not to consent to evil because of fear of evil. 3. For in the former the good is willed, whereas in the latter it is as it were coerced and violently forced out of someone who is unwilling, whether by fear of punishment or by desire for rewards. For the person who resists the blandishments of vice by reason of fear will return to what he loves when the obstacle of fear has been removed, and consequently he will not attain to constant steadfastness in good; on the contrary, he will never be free of attack, because he will not possess the firm and unceasing peace of purity. 4. For where battles rage there cannot but be the danger of wounds as well. Whoever is placed in conflict must occasionally be grazed by the enemy's sword even if he is a warrior and, fighting bravely, frequently inflicts deadly wounds on his adversaries. But the person who has overcome the onslaught of vice, who now enjoys a secure peace and has passed to a disposition for the virtuous itself will hold constantly to that state of goodness which now possesses him entirely, because he believes that nothing is more damaging than damage done to inner chastity. 5. For he to whom the wicked transgression of virtue and the poisonous contagion of vice itself are a serious punishment does not consider anything dearer and more precious than present purity. In his case, I say, awareness of the presence of another human being does not add anything to his goodness nor does solitude detract from it. Rather, always and everywhere he bears about with himself as his witness the consciousness not only of his deeds but also of his thoughts, and he strives above all to please it, which he knows that he cannot cheat or deceive or escape from.

IX.1. "If, by God's help and not relying on his own laborious effort, anyone deserves to possess this state, he will begin to pass from the condition of a slave, in which there is fear, and from a hireling's hopeful desire, in which it is not so much the goodness of the giver but rather the payment of a wage that is looked for, to adopted sonship, where there is no longer any fear or greed but rather that love which never fails and always abides. Concerning this fear and love the Lord reproves some and shows them what is appropriate to each person: 'A son honors his father and a slave fears his master. But if I am a father, where is my honor? And if I am a master, where is my fear?'[16] 2. For a slave must fear, because 'if he knows the will of his master and does what is worthy of stripes, he shall be badly beaten.'[17]

"And so, whoever attains by way of this love to the image and likeness of God will take delight in the good because of pleasure in the good itself. Since he likewise possesses a similar disposition of patience and mildness he will no longer be angered by the vices of sinners. On the contrary, with sorrow and compassion he will beg pardon for their frailty. Remembering that he himself was for a long time assailed by the urges of similar passions until he was saved by the Lord's pity, he will realize that, since he was not freed from assaults of the flesh by his own effort but was saved by the protection of God, it is not wrath but mercy which must be shown to those in error, and he will repeat this verse to God with utter tranquillity of heart: 'You have broken my chains. To you will I offer a sacrifice of praise.'[18] And: 'Unless the Lord had helped me, my soul would soon have dwelt in hell.'[19] 3. Possessing this humility of mind, he will also be able to fulfill the gospel command of perfection: 'Love your enemies, do good to those who hate you, and pray for those who persecute and calumniate you.'[20]

"Thus we shall deserve to attain to the concomitant reward, by which we shall not only manifest the image and likeness of God but shall also be called his sons: 'So that you might be,' he says, 'sons of your Father who is in heaven, who makes his sun rise on the good and the bad and who rains on the just and the unjust.'[21] The blessed John knew that he had acquired this disposition and he said: 'That we might have confidence on the day of judgment, because as he is so are we also in this world.'[22] 4. For how can a weak and frail human nature be like him unless, in peaceful imitation of God, it always bestows the love of its own heart on the good and the bad, the just and the unjust? Thus it does good out of a disposition toward goodness itself, attaining to that true adoption of the sons of God about which the same blessed apostle declares: 'No one who has been born of God commits sin, because his seed is in him, and he cannot sin, for he has been born of God.'[23] And again: 'We know that no one who has been born of God sins, but his having been begotten by God preserves him, and the evil one does not touch him.'[24]

5. "This must be understood to refer not to every kind of sin but only to capital crimes. In another place the aforesaid apostle declares that whoever does not wish to avoid these or cleanse himself of them must not even be prayed for: 'Whoever knows that his brother is committing a sin that is not unto death, let him ask, and he will give life to those not sinning unto death. There is a sin unto death. I do not say that you should ask for it.'[25] But with regard to those which he declares are not unto death, from which even persons who faithfully serve Christ cannot be immune, however carefully they may conduct themselves, it is said: 'If we say that we have no sin, we deceive ourselves and there is no truth in us.'[26] And again: 'If we say that we have no sin, we make him a liar and his word is not in us.'[27] 6. For it is impossible for any of the holy ones not to fall into those small sins that are committed by word, by thought, by ignorance, by forgetfulness, by necessity, by will, and by surprise. Although these may be different than the sin which is said to be unto death, nonetheless they cannot be without guilt and blame.

X.1. "Consequently, when someone has attained to a disposition of goodness and to the imitation of God that we have spoken about, he has made his own the Lord's compassion and will also pray for his persecutors in the same way, saying: 'Father, forgive them, for they do not know what they are doing.'[28] But it is a clear indication that the soul is not yet cleansed of the dregs of vice when it does not mourn over others' sins out of a disposition of mercy but is inflexibly judgmental. For how will someone be able to obtain perfection of heart when he does not have what, according to the Apostle, can carry out the law completely, when he said: 'Bear one another's burdens, and so you will fulfill the law of Christ'?[29] He does not possess the virtue of love, which 'is not angry, not boastful, does not think evil,' which 'suffers all things, endures all things.'[30] For 'the one who is righteous has mercy on the souls of his beasts, but the heart of the wicked is without mercy.'[31] Therefore a monk is most certain to fall into the same vices that he condemns in others with a pitiless and cruel severity. For 'an unyielding king brings evil upon himself,'[32] and 'one who stops his ears from hearing the weak will himself cry out, and there will be no one to answer him.'"[33]

XI. GERMANUS: "You have indeed spoken powerfully and splendidly about the perfect love of God. But it disturbs us that, although you mentioned this with such praise, you said that the fear of God and the hope of an eternal reward are imperfect, for it seems that the prophet has a much different opinion of them when he says: 'Fear the Lord, all his holy ones, for nothing is lacking to those who fear him.'[34] And again, in carrying out the righteous deeds of God, he admits that he has done them with a view to being rewarded when he says: 'I have inclined my heart to do your righteous deeds forever, for the reward.'[35] And the Apostle says: 'By faith Moses, when he was grown up, denied that he was the son of Pharaoh's daughter. He chose to be afflicted with the people of God rather than to have the pleasure of sin for a short while, and he considered the reproach of Christ greater riches than the treasures of the Egyptians, for he looked to the reward.'[36] Why, then, must these be thought to be imperfect when the blessed David boasts that he has done the righteous deeds of the Lord with the idea of being rewarded, and the Lawgiver is said to have spurned the adoption of royal dignity and to have preferred the harshest affliction to the treasures of the Egyptians because he foresaw future rewards?"

XII.1. CHAEREMON: "Divine Scripture arouses the freedom of our will to different degrees of perfection in keeping with the condition and measure of each mind. For an identical crown of perfection could not be offered to everyone because not everyone has the same virtue or will or ardor. Therefore the divine word has in some way established different ranks and different measures of perfection itself.

2. "The various gospel beatitudes clearly demonstrate that this is so. For although they are called blessed who possess the kingdom of heaven, and blessed who will possess the earth, and blessed who will receive consolation, and blessed who will be satisfied, nonetheless we believe that there is a great difference between inhabiting the kingdom of heaven and possessing the earth, whatever that may be, and between receiving consolation and being filled and satisfied with righteousness, and there is a great distinction between those who will receive mercy and those who will deserve to enjoy the most glorious vision of God.[37] 3. For 'there is one glory of the sun, and another glory of the moon, and another glory of the stars, for star differs from star in glory. So also is the resurrection of the dead.'[38]

"It is true, therefore, that divine Scripture praises those who fear God in this way and says: 'Blessed are all who fear the Lord,'[39] thus promising them complete blessedness. Yet it also says: 'There is no fear in love, but perfect love casts out fear. Since fear has punishment, the one who fears is not perfect in love.'[40] 4. And again, it is true that to serve God is glorious and that it is said: 'Serve the Lord in fear.'[41] And: 'It is a great thing for you to be called my servant.'[42] And: 'Blessed is that servant whom, when his master comes, he finds so doing.'[43] Yet it is said to the apostles: 'I no longer call you servants, because a servant does not know what his master is doing. But I call you friends, because I have made known to you everything that I have heard from my Father.'[44] And again: 'You are my friends if you do what I command you.'[45]

5. "You see, then, that there are different degrees of perfection and that we are challenged by the Lord to go from the heights to still higher places in such a way that the one who is blessed and perfect in the fear of God and who proceeds, as it is written, 'from strength to strength'[46] and from one perfection to another—that is, who mounts with eager mind from fear to hope—is invited again to a more blessed state, which is love, and the one

who was 'a faithful and prudent servant'[47] passes over to the intimacy of friendship and to adopted sonship.

6. "It is in this sense, then, that our words should be understood—not that we declare that an awareness of everlasting punishment or of the blessed reward which is promised to the holy ones is of no importance. These things are helpful and introduce those who reflect on them to the beginnings of blessedness. But love, in which there is a fuller confidence and already an enduring joy, takes them from a servile fear and a hireling's hope, brings them to the love of God and to adopted sonship, and, from being perfect, makes them somehow more perfect. For, as the Savior says, 'there are many dwelling places in my Father's house.'[48] And although the stars are all seen to be in the sky, nonetheless between the brightness of the sun and the moon and between that of the morning star and the other stars there is a great distinction.

7. "Therefore the blessed Apostle prefers the way of love not only to fear and hope but even to all the charisms which are considered to be great and marvelous, and he shows that it is far more excellent than anything else. For when he had completed the entire list of the spiritual charisms of the virtues and wanted to describe aspects of it, he began thus: 'I will show you a still more excellent way. If I should speak with the tongue of men and of angels, and if I had prophecy and knew all mysteries and all knowledge, and if I had all faith such that I could move mountains, and if I distributed all my wealth as food for the poor and gave my body to burn, but did not have love, it would profit me nothing.'[49] 8. You see, then, that nothing is more precious, nothing more perfect, nothing more sublime, and—as I might say—nothing more enduring than love. For, 'whether there are prophecies, they shall come to naught; or tongues, they shall cease; or knowledge, it shall be destroyed,' but 'love shall never disappear.' Without it not only the most excellent kinds of charisms but even the glory of martyrdom itself comes to naught.

XIII.1. "Whoever, therefore, has been established in the perfection of this love will certainly mount by a degree of excellence to the more sublime fear of love, which is begotten not by dread of punishment or by desire for rewards but by the greatness of one's love. It is with this anxious disposition that a son fears his very indulgent father or a brother his brother or a friend his friend or a wife her husband, inasmuch as they are afraid not of blows or of insults but of the slightest offense against love. And so they are always preoccupied with a concerned devotion not only in every action but also in every word, lest the ardor of the other's love for them become to the slightest extent lukewarm.

2. "One of the prophets neatly expressed the grandeur of this fear when he said: 'Wisdom and knowledge are the riches of salvation. The fear of the Lord is his treasure.'[50] He could not express more clearly the dignity and the worth of this fear than by saying that the riches of our salvation, which consist in true wisdom and in the knowledge of God, cannot be preserved except by the fear of the Lord. As the psalmist says, it is not sinners but holy persons who are urged to this fear by the prophetic words: 'Fear the Lord, all his holy ones, for nothing is lacking to those who fear him.'[51] 3. For it is certain that nothing is lacking to the perfection of one who fears God with this fear. The apostle John says clearly with respect to the fear of punishment: 'Whoever fears is not perfect in love, since fear has punishment.'[52]

"There is a great distinction, then, between the fear that lacks for nothing, which is the treasure of wisdom and knowledge, and the one that is imperfect, which is called 'the beginning of wisdom.'[53] This latter has punishment in itself, and it is cast out from the hearts of the perfect upon the advent of the fullness of love. For 'there is no fear in love, but perfect love casts out fear.'[54] 4. And in fact if the beginning of wisdom consists in fear, what but the love of Christ will be its perfection, which contains in itself the fear of perfect love and which is no longer called the beginning but rather the treasure of wisdom and knowledge?

"Therefore there are two degrees of fear. The one is for beginners—that is, for those who are still under the yoke and under servile dread. In regard to this it is said: 'The slave shall fear his master.'[55] And in the Gospel: 'I no longer call you servants, because a servant does not know what his master is doing.'[56] 5. And consequently he says: 'The slave does not remain in the house forever; the son remains forever.'[57] For he is instructing us to pass from the fear of punishment to the fullest freedom of love and to the confidence of the friends and sons of God. And the blessed Apostle, who had long since passed beyond the degree of servile fear, thanks to the power of the Lord's love, disdains lower things and professes that he has been endowed with greater goods. 'For,' he says, 'God has not given us a spirit of fear but of power and love and self-control.'[58] 6. Those who burned with perfect love of the heavenly Father and whom, from slaves, the divine adoption had already made sons he also exhorts in these words: 'You have not received a spirit of slavery again in fear, but you have received a spirit of adoption, in which we cry out: Abba, Father.'[59]

"When the prophet was describing the sevenfold spirit that without a doubt came down upon the Lord in human form, according to the plan of the incarnation, he said concerning this fear: 'The spirit of the Lord shall rest upon him—a spirit of wisdom and understanding, a spirit of counsel and fortitude, a spirit of knowledge and piety.'[60] Lastly, as if referring to something special, he says: 'And a spirit of fear of the Lord shall fill him.'[61] 7. It should first be carefully noted that he did not say: And a spirit of fear of the Lord shall rest upon him, as he did when speaking of those others, but rather: 'A spirit of fear of the Lord shall fill him.' For so very overwhelming is it that it lays hold not of part of the mind but of all of it in the person whom it has once possessed by its power. Not without reason. Since it clings to that love which 'never fails,' it not only fills but also possesses everlastingly and inseparably the person whom it has seized. It is not weakened by any of the delights of temporal joy or pleasure, which is sometimes the case with that fear which is cast out.

8. "This, then, is the perfect fear with which the Lord, in human form, who came not only to redeem the human race but also to offer a way of perfection and an example of virtue, is said to have been filled. For the true Son of God, 'who did not sin, nor was deceit found in his mouth,'[62] was unable to have a servile fear of punishment."

XIV. GERMANUS: "Since you have finished speaking about perfect love, we also want to ask something more freely about the end of chastity. For we have no doubt that the splendid dignity of love—by which, as has been discussed up to this point, one may mount to the image and likeness of God—cannot at all exist without perfect chastity. But we want to know whether it can be obtained in a lasting way in order that wanton titillation may never assail the integrity of our heart and in order that we may sojourn far from this carnal passion while living in the flesh, so as never to burn with seething emotions and impulses."

XV. CHAEREMON: "Continually to learn and to teach the disposition by which we may cling to the Lord is a mark of the highest blessedness and of singular worth. Thus, in the opinion of the psalmist, meditating on it should consume all the days and nights of our life,[63] and by always chewing on this heavenly food it should sustain our mind, which insatiably hungers and thirsts for righteousness.

"But, in keeping with the most gracious providence of our Savior, care should also be had for the beast of burden which is our body, lest it faint on the way,[64] for 'the spirit is willing, but the flesh is weak.'[65] This should be attended to right now with a little something to eat, so that after eating the attention of our mind may be given over to what you desire to investigate more carefully."

TEXUAL REFERENCES

1. Cf. Mt 13:45–46.
2. Ps 107:33–34.
3. Prv 8:13.
4. Ps 34:22.
5. 1 Cor 13:8.
6. 1 Pt 4:8.
7. 1 Cor 13:13.
8. Prv 16:4.
9. Lk 17:10.
10. Lk 15:19a.
11. Lk 15:17–19.
12. Jn 16:15.
13. 1 Cor 3:22.
14. Mt 5:48.
15. 1 Jn 4:18–19.
16. Mal 1:6 LXX.
17. Lk 12:47.
18. Ps 116:16–17.
19. Ps 94:17.
20. Mt 5:44.
21. Mt 5:45.
22. 1 Jn 4:17.
23. 1 Jn 3:9.
24. 1 Jn 5:18.
25. 1 Jn 5:16.
26. 1 Jn 1:8.
27. 1 Jn 1:10.
28. Lk 23:34.
29. Gal 6:2.
30. 1 Cor 13:4–7.
31. Prv 12:10 LXX.
32. Prv 13:17 LXX.
33. Prv 21:13 LXX.
34. Ps 34:9.
35. Ps 119:112.
36. Heb 11:24–26.
37. Cf. Mt 5:3–8.
38. 1 Cor 15:41–42.

39. Ps 128:1.
40. 1 Jn 4:18.
41. Ps 2:11.
42. Is 49:6 LXX.
43. Mt 24:46.
44. Jn 15:15.
45. Jn 15:14.
46. Ps 84:7.
47. Mt 24:45.
48. Jn 14:2.
49. 1 Cor 12:31–13:3.
50. Is 33:6.
51. Ps 33:10.
52. 1 Jn 4:18.
53. Ps 111:10.
54. 1 Jn 4:18.
55. Mal 1:6a LXX.
56. Jn 15:15a.
57. Jn 8:35.
58. 2 Tm 1:7.
59. Rom 8:15.
60. Is 11:2a.
61. Is 11:2b.
62. 1 Pt 2:22.
63. Cf. Ps 1:2.
64. Cf. Mt 15:32.
65. Mt 26:41.

11.1 Syria is understood as including the smaller region of Palestine. The cenobium in question was located in Bethlehem, as we learn in 11.5.

Thennesus was a town in Augustamnica Prima in the ancient diocese of Egypt, and it was located on the southern shore of Lake Thennesus. The site is presently known as Tell Tennis.

11.2.1 On Archebius cf. the note at 7.26.3. It is significant that he became a bishop against his will. Involuntary ordinations were not uncommon in antiquity. Cf. Paulinus, *V. Ambrosii* 3.6ff.; Gregory Nazianzen, *Or.* 2; Epiphanius, ap. Jerome, *Ep.* 51.1; Possidius, *V. Augustini* 4; Theodoret of Cyrus, *Hist. relig.* 13.4; *V. Danielis Styl.* (ed. by Delehaye, Brussels, 1923, 38–41). Cf. also the note at 1.20.5. Archebius's maintenance of monastic customs after his episcopal ordination is paralleled in Sulpicius Severus, *V. S. Martini* 10; Cyril of Scythopolis, *V. Ioann. Hesych.* 3 (ed. by Schwartz, Leipzig, 1939, 202).

On Panephysis cf. 7.26.2 and the relevant note.

11.2.2 On the radiant faces of the elders here, and on Chaeremon's in particular in 11.4.2, cf. the note at 7.1.

That a teacher's authority depends on his deeds at least as much as on his words is a theme that recurs in 11.4.3, 14.9.5ff., 23.2.2, 24.26.19; *Inst.* 12.13, 12.15.1. It is a commonplace in ancient literature, pagan and Jewish as well as Christian. For a collection of pertinent texts cf. André-Jean Festugière, "Lieux communs littéraires et thèmes de folk-lore dans l'hagiographie primitive," *Wiener Studien* 73 (1960): 140–142.

11.3.2 Chaeremon, Nesteros, and Joseph are the elders whose conferences occupy the second part. Each is discussed in his own place.

11.4.1 On the use of the term "monastery" for the dwelling of a single monk, as here, cf. 18.10 and the relevant note.

Chaeremon, at more than a hundred years of age, is the oldest of the abbas whom Cassian and Germanus encounter. Only Paphnutius, of whom it is said in 3.1.1

that he was more than ninety years old, approaches him, although many of the other abbas are characterized as old too, but of indeterminate age. Other centenarians in the desert appear in Athanasius, *V. S. Antonii* 89; Jerome, *V. S. Pauli* 7; Palladius, *Hist. laus.* 6.7; *Hist. monach. in Aegypto* 20.13; Besa, *The Life of Shenoute* 174f. (trans. by Bell, CS 73, 1983, 89); John Moschus, *Pratum spirituale* 95. On old age as symbolic of virtue cf. Philo, *De sobrietate* 4ff.; Origen, *Hom. in Gen.* 3.3; idem, *Hom. in Iesu Nave* 16.1; Evagrius, *Ep.* 49 (ed. by Frankenberg, Berlin, 1912, 598).

11.5 According to *Inst.* 4.31, Cassian's and Germanus's cenobium at Bethlehem was located not far from the cave where Christ was born. Cf. also 17.5.2. *Inst.* 3.4, as here, simply alludes to the Bethlehem site of the monastery.

11.6.3 In patristic thought "image" sometimes has static and "likeness" sometimes has dynamic connotations, and sometimes, on the other hand, the terms are used interchangeably. Cf. Walter J. Burghardt, *The Image of God in Man according to Cyril of Alexandria* (SCA 14 [1957]: 1–11). Here–as in 11.7.3, 11.9.2f., and 11.4–no distinction is made between the two and both appear to have a dynamic thrust: i.e., the image and likeness of God are seen as being received as the result of the practice of virtue rather than as givens. In 11.7.4, however, "likeness" is used by itself. Cf. also 9.6.5 and the relevant note.

11.7.2 The husks of the swine also have a negative meaning in Origen, *Frag. in Luc.* 216 (GCS 49.321), where they appear as carobs, and in Ambrose, *Exp. evang. sec. Luc.* 7.217f.

11.9.2 On the necessity of divine protection, or grace, cf. the note at 2.1.3f.

11.9.5 The sins from which those "who faithfully serve Christ cannot be immune" are also spoken of in 20.12.1ff., 22.7.2ff., 22.13.1ff., 23 passim. Involuntary sins of this sort are mentioned by Philo. Cf. Harry Austryn Wolfson, *Philo* (rev. printing, Cambridge, Mass., 1948) 1.438–441. They also appear in Origen, *De princ.* 3.2.2; Augustine, *Ep.* 177.18; idem, *De peccat. merit. et remis.* 2.10.12ff.; idem, *Enchir.* 19.71.

11.10 On falling into vices that one condemns in others cf. 2.13.4ff. and the relevant note.

11.12.8 That martyrdom must be accompanied by love is drawn with particular force in Cyprian, *De un. cath. eccl.* 14.

11.13.6 "The Lord in human form" is an expression that reappears in 11.13.8 and then again in *De incarn.* 5.5 and 6.22 (twice). The term translates *dominicus homo*, which could be more literally rendered as "Lordly man." It is used by several ancient authors, including Augustine in *De serm. Dom. in monte* 2.6 and *Enarr. in Ps.* 1.1, 8.13; he, however, later rejects it in *Retract.* 1.18.8. Cf. Alois Grillmeier, "Jesus Christ, the *Kyriakos Anthropos*," *Theological Studies* 38 (1977): 275–293; idem, Ο κυριακος ανθροπος: Eine Studie zu einer christologischen Bezeichnung der Väterzeit," *Traditio* 33 (1977): 1–63. In the former article, p. 292, Grillmeier suggests the translation "the man of the Lord" and says that, as Cassian uses it, the term is acceptable and "colorless."

TWELFTH CONFERENCE
THE SECOND CONFERENCE OF ABBA CHAEREMON: ON CHASTITY

TRANSLATOR'S INTRODUCTION

At the conclusion of the eleventh conference Germanus had asked Abba Chaeremon about chastity and, more specifically, about the control of genital movements (the *libidinis titillatio* or "wanton titillation" of 11.14). The twelfth conference, which takes up many of the points that had already made an appearance in the sixth book of *The Institutes,* "On the Spirit of Fornication," is Chaeremon's response to this request. Germanus had himself drawn the connection between perfect love and chastity, and the old man begins by alluding to this link, thus providing the perspective from which the conference should be approached, however obscured it may be at times.

The initial segment of the discussion concerns the body of sin and its members. After briefly describing the different members in question, which are enumerated in Colossians 3:5, Chaeremon notes that, just as it is possible to cut off avarice and other sinful members, so also is it possible to eradicate impurity of whatever sort. This, however, is accomplished not merely by the usual ascetic practices but in particular by divine grace, which Cassian emphasizes several times in the conference.

When in 12.4.3 Chaeremon speaks of the powerful yearning for chastity that must characterize the person who wishes to possess it, he has recourse to the language of love between a man and a woman. This is an interesting use of the principle of compensation (strikingly paralleled in the erotic description of the vision of chastity in Augustine, *Conf.* 8.11.27), and Cassian's grasp of this principle, as evidenced here and in 12.5.3, is but one more proof of his fine understanding of human psychology.

The control of the mind, Chaeremon continues, is the key to the control of the body. Growth in mildness and patience, especially, brings with it an increase of chastity. But if a person were so foolish as to slip into pride by reason of his physical integrity, the consequence would certainly be a corporeal reminder of his physical frailty—namely, nocturnal fantasies followed by an emission of semen.

With this Chaeremon lists the six degrees of chastity by which one may mount to perfect purity. They range from not succumbing to carnal attacks when one is awake to, finally, not producing seductive female images when one is asleep. The existence of such images, while not sinful, nonetheless indicates that deeply rooted desires are present in a person; these images, according to Cassian, depend for their content on the sexual experience, or lack of it, that a person may have had. There is also a seventh degree of chastity, but it is so rare and so far above the others that it must be mentioned apart from them. This degree is the condition whose possible attainment had already been referred to by Germanus at the end of the previous conference—namely, the control of genital movements during sleep, including the discharge of semen.

There is considerable space devoted to this most exalted level of chastity, and part of the discussion is of biological factors. Cassian, in any event, rejects the view (represented by a certain Dioscorus in *Hist. monach. in Aegypto* 20.2) that nature alone is responsible for genital movements. An unpurged heart, rather, is their cause in most instances. "For the character of our thoughts," he writes very clearly in *Inst.* 6.11, "which is rather negligently paid heed to in the midst of the day's distractions, is made trial of in the calm of night. Consequently, when some delusion of this sort occurs, guilt must not be imputed to sleep. This is, rather, the result of past negligence and the manifestation of a disease hidden within. The night was not the first to give it birth, but the relaxation of sleep brought it forth to the surface from the hidden depths of the soul." Nature demands its due, to be sure, but a pure heart can reduce movements of this kind to a bare few. It is in this context that Cassian distinguishes, as he had previously done in *Inst.* 6.4.1, between chastity and abstinence. Abstinence, he avers, is a consequence of struggle, and it implies a nagging delight in the thing struggled against; hence it can hardly succeed in governing unconscious yearnings. But chastity, on the other hand, is a love of purity for its own sake, which penetrates into the unconscious and which can act to control even "involuntary" bodily movements. Those who possess it no longer experience the struggle between flesh and spirit. The wonder of this state, which is achieved as the result of God's prodigious gift, can only be told by those who have themselves experienced it, and it must ultimately be described in ecstatic language.

Germanus's response to all this is to ask about the wherewithal for acquiring such chastity and about the period of time in which it might be acquired. Chaeremon replies by mentioning some canonized ascetical practices and by emphasizing an explicit dependence on grace. If the asceticism in question is practiced, then it is possible to attain to this chastity in six months.

The conference concludes late at night with a reiteration of the ideals of chastity.

Unlike Fathers such as Gregory of Nyssa (cf. *De virg.*, passim), Ambrose (cf. *De virginibus* 1.3.11ff.), and Jerome (cf. *Ep.* 22.25), for whom chastity is a superlative virtue that places its practitioners in immediate contact with God or Christ, Cassian does not speak of it in those terms. For him it is simply a means to an end and not the summit of perfection or, rather, it is at best an indication of and an accompaniment to that perfection which may be characterized as love or inner tranquillity or purity of heart. Hence Cassian's focus on genital movements and nocturnal emissions here and in the twenty-second conference, despite its appearance of concentrating embarrassingly on externals, is in fact (as has already been suggested above) only a discussion of the mechanism of the barometer of an internal state. This is particularly evident from what is related in 15.10.3, where we read that a dangerous but presumably hypothetical sexual experiment was proposed as a gauge of Abba Paphnutius's inner calm, which is ultimately understood more broadly than simply as chastity.

Indeed, sexuality in and of itself is not the preoccupation for Cassian and the Desert Fathers that it is sometimes imagined to be (although cf. Athanasius, *Ep.* 48, addressed to the monk Amoun, who seems to have been taxed with worry about his bodily excretions). The great monastic preoccupation is really food (cf. the perceptive commentary in Peter Brown, *The Body and Society: Men, Women, and Sexual Renunciation in Early Christianity* [New York, 1988], 213–240).

For studies on the material contained in this conference, and also in the twenty-second, cf. Terrence Kardong, "John Cassian's Teaching on Perfect Chastity" (*The American Benedictine Review* 30 [1979]: 249–263); Kenneth Russell, "Cassian on a Delicate Subject" (*Cistercian Studies Quarterly* 27 [1992]: 1–12); and David Brakke, "The Problematization of Nocturnal Emissions in Early Christian Syria, Egypt, and Gaul" (JECS 3 [1995]: 419–460, esp. 446–458).

XII. The Second Conference of Abba Chaeremon: On Chastity

Chapters

I.1. Once we had taken our meal—which, to us who desired the food of teaching, seemed more burdensome than pleasant—the old man understood that we were waiting then and there for him to fulfill his promise of a talk.

"I am pleased," he said, "not only by how intensely your mind is set upon learning but also by the way that you posed your question. For you have in fact observed a reasonable ordering in your question. For the immeasurable rewards of a perfect and perpetual chastity will inevitably accompany the fullness of so lofty a love, and there will be an equal joy in receiving two such equal palms. 2. For they are so closely united to one another that one cannot be possessed without the other.

"What you ask in this regard is difficult—that in a similar discourse we should discuss whether the fire of lust, whose heat this flesh senses as something inborn, can be completely extinguished. Concerning this we should first inquire carefully as to the view of the blessed Apostle. 'Put to death,' he says, 'your members that are on earth.'[1] Before pursuing anything else, then, we should investigate what these members are that he ordered to be put to death. For the blessed Apostle is not forcing us by a cruel command to cut off our hands or our feet or our genitals. He desires, rather, that the body of sin, which indeed consists in members, be destroyed as quickly as possible by a zeal for perfect holiness.

"He speaks about this body elsewhere: 'In order that the body of sin may be destroyed.'[2] And what its destruction is he explains next: 'So that we may no longer be enslaved to sin.'[3] He also begs to be freed from it when he says with groaning: 'Wretched man that I am! Who will free me from the body of this death?'[4]

II.1. "This body of sin, then, is shown to be constructed out of the many members of the vices, and to it belongs whatever sin is committed by deed or word or thought. Its members are very correctly said to be upon the earth. For those who do not make use of them can truly profess: 'Our way of life is in the heavens.'[5] The Apostle describes the members of this body when he says in this place: 'Put to death your members that are on earth–fornication, impurity, wantonness, evil desire and avarice, which is slavery to idols.'[6]

2. "He believed that in the first place he should mention fornication, which occurs in carnal union. He called the second member impurity, which sometimes creeps up on those who are sleeping or awake, without even touching a woman, due to the negligence of a heedless mind. Therefore it is noted and forbidden in the law, which not only deprived everyone who was impure of eating consecrated meat but also ordered them to be put outside the camp, lest holy things be polluted by contact with them. As it says: 'Whatever soul in which there is uncleanness eats of the meat of the saving sacrifice, which is the Lord's, shall perish before the Lord, and whatever an unclean person touches shall be unclean.'[7] 3. Likewise in Deuteronomy: 'If there is among you a man who has been polluted at night in a dream, he shall leave the camp and shall not return until he has washed himself in water at eventide, and after sunset he shall come back to the camp.'[8] Then, as the third member of sin he mentions wantonness, which grows in the recesses of the soul and which can even occur in a person without bodily passion. For there is no doubt that wantonness takes its name from what is pleasing.

4. "After this he descends from greater sins to lesser ones, bringing up evil desire as the fourth member. This can refer not only to the aforementioned passion of lewdness but also in general to every wicked lust; it is but the sickness of a corrupt will. The Lord says about it in the Gospel: 'Whoever looks at a woman with lust has already committed adultery with her in his heart.'[9] For it is a much greater thing to contain the desire of a wandering mind when an attractive appearance happens to present itself. 5. Hence it is clearly proven that the chastity of bodily abstinence alone is insufficient for perfect purity unless integrity of mind is also present.

"After all of these he speaks of avarice as the last member of that body, demonstrating beyond a doubt not only that the mind must be preserved from a desire for others' property but also that one's own must be high-mindedly disdained. For we read in the Acts of the Apostles that this was also done by the multitude of the believers, of whom it says: 'The multitude of believers had one heart and one soul, and none of them said that anything that he possessed was his own, but all things were common to them. For as many as owned fields or houses sold them and brought the price of what they sold and laid it at the feet of the apostles, and this was distributed to each just as each had need.'[10] 6. And lest this perfection seem to be for just a few, he declares that avarice is slavery to idols. Not without reason. For whoever does not contribute to the needs of the poor and sets his own money, which he holds onto with a faithless grasp, above the commands of Christ commits the crime of idolatry by preferring the love of worldly goods to divine love.

III.1. "We see that many people have so abandoned what is theirs for the sake of Christ that it is clear to us that they have forever cut out from their hearts not only the possession of money but even the desire for it. If this is so, it follows that we should believe that the fire of fornication can be extinguished in the same way. For the Apostle would not have joined something impossible to something possible, but he knew that both were possible and he decreed that they should be put to death in like fashion. 2. And so confident is the blessed Apostle that fornication and impurity can be rooted out of our members that he declares that not only must they be put to death but that they should not even be mentioned among us. As he says: 'Fornication and every impurity or avarice should not be mentioned among you, nor filthiness nor foolishness nor buffoonery, which are not fitting.'[11] He also teaches in similar fashion that these things are equally destructive and cut us off from the kingdom of God when he says: 3. 'Know this, that no fornicator or impure or avaricious person (which is slavery to idols) has an inheritance in the kingdom of Christ and God.'[12] And again: 'Do not be mistaken: No fornicators or idolaters or adulterers or effeminate persons or those who sleep with men or thieves or avaricious persons or drunkards or abusive talkers or robbers shall possess the kingdom of God.'[13]

"Hence there must be no doubt that the contagion of fornication and impurity can be done away with in our members, since he has not commanded that they should be cut off in some other way than avarice, foolishness, buffoonery, drunkenness, and thievery, which are easily cut off.

IV.1. "Yet we should be certain that although we undergo all the rigors of abstinence—namely, hunger and thirst, along with vigils and constant work and an unceasing pursuit of reading—we are still unable to acquire the perpetual purity of chastity through these efforts unless, while exerting ourselves constantly in them, we are taught in the school of experience that its incorruption is granted to us by the bounty of divine grace. 2. For this reason alone everyone should realize that he must persevere tirelessly in these practices. Thus, once he has obtained the mercy of the Lord through being afflicted with them, he will deserve to be freed from the assault of the flesh and from the domination of the ruling vices, thanks to the divine gift. But he must not believe that through these things he will attain by himself the unspoiled bodily chastity that he seeks.

3. "Like someone who very avidly goes after money, so afire with desire and love should a person be in his pursuit of chastity. Like someone who strains ambitiously after the highest honors, or someone who is seized with an unbearable love for a beautiful woman, he wants to consummate his desire with the most impatient ardor. And so it happens that, as long as he is aflame with insatiable yearning for perpetual integrity, desirable food is disdained, necessary drink is disgusting, and the very sleep that is owed to nature is spurned, or at least it is considered by the ecstatic but suspicious mind as a fraudulent deceiver of purity, as jealous of and opposed to chastity. Thus, whoever is aware each morning of his integrity should rejoice at the purity that has been bestowed upon him and should understand that he has acquired it not by his own efforts and vigilance but by the protection of the Lord, and he should realize that his body will persevere in this as long as the Lord mercifully permits it.

4. "The one who possesses this faith in a stable way will not trust proudly in the knowledge of his own virtue. Nor, lulled by a prolonged quiescence of the disgusting fluid, will he be weakened by a flattering sense of security, for he knows that he will immediately be sullied by a wetting from the unclean discharge if the divine protection departs from him even for a very little while.

Therefore, in all contrition and humility of heart, one must pray ceaselessly for perseverance in this.

V.1. "But do you want a clear demonstration of the truth of what we are talking about, by which you may be sure of what has been said and may learn that this bodily struggle, which seems hostile and harmful to us, has been placed in our members for our benefit? Consider, please, those who are eunuchs in body. Is it not this above all that renders them apathetic and lukewarm in the pursuit of virtue—that they believe themselves to be free of the danger of ruining their chastity? 2. But no one should believe that I am declaring that none of them are utterly aglow with perfect renunciation. On the contrary, they would overcome their nature in some fashion if some of them happened to struggle with a very disciplined mind for the palm of perfection that is set before them. The ardent desire for this would once for all enkindle him whom it had compelled to withstand hunger, thirst, vigils, poverty, and all sorts of bodily labors not only patiently but even gladly. For 'a man in sorrow labors for himself and forcibly prevents his own ruin.'[14] And again: 'To the needy soul even bitter things seem sweet.'[15]

3. "For desires for present things cannot be repressed or plucked out unless salutary dispositions have been introduced to replace the harmful ones that we want to cut off. In no way can the mind's vitality subsist without some feeling of desire or fear, joy or sadness, which must be turned to good use. Therefore, if we want to cast carnal desires from our hearts, we should at once plant spiritual pleasures in their place, so that our mind, always bound to them, might have the wherewithal to abide in them constantly and might spurn the allurements of present and temporal joys.

4. "And when our mind has been trained by daily discipline and has arrived at this state, it will understand, having been taught by experience, the sentiment of that verse which we all sing in the accustomed tone, to be sure, but whose power only a few experienced persons understand: 'I kept the Lord ever in my sight. Since he is at my right hand I shall not be moved.'[16] He alone will really attain to the force and understanding of this song who, arriving at the purity of body and soul which we are speaking of, understands that at every moment the Lord is keeping him from

falling away from it again, and that his right hands—that is, his holy deeds—are constantly protected by him. 5. For the Lord is never present to his holy ones on their left, because a holy person has nothing that is left, but on their right. He is not seen by sinners and by the wicked because they do not have those right hands where the Lord is usually present, and they cannot say with the prophet: 'My eyes are always on the Lord, for he himself will snatch my feet from the snare.'[17] No one will be able to profess this truthfully except the person who considers everything in this world to be either harmful or unnecessary or at least inferior to the highest virtues, and who fixes his whole gaze, all his effort, and all his concern on the cultivation of his heart and on the purity of chastity. Thus the mind, polished by these practices and refined by its progress, will arrive at perfect holiness of body and soul.

VI.1. "For as a person progresses in mildness and patience of heart, so also does he in purity of body; and the further he has driven away the passion of anger, the more tightly will he hold on to chastity. The body's seething heats will not lessen if one has not previously suppressed the mind's movements. The beatitude commended by the mouth of our Savior declares this very plainly: 'Blessed are the meek, for they shall possess the earth.'[18] 2. We shall not possess our own earth—that is, the earth of this rebellious body will not be placed under our sway—unless our mind has first been fixed in patient mildness. Likewise, a person will be unable to restrain the revolts of wantonness against his own flesh unless he has first been supplied with the weapons of gentleness, for 'the gentle shall possess the earth,'[19] and 'they shall dwell upon it forever.'[20] Later in that very psalm the same prophet teaches us how to acquire this earth: 'Wait for the Lord and keep to his way, and he will exalt you so that you may have the earth for your inheritance.'[21]

3. "It is obvious, then, that no one can rise to acquiring firm possession of this earth except those who, through an unchangeable patient mildness, have kept to the hard ways of the Lord and to his commands and have been raised up from the filth of the carnal passions, out of which he himself has drawn them. 'The gentle shall possess the earth,' then, and not only shall they possess it but they shall also 'delight in an abundance of peace.'[22] No one will enjoy this enduringly in whose flesh there still rage the battles of

lust. Such a person is inevitably assailed by the savage attacks of the demons and, wounded by the fiery darts of dissipation, must lose possession of his earth, until the Lord 'makes wars cease to the ends of his earth, destroys the bow and shatters the weapons and burns the shields with fire.'[23] That is to say, with that fire which the Lord came to cast upon the earth[24] he shatters the bows and weapons with which the evil spirits, struggling day and night, were transfixing his heart with the fiery darts of the passions.

4. "Thus, when the Lord has destroyed wars and freed that person from every seething emotion and impulse, he shall attain to the state of purity. Then, no longer distressed by the horror that he felt for himself–that is, for his flesh–when he was being assailed, he will begin to be delighted by it as if it were the purest tabernacle, for 'no evils shall befall him, and no scourge shall approach his tent.'[25] He will fulfill that prophecy by the virtue of patience, so that, thanks to his gentleness, he will not only possess his earth but will also 'delight in an abundance of peace.'

5. "But where there is still uncertainty about the struggle there can be no abundance of peace. For it does not say that they shall delight in peace, but rather 'in an abundance of peace.' From this it is quite evident that the heart's most effective medicine is patience. According to the words of Solomon: 'The gentle man is the physician of the heart.'[26] So true is this that it uproots not only all the vices of anger, sadness, acedia, vainglory, and pride, but also that of wantonness along with them. For, as Solomon says: 'In long-suffering is the prosperity of kings.'[27] Whoever is always meek and tranquil is not inflamed by the disturbance of anger, nor consumed by the anguish of acedia and sadness, nor distracted by the emptiness of vainglory, nor lifted up by the swelling of pride. For 'there is much peace for those who love the name of the Lord, and for them there is no stumbling block.'[28] 6. Therefore it is declared with good reason: 'Better is the one who is patient than the one who is strong, and the one who restrains his anger than the one who captures a city.'[29]

"Until we deserve to acquire this firm and perpetual peace we shall inevitably be assailed by numerous attacks and frequently repeat this verse with groaning and tears: 'I have become wretched, and I am afflicted beyond measure. All the day I went about mournfully, for my loins are filled with illusions.'[30] And: 'There is no health in my flesh in the face of your anger. There is no peace in my bones in the face of my foolishness.'[31]

7. "We shall bewail these things well and truly when, after long-standing purity of body and after hoping that we had already completely escaped fleshly contagion, we see that the urges of the flesh are once more asserting themselves against us on account of our pride of heart or even that the impurity of an erstwhile discharge is wetting us through deceitful dreams. For when someone has begun to rejoice over an extended period of purity of heart and body, believing that he can no longer fall away from that virtuousness, he will surely boast within himself somehow and say: 8. 'I said in my prosperity: I shall never be moved.'[32] But when, having been abandoned by the Lord for his own good, he realizes that the state of purity in which he placed his confidence is abandoning him and he sees himself faltering in his spiritual progress, let him return at once to the Author of his integrity. Acknowledging his frailty, let him confess and say: 'Lord,' not in mine but 'in your will you gave strength to my comeliness. You turned away your face and I was dismayed.'[33] There are also the words of blessed Job: 'If I had washed in snow water and my hands gleamed immaculately, still you would plunge me in filth, and my garments would horrify me.'[34] 9. But one who plunged himself in filth by his own sinfulness could not say this to his Creator.

Until a person arrives at the state of perfect purity, then, he has to be trained frequently by these discrepancies until, confirmed by the grace of God in the purity that he is seeking, he is worthy to say in truth: 'I have waited, I have waited for the Lord, and he turned to me and he heard my plea. He drew me out of the pit of wretchedness and from the miry bog. He set my feet upon a rock and he guided my steps.'[35]

VII.1. "For many are the degrees of chastity by which one may mount to inviolable purity. Although our ability is inadequate to pick them out and to speak of them as they deserve, nonetheless, since the plan of our discourse demands it, we shall try to expose them as well as we can, to the extent of our slender experience. We shall leave to the perfect the things that are more perfect and we shall not jump to conclusions about those who, thanks to their more fervent efforts, possess a purer chastity and who excel by reason of the force of their clearsightedness, the more zealous they are.

2. "Accordingly, although there is a great difference in sublimity among the degrees, I would distinguish six lofty summits of chastity. But I shall leave out the intermediate degrees which are numerous and whose subtlety so escapes human comprehension that neither the mind can grasp it nor the tongue express it. By them the perfection of chastity grows gradually and by daily progress. For strength of soul and mature chastity are acquired according to the likeness of earthly bodies, which imperceptibly increase in size day by day and thus achieve their proper state all unawares.

3. "So, the first degree of chastity is that the monk not be undone by carnal attacks while awake. The second is that his mind not dwell upon pleasurable thoughts. The third is that he not be moved to desire, even slightly, by looking upon a woman. The fourth is that he not permit a movement of the flesh, however simple, while awake. The fifth is that, when a discussion or some necessary reading evokes the thought of human generation, a very subtle assent to the pleasurable action not come upon the mind. Rather, it should look upon this with the gaze of a tranquil and pure heart, as a kind of simple act and as a ministry that is unavoidably part of human nature. Let it make nothing more of this recollection, which it should think of like brickmaking or some other task.

4. "The sixth degree of chastity is that he not be deluded by the alluring images of women even when asleep. For although we do not believe that this delusion is sinful, nonetheless it is an indication of a desire that is still deeply ingrained. It is evident that this delusion can occur in a number of ways. For each person is tempted, even while asleep, according to how he behaves and thinks while awake. Those who have known sexual intercourse are led astray in one way, those who have had no part in union with a woman in another way. The latter are usually disturbed by simpler and purer dreams, such that they can be cleansed more easily and with less effort. 5. But the former are deceived by filthier and more explicit images until, gradually and according to the measure of

chastity for which each is struggling, even the mind that has fallen asleep learns to hate what it used to find pleasurable, and, through the prophet, the Lord grants it what is promised to brave men as the highest reward for their labors: 'I will destroy the bow and the sword and war from your land, and I will make you sleep securely.'[36]

6. "And so finally a person will arrive at the purity characteristic of blessed Serenus and of a few other men like him. This I have set aside from the aforementioned six degrees of chastity because not only can it not be possessed but it cannot even be believed except by the most extraordinary persons, and because what was granted in particular to him by the graciousness of the divine gift cannot be proposed as a kind of general precept—namely, that our mind would be so stamped with the purity of chastity that even the natural movement of the flesh would have died and one would not produce any disgusting fluid at all.

7. "I must by no means be silent about the opinion of some people, who say with regard to this discharge of the flesh that it happens to those who are asleep not because an illusion caused by dreams produces it but rather because an excess of that moisture makes something alluring arise in a sickly heart. They say that when this buildup ceases, the deception also quiets down along with the emission.

VIII.1. "But no one can conceive these things or prove them and know for certain whether they are possible or impossible except the person who, through long experience and purity of heart, has arrived at the boundaries of flesh and spirit under the guidance of the Lord's word. The blessed Apostle says about this: 'The word of God is alive and active and sharper than any two-edged sword, piercing to the division of soul and spirit, of joints and marrow, and discerning the thoughts and intentions of the heart.'[37]

2. "Placed thus, as it were, at the boundaries of those realities, he will discern by a just assessment, like an observer and a judge, what is necessarily and ineluctably part of the human condition and what has been introduced by bad habits and by youthful heedlessness. Concerning their effect and their nature he will not be led astray by the false opinions of the crowd nor will he give in

to the untried assertions of the inexperienced. Rather, weighing the measure of purity in the sure balance of his own experience and after a careful examination, he will never be deceived by the error of those who excuse themselves for their natural condition which, due to their own sinful negligence, nature drives into filthy behavior by ever more frequent necessity, when he sees them speaking in terms of the force of nature and twisting out of it a pollution for which it is not responsible, referring their own immoderation to the necessity of the flesh, or rather to its Creator, and making their own faults into nature's shame. 3. Of these people it is well expressed in Proverbs: 'A man's foolishness corrupts his ways, but he blames God in his heart.'[38]

"If someone cannot give credence to what I have said, I beg that he not argue with us from a predetermined position, before having taken upon himself the institutes of this discipline. And when he has observed these for a very few months, with the customary moderation, he will certainly be able to make a responsible judgment about what we have spoken of. But whoever has not first pursued with the greatest effort and strength all that pertains to the mastery of a particular art or discipline will struggle in vain to make it completely his own. 4. It is as if, for example, I should declare that something like honey could be produced from grain just as the mildest oil is produced from the seed of radishes and flax. If there were someone present who was completely ignorant of this, would he not cry out that it runs contrary to the nature of things and laugh at me as the author of a patent untruth? Suppose I were to set before him innumerable witnesses who would testify that they had seen and tasted and done this, and in addition suppose I were to explain the method and the manner in which those sorts of things are transformed into the richness of oil or the sweetness of honey. But if he persisted in the obstinacy of his foolish position and denied that anything sweet or unctuous could be produced from those seeds, would not his irrational and stubborn contention be more remarkable than the truth of what I said would be laughable, given that it is supported by the weighty testimony of many trustworthy persons, by clear documentation, and, what is more, by the proof of experience?

5. "Therefore, when a person, by constant attentiveness of

heart, arrives at the state of purity where his mind is already completely free of this passion's titillation but his flesh expels something like an excess of moisture during sleep, he will recognize with utter certainty that nature is at work. Thus, when he wakes up and discovers that his flesh has been polluted after a long period of time, without his having been aware of it at all, let him then—and only then—blame the needs of nature. He has without a doubt arrived at the state where he is the same at night as during the day; the same in reading as at prayer; the same alone as when surrounded by crowds of people; so that, finally, he never sees himself in secret as he would blush to be seen by men, and that inescapable eye does not see anything in him that he would wish to be hidden from human gaze.

6. "And so, once he has begun to take constant pleasure in the most sweet light of chastity, he will be able to say with the prophet: 'The night is bright in my delights. For the darkness shall not be dark to you, and the night shall be as bright as the day. As its darkness is, so also is its light.'[39] Then the same prophet adds how this may be acquired, since it seems beyond the condition of human nature, and he says: 'For you possessed my reins.'[40] That is to say, I have not earned this purity by my own effort or virtue but because you put to death the fire of wanton pleasure that was implanted in my reins."

IX. GERMANUS: "We have experienced that in some way perpetual purity of body can indeed be possessed by those who are awake, thanks to the grace of God, and we do not deny that it is possible for a disturbance of the flesh not to befall the wakeful by reason of rigorous strictness and a determination to resist it. But we want to learn whether we can also be free of this disturbance while we are sleeping. We do not believe that this is possible for two reasons. Although we are unable to express them without shame, nonetheless, since the need for a remedy demands it, we beg that you will be forgiving if they be spoken of in somewhat shameless fashion. The first reason, then, is that the surreptitiousness of this disturbance can never be observed during the repose of sleep, when the mind's alertness is relaxed. The second reason is that when an accumulation of urine has completely filled the bladder with a ceaseless flow of internal fluid, which occurs while we are sleeping, it arouses the relaxed members. By force of the same law this even happens to children and to eunuchs. Hence it is that if wanton pleasure does not damage the mind's assent, still the baseness of one's members humiliates it by this disorder."

X.1. CHAEREMON: "It appears that you have not yet recognized the virtue of true chastity, since you believe that it can be maintained solely by the wakeful with the help of strict discipline. Therefore you think that integrity cannot be preserved by those who are asleep, as if by a rigorously determined mind. But chastity subsists not—as you think—thanks to a rigorous defense but rather by love of itself and by delight in its own purity. For it is not chastity but abstinence when adverse pleasure still offers some resistance.

2. "You see, then, that the cessation of strictness during sleep is not injurious to those who by the grace of God have interiorly received the disposition of chastity. This is proven in the most certain fashion to be untrustworthy even in those who are awake. For, when something is restrained with an effort, the relief that is offered to the one struggling is only temporary, and there is still no enduring and secure peace after the effort. But when something has been conquered by deeply rooted virtue, there is a calm without any hint of disturbance, and a steady and firm peace is granted the victor.

3. "Hence, as long as we feel that we are being afflicted by a disturbance of the flesh, we know that we have not yet arrived at the heights of chastity but are still toiling under a frail abstinence, engaged in battles whose outcome is always inevitably doubtful.

"But you wanted to establish that the disturbance of the flesh was unavoidable, and to do so by this fact—namely, that the eunuchs themselves, who have no genitals, because they have been removed, are unable to be free of it. It should be known that they lack neither the seething emotions of the flesh nor the effects of lust but only the power of generation. 4. Therefore it is clear that even they must not relax their humility and contrition of heart and the rigor of their abstinence if they want to attain to the chastity for which we are striving, even if it must not at all be disbelieved that they can lay hold of chastity with less effort and exertion.

XI.1. "For this reason perfect chastity is distinguished from the toilsome rudiments of abstinence by its perpetual tranquillity. For this is the consummation of true chastity, which does not fight the movements of carnal lust but detests them with utter horror, maintaining a constant and inviolable purity for itself. This can be nothing else than holiness.

"But, once the flesh has stopped lusting against the spirit and has given in to its desires and to virtue, they begin to be mutually joined to one another by a most stable peace, and they dwell as 'brothers in unity,'[41] according to the words of the psalmist. They possess the blessing promised by the Lord, about which he says: 'If two of you agree on earth about asking for anything whatsoever, it shall be done for them by my Father who is in heaven.'[42] 2. Whoever, therefore, passes beyond the degree of that spiritual Jacob—that is, the supplanter—will mount by the steady inclination of his heart from the struggle of abstinence and from the supplanting of the vices to the dignity of Israel, once the nerve in his thigh has been numbed.[43]

"Through the prophetic action of the Holy Spirit the blessed David also distinguished this order of things when he said first: 'God is known in Judah'[44]—that is, in the soul that is still held under the confession of sin, since Judah means confession. But 'in Israel'—that is, in the one who sees God or, as some people interpret it, God's most righteous one—he is not only known but also 'his name is great.'[45] 3. Then he calls us to sublimer things and even wishes to show us the place wherein the Lord delights, saying: 'His place is in peace'[46]—that is, not in the struggle of conflict and in the battle of vice but rather in the peace of chastity and in perpetual tranquillity of heart. If anyone has deserved to arrive at this place of peace through the extinction of his carnal passions, proceeding from this degree he will become a spiritual Zion—that is, the observation of God—and will also be his dwelling place. For the Lord dwells not in the struggle of abstinence but rather in the continual observation of virtue. There he does not fight back or suppress the power of the bows from which the fiery darts of wantonness were once aimed against us; instead he destroys them forever. 4. You see, then, that the Lord's place is not in the battle of abstinence but in the peace of chastity, so that his dwelling is in the observation and contemplation of virtue. Hence not without reason are the gates of Zion preferred to all the tents of Jacob, for 'the Lord loves the gates of Zion above all the tents of Jacob.'[47]

"You assert that a disturbance of the flesh is unavoidable because the urine, once it has filled the bladder by constantly trickling into it, arouses the recumbent members, although this disturbance does not hinder the true pursuers of purity from acquiring it, since only an occasional need provokes it, and then only during sleep. Yet it should be known that if they have been disturbed they can be restored to their appropriate recumbency by the command of chastity, in such a way that they are calmed not only with no tingling sensation but not even with any recollection of lust. 5. Therefore, in order that the law of the body may conform with the law of the mind, an excessive drinking even of water itself should be curbed, so that the daily volume of liquid which flows more slowly into the dry members may render that bodily movement–which you consider unavoidable–not only extremely infrequent but even phlegmatic and dull. In the manner of that wonderful vision of Moses,[48] it will enkindle what I would call a cold flame and cause moisture without any fiery heat, so that the bush of our flesh may not burn, surrounded as it is with a harmless fire. Or it will be like those three young men for whom the flames of the Chaldean furnace were so scattered by the dew-bearing Spirit that the smell of the fire did not touch their hair or the hems of their garments.[49] Thus we shall somehow begin to possess in this body what is promised to holy persons by the prophet: 'When you walk through fire you shall not burn, and the flames shall not set you afire.'[50]

XII.1. "These great and truly marvelous things, completely unknown to anyone except to those who have experienced them, are given with unspeakable generosity by the Lord to his faithful ones who are still living in this vessel of corruption. The prophet, shining forth in his purity of mind, proclaims this as much in his own person as in the person of those who attain to this state and disposition: 'Wonderful are your works, and my soul knows them exceedingly.'[51] The prophet is understood to have said nothing new or great if he is believed to have declared this merely about another disposition of the heart or about some other works of

God. 2. For there is no one who does not know from the vastness of creation itself that the works of God are marvelous. But what he accomplishes in his holy ones by his daily activity and abundantly pours into them by his particular munificence—this no one knows but the soul which enjoys it and which, in the recesses of its conscience, is so uniquely the judge of his benefits that it cannot only not speak of them but cannot even seize them in understanding or thought when, leaving behind its fiery ardor, it falls back to gazing upon material and earthly realities.

3. "For who would not wonder at the works of the Lord in himself when he sees the stomach's insatiable voracity and the sumptuous and ruinous luxury of gormandizing so suppressed in himself that he hardly eats a minimum of unsavory food, and that but rarely and unwillingly? Who would not be struck dumb at the works of God when he notices that the fire of wantonness, which he previously believed was natural and as it were inextinguishable, has grown so cold that he does not feel himself aroused even by a simple movement of the body? How would one not tremble before the power of the Lord when he sees that people who once were harsh and cruel and who used to fall into an ungovernable rage even at the most cringing submission of their inferiors have become so gentle that they are not only unmoved by any insults but even rejoice with the loftiest high-mindedness when they suffer them? 4. Who would not wonder thoroughly at the works of God and cry out with his whole being: 'I know that the Lord is great,'[52] when he sees that he or someone else has gone from grasping to generous, from wasteful to abstinent, from proud to humble, from delicate and refined to filthy and rough, even gladly enjoying poverty and the scarcity of temporal things?

"These are truly the marvelous works of God, which the soul of the prophet and of others like him knows specially by the dumbstruck gaze of a wondering contemplation. These are the prodigies that he has wrought upon the earth, which the same prophet, reflecting upon them, calls all people to admire when he says: 'Come and see the works of God, the prodigies that he has wrought upon the earth, making wars cease to the ends of the earth. He destroys the bow and shatters the weapons and burns the shields with fire.'[53]

5. "What could be a greater prodigy than that in a brief moment grasping tax-collectors would become apostles and harsh persecutors would be turned into the most patient preachers of the Gospel, such that they would spread the faith which they used to persecute even to the shedding of their own blood? These are the works of God which the Son declares that he does every day, together with his Father, when he says: 'My Father is working until today, and I am working.'[54] The blessed David, singing in spirit, says of these works of God: 'Blessed be the Lord, the God of Israel, who alone does great marvels.'[55] The prophet Amos says about them: 'He does all things and changes them. He changes the shadow of death into morning.'[56] This, namely, is the 'changing of the right hand of the Most High.'[57] 6. Concerning this saving work of God the prophet prays to the Lord and says: 'Confirm, O God, what you have worked in us.'[58]

"Let me pass over those secret and hidden dispensations of God which each holy person's mind sees operative in a special way within itself at given moments; over that heavenly inpouring of spiritual gladness by which the downcast mind is uplifted by an inspired joy; over those fiery ecstasies of heart and the joyful consolations at once unspeakable and unheard of, by which those who occasionally fall into a listless torpor are raised as out of the deepest sleep to the most fervent prayer. 7. This indeed is the joy which, the blessed Apostle says, 'eye has not seen nor ear heard nor has it entered into the heart of man'[59]—namely, of the person who is still a human being dulled by earthly vices, who clings to human feelings and who sees nothing of the gifts of God. Then the same Apostle, speaking both for himself and for those like him who had already broken away from a human way of life, adds: 'But God has revealed this to us through his Spirit.'[60]

XIII.1. "In all these instances, then, the more the mind has advanced to a more refined purity, the more sublimely it will see God, and it will grow in wonder within itself rather than find the ability to speak of it or a word to explain it. For just as the inexperienced person will be unable to grasp in his mind the power of this gladness, neither will the person who has experienced it be able to explain it in words. It is as if someone wished to describe in words the sweetness of honey to a person who had never tasted anything sweet. The one will in fact not grasp with his ears the agreeable flavor that he has never had in his mouth, while the other will be unable to give any indication in words of the sweetness that his taste knows from its own enjoyment. Only by his personal knowledge of the attractive sweetness can he wonder silently within himself at the pleasant flavor that he has experienced.

2. "So, then, whoever has deserved to arrive at that state of virtue which we have been speaking of, after examining in the silence of his mind all the things that the Lord works in those who are his own by his special grace, and aflame with astonished reflection on them all, will cry out with the deepest emotion of his heart: 'Wonderful are your works, and my soul knows them exceedingly.' This, then, is the wondrous work of God—that a fleshly human being, dwelling in flesh, would have rejected fleshly desires, would hold to one state of mind in the midst of so many different affairs and assaults and would remain changeless in every changing happenstance.

3. "Once a certain old man who was practiced in this virtue was surrounded by crowds of infidels when he was in Alexandria. He was pressed upon not only with reviling but even with the most grievous insults by those who were jostling him, and his mockers said to him: 'What miracle has your Christ, whom you worship, performed?' He said: 'That I not be disturbed or offended by these or by greater insults, if you offer them.'"

XIV. GERMANUS: "Since admiration for this not human or earthly but clearly heavenly and angelic chastity stupefies and amazes us so suddenly as to inspire a dreadful hopelessness rather than to challenge our minds to ask this for themselves, we beg you to teach us by the most comprehensive instruction about the character of the discipline and the length of time in which it could be acquired and perfected, in order that we may both believe that this can be achieved and be encouraged to ask for it after a little while. For we are somewhat of the opinion that this is ungraspable by those who dwell in this flesh, unless a certain method and approach are suggested to us by which it can be arrived at in sure fashion."

XV.1. CHAEREMON: "It is rather rash to impose a set period of time for the achievement of this chastity that we have been speaking about, particularly since there is a great diversity of wills and strengths. Such a thing cannot be easily determined even in material arts and visible disciplines. For of necessity they are grasped, whether more quickly or more slowly, by each individual in accordance with the attentiveness of his mind and the character of his abilities. Nonetheless we can firmly fix a form of discipline and a length of time within the context of which its possibility may be realized.

2. "Whoever, then, has withdrawn from every useless conversation; has put to death all anger and concern and worldly care; is satisfied with just two loaves for his daily meal; does not drink his fill of water; wakes up after three hours of sleep or, as others have established, after four hours; yet does not believe that he will obtain it due to these efforts or this abstinence but rather by the mercy of the Lord, because without this belief every intense human effort is in vain—that person will know in not more than six months that perfection in this is not impossible for him.

3. "To begin not to hope for it by one's own laborious efforts is a clear sign that purity is already near. For if someone has truly grasped the force of the verse: 'Unless the Lord has built the house, those who are building it have labored in vain,'[61] it follows that he should not glory in the deserts of his purity, since he realizes that he has obtained it not by his own toil but by the Lord's mercy. Nor should he be moved against others with a harsh severity, since he knows that there is no human virtue if the divine virtue has not commanded it.

XVI.1. "Hence, for each one of us who contends against the spirit of fornication with all his strength, it is a notable victory not to expect relief through his own efforts. Although this belief seems easy and evident to all, yet it is seized with as much difficulty by beginners as is the perfection of chastity itself. For when purity smiles on them ever so slightly, they immediately flatter themselves in the depths of their conscience by a pride that subtly slips in. They think that they have achieved this by their own diligent zeal. Thus it is necessary for them to be gradually deprived of heavenly protection and to be oppressed by those passions which the divine power had extinguished until they realize by experience that they are unable to obtain the good of purity by their own strength and toil.

2. "And, so as to conclude quickly our night-long discourse on the end of the fullness of chastity, let us put together everything that has been said at length and in scattered fashion. This is the consummation of chastity—that no wanton pleasure would touch a monk when he is awake and that no illusory dreams would lead him astray when he is asleep, but that when a disturbance of the flesh creeps up on him while sleeping, due only to the carelessness of a weary mind, then, just as it was aroused without any pleasurable titillation, so likewise it would return to calm without any bodily sensuality.

3. "We have expressed these things about the end of chastity to the best of our ability not with words but with experience as our teacher. Although I think that they will probably be considered impossible by the lazy and the negligent, nonetheless I am sure that they will be accepted and approved by zealous and spiritual men. As much as human beings are different from one another, so also the things to which their minds incline are different—namely, heaven and hell and Christ and Belial, following the words of the Lord, the Savior: 'If anyone serves me, let him follow after me, and where I am, there also will my servant be.'[62] And again: 'Where your treasure is, there also will your heart be.'"[63]

4. Thus far did the blessed Chaeremon speak about perfect chastity, and in words of this sort he concluded his wonderful teaching on the most sublime purity. Then he persuaded us, stupefied and anxious as we were, not to deprive our members of the natural food of sleep, since the greater part of the night had already slipped by and it had gradually become more quiet. Otherwise even the mind, wearied by the sluggishness of its body, would lose its holy and intense vigor.

Textual References

1. Col 3:5a.
2. Rom 6:6a.
3. Rom 6:6b.
4. Rom 7:24.
5. Phil 3:20.
6. Col 3:5.
7. Lv 7:20 LXX; Nm 19:22.
8. Dt 23:11–12.
9. Mt 5:28.
10. Acts 4:32, 34–35.
11. Eph 5:3–4.
12. Eph 5:5.
13. 1 Cor 6:9–10.
14. Prv 16:26 LXX.
15. Prv 27:7 LXX.
16. Ps 16:8.
17. Ps 25:15.
18. Mt 5:4.
19. Ps 37:11a.
20. Ps 37:29.
21. Ps 37:34.
22. Ps 37:11b.
23. Ps 46:9.
24. Cf. Lk 12:49.
25. Ps 91:10.
26. Prv 14:30 LXX.
27. Prv 25:15 LXX.
28. Ps 119:165.
29. Prv 16:32 LXX.
30. Ps 38:6–7.
31. Ps 38:3.
32. Ps 30:6.
33. Ps 30:7.
34. Jb 9:30–31.
35. Ps 40:1–2.
36. Hos 2:20.
37. Heb 4:12.
38. Prv 19:3 LXX.

39. Ps 139:11–12.
40. Ps 139:13.
41. Ps 133:1.
42. Mt 18:19.
43. Cf. Gn 32:26–29.
44. Ps 76:1a.
45. Ps 76:1b.
46. Ps 76:2.
47. Ps 87:2.
48. Cf. Ex 3:2.
49. Cf. Dn 3:27.
50. Is 43:2.
51. Ps 139:14.
52. Ps 135:5.
53. Ps 46:8–9.
54. Jn 5:17.
55. Ps 72:18.
56. Am 5:8 LXX.
57. Cf. Ps 77:10.
58. Ps 68:28.
59. 1 Cor 2:9.
60. 1 Cor 2:10.
61. Ps 127:1.
62. Jn 12:26.
63. Mt 6:21.

12.1.2 Voluntary castration was not unknown in Christian antiquity. Cf. Justin, *1 Apol.* 29 (an attempted castration); *Acta Ioannis* 53 (CCSA 1.237); Eusebius, *Hist. eccl.* 6.8.1f. (Origen's self-mutilation); Council of Nicaea, canon 1; Epiphanius, *Panarion* 58.

12.2.3 Wantonness takes its name from what is pleasing: *Libidinem enim ab eo quod libeat dictam esse.*

12.3.1ff. On Cassian's understanding of fornication cf. 5.11.4 and the relevant note.

12.4.1ff. On the necessity of grace here and in 12.8.6, 12.12, and 12.15.2ff., cf. the note at 2.1.3f.

12.4.1 On being taught by experience here and in 12.5.4, 12.8.1ff., 12.12.1f., 12.13.1, and 12.16.1, cf. the note at 3.7.4.

12.5.1f. On the eunuchs' lukewarmness cf. the note at 4.17.

12.5.4f. On the two right hands of the holy person cf. 6.10 and the relevant note.

12.6.2 On the earth as an image of the body cf. Augustine, *De serm. Dom. in monte* 2.6.23; idem, *Enarr. in Ps.* 36, serm. 3.13.

12.6.3 On the demons' fiery darts here and in 12.11.3f. cf. the note at 2.13.7f.

12.6.4 Tabernacle...tent: *Tabernaculo...tabernaculo.*

12.6.7f. On pride leading to a rude reminder of one's carnality cf. the note at 4.15ff.

12.7.3 The use of "simple" with reference to a sexual movement of the flesh here and in 12.12.3 is unclear. Cf. the note at 22.3.5.

12.7.4 The idea that one is not morally responsible for what occurs during one's sleep, when no sinful provocation has preceded, was not universally held in antiquity. Cf. Caesarius of Arles, *Serm.* 177.4.

12.7.4f. On the relation of the memory of past experiences to the production of images cf. Evagrius, *Prac.* 34;

Augustine, *Conf.* 10.30.41; Maximus the Confessor, *Cap. de caritate* 1.63.

12.7.6 The Serenus in question is the abba of the seventh and eighth conferences. On his extraordinary chastity cf. 7.1f.

12.8.4 The examples here and in 12.13.1 of an unwillingness to believe what lies outside of one's own range of experience recall another such example in 7.4.1. There is a similar passage in Origen, *C. Celsum* 6.73. On the salubrious qualities of an oil made from radishes, mentioned as being particularly familiar to the Egyptians, cf. Pliny, *Hist. nat.* 15.17.

12.11.2 Spiritual Jacob...dignity of Israel: Cf. the note at 1 praef. 5.

12.11.4f. On limiting one's intake of water in this context cf. 22.3.2, 22.6.4f.; Evagrius, *Prac.* 17. Cf. also the note in SC 171.543–545; Weber 84–85. Tertullian, *De ieiun.* 1 and 9, mentions a restricted use of water by the Montanists and establishes a general connection between fasting and the restraint of sexual desire. On fasting as helpful in controlling nocturnal emissions cf. 2.23.1, 22.3.2, 22.6.4f. The linkage is tentatively affirmed in A. W. Richard Sipe, *A Secret World: Sexuality and the Search for Celibacy* (New York, 1990), 149–150.

12.13.3 The incident described here cannot be dated more precisely than sometime in the fourth century–if indeed it happened at all. In any event, the pagan (spoken of here as "infidel") population of Alexandria remained significant and influential into the fifth century. The assassination of the pagan philosopher Hypatia in 415 perhaps marks the effective terminal point of this influence.

12.15.2 Two loaves: Cf. 2.18ff.

THIRTEENTH CONFERENCE THE THIRD CONFERENCE OF ABBA CHAEREMON: ON GOD'S PROTECTION

TRANSLATOR'S INTRODUCTION

The present conference, the last of Chaeremon's three, is by far the most controversial of all twenty-four. It was this conference that prompted Prosper of Aquitaine to write his treatise *Contra collatorem,* or *Against the Author of the Conferences,* about the year 432, and this conference, almost certainly, is responsible for the fact that Cassian hardly enjoys the title of saint in the West, despite his vast influence.

The controversial material is introduced quite unremarkably approximately a third of the way through the conference with the words: "When [God] notices good will making an appearance in us, he at once enlightens and encourages it and spurs it on to salvation, giving increase to what he himself planted and saw arise *from our own efforts*" (13.8.4, emphasis added). With this we are in the realm of what later came to be called Semi-pelagianism and which more recently, and probably more correctly, has been referred to as Semi-augustinianism—namely, the belief that it is possible for the human person, thanks to the God-bestowed goodness of human nature, to accomplish something virtuous preliminary to having received grace to do so. The remaining two-thirds of the conference represents a development of this semi-Pelagian or semi-Augustinian tendency.

The first chapters of the conference do not at all suggest what is to follow. They begin with Germanus's bewilderment over Chaeremon's absolutizing of grace in the previous conference on chastity. Can nothing, he asks, be attributed to one's own efforts? Chaeremon's response is to insist once again on the need for divine assistance, or grace, in order to achieve any good whatsoever. Germanus objects that some pagans are said to have been particularly chaste as a result of their own efforts. In reply Chaeremon contrasts pagan chastity with the Christian ideal presented in the twelfth conference. Using Socrates and Diogenes as examples, he shows that pagans such as these were at best only capable of external purity but could not attain to the control of their erotic desires. Having established this, the old man continues with a lengthy affirmation of his previous assertions on the absolute necessity of grace in all circumstances.

It is near the beginning of this section, however, that Chaeremon adduces the significant qualification that, whereas indeed grace is always necessary for the doing of good, in some cases it bolsters an option for the good that had already been made, thanks to free will. The succeeding pages are taken up with giving both grace and free will their due. Cassian accomplishes this, at least to his own satisfaction, first, by asserting the goodness of human nature, "which has been bestowed by the kindness of the Creator" (13.9.5), thus setting the possibility for the will's right orientation; and, second, by demonstrating from Scripture that sometimes grace and sometimes free will is at the root of a particular good action, although both are required to bring it to completion. But his analysis of the working of the two leaves something to be desired because he simply juxtaposes them without seeking to explain their interaction in any significant way. In other words, Cassian does not explore the influence of grace upon the will; he merely says that such influence exists. And he is inconsistent with his previous statements to the effect that grace is an absolute and universal necessity, because for him it is not always such with regard to the orientation and purification of the will.

The immediate historical background to Cassian's position here deserves a brief retelling. Augustine's teaching on grace and free will, elaborated in the face of the Pelagian heresy during the second decade of the fifth century, had made its way to southern Gaul by the early 420s. While Pelagius had taught that human beings were able to perform virtuous acts that would merit salvation thanks to their natural gifts alone, and that in fact they were obliged to perform what they were capable of doing, Augustine had denied the power of such gifts to accomplish anything whatsoever of enduring value, and he had placed this denial in the context of an understanding of divine predestination that suggested the valuelessness of all human effort to be virtuous. Some monks of southern Gaul, while not drawn to Pelagius (although they were sympathetic to the asceticism that his system implied and even demanded), found themselves also unattracted to Augustine's views. In their estimation his pessimism concerning human effort and his doctrine of predestination undercut the whole possibility of conversion and the necessity of the ascetical practices that were at the heart of monasticism. Despite Augustine's attempts in 426 to clarify his position with two treatises entitled *De gratia et libero arbitrio* and *De correptione et gratia,* a large number of monks, including Cassian, remained unmoved; for clarification in this instance did not mean a change of stance. The thirteenth conference, then, was produced in order to address the problem raised by Augustine, and it had for its goal the restoration of free will and human effort to what its author believed to be their rightful place.

Although Cassian does not mention Augustine by name in the present conference, there are at least two allusions to him and to his teaching in addition to what the general tenor of the conference presupposes. There is a rejection of Augustine's pessimism regarding salvation (well expressed in his narrow interpretation of 1 Timothy 2:4 in *Enchir.* 27.103 and *De correp. et gratia* 14.44) in 13.7, with its stress on God's universal call to salvation. More particularly, Cassian here seems to take a different position than does Augustine with reference to the salvation of unbaptized infants. Whereas Augustine claimed that they were damned (cf. *De peccat. meritis et remis.* 1.16.21, 1.23.33; *De natura et gratia* 8.9; *De anima et eius origine* [1.9.11]), Cassian's emphasis on Matthew 18:14 ("It is not the will of your Father in heaven that one of these little ones should perish") suggests that he finds such a view untenable. And in 13.11.1 there is a reference to those persons–presumably Pelagius on the one hand and Augustine on the other–who maintain too unyieldingly the preeminence of either grace or free will:

"For many who hold to one of these alternatives and assert it more freely than is right have fallen into different self-contradictory errors." It is clear, incidentally, from Cassian's refusal, in his own eyes, to overstress the capability of free will that he sees himself fighting against not only Augustine but also Pelagius. The Pelagian theology of earned grace is firmly rejected in 13.16.1: "But no one should think that we have suggested these things in an attempt to say that the whole of salvation is entirely dependent on our faith, according to the godless opinion of some, who ascribe everything to free will and understand that the grace of God is dispensed to each person in conformity with his deserts."

That Cassian takes his own views with the utmost seriousness and as fully warranted is evident from his unaccustomed appeals to the tradition and authority of the Church at large, which are found in 13.11.4, 13.12.2, and 13.18.4, as well as from the polemical tone that marks 13.18.5: "If something cleverly gleaned from human argumentation and reasoning seems contrary to this understanding, it should be avoided rather than called forth to the destruction of the faith."

This thirteenth of Cassian's conferences provides an excellent example of how a controversial theological position can generate an opposing position on the same subject. The passages in the other conferences in which he speaks of grace and human effort (cf. the note at 2.1.3f.) can usually be construed without any difficulty whatsoever in the most unobjectionable fashion; they are fairly clear about the primacy of grace while at the same time declaring the necessity of human exertion. The same thing can even be said about the first third of the present conference, which in turn suggests the possibility, however unlikely it may be, that Cassian changed his mind with respect to the proper balance between the two elements in the very process of writing it, and that he never subsequently made the appropriate corrections in the earlier part. This is not to say that Cassian had ever thought very deeply about the relationship between the two components before he opted to take the position that he did in 13.8.4ff.; he was simply handing on the wisdom that he had received. But, having been made aware of Augustine's views on a matter to which he himself had probably given rather little thought, he saw in those views a threat to an understanding of grace and free will that he had never had the occasion to question. If now, in Cassian's estimation, Augustine had overstressed the seemingly arbitrary aspect of a grace that was incommensurable with any human activity, it devolved on him to re-stress free will and human effort. In re-stressing these elements, however, it would appear that he overstressed them, for merely giving them a nearly equal place with grace was to give them too great a place.

For analyses of Cassian's understanding of grace and related issues cf. Alexander Hoch, *Die Lehre des Johannes Cassianus von Natur und Gnade: Ein Beitrag zur Geschichte des Gnadenstreits im 5. Jahrhundert* (Freiburg, 1894); Joseph Laugier, *S. Jean Cassien et sa doctrine sur la grâce* (Lyon, 1908); DTC 14.1802–1808; Léon Christiani, *Jean Cassien: La spiritualité du désert* (S. Wandrille, 1946), 2.237–268; Peter Munz, "John Cassian," *The Journal of Ecclesiastical History* 11 (1960): 15–17; Chadwick, 110–136; D. J. Macqueen, "John Cassian and Grace and Free Will, with Particular Reference to Institutio XII and Collatio XIII," *Recherches de théologie ancienne et médiévale* 44 (1977): 5–28 (probably the most interesting approach to the issue; the author seeks to demonstrate that Cassian is not inconsistent with himself and that he can be reconciled to Augustine); Marianne Djuth, *The Problem of Free Choice of Will in the Thought of Augustine, John Cassian, and Faustus of Riez* (Ph.D. diss., Toronto, 1988), 105–147; Robert A. Markus, *The End of Ancient Christianity* (Cambridge, 1990), 177–179 (the author claims that Cassian is aiming not at Augustine but at Pelagius in the thirteenth conference, although he does so "from a point of view more in line with a pre-Augustinian theological tradition than with Augustine's anti-Pelagian theology").

XIII. The Third Conference of Abba Chaeremon: On God's Protection

Chapters

I. When we returned to the morning synaxis after a short sleep and were waiting for the old man, Abba Germanus was struck with bewilderment by the fact that in the previous discussion, whose power had filled us with the highest desire for an as yet untried chastity, the blessed old man had in a single assertion nullified the value of human effort. He had stated that a human being, although striving with all his strength for a good result, would nonetheless be unable to possess the good unless he had received it through the generosity of a divine bestowal rather than by his own zealous toil. As we were puzzling over this question, then, the blessed Chaeremon arrived at our cell. When he noticed that we were speaking quietly together about something, and after the ceremony of prayers and psalms had been gone through more quickly than usual, he asked what the matter was.

II. Then GERMANUS said: "By reason of the sublimity of the most excellent virtue that was analyzed during our nighttime discussion, we are, I would say, virtually excluded from believing in its feasibility. Hence it seems absurd to us (if you will excuse me for saying it) that the labor's reward–namely, the perfection of chastity, which is acquired by the intensity of one's own efforts–is not attributed directly to the laborer's toil. For, if for example we see a farmer constantly hard at work tilling the soil, it is ridiculous not to ascribe the harvest to his diligence."

III.1. CHAEREMON: "From the very example that you have given it is all the more clear that the laborer's toil can accomplish nothing without the help of God. For a farmer, when he has expended all his efforts in tilling the soil, would not then be able to attribute the produce of his fields and his abundant yield to his own toil, which he often saw was useless, if adequate rainfall and a quietly peaceful winter had not played their part. For we have frequently seen fruit already ripe and perfectly mature snatched as it were out of the hands of those holding it, and a continual intense effort conferring nothing on the toilers, because it was not assisted by the Lord's guidance.

2. "Consequently, just as the divine goodness does not bestow an abundant yield on sluggish farmers who do not plow their fields frequently, so neither will night-long anxiety be profitable to those who labor if it has not been smiled upon by the Lord's mercy. Yet human pride should never strive herein to put itself on the same level as or to interfere with the grace of God, nor should it try to make itself a sharer in the gifts of God in such a way as to think that its own efforts have brought upon it the divine generosity, boasting that its own deserving toil has been responded to with an abundant harvest. 3. For a person should consider and reflect in all honesty upon the fact that by his own power he would have been unable to expend the efforts that he did when he was intently working out of a desire for an abundance if the Lord's protection and mercy had not fortified him to endure all the burdens imposed by farming. Likewise, his will and strength would have been useless if the divine mercy had not provided the wherewithal for producing the plenty that too much dryness or rain sometimes deprive him of. 4. For although the Lord has granted strong cattle, bodily health, a successful outcome to every activity, and prosperous deeds, prayer must still be offered lest, as it is written, there be 'a heaven of brass and an earth of iron,'[1] and lest 'the swarming locust eat what the cutting locust has left, and the caterpillar devour what the swarming locust has left, and the blight consume what the caterpillar has left.'[2] Not in this alone does the effort of the toiling farmer stand in need of the Divinity's assistance. It must also fend off unexpected accidents by which, even if a field is loaded with the desired fruitful yield, he will not only be frustrated by waiting in vain for what he has hoped for but will even be deprived of the abundant crop that has already been harvested and that is stored on the threshing floor or in the barn.

5. "From this it is clear that the origin not only of good acts but even of good thoughts is in God. He both inspires in us the beginnings of a holy will and grants the ability and the opportunity to bring to fulfillment the things that we rightly desire. For 'every good gift and every perfect benefit is from above, coming down from the Father of lights.'[3] He it is who begins what is good and carries out and fulfills it in us, as the Apostle says: 'He who gives

seed to the sower will also provide bread to eat and will multiply your seed and make the fruit of your righteousness increase.'[4]

6. "But it is up to us to conform humbly to the grace of God that daily draws us on. Otherwise, if we resist it with a stiff neck and uncircumcised ears,[5] as it is written, we shall deserve to hear what Jeremiah says: 'Shall the one who falls not rise again, and the one who has turned away not turn back? Why, then, has this people in Jerusalem turned away with a contentious turning? They have stiffened their necks, they have not wished to return.'"[6]

IV. GERMANUS: "This tends toward the destruction of free will and seems to stand in opposition to a good understanding of it that we cannot hastily reject. For we see that many Gentiles, who certainly do not deserve the grace of divine assistance, shine with the virtues not only of temperance and patience but even–which is more wonderful–with that of chastity. How can it be believed that their free will was fettered and that these things were bestowed on them by the gift of God when they were in fact followers of worldly wisdom and not only completely ignorant of the grace of God but even of the true God himself, as we know from the course of our reading and from the teaching of certain persons? They are said to have possessed the purest chastity thanks to their own laborious efforts."

V.1. CHAEREMON: "I am pleased that, although you are inflamed with the greatest love for a truth that should be known, you nonetheless propose some foolish things, the response to which will make the power of the Catholic faith more evident and–as I would say–more firmly established. For what wise person would make such contradictory statements, asserting as you did yesterday that the heavenly purity of chastity could not be bestowed on any mortal, and now believing that even the Gentiles have possessed it by their own power? 2. But since you are doubtlessly–as has been said–suggesting these things out of a zeal to uncover the truth, pay attention to what we should hold in this regard.

"First, it should never be believed that the philosophers attained to the kind of chastity of mind that is demanded of us, who are enjoined against mentioning not only fornication but even impurity among ourselves.[7] They had a certain μερικη, or small portion of chastity–that is, abstinence of the flesh–whereby they merely curbed their wanton desire from sexual intercourse. They were unable, however, to attain to an interior purity of mind and an enduring purity of body either in act or—I would say—in thought. 3. Socrates, the most famous of them, did not blush to confess this about himself, as they themselves assert. For one time a certain expert in physiognomy saw him and said: ομματα παιδεραστοι—that is: These are the eyes of a corruptor of boys. When his disciples rushed upon the man, wanting to avenge the insult to their teacher, it is said that he restrained their anger with these words: παυσασθε, εταιροι. ειμι γαρ, επεχω δε—that is: Calm yourselves, my friends. For I am such, but I contain myself. It is very clear, then, not only from our assertion but even from their own say-so that they only repressed actual immoral behavior—that is, wicked intercourse—by main force, but that desire for and delight in this passion had not been cut out from their hearts.

4. "With what horror should the words of Diogenes be recounted: For what he did, which the philosophers of this world are not embarrassed to recount as something memorable, can be neither spoken of nor listened to by us without shame. As the story is told, he said to a person who was to be punished for the crime of adultery: το δωρεαν πωλοιμενον θανατω μη αγοραζε—that is: You should not purchase with your death what is freely sold. It is obvious, then, that they did not know the virtue of true chastity to which we aspire. Therefore, it is quite certain that our circumcision, which is in the spirit, can only be possessed by the gift of God, and that it only exists in those who are devoted to God with utter contrition of spirit.

VI.1. "Consequently, although it can be shown that human beings and that by itself alone—that is, without the help of God—human frailty can accomplish nothing which pertains to salvation, this is still nowhere more evident than in acquiring and maintaining chastity. For since the discussion on the difficulty concerning its integrity has been put off for so long, now let us briefly discuss its means.

2. "Who, I ask, no matter how fervent in spirit, would be able to endure on his own, with no support from human praise, the harshness of the desert and even an abundance of dry bread, to say nothing of a daily lack of it? Who could, as a rule, tolerate a

constant thirst for water without the Lord's consolation and deprive his human eyes of that sweet and delightful morning repose, compressing the whole period of sleep within the space of four hours? Who would be capable without the grace of God of pursuing continual intense reading or unremitting and assiduous work, receiving no profit of present gain? 3. Just as none of these things can be constantly desired by us without the divine inspiration, so neither can they at all be brought to fulfillment without his assistance.

"Now let us not only prove these same things to ourselves by the teaching of experience but also make them clearer by irrefutable indications and arguments. Does not in many instances a certain frailty enter in and destroy plans that we have made and that we wish to carry out for a good reason, even though there is no lack of an ardent desire and a perfect will? Does not the projected result come to naught unless the power of bringing it to fulfillment has been granted by the Lord's mercy? Thus, although there is an innumerable multitude of people who would desire to adhere faithfully to the pursuit of virtue, nonetheless you find that those who can bring it off or put up with it are extremely rare. 4. I am not even speaking of the cases where no sickness at all hinders us but the ability to do everything that we want does not lie in our grasp. For we do not keep to solitary silence or strict fasting or intense reading by our own will even when we are able to, but even against our own will we are frequently distracted from beneficial practices by conflicting interests, so that we are obliged to beseech the Lord for ample space or time in which to carry out these things.

5. "And certainly it is not enough for us to have the ability unless the Lord also grants us the opportunity of doing the things that in fact we can. About this the Apostle says: 'We wanted to come to you time and again, but Satan hindered us.'[8] Thus we sometimes feel ourselves called away for a good reason even from spiritual concerns, so that, as the intensity of our pursuit is unwillingly interrupted and we give in somewhat to the weakness of our flesh, we may learn—even against our will—a salutary patience. The blessed Apostle says something similar about this plan of God: 'Therefore I asked the Lord three times that this would

leave me. And he said to me: My grace is sufficient for you, for strength is perfected in weakness.'[9] And again: 'We do not know what to pray for as we ought.'[10]

VII.1. "For God's purpose, according to which he did not make the human being to perish but to live forever, abides unchanging. When his kindness sees shining in us the slightest glimmer of good will, which he himself has in fact sparked from the hard flint of our heart, he fosters it, stirs it up, and strengthens it with his inspiration, 'desiring all to be saved and to come to the knowledge of the truth.'[11] For, he says, 'it is not the will of your Father who is in heaven that one of these little ones should perish.'[12] And again he says: 'God does not wish a soul to perish, but he withdraws and reflects, lest one who has been cast down perish utterly.'[13]

2. "For he is truthful and does not lie when he sets down with an oath: 'As I live, says the Lord God, I do not wish the death of the sinner but that he turn from his way and live.'[14] How can it be thought without great sacrilege of him who does not want a single little one to perish that he does not wish all to be saved universally, but only a few instead of all? Those who perish, therefore, perish against his will, as he daily cries out to each one of them: 'Turn from your wicked ways. And why will you die, O house of Israel?'[15] And again: 'How often have I wanted to gather your sons as a hen gathers her chicks under her wings, and you would not.'[16] And he says: 'Why has this people in Jerusalem turned away with a contentious turning? They have hardened their faces, they have refused to return.'[17]

3. "Therefore the grace of Christ is at hand every day. It calls out and says to everyone without exception: 'Come to me, all you who labor and are burdened, and I will give you rest,'[18] because he desires 'all to be saved and to come to the knowledge of the truth.' But if he does not call all universally but only a few, it follows that not all are burdened by original sin and by present sin and that these words are not true: 'All have sinned and fall short of the glory of God.'[19] Nor would it be believed that 'death has passed through all men.'[20] 4. And so true is it that all who perish do so contrary to God's will that God is said not to have made death

itself, as Scripture testifies: 'God did not make death, nor does he rejoice in the loss of the living.'[21]

"This is very frequently the reason for the fact that, when we ask for bad things instead of good, our prayer is heard either after a delay or not at all. On the other hand, what we consider bad, the Lord, like a most gracious physician, deigns to apply to us for our benefit even against our will. And sometimes he impedes and restrains our evil inclinations and our fatal impulses from a detestable outcome, drawing us back to salvation as we hasten to our death and extricating us, unbeknownst to ourselves, from the jaws of hell.

VIII.1. "Through the prophet Hosea the divine word well expressed this concern and providence of his in our regard by way of the image of Jerusalem as a prostitute who is drawn with wicked ardor to the worship of idols. She says: 'I will go after my lovers, who give me my bread and my water, my wool and my flax, my oil and my drink.'[22] The divine condescension replies, with a view to her salvation and not to her will: 'Behold, I will hedge in her paths with thorns, and I will hedge her in with a wall, and she will not find her ways. And she will pursue her lovers and not lay hold of them, and she will seek them and not find them, and she will say: I will return to my first husband, because then it was better for me than it is now.'[23]

2. "Again, the obstinacy and contempt with which we rebelliously disdain him when he urges us to return for our own salvation is described in this way: 'I said that you shall call me Father,' he says, 'and that you shall not cease to come after me. But just as a woman despises her lover, so the house of Israel has despised me, says the Lord.'[24] Since he had compared Jerusalem to an adultress abandoning her spouse, he has also quite appropriately compared his love and abiding kindness to a man who is desperately in love with a woman. 3. For the graciousness and love of God, which he always shows to the human race and which is never extinguished by hurt, such that it would lose concern for our salvation and withdraw from his original intention as if overcome by our wickedness, could not be expressed by a better comparison than the example of a man who is passionately in love with a

woman and who is all the more vehemently inflamed with desire for her the more he feels that he is neglected and despised by her.

"The divine protection, then, is always inseparably present to us, and so great is the love of the Creator for his creature that his providence not only stands by her but even goes constantly before her. The prophet, who has experienced this, confesses it very clearly when he says: 'My God will go before me with his mercy.'[25] 4. When he notices good will making an appearance in us, at once he enlightens and encourages it and spurs it on to salvation, giving increase to what he himself planted and saw arise from our own efforts. For, he says, 'before they cry, I will hear them. I will hear them when they are still speaking.'[26] And again: 'As soon as he hears the voice of your cry, he will respond to you.'[27] Not only does he graciously inspire holy desires, but he also arranges favorable moments in one's life and the possibility of good results, and he shows the way of salvation to those who are straying.

IX.1. "Hence human reason does not easily discern how the Lord gives to those who ask, is found by those who seek, and opens to those who knock,[28] and on the other hand how he is found by those who do not seek, appears openly among these who were not asking for him, and stretches out his hands the whole day to a people who do not believe in him and who gainsay him,[29] calls those who resist and are far away, draws the unwilling to salvation, removes from those who want to sin the means of fulfilling their desire, and graciously hinders those who are hastening on to what is evil.

2. "But who understands clearly how the sum of salvation is attributed to our will, about which it is said: 'If you wish, and you hear me, you shall eat the good things of the land'?[30] And how is it 'not of the one who wills or of the one who runs, but of God who is merciful'?[31] What, moreover, does it mean that God 'renders to each one according to his works'?[32] And: 'It is God who works in you both to will and to accomplish, for the sake of his good pleasure'?[33] And: 'This is not from you, but it is a gift of God, not because of works, lest anyone boast'?[34] And what do these words mean: 'Draw near to the Lord, and he will draw near to you'?[35] And what is said elsewhere: 'No one comes to me unless the Father who sent me draws him'?[36] 3. What is this: 'Make straight

paths for your feet, and direct your ways'?[37] And what is it that we say when we pray: 'Direct my way in your sight'?[38] And: 'Make my steps perfect in your paths so that my footsteps may not slip'?[39] Why, again, are we admonished: 'Make yourselves a new heart and a new spirit'?[40] And what is it that is promised: 'I will give them one heart, and I will place a new spirit in their bowels, and I will remove the stony heart from their flesh, and I will give them a heart of flesh so that they may walk in my precepts and keep my laws'?[41] 4. What does the Lord command when he says: 'Wash your heart of iniquity, Jerusalem, so that you may be saved'?[42] And what does the prophet ask of the Lord when he says: 'Create in me a clean heart, O God'?[43] And again: 'You will wash me, and I shall be whiter than snow'?[44] What is it that is said to us: 'Enlighten yourselves with the light of knowledge'?[45] And what is it that is said of God: 'Who teaches man knowledge'?[46] And: 'The Lord enlightens the blind'?[47] Or what we say when we pray with the prophet: 'Enlighten my eyes that I may never fall asleep in death'?[48]

"What does this all mean except that in each of these cases both the grace of God and our freedom of will are affirmed, since even by his own activity a person can occasionally be brought to a desire for virtue, but he always needs to be helped by the Lord? 5. For a person does not enjoy good health whenever he wishes, nor is he freed from illness at the desire of his will. What is the point of having longed for the grace of good health if God, who has bestowed the use of life itself, does not also impart vigorous well-being? But so that it might be still more evident that out of a good nature, which has been bestowed by the kindness of the Creator, the beginnings of a good will sometimes spring up, although they cannot attain to the perfection of virtue unless they are guided by the Lord, here is the witness of the Apostle, who says: 'To will is present to me, but I find no way to perform the good.'[49]

X.1. "For divine Scripture corroborates the freedom of our will when it says: 'Guard your heart with all care.'[50] But the Apostle lays bare its weakness when he says: 'May the Lord guard your hearts and your understanding in Christ Jesus.'[51] David proclaims the power of free will when he says: 'I have inclined my heart to do your righteous deeds.'[52] But he also teaches its weakness when he prays and says: 'Incline my heart to your testimonies and not to avarice.'[53] Solomon says as well: 'May the Lord incline our hearts to himself, so that we may walk in all his ways, and keep his commands and his ceremonies and his judgments.'[54] 2. The psalmist refers to the power of our will when he says: 'Keep your tongue from evil, and let your lips not speak falsehood.'[55] Our own prayer testifies to its weakness when we say: 'Place, O Lord, a guard at my mouth and a gate at my lips.'[56] The ability of our will is declared by the Lord when it is said: 'Break the chains of your neck, O captive daughter of Zion.'[57] The prophet chants its frailty when he says: 'The Lord looses those who are bound.'[58] And: 'You have broken my chains. To you will I offer a sacrifice of praise.'[59] 3. We hear the Lord calling us in the Gospel to hasten to him by our free will: 'Come to me, all you who labor and are burdened, and I will give you rest.' But the same Lord testifies to its weakness when he says: 'No one can come to me unless the Father who sent me draws him.' The Apostle refers to our free will when he says: 'Run in such a way as to obtain.'[60] But John the Baptist bears witness to its weakness when he says: 'No one can receive anything of himself unless it is given him from heaven.'[61] 4. We are ordered to guard our souls carefully by one prophet when he says: 'Guard your souls.'[62] But another prophet declares by the same Spirit: 'Unless the Lord guard the city, in vain has he who guards it kept watch.'[63] The Apostle writes to the Philippians and refers to their free will when he says: 'Work out your salvation with fear and trembling.'[64] But in order to show its weakness he adds: 'It is God who works in you both to will and to accomplish, for the sake of his good pleasure.'

XI.1. "These things are mixed together and fused so indistinguishably that which is dependent on which is a great question as far as many people are concerned—that is, whether God has mercy on us because we manifest the beginnings of a good will, or we acquire the beginnings of a good will because God is merciful. For many who hold to one of these alternatives and assert it more freely than is right have fallen into different self-contradictory errors. For if we said that the beginning of free will was up to us, what was there in Paul the persecutor and in Matthew the tax-collector, one of whom was drawn to salvation while intent upon the blood and torment of the innocent,[65] the other upon violence and the plunder of public property?[66] 2. But if we said that the beginnings of a good will were always inspired by the grace of God, what should we say about the faith of Zacchaeus[67] and about the devotion of the thief on the cross?[68] By their own desire they brought a certain force to bear on the heavenly kingdom[69] and anticipated the particular signs of their calling. But if we attributed the perfection of virtue and the carrying out of the commandments of God to our will, how do we pray: 'Confirm, O God, what you have worked in us'?[70] And: 'Direct upon us the work of our hands'?[71] We know that Balaam was brought to curse Israel, but we see that it was not permitted him to curse when he wanted to.[72] Abimelech was prevented from touching Rebekah and sinning against God.[73]

"Joseph was led away because of his brothers' envy, so that the progeny of the children of Israel would be in Egypt and remedies for future famine would be made ready for those who plotted their brother's death. 3. This same Joseph made this plain when he disclosed himself to his brothers and said: 'Do not be afraid, and let it not seem hard to you that you sold me into these parts. For God sent me ahead of you for your salvation.'[74] And then: 'God sent me on before so that you would be preserved upon the earth and would be able to have food to live. I was sent not by your own design but by the will of God, who made me as it were the father of Pharaoh, the master of all his house and a prince in the whole land of Egypt.'[75] And when his brothers were frightened after the death of their father and he removed their anxious fear, he said: 'Fear not. Can we resist the will of God? You contrived evil against me, but God turned it into good, in order to exalt me, as you see at present, so that he might save many peoples.'[76] 4. The blessed David likewise declared in the hundred and fourth psalm that this was done providentially at that time when he says: 'He called a famine upon the land, and he broke the whole staff of bread. He sent before them a man, Joseph, who was sold as a slave.'[77]

"These two things—that is, the grace of God and free will—certainly seem mutually opposed to one another, but both are in accord, and we understand that we must accept both in like manner by reason of our religion, lest by removing one of them from the human being we seem to contravene the rule of the Church's faith. 5. For when God sees us turning in order to will what is good, he comes to us, directs us, and strengthens us, for 'as soon as he hears the voice of your cry, he will respond to you.' And: 'Call upon me,' he says, 'on the day of distress, and I will save you, and you shall glorify me.'[78] On the other hand, if he sees us unwilling or growing lukewarm, he brings to our hearts salutary exhortations by which a good will may be either repaired or formed in us.

XII.1. "For it must not be believed that God made the human being in such a way that he could never will or be capable of the good. He has not allowed him a free will if he has only conceded that he will what is evil and be capable of it but not of himself either will the good or be capable of it. And how will those words of the Lord stand, which he spoke after the sin of the first man: 'Behold, Adam has become like one of us, knowing good and evil'?[79] 2. For we must not think that he was such as to have been completely ignorant of the good previously. Otherwise it will have to be said that he was fashioned like a kind of irrational and senseless animal, which is quite absurd and utterly foreign to the Catholic faith. Rather, in the words of the most wise Solomon: 'God made man upright'[80]—that is, so that he would continually enjoy knowledge only of the good. But 'they sought out many thoughts,'[81] for they came to know, as has been said, good and evil. After his sin, therefore, Adam conceived a knowledge of evil that he had not had, but he did not lose the knowledge of good that he had received. 3. Finally, in the words of the Apostle it is very clearly stated that after Adam's sin the human race did not lose the knowledge of the good: 'When the Gentiles, who do not have the law, naturally do the things of the law, they who do not have the law are a law unto themselves. They show the work of the law written in their hearts, their conscience bearing witness to them and their thoughts within them accusing or defending them, on the day when God will judge the secrets of men.'[82]

"It is with this understanding that through the prophet the Lord also rebukes the willful—not natural—blindness of the Jews, which they brought upon themselves by their own obstinacy. 'Listen, you deaf,' he says, 'and look, you blind, so that you may see. Who is deaf but my servant? And who is blind but the one to whom I have sent my messengers?'[83] 4. And so that no one would be able to ascribe this blindness of theirs to nature and not to will, he says elsewhere: 'Lead out the people who are blind and who have eyes, who are deaf and who have ears.'[84] And again he says: 'You who have eyes and do not see, and ears and do not hear.'[85] The Lord says in the Gospel too: 'Seeing they do not see, and hearing they do not hear, nor do they understand.'[86] In them there is fulfilled the prophecy of Isaiah that says: 'Hearing you shall hear, and you shall not understand, and seeing you shall see, and you shall not see. For the heart of this people has grown heavy, and their ears are dull of hearing, and they have shut their eyes, lest at some time they see with their eyes and hear with their ears and understand with their heart and be converted and I heal them.'[87] 5. Finally, in order to indicate that the possibility for good lay in them, he said when he rebuked the Pharisees: 'Why do you not of yourselves judge what is just?'[88] He certainly would not have said this to them if he had not known that they could discern what was correct by natural judgment.

"Therefore, we must be on the watch lest we attribute all the good works of holy persons to the Lord in such a way that we ascribe nothing but what is bad and perverse to human nature. Herein, indeed, we are refuted by the testimony of the most wise Solomon, or rather by that of the Lord, whose words these are. For when the building of the Temple was finished, he prayed and said: 'David my father wished to build a house to the name of the Lord God of Israel. And the Lord said to David my father: You have done well to think in your heart about building a house to my name, and to reflect on this in your mind. But you shall not build a house to my name.'[89] 6. Should it be said, then, that this thought and this reflection of King David was good and from God or bad and from man? For if this thought was good and was from God, why was its being brought to fulfillment denied by the one by whom it was inspired? But if it was bad and was from man, why was it praised by the Lord? It remains, then, that it should be believed to be both good and from man.

"This is the way that we too can judge our daily thoughts. For it was not given to David alone to think good of himself, nor is it denied us by nature ever to perceive or to think what is good. 7. It cannot be doubted, therefore, that the seeds of virtue exist in every soul, having been placed there by the kindness of the Creator. But unless they have been germinated by the help of God they will not be able to increase in perfection, because, according to the blessed Apostle, 'neither is the one who plants anything, nor the one who waters, but God who gives the increase.'[90] The book entitled *The Shepherd* also teaches very clearly that freedom of will is at a human being's disposal to a certain degree. In it two angels—that is, a good one and a bad one—are said to be attached to each one of us, but it is up to the human being to choose which to follow.[91]

8. "Consequently there always remains in the human being a free will that can either neglect or love the grace of God. For the Apostle would not have commanded and said: 'Work out your salvation with fear and trembling,' if he had not known that it could be either tended or neglected by us. But lest they believe that they do not stand in need of the divine help for the work of salvation, he adds: 'It is God who works in you both to will and to accomplish, for the sake of his good pleasure.' And therefore he warns Timothy, saying: 'Do not neglect the grace of God that is in you.'[92] And again: 'For this reason I exhort you to stir up the grace of God that is in you.'[93] 9. Hence he also writes to the Corinthians, encouraging and admonishing them not to show themselves unworthy of the grace of God because of fruitless works, saying: 'We, helping, exhort you not to receive the grace of God in vain.'[94] Doubtless the reception of saving grace was of no value to Simon because he had received it in vain. For he did not choose to obey the precepts of the blessed Peter, who said: 'Repent of your wickedness, and pray God if perhaps this thought of your heart may be forgiven you. For I see that you are in the gall of bitterness and in the fetters of iniquity.'[95]

10. "It anticipates a human being's will, then, since it is said: 'My God will go before me with his mercy.'[96] On the other hand, our will anticipates God when he lingers and as it were stands still with the salutary intent of testing our will, as it says: 'In the morning my prayer shall come before you.'[97] And again: 'I anticipated the dawn, and I cried out.'[98] And: 'My eyes have anticipated the break of day.'[99]

11. "He also calls and invites us when he says: 'The whole

day I have stretched out my hands to a people who do not believe in me and who gainsay me.'[100] And he is invited by us when we say to him: 'The whole day I have stretched out my hands to you.'[101] He waits for us, as is said through the prophet: 'Therefore the Lord waits to have mercy on you.'[102] And he is waited for by us when we say: 'I have waited, I have waited for the Lord, and he turned to me.'[103] And: 'I have waited for your salvation, Lord.'[104] He strengthens us when he says: 'I instructed and strengthened their arms, and they devised evil against me.'[105] And he exhorts us to strengthen ourselves when he says: 'Strengthen your weak hands and steady your feeble knees.'[106] 12. Jesus cries: 'If anyone thirsts, let him come to me and drink.'[107] The prophet also cries to him: 'I have labored with crying, my throat has become hoarse. My eyes have grown weak as I hope in my God.'[108] The Lord seeks us when he says: 'I sought, and there was no man. I called, and there was no one who responded.'[109] And he himself is sought by his bride, who mourns tearfully: 'In my chamber at night I sought him whom my soul loved. I sought him and I did not find him, I called him and he did not answer me.'[110]

XIII.1. "And so the grace of God always works together with our will on behalf of the good, helping it in everything and protecting and defending it, so that sometimes it even demands and expects from it certain efforts of a good will, lest it seem to bestow its gifts wholly on one who is asleep or relaxed in lazy sluggishness. It seeks occasions whereby the torpor of human slothfulness may be shattered and its own munificent generosity may not appear unreasonable, dispensing it under the pretext of a certain desire and toil. But the grace of God nonetheless remains free, since with inestimable generosity it confers on meager and small efforts such immortal glory and such gifts of everlasting blessedness.

2. "For because the faith of the thief on the cross came first, it must not therefore be asserted that a blessed life in paradise was not freely promised him. Nor should it be believed that it was the repentance of King David—expressed in the brief phrase: 'I have sinned against the Lord'[111]—that removed those two so very serious sins of his, and not rather the mercy of God, so that he deserved to hear through the prophet Nathan: 'The Lord has removed your iniquity. You shall not die.'[112] That he added murder to adultery

was indeed due to free will, but that he was reproached by the prophet was a matter of the grace of divine condescension. 3. Again, that he humbly acknowledged his sin was his doing, but that he was so quickly promised forgiveness for such great crimes was a gift of the merciful Lord.

"And what shall we say of this very brief confession and of the incomparable immensity of the divine reward, when it is so easy to reflect on the blessed Apostle as he gazes on the vastness of his future reward and speaks about his innumerable persecutions? 'For this momentary and light tribulation of ours,' he says, 'works in us an immeasurable and incomparable eternal weight of glory.'[113] About this he also speaks firmly elsewhere when he says: 'The sufferings of the present time are not worthy of the future glory that will be revealed in us.'[114] 4. However much human weakness may strive, then, it will be unable to reach the level of the future reward, nor will it diminish divine grace by its own labors in such a way that it would not always remain free. Therefore, the aforesaid teacher of the Gentiles, although testifying that he has received the rank of an apostle by the grace of God when he says: 'By the grace of God I am what I am,'[115] nonetheless also declares that he has responded to divine grace when he says: 'His grace in me was not in vain, but I have labored more abundantly than all of them–yet not I, but the grace of God with me.'[116] 5. When he says: 'I have labored,' he is indicating the effort of his own will. When he says: 'Yet not I, but the grace of God,' he is pointing to the power of the divine protection. When he says: 'With me,' he is declaring that it has worked together not with a lazy or careless person but with one who labors and toils.

XIV.1. "We read that the divine righteousness also provided for this in the case of Job, his very experienced athlete, when the devil sought him out for single combat. For if he had engaged the enemy not by his own strength but with the protection of God's grace alone, and if he had borne that manifold burden of trial and destruction, refined by all the enemy's cruelty, supported not by any patient virtuousness of his own but only by the divine assistance, how would the devil not have repeated justly those slanderous words that he had uttered against him previously: 'Does Job worship God for nothing? Have you not hedged him and all his property round about? But remove your hand'—that is, let him fight against me by his own strength—'and he will curse you to your face.'[117] 2. But since the slanderous enemy did not dare to repeat any complaint of this sort after the conflict, he confessed that he had been conquered not by God's power but by Job's. Yet it must not be believed that the grace of God was in any way wanting to him either: It gave the one who tried him as much power to try him as he also knew that he had the strength to resist, without protecting him from his attack in such a way that there would be no room for human virtue. Instead it only provided that the raging enemy would not drive him mad and overcome him in his weakened condition by the unequal and wicked burden of the struggle.

3. "We are taught by the story of the centurion in the Gospel that the Lord occasionally tries our faith, so that it may become stronger and more glorious. Although the Lord certainly knew that he was going to heal his servant by the power of his word, he chose rather to offer his bodily presence, saying: 'I will come and heal him.'[118] But the ardent fervor of the man's faith transcended his offer, and he said: 'Lord, I am not worthy that you should enter under my roof, but only say a word and my servant shall be healed.'[119] At this the Lord marveled at him and praised him, singling him out from all the people of Israel who had believed, saying: 'Amen, I say to you, I have not found such great faith in Israel.'[120] 4. It would not have been praiseworthy or meritorious if Christ had singled out in him what he himself had given.

"We read that the divine righteousness also probed the faith of that most magnificent patriarch, when it is said: 'It happened that after these words God tried Abraham.'[121] For the divine righteousness wished to test not the faith that the Lord had inspired in him but that which he who had once been called and enlightened by the Lord could display by his own free will. Hence it was not without reason that the steadfastness of his faith was proved. And when the grace of God, which had left him for a time so that he might be tried, came to help him, he was told: 'Do not lay your hand on the boy or do anything to him, for now I know that you fear the Lord and that for my sake you did not spare your beloved son.'[122]

5. "It is foretold quite clearly by the Lawgiver in Deuteronomy that this kind of trial can befall us as well for the

sake of proving us: 'If a prophet or someone who says that he has seen a dream arises among you and he foretells a sign and a wonder, and what he has spoken comes to pass, and he tells you: Let us go and serve foreign gods that you do not know, do not listen to the words of that prophet or dreamer. For the Lord your God is trying you with a trial, to see whether you love him with all your heart and are keeping his commandments or not.'[123] 6. What then? When God permits this prophet or dreamer to arise, should it be believed that he is going to protect those whose faith he plans to test, such that he leaves to their free will no room whatsoever wherein they may confront with their own strength the one who is trying them?

"And why must those be tried at all who he knows are so weak and frail that they are utterly unable to resist by their own power the one who is trying them? But the righteousness of the Lord would certainly not have permitted them to be tried if he had not known that there was a commensurate power of resistance in them, whereby they could be fairly judged in either case as guilty or praiseworthy. 7. Such is what is said by the Apostle: 'Therefore, whoever thinks that he is standing should see that he not fall. No trial has seized you except what is common to humanity. But God is faithful, who will not permit you to be tried beyond your capacity. But with the trial he will also provide a way out, so that you may be able to endure.'[124] When he says: 'Whoever is standing should see that he not fall,' he is alerting free will, which he had certainly known could, once it had received grace, either stand by its own effort or fall by its own negligence. But when he says: 'It is nothing but a human trial that has overtaken you,' he is reproaching the weakness and inconstancy of their as yet frail mind, with which they were still unable to resist the throngs of evil spirits, against which he knew that he himself and those who are perfect are in daily combat. About them he says to the Ephesians: 'Our struggle now is not against flesh and blood but against principalities, against powers, against the world rulers of this darkness, against spirits of evil in heavenly places.'[125] But when he adds: 'But God is faithful, who will not permit you to be tried beyond your power,' he certainly does not want the Lord not to permit them to be tried, but rather that they not be tried more than they are able to bear. 8. The former indicates the power of free will, whereas the latter refers to the grace of the Lord, who arbitrates the struggles brought on by trials.

"In all these instances, then, it is proved that divine grace always rouses a human being's will in such a way as not to protect and defend it in everything. Thus it does not make him fight his spiritual enemies by his own efforts, so that he may appreciate the grace of God when he is the victor and his own weakness when he has been vanquished, and so that he may learn not to hope in his own strength but always in the divine assistance, and ever to turn to his protector. And in order that this might be verified not by our own interpretation but by the still clearer testimonies of divine Scripture, let us recall what is read in Joshua the son of Nun: 'The Lord,' it says, 'left these nations and did not want to disperse them, so that by them he might test Israel, to see whether it kept the commands of the Lord its God, and so that they might grow accustomed to fighting with their enemies.'[126]

9. "Now let us compare something mortal to the incomparable mercy of our Creator, not because it is equally good but because there is some similarity as far as lovingkindness is concerned. Imagine a good and careful nurse, who carries a small child in her bosom for a long while, so that eventually she might teach him to walk. First she lets him crawl, then holds him upright with her hand so that he will be supported at each step, then leaves him for a little while, only to grasp him at once when she sees that he is wavering, steadies him when he is tottering, picks him up when he has fallen down, and either prevents him from falling or lets him fall lightly and lifts him up after a tumble. But when she has brought him to boyhood or to the strength of adolescence and young manhood, she lays upon him some burdens and hardships by which he will not be oppressed but exercised, and she lets him brave his peers. How much more does the heavenly Father of all know whom to carry in the bosom of his grace and whom to exercise in his sight for virtue's sake by a decision of free will, yet helping him as he struggles, hearing him when he calls, not abandoning him when he looks for him, and occasionally snatching him from danger even unbeknownst to him.

XV.1. "Hence it is quite clear that 'inscrutable are the judgments of God and unsearchable his ways'[127] by which he draws the human race to salvation. We can prove this as well by examples of gospel callings. For by the voluntary condescension of his grace he chose Andrew and Peter and the other apostles, who were not at all thinking of healing and salvation. He not only accepted Zacchaeus, who in his faithfulness was eager to catch a glimpse of the Lord and was making up for his short stature on the sycamore's height, but he even honored him with the blessing of a visit.[128] 2. Paul he drew unwilling and opposed. Another he ordered to join him so inseparably that he did not give him the briefest respite when he asked to bury his father.[129] To Cornelius, who was ever intent on prayer and almsgiving, the way of salvation was shown as a reward, and through the visitation of an angel he was ordered to summon Peter and to hear the words of salvation from him, so that he and all his household would be saved.[130]

"And so the manifold wisdom of God dispenses the salvation of human beings by numerous and inscrutable kindnesses and imparts its generous grace according to the capacity of each person, so that he wills to administer healing not according to the uniform power of his majesty but according to the degree of faith that he finds in each person or that he himself has bestowed on each person. 3. For when someone believed that the will of Christ alone was enough to cleanse him of his leprosy, he cured him by the mere assent of his will, saying: 'I will it. Be clean.'[131] When someone else begged him to come and raise his dead daughter by laying his hand on her, he entered his house and granted what he was asking for in conformity with his expectations.[132] When another believed that the sum of well-being consisted in his oral command and responded: 'Only say a word and my servant shall be healed,'[133] he restored the weakened limbs to their former strength by a word of command, saying: 'Go, and be it done to you as you have believed.'[134] 4. When others hoped for healing by touching the hem of his garment, he bestowed the gifts of health abundantly.[135] To others he granted healing for their sickness when he was asked. To others he voluntarily offered healing. He encouraged others to hope when he said: 'Do you wish to be well?'[136] To others who were without hope he brought help. He searched out the desires of others before he satisfied their need, saying: 'What do you wish me to do for you?'[137] To another who did not know how to obtain what he desired he kindly showed it when he said: 'If you believe, you shall see the glory of God.'[138] 5. So abundantly did he pour forth his healing power among others that the evangelist recalls of them: 'He healed all their sick.'[139] But among others that immense abyss of Christ's good deeds was so stopped up that it is said: 'Jesus could do among them no powerful deeds because of their lack of faith.'[140] And God's generosity is shaped according to the capacity of human faith in such a way that he can say to one person: 'Be it done to you according to your faith';[141] but to another: 'Go, and be it done to you as you have believed'; while to another: 'Be it done to you as you wish';[142] and to still another: 'Your faith has saved you.'[143]

XVI1. "But no one should think that we have suggested these things in an attempt to say that the whole of salvation is entirely dependent on our faith, according to the godless opinion of some, who ascribe everything to free will and understand that the grace of God is dispensed to each person in conformity with his deserts. We, however, declare firmly and clearly that the grace of God sometimes even overflows and surpasses the limits of human faithlessness. 2. We recall that this was so in the case of that ruler in the Gospel who believed that his sick son could more easily be healed than raised when he was dead, and who in haste beseeched the Lord to come, saying: 'Come down before my son dies.'[144] Although Christ rebuked his lack of faith with these words: 'Unless you see signs and wonders, you do not believe,'[145] still he did not exercise his divine grace in conformity with the man's weak faith; he expelled the deadly feverish disease not by his bodily presence, according to the man's belief, but by his powerful word, when he said: 'Go, your son lives.'[146]

3. "We also read that the Lord poured out his overflowing grace in the case of the healing of the paralytic, when he first brought health of soul to one who was only asking for a cure of the sickness with which his body was afflicted. 'Son, be of good cheer,' he said, 'your sins are forgiven you.'[147] Whereupon, when the scribes did not believe that he could forgive human sins, he also unbound the man's limbs with a word and destroyed the power of the paralysis in order to confound their unbelief, saying:

'Why do you think evil in your hearts? What is easier, to say: Your sins are forgiven, or to say: Arise and walk? But that you may know that the Son of Man has power on earth to forgive sins, he said then to the paralytic: Arise, take your bed and go home.'[148]

4. "He also displayed the breadth of his spontaneous generosity in the case of the man who for thirty-eight years had been lying helpless by the side of the pool, hoping for healing from the movement of the water. He wished to arouse in him a desire for the healing of salvation, and so he said to him: 'Do you wish to be well?' And when the man complained about the lack of human assistance and said: 'I have no one to put me in the pool when the water has been stirred up,'[149] the Lord forgave his unbelief and ignorance and in his mercy restored to him his former health, not in the way that he had expected but as he himself willed, saying: 'Arise, take your bed and go home.'[150]

5. "What is so wonderful if these deeds accomplished by the Lord's power are told of, when divine grace also worked similar things through his servants? When Peter and John were going into the Temple and the man who was lame from his mother's womb, who could not walk a single step, asked for an alms, they did not give the paltry coins that the sick man requested but rather the ability to walk, and one who was hoping for the relief provided by a small offering they enriched with the prize of an unhoped-for well-being. In the words of Peter: 'Silver and gold I do not have, but what I have I give to you. In the name of Jesus Christ of Nazareth, rise and walk.'[151]

XVII.1. "From these examples which we have produced from the gospel writings we shall be able to perceive very clearly that God provides for the salvation of the human race in numberless different manners and in inscrutable ways. He inspires some, who wish it and thirst for it, to a greater ardor, while some others, who do not even wish it, he compels against their will. Sometimes he helps to accomplish the things that he sees we desire for our own good, and at other times he inspires the beginnings of that holy desire and bestows both the commencement of a good work and perseverance in it. 2. Hence it is that when we pray we proclaim that the Lord is not only our protector and savior but also our helper and supporter. For, inasmuch as he first calls us and draws us to salvation unaware and unwilling, he is our protector and savior, but inasmuch as he provides us with help in our struggle and supports and defends us when we seek refuge, he is called our supporter and our refuge.

"Finally, the blessed Apostle, reflecting on the manifold bounty of God's design and seeing that he has fallen into the vast and boundless sea as it were of God's goodness, exclaims: 'Oh, the depth of the riches of the wisdom and knowledge of God! How inscrutable are the judgments of God and how unsearchable his ways! For who has known the mind of the Lord?'[152] 3. Whoever believes that he can sound the depths of that immeasurable abyss by human reason is trying to nullify the marvelous aspect of this knowledge, then, which struck with awe the great teacher of the Gentiles. For the person who is sure that he can conceive in his mind or discuss at length the designs whereby God works salvation in human beings is certainly resisting the truth of the Apostle's words and declaring with impious audacity that the judgments of God are not inscrutable and that his ways are traceable.

4. "This design and love of his, which the Lord deigns with unwearying kindness to benefit us with and which he wishes to express by an act of human affection, although he discovers no such loving disposition in his creation to which he could worthily compare it, he has compared to the most tender heart of a loving mother. He uses this example because he can find nothing dearer in the nature of human beings, and he says: 'Can a mother forget her baby, so as not to have compassion on the son of her womb?'[153] Not satisfied with this comparison, however, he immediately goes beyond it and adds to it, saying: 'And though she may forget, yet I will not forget you.'[154]

XVIII.1. "From this it is clearly understood by those who measure the vastness of grace and the smallness of the human will not by vain talk but under the guidance of experience that 'the race is not to the swift, nor the battle to the strong, nor bread to the wise, nor wealth to the prudent, nor grace to the learned, but one and the same Spirit accomplishes all these things, distributing to each person as he wishes.'[155] 2. Therefore it is evident from indubitable faith and from—as I would say—palpable experience that the God of the universe, like a most loving father and a most gracious physician, works all things evenhandedly in everyone, according to the Apostle. Sometimes he inspires the beginnings of salvation and places in each person a fervent good will, while sometimes he grants the performance of the work and the perfection of virtuousness. Sometimes he calls back from near ruin and a sudden fall even the unwilling and the unaware, while sometimes he provides occasions and opportunities for salvation and withholds heedless and violent efforts from deadly outcomes. Some he supports as they hasten and run, while others he draws unwilling and resisting and compels them to a good will.

3. "But we are taught in the very words of the Lord that everything is granted us by the Divinity when we are not always resisting and constantly unwilling, and that the whole of our salvation must be ascribed not to our deserving works but to heavenly grace. Thus: 'You shall remember your ways and all your evil deeds with which you have been polluted, and you shall be displeased with yourselves in your own sight for all your wickedness which you have done. And you shall know that I am the Lord when I do good to you for my name's sake, not according to your evil ways nor according to your most wicked deeds, O house of Israel.'[156]

4. "Therefore it is understood by all the Catholic fathers, who have taught perfection of heart not by idle disputation but in fact and in deed, that the first aspect of the divine gift is that each person be inflamed to desire everything which is good, but in such a way that the choice of a free will faces each alternative fully. Likewise, the second aspect of divine grace is that the aforesaid practice of virtue bear results, but in such a way that the possibility of choice not be extinguished. The third aspect is that it pertains to the gifts of God that one persevere in a virtue that has been acquired, but not in such a way that a submissive freedom be taken captive. 5. Thus it is that the God of the universe must be believed to work all things in all, so that he stirs up, protects, and strengthens, but not so that he removes the freedom of will that he himself once granted. If something cleverly gleaned from human argumentation and reasoning seems contrary to this understanding, it should be avoided rather than called forth to the destruction of the faith. For we do not acquire faith from

understanding but understanding from faith, as it is written: 'If you do not believe, you will not understand.'[157] For how God works all things in us on the one hand and how everything is ascribed to free will on the other cannot be fully grasped by human intelligence and reason."

Strengthened as we were with this food, the blessed Chaeremon did not let us feel the burden of the difficult journey.

Textual References

1. Dt 28:23.
2. Jl 1:4.
3. Jas 1:17.
4. 2 Cor 9:10.
5. Cf. Acts 7:51.
6. Jer 8:4–5.
7. Cf. Eph 5:3.
8. 1 Thes 2:18.
9. 2 Cor 12:8–9.
10. Rom 8:26.
11. 1 Tm 2:4.
12. Mt 18:14.
13. 2 Sm 14:14.
14. Ez 33:11a.
15. Ez 33:11b.
16. Mt 23:37.
17. Jer 8:5, 5:3.
18. Mt 11:28.
19. Rom 3:23.
20. Rom 5:12.
21. Wis 1:13.
22. Hos 2:7.
23. Hos 2:8–9.
24. Jer 3:19–20.
25. Ps 59:10.
26. Is 65:24.
27. Is 30:19.
28. Cf. Mt 7:7.
29. Cf. Rom 10:20–21.
30. Is 1:19.
31. Rom 9:16.
32. Rom 2:6.
33. Phil 2:13.
34. Eph 2:8–9.
35. Jas 4:8.
36. Jn 6:44.
37. Prv 4:26 LXX.
38. Ps 5:8.

39. Ps 17:5.
40. Ez 18:31.
41. Ez 11:18–20.
42. Jer 4:14a.
43. Ps 51:10.
44. Ps 51:7.
45. Hos 10:12 LXX.
46. Ps 94:10.
47. Ps 146:8.
48. Ps 13:3.
49. Rom 7:18b.
50. Prv 4:23.
51. Phil 4:7.
52. Ps 119:112.
53. Ps 119:36.
54. 1 Kgs 8:58.
55. Ps 34:13.
56. Ps 141:3.
57. Is 52:2.
58. Ps 146:7.
59. Ps 116:16–17.
60. 1 Cor 9:24.
61. Jn 3:27.
62. Jer 17:21.
63. Ps 126:1 LXX.
64. Phil 2:12.
65. Cf. Acts 9:1–6.
66. Cf. Mt 9:9.
67. Cf. Lk 19:2–10.
68. Cf. Lk 23:40–43.
69. Cf. Mt 11:12.
70. Ps 68:28.
71. Ps 90:17.
72. Cf. Nm 22:5–24:25.
73. Cf. Gn 20:6.
74. Gn 45:5.
75. Gn 45:7–8.
76. Gn 50:19–20.

77. Ps 105:16–17.
78. Ps 50:15.
79. Gn 3:22.
80. Sir 7:29a LXX.
81. Sir 7:29b LXX.
82. Rom 2:14–16.
83. Is 42:18–19.
84. Is 43:8.
85. Jer 5:21.
86. Mt 13:13.
87. Is 6:9–10 LXX.
88. Lk 12:57.
89. 1 Kgs 8:17–19.
90. 1 Cor 3:7.
91. Cf. Hermas, *Pastor,* mand. 6.2.
92. 1 Tm 4:14.
93. 2 Tm 1:6.
94. 2 Cor 6:1.
95. Acts 8:22–23.
96. 2 Tm 1:6; Ps 59:11.
97. Ps 88:13.
98. Ps 119:147.
99. Ps 119:148.
100. Rom 10:21.
101. Ps 88:9.
102. Is 30:18.
103. Ps 40:1.
104. Ps 119:166.
105. Hos 7:15.
106. Is 35:3.
107. Jn 7:37.
108. Ps 69:3.
109. Sg 5:6.
110. Sg 3:1 LXX.
111. 2 Sm 12:13a.
112. 2 Sm 12:13b.
113. 2 Cor 4:17.
114. Rom 8:18.

115. 1 Cor 15:10a.
116. 1 Cor 15:10b.
117. Jb 1:9–11 LXX.
118. Mt 8:7.
119. Mt 8:8.
120. Mt 8:10.
121. Gn 22:1 LXX.
122. Gn 22:12.
123. Dt 13:2–4.
124. 1 Cor 10:12–13.
125. Eph 6:12.
126. Jgs 3:1–2, 2:22.
127. Rom 11:33.
128. Cf. Lk 19:2–6.
129. Cf. Mt 8:21–22.
130. Cf. Acts 10.
131. Mt 8:3.
132. Cf. Mt 9:18–25.
133. Mt. 8:8b.
134. Mt 8:13.
135. Cf. Mt 9:20–22.
136. Jn 5:6.
137. Mt 20:32.
138. Jn 11:40.
139. Mt 14:14.
140. Mk 6:5–6.
141. Mt 9:29.
142. Mt 15:28.
143. Lk 18:42.
144. Jn 4:49.
145. Jn 4:48.
146. Jn 4:50.
147. Mt 9:2.
148. Mt 9:4–6.
149. Jn 5:7.
150. Jn 5:8.
151. Acts 3:6.
152. Rom 11:33–34.

153. Is 49:15a.
154. Is 49.15b.
155. Eccl 9:11 LXX; 1 Cor 12:11.
156. Ez 20:43–44.
157. Is 7:9 LXX.

13.1 The single assertion spoken of here is made in 12.15.2ff.

13.3.1ff. For other imagery taken from farming cf. 1.2ff and the note at 1.2.

13.4f. The possibility of the existence of virginity among the Gentiles, or pagans, is also raised in Ambrose, *De virginibus* 1.6; Chrysostom, *De virg.* 1.1; idem, *Quod regulares feminae* 1.5 (PG 47.514). It is also dismissed in these writings.

13.5.3 The story told of Socrates (c. 470 B.C.–399 B.C.) here is also recounted in Cicero, *Tusc.* 4.37.80, but there it occurs in a context that is complimentary to the great philosopher. The "unnamed expert in physiognomy" was a certain Zopyrus, according to Cicero. The source of the present Greek text is unknown. Cassian's attitude toward Socrates is rather unusual inasmuch as he is ordinarily very well spoken of in ancient Christian literature. Cf. Giuseppina Melinossi, "Socrate nella tradizione cristiana dei primi secoli," in *Didaskaleion* 9.3 (1930): 125–176; Ernst Benz, "Christus und Sokrates in der alten Kirche: Ein Beitrag zum altkirchlichen Verständnis des Märtyrers und des Martyriums," in *Zeitschrift für die Neutestamentliche Wissenschaft* 43 (1950/1951): 195–224; Anne-Marie Malingrey, "Le personnage de Socrate chez quelques auteurs chrétiens du IVe siècle," in *Forma Futuri: Studi in onore del Cardinale Michele Pellegrino* (Turin, 1975), 159–178.

13.5.4 These words of Diogenes (d. c. 320 B.C.), the founder of the Cynic movement, are otherwise unknown.

13.7.3 The precise term "original sin" *(peccatum originale),* which Cassian uses here, appears for the first time in Augustine's writings, although it had many precedents in other terms. Cf. DTC 12.1.317–406.

13.7.4 On the image of Christ as physician here and of God as physician in 13.18.2 cf. the note at 2.13.7.

13.13.1 Grace...free: *Gratia...gratuita*. Cf. also 13.13.4.

13.14.1 His very experienced athlete: Cf. the note at 7.20. Job is also spoken of in terms of an athlete in Origen, *Selecta in Iob* ad 19.1 and 7 (PG 12.1031–1034); Athanasius, *Frag. in Iob* (PG 27.1345); Didymus, *Frag. in Iob* ad 2.6 (PG 39.1129); Ambrose, *De interpel. Iob et David* 1.2.4; Chrysostom, *De laudibus Pauli* 1.10; Gregory the Great, *Moralia in Iob* 1.3.4.

13.14.8 The citation is incorrectly said to be from Joshua.

13.14.9 Nurse: *Nutrix*. The word is translated as "nurse" by Gibson and as *mère* by Pichery. There is a remarkably similar illustration of grace, this time compared unmistakably with a mother, in Ps.-Macarius, Coll. 3, *Hom.* 27.3 (SC 275.320–322).

13.17.2 The citation of Rom 11.33–34 is very frequent in Augustine's anti-Pelagian writings. But whereas Cassian uses it here in the context of reflecting on God's goodness in drawing human beings to salvation "in numberless different manners and in inscrutable ways" (13.17.1), Augustine quotes it in reference to the mystery of the seeming arbitrariness in the fact that some are saved while others are lost. Cf. *De peccat. meritis et remis.* 1.21.29; *De spir. et litt.* 34.60; *C. duas epp. Pelag.* 4.6.16; *De gratia et libero arbitrio* 22.44; *De correp. et gratia* 8.17, 8.19; *De praedest. sanct.* 8.16; *De dono persev.* 12.30.

13.18.1f. On experience as a sure guide cf. the note at 3.7.4.

13.18.5 That faith (or authority) precedes understanding is a favorite theme of Augustine. Cf. *De mor. eccl. cath.* 2.3; *De util. cred.* 10.23ff.; *De symb. ad cat.* 4. It would be ironic if Cassian concluded this particular conference with an idea that he had taken from Augustine–if indeed it came from that source.

FOURTEENTH CONFERENCE
THE FIRST CONFERENCE
OF ABBA NESTEROS:
ON SPIRITUAL KNOWLEDGE

TRANSLATOR'S INTRODUCTION

Nesteros, the second of the three abbas of this second part of *The Conferences,* is perhaps identical with Nisteros ("the Great") of the *Apophthegmata patrum.* It is unlikely, in any event, that he is the same as Nistheros the Cenobite, also of the *Apophthegmata patrum,* in view of the fact that the Nesteros of the present conference is referred to as an anchorite in 11.3.2. After an extremely brief introduction, and after we are told that the old man has heard of Cassian's and Germanus's desire to understand certain scriptural passages that they have committed to memory, he at once proceeds to speak on the topic of knowledge.

He begins by dividing religious knowledge into two kinds—practical (πρακτικη) and contemplative or spiritual (θεωρητικη). In its present form this distinction may be traced to Aristotle (*Metaph.* 2.1): "Philosophy is rightly called a knowledge of truth. The end of contemplative [knowledge] is truth, but that of practical [knowledge] is action." Less remotely, though, the idea is Evagrian (cf. SC 170.38–56). This is but the first of numerous distinctions that make the fourteenth conference one of the most analytic of all the conferences. Practical knowledge, which must precede its contemplative counterpart, itself exists in twofold form: It both understands the working of the vices and forms the mind according to the virtues, in such a way that the mind delights in these latter. The words of Jeremiah 1:10 suggest to Nesteros, however, that expelling vice is twice as hard as acquiring virtue.

Practical knowledge is to be found in many different contexts—among solitaries and cenobites, among monks and secular persons. Indeed, Cassian implies that such knowledge *is* whatever profession a man or woman may take up and pursue in Christian fashion. And whatever profession a person may embrace, he should stick to it and therein discover perfection for himself. The insistence on being faithful to one's profession is reminiscent of the insistence, found elsewhere in *The Conferences* and throughout desert literature (cf. 6.15 and the relevant note), on being faithful to one's cell and to the place where one has established one's monastic career.

It is only when he begins to speak of contemplative or spiritual knowledge that Nesteros finally addresses himself directly to the concern of his two listeners, for it is clear that this knowledge pertains exclusively to the understanding of Scripture. Like practical knowledge, it is twofold, having to do with both the historical interpretation and the spiritual understanding of Scripture. While the former deals simply with historical facts or assertions, the latter is occupied with the possible deeper meaning or meanings of a given text. In an elaboration of 8.3, Cassian here divides the spiritual senses of Scripture into three—namely, allegory, anagogy, and tropology. Roughly speaking, allegory has to do with Christ, the Church, and the sacraments—in other words, with historical or visible things that are, however, charged with spiritual significance. Anagogy has to do with invisible, eternal, heavenly realities. Tropology, finally, bears a certain moral weight. To the four senses of Scripture (including the historical) there correspond the four terms that Paul employs in 1 Corinthians 14:6: The historical is linked with instruction, the allegorical with revelation, the anagogical with prophecy, and the tropological with knowledge. Cassian's complex structure here is a masterpiece of hermeneutical literature. Both Ambrose (*Exp. evang. sec. Luc.*, prol. 2) and Augustine (*De util. cred.* 3.5ff.) had proposed four possible levels on which Scripture could be understood, but they differ from Cassian's scheme, which is original to him.

Hereupon Nesteros returns to the practical, for in order for a person to acquire spiritual understanding he must first have acquired virtue. Once worldly cares have been stilled, an assiduous program of reading the Bible must be undertaken. Reading, though, brings with it the danger of pride, and consequently the exercise of humble discretion is urgently recommended as well. Reading in turn suggests memorization, and Nesteros does not hesitate to say that the reader must eventually memorize the Bible in its entirety. Scripture will thus form the subject of continual meditation, which will then both drive out other thoughts and gradually reveal the beauty of what has been memorized. But whatever a person may derive from Scripture is shaped according to his capacity to understand it, and a passage as apparently simple, for example, as Exodus 20:14 ("You shall not commit fornication") can yield a multitude of deeper meanings.

One such deeper meaning is the identification of fornication with wandering thoughts. On hearing Nesteros offer this interpretation, Cassian himself, in one of the few passages where he and not Germanus speaks, laments his boyhood schooling in literature, which has given him the wherewithal for his distractions: He cannot sing a psalm without seeing the heroes of pagan mythology with his mind's eye. Nesteros replies by observing that worldly tales and poems can be expelled from the imagination by reading and meditating on the Bible. Once a person has done this over a certain period of time, spiritual thoughts will begin to well up in him of their own accord. But, again, for such a thing to happen a person must have overcome his vices: The contemplative must be preceded by the practical.

Now it is Germanus who intervenes with the objection that some who have not attained to virtue are nonetheless more knowledgeable about Scripture than many holy persons. Nesteros responds by distinguishing between a rhetorical skill that passes for spiritual knowledge on the one hand and holiness that provides true spiritual insight on the other. This kind of rhetorical skill is merely pseudo-knowledge. It is important to note here that Cassian's view in this matter cannot be characterized as anti-intellectual. In contrast to many Egyptian monks who condemned learning *tout court,* Cassian rejects only the abuse of learning. On Egyptian anti-intellectualism cf. the note at 10.2.2.

Having encouraged his two listeners to read and memorize Scripture, Nesteros warns them not, out of a desire for human praise, to teach those who are unworthy to learn. But attempts at spiritual teaching will fail in two instances–namely, when the teacher himself speaks without experience in spiritual matters, and when the hearer obdurately refuses to accept the teaching. Yet sometimes God will even give the grace of teaching to persons who theretofore had resisted all grace.

The conference concludes with Nesteros's promise to discuss the gifts of healing that evening.

XIV. The First Conference of Abba Nesteros: On Spiritual Knowledge

Chapters

I.1. Both our promise and the sequence of our itinerary demand that the instruction of Abba Nesteros, a man of the highest knowledge and outstanding in every regard, should follow. When he heard that we had committed some parts of Holy Scripture to memory and desired to understand them, he addressed us in words like these:

2. "There are indeed as many kinds of knowledge in this world as there are different sorts of arts and disciplines. But, although all are either completely useless or contribute something of value only to the present life, still there is not one that does not have its own order and method of instruction by which it can be grasped by those who are interested in it. 3. If, then, those arts follow their own defined principles when they are taught, how much more does the teaching and profession of our religion, which is directed to contemplating the secrets of invisible mysteries rather than to present gain and which seeks instead the reward of eternal prizes, consist in a defined order and method. Its knowledge is in fact twofold. The first kind is πρακτικη, or practical, which reaches its fulfillment in correction of behavior and in cleansing from vice. The other is θεωρητικη, which consists in the contemplation of divine things and in the understanding of most sacred meanings.

II. "Whoever, therefore, wishes to attain to the θεωρητικη must first pursue practical knowledge with all his strength and power. For the πρακτικη can be possessed without the theoretical, but the theoretical can never be seized without the practical. For certain steps have been arranged and distinguished in such a way that human lowliness can mount to the sublime. If these follow one another according to the method that we have mentioned, a person can attain to a height to which he cannot fly if the first step has not been taken. In vain, therefore, does someone who does not reject the contagion of vice strive for the vision of God. 'For the Spirit of God hates deception, and it does not dwell in a body subject to sin.'[1]

III.1. "Now this practical perfection exists in a twofold form. Its first mode is that of knowing the nature of all the vices and the method of remedying them. The second is that of discerning the sequence of the virtues and forming our mind by their perfection in such a way that it is obedient to them not as if it were coerced and subjected to an arbitrary rule but as taking pleasure in and enjoying what is so to say a natural good, thus mounting with delight the hard and narrow way. For how will a person who does not understand the nature of his vices and has not striven to uproot them be able to attain either to the method of the virtues, which is the second step in practical discipline, or to the mysteries of spiritual and heavenly realities, which are found on the higher step of theoria?

2. "It follows that a person who has not conquered the level places cannot progress to the heights, and much less will he grasp things that are outside himself if he has been unable to understand things that are within himself. Yet we should know that we must exert ourselves twice as hard to expel vice as to acquire virtue. We do not come to this by our own guesswork, but we are taught by the words of him who alone knows the ability and intelligence of what he has made: 'Behold,' he says, 'today I have set you over nations and over kingdoms, to root up and to pull down and to disperse and to scatter and to build and to plant.'[2] 3. He has pointed out that four things are necessary for expelling what is harmful–namely, rooting up, pulling down, dispersing, and scattering. But for perfecting the virtues and for acquiring what pertains to righteousness there are only building and planting. Hence it is quite clear that it is more difficult to pluck out and eradicate the ingrown passions of body and soul than it is to gather and plant spiritual virtues.

IV.1. "This πρακτικη, then, which–as has been said–exists in two modes, is divided among many professions and pursuits. For some people are completely set upon the remoteness of the desert and on purity of heart, as we know Elijah and Elisha were in times past and the blessed Antony and others were in our own day, pursuing the same chosen orientation and attaching themselves very closely to God by the silence of the desert. 2. Some have devoted every painstaking effort of theirs to the instruction of the brothers and to the constant care of the cenobia, as we recall was the case lately with Abba John, who presided over a large cenobium near the town called Thmuis; and there were some other men who were equally worthy and who also shone forth with apostolic signs. The kindly duty of welcoming strangers is attractive to some. This was how, also in times past, the patriarch Abraham and Lot pleased the Lord,[3] and lately there was the blessed Macarius, a man of extraordinary gentleness and patience. He presided over a hostel in Alexandria in such a way that he should not be considered inferior to any of those who pursued the remoteness of the desert. 3. Some choose the care of the sick, others carry out the intercession that is owed to the downtrodden and the oppressed, some are intent upon teaching, and others give alms to the poor, and among great and noble men they have flourished by reason of their love and their goodness.

V.1. "Therefore it is beneficial and proper for each person, in accordance with the orientation that he has chosen and the grace that he has received, to strive most zealously and diligently to attain to perfection in the work that he has undertaken. He may praise and admire the virtues of others, but he should never depart from the profession that he has once chosen, knowing that, according to the Apostle, the body of the Church is indeed one, although its members are many,[4] and that it has 'gifts differing according to the grace which has been given us, whether prophecy according to the degree of faith, or ministry in ministering, or the one who teaches in doctrine, or the one who exhorts in exhortation, or the one who gives in simplicity, or the one who presides in carefulness, or the one who shows mercy in cheerfulness.'[5] Some members cannot claim for themselves the ministries of other members, for the eyes cannot perform the function of the hands nor the nose of the ears. Therefore not all are apostles, not all are prophets, not all are teachers, not all have the grace of healing, not all speak in tongues, not all interpret.[6]

VI. "Those who are not yet established in the profession that they have undertaken are accustomed, when they hear some people commended for their different concerns and virtues, to be so taken up with their praise that they immediately desire to imitate their practices. In such cases human frailty inevitably expends its efforts in vain. For it is impossible for one and the same person to shine simultaneously in all the virtues that I have listed above. If someone wants to strive after all of them together, in his pursuit of them he will of necessity not possess a single one completely, and he will suffer loss rather than make gain as a result of this diversity and variation. For there are many ways that lead to God, and therefore each person should finish the one that he has taken up, intent upon his course, so that he may be perfect in his profession, whatever it may be.

VII.1. "For, apart from the loss that befalls a monk who, as we have said, in his fickleness of mind wants to pass from one pursuit to another, he also runs the risk of death in this respect–in that occasionally things that are correctly done by some are taken by others as a bad example, and things that had turned out well for some are thought by others to be wicked. For example, suppose someone wished to imitate the virtue of that man whom Abba John is in the habit of mentioning, not as a model to imitate but only as one to admire.

"Now, someone dressed in worldly attire came up to the aforesaid old man and, when he had offered him some of the first-fruits of his harvest, he found someone there who was possessed by a raging demon. 2. Although the latter disdained Abba John's adjurations and commands and swore that he would never obey his injunction and leave the body that he had possessed, he was utterly terrified at the coming of this man and departed, very reverently calling out his name. The old man wondered greatly at such obvious grace and, all the more astonished because he noticed that he was in worldly attire, he began to ask him carefully about his state of life and profession. 3. And when he said that he was in the world and bound by the ties of marriage, the blessed John reflected on the excellence of his virtue and grace and inquired attentively as to his way of life. The man testified that he came from the country, that he earned his living by the daily work of his hands, and that he was not aware of anything good about himself except that he never went out to his work in the fields in the morning or returned home in the evening without having thanked God beforehand in church for having provided him with his daily bread. Nor did he ever take any of his own produce without first having offered God the firstfruits and a tithe, and he never led his cattle through someone else's harvest without first having muzzled them, lest his neighbor suffer even the slightest loss through his carelessness. 4. And when these things still did not seem sufficient to Abba John to obtain the great grace with which he saw that he was endowed, he probed and asked him what it was that he did to deserve such grace. The man felt himself obligated by the respect with which so anxious an inquiry was made, and he confessed that twelve years previously he had been forced by the pressure and command of his parents to take a wife, although he had wanted to profess the monastic life. Although even now no one was aware of it, he kept her a virgin and treated her as a sister. When the old man heard this he was so struck with admiration that he proclaimed publicly, in the man's presence, that not without reason had the demon who had disdained him not been able to endure the presence of a man whose virtue he himself would not dare to seek not only in the heat of youth but even now without endangering his chastity.

5. "Although Abba John would speak of this situation with the highest admiration, nonetheless he did not encourage any of the monks to try it out, knowing that many things which have been rightly practiced by some have led others who imitated them into great danger, and that what the Lord has bestowed by a special favor upon a few cannot be seized upon by all.

VIII.1. "But let us return to discussing the knowledge that was spoken of at the beginning. As we said previously, the πρακτικη is dispersed among many professions and pursuits. The θεωρητικη, on the other hand, is divided into two parts—that is, into historical interpretation and spiritual understanding. Hence, when Solomon had enumerated the different forms of grace in the Church, he added: 'All who are with her are doubly clothed.'[7] Now, there are three kinds of spiritual knowledge—tropology, allegory, and anagogy—about which it is said in Proverbs: 'But you describe those things for yourself in threefold fashion according to the largeness of your heart.'[8]

2. "And so history embraces the knowledge of past and visible things, which is repeated by the Apostle thus: 'It is written that Abraham had two sons, one from a slave and the other from a free

woman. The one from the slave was born according to the flesh, but the one from the free woman by promise.'[9] The things that follow belong to allegory, however, because what really occurred is said to have prefigured the form of another mystery. 'For these,' it says, 'are two covenants, one from Mount Sinai, begetting unto slavery, which is Hagar. For Sinai is a mountain in Arabia, which is compared to the Jerusalem that now is, and which is enslaved with her children.'[10] 3. But anagogy, which mounts from spiritual mysteries to certain more sublime and sacred heavenly secrets, is added by the Apostle: 'But the Jerusalem from above, which is our mother, is free. For it is written: Rejoice, you barren one who do not bear, break out and shout, you who are not in labor, for the children of the desolate one are many more than of her who has a husband.'[11] Tropology is moral explanation pertaining to correction of life and to practical instruction, as if we understood these same two covenants as πρακτικη and as theoretical discipline, or at least as if we wished to take Jerusalem or Zion as the soul of the human being, according to the words: 'Praise the Lord, O Jerusalem; praise your God, O Zion.'[12]

4. "The four figures that have been mentioned converge in such a way that, if we want, one and the same Jerusalem can be understood in a fourfold manner. According to history it is the city of the Jews. According to allegory it is the Church of Christ. According to anagogy it is that heavenly city of God 'which is the mother of us all.'[13] According to tropology it is the soul of the human being, which under this name is frequently either reproached or praised by the Lord. Of these four kinds of interpretation the blessed Apostle says thus: 'Now, brothers, if I come to you speaking in tongues, what use will it be to you unless I speak to you by revelation or by knowledge or by prophecy or by instruction?'[14]

5. "Now, revelation pertains to allegory, by which the things that the historical narrative conceals are laid bare by a spiritual understanding and explanation. Suppose, for example, that we tried to make clear how 'all our fathers were under the cloud, and all were baptized in Moses in the cloud and in the sea, and [how] all ate the same spiritual food and drank the same spiritual drink from the rock that followed them. But the rock was Christ.'[15] This expla-

nation, which refers to the prefiguration of the body and blood of Christ that we daily receive, comprises an allegorical approach.

6. "But knowledge, which is also mentioned by the Apostle, is tropology, by which we discern by a prudent examination everything that pertains to practical discretion, in order to see whether it is useful and good, as when we are ordered to judge for ourselves 'whether it befits a woman to pray to God with unveiled head.'[16] This approach, as has been said, comprises a moral understanding.

"Likewise, prophecy, which the Apostle introduced in the third place, bespeaks anagogy, by which words are directed to the invisible and to what lies in the future, as in this case: 'We do not want you to be ignorant, brothers, about those who are asleep, so that you may not be saddened like others who have no hope. For if we believe that Christ has died and has arisen, so also God will bring those who have fallen asleep in Jesus with him. For we say this to you by the word of the Lord, that we who are alive at the coming of the Lord shall not anticipate those who have fallen asleep in Christ, for the Lord himself shall descend from heaven with a command, with the voice of an angel and with the trumpet of God, and the dead who are in Christ shall arise first.'[17] 7. The figure of anagogy appears in this kind of exhortation.

"But instruction lays open the simple sequence of a historical exposition in which there is no more hidden meaning than what is comprised in the sound of the words, as in this case: 'I delivered to you first what I also received, that Christ died for our sins according to the Scriptures, that he was buried, that he rose on the third day, and that he was seen by Cephas.'[18] And: 'God sent his Son, made of a woman, made under the law, to save those who were under the law.'[19] And this: 'Hear, O Israel: The Lord your God is one Lord.'[20]

IX.1. "Therefore, if you are concerned to attain to the light of spiritual knowledge not by the vice of empty boastfulness but by the grace of correction, you are first inflamed with desire for that blessedness about which it is said: 'Blessed are the pure of heart, for they shall see God,'[21] so that you may also attain to that about which the angel said to Daniel: 'Those who are learned shall shine like the splendor of the firmament, and those who instruct many in righteousness like the stars forever.'[22] And in another prophet: 'Enlighten yourselves with the light of knowledge while there is time.'[23]

2. "Maintaining the diligence in reading that I think you have, then, make every effort to get a complete grasp of practical—that is, ethical—discipline as soon as possible. For without this the theoretical purity that we have spoken of cannot be acquired. The only people who attain to it, possessing it as a reward after the expenditure of much toil and labor, are those who have found perfection not in the words of other teachers but in the virtuousness of their own acts. Obtaining this understanding not from meditating on the law but as a result of their toil, they sing with the psalmist: 'From your commandments I have understood.'[24] And after all their passions have been purified they say with confidence: 'I will sing and I will understand in the undefiled way.'[25] 3. For the one who is singing the psalm, who is moving forward in the undefiled way with the stride of a pure heart, will understand what is sung.

"Therefore, if you wish to prepare a sacred tabernacle of spiritual knowledge in your heart, cleanse yourselves from the contagion of every vice and strip yourselves of the cares of the present world. For it is impossible for the soul which is even slightly taken up with worldly distractions to deserve the gift of knowledge or to beget spiritual understanding or to remember the sacred readings.

4. "Take care first of all, then (especially you, John, who should be more heedful of observing what I am going to speak of, since you are somewhat younger), that your lips maintain strict silence, lest your pursuit of reading and the intensity of your desire come to naught because of empty pride. This is the first beginning of practical discipline—that with attentive heart and as it were silent tongue you receive the institutes and words of all the elders, preserve them carefully in your breast, and strive to fulfill them rather than to teach them. For from the latter the dangerous presumption of vainglory will spring, but from the former the fruit of spiritual knowledge. 5. Consequently, do not dare to put anything forward during a conference of the elders unless either a harmful ignorance or the need to know something compels you to ask a question, since some people who are puffed up with the

love of vainglory make up questions about things that they know very well in order to show off their learning. For it is impossible for a person who pursues reading persistently with the intention of winning human praise to deserve the gift of true knowledge. Whoever has been overcome by this passion is invariably entangled in other vices too, and especially in pride. Thus, having come to ruin with the practical and ethical, he will not acquire the spiritual knowledge that springs from it. Be in every respect, therefore, 'quick to hear, but slow to speak,'[26] lest there befall you what Solomon mentions: 'If you see a man who is quick with words, know that a fool has more hope than he.'[27]

"Nor should anyone presume to teach in words what he has not previously done in deed. 6. Our Lord taught us by his own example that we should follow this order, as it is said: 'Which Jesus began to do and teach.'[28] Be careful, therefore, that you not jump to teaching before you have acted and be counted among those of whom the Lord speaks to his disciples in the Gospel: 'Observe and do what they say, but do not do according to their works. For they bind heavy burdens, hard to carry, and place them on people's shoulders, but they themselves do not move them with their finger.'[29] For if the person 'who breaks the least commandment and teaches people so shall be called least in the kingdom of heaven,'[30] it follows that whoever neglects many great things and dares to teach is certainly not merely least in the kingdom of heaven but should be considered greatest in the punishment of Gehenna.

7. "Therefore you should be careful lest you be stirred to teach by the example of those who have acquired skill in speaking and a fluent tongue and who are believed by those who are unable to discern its power and character to possess spiritual knowledge because they can say whatever they want elaborately and at length. For it is one thing to speak with ease and beauty and another to enter deeply into heavenly sayings and to contemplate profound and hidden mysteries with the most pure eye of the heart, because certainly neither human teaching nor worldly learning but only purity of mind will possess this, through the enlightenment of the Holy Spirit.

X.1. "If you wish to attain to a true knowledge of Scripture, then, you must first hasten to acquire a steadfast humility of heart which will, by the perfection of love, bring you not to the knowledge which puffs up[31] but to that which enlightens. For it is impossible for the impure mind to receive the gift of spiritual knowledge. Therefore, avoid this very carefully, lest by zealous reading there arise in you, out of arrogant vanity, not the light of knowledge or the everlasting glory that is promised by the enlightenment of teaching but rather the means of your own destruction.

2. "Then, once all worldly cares and preoccupations have been cast out, you must strive in every respect to give yourself assiduously and even constantly to sacred reading. Do this until continual meditation fills your mind and as it were forms it in its likeness, making of it a kind of ark of the covenant,[32] containing in itself two stone tablets—that is, constant steadfastness under the aspect of a twofold Testament; a golden jar too—that is, a pure and sincere memory, which preserves safely and lastingly the manna that is contained in it—namely, the enduring and heavenly sweetness of spiritual understandings and of the angelic bread; and also the rod of Aaron—that is, the banner of salvation of our true high priest Jesus Christ, ever green with undying remembrance, 3. for this is the rod which had been cut from the root of Jesse[33] and which, having died, flourishes again with still greater life. All of these are guarded by two cherubim—that is, by the fullness of historical and spiritual knowledge, for the cherubim are interpreted as the breadth of knowledge. They constantly guard the propitiatory of God—that is, your interior calm—and protect it from every assault of the evil spirits. Thus your mind, having advanced not only as far as the ark of the divine covenant but even as far as the priestly kingdom, and by its unshakable love of purity being as it were absorbed in spiritual discipline, will fulfill the priestly command that is laid down in this way by the Lawgiver: 'He shall not go forth from the holy places, lest he pollute the sanctuary of God'[34]—that is, his own heart, in which the Lord promises that he will always dwell when he says: 'I will dwell in them and walk among them.'[35]

4. "Hence the successive books of Holy Scripture must be diligently committed to memory and ceaselessly reviewed. This continual meditation will bestow on us double fruit. First, inasmuch as the mind's attention is occupied with reading and with preparing to

read, it cannot be taken captive in the entrapments of harmful thoughts. Then, the things that we have not been able to understand because our mind was busy at the time, things that we have gone through repeatedly and are laboring to memorize, we shall see more clearly afterward when we are free from every seductive deed and sight, and especially when we are silently meditating at night. Thus, while we are at rest and as it were immersed in the stupor of sleep, there will be revealed an understanding of hidden meanings that we did not grasp even slightly when we were awake.

XI.1. "But as our mind is increasingly renewed by this study, the face of Scripture will also begin to be renewed, and the beauty of a more sacred understanding will somehow grow with the person who is making progress. For its form is also adapted to the capacity of the human intelligence, and it will appear as earthly to carnal persons and as divine to spiritual persons, such that those to whom it previously seemed wrapped in thick clouds will be unable to grasp its subtlety or endure its splendor. But in order that what we are trying to say may be made clearer by an example, it is enough to mention one passage from the law by which we can demonstrate that all the heavenly commands are shaped for the whole human race according to the measure of our condition.

2. "It is written in the law: 'You shall not commit fornication.'[36] This is kept in a beneficial way according to the simple sound of the letter by the person who is still entangled in the passions of fleshly impurity. It is necessarily observed in spiritual fashion, however, by one who has already left behind this filthy behavior and impure disposition, so that he also rejects not only all idolatrous ceremonies but also every superstition of the Gentiles and the observance of auguries and omens and of all signs and days and times, and is certainly not engaged in the divination of particular words or names, which befouls the wholesomeness of our faith. 3. Jerusalem herself is said to have been debauched by this fornication, having fornicated 'on every high hill and under every green tree.'[37] And the Lord, rebuking her, says by the prophet: 'Let the astrologers stand and save you, who gazed on the stars and counted the months, so that from them they might announce the things that are to happen to you.'[38] Concerning this fornication the Lord reproaches them elsewhere

when he says: 'The spirit of fornication has deceived them, and they went fornicating away from their God.'[39]

"But whoever has left behind these two fornications will have a third kind to avoid, which is contained in the superstitions of the law and of Judaism. 4. The Apostle says of these: 'You observe days and months and seasons and years.'[40] And again: 'Do not touch or taste or handle.'[41] There is no doubt that these things were said about the superstitions of the law. If anyone falls into them he has doubtless committed adultery with respect to Christ and does not deserve to hear from the Apostle: 'I have espoused you to one husband, to show you as a chaste virgin to Christ.'[42] Instead there will be addressed to him what follows, in the words of the same Apostle: 'I fear lest, as the serpent seduced Eve by his cunning, so your minds may be corrupted away from the simplicity that is Christ Jesus.'[43]

5. "But if a person has escaped from the uncleanness of this fornication too, there is still a fourth, which is perpetrated by the adultery of heretical teaching. About this the same blessed Apostle says: 'I know that after my departure fierce wolves will enter in among you, not sparing the flock, and from you yourselves there will arise men who speak wicked things, in order to lead astray the disciples.'[44]

"Whoever has been able to avoid this should beware lest by a more subtle sin he fall into the vice of fornication which consists in wandering thoughts, for every thought that is not only wicked but even idle and that to some degree departs from God is considered the most impure fornication by the perfect man."

XII.1. Upon hearing these things I was at first very moved by a hidden compunction, and then I groaned deeply and said: "All these things that you have discussed at great length have brought upon me a greater despair than I had previously endured. For, besides those general captivities of the soul by which I have no doubt that the weak are afflicted from without, there is a particular stumbling block to salvation that comes from the knowledge of literature which I seem to have acquired to a slight degree. In this respect the insistence of my teacher and the constant attention paid to reading have so weakened me that now my mind, infected as it were with those poems, meditates even during the time for prayer on the silly fables and narratives of wars with which it was filled when I was a boy and had begun my studies. The shameless recollection of poetry crops up while I am singing the psalms or asking pardon for my sins, or a vision of warring heroes passes before my eyes. Daydreaming about such images constantly mocks me, and to such an extent does it prevent my mind from attaining to higher insights that it cannot be gotten rid of even with daily weeping."

XIII.1. NESTEROS: "From this very fact, which has given rise to your immense despair of being cleansed, there can come quite a speedy and effective remedy if you wish to transfer the same diligence and urgency, which you said that you had in those worldly studies, to the reading of and meditation upon spiritual writings. For your mind will inevitably be taken up with those poems until it harvests for itself other things within itself, pursues them with similar zeal and interest, and bears spiritual and divine realities in place of those fruitless and earthly ones. 2. When it has grasped their depth and their height and has been nourished by them, the former thoughts will be able to be gradually cast out and completely abolished. For the human mind cannot be open to every thought, and therefore as long as it is not occupied with spiritual pursuits it will inevitably be wrapped up in those that it had learned some time before. As long as it has nothing to return to and to exercise itself tirelessly on it will inevitably fall back on what it had been imbued with in childhood, and it will constantly reflect on what it has conceived after long habituation and meditation.

3. "This spiritual knowledge must be strengthened in you firmly and lastingly. It is not for you to enjoy it only temporarily, like those who lay hold of it not by their own efforts but by way of another person and who snatch at it as if it were a kind of ethereal scent; rather, it should be stored deep in your mind and be made as it were visible and palpable. In order to accomplish this it behooves you to see to it with great care that, even should you hear mentioned in a conference what you know very well, you should not on that account treat disdainfully and haughtily what is already known to you. Instead, you should accept it in your heart with the same eagerness with which the long-desired words of salvation should be ceaselessly poured into our ears and ever spoken

by our lips. 4. For even if there is a frequent repetition of holy things, still satiety will never beget disgust in the soul of one who has a thirst for true knowledge. Rather, it takes those things in every day as if they were new and sought-after, and the more often it imbibes them the more eagerly it will hear and speak of them, and from their repetition it will be strengthened by the knowledge that has been gained instead of being bored by frequent conferences. For it is a clear indication of a lukewarm and proud mind if it receives the medicine of saving words haughtily and heedlessly, even when it has been offered with an overzealous frequency. For 'the soul that is full jeers at a honeycomb, but to the needy soul even bitter things seem sweet.'[45]

5. "If, then, these things have been diligently listened to, stored in the recesses of the mind, and sealed by deep silence, afterward, like certain sweet-smelling wines that 'rejoice the heart of man,'[46] when they have been warmed by reverent thoughts and by a long-standing patience and have been brought forth from the vessel of your breast with a strong aroma, they will bubble up like an unceasing fountain out of the springs of experience and the watercourses of virtue, and they will pour forth continual streams as it were from the abyss of your heart. 6. There will take place in you what is said in Proverbs to one who has accomplished these things in his work: 'Drink water from your own vessels and from the fountain of your own wells. Let water from your own fountain flow abundantly for you, but let your water pass through into your streets.'[47] And according to the prophet Isaiah: 'You shall be like a watered garden and like a fountain of water whose water will not fail. And places desolate for ages shall be rebuilt in you. You shall raise up foundations of generation upon generation, and you shall be called the repairer of fences, turning paths into rest.'[48] 7. For the blessedness that the same prophet promises shall come to you: 'The Lord will not make your teacher flee from you any more, and your eyes shall see your teacher. And your ears shall hear the words of one admonishing you behind your back: This is the way; walk in it and go neither to the right nor to the left.'[49] And thus it will come about that not only every aim and meditation of your heart but also every wandering and digressive thought of yours will be for you a holy and continuous reflection on the divine law.

XIV.1. "But it is impossible, as we have already said, for someone who is inexperienced to know or teach this. For if someone is really incapable of receiving something, how will he be fit to pass it on? Yet even if he presumes to teach something about these matters, his words will only get as far as his hearers' ears, and they will be ineffective and useless. Produced out of inactivity and barren vanity, they will be unable to penetrate their hearts because they come not from the treasury of a good conscience but from vain and arrogant boastfulness. 2. For it is impossible for the impure soul, with whatever effort it may have toiled in reading, to acquire spiritual knowledge. No one pours a choice ointment or the finest honey or any kind of precious liquid into a foul-smelling and filthy vessel. A pot that has once been filled with horrid foul-smelling odors spoils the most aromatic myrrh more easily than it receives any sweetness or pleasantness from it, for clean things are more quickly filthied than filthy things are made clean. 3. Likewise, therefore, unless the vessel of our heart has first been cleansed of every foul-smelling vice it will not deserve to receive the oil of blessing that is spoken about by the prophet: 'Like oil on the head, which ran down to Aaron's beard, which ran down to the edge of his garment.'[50] Nor will it preserve unspoiled that spiritual knowledge and the words of Scripture that are 'sweeter than honey and the honeycomb.'[51] 'For what do righteousness and wickedness have in common? Or what fellowship is there between light and darkness? Or what agreement is there between Christ and Beliel?'"[52]

XV. GERMANUS: "This understanding does not at all seem to us to be based on truth or to be supported by credible reasoning. For although it is clear that all who either never receive the faith of Christ or corrupt it by blasphemous and wicked teaching are unclean of heart, how is it that many Jews and heretics and also Catholics who are entangled in different vices have acquired a perfect knowledge of Scripture and boast of their extensive spiritual learning, whereas an innumerable multitude of holy men, whose hearts are cleansed of every stain of sin, is content with a devout and simple faith and is ignorant of the secrets of a deeper knowledge? How, then, will this opinion stand, which attributes spiritual knowledge solely to purity of heart?"

XVI.1. NESTEROS: "One who does not carefully weigh all the words of an opinion that has been expressed does not rightly perceive the thrust of the statement. For we said before that people of this kind only have skill in disputation and an ornate style, but that they are unable to penetrate the depths of Scripture and the secrets of spiritual meanings. True knowledge is possessed only by true worshipers of God, and the people to whom this is said certainly do not have it: 'Hear, O foolish people, who have no heart, who have eyes and do not see, and ears and do not hear.'[53] And again: 'Because you have rejected knowledge, I also will reject you from acting as my priest.'[54] 2. For when it is said that 'all the treasures of wisdom and knowledge are hidden' in Christ,[55] how can a person who has scorned to find Christ or who blasphemes him with sacrilegious tongue when he is found or who has at least stained the Catholic faith with unclean works be believed to have acquired true knowledge? 'For the Spirit of God will flee from deception, and it does not dwell in a body subject to sin.'

"Therefore, there is no other way of attaining to spiritual knowledge except by following this order, which one of the prophets has neatly expressed: 'Sow for yourselves unto righteousness; reap the hope of life; enlighten yourselves with the light of knowledge.'[56] 3. First, then, we must sow for ourselves unto righteousness–that is, we must increase practical perfection by works of righteousness. Then we must reap the hope of life–that is, we must gather the fruit of spiritual virtues by expelling our carnal vices. Thus we shall be able to enlighten ourselves with the light of knowledge. The psalmist also concludes that this is the order that must be followed when he says: 'Blessed are the undefiled in the way, who walk in the law of the Lord. Blessed are those who search his testimonies.'[57] He did not say first: 'Blessed are those who search his testimonies,' and add afterward: 'Blessed are the undefiled in the way.' Rather, he says first: 'Blessed are the undefiled in the way.' By this he clearly shows that no one can properly arrive at searching into the testimonies of God unless he first enters undefiled upon the way of Christ by his practical way of life.

4. "Those unclean persons whom you spoke of, therefore, cannot have this. Instead, they possess a knowledge that is ψευδώνυμον–that is, which is in name only and about which the

blessed Apostle says: 'O Timothy, guard what has been placed in your care, avoiding profane novelties of words and the antagonism of knowledge in name only.'[58] This appears in Greek as: τας αντιθεσεις της ψευδωνυμον γνωσεως. Of those who seem to acquire a certain veneer of knowledge and who, although they diligently pursue the reading of the sacred books and the memorization of Scripture, nonetheless do not abandon carnal vice, it is well put in Proverbs: 'Like a golden ring in the snout of a swine, so is the beauty of an evil-tempered woman.'[59] 5. For what does it profit someone to have acquired the ornamentation of heavenly words and the most precious beauty of Scripture if, by clinging to filthy deeds and thoughts, he ruins it, so to say, by rooting around in the foulest soil, or stains it in the dirty mire of his wanton desires? For what happens is that what was supposed to be an ornament for those who used it properly will not only not be able to adorn them but in fact gets stained from contact with more filth. For 'from the mouth of a sinner praise is unseemly.'[60] To such a person it is said by the prophet: 'Why do you recount my righteous deeds, and why do you take my covenant in your mouth?'[61] 6. Of souls of this kind, who do not at all posses an unwavering fear of the Lord (about which it is said: 'The fear of the Lord is instruction and wisdom'[62]) and who strive to attain to an understanding of Scripture by constantly meditating on it, it is well noted in Proverbs: 'Of what use are riches to the fool? For a senseless person cannot possess wisdom.'[63]

"But to such an extent is this true and spiritual knowledge removed from that worldly learning, which is stained by the filth of fleshly vice, that we know that it occasionally flourishes in wondrous fashion in some rustic and nearly illiterate persons. 7. This is very clearly demonstrated in the case of the apostles and of many holy men, who did not spread themselves out with an empty abundance of leaves but who were weighed down with the true fruit of spiritual knowledge. It is written about them in the Acts of the Apostles: 'When they saw the boldness of Peter and John and had found out that they were illiterate and unlearned men, they were astonished.'[64]

"Therefore, if you are anxious to acquire the unfading fragrance of that knowledge, make every effort first of all to obtain a chaste purity from the Lord. 8. For no one in whom there still dominates a love of fleshly passions and especially of fornication will be able to possess spiritual knowledge. For 'wisdom will repose in a good heart.'[65] And: 'Whoever fears the Lord will find knowledge with righteousness.'[66] The blessed Apostle also teaches that by following this order, which we have spoken of, spiritual knowledge can be acquired. For when he wished not only to draw up a list of all his virtues but also to set out their sequence, in order to express which followed which and which sprang from which, he mentioned after some other things: 'In watching, in fasting, in chastity, in knowledge, in long-suffering, in gentleness, in the Holy Spirit, in unfeigned love.'[67] 9. With this concatenation of virtues he very obviously wished to teach us that one proceeds from watching and fasting to chastity, from chastity to knowledge, from knowledge to long-suffering, from long-suffering to gentleness, from gentleness to the Holy Spirit, and from the Holy Spirit to the reward of unfeigned love. When, therefore, by this discipline and in this sequence you yourself attain to spiritual knowledge, you will certainly have, as we have said, a learning that is not barren and worthless but one that is alive and fruitful. Thereupon an abundant downpour of the Holy Spirit will germinate the seed of the saving word that has been commended by you to the hearts of your hearers and, according to what the prophet promised, 'rain will be given to your seed, wherever you sow on the land, and the bread of the fruit of your land shall be most abundant and rich for you.'[68]

XVII.1. "Beware also lest, seduced by love of vainglory, you tell impure persons at random about these things, which you have learned not so much from reading as from toilsome experience, once a more mature age has drawn you to teach. Thus you will bring upon yourself what the most wise Solomon forbade: 'Do not attach a wicked person to the pastures of the righteous, and do not let yourself be seduced by a full stomach.'[69] For 'pleasures are not fitting for a fool, nor is wisdom necessary where sense is lacking. 2. For foolishness is the more led on because a stubborn servant will not be corrected by words; even if he understands, he will not obey.'[70] And: 'Do not say anything in the hearing of an imprudent person, lest perchance he laugh at your wise words.'[71]

And: 'Do not give what is holy to dogs, and do not cast your pearls before swine, lest perchance they trample them underfoot and turn and rend you.'[72]

"It is fitting, then, that you hide the mysteries of spiritual meanings from such persons, so that you may sing effectively: 'I have hidden your words in my heart, so that I might not sin against you.'[73] 3. But perhaps you will say: To whom are the mysteries of Divine Scripture to be dispensed? The most wise Solomon teaches you: 'Give,' he says, 'intoxicating drink to those who are in sorrow, and wine to drink to those who are in pain, that they may forget their poverty and remember their pains no longer.'[74] That is to say, pour out abundantly the joy of spiritual knowledge, like wine that 'rejoices the heart of man,' for those who are cast down with bitterness and sorrow on account of being punished for their former deeds, and restore them with the inebriation of a saving word, lest perchance, overcome by constant bitterness and deathly hopelessness, people of this sort 'be swallowed up by too much sorrow.'[75] 4. But concerning those who are lukewarm and negligent and afflicted with no sorrow of heart it is said: 'One who is carefree and without sorrow shall be in need.'[76]

"Be as careful as you can, therefore, not to be puffed up with the love of vainglory, lest you be unable to have any part with the one whom the prophet praises, 'who has not loaned his money at interest.'[77] 5. For everyone who dispenses the words of God (of which it is said: 'The words of the Lord are pure words, silver tried in the fire, refined from the earth, seven times refined'[78]) out of love of human praise lends his money out at interest, and for this he will deserve not praise but punishment. For he has chosen to waste the Lord's money for the sake of making temporary gain out of it, not so that, as it is written, when the Lord comes 'he will receive what is his with interest.'[79]

XVIII. "But it is clear that the teaching of spiritual matters is ineffective under two conditions. Namely, either the person who is teaching recommends things that he has not experienced and attempts to instruct his hearer with empty phrases, or the hearer, full of wickedness and vice and hard of heart, does not accept the saving and holy teaching of the spiritual man. Of the latter it is said by the prophet: 'The heart of this people is blinded, and their ears are dull of hearing, and they have shut their eyes, lest at some time they see with their eyes and hear with their ears and understand with their heart and be converted and I heal them.'[80]

XIX.1. "Yet sometimes it is granted by the bountiful generosity of our God, who so ordains it and 'who desires all to be saved and to come to the knowledge of the truth,'[81] that a person who has not shown himself worthy of the preaching of the Gospel by reason of his blameless way of life acquires the grace of spiritual teaching for the salvation of many.

"It makes sense that we should explain by a similar discussion how the gifts of healing are granted by the Lord for the purpose of casting out demons. But, since we are getting up to eat, we shall reserve this for the evening, because whatever is assimilated gradually and without too much bodily labor is always more effectively grasped by the heart."

Textual References

1. Wis 1:5, 4.
2. Jer 1:10.
3. Cf. Gn 18:1–8, 19:1–3.
4. Cf. Rom 12:4–5.
5. Rom 12:6–8.
6. Cf. 1 Cor 12:28.
7. Prv 31:21 LXX.
8. Prv 22:20 LXX.
9. Gal 4:22–23.
10. Gal 4:24–25.
11. Gal 4:26–27.
12. Ps 147:12.
13. Gal 4:26.
14. 1 Cor 14:6.
15. 1 Cor 10:1–4.
16. 1 Cor 11:13.
17. 1 Thes 4:13–16.
18. 1 Cor 15:3–5.
19. Gal 4:4–5.
20. Dt 6:4.
21. Mt 5:8.
22. Dn 12:3.
23. Hos 10:12b LXX.
24. Ps 119:104.
25. Ps 101:1–2.
26. Jas 1:19.
27. Prv 29:20 LXX.
28. Acts 1:1.
29. Mt 23:3–4.
30. Mt 5:19.
31. Cf. 1 Cor 8:1.
32. Cf. Heb 9:4–5.
33. Cf. Is 11:1.
34. Lv 21:12.
35. 2 Cor 6:16.
36. Ex 20:14.
37. Jer 3:6.
38. Is 47:13.

39. Hos 4:12.
40. Gal 4:10.
41. Col 2:21.
42. 2 Cor 11:2.
43. 2 Cor 11:3.
44. Acts 20:29–30.
45. Prv 27:7 LXX.
46. Ps 104:15.
47. Prv 5:15–16 LXX.
48. Is 58:11–12.
49. Is 30:20–21.
50. Ps 133:2.
51. Ps 19:10.
52. 2 Cor 6:14–15.
53. Jer 5:21.
54. Hos 4:6.
55. Col 2:3.
56. Hos 10:12 LXX.
57. Ps 119:1–2.
58. 1 Tm 6:20.
59. Prv 11:22 LXX.
60. Sir 15:9.
61. Ps 50:16.
62. Prv 15:33 LXX.
63. Prv 17:16 LXX.
64. Acts 4:13.
65. Prv 14:33.
66. Sir 32:16.
67. 2 Cor 6:5–6.
68. Is 30:23.
69. Prv 24:15 LXX.
70. Prv 19:10 LXX; 18:2 LXX; 29:19 LXX.
71. Prv 23:9 LXX.
72. Mt 7:6.
73. Ps 119:11.
74. Prv 31:6–7 LXX.
75. 2 Cor 2:7.
76. Prv 14:23 LXX.

77. Ps 15:5.
78. Ps 12:6.
79. Mt 25:27.
80. Is 6:10 LXX.
81. 1 Tm 2:4.

14.1.2f. The reference to the different arts and disciplines recalls 1.2.

14.4.1 Elijah and also Elisha (the latter to a lesser degree) were canonized models of the ascetical life. Cf. 18.6.2, 21.4.2 (with the relevant note); *Inst.* 1.1.2; Eucherius, *De laude heremi* 18f. On Elijah's paradigmatic role in particular cf. DS 4.567-571. Comparisons of holy individuals with one or more of these two Old Testament figures were a commonplace in antiquity. Cf. 15.3.6; Jerome, *V. S. Pauli* 13; *V. prima gr. Pachomii* 2; *Hist. monach. in Aegypto* 2.9, 7.1, 8.46; Palladius, *Hist. laus.* 14.4; Theodoret of Cyrus, *Hist. relig.* 3.1, 13.17, 17.6, 26.7; Besa, *The Life of Shenoute* 10, 19 (trans. by Bell, CS 73 [1983]: 44, 45, 48); Gregory the Great, *Dial.* 2.8.

The Antony mentioned here is the subject of Athanasius's *V. S. Antonii.*

14.4.2 The John who appears here and in 14.7 may be any one of several of this name.

Thmuis was a town of Augustamnica Secunda in the ancient diocese of Egypt, on the banks of the Mendesian branch of the Nile. Serapion, the bishop and writer, who died after 362, was its most renowned inhabitant.

Abraham's and Lot's hospitality were exemplary in Christian antiquity. Cf. Heb 13:2; *1 Clem.* 10.7f.

The Macarius spoken of here also appears in Palladius, *Hist. laus.* 6.5ff.

14.6 On the impossibility of acquiring perfection in all the virtues cf. *Inst.* 5.4.

14.7 This story of a holy layman is reminiscent of that told in *Apophthegmata patrum,* de Eucharisto homine saeculari. Cf. Weber 35–38. The account of the initially unimpressive layperson who is in fact often as holy as or even holier than the professional ascetic is a common one in desert literature. Cf. *Hist. monach. in Aegypto* 14.2ff. (which contains three such accounts); *Verba seniorum* 20.13, 20.17; Regnault 37–38, N67;

ibid. 79–80, N490; ibid. 148–149, N628; ibid. 219–220, Bu I 104; John Moschus, *Pratum spirituale* 154. Accounts like these, however, are not necessarily to be taken as promoting holiness "in the world," since so many of the laypeople whom they are about are really monks (or nuns) in everything but name. The purpose of such stories, rather, is to show grace at work in unexpected places and to humble the professional ascetics; in this respect they recall, mutatis mutandis, the narrative of the centurion of Capernaum in Mt 8:5–13 par.

14.7.1 The offering of firstfruits, as well as tithing (mentioned in 14.7.3), is also spoken of in 21.1.3. On this practice in early Christianity cf. DACL 4.995–1003. There is no indication in *The Conferences* that these offerings were obligatory, although this is implied ibid. 997.

14.7.4 Marriages in which sexual union is either never practiced or its practice ceases occur with some regularity in desert literature. Cf. 21.8.2ff. (where a cessation of sexual relations is proposed, but to no avail), 24.26.3 (where this is suggested as an ideal), 24.26.6; Palladius, *Hist. laus.* 8.1ff., 61.2f.; *Apophthegmata patrum,* de Eucharisto homine saeculari.

14.8 On the historical and spiritual understanding of Scripture cf. also 8.3 and the relevant note. Examples of the tropological understanding of Scripture are to be found in 7.5.1 and *Inst.* 8.10.

14.8.4 The fourfold interpretation of Jerusalem, as Cassian understands it, can be traced back to Origen and was a commonplace by the time of our author. Cf. Henri DeLubac, *Exégèse médiévale: Les quatre sens de l'Ecriture* 1/2 (Paris, 1959), 645–646.

14.8.5 On the daily reception of Holy Communion cf. the note at 7.30.2.

14.9.2 The frequent mentions of reading, which begin here, must probably be taken as referring primarily to the reading of Scripture. But books other than the Bible were also read in the desert. Cf. Palladius, *Hist. laus.* 55.3; *Apophthegmata patrum,* de Epiphanio episcopo Cypri 8; John Moschus, *Pratum spirituale* 46, 55, 172. On "spiritual reading" in early monasticism in general cf. Louis Leloir, "La lecture de l'Ecriture selon les anciens Pères," in RAM 47 (1971): 183–199; DS 9.475–478; and on Cassian in particular cf. Franz Bauer, "Die Heilige Schrift bei den Mönchen des christlichen Altertums nach den Schriften des Johannes Cassianus," in *Theologie und Glaube* 17 (1925): 512–532.

14.9.4 The remark about John's relative youth is one of the few references to Cassian himself in *The Conferences.* Only here and in *Inst.* 5.35 is he called simply John.

The connection between reading—even (or especially) the reading of Scripture—and pride helped to contribute to the anti-intellectualism of the desert. One of the ways of dealing with the tempation to pride of this sort was to pretend that one knew nothing about Scripture when one was asked. Cf. *Apophthegmata patrum,* de abbate Poemene 8, de abbate Pambo 9. The most considered warning against an excessive familiarity with secular literature is found in Augustine, *De doct. christ.* 2.39.58ff.

14.9.5 Knowledge is briefly spoken of here as threefold—namely, not only as practical and as spiritual but also as ethical. The distinction between the ethical and the other two is not explained. Origen, citing unnamed sources in Greek philosophy, also divides knowledge into three parts—*moralis, naturalis,* and *inspectiva* (with a fourth, *rationalis,* mentioned in passing). The *moralis* corresponds to the ethical and the practical, the *inspectiva* to the spiritual, but the *naturalis* is equivalent to natural philosophy. Cf. Origen, *Comm. in Cant. Cant.,* prol. (GCS 33.75–79). On this division of knowledge cf. also Evagrius, *Schol. in Prov.* 247 (SC 340–342), with the commentary in SC 340.28–30 and the note ibid. 343. Cf. also 5.21.3 and the note at 3.6.4.

14.9.5ff. On the necessity of teaching by example as well as by word cf. the note at 11.2.2.

14.9.7 On the pure heart needed to understand Scripture cf. *Inst.* 5.34; Athanasius, *De incarn.* 57; Chrysostom, *Serm. in Act. Apost.* 55.2 ad fin.

14.10.2f. Similar ark of the covenant imagery as applied to the inner person may be found in Origen, *Hom. in Exod.* 9.4.

14.10.2 A twofold Testament: *Duplicis instrumenti.* On the use of *instrumentum* in this context cf. Tertullian, *Adv. Marcionem* 4.1: "Dividing the gods into two beings that are in fact different, one for each instrument–or, as is more usually said, Testament." On "instrument" as referring to the whole of Scripture cf. 10.10.3; and to the Old Testament alone cf. 17.19.2; *Inst.,* praef. 1.

14.10.4 Nesteros's recommendation that Cassian and Germanus memorize the whole Bible is not as outrageous as it may seem, given the alleged prodigious memories of many of the desert monks. Cf. Pachomius, *Praecepta* 140; Athanasius, *V. S. Antonii* 3; Jerome, *V. S. Hilarionis* 10; *Verba seniorum* 4.57, 10.91, 10.94, 10.96; Palladius, *Hist. laus.* 11.4 (where Ammonius is said to have memorized not only the entire Bible but also six million verses from different theological writings!), 18.25, 26.3, 32.12, 37.1, 58.1; *Hist. monach. in Aegypto* 2.5, 8.50, 10.7; Regnault 88–89, N518; ibid. 281–282, Ch250; Besa, *The Life of Shenoute* 96 (trans. by Bell, CS 73 [1983]: 70–71). There is a passing reference to memorizing the Gospels in 8.23.4.

That things constantly meditated upon while one is awake will form the subject matter of one's dreams when asleep is an idea that appears in Aristotle, *Eth. nicomach.* 1.13; Gregory Thaumaturgus, *Panegyricus* 16.196 (SC 148.178); Augustine, *Conf.* 10.30.41.

14.11 That Scripture adapts itself to the understanding of the reader is similar to the notion that Christ appears to different persons according to their ability to receive him. Cf. 10.6.1ff. and the relevant note. Parallel to this is the concept of the inexhaustibility of Scripture. Cf. Ephrem, *Comm. in Diatessaron* 1.19 (SC 121.53).

14.11.5ff. On wandering thoughts cf. the note at 1.5.4. On such thoughts characterized as fornication cf. 1.13.1 and the relevant note.

14.13.3f. The conference mentioned here seems to be a gathering of monks for instruction, undoubtedly by an elder.

14.14.1 On the inability of the impure soul either to receive spiritual knowledge or to pass it on cf. 21.36.3f.; Evagrius, *Schol. in Prov.* 178 (SC 340.272). On the impropriety of instructing the unworthy cf. 1.1 (and the relevant note) and 14.17.

14.14.2f. The image of the unclean vessel that must first be cleaned before being filled with some precious fluid is paralleled in Augustine, *Tract. in Ep. Ioann.* 4.6.

14.14.3 On vice as foul smelling cf. the note at 2.11.5.

14.16.7 The ignorance and simplicity of the apostles is a common theme in early Christian literature. Cf. Origen, *C. Celsum* 1.62; Athanasius, *De incarn.* 47; Chrysostom, *Serm. in 1 Cor.* 4.3.6; Augustine, *De civ. Dei* 22.5.

On spiritual knowledge as fragrant cf. the note at 1.1.

14.17.1 On the necessity of experience for learning spiritual truths (and for teaching them, as in 14.18) cf. the note at 3.7.4.

FIFTEENTH CONFERENCE THE SECOND CONFERENCE OF ABBA NESTEROS: ON DIVINE GIFTS

TRANSLATOR'S INTRODUCTION

Abba Nesteros's second conference, which deals with the charism of healing, is the shortest of all twenty-four conferences. Nesteros begins by distinguishing among three kinds of healing that differ by reason not of their object or their effect but by reason of the character and disposition of the healer. Thus there are healings performed by holy persons; by sinners and by other unworthy persons to whom, nonetheless, power has been given by God; and by demons who work through public sinners and who are thereby seeking to undermine the respect in which religion is held. Therefore it is not miracles themselves that are admirable, since the wicked can sometimes perform them, but rather a virtuous life. Above all, it is love that counts, and this is equivalent to that practical knowledge that had been discussed in 14.1.3ff.

The great men of the desert were in fact hesitant to work miracles, and they only did so when it seemed that they were compelled to it. As an illustration of this reluctance, Nesteros recounts the stories of three abbas who enacted miracles either to defend the faith in some way or as a merciful response to an urgent request. These men gave no credit to themselves for their gift but humbly acknowledged God as its source.

It is humility that particularly marks the Christian and that is capable of being learned by all, whereas miracle-working is for the few and is, in any event, conducive to vainglory. Indeed, it is a greater miracle to control one's own passions than to work miracles for others.

As a proof of this, and in conclusion, Nesteros relates an incident in the life of Abba Paphnutius. Paphnutius prided himself on his perfect chastity, but once, when he was cooking his meal, he burned his hand, which upset him. This in turn led him to reflect, despite his conviction of being pure, on the fires of hell. As he was musing on these thoughts and slowly drowsing off, an angel appeared to him and gently rebuked him for believing that he was pure, when in fact he was not completely in control of himself. If he wanted to demonstrate this to himself, he should take a naked maiden and embrace her and see if he remained unmoved. Paphnutius wisely realized that he could not survive such a test, and Nesteros ends the conference by observing that perfect purity is a higher gift than expelling demons.

Cassian's express relegation of miracles and extraordinary charisms to a very secondary level in comparison with a virtuous life is consonant with his words in *Inst.* praef. 8: "My plan is to say a few things not about the marvelous works of God but about the improvement of our behavior and the attainment of the perfect life, in keeping with what we have learned from our elders." The same sentiment appears later in *Conlat.* 18.1.3, when Cassian declares himself unwilling to expatiate on the miracles of Abba Piamun; his purpose is to "offer to our readers only what is necessary for instruction in the perfect life and not a useless and vain object of wonderment without any correction for faults." Nonetheless there is enough of the miraculous in the present conference, and throughout *The Conferences* in general, for the reader to grasp quickly that wonders were not necessarily infrequent in the desert. This is in turn intended to accomplish the further end of implanting in the reader an awe of the abbas whose teaching is being transmitted. Their miracles thus give authority to their words.

XV. The Second Conference of Abba Nesteros: On Divine Gifts

Chapters

I.1. After the evening synaxis we sat down together on the mats as usual, eager for the promised conference. And when we had kept silence for a little while out of respect for the old man, he anticipated our reverent stillness with words of this sort:

2. "The course of our previous discussion had gotten as far as broaching the subject of the arrangement of the spiritual gifts, which we have understood from the tradition of our forebears to be threefold. The first kind is for the purpose of healing, when the grace of miracles accompanies certain chosen and righteous men because of their holiness, as is clear in the case of the apostles and many holy persons, who worked signs and wonders in accordance with the authority of the Lord, who said: 'Cure the sick, raise the dead, cleanse lepers, cast out demons. You have freely received; freely give.'[1]

3. "The second is when, for the sake of the upbuilding of the Church or because of the faith of those who bring their sick or of those who must be healed, a health-giving power comes forth even from sinners and unworthy persons. Of these the Savior says in the Gospel: 'Many will say to me on that day: Lord, Lord, did we not prophesy in your name, and cast out demons in your name, and do many mighty deeds in your name? And then I will confess to them: I never knew you. Depart from me, you workers of wickedness.'[2] 4. On the other hand, if the faith of the petitioners or of the sick is wanting, he does not permit those to whom the gifts of healing have been granted to exercise their health-giving power. Luke the evangelist says about this: 'Jesus could do no powerful deeds among them because of their lack of faith.'[3] Hence the Lord also says: 'There were many lepers in Israel in the time of Elisha the prophet, and none of them was cleansed but Naaman the Syrian.'[4]

5. "The third type of healing is aped by the deceitful workings of the demons, so that, when a person who is entangled in obvious sins is believed to be holy and a friend of God out of admiration for his miracles, the imitation of his vices might also

appear desirable. Thus the sanctity of religion will be damaged when access has been given to disparagement, and certainly the person who believes that he has the gifts of healing will be all the more seriously hurt when he is puffed up with pride of heart. Hence, invoking the names of such people, who they know have neither the deserts of holiness nor any spiritual fruits, they make believe that they are being harassed by their worthiness and are fleeing from the bodies that they have possessed. 6. Of these it says in Deuteronomy: 'If a prophet or someone who says that he has seen a dream arises in your midst and he foretells a sign and a wonder, and what he has spoken comes to pass, and he tells you: Let us go and follow foreign gods that you do not know, and let us serve them, you shall not listen to the words of that prophet or dreamer, for the Lord your God is trying you, so that it might be clear whether you love him or not with all your heart and with all your soul.'[5] And in the Gospel it says: 'False Christs and false prophets will arise and will produce great signs and wonders, so that if possible even the elect might be led into error.'[6]

II.1. "Therefore we must never admire those who feign these things by such miracles. Rather, we should see whether they have been made perfect by the uprooting of all their vices and the correction of their behavior, for when the grace of God is dispensed it is certainly not bestowed because of someone else's faith or for any number of reasons but because of the person's own zeal. 2. For this is the practical knowledge which is also given the name of love by the Apostle and which on apostolic authority is preferred to all the tongues of men and angels, to the fullness of faith that even moves mountains, to all knowledge and prophecy, to the distribution of one's property, and even, lastly, to a glorious martyrdom.[7] For after he has enumerated all the different kinds of gifts and has said: 'To one is given a word of wisdom by the Spirit, to another a word of knowledge, to another faith, to another the grace of healing, to another the working of miracles,'[8] and so forth, and is on the verge of speaking about love, notice how in a few words he sets it as it were above all the gifts: 'I will show you a still more excellent way.'[9] 3. From this it is clearly evident that the whole of perfection and blessedness consists not in the working of those wonders but in the purity of love. Rightly so.

For all those things are going to be abolished and destroyed, but love will remain forever.[10] We see, therefore, that the working of signs was never made much of by our fathers. On the contrary, although they possessed this by the grace of the Holy Spirit, they never wanted to exercise it unless perchance an extreme and unavoidable necessity forced them.

III.1. "It is thus that we remember a dead man being raised by Abba Macarius, who was the first to make his dwelling in the desert of Skete. When a certain heretic who followed the perfidy of Eunomius was trying to subvert the purity of the Catholic faith by dialectical arts and had already deceived a vast number of people, the blessed Macarius was asked by some Catholic men who were very greatly troubled by this ruinous subversion if he would free Egypt in all its simplicity from the shipwreck of unbelief, and so he came. 2. When the heretic had accosted him with his dialectical arts and was wishing to entangle him, unwitting, in Aristotelian subtleties, the blessed Macarius put an end to his talkativeness with apostolic brevity, saying: '"The kingdom of God is not in word but in power."[11] Let us go to the tombs, then, and invoke the name of the Lord over the first dead man that we find. As it is written, let us show our faith by our works,[12] so that by his testimony the clearest proofs of a correct faith might be displayed, and we might confirm the plain truth not by a foolish and wordy discussion but by the power of signs and by that judgment which cannot be mistaken.' 3. On hearing this, the heretic was struck with shame in the presence of the bystanders. He made believe that he had agreed to be present under the established conditions and promised that he would be there on the next day. Yet that following day, when out of curiosity to see the spectacle all the people had eagerly thronged to the appointed location and were waiting, he became terrified at the awareness of his unbelief and fled at once, leaving Egypt completely behind. When the blessed Macarius had waited until the ninth hour with the crowd and realized that the man had not shown up because of his conscience, he took the people who had been corrupted by him and went to the designated tombs.

4. "Now, the overflowing of the River Nile is responsible for the practice among the Egyptians that the bodies of the dead are

embalmed with aromatic unguents and kept in little cells, which are somewhat raised, since the entire surface of that region is covered like an immense sea with the usual inundation for no small part of the year, such that there is no way for anybody to go anywhere except by taking a boat. The ground of that region, which is always very damp, prevents the carrying out of burials. For if corpses have been buried in it, the excessive moisture forces them to the surface. 5. So, when the blessed Macarius came to a certain very old corpse, he said: 'O man, if that heretic and son of perdition had come here with me and were himself standing by, and if I had cried out and invoked the name of Christ my God, say whether you would have arisen in the presence of these persons, who were nearly subverted by his deception.' Then he arose and responded with a word of assent. Abba Macarius asked him what he had been when he enjoyed this life, in what era he had lived, and whether he had known the name of Christ then. He replied that he had lived under the kings of remote antiquity, and he declared that he had not heard the name of Christ at that time. 6. Abba Macarius said to him again: 'Sleep in peace with the others of your condition, to be raised up by Christ at the end of time.'

"This power and grace of his, great as it was in him, would perhaps always have been hidden if the need of a whole imperiled province and an encompassing devotion to Christ and a sincere love had not compelled him to perform this miracle. It was certainly not a display of pride but rather a love of Christ and the well-being of a whole people that extracted this from him, as a reading from Kings shows was also the case with the blessed Elijah. He called for fire to come down from heaven upon the offerings laid on the pyre, so that he might free the imperiled faith of a whole people from the cunning of false prophets.[13]

IV. "And what shall I say of the deeds of Abba Abraham, who is named απλους, or 'the simple one,' on account of his simplicity of behavior and innocence? When, for the sake of the harvest, he had gone from the desert to Egypt for the days of Pentecost and been tearfully pestered by a woman who brought her infant, already wasting away and half dead for want of milk, he gave her a cup of water to drink that he had signed with the sign of the cross. When she had drunk of this, her breasts, which had been completely dry up until then, suddenly flowed with an abundant amount of milk.

V. "Or what about when the same man came to a village and was surrounded by a crowd of mockers who scoffingly showed him a certain man who, on account of a contracted knee, had for many years been deprived of the ability to walk and was crawling along because of his long-standing infirmity? Testing him, they said: 'Show us if you are a servant of God, Abba Abraham, and restore this man to his former health, so that we may believe that the name of the Christ whom you worship is not meaningless.' Then he immediately called on the name of Christ, bent over, grasped the man's withered foot, and stretched it. Instantly, at his touch, the dry and crooked knee was straightened out. Having regained the ability to walk which his years-long infirmity had made him forget, the man departed happy.

VI.1. "These men took no credit for themselves for being able to perform such marvels, because they acknowledged that they accomplished them not by their own virtuousness but by the Lord's mercy, and with the words of the apostles they rejected the human glory that arose from admiration for their miracles: 'Men and brothers, why do you marvel at this, or why do you look at us as if we had made this man walk by our own power or holiness?'[14] They considered that a person should not be praised for God's gifts and marvels but rather for the fruits of his own virtue, which are brought forth by an effort of one's mind and by the power of one's deeds. 2. For there are many people, as has already been said before, who are corrupt in mind and reprobate in faith but who cast out demons and work mighty deeds in the name of the Lord. It is true that when the apostles were talking about these and saying: 'Teacher, we saw someone casting out demons in your name, and we forbade him because he does not follow us,'[15] Christ replied to them at the time: 'Do not forbid him, for the one who is not against you is for you.'[16] Nonetheless, to those who say: 'Lord, Lord, did we not prophesy in your name, and cast out demons in your name, and do many mighty deeds in your name?' it is testified that he will reply: 'I never knew you. Depart from me, you workers of wickedness.' 3. Therefore he warns those upon whom he has bestowed the glory of signs and mighty deeds because of their holiness that they should not vaunt themselves on account of them, when he says: 'Do not rejoice because the demons are subject to you, but rejoice because your names are written in heaven.'[17]

VII.1. "Finally, when the very Author of all signs and mighty deeds was proposing his teaching to his disciples, he showed clearly what his true and most intimate followers should learn from him in particular. 'Come,' he said, 'and learn from me'[18]—not, to be sure, how to cast out demons with heavenly power, nor how to cleanse lepers, nor how to enlighten the blind, nor how to raise the dead. For even if I perform these things through some of my disciples, the human condition cannot make its own the praises of God, nor can a minister and servant claim for himself any part in this, where the glory is the Divinity's alone. But you, he says, 'learn from me, for I am meek and humble of heart.'[19] 2. For this can be learned and practiced by everyone in general, whereas the works of signs and mighty deeds are neither always necessary and appropriate for everyone, nor are they bestowed on everyone.

"Humility, then, is the teacher of all the virtues; it is the most firm foundation of the heavenly edifice; it is the Savior's own magnificent gift. For a person may perform without danger of pride all the miracles that Christ worked if he strains after the meek Lord not because of his exalted signs but because of his patience and humility. 3. But a person who itches to command unclean spirits, to bestow the gift of health on the sick, or to show some wondrous sign to the people is far from Christ even though he invokes the name of Christ in his displays, because by reason of his proud mind he does not follow the Teacher of humility. Even when he was returning to his Father he prepared what I might call his testament, and he left this to his disciples: 'A new commandment I give you,' he said, 'that you love one another; as I have loved you, you must also love one another.'[20] And immediately he added: 'By this all will know that you are my disciples, if you have love for one another.'[21] 4. He did not say: If you also perform signs and mighty deeds, but: 'If you have love for one another.' Certainly no one can observe this but the gentle and the humble.

"Therefore our forebears never considered those monks to be upright or free of the disease of vainglory who presented themselves as exorcists before men and who, in the midst of admiring crowds, proclaimed by a boastful display this grace that they had either deserved or arrogated to themselves. 5. They did this to no purpose. For 'the one who trusts in lies feeds the winds; he follows after birds that fly away.'[22] Surely what is spoken of in Proverbs is true in the case of these persons: 'As the winds and clouds and rain are very manifest, so also are those who boast of a false gift.'[23] Hence, if someone does one of these things in our presence, we should think him praiseworthy not for his wonderful signs but for his splendid behavior, and we should not ask whether demons are subject to him but whether he possesses the parts of love that the Apostle describes.[24]

VIII. "And indeed it is a greater miracle to tear out the remains of lasciviousness from one's own flesh than to cast out unclean spirits from the bodies of others. It is a more magnificent sign to control fierce movements of anger by the virtue of patience than to command the princes of the air. It is better to have kept devouring sadness from one's own heart than to have expelled bodily illness and fever from another's. Finally, it is in many respects a more splendid virtue and a more sublime accomplishment to cure the diseases of one's own soul than those of another's body. For to the extent that it is more sublime than the flesh, its well-being is the more important, and to the extent that its substance is more precious and excellent, its destruction is the more serious and dangerous.

IX. "Concerning those healings it is said to the most blessed apostles: 'Do not rejoice because the demons are subject to you.' For it was not their own power that wrought this but rather the power of the name that had been invoked. Therefore they are warned that they should not dare to claim for themselves from it any of the blessedness or glory that comes from the might and power of God alone. Instead they may claim that inner purity of life and heart on account of which they deserve to have their names inscribed in heaven.

X.1. "And in order that we may prove what we have just said from the testimonies of the ancients and from the divine oracles, we rightly tell in his own words and from his own experience what the blessed Paphnutius thought about marvelous signs and about the grace of purity, or rather what he knew from the revelation of an angel. He lived for many years under such strict discipline that he believed that he was completely free of the snares of carnal desire, for he felt that he was beyond all the attacks of the demons that he had been openly fighting over a long period. Now, as he was preparing a lentil relish—which they call *athera*—for some holy men who had arrived, his hand, as is wont to happen, was burned in the oven by a flame that darted up. 2. Aggrieved at this, he began to reflect at great length quietly within himself: 'Why,' he said, 'does this fire give me no peace, when the more savage struggles with the demons have ceased for me? And how will the inextinguishable fire, the searcher of all deserts, pass me by and not hold me fast on that fearful day of judgment, when this temporal and small external thing has not spared me now?' And when drowsiness suddenly crept up on him as he was troubled with thoughts of this kind and with sadness, an angel of the Lord approached him and said: 'Why are you sad, Paphnutius, that this earthly fire is not yet at peace with you, when there still resides in your members a disturbance of fleshly movements that has not yet been completely purified? 3. As long as its roots flourish deep within you, they will never allow this material fire to give you any peace. You will certainly not be able to consider it harmless until by signs of this sort you see that all these internal movements are extinct: Go, take a naked and very beautiful virgin. If while you hold her you notice that the tranquillity of your heart is untouched and that seething carnal emotions do not disturb you, neither will the touch of this visible flame, gentle and harmless like that of the three young men in Babylon,[25] come in contact with you.' 4. And so the old man, struck by this revelation, did not, to be sure, take upon himself the dangers of the divinely revealed test. Instead he probed his conscience, examined his purity of heart, and, concluding that his chastity would not yet bring him through this trial, said: 'It is not surprising if, when the unclean spirits battle me, I should still feel raging against me that burning fire which I used to believe was less than the most savage encounters with the demons.' 5. In fact it is a greater virtue and a sublimer grace to extinguish the inner lust of the flesh than by a miracle of the Lord and by the power of the Most High to subdue the wicked attacks of the demons and to expel them from the bodies of the possessed by invoking the divine name."

With this Abba Nesteros concluded his account of the true operation of the gifts and, as we hastened to the cell of the old man Joseph, which was nearly six miles away, he accompanied us by the instruction of his teaching.

TEXTUAL REFERENCES

1. Mt 10:8.
2. Mt 7:22–23.
3. Mk 6:5–6.
4. Lk 4:27.
5. Dt 13:2–4.
6. Mt 24:24.
7. Cf. 1 Cor 13:1–3.
8. 1 Cor 12:8–10.
9. 1 Cor 12:31.
10. Cf. 1 Cor 13:8.
11. 1 Cor 4:20.
12. Cf. Jas 2:14–26.
13. Cf. 1 Kgs 18:20–40.
14. Acts 3:12.
15. Lk 9:49.
16. Lk 9:50.
17. Lk 10:20.
18. Mt 11:28–29.
19. Mt 11:29.
20. Jn 13:34.
21. Jn 13:35.
22. Prv 10:4.
23. Prv 25:14 LXX.
24. Cf. 1 Cor 13:4–7.
25. Cf. Dn 3.

15.1.1 On the mats used for sitting cf. the note at 1.23.4.

15.2.1 That "the grace of God is dispensed...because of a person's own zeal" is an idea reminiscent of the teaching of the thirteenth conference.

15.3 Similar incidents involving Macarius are recounted in *Hist. monach. in Aegypto* 21 (PL 21.452: an addition of Rufinus); Palladius, *Hist. laus.* 17.11; Sozomen, *Hist. eccl.* 3.14. Cf. Weber 93–96. The sources indicate that this Macarius was the one known as "the Egyptian."

15.3.1 On Eunomius cf. the note at 7.32.3.

On the image of unbelief as shipwreck cf. 3.16.2 and the relevant note.

15.3.1f. "Dialectical arts" and "Aristotelian subtleties" were the bane of orthodox belief in the view not only of the simple but even in that of some of the most sophisticated theologians of the early Church. Aristotle, unlike Plato, did not for the most part enjoy a good reputation in Christian antiquity. For an evaluation of his place in the estimation of the Greek Fathers in particular up until the time of Theodoret of Cyrus cf. André-Jean Festugière, *L'idéal religieux des grecs et l'évangile* (Paris, 1932), 221–263. Note also the contrast between heretical "talkativeness" and "apostolic brevity." That heretics talk too much is a commonplace and is understood to be the result of the "Aristotelian" tendency to want to know–or at least express–too much. Cf. Gregory Nazianzen, *Or.* 27.1ff. Cassian declares his suspicion of "dialectical syllogisms and Ciceronian eloquence," contrasting these with the simplicity of the apostles, in *Inst.* 12.19. On the related issue of the elegance of philosophy and its ability to lead the monk astray cf. 1.20.3.

15.3.4 On the practice of embalming the dead (which seems to be identical with mummifying in the present context) in Christian Egypt cf. Alfred C. Rush, *Death and Burial in Christian Antiquity* (SCA 1) (1941): 119–121; ACW 10.136, n. 291.

15.3.6 Macarius's final words to the corpse seem to indicate that the dead man would be saved at the last judgment. This suggests an optimistic belief, rare among the Fathers, in the possibility of salvation for pagans who, through no fault of their own, did not know Christ.

On the comparison with Elijah cf. the note at 14.4.1.

It is uncertain with whom this Abba Abraham is to be identified. The name occurs elsewhere in desert literature, and the twenty-fourth conference is built around a certain Abraham. The present Abraham, in any case, was not the only one who was designated "simple." There was also a Paul the Simple. Cf. *Hist. monach. in Aegypto* 24; Palladius, *Hist. laus.* 22.

15.4.1 From the desert to Egypt: "Egypt" in this instance refers to the fertile region around the Nile delta. For a similar distinction cf. *Inst.* 2.3.1, 2.4, 4.1.

The days of Pentecost are the days from the feast of Easter to that of Pentecost.

15.6.1 Note the distinction between "God's gifts and marvels" and "the fruits of [one's] own virtue, which are brought forth by an effort of one's mind and by the power of one's deeds."

15.10 The Paphnutius who appears here is perhaps the same as the one who presides over the third conference.

15.10.1 On the term *athera* cf. Gazet's commentary in PL 49.1010.

15.10.2 The "disturbance of fleshly movements" refers to those involuntary genital movements whose control is the subject of much of the twelfth conference.

15.10.3 The perilous experiment that the angel describes (also suggested to be pursued in imaginary fashion in 19.16.4) may have had a precedent in ancient pagan literature. Georg Luck, "The Doctrine of Salvation in the Hermetic Writings," *The Second Century* 8 (1991): 36, says that some philosophers "seem to have encouraged their disciples to create in their imagination certain situations as a challenge, so to speak, or as an opportunity to test their self-control, their inner resources." But he does not specify. This particular act of imagination also recalls the early Christian practice of celibate men who lived with *virgines subintroductae* (lit. "virgins admitted in secret," also known as *synesaktoi* and *agapetae*). According to such celibates, the practice was justifiable because it offered the opportunity of testing one's chastity by a struggle. Cf. esp. the anonymous third-century treatise *De singularitate clericorum* 9. The angel makes his recommendation, however, for the sake of proving to Paphnutius that he is not beyond the struggle. It is almost certainly not intended to be taken seriously. On *virgines subintroductae* cf. Hans Achelis, *Virgines Subintroductae: Ein Beitrag zum VII. Kapitel des I. Korintherbriefs* (Leipzig, 1902); Pierre DeLabriolle, "Le mariage spirituel dans l'antiquité chrétienne," in *Revue historique* 137 (1921): 204–225; DACL 10.2.1881–1888; Roger E. Reynolds, "*Virgines Subintroductae* in Celtic Christianity," in *Harvard Theological Review* 61 (1968): 547–566.

SIXTEENTH CONFERENCE THE FIRST CONFERENCE OF ABBA JOSEPH: ON FRIENDSHIP

TRANSLATOR'S INTRODUCTION

The Joseph who presides over this and the following conference is probably the same as the Joseph of Panephysis to whom some eleven sentences are dedicated in the *Apophthegmata patrum*. Archebius, who introduced Germanus and Cassian to him, was bishop of Panephysis. Abba Joseph's distinguished background (he came from an important family of Thmuis) and his fluency in Greek are worth noting, as Cassian does, because they were unusual characteristics in the desert.

Some preliminary conversation about the relationship between Cassian and Germanus provides the occasion for Joseph to raise the topic of the different kinds of friendship. After speaking of friendships founded on utility, kinship, and the like, he observes that they are subject to disintegration for one reason or other. Only a friendship based on a mutual desire for perfection is capable of surviving, and this desire must be strong in each friend; each must, in a word, share a common yearning for the good.

When Germanus asks whether one friend should pursue what he perceives as good even against the wishes of the other friend, Joseph replies by saying that friends should never or rarely think differently about spiritual matters. Certainly they should never get into arguments with one another, which would indicate that in fact they were not of one mind in the first place. With this Joseph sets out six rules for maintaining friendship. It is interesting to see that these rules treat the subject more from the negative than from the positive side; that is, they aim more at preserving a friendship from collapse than at promoting it, although of course the former implies the latter. The final three rules, thus, touch upon controlling anger. Indeed, much of the rest of the conference has precisely this for its theme. The practice of humility and discretion—even to the point of seeking counsel from those who appear slow-witted, although actually they are more perceptive—is a major antidote to that divisiveness of will among friends from which anger springs. For the space of three chapters, the tenth to the twelfth, the discussion is so focused on discretion as to be particularly reminiscent of the second conference.

Following these chapters Cassian distinguishes between love and affection: The former is a disposition that must be shown to all, whereas the latter is reserved to only a few. Affection itself exists in almost limitless variety: "For parents are loved in one way, spouses in another, brothers in another, and children in still another, and within the very web of these feelings there is a considerable distinction, since the love of parents for their children is not uniform" (16.14.2).

The remaining half of the conference returns to the topic of dealing with anger, and in it Cassian demonstrates, as he did in previous conferences, his fine grasp of the workings of the human mind. He had already alluded in the ninth chapter to unacceptable conduct being concealed under the guise of "spiritual" behavior, and with the fifteenth chapter he takes this up again. There are brothers, for example, who cultivate the exasperating habit of singing psalms when someone is angry with them or they are angry with someone; they do this instead of seeking reconciliation and, undoubtedly, in order to manifest to any who might be looking on that they are superior to their own and others' emotions. Other brothers find it easier to treat pagans mildly and with restraint than to act in such wise toward their fellows; Cassian can only shake his head at this attitude. Still others give those who have irritated them the "silent treatment" or make provoking gestures that are more injurious than words; these persons deceive themselves by claiming that they have spoken nothing to disturb their confrères. (At this point Cassian distinguishes between deed and intention, which is a nuance that will assume a certain prominence in the next conference.) There are others, again, few though they may be, who stop eating when they are angry, although ordinarily they are able to endure fasting only with difficulty; persons of this sort must be qualified as sacrilegious for doing out of pride what they cannot do out of piety. Finally, there are some who knowingly set themselves up for a blow because of their all too artificially patient demeanor, to which they add insulting language; this patent abuse of the gospel injunction to turn the other cheek in fact indicates a wrathful spirit.

Only the person who is strong, Cassian informs the reader, can sustain one who is weak without losing his temper. The weak, on the other hand, are easily moved to anger and to harsh words. To sum up, anger must never be surrendered to, and when discord has arisen reconciliation must be speedy.

The concentration on anger in these pages that treat of friendship must at first appear startling, and Cassian may be criticized for not presenting a more optimistic vision of his subject. Where are the beautiful sentiments that lie scattered throughout much of Augustine's *Confessions,* say, or that can be found in Gregory Nazianzen, Paulinus of Nola, and others? Does friendship consist in nothing more than swallowing one's gorge? Yet Cassian is being painfully realistic: Anger is in fact one of the greatest threats, if not the greatest, to the very intimate relationship that he suggests in the opening pages of the conference. For a more idealized picture of friendship we must go to the first lines of the present conference or to those of the very first conference, in which Cassian describes his bond with Germanus. This is certainly the ideal, and we may only wish that its portrayal had been a little longer drawn out. A perhaps more important criticism is that most of what Cassian says is not really specific to friendship but can apply to almost any relationship. If the reader senses a slight unfocusing of the conference, it is probably for this reason.

The conference concludes with some perhaps unexpected words about friendships founded on magic, which are bound not to survive.

On Cassian's view of friendship and its sources, especially Basil and Evagrius, cf. A. Fiske, "Cassian and Monastic Friendship," in *The American Benedictine Review* 12 (1961): 190–205, and on the present conference in particular cf. 198–203; for Stoic influences cf. Colish 120–121; and for the best overall treatment cf. Karl August Neuhausen, "Zu Cassians Traktat De amicitia (Coll. 16)," in Christian Gnilka and Willy Schetter, eds., *Studien zur Literatur der Spätantike* (Bonn, 1975), 181–218. For other studies cf. Brian Patrick McGuire, *Friendship and Community: The Monastic Experience,* 350–1250, CS 95.77–82; David Konstan, "Problems in the History of Christian Friendship," in JECS 4 (1996): 87–113, esp. 104–106.

XVI. The First Conference of Abba Joseph: On Friendship

Chapters

I. The blessed Joseph, whose institutes and precepts must now be related, was one of the three whom we mentioned in the first conference. He came from a very distinguished family and was the leading man of his town in Egypt, which is called Thmuis. So utterly fluent was he not only in the Egyptian but also in the Greek language that he would speak very beautifully both with us and with those who were completely ignorant of the Egyptian tongue by himself and not through an interpreter, as others did.

When he noticed that we were eager for his instruction, he asked first whether we were blood brothers. Then, having heard from us that we were joined not by a fleshly but by a spiritual brotherhood, and that we had always been linked by an indivisible bond from the beginning of our renunciation both in the journey which the two of us had undertaken for the sake of our spiritual soldiery and in the pursuits of the cenobium, he started with these words:

II.1. "There are many kinds of friendship and companionship which, in different ways, bind the human race by the fellowship of love. For a good reputation is sufficient for some people to enter upon a relationship of acquaintance first and afterward of friendship as well. In the case of others, a contract or agreement about something given and received forges a bond of love. Similar interest and sharing with regard to business or soldiering or art or study fastens still others together by the cords of friendship, and in this way even savage hearts grow so gentle toward one another that even those who live in forests and on mountains and who take pleasure in robbery and delight in the shedding of human blood embrace and cherish those who participate in their crimes.

2. "There is another kind of love, too, which is founded on a natural instinct and on the law of kinship, in accordance with which one's tribesmen and spouse and parents and brothers and children are naturally preferred to others. This appears to be the case not only with the human race but with every winged creature and animal. For at the urging of a natural disposition they so protect and defend their chicks and their young that frequently they are not

even afraid to expose themselves to dangers and to death on behalf of them. And even those kinds of beasts and serpents and winged creatures whose unbearable ferocity and deadly poison separate them and set them apart from all the others, like basilisks and unicorns and griffins, remain peaceful and harmless among themselves because of their common origin and feeling, even though the very sight of them is said to be dangerous to all others.

3. "But inasmuch as all these kinds of love that we have spoken about are common, as we see, to bad and good and even to wild animals and serpents, it is certain that they cannot endure as such forever. For distance, the forgetfulness brought on by time, business agreements, and concerns over words and affairs frequently end them. Since they are usually based on various relationships of gain or lust or kinship or different needs, they are broken off when some reason for severing them arises.

III.1. "Among all of these there is one kind of love that is indestructible and that is founded not on a good reputation or on the greatness of one's title or one's gifts or on some business obligation or on natural need but on likeness of virtue alone. This, I say, can never be cut off for any reason: Not only are distance and time unable to undo and destroy it, but even death itself does not sunder it. 2. This is the true and indissoluble love that grows by the combined perfection and virtue of the friends. Once the relationship has begun, neither a difference in desires nor a contentious clash can do it damage.

"But we have known many who lived out this chosen orientation and who, although they were linked by the most ardent companionship for the sake of Christ's love, were unable to maintain it constant and unshaken. The reason for this is that, even though the foundation of their fellowship was good, nonetheless they did not hold with one and the same zeal to the orientation that they had chosen and agreed upon, and since this was not striven after with equal effort by both but only one persisted in it, the affection between them was of a temporary sort. Despite the fact that one person keeps to this boldly and unweariedly, it is inevitably ruined by the other person's faintheartedness.

3. "For the infirmities of those who lukewarmly desire the health of perfection are unbearable to those who are sick, how-

ever perseveringly they may be sustained by the strong. The causes of their disorders, which give them no peace, are rooted in them. They are like those who are annoyed by an upset stomach and who are in the habit of attributing their nausea to the negligence of their cooks and servants. Whatever concern may be shown them by those who wait on them, they still blame the healthy for the causes of their disorder, which they fail to realize resides within themselves due to the defect of their weakness.

4. "Hence, as we have said, only the ties of a friendship which is founded upon similarity of virtuousness are trustworthy and indissoluble, for 'the Lord makes those of one mind to dwell in the house.'[1] Therefore love can abide unbroken only in those in whom there is one chosen orientation and one desire, one willing and one not willing. If you also wish to preserve this inviolable, you must first strive, after having expelled your vices, to put to death your own will and, with common earnestness and a common chosen orientation, to fulfill diligently what the prophet takes such great delight in: 'Behold, how good and how pleasant it is for brothers to dwell in unity.'[2] 5. This should be understood not in terms of place but spiritually. For it profits nothing if those who disagree about behavior and chosen orientation are together in one dwelling, nor is it a drawback to those who are of like virtue to be separated by distance. With God it is common behavior rather than a common location that joins brothers in a single dwelling, and the fullness of peace can never be maintained where there is a difference of wills."

IV. GERMANUS: "What if one person wishes to do something that he sees as useful and beneficial from God's perspective, but the other does not give his assent? Should this be pursued even against the wish of that brother or should it be abandoned for his sake?"

V. JOSEPH: "It was for this reason that we said that the grace of friendship in its fullness and perfection can only survive among perfect men of like virtue. Their similar will and their common chosen orientation either never or certainly very rarely let them think differently or disagree about what pertains to progress in the spiritual life. But if they start to get into excited and heated arguments, it is clear that they have never been at one according to the rule that we have spoken of. But since no one can start with perfection except the person who has begun from its very foundation, and since you are inquiring not about its greatness but rather about how one can attain to it, I think it necessary to explain to you, in a few words, its rule and the path that your steps must take in order for you to be able to obtain more easily the good of patience and peace.

VI.1. "The first foundation of true friendship, then, consists in contempt for worldly wealth and disdain for all the things that we possess. For it is unrighteous and blasphemous indeed if, after having renounced the vanity of the world and of everything in it, we should prefer the paltry household articles that remain to the most precious love of a brother.

"The second is that each person should so restrain his will as not to consider himself wise and learned, preferring to follow his own point of view rather than his neighbor's.

2. "The third is that he should realize that all things, even those which he considers useful and necessary, must be subordinated to the good of love and peace.

"The fourth is that he should see that he must never be angered for any reason, whether just or unjust.

"The fifth is that he should desire to calm the anger that a brother may have conceived against him, even if it is groundless, just as he would his own, knowing that another's annoyance will be as dangerous for him as if he were himself moved against another, if he has not, as far as possible, expelled it from his brother's mind.

"The last is what is certainly decisive in regard to all vices in general—namely, that a person reflect daily on the fact that he is going to depart from this world. 3. This conviction not only does not permit any annoyance to remain in the heart, but it even suppresses all the movements of every wrongful desire and sin. Whoever holds to this, therefore, will neither suffer nor inflict the bitterness of anger and discord.

"But when these things are lacking, as soon as he who is jealous of love has gradually injected the poison of annoyance into the hearts of his friends, it is inevitable that, little by little, with frequent quarrels and an ever more lukewarm love, he will finally separate the hearts of those who love one another, which have over the course of time been sorely hurt.

4. "For how will the one who takes the path that has previously been pointed out ever be able to differ from his friend if he completely removes the underlying cause of disputes, which is usually occasioned by the most insignificant things and the paltriest matters, and claims nothing for himself? In this way he observes with all his strength what we read about in the Acts of the Apostles with regard to the unity of the believers: 'The multitude of believers had one heart and one soul, and none of them said that what he possessed was his own, but all things were common to them.'[3] And how will the seeds of dissension germinate in a person who follows the will of his brother rather than his own and who has become the imitator of his Lord and Creator, who said, speaking in the person of the man whom he bore: 'I have not come to do my own will but the will of him who sent me'?[4] 5. How will a person arouse any discord at all if he has determined, based on his own knowledge and understanding, to trust not so much his own decision as his brother's judgment, in accordance with his will either approving or disapproving his own perceptions, thereby fulfilling with a devout and humble heart the gospel words: 'Not as I will but as you do'?[5] Or how will a person allow anything to provoke his brother if he considers nothing more precious than the good of peace, not forgetting those words of the Lord: 'By this all will know that you are my disciples, if you have love for one another'?[6] It was by this particular sign that Christ wanted his flock of sheep to be recognized in this world, and by this characteristic, as it were, to be distinguishable from all others. 6. And how will a person let an annoying grudge burden him or remain with someone else if his guiding principle is that there can be no just reason for anger, which is wicked and impermissible, and that likewise, when a brother is angered against him, just as when he himself is angered against his brother, he cannot pray? For he always keeps in his heart the words of the Lord, his humble Savior: 'If you are offering your gift at the altar and there remember that your brother has something against you, leave your gift there at the altar, go first to be reconciled with your brother, and then come and offer your gift.'[7] 7. It will be of no use to you if you

say that in fact you are not angry and you believe that you are fulfilling the command which says: 'The sun should not go down on your anger,'[8] and: 'Whoever is angry with his brother shall be liable to judgment,'[9] but you disdain with a stubborn heart someone else's annoyance, which you would have been able to soothe by your own graciousness. You will be punished in the same way for having transgressed the Lord's command. For he who said that you must not be angry with another person also said that another's annoyance must not be disdained, because God, 'who desires all to be saved,'[10] makes no distinction between destroying yourself and destroying someone else. 8. For the destruction of anyone results in loss for him, and in the same way the ruin of all is delightful to the one who profits from your death and your brother's. Finally, how will a person who is convinced every day—and indeed constantly—that he is going to depart from this world be able to stay annoyed with his brother?

VII. "Just as nothing is to be preferred to love, then, so also, on the other hand, nothing is to be less esteemed than rage and wrath. For everything, however beneficial and necessary it may appear, should nonetheless be put aside in order to avoid the disturbance of anger, and everything that may seem inimical should be put up with and tolerated in order to maintain unharmed the tranquillity of love and peace, for it must be believed that nothing is more destructive than anger and annoyance and nothing more beneficial than love.

VIII. "For as the enemy separates brothers who are still carnal and weak by a flare-up over some paltry and earthly thing, so also he produces discord between spiritual persons on account of a difference of perceptions, and from this there certainly arise with frequency the disputes and arguments that the Apostle condemns.[11] Hence, as a result, the jealous and wicked enemy sows division between brothers living in harmony. For the words of the most wise Solomon are true: 'Contention arouses hatred, but friendship will defend all those who do not contend.'[12]

IX. "For this reason, in order to maintain an enduring and undivided love, it is of no value to have removed the first cause of dissension, which usually springs from vain and worldly things, to have despised everything carnal, and to have allowed our brothers complete access to everything that we need unless we have also cut off the second cause, which usually appears under the guise of spiritual thoughts, and in every respect acquired humble thoughts and harmonious wills.

X. "For I remember that, when my youthfulness was still encouraging me to get married, the awareness of this frequently inserted itself into our studies in morality and Holy Scripture, so that we believed that nothing was more realistic and nothing more reasonable than this. But when we came together and began to disclose our feelings, some things were considered false and harmful by another person during the course of the general discussion, and soon afterward they were pronounced wicked by the common judgment and condemned. So luminously radiant were they, so to speak, when they were first suggested by the devil, that they would easily have been able to generate discord if the command of the elders, which was observed like a kind of divine oracle, had not kept us from all contention. It was thus decreed by them, with a kind of legal force, that neither of us should trust his own judgment more than his brother's if we wished never to be deceived by the cleverness of the devil.

XI.1. "For what the Apostle says is frequently proven to be the case: 'Satan himself transforms himself into an angel of light.'[13] In this way he fraudulently pours a dark and foul obscurity over our thoughts in place of the true light of knowledge. Unless they have been received by a humble and gentle heart and kept for examination by a very mature brother or a very approved elder and are rejected or accepted by us only after having been carefully subjected to their scrutiny, we shall certainly in our thoughts venerate an angel of darkness instead of an angel of light and suffer most serious ruin. It is impossible for a person who trusts in his own judgment to escape this calamity unless he loves and practices true humility and carries out with utter contrition of heart what the Apostle so greatly beseeches: 2. 'If there is any consolation in Christ, then, if there is any comfort of love, if there are any bowels of compassion, complete my joy: Be of the same mind, have the same love, be of one accord, thinking the same thing, doing nothing contentiously or vaingloriously, but in humility considering the others superior to yourselves.'[14] And this: 'Outdo one another in honor,'[15] so that each person may ascribe more knowledge and holiness to his fellow and may believe that the height of true discretion lies in another's judgment rather than in one's own.

XII. "But by an illusion of the devil or by the intervention of human error, by which no one in this flesh goes undeceived, as is the way of men, it often happens that a person who has a sharper wit and a broader knowledge sometimes conceives something false in his mind, while a person who has a slower wit and less prestige perceives something more correctly and truly. Therefore no one, however well endowed with knowledge, should persuade himself with empty pride that he does not need anyone else's advice. For even if a diabolical illusion does not cloud his judgment, he will still not escape the more serious snares of haughtiness and pride. For who could arrogate this to himself without great danger when the vessel of election,[16] in whom Christ spoke, as he himself declared,[17] said that he had gone up to Jerusalem solely in order to deliberate in private with his fellow apostles about the Gospel which he was preaching to the Gentiles and which the Lord had revealed and was helping him with?[18] From this it is clear not only that unanimity and concord are maintained by these precepts but also that none of the traps of our adversary the devil and the snares of his illusions are to be feared.

XIII. "Finally, the virtue of love is so greatly extolled that blessed John the apostle declares that it is not merely something belonging to God but is in fact God himself when he says: 'God is love. The one who abides in love abides in God and God in him.'[19] To such an extent do we experience its divinity that we clearly see flourishing in us what the Apostle speaks of: 'The love of God has been poured out in our hearts by the Holy Spirit, who dwells in us.'[20] It is as if he were saying that God has been poured out in our hearts by the Holy Spirit who dwells in us. He himself, even when we do not know what we ought to pray, 'intercedes for us with unspeakable groans. But he who searches hearts knows what the Spirit desires, because he asks on behalf of the holy ones according to God.'[21]

XIV.1. "It is possible for this love, then, which is called αγαπη, to be shown to all. The blessed Apostle says about it: 'Therefore, while we still have time, let us do good to all, but especially to the household of the faith.'[22] So much is it the case that it must be shown to all in general that we are commanded by the Lord to bestow it even on our enemies. For he says: 'Love your enemies.'[23]

"But διαθεσις, or affection, is shown to very few, to those who are linked by a similarity of behavior and by the fellowship of virtue. Yet even διαθεσις itself seems to have many divisions. 2. For parents are loved in one way, spouses in another, brothers in another, and children in still another, and within the very web of these feelings there is a considerable distinction, and not even the love of parents for their children is uniform. This is proven by the example of the patriarch Jacob, who, although he was the father of twelve sons and loved all of them with a fatherly love, nonetheless loved Joseph with a particular affection, so that Scripture recalls quite clearly of him: 'His brothers envied him because his father loved him.'[24] That is to say, it was not that this righteous man and father did not really love his other offspring as well, but rather that he clung more sweetly and tenderly as it were to his affection for this one, preferring him as a type of the Lord.

3. "We read very plainly that this was also the case with John the evangelist, when it is said of him that he was 'the disciple whom Jesus loved.'[25] Yet, to be sure, he also included the other eleven, since they were similarly chosen, in so special a love that he distinguishes it with a gospel attestation: 'As I have loved you, you must also love one another.'[26] About them it is also said elsewhere: 'Loving his own who were in the world, he loved them to the end.'[27] But in this instance an affection for one did not imply a lesser love for the other disciples but rather a larger and more abundant love for that one, which was bestowed on him because of the privilege of his virginity and his unsullied flesh. 4. It is singled out as something sublime inasmuch as it is set apart not by an odious comparison but by the overflowing favor of a most abundant love. Such is also what we read in the Song of Songs in the person of the bride, when she says: 'Set in order love in me.'[28] For this is a properly ordered love which, while hating no one, loves certain persons more by reason of their good qualities. Although it loves everyone in a general way, nonetheless it makes an exception for itself of those whom it should embrace with a particular affection. And, again, among those who are highest and chiefest

in this love it chooses for itself some who are set apart from the others by an extraordinary affection.

XV. "On the other hand we know that some brothers (would that we did not know them!) are so stubborn and unyielding that, when they sense that they are angry with a brother or that a brother is angry with them, they withdraw from those whom they should be soothing by a humble act of reparation and by conversation, and they begin to sing some verses of the psalms in order to conceal the mental annoyance that has arisen from the anger caused by whatever the disturbance may have been. Although they think that they are calming the bitterness that has sprung up in their heart, by their scorn they are increasing what they would have been able to get rid of at once if they had had a mind to be more considerate and humble, by a timely compunction both healing their own hearts and calming their brothers' minds. For by pettiness of this sort they are in fact encouraging and nurturing the vice of pride instead of eliminating the grounds for dispute, and they are heedless of the command of the Lord which says: 'Whoever is angry with his brother shall be liable to judgment.' And: 'If you remember that your brother has something against you, leave your gift there at the altar, go first to be reconciled with your brother, and then come and offer your gift.'

XVI.1. "So greatly, then, does our Lord wish us not to treat someone else's annoyance as if it were nothing that, if our brother has anything against us, he will not accept our gifts—that is, he will not permit us to offer him our prayers—until by a speedy act of reparation we remove the annoyance from his mind, whether it has been conceived justly or unjustly. For he does not say: If your brother has a real quarrel with you, leave your gift at the altar and go first to be reconciled with him, but rather: 'If you remember that your brother has anything against you'—that is, even if there is something light and trivial that has aroused your brother against you, and you suddenly remember it, you should realize that you ought not to offer the spiritual gifts of your prayers if you have not first, by a gracious act of reparation, removed from your brother's heart the annoyance that has arisen for whatever reason.

2. "If, then, the words of the Gospel command us to make reparation to those who are angry even for a past and slight dis-

sension and for one that has arisen for the most insignificant of reasons, what will become of us wretched persons who with obstinate dissimulation make nothing of recent and very serious sins that were committed by our own wrongdoing, and, puffed up with diabolical pride, are ashamed to be humbled, denying that we are responsible for our brother's annoyance, with rebellious spirit disdaining to submit to the Lord's precepts, and contending that they need never be observed and can never be fulfilled? And so it happens that, in judging that he has commanded something impossible and inappropriate, we become, according to the apostle, 'not doers but judges of the law.'[29]

XVII.1. "It is also cause for tears when some brothers are inflamed by some kind of insulting word and are wearied by the pleas of another person who wants to smooth it over, and when they hear that they must never get annoyed with a brother and remain so, according to what is written: 'Whoever is angry with his brother shall be liable to judgment.' And: 'The sun should not go down on your anger.' Thereupon they declare 2. that, if a pagan or a person living in the world had done this or said such things, it would rightly have to be endured. But who could put up with a brother who was guilty of so serious a fault and who expressed such a bizarre reproach! As if patience must be shown only to unbelievers and to sacrilegious persons and not to everyone in general, and as if wrath must be considered harmful for a Gentile and beneficial for a brother, when in fact the stubborn disturbance of an irritated mind inflicts the same loss on oneself, whomever it may have been aroused against. 3. How stubborn and indeed senseless it is that in their dull and brutish minds they do not make out the meaning of those words, for it is not said that everyone who is angry with a stranger shall be liable to judgment. This would perhaps, according to their understanding, have excepted those who share our faith and way of life. But the gospel words express it clearly when they say: 'Everyone who is angry with a brother shall be liable to judgment.' And so, although according to the rule of truth we must accept everyone as our brother, nonetheless in this text it is the believer and the one sharing in our way of life rather than the heathen who is designated by the particular word 'brother.'

XVIII.1. "But what sort of a thing is it that we sometimes think that we are patient because, when we are aroused, we disdain to respond but mock our irritated brothers by a bitter silence or by a derisory movement or gesture in such a way that we provoke them to anger more by our taciturn behavior than we would have been able to incite them by passionate abuse, in this respect considering ourselves utterly blameless before God, since we have voiced nothing that could brand or condemn us according to the judgment of human beings? As if it were words alone and not the will in particular that is declared guilty in the sight of God, and just the sinful deed and not also the wish and the intention that should be considered wrong, and only what each person has done and not also what he wanted to do that should be submitted to judgment. 2. For it is not only the nature of the disturbance that has occurred which is criminal but also the intention of the one causing the irritation. Therefore the probing examination of our Judge will not seek out how a quarrel arose but rather by whose fault it flared up, for it is the purpose of the sin and not the sequence of the wrongdoing that must be taken into account. For what difference does it make whether someone slays his brother personally with a sword or drives him on to his death by some sort of deception when, whether by cunning or lawlessness, it is clear that he is dead? As if it were enough not to have knocked a blind man down with one's own hand, when he who scorned to help him when he was lying near the ditch, although he could have, is just as guilty. Or as if only the person who ensnared someone with his hand were wrong and not also the one who prepared or set up the snare or at least was unwilling to remove it when he could have.

3. "It is of no value not to speak, then, if we enjoin silence on ourselves in order to do by silence what would have been done by an outcry, feigning a kind of behavior by which both the person who should be healed is aroused to a more violent wrath and we are praised for all these things by his loss and perdition. As if a person would not be more criminal from the very fact of his wishing to acquire glory for himself from his brother's perdition. For such silence is equally harmful to both because, just as it builds up annoyance in another's heart, it does not permit that which is in one's own to be calmed. 4. Against persons of this sort the

prophet's curse is quite properly directed: 'Woe to the one who gives drink to his friend and who puts in his gall, making him drunk so that he looks on his nakedness. He is filled with shame instead of glory.'[30] And another says this about such persons: 'Every brother will utterly supplant, and every friend will go about deceitfully. And a man will mock his own brother, and they will not speak the truth.'[31] For 'they bend their tongue like a bow of falsehood and not of truth.'[32]

"Often a feigned patience arouses a still more bitter wrath than does a word, and a spiteful silence surpasses the harshest verbal abuse, and the wounds of enemies are more easily borne than the sly compliments of mockers. 5. Of these it is well said by the prophet: 'Their words are smoother than oil, but they are darts.'[33] And elsewhere: 'The words of the clever are smooth, but they bore into the depths of the belly.'[34] This too can be well applied to them: 'With his mouth he speaks peace to his friend, but secretly he sets traps for him.'[35] Yet the one who deceives by these is deceived himself instead, for 'he who prepares a net before his friend spreads it at his own feet.'[36] And: 'The one who digs a ditch for his neighbor will fall into it himself.'[37]

"Finally, when a great multitude had come with swords and clubs to seize the Lord, no one was more conspicuous by his cruelty to the Author of our life than that parricide who preceded everyone with the obeisance of a feigned greeting and offered a kiss of deceitful love. 6. To him the Lord said: 'Judas, do you betray the Son of Man with a kiss?'[38] That is to say: The bitterness of your persecution and hatred has taken on this guise, whereby it is expressed as the sweetness of true love. He expounds more openly and vehemently on the force of this sorrow through the prophet when he says: 'If my enemy had cursed me I would certainly have borne it. And if he who hated me had spoken great things against me I would certainly have hidden myself from him. But it was you, a man of one mind, my guide and my friend, who used to eat pleasant food together with me. We walked in the house of God with one accord.'[39]

XIX.1. "There is another unholy kind of annoyance that would not have been worth mentioning if we did not know that it was being practiced by some brothers. When they have been annoyed or angered they stubbornly refrain from eating, such that (which we are unable to say without being ashamed) those who say that they are unable to postpone eating until the sixth hour or at most the ninth when they are in good humor do not even feel two-day fasts and are able to put up with a considerable loss of food, thanks to their being sated with anger, when they are full of annoyance and wrath. 2. In this it is clear that they bring on themselves the crime of sacrilege by enduring fasts out of diabolical pride which should be offered to God alone specifically out of humility of heart and as a cleansing from sin. It is as if they are making their prayers and sacrifices not to God but to the demons, and so they deserve to hear the rebuke of Moses: 'They have sacrificed to demons and not to God, to demons that they did not know.'[40]

XX. "Nor are we ignorant of that other kind of madness which is to be found in some brothers under the guise of a counterfeit patience. For them it is not enough to have aroused contention unless they also irritate others with provocative words so as to get hit. And when they have been hit a light blow, they offer another part of their body to be struck, as if by this they were going to fulfill perfectly the command which says: 'If anyone strikes you on your right cheek, offer him the other as well.'[41] But they are completely ignorant of the meaning and the intention of Scripture, for they think that they are practicing gospel patience by way of the sin of wrath, for the utter eradication of which not only are mutual retaliation and wrangling forbidden but we are even commanded to calm the rage of the striker by putting up with redoubled mistreatment."

XXI. GERMANUS: "Why must someone be blamed who carries out the gospel precept and not only does not make retaliation but is even prepared to undergo redoubled mistreatment?"

XXII.1. JOSEPH: "As was said a short while ago, it is not merely the thing itself which is done but also the character of the mind and the intention of the doer that must be looked at. Therefore, if by careful scrutiny you weigh what is accomplished by each person, with what mind it is done and from what inmost disposition it proceeds, you will see that the virtue of patience and mildness can never be exercised by a contrary spirit—that is, by one of impatience and rage.

2. "Our Lord and Savior instructed us thoroughly in the virtue of patience and mildness—that is, so that we would not promote it by mere lip service but would lay it up in the deepest recesses of our soul—and gave us this formula for gospel perfection when he said: 'If anyone strikes you on your right cheek, offer him the other as well.' (Without doubt one on the right is to be understood, and this other right one cannot be understood except as being, in my estimation, on the face of the inner man.) In so doing he desired to remove completely the dregs of wrath from the inmost depths of the soul. Thus, if your outer right cheek has received a blow from the striker, the inner man should offer his right cheek to be struck as well in humble accord, suffering along with the outer man and as it were submitting and subjecting its own body to the injustice of the striker, so that the inner man may not be disturbed even silently within itself at the blow dealt the outer man.

3. "You see, then, that they are far from that gospel perfection which teaches that patience must be observed not by words but by the inner tranquillity of the heart, and which commands that we must hold to it when something adverse occurs in such a way that we not only keep ourselves far from wrathful disturbance but also, by submitting to their mistreatment, urge those who have been aroused by their wickedness to return to calm, now that they are sated with their blow. Thus we shall conquer their rage with our mildness, and thus we shall also fulfill the apostolic words: 'Do not be overcome by evil, but overcome evil with good.'[42]

4. "This can by no means be fulfilled by those who utter words of mildness and humility in a proud spirit. They not only do not calm the fiery rage that has been conceived; on the contrary, they cause it to flare up more in their own mind than in that of their brother who has been aroused. Yet, even if in some way they could remain gentle and calm, they would never receive any fruits of righteousness thereby because they are claiming the glory of patience for themselves by way of their neighbor's loss, and thus they are very far indeed from that apostolic love which 'does not seek what is its own'[43] but rather what belongs to others. For it does not want riches in such a way as to make a profit for itself at

its neighbor's expense, nor does it desire to acquire anything to someone else's impoverishment.

XXIII. "It should certainly be known that, as a rule, he who submits his own will to his brother's will acts the stronger part than he who is more obstinate in defending and holding on to his own opinions. For the former, in putting up with and tolerating his neighbor, obtains the status of one who is healthy and strong, whereas the latter that of one who is somehow weak and sickly, who must be so flattered and coaxed that occasionally it is good that some adjustments be made even with respect to necessary things for the sake of his calm and peace. In this, to be sure, he should not believe that his perfection is at all diminished, although by giving in he has somewhat mitigated his intended strictness. On the contrary he should realize that he has gained much more by his forbearance and patience. For the apostolic precept has it: 'You who are strong should put up with the infirmities of the weak.'[44] And: 'Bear one another's burdens, and so you will fulfill the law of Christ.'[45] For one weak person never puts up with another weak person, nor will someone who is sick be able to endure or heal someone else who is ailing in the same way. Rather, it is he who is himself not subject to infirmity who bestows healing on the infirm. Rightly is it said to him: 'Physician, heal yourself.'[46]

XXIV. "It should also be noted that the character of the weak is consistently of this sort: They quickly and easily pour out abuse and sow discord, but they themselves do not wish to put up with the slightest mistreatment, and although they carry on violent arguments and get on their high horse without any fear of the consequences, they are unwilling to bear small and indeed very minor things. Therefore, according to the aforesaid opinion of the elders, a stable and unbroken love cannot endure except among men of the same virtue and chosen orientation. For it is bound to be rent at some time or other, however carefully it may be maintained by one of the persons involved."

XXV. GERMANUS: "How, then, can the patience of the perfect man be praiseworthy if he cannot always tolerate the weak?"

XXVI.1. JOSEPH: "I did not say that the strength and tolerance of the person who is strong and robust was going to be overcome but rather that the great frailty of the weak, which is sustained by the forbearance of the person who is well and which is daily declining to a worse state, was going to lead him to the conclusion that he himself ought no longer to be put up with or else that it would be better for him to depart at some time or other, once he has become aware of his neighbor's remarkable patience and the deterioration caused by his own impatience, rather than to be constantly put up with because of someone else's magnanimity.

2. "We are of the opinion, therefore, that these are the most important things to be observed by those who wish to keep a companionable disposition inviolable. First, the monk who has been aroused by any mistreatment whatsoever must preserve the calm not only of his lips but also of the depths of his heart. Yet, if he feels that they have been even slightly disturbed, he must compose himself in utter silence and carefully observe what the psalmist says: 'I was troubled and did not speak.'[47] And: 'I said: I will guard my ways lest I sin with my tongue. I set a guard at my mouth when the sinner stood against me. I was dumb and was humbled, and I did not speak of good things.'[48] Nor should he think of his present state and utter the things that rage suggests to him and his aggrieved mind broods over when he is upset. Instead, he should recall the joy of past love and in his mind look forward to the restoration of a peace fashioned anew, seeing it, even at the very moment of distress, make a speedy return. 3. And in foreseeing for himself the sweetness of a soon-to-be amity in the future, he will not feel the bitterness of present contention, and he will respond particularly in such a way that, once love has been restored, he cannot either blame himself or be reproached by another. Thus he will fulfill the prophetic words: 'In anger you will remember mercy.'[49]

XXVII.1. "It behooves us, therefore, to contain every movement of wrath and to temper it with discretion as our guide lest, overcome with rage, we be swept up into what is condemned by Solomon: 'The wicked person expends his anger all at once, but the wise person dispenses it gradually.'[50] That is to say, in the heat of his anger the fool is inflamed to revenge himself, but by mature deliberation and moderation the wise man slowly diminishes and gets rid of his.

2. "This is what the Apostle says too: 'Do not avenge your-

selves, beloved, but give place to anger.'[51] That is to say, you should never incline to vengeance under the influence of wrath, but give place to anger. This means that your hearts should not be confined within the narrow limits of impatience and faintheartedness, so that they will be unable to endure a violent and tempestuous disturbance when that occurs. Rather, you should be enlarged in your hearts, receiving the adverse waves of wrath in the broad harbor of love, which 'suffers all things, endures all things.'[52] Thus your mind, enlarged by a breadth of forbearance and patience, will have within itself salutary recesses of counsel wherein the foul vapor of wrath, once having been taken in somehow and having spread, will immediately disappear. 3. Or else it is to be understood thus: We give place to anger as often as we give in with humble and tranquil mind to another's upsetting behavior, acknowledging that we are in some way worthy of mistreatment, and yield to his fierce impatience.

"But those who so twist the meaning of apostolic perfection as to think that people who leave the angry person are giving place to anger seem to me not to be cutting off but rather to be nurturing the root of discord. 4. For unless one's neighbor's wrath is immediately overcome by a humble act of reparation, flight inflames it rather than diminishes it. There is something like this in what Solomon says: 'Do not hasten to be angered in your spirit, because anger reposes in the bosom of fools.'[53] And: 'Do not rush quickly into a quarrel, lest you be sorry in the end.'[54] When he blames hastiness in quarreling and wrath he does not do it in such a way as to approve slowness in their regard. Likewise there are these words to be attended to: 'The fool declares his anger at that very moment, but the one who is clever conceals his shame.'[55] 5. He does not declare that the shameful passion of wrath should be concealed by the wise in such a way that he blames quickness of wrath and does not forbid its slowness. Indeed, he holds that it must be concealed if it should arise due to the pressure of human weakness, so that, being wisely hidden at the moment, it may forever be destroyed. For the nature of anger is such that when it has been checked it weakens and perishes, but when it has been brought out into the open it flares up more and more.

"Our heart, therefore, should be enlarged and expanded,

lest by being confined within the narrow limits of fainthearted-ness it be completely filled with the turbulent emotions of wrath and we be able neither to receive in our narrow hearts, in the words of the prophet, the exceedingly broad command of God[56] nor to say with the prophet: 'I have run the way of your commands, since you enlarged my heart.'[57] 6. For we are taught by the very clear testimony of Scripture that forbearance is wisdom: 'A forbearing man is great in prudence, but a fainthearted man is foolish indeed.'[58] Therefore Scripture says of him who praise-worthily asked the Lord for the gift of wisdom: 'God gave Solomon exceedingly great wisdom and prudence, and a breadth of heart like the countless sands of the sea.'[59]

XXVIII. "It has also been very frequently shown by a considerable amount of experience that those who enter the ties of friendship founded on magic have never been able to preserve their harmony unbroken, either because they have tried to keep it up not out of a desire for perfection nor by reason of the demand of apostolic love but rather out of an earthly love and under the pressure and obligation of a pact, or because that most clever enemy quickly pushes them to break the bonds of friendship, so that he may make them transgressors of their own oath. That opinion of very prudent men is most trustworthy, then, which says that true harmony and an indivisible fellowship cannot exist except among men of faultless behavior, who share the same virtue and chosen orientation."

Blessed Joseph discussed these things about friendship in his spiritual discourse, inspiring us all the more ardently to make enduring the love of our companionship.

Textual References

1. Ps 68:6.
2. Ps 133:1.
3. Acts 4:32.
4. Jn 6:38.
5. Mt 26:39.
6. Jn 13:35.
7. Mt 5:23–24.
8. Eph 4:26.
9. Mt 5:22.
10. 1 Tm 2:4.
11. Cf. Gal 5:20.
12. Prv 10:12 LXX.
13. 2 Cor 11:14.
14. Phil 2:1–3.
15. Rom 12:10.
16. Cf. Acts 9:15.
17. Cf. 2 Cor 13:3.
18. Cf. Gal 2:1–2.
19. 1 Jn 4:16.
20. Rom 5:5.
21. Rom 8:26–27.
22. Gal 6:10.
23. Mt 5:44.
24. Gn 37:4.
25. Jn 13:23.
26. Jn 13:34.
27. Jn 13:1.
28. Sg 2:4 LXX.
29. Jas 4:11.
30. Hb 2:15–16.
31. Jer 9:3–4.
32. Jer 9:2.
33. Ps 55:21.
34. Prv 26:22 LXX.
35. Jer 9:7.
36. Prv 29:5 LXX.
37. Prv 26:27 LXX.
38. Lk 22:48.

39. Ps 55:12–14.
40. Dt 32:17.
41. Mt 5:39.
42. Rom 12:21.
43. 1 Cor 13:5.
44. Rom 15:1.
45. Gal 6:2.
46. Lk 4:23.
47. Ps 77:4.
48. Ps 39:1–2.
49. Hb 3:2 LXX.
50. Prv 29:11 LXX.
51. Rom 12:19.
52. 1 Cor 13:7.
53. Eccl 7:9 LXX.
54. Prv 25:8 LXX.
55. Prv 12:16 LXX.
56. Ps 119:96.
57. Ps 119:32.
58. Prv 14:29 LXX.
59. 1 Kgs 5:9.

16.1 On Thmuis cf. the note at 14.4.2.

Spiritual soldiery: Cf. the note at 1.1.

16.2.2 Basilisks and unicorns and griffins: Other such beasts (basilisks among them) appear in 7.32.4, where they have demonic connotations. On the danger of looking at basilisks cf. Pliny, *Hist. nat.* 29.19.66. Regarding unicorns cf. Ps.-Jerome, *Comm. in Iob* 39 (PL 26.770): "There are beasts of this sort in the desert of the East, but they are never seen by human beings or captured by them." Perhaps the fact that, according to at least one opinion, they were never seen suggested to Cassian that they would be dangerous if ever they were. A confusion of all three animals is noted as a possibility in RAC 12.976.

16.3ff. Ideal friendship, founded on similarity of virtue, is discussed in Aristotle, *Eth. nicomach.* 8.3; Cicero, *De amicitia* 6.20 ("Friendship is nothing else than agreement in all matters, divine and human, along with benevolence and love....Without virtue there can be no friendship at all").

16.6.1 On the irony of having renounced everything only to make much of some insignificant object, which is an idea that recurs in 16.6.4, cf. 1.6.1f. and the relevant note.

16.6.2ff. The term "annoyance" here and in the following pages is a translation of *tristitia,* usually rendered as "sadness." Sadness seems too mild an expression for the emotion suggested here. Cf. also 19.12.2f.

16.6.3 "He who is jealous of love" is the devil.

16.6.4 In the person of the man whom he bore: *Ex persona hominis quem gerebat.* The expression is doctrinally ambiguous. Cf. the note at 7.22.2.

16.6.8 "The one who profits from your death and your brother's" is the devil.

16.14.2 On the variations of love within the context of consanguinity cf. Aristotle, *Eth. nicomach.* 8.12.

That Joseph was a type of Christ was a commonplace in patristic literature. Cf. Melito, *Hom. pasch.* 69; Paulinus of Nola, *Ep.* 38.3; Asterius of Amasea, *Hom.* 19, in Ps. 5 (PG 40.433–444).

16.14.3 That Christ loved John particularly because of his virginity is an idea that is traceable to *Acta Ioannis* 113 (CCSA 1.311–313). Cf. Jerome, *C. Iovinianum* 1.26; Augustine, *Tract. in Ioann.* 124.7.

16.14.4 Sg 2:4 (LXX)—"Set in order love in me"—is similarly understood as applying to a hierarchy of those who are to be loved in Origen, *Comm. in Cant. Cant.* 3 (GCS 33.189–191); idem, *Hom. in Cant. Cant.* 2.8.

16.19 Basil, *Reg. brev. tract.* 134, is also aware of the tactic of not eating out of anger; Basil refuses food to such persons when finally they want to eat. Cf. Weber 86–87.

16.22.2 On the image of the two right cheeks cf. Origen, *Frag. in Matth.* 108 (GCS 41.1.60); Jerome, *Comm. in Matth.* 1 (Mt 5:39–40). The latter observes: "According to the mystical understanding, when our right [cheek] has been struck we are ordered not to offer our left one but our other one—namely, our other right one. For the righteous person does not have a left one." Cf. also 6.10 and the relevant note.

SEVENTEENTH CONFERENCE THE SECOND CONFERENCE OF ABBA JOSEPH: ON MAKING PROMISES

TRANSLATOR'S INTRODUCTION

Abba Joseph's second conference begins with a discussion between Cassian and Germanus as to whether they should keep their promise to return to the monastery in Palestine whence they came or whether they should remain in Egypt. The second alternative, in their view, offered the possibility of increased spiritual growth, but they felt bound by their promise to go back to a place that now seemed to them to be characterized by mediocrity. Cassian suggests that they bring their problem to Abba Joseph, and the conclusion of the conference tells us that they finally decided to stay for another seven years in Egypt. Then they returned to Palestine, only to obtain permission shortly thereafter from their superiors for a second sojourn in Egypt. It is Joseph's understanding of the nature of a promise (which leads into an important discussion on lying as well) that provides them with the basis for their decision.

In a word, the present conference is a justification, in specified circumstances, both for breaking promises and for lying, and it is this teaching that has gained the conference whatever notoriety it may have. But it also serves, whether intentionally or not, as propaganda for the practice of monasticism in Egypt or, perhaps more appositely, for the practice of monasticism according to the Egyptian model. The upshot of the conference, after all, is that a promise to return to a monastery in Palestine can be broken in favor of staying in Egypt and sitting at the feet of the elders there.

Moreover, scattered throughout the conference are remarks at least implicitly demeaning of Palestinian monasticism, including one rather forceful comment by Joseph himself that suggests a certain acquaintance on his part with the mentality of the monks in Palestine: "Their leaders are in the habit of preferring their own will to the brothers' meals, and they obstinately pursue what they have once conceived of in their minds. But our elders..." (17.23). The difference between Palestine and Egypt is, among other things, the difference between rigidity and flexibility, which in this case is another way of describing discretion, as is clear in 17.26: "It is better to go back on our word than to suffer the loss of something that is salutary and good. We do not recall that the reasonable and proven fathers were ever hard and inflexible in decisions of this sort but that, like wax before a fire, they were so softened by reason and by the intervention of more salutary counsel that they unhesitatingly yielded to what was better. But those whom we have seen cling obstinately to their own decisions we have always experienced as unreasonable and bereft of discretion."

The substance of the conference begins after Cassian and Germanus have presented their dilemma to Joseph. He replies by observing that monks should not make hasty promises. But, if such a promise has been made, which leaves the monk (or any other person) facing the undesirable alternatives of either breaking the promise or incurring some spiritual loss, the course that is the less inopportune should be followed. Thus, a promise may be broken or a lie may be told for the sake of a greater spiritual good. In order to buttress his argument, Joseph offers examples from the New Testament that show where breaking a bad promise was beneficial, whereas keeping one was disastrous. Germanus objects with the words of Matthew 5:37: "Let your speech be yes, yes, no, no...."

Joseph's response never really addresses this crucial gospel verse, but he does at this point lay down the principle under which lying and breaking promises may be admitted–namely, that the intention of the doer, rather than the nature of the deed itself, determines the morality of the deed. Scriptural instances intending to demonstrate the validity of this view follow. As far as Cassian's and Germanus's own promise is concerned, it is manifest that their good intention of acquiring perfection endures even though their means of acquiring it have changed. In words that recall the first conference's emphatic subordination of everything to purity of heart or perfection, Joseph avers that any promise may be set aside if, when one does so, the aim of a pure heart is advanced. And if such a policy seems to offer a handle for immoral behavior to weaker persons, then so be it, for those who want to lie or break their promises for immoral reasons will always find excuses for such behavior anyway. Toward the end of the conference Joseph remarks conversely, once again in a fashion reminiscent of the hierarchization of values in the first conference, that only promises that touch on secondary matters can be broken but that nothing that has to do with the principal virtues can be. Fasting, abstinence, reading, and the like are secondary, but love, purity, righteousness, and the like are principal.

Although Joseph's approach to the topic in question is fairly sanguine, he nonetheless indicates a certain appreciation of the ethical ambiguity of lying in the seventeenth chapter in particular. Here he states that a lie is like hellebore, which means that it can be used only in extreme circumstances without causing damage. Indeed, when it is used, the one who resorts to the remedy will be "bitten by the healthful guilt of a humbled conscience" (17.17.3). In the nineteenth chapter he admits that lying is contrary to the liar's spiritual well-being, but that that must sometimes be sacrificed for the sake of others' well-being. Thus lying is, so to say, a permissible sin, a concession to human frailty in the face of the ineluctable complications of human existence.

Germanus often appears leery of Joseph's arguments, but he does concede outright that a lie is admissible to prevent another person from learning that one is fasting, so that one's own virtue may remain hidden.

Joseph concludes by warning against hasty promises, which succeed only in binding a monk to a form of slavery. It is better to pursue secondary practices as the need arises rather than to obligate oneself to them by a promise.

Cassian's teaching on breaking promises and lying, it is obvious from the whole thrust of the seventeenth conference, falls under the heading of discretion. It involves making correct choices, as is typical of discretion–in this case between the real good of spiritual progress and the apparent good of a spiritual perfection that is characterized by a freedom from the moral ambiguity represented by the "necessary" breaking of a promise and the "necessary" lie. The behavior of Joseph, Cassian, and Germanus, moreover, provides an illustration of the practice of discretion: The two friends take a dilemma to Joseph, with the realization that its resolution will possibly involve setting aside the authority of their superiors in Palestine; Joseph in turn has recourse to Scripture, founding his own judgment on that irrefutable authority. Thus any act of true discretion is ultimately grounded on and validated by the divine word, before which all other words give way. But it is ironic to see here how that word, which is truth, is used to validate an occasional untruth!

Cassian's view of lying, unfamiliar as it may seem, was, however, by no means a singular one in Christian antiquity. Numerous other fathers of the Church—notably Clement of Alexandria, Origen, Hilary of Poitiers, and John Chrysostom—also believed that lying was justified in some circumstances, and Augustine was the first to take the contrary position in any systematic way, with his treatises *De mendacio* and *Contra mendacium,* written respectively in 394–395 and 419. (Cf. Boniface Ramsey, "Two Traditions on Lying and Deception in the Ancient Church," in *The Thomist* 49 [1985]: 504–533.) What Cassian has to say on this topic represents at most a slight elaboration on the insights of those who preceded him; like them, he is a proponent of a kind of limited consequentialism. We may wonder whether his broad and humane approach to the subject of lying was at least in part intended as a critique of Augustine's rigorous and unrelenting (and philosophically and theologically far more tenable) position, just as his thirteenth conference is a critique of Augustine's understanding of grace. (Cf. Z. Golínski, "Doctrina Cassiani de mendacio officioso," in *Collectanea Theologica* (Lwów) 17 (1936): 491–503, esp. 497–501.)

The present conference ends with a brief account of Cassian's and Germanus's subsequent history, which included the decision to break their promise, and an apologetic conclusion to the entire second part of the work.

XVII. The Second Conference of Abba Joseph: On Making Promises

Chapters

I. On the vigils that we carried out.
II. Abba Germanus's concern about remembering our promise.
III. What occurred to me in this respect.
IV. Abba Joseph's question and our reply about how our concern arose.
V. Abba Germanus's explanation about why we preferred to remain in Egypt but were also drawn back to Syria.
VI. Abba Joseph's question as to whether we would make more progress in Egypt than in Syria.
VII. The reply, on the difference in the instruction in each province.
VIII. That perfect men should promise nothing at all, and whether they can go back on promises without sinning.
IX. That very often it is more beneficial to alter one's decisions than to stick to them.
X. Our question about our anxiety over the vow that was made in the cenobium in Syria.
XI. The reply, that the intention of the doer rather than the outcome of the affair must be considered.
XII. That good results are of no benefit to those who have started off wickedly, nor do bad actions harm the good.
XIII. Our reply, about why a vow was demanded of us.
XIV. The old man's discourse, to the effect that the sequence of one's activity may be altered without blame, provided that the intention of a good desire is maintained.
XV. A question as to whether it is sinful that our knowledge offers an occasion for lying to those who are weak.
XVI. The reply, that the truth of Scripture should not be altered because of scandal taken by the weak.
XVII. That holy persons have made good use of lying as if it were hellebore.
XVIII. An objection, that only those who lived under the law used lying blamelessly.

XIX. The reply, that permission to lie, which was not granted even in the Old Testament, was uprightly made use of by many.

XX. That very often the apostles themselves considered a lie beneficial and the truth harmful.

XXI. Whether one's hidden abstinence should be divulged to questioners without lying, and whether what has once been refused should be accepted.

XXII. An objection, that one's abstinence should indeed be concealed, but that what has once been refused must not be accepted.

XXIII. The reply, that obstinacy with regard to this decision is unreasonable.

XXIV. How Abba Piamun chose to conceal his abstinence.

XXV. Texts from Scripture concerning promises that have been changed.

XXVI. That holy men are unable to be obstinate and hard.

XXVII. A question as to whether the words "I have sworn and have determined" are contrary to the aforesaid opinion.

XXVIII. The reply: Under what conditions a promise should be kept unchanged, and under what conditions, if necessary, it should be revoked.

XXIX. How to keep concealed what must be concealed.

XXX. Nothing should be promised beyond what concerns the good of the common life.

I. After the previous conference had ended, then, and nocturnal silence had fallen, we were brought by the holy Abba Joseph to a distant cell in order to get some rest. But his words had stirred up a kind of fire in our hearts and, having passed the whole night without sleep, we left the cell, went off about a hundred paces from it, and sat down together in a still more remote spot. And when the opportunity for speaking with one another in a quiet and friendly fashion was offered us by the shades of night, Abba Germanus groaned heavily as we sat there.

II.1. "What are we doing?" he said. "For we see ourselves at a critical point and hindered by our extremely wretched condition. Reason itself and the way of life of holy persons are effectively teaching us what is more beneficial for making progress in the spiritual life, yet the promise that we made to the elders does not permit us to choose what is expedient. 2. For our life and chosen orientation could be more perfectly shaped by the examples of these great men except for the fact that the obligation of what was promised compels us to return at once to the cenobium. If we went back there, no means of returning here would ever again be offered us. But if we stay here and choose to satisfy our desire, what about the fidelity to our vow which we know that we made to our elders, promising to go back as soon as possible after having been permitted to travel around quickly to the holy men and monasteries of this region?"

3. And as we were thus in turmoil over this and were unable to decide what to do for the sake of our salvation, we bore witness by groans alone to the distress of our most difficult situation. We cast blame on the weakness of our audacity and cursed our innate bashfulness, weighed down by the burden of which, even contrary to our own benefit and chosen orientation, we were unable to resist the pleas of those holding us back except by a swift return, in accordance with our promise, and we bemoaned the fact that we labored under the evil of that shame, of which it is said: "There is a shame that brings sin."[1]

III. Then I said: "Let the advice—or rather the authority—of the old man resolve our dilemma. We ought to bring our troubles to him, and whatever he decides should, as if it were a divine and heavenly response, put an end to all our turmoil. We should have no doubts at all, indeed, about what will be given us by the Lord through the mouth of this holy man, by reason both of his worthiness and our faith. For by the Lord's gift believers have often obtained beneficial advice from the unworthy, and unbelievers from holy persons, since it is he who bestows it in keeping with both the worthiness of those who answer and the faith of those who ask."

The holy Abba Germanus heard these words with eagerness, as if I had uttered them not of myself but at the Lord's inspiration, and we waited a short while for the arrival of the old man and for the already approaching hour of the evening synaxis. After we had received him with the customary greeting and the correct number of prayers and psalms had been fulfilled, we sat down once more in our usual fashion on the same mats on which we had composed ourselves for sleep.

IV. Then the venerable Joseph, noticing that we were rather downcast in mind and conjecturing that we were not this way without reason, addressed us in the words of the patriarch Joseph: "Why are your faces sad today?"[2] To which we said: "It is not that we have had a dream and that there is no one to interpret it, as was the case with those imprisoned servants of Pharaoh.[3] But I admit that we have passed a sleepless night, and there is no one to lift the weight of our distress, unless the Lord removes it through your discernment." Then he who recalled the patriarch's virtue in both dignity and name said: "Does not the healing of human thoughts come from the Lord? Let them be brought to the fore, for the divine mercy is able, in accordance with your faith, to provide a remedy for them by way of our advice."

V.1. To this GERMANUS said: "We thought that, after having seen your blessedness, we were going to return to our cenobium not only abundantly filled with spiritual joy but also having made great progress, and that after our return we were going to adhere to what we had learned from you by the closest imitation. For love for our elders as well obliged us to promise this to them, since we thought that we could imitate to some degree the sublimity of your life and teaching in that cenobium. Hence, having judged that complete joy would be bestowed on us from this, we are contrariwise consumed with unbearable sorrow when we reflect on the fact that in following this arrangement we know that we shall be unable to acquire what is beneficial for ourselves.

2. "Therefore, we are now pressed on both sides. For if we wish to fulfill the promise that we made in the presence of all the brothers in the cave in which our Lord shone forth from out of the royal court of the virgin's womb, and to which he himself was a witness, we are incurring the highest loss to our spiritual life. But if we are heedless of our promise and remain in these parts, intending to disregard those vows for the sake of our perfection, we fear the dizzying perils of lying and perjury. 3. We are unable to relieve our distress even by this plan—that, after the terms of our oath have been accomplished by a hasty return, we quickly come back here again. For although even a slight delay is dangerous and harmful to those who are pursuing progress in spiritual matters and virtue, still we would hold to our promise and our fidelity even by a fretful return, except that we realize that we would be inextricably bound not only by the authority of our elders but also by love of them, such that thenceforth no possibility of coming back here would ever be given us."

VI. At this the blessed JOSEPH said, after some period of silence: "Are you certain that greater progress in spiritual matters can be conferred on you in this region?"

VII. GERMANUS: "Even though we ought to be extremely grateful for the teaching of those men who have taught us from our youth to attempt great things and who have, by offering a taste of their own goodness, placed in our heart an extraordinary thirst for perfection, nonetheless, if our judgment is to be trusted, we find no comparison between these institutes and the ones that we received there. This is to say nothing of the inimitable purity of your way of life, which we believe was conferred on you not merely by the strictness of your mind and of your chosen orientation but also by the favorable circumstances of the place. Hence we have no doubt that this splendid teaching, which has been hastily passed on, will not suffice for the imitation of your perfection unless we also have the support of actually staying here and the slackness of our heart has been removed by the discipline of daily instruction over a long period of time."

VIII.1. JOSEPH: "It is indeed good and perfect and altogether in keeping with our profession that we carry out adequately the things that we have determined upon in accordance with some promise. For this reason a monk should promise nothing on the spur of the moment, lest either he be forced to carry out what he has carelessly promised or, having reconsidered with a clearer insight, he appear as a breaker of his own promise. 2. But, inasmuch as our concern now is not so much for the state of your well-being as it is for the healing of your infirmity, what must be submitted to kindly counsel is not what you ought to have done in the first place but rather how you can escape the perils of this dangerous shipwreck.

"When, therefore, no bonds restrain us and no circumstances hinder us, and when advantageous things are placed before us and a choice is offered, we should select what is better. But when some adverse complication stands in the way, and when harmful things are placed before us, we should strive after what is subject to fewer drawbacks. 3. Accordingly, as your own assertion has made clear, when a thoughtless promise has brought you to this pass, so that in either case you will have to suffer serious loss, the choice should incline in the direction where the damage is more tolerable and may more easily be compensated for by the remedy of reparation.

"If, then, you believe that by staying here a greater gain will be conferred on your spirit than what you found in the way of life of that cenobium, and that the terms of your promise cannot be fulfilled without the loss of very significant goods, it is better for you to assume the damage of a lie or of an unfulfilled promise (which, once it is past, will neither be repeated again nor be able to beget other sins of itself), than to fall into the situation wherein a somewhat lukewarm life-style, as you say, will cause you daily and lasting harm. 4. For a thoughtless promise is pardonably and even praiseworthily altered if it is turned to something better, nor should it be believed that it is a betrayal of fidelity rather than a correction of rashness whenever a wicked promise is corrected. It can all be very plainly proven, too, from texts of Scripture, for how many persons the fulfillment of promises has turned out to be a deathly thing, and for how many, on the other hand, breaking them has been useful and beneficial.

IX. "The examples of the holy apostle Peter and of Herod bear very clear witness to each of these situations. For the former, in departing from the words of the promise that he had made with something like the force of an oath when he said: 'You shall never wash my feet,'[4] was promised undying fellowship with Christ, whereas he would certainly have been deprived of the grace of this blessedness had he clung obstinately to his words. But the latter, very cruelly insisting on holding to his thoughtless oath, was the murderer of the Lord's precursor and, in the vain fear of breaking his oath, brought upon himself damnation and the torment of everlasting death.[5]

"In every case, then, the end is the thing to be taken into account, and in accordance with it the direction of our chosen orientation is to be set. If, thanks to having received better advice, we saw that we were on the wrong course, it would be preferable to eliminate the unsuitable situation and to move toward what was better rather than, by sticking persistently to what we have promised, to involve ourselves in more serious sins."

X. GERMANUS: "Inasmuch as this touches on our desire, which came upon us for the sake of a spiritual good, we wished to be edified by your constant companionship. For if we returned to our cenobium we would not only fall away from this sublime orientation but it is certain that, because of the mediocrity of that way of life, we would suffer numerous losses as well. But the gospel command frightens us terribly: 'Let your speech be yes, yes, no, no. Whatever is more than these is from the evil one.'[6] For we believe that the transgression of so great a precept can be compensated for by no righteous act, and that what has once been badly begun cannot come out right in the end."

XI. JOSEPH: "In every affair, as we have said, it is not the outcome of the work but rather the will of the worker that must be looked at, nor should who has done what be the first thing to be inquired into but rather with what intention he did it. Thus we shall find that some people have been condemned for deeds out of which good later arose and, by the same token, that certain others have attained to the highest righteousness by blameworthy actions. And neither has a beneficial result been of any use to the person who, having approached a thing with a bad intention, did not wish to bring about the good that ensued but something different, nor has a blameworthy beginning been harmful to the person who accepted the necessity of a faulty start not out of disdain for God or with the intention of wrongdoing but for the sake of a necessary and holy end.

XII.1. "And, by way of casting light on these matters with examples from Holy Scripture, what could have been of greater value to the whole world than the saving remedy of the Lord's passion? And yet not only was it useless to the traitor at whose connivance it is known to have occurred but it was so prejudicial to him that it is unhesitatingly declared of him: 'It would have been good for him if that man had not been born.'[7] For the fruit of his work was not to be repaid him in accordance with what resulted but in accordance with what he wanted to do and believed that he was going to accomplish. 2. Again, what is more wicked than a deceptive act and a lie perpetrated even against a stranger, to say nothing of one's brother or father? Yet not only did the patriarch Jacob incur no condemnation or blame for these things, but he was even rewarded with a blessed and everlasting inheritance.[8] Quite rightly so, because he sought the blessing intended for the firstborn not out of covetousness for present gain but in the expectation of everlasting holiness, while the other one handed over to death the Redeemer of all not with a view to human salvation but because of the sin of avarice.

3. "Therefore, the fruit of each one's activity was ascribed to him in accordance with the aim of his mind and the intention of his will, by which neither the one had determined to bring about a fraud nor the other salvation. For there is justly repaid to each one by way of recompense what he was principally thinking of in his mind, not what resulted from that, whether for good or for ill, contrary to the will of the doer. Hence the most righteous Judge considered excusable and even praiseworthy the perpetrator of that lie, because without it he would have been unable to acquire the blessing of the firstborn. Nor should what arose out of a

desire for a blessing be referred to as a sin. 4. Otherwise the aforesaid patriarch would have been not only wicked with regard to his brother but also deceptive and sacrilegious with regard to his father if, having had another way of acquiring the grace of that blessing, he had preferred to seek this one, to the ruin and harm of his brother. You see, then, that God does not search into the outcome of the work but into the aim of the mind.

"Now that these preliminaries have been dealt with, so that we may return to the question that was posed (which is why we have gone through all these things), I want you to tell me first why you tied yourselves down by this promise."

XIII. GERMANUS: "As we have said, the first reason is that we feared to sadden our elders and to resist their precepts. The second is that, if we had received anything perfect or excellent from you, whether by seeing or hearing, we believed in a very thoughtless way that we would have been able to pursue it when we had returned to the cenobium."

XIV.1. JOSEPH: "As we said before, the aim of the mind either rewards or condemns a person, according to the words: 'Their thoughts within them either accusing or defending them, on the day when God will judge the secrets of men.'[9] And also these: 'I am coming to gather their works and thoughts together with all nations and tongues.'[10] Therefore, as I see it, you bound yourselves by the fetters of this oath out of a desire for perfection, inasmuch as you believed that in this way it could be seized, whereas now, after a fuller reflection, you realize that its heights cannot thus be scaled. 2. Whatever differs from that arrangement, then, does not prejudice what may seem to have happened, as long as no change occurs in the principal intention. For changing a tool is not the same as abandoning a project, nor does choosing a shorter and more direct path prove that a traveler is lazy. Likewise, then, the correction of a careless decision must not be judged as if it were a transgression of a spiritual vow. For whatever is done for the sake of the love of God or the love of devotion, which 'holds the promise of the life that now is and of the one that is to come,'[11] is not only not blameless but also most praiseworthy, even though it seems to have had a rough and bad start. 3. Consequently the setting aside of a thoughtless promise is harmless if only in every case the scopos—that is, the intended religious goal—is held to. For we do everything in order that we might be able to present a pure heart to God. If the achievement of this is considered easier in this place, the alteration of the promise that was wrested from you will not hurt you as long as the perfection of purity, which is overriding and for which your promise was made, is the more quickly obtained in accordance with the Lord's will."

XV. GERMANUS: "As far as the force of the words (which were reasonably and carefully weighed) is concerned, we could have dispelled the scruple about our promise without any difficulty whatsoever, except that we are terribly frightened by the fact that by these examples an occasion for lying seems to be offered to weaker persons if they should ever find out that a trust could legitimately be broken, especially since this very thing is forbidden in such menacing language by the prophet, when he says: 'You will destroy all those who speak a lie.'[12] And: 'The mouth that lies will slay the soul.'"[13]

XVI.1. JOSEPH: "There can be no lack of occasions and causes of destruction for those who are going to be destroyed and who, indeed, desire to perish. For the texts whereby the wickedness of heretics is encouraged, the infidelity of the Jews is hardened, and proud Gentile wisdom is offended must not be set aside and utterly eradicated from the body of Scripture. Rather, to be sure, they must be devoutly believed, firmly maintained, and preached according to the rule of truth.

2. "Therefore we must not, because of another's infidelity, reject the οικονομιαι—that is, the dispensations—of the prophets and holy persons which Scripture contains. Otherwise, while believing that we must descend to their weakness, we shall be stained by the crime not only of lying but even of sacrilege. But, as we have said, we should acknowledge those things as historically true and explain how they were devoutly accomplished. 3. For those, however, who are of a wicked disposition, the possibility of lying will not hereby be impeded, even if we should make an effort either to deny completely or to weaken with allegorical interpretations the truth of the things that we are going to say or that we have said. For how will the authority of these texts harm those for whom the corruption of the will alone is enough for sinning?

XVII.1. "And so a lie is to be thought of and used as if it were hellebore. If it is taken when a deadly disease is imminent it has a healthful effect, but taken when there is no urgent need it is the cause of immediate death. For we read that even men who were holy and most approved by God made such good use of lying that they not only did not commit sin thereby but even acquired the highest righteousness. If deceit were capable of conferring glory on them, would truth, on the other hand, have brought them anything but condemnation?

"This was the case with Rahab. Scripture not only recalls nothing virtuous about her but even speaks of her immorality. Yet for her lie alone, whereby she chose to conceal the spies rather than betray them, she deserved to share an eternal blessing with the people of God.[14] 2. If she had chosen to speak the truth or to be concerned for the safety of her people, there is no doubt that she and her whole household would not have escaped the approaching destruction and that she would not have deserved to be included among those responsible for the Lord's birth, to be numbered on the roll of the patriarchs,[15] and, through her offspring, to beget the Savior of all. Then there is Delilah, who was concerned for the well-being of her people and who betrayed the truth that she had spied out. She obtained everlasting perdition in exchange for this, and left to everyone nothing but the memory of her sin.[16]

3. "When some grave danger is connected with speaking the truth, therefore, the refuge of lying must be resorted to, yet in such a way that we are bitten by the healthful guilt of a humbled conscience. But when no circumstance of great urgency presses, every precaution must be taken to avoid lying as if it were something deadly. It is like the potion of hellebore that we were speaking of, which is healthful indeed if it is only taken when an unavoidable and deadly sickness is imminent. But if it is taken when the body is enjoying complete and undisturbed health, its destructive force immediately seeks out and possesses the vitals.

4. "This is very clearly evident with respect to Rahab of Jericho and the patriarch Jacob. Of the two of them, she would have been unable to escape death and he to attain the blessing of the firstborn otherwise than by this remedy. For God is not the overseer and judge of our words and deeds alone but also the one

who looks into our intention and aim. 5. If he sees that something has been done or promised by someone for the sake of eternal salvation or with a view to divine contemplation, even if it appears to human beings to be hard and wicked, he nonetheless perceives the inner devotion of the heart and judges not the sound of the words but the intent of the will, because it is the end of the work and the disposition of the doer that must be considered. In accordance with this, as has already been said, one person can be justified even when lying, whereas another can commit a sin deserving everlasting death by telling the truth.

"With this end in mind the patriarch Jacob himself was not afraid to counterfeit his brother's hairy body by wrapping himself up in skins, praiseworthily going along with the lie that his mother inspired. 6. For he saw that in this way greater benefits would be conferred on him—those of a blessing and of righteousness—than by holding to candor. He had no doubt that the stain of this lie would be instantly washed away by the outpouring of his father's blessing, that it would be quickly removed like a kind of little cloud by the breath of the Holy Spirit, and that more abundant and worthy rewards would be conferred on him by this dissimulation than by the unvarnished truth."

XVIII.1. GERMANUS: "No wonder that these dispensations were uprightly made use of in the Old Testament and that holy men sometimes lied in praiseworthy or at least in pardonable fashion, since we see that far greater things were permitted them because it was a time of beginnings. For what is there to wonder at that when the blessed David was fleeing Saul and Ahimelech the priest asked him: 'Why are you alone, and no one is with you?'[17] he replied and said: 'The king gave me a commission and said: Let no one know the reason why you were sent, for I have also appointed my servants to such and such a place'?[18] And again: 'Do you have a spear or a sword at hand? For I did not bring my sword and my weapons with me because the king's business was urgent'?[19] Or what happened when he was brought to Achish, the king of Gath, and made believe that he was insane and raging, and 'changed his countenance before them, and fell down between their hands, and dashed himself against the door of the gate, and his spittle ran down his beard'?[20] For, after all, they lawfully enjoyed flocks of wives and concubines, and no sin was imputed to them on this account. Besides that, they also frequently spilled their enemies' blood with their own hands, and this was held not only to be irreprehensible but even praiseworthy.

2. "We see that, in the light of the Gospel, these things have been utterly forbidden, such that none of them can be committed without very serious sin and sacrilege. Likewise we believe that no lie, in however pious a form, can be made use of by anyone in a pardonable way, to say nothing of praiseworthily, according to the words of the Lord: 'Let your speech be yes, yes, no, no. Whatever is more than these is from the evil one.' The Apostle also agrees with this: 'Do not lie to one another.'"[21]

XIX.1. JOSEPH: "Now that the end of the ages is at hand and the multiplication of the human race has been completed, that ancient freedom with regard to many wives and concubines had rightly to be cut off as quite unnecessary, thanks to gospel perfection. For up until the coming of Christ it was proper for the blessing of those primordial words to be in force, according to which it was said: 'Increase and multiply and fill the earth.'[22] 2. Therefore it was most just that from the stock of human fruitfulness, which flourished advantageously in the Synagogue in accordance with the dispensation of the age, blossoms of angelic virginity should spring forth and the aromatic fruits of chastity should grow sweetly in the Church.

"The whole text of the Old Testament shows clearly, however, that lies were condemned even then, when it says: 'You will destroy all those who speak a lie.' And again: 'The bread of lying is sweet to a person, but afterward his mouth will be filled with gravel.'[23] And the Lawgiver himself says: 'You shall avoid a lie.'[24]

3. "But we have said that it was made use of in upright fashion only when some need or saving dispensation was linked to it, for which reason it was not to be condemned. Such is what you recalled in connection with King David, when he was fleeing the unjust persecution of Saul and used lying words to Ahimelech the priest, not with the intention of gain or with the desire to harm anyone but only in order to save himself from that most wicked persecution of his. For, indeed, he did not wish to stain his hands with the blood of the hostile king, who had so often been deliv-

ered over to him. As he said: 'May the Lord be gracious to me, lest I do this thing to my lord, the anointed of the Lord, and lay my hand on him, for he is the Lord's anointed.'[25]

4. "Therefore, we ourselves cannot forgo these dispensations, which we read that holy men in the Old Testament practiced for the sake of the will of God or for the prefiguring of spiritual mysteries or for the salvation of some people, when necessity compels it, since we see that even the apostles themselves did not draw back from them when the consideration of some benefit demanded it. Leaving these latter aside for a short while, and after having first discussed what we still want to bring up from the Old Testament, we shall introduce them afterward in more appropriate fashion, so that it may the more easily be demonstrated that the righteous and holy men of both the New and the Old Testaments were in complete agreement with one another with respect to these devices.

5. "For what shall we say about Hushai's pious deception of Absalom for the sake of King David's safety which, although formulated with good will by the deceiver and cheater and opposed to the well-being of the questioner, is approved by the text of divine Scripture that says: 'By the will of the Lord the useful advice of Ahitophel was undone, so that the Lord might bring evil upon Absalom'?[26] For what was accomplished with a right intention and pious judgment for a good purpose and conceived for the safety and religious victory of a man whose piety was pleasing to God, all by way of deception, could not be blamed.

6. "And what shall we say about the deed of the woman who received those who had been sent to King David by the aforementioned Hushai and who hid them in a well, spreading a cover over the mouth of it and making believe that she was drying barley? 'They went on,' she said, 'after having drunk a little water,'[27] and by this trick she saved them from the hands of their pursuers. Tell me, then, I ask you, what you would have done if a similar situation had arisen for you who now live under the Gospel. Would you have chosen to conceal them by a similar lie, saying in the same way: 'They went on after having drunk a little water,' thus fulfilling what is commanded: 'Spare not to save those who are being led to death and to redeem those who are being slain'?[28] Or by speaking

the truth would you have given over those who were hidden to those who were going to kill them? 7. What, then, of the Apostle's words? 'Let no one seek what is his own but rather what is another's.'[29] And: 'Love does not seek what is its own but rather what belongs to others.'[30] And what he says about himself: 'I do not seek what is beneficial to me but what is beneficial to the many, so that they may be saved.'[31] For if we seek what is ours and wish to hold on obstinately to what is beneficial to us, we shall have to speak the truth even in difficulties of this sort, and we shall become guilty of another's death. But if we fulfill the apostolic command by placing what is helpful to others ahead of our own well-being, without a doubt the necessity of lying will be imposed upon us. 8. And therefore we shall be able neither to possess the bowels of love in their entirety nor to seek, according to the apostolic teaching, what belongs to others unless we choose to relax somewhat the things that pertain to our own strictness and perfection and to accommodate ourselves with a willing disposition to what is beneficial for others. Thus, along with the Apostle, we shall be weak to the weak, in order to be able to gain the weak.[32]

XX.1. "Instructed by these examples, the blessed apostle James as well and all the chief rulers of the primitive Church urged the apostle Paul to stoop to simulation for the sake of the infirmity of the weak. They compelled him to be purified in accordance with the observance of the law, to shave his head and to offer vows, considering the short-term damage that arose from this hypocrisy to be nothing, and looking forward instead to the gains that would be made from his long career of preaching. 2. For the gain conferred on the apostle Paul by this strictness of his would not have been as great as the loss that all the pagans would have incurred by his sudden death. This is what certainly would have happened to the whole Church then if this beneficial and salutary hypocrisy had not saved him for the preaching of the Gospel. For out of necessity one may pardonably acquiesce in the evil of a lie when, as we have said, the damage done by speaking the truth and the benefit conferred on us from the truth could not offset the harm that would be caused.

3. "The same blessed Apostle testifies in other words that he held to this point of view everywhere and always when he says: 'To

the Jews I became as a Jew, in order to gain the Jews. To those who were under the law I was as one under the law, although I myself was not under the law, in order to gain those who were under the law. To those who were without the law I was as one without the law, although I was not without the law of God but under the law of Christ, in order to gain those who were without the law. To the weak I became weak, in order to gain the weak. I became all things to all people, in order to save all people.'[33] What is he demonstrating by this if not that he always accommodated himself and relaxed something of his rigorous perfection in accordance with the degree of weakness of those who were being instructed, and that he did not hold on to what his strictness seemed to demand but, instead, preferred what the well-being of the weak required?

4. "And–in order to examine these same matters more carefully and to go over the signs of apostolic virtue one by one–suppose someone should ask how the blessed Apostle may be shown to have adapted his person to all people in all respects, and when he became as a Jew to the Jews. At the very moment when, while maintaining in his inmost being the point of view that he had declared to the Galatians, saying: 'Behold, I, Paul, tell you that, if you are circumcised, Christ will profit you nothing,'[34] he nonetheless took on the aspect of Jewish superstition, so to speak, by circumcising Timothy.[35]

5. "Again, when did he become to those who were under the law as one who was under the law? Namely, when James and all the elders of the Church were afraid lest the multitude of Jewish believers–indeed, of Judaizing Christians–that had received the faith of Christ in such a way as still to be held by the ritual of legal ceremonies might attack him. They aided him in his danger with this advice and counsel, and they said: 'You see, brother, how many thousands of Jews there are who have believed, and all of these are zealous for the law. But they have heard of you that you are teaching the Jews who are among the Gentiles to depart from Moses, saying that they ought not to circumcise their sons.'[36] And further on: 'Do what we tell you, therefore. There are four men among us who have a vow. Take them and sanctify yourself with them and pay for them to shave their heads, and everyone will know that

what they have heard about you is false, and that you yourself walk in keeping with the law.'[37] 6. Thus, for the salvation of these who were under the law he trampled for a while on his strict attitude, in keeping with which he had said: 'Through the law I am dead to the law, so that I may live to God,'[38] and he was obliged to shave his head, to be purified in accordance with the law, and, following the Mosaic ritual, to offer his vows in the Temple.

"Do you also want to know when he became as one without the law for the salvation of those who were completely ignorant of God's law? Read how he began his preaching when he was in the city of Athens, where the wickedness of the Gentiles flourished: 'As I was passing by,' he said, 'I saw your idols and an altar on which was written: To an unknown god.'[39] 7. And when he had spoken of their superstition as if he were himself also without the law, he used that profane inscription as an opportunity to introduce faith in Christ, and he said: 'What you are worshiping unawares, then, I announce to you.'[40] After a few words, as if he were utterly ignorant of the divine law, he chose to bring forth a verse from a Gentile poet rather than a phrase from Moses or Christ, and he said: 'Just as some of your own poets have said: We are also his offspring.'[41] And when he had thus approached them with their own texts, which they were unable to refute, thus confirming what was true from what was false, he went on and said: 'Since we are the offspring of God, then, we should not consider that the Divinity is like gold or silver or stone, a statue produced by the skill and reflection of a human being.'[42]

8. "He became weak to the weak, though, when, by way of concession and not by way of command, he permitted those who could not contain themselves to come together again,[43] and when he fed the Corinthians with milk rather than solid food[44] and said that he was among them in weakness, fear, and great trembling.[45]

"But he became all things to all people, in order to save all people, when he said: 'The one who eats should not despise the one who does not eat, and the one who does not eat should not judge the one who does eat.'[46] And: 'The one who gives his virgin in marriage does well, and the one who does not give her does better.'[47] And elsewhere he says: 'Who is weak and I am not weak? Who is offended and I do not burn?'[48] 9. And in this way he fulfilled what he had commanded the Corinthians when he said: 'Be without offense to the Jews and the Greeks and to the Church of Christ, just as I myself please everyone in all respects, not seeking what is beneficial to me but what is beneficial to the many, so that they may be saved.'[49] For it certainly would have been beneficial not to circumcise Timothy, not to shave his head, not to undergo Jewish purification, not to walk barefoot, not to offer the law's vows. But he did all these things because he sought not what was beneficial to himself but to the many. Although this was done with a view to God, nonetheless deception was involved. 10. For he who through the law of Christ had died to the law in order to live to God, and who had without complaint treated as loss the righteousness of the law in which he had lived, considering it like dung, in order to gain Christ,[50] could not offer the things of the law with the correct disposition of heart. Nor is it right to believe that he fell into what he himself had condemned when he said: 'If I again rebuild what I have destroyed, I make myself a transgressor.'[51]

"To such an extent is the disposition of the doer given more weight than the thing which is done that, contrariwise, the truth is found to have harmed some people and a lie to have helped them. 11. For one time King Saul was complaining in the presence of his retainers about David's flight, saying: 'Will the son of Jesse give all of you fields and vineyards, and make all of you tribunes and centurions, since you have all conspired against me, and there is no one to inform me?'[52] What but the truth did Doeg the Edomite tell him when he said: 'I saw the son of Jesse in Nob, with Ahimelech the son of Ahitub the priest. He consulted the Lord on his behalf, and he gave him provisions, and he gave him the sword of Goliath the Philistine as well'?[53] For this truth he deserved to be uprooted from the land of the living, and of him it is said by the prophet: 'Therefore God shall destroy you forever, pluck you up and remove you from your tent and uproot you from the land of the living.'[54] 12. For indicating the truth, then, he was everlastingly uprooted from the land in which Rahab the harlot was planted, along with her family, because of her lie. In the same way we remember that Samson in most ruinous fashion delivered over to his wicked wife a truth that had long been concealed by a lie. Therefore the truth that he had very heedlessly disclosed to her brought about his own undoing, because he failed to keep that prophetic command: 'Keep the doors of your mouth from her who sleeps on your breast.'[55]

XXI.1. "And now let us offer some examples as well from our unavoidable and almost daily needs, which we are never able to guard against, however careful we may be, in such a way that we are not obliged to cater to them whether we want to or not. What, I ask, should be done when we have decided to postpone our meal and a brother who arrives at nightfall inquires whether we have eaten? Should our fasting be concealed and our virtuous frugality be covered over, or should it be disclosed by speaking the truth? 2. Suppose that we hide it in order to fulfill the Lord's command, which says: 'When you are fasting, do not let yourself be seen by men but by your Father, who is hidden.'[56] And again: 'Your left hand should not know what your right hand is doing.'[57] Then we would certainly be lying. But if we publicize our virtuous abstinence, the gospel words would justifiably daunt us: 'Amen, I say to you, they have received their reward.'[58]

3. "What if someone has decisively declined a drink that was offered him by a brother, utterly refusing to take what he who rejoices at his coming humbly entreats him to receive? Is it right that he should submit, even with an effort, to the brother who has fallen on his knees and is prostrate on the ground, and who believes that he can act in a loving way only by performing this service, or should he persevere in the obstinacy of his word and his intention?"

XXII. GERMANUS: "In the former example, to be sure, there is no doubt that, as we believe, it is better for our abstinence to be hidden than to be disclosed to inquirers, and we concede as well that a lie for reasons of this sort is unavoidable. In the second case, however, no necessity of lying presses upon us—first, because we are able to decline what is offered by the ministry of our brothers in such a way as not to involve ourselves in the restrictions of a promise; and then because, once we have declined, we can keep our resolution fixed."

XXIII.1. JOSEPH: "There is no doubt that these promises were made in those monasteries in which, as you say, the first steps of your renunciation were taken. Their leaders are in the habit of preferring their own will to their brothers' meals, and they obstinately pursue what they have once conceived of in their minds. But our elders, whose faith has been borne witness to by the signs of apostolic virtues and who do everything in accordance with the judgment and discretion of the Spirit rather than by following their own rigidly obstinate mind, have determined that those who adapt themselves to others' weaknesses gain much richer fruits than those who hold fast to their own promises, and they have declared that it is more sublimely virtuous to conceal one's abstinence by this necessary and humble lie, as has been said, than to reveal it by proudly indicating the truth.

XXIV.1. "Finally there is Abba Piamun, who, after twenty-five years, unhesitatingly took some grapes and wine that were offered him by a certain brother and, against his own custom, preferred to taste at once what had been brought to him rather than to publicize the virtue of his abstinence, which was not known to anyone. For if we also wish to consider what we recall our elders used to do unhesitatingly, making believe that their miraculous powers and their own deeds, which had to be mentioned in conferences for the sake of the younger men, were other people's doing–what other judgment can we make of these things than that they were downright lies? 2. And would that we too had something worthy that could be set before the young men to stimulate their faith! Certainly we should not fear to follow the deceptions of men of that sort. For it is more justifiable to lie by this kind of deception than either to conceal by an inappropriate silence things that could edify our listeners or to brag with harmful vanity by speaking truthfully about ourselves. 3. The teacher of the Gentiles has also instructed us clearly in this regard by his own teaching, when he preferred to speak of the greatness of his revelations as if he were someone else, saying: 'I know a man in Christ, whether in the body or out of the body I do not know, God knows, who was caught up to the third heaven. And I know that this man was caught up in paradise and heard unspeakable words, which it is not permitted for a man to utter.'[59]

XXV.1. "It is impossible for us to run through everything in a short space. For who could count all the almost innumerable patriarchs and holy persons who have sought protection, so to speak, in lying—some in order to save their lives, some out of desire for a blessing, some out of mercy, some in order to conceal a mystery, some out of zeal for God, and some in probing the truth? Just as all of these cannot be numbered, so neither should they all be completely omitted.

2. "For piety compelled the blessed Joseph to fasten a false crime on his brothers, even with an oath by the king's life, when he said: 'You are spies. You have come to look at the weaker parts of the land.'[60] And further on he said: 'Send one of you, and bring your brother here. But you shall be kept here while your words become clear, whether what you say is true or not. But if not, by Pharaoh's life, you are spies.'[61] If he had not frightened them with this merciful lie he would have been unable to see his father and his brother again or to feed them when they were so endangered by want or, finally, to purify his brothers' conscience of the guilt of having sold him. 3. It was not so blameworthy, then, for him to have struck fear in his brothers by way of a lie as it was holy and praiseworthy to have driven his enemies and sellers to a beneficial repentance by way of a feigned danger. When they were suffering under the weight of that very serious charge, they were crushed by an awareness not of what was falsely brought up but of their previous crime, and they said to one another: 'We are rightly suffering these things, because we sinned against our brother, because we despised the tribulation of his soul when he called out to us and we did not listen to him. Therefore all this tribulation has come upon us.'[62] This confession, as we believe, expiated not only the sin against their brother, which they committed with wicked cruelty, but also that against God, thanks to their most salutary humility.

4. "What about Solomon, who received the gift of wisdom from God and who made his first judgment with the help of a lie? For, in order to elicit the truth that was hidden by a woman's lie, he himself also made use of a very cleverly thought-out lie when he said: 'Bring me a sword, and cut the living infant in two pieces, and give half to one and half to the other.'[63] When this semblance of cruelty profoundly shook the real mother but was praised by the one who was not the mother, he at once, as a result of this most astute discovery of the truth, handed down the sentence that everyone believes was inspired by God: 'Give the living

infant to this woman,' he said, 'and do not let it be slain. This is its mother.'[64]

5. "Further, we are taught at considerable length by other texts of Scripture, too, that we neither should nor can fulfill everything that we decide upon whether with tranquil or upset mind. In them we frequently read that holy men or angels or even Almighty God himself altered the things that they had promised. For blessed David determined with the promise of an oath and said: 'May God do this and add more to the enemies of David if, of all that belongs to Nabal, I leave one male until morning.'[65] 6. But when his wife Abigail interceded and entreated on his behalf, he immediately ceased his threats, softened his words, and preferred to be considered a transgressor of his own intention than to be true to his oath by cruelly carrying it out, and he said: 'As the Lord lives, unless you had come quickly to meet me, there would not have been left to Nabal one male until the morning light.'[66] As we do not at all consider the promptness of his rash vow, which proceeded from an upset and disturbed mind, as something to be imitated, so likewise we judge that the cessation and correction of the thing that was decided on is to be pursued.

7. "In writing to the Corinthians, the vessel of election[67] promised unconditionally that he would return, saying: 'I will come to you when I pass through Macedonia, for I will pass through Macedonia. But I will stay with you or even pass the winter with you, so that you may take me wherever I shall be going. For I do not want to see you now in passing, since I hope to spend some time with you.'[68] He recalls this matter even in his second letter, as follows: 'In this confidence I wanted to come to you first, so that you might have a second favor, and by you to go over to Macedonia, and to return to you from Macedonia and to be taken by you to Judea.'[69] But he thought better about it and openly confesses that he will not carry out what he had promised. 'When I intended this,' he says, 'was I careless? Or do I think what I think according to the flesh, so that there is a yes, yes and a no, no with me?'[70] 8. Finally, he declares with an oath that he preferred to break his word than to submit his disciples to an annoying burden by his coming: 'I invoke God as a witness against my soul that I did

not go as far as Corinth in order to spare you. For I decided this with myself, that I would not come to you in sorrow.'[71]

"Although the angels had refused to enter Lot's house at Sodom and had said to him: 'We will not enter, but we will remain in the street,'[72] they were at once obliged to alter their stated word because of his prayers, as Scripture adds: 'And Lot compelled them, and they turned in to him.'[73] 9. Certainly, if they had known that they were going to turn in to him, they refused their host's request with a feigned excuse. But if their excuse was real, they are clearly shown to have altered their word. Indeed, we believe that the Holy Spirit inserted these things in the sacred volumes for no other reason than that we might be instructed by these examples not to hold obstinately to our promises but to subject them to our will and to keep our judgment free from every constraint of law, such that it might be ready to go wherever good counsel directs it and not postpone or refuse to pass on without delay to what a salutary discernment may find to be more beneficial.

10. "Now let us rise to still more sublime examples. Speaking in the person of God, the prophet Isaiah addressed King Hezekiah as he was lying in bed and laboring under a grave illness: 'The Lord says this: Set your house in order, because you shall die, and you shall not live. And Hezekiah,' it says, 'turned his face to the wall and prayed to the Lord and said: I beseech you, Lord, remember, I pray, how I walked before you in truth and with a perfect heart, and did what was good in your sight. And Hezekiah wept with much weeping.'[74] After this it was said to him again: 'Turn back and speak to Hezekiah, king of Judah, and say: The Lord, the God of David your father, says this: I have heard your prayer, I have seen your tears, and behold, I will add fifteen years to your days, and I will free you from the hand of the king of the Assyrians, and I will defend this city for my own sake and for the sake of my servant David.'[75] 11. What is clearer than this text, according to which the Lord, with a view to mercy and kindness, chose to break his own word and to extend the life of the one praying by fifteen years beyond the appointed time of his death rather than show himself inexorable because of an inflexible decree?

"The divine judgment spoke in similar fashion to the Ninevites as well: 'Yet three days and Nineveh shall be overthrown.'[76] And at once, due to their repentance and fasting, the sentence that was so threatening and abrupt was softened and, through love, made merciful. But if anyone asserts that the Lord was already aware, as it were, of their conversion and threatened them with the overthrow of their city in order to incite them to a salutary repentance, the consequence would be that those who are set over their brothers may, if need be and without any of the blame attached to a lie, threaten those who stand in want of correction with something more stringent than they are going to carry out. 12. But he may say that God revoked that severe sentence of his out of consideration for their repentance, in keeping with what is said through Ezekiel: 'If I say to the wicked: You shall surely die, and he repents of his sin, and does judgment and righteousness, he shall surely live, he shall not die.'[77] If that is so, then we are taught that we must not hold obstinately to our promises but with gentle mercy must soften threats that are made out of some necessity.

13. "So that the Lord may not be believed to have shown this only to the Ninevites in particular, he continually declares by Jeremiah that he is going to act in the same way toward everyone in general, and he promises that, because of our deserts, he will unhesitatingly alter his word if need be. As he says: 'I will suddenly speak against a nation and against a kingdom, to root up and to tear down and to destroy it. If that nation repents of the evil which I have spoken against it, I also will repent of the evil which I thought to do to it. And I will suddenly speak of a nation and a kingdom, to build it up and to plant it. If it does evil in my sight, so as not to hear my voice, I will repent of the good which I spoke of doing for it.'[78] To Ezekiel as well: 'Do not hold back a word, if perchance they hear and everyone be turned from his evil way. And I will repent of the evil which I thought to do to them because of the wickedness of their deeds.'[79]

14. "These texts declare that we should not cling stubbornly to our promises, but that they should be tempered by reason and judgment, that what is better should always be chosen and preferred and that we should pass over without any hesitation to whatever is proven to be more beneficial. This invaluable judgment also teaches us above all that, although each person's end

may be known to him before he was born, he so disposes everything with order and reason and, so to say, human feelings, that he determines all things not by his power or in accordance with his ineffable foreknowledge but, based upon the deeds of human beings at the time, either rejects them or draws them or daily pours out grace upon them or turns them away.

15. "The choosing of Saul also demonstrates that this is so. Although, indeed, the foreknowledge of God could not be ignorant of his miserable end, he chose him from among many thousands of Israelites and anointed him king.[80] In doing this he rewarded him for his deserving life at the time and did not take into consideration the sin of his future transgression. And so, after he became reprobate, God as it were repented of his choice and complained of him with, so to speak, human words and feelings, saying: 'I repent that I set up Saul as king, because he has forsaken me and not carried out my words.'[81] And again: 'Samuel grieved over Saul, because the Lord repented that he had set up Saul as king over Israel.'[82]

16. "There is also this, which the Lord carried out afterward, when he declared by Ezekiel the prophet how he would act with everyone according to his daily judgment: 'Even if I say,' he says, 'to the righteous that he shall surely live, and he acts wickedly, trusting in his righteousness, all of his righteousness shall be forgotten, and he shall die in the very wickedness that he worked. But if I say to the wicked: You shall surely die, and he repents of his sin, and does judgment and righteousness, and if that wicked man restores the pledge, returns what he has robbed, walks in the commands of life, and does not do anything unjust, he shall surely live, he shall not die. None of the sins that he committed shall be imputed to him.'[83]

17. "And when, because of their sudden transgression, the Lord had turned away the gaze of his mercy from the people that he had selected from all the nations, the Lawgiver interceded for them and cried out: 'I beseech you, O Lord. This people has committed a great sin, they have made for themselves gods of gold. And now, if you forgive their sin, forgive it. Otherwise, blot me out from your book, which you have written. The Lord said to him: If anyone has sinned in my sight, I will blot him out from my book.'[84]

"Likewise David, when he was complaining in prophetic spirit about Judah and about the persecutors of Christ, said: 'Let them be blotted out of the book of the living.'[85] And because they did not deserve to attain to a salutary repentance for such a great criminal offense, he adds: 'And let them not be enrolled with the righteous.'[86]

18. "Finally, in the case of Judas himself, the power of the prophetic curse was clearly fulfilled. For, once he had committed the crime of betrayal, 'he killed himself by hanging,'[87] lest after his name was blotted out he turn again to repentance and deserve to be enrolled with the righteous in heaven. For there is no doubt that even the name of Judas was written in the book of the living at the time when he was chosen by Christ and appointed to the rank of an apostle, and that he heard along with the others: 'Do not rejoice because the demons are subject to you, but rejoice because your names are written in heaven.'[88] 19. But since he was corrupted by the plague of avarice and was cast down from a heavenly enrollment to earthly things, it is appropriately said of him and of others like him by the prophet: 'Lord, let all those who abandon you be confounded. Let those who depart from you be written in the earth, because they have abandoned the Lord, the vein of living waters.'[89] And elsewhere: 'They shall not be in the council of my people, nor enrolled in the book of the house of Israel, and they shall not enter into the land of Israel.'[90]

XXVI. "Nor should we keep silent about the beneficial nature of that precept. For even if we have bound ourselves by a vow at the instigation of anger or some other passion, which indeed must never be the case with a monk, nonetheless the alternatives should be weighed with a most judicious mind, and the thing that we have decided upon should be compared with the thing that we are moved to go over to, and after more mature reflection we should unhesitatingly go over to what has been indicated as being preferable. For it is better to go back on our word than to suffer the loss of something that is salutary and good. We do not recall that the reasonable and proven fathers were ever hard and inflexible in decisions of this sort but that, like wax before a fire, they were softened by reason and by the intervention of more salutary counsel and unhesitatingly yielded to what was better. But those whom we have seen cling obstinately to their own promises we have always experienced as unreasonable and bereft of discretion."

XXVII. GERMANUS: "In view of what has been laid out, which has been clearly and lengthily discussed, a monk should not make a promise, lest he be found either a transgressor or obstinate. But how shall we view the word of the psalmist: 'I have sworn and have determined to keep the judgments of your righteousness'?[91] What does it mean to swear and to determine other than to hold unyieldingly to what has been promised?"

XXVIII.1. JOSEPH: "We are not laying down these things with respect to the principal commands without which we can never be saved, but with respect to what we are able to let go or to keep hold of without endangering our situation—for example, unbroken and strict fasting, perpetual abstinence from wine or oil, absolute confinement in one's cell, and unceasing reading or meditation. These can be practiced at will without harming our profession and our chosen orientation, and they can be blamelessly omitted if necessary.

2. "But a very firm promise is to be made concerning those principal commands, and for their sake even death, if need be, must not be avoided. With regard to them it must be said in unalterable fashion: 'I have sworn and have determined.' This we must do for the maintaining of love, for which all things are to be disdained, lest the good of tranquillity and its perfection be blemished. We must likewise swear for the sake of the purity of chastity, and it behooves us to do the same for the sake of faith, sobriety, and righteousness, all of which are to be held to with an unchangeable perseverance, and to withdraw from which even slightly is worthy of condemnation.

3. "Concerning those bodily disciplines, however, which are spoken of as beneficial for a few things,[92] decisions must be made in such a way that, as we have said, if a more realistic possibility for goodness occurs which suggests that they should be let go, we should not be bound by any rule in their regard but should leave them behind and freely move on to what is more beneficial. For there is no danger in leaving off these bodily disciplines for a while, but it is fatal to cease from the others even for a moment.

XXIX. "Precaution should likewise be taken so that, if perchance a word that you wish to be hidden has slipped from your mouth, no obligation to secrecy may trouble your hearer. For a thing will be better concealed if it is carelessly and unobtrusively let pass, because the brother, whoever he may be, will not be racked by a temptation to divulge it. He will consider it an insignificant matter that has been revealed in a passing conversation, which is not important precisely because it has not been presented to the ears of the listener in the context of a need to be specially careful. For if you bind him to an oath, you may be certain that it will be betrayed all the more quickly, inasmuch as the force of the diabolical onslaught that will attack him will be greater, so that you will be saddened and betrayed on the one hand and he will more speedily transgress his oath on the other.

XXX.1. "Therefore a monk should never promise anything hastily with regard to what pertains to bodily disciplines, lest instead he incite the enemy to attack the things that he is holding to as it were under the obligation of law and be quickly forced to violate them. For whoever lives under the grace of liberty and sets up a law for himself binds himself to a ruinous slavery, with the result that he is compelled to observe, as a transgressor and in a state of sin, things that he would have been able to undertake lawfully and even praiseworthily, with thanksgiving, whenever the need arose. 'For where there is no law, neither is there transgression.'"[93]

2. Strengthened as by a divine oracle by this instruction and teaching of the most blessed Joseph, we chose to remain in Egypt. But although from then on we were not particularly troubled by our promise, nonetheless we fulfilled our promise gladly at the end of seven years. For we hastened to our cenobium at a time when we were confident of obtaining a return to the desert, and first we paid our due respects to our elders. Then we restored their former love to the souls of those who, out of an ardent love, had not in the least been appeased by the frequent excuses contained in our letters. And at length, after the sting of our promise had been completely plucked out, we returned to the depths of the desert of Skete, while they urged us on with joy.

3. Our ignorance, O holy brothers, has cast as much light for you as it could on the knowledge and teaching of the illustrious

fathers. Even if perchance our unskilled language has confused it instead of clarifying it, I pray that our blameworthy rudeness not nullify the renown of these remarkable men. For it seemed safer to us in the sight of our Judge to lay bare this magnificent teaching, even in awkward language, than to keep silent about it. Indeed, if one reflects upon its sublime insights, the offensive boorishness of our words cannot hinder the reader's profit. And we ourselves are concerned more about usefulness than renown. To be sure, I advise all into whose hands these little works may fall to realize that whatever is pleasing in them is from the fathers, whereas whatever is displeasing is ours.

TEXTUAL REFERENCES

1. Prv 26:11 LXX.
2. Gn 40:7 LXX.
3. Cf. Gn 40:8.
4. Jn 13:8.
5. Cf. Mt 14:3–10.
6. Mt 5:37.
7. Mt 26:24.
8. Cf. Gn 27.
9. Rom 2:15–16.
10. Is 66:18.
11. 1 Tm 4:8.
12. Ps 5:6.
13. Wis 1:11.
14. Cf. Jos 2:1–21; 6:17–25.
15. Cf. Mt 1:5.
16. Cf. Jgs 16:4–21.
17. 1 Sm 21:2.
18. 1 Sm 21:3.
19. 1 Sm 21:9.
20. 1 Sm 21:14.
21. Col 3:9.
22. Gn 1:28.
23. Prv 20:17.
24. Ex 23:7.
25. 1 Sm 24:7.
26. 2 Sm 17:14.
27. 2 Sm 17:20.
28. Prv 24:11 LXX.
29. 1 Cor 10:24.
30. 1 Cor 13:5; Phil 2:4.
31. 1 Cor 10:33.
32. Cf. 1 Cor 9:22.
33. 1 Cor 9:20–22.
34. Gal 5:2.
35. Cf. Acts 16:3.
36. Acts 21:20–21.
37. Acts 21:23–24.
38. Gal 2:19.

39. Acts 17:23a.
40. Acts 17:23b.
41. Acts 17:28.
42. Acts 17:29.
43. Cf. 1 Cor 7:5.
44. Cf. 1 Cor 3:2.
45. Cf. 1 Cor 2:3.
46. Rom 14:3.
47. 1 Cor 7:38.
48. 2 Cor 11:29.
49. 1 Cor 10:32–33.
50. Cf. Phil 3:6–8.
51. Gal 2:18.
52. 1 Sm 22:7–8.
53. 1 Sm 22:9–10.
54. Ps 52:5.
55. Mi 7:5.
56. Mt 6:18.
57. Mt 6:3.
58. Mt 6:2.
59. 2 Cor 12:2–4.
60. Gn 42:9 LXX.
61. Gn 42:16 LXX.
62. Gn 42:21 LXX.
63. 1 Kgs 3:24–25.
64. 1 Kgs 3:27.
65. 1 Sm 25:22.
66. 1 Sm 25:34.
67. Cf. Acts 9:15.
68. 1 Cor 16:5–7.
69. 2 Cor 1:15–16.
70. 2 Cor 1:17.
71. 2 Cor 1:23, 2:1.
72. Gn 19:2.
73. Gn 19:3 LXX.
74. 2 Kgs 20:1–3 LXX.
75. 2 Kgs 20:5–6 LXX.
76. Jon 3:4 LXX.

77. Ez 33:14–15.
78. Jer 18:7–10.
79. Jer 26:2–3.
80. Cf. 1 Sm 8–10.
81. 1 Sm 15:11.
82. 1 Sm 15:35.
83. Ez 33:13–16.
84. Ex 32:31–33 LXX.
85. Ps 69:28a.
86. Ps 69:28b.
87. Mt 27:5.
88. Lk 10:20.
89. Jer 17:13.
90. Ez 13:9.
91. Ps 119:106.
92. Cf. 1 Tm 4:8.
93. Rom 4:15.

17.2.1 Cassian uses four words to express the notion of promise in the present conference—*sponsio,* as here; *promissio,* as in 17.5.2; *pollicitatio,* as in 17.5.3; and *definitio,* as in 17.8.4. Among the first three there seems to be little difference, but the last, which is by far the most frequent, suggests a decision that is viewed as binding by the one making it, although intrinsically it has no claim to be such.

17.5.2 On Cassian's and Germanus's relationship to Bethlehem cf. the note at 11.5. A basilica existed on the supposed site of Christ's birth from the time of Constantine, toward the beginning of the fourth century. The cave itself (which is mentioned already in the 140s in Justin, *Dial. c. Tryph.* 78) was surmounted by a large octagonal structure, which was somewhat separate from the basilica. The cave was visible to pilgrims but usually not accessible to them; certainly, however, access would have been given to local monks in the event of such a solemn occasion as Germanus describes here. For a brief description of the ensemble of basilica and octagon cf. Richard Krautheimer, *Early Christian and Byzantine Architecture* (Baltimore, 1975), 60–62. There is a description of the adornments in the cave of the Nativity in Cassian's time in Jerome, *De nativ. Dom.* (CCSL 78.524–525). In general, for mentions of the cave in patristic literature cf. Origen, *Contra Celsum,* trans. by Henry Chadwick (Cambridge, England, 1953), 47, n. 5.

The royal court of the virgin's womb: This imagery is used by Ambrose. For a commentary cf. Peter Brown, *The Body and Society: Men, Women, and Sexual Renunciation in Early Christianity* (New York, 1988), 354–356.

17.9 On the example of Herod in the same context, with a passing reference to Peter, cf. John Moschus, *Pratum spirituale* 216.

17.12 For Judas's betrayal as an example of a badly intended act with a good result cf. 6.9.1; Augustine, *In Ep. Ioann.* 7.7.

17.12.2 Joseph's description, which is recounted in Gn 27 and which Cassian mentions again in 17.17.5f., is referred to in Augustine, *C. mendacium* 24, with the famous words: "Non est mendacium, sed mysterium"—"It is not a lie but a mystery."

17.14.3 On the term "scopos" cf. the note at 1.2.1. On the scopos or goal as purity of heart cf. the first conference, *passim*.

17.17.1 On the properties of hellebore cf. Pauly-Wissowa 8.163–170, esp. 165–170. The sources cited suggest many curative properties but relatively few hurtful ones. Dorotheus of Gaza, *Instruc.* 9.102 (SC 92.330), also compares "unnecessary" lying to employing an excessive amount of medicinal herbs.

17.18.1ff. The fact that the patriarchs had concubines was occasionally adduced by Manicheans and others to show that the New Testament had utterly superseded the Old, or even that the Old was completely immoral. Cf. Faustus *ap.* Augustine, *C. Faustum* 22.5, which is answered by Augustine, ibid. 22.47ff.

17.19.1f. The idea that the practice of sexuality was typical of the Old Testament while virginity was typical of the era of the Church is found in Methodius of Olympus, *Symposium* 1.2ff.; Ambrose, *De virginibus* 1.3.13.

17.19.2 The aromatic fruits of chastity: Cf. 10.10.9 (with relevant note) and the note at 1.1.

The whole text of the Old Testament: *Totius veteris instrumenti textus.* Cf. the note at 14.10.2.

17.20.12 His wicked wife: The narrative of Samson in Jgs 16 nowhere says that Delilah was his wife.

17.21f. That a lie to dissemble one's fasting is justifiable testifies to the high valuation of humility in the desert.

That fasting should be concealed from others is also stated in *Inst.* 5.23.3.

17.24.1 The Abba Piamun mentioned here is almost certainly the same as the one who leads the eighteenth conference.

17.25.14 Cassian's view of divine providence, as expressed in the latter half of this paragraph, is similar to that found in Origen, *De orat.* 6.3ff. Both subordinate the divine plan to human behavior by accommodating that plan somehow to human activity. Thus Cassian, like Origen, gives the initiative to human activity, which is in keeping with his understanding of the interrelationship of grace and free will, which is elaborated in the thirteenth conference.

17.26 Contrast this image with the one in 6.12, where a mind like wax is deplored.

17.30.3 On Cassian's disclaimer of writing ability cf. the note at 1 praef. 3.

The Third Part of the Conferences of John Cassian

◆

CONFERENCES XVIII–XXIV

TRANSLATOR'S NOTE TO THE THIRD PART

This short preface introduces the final seven conferences, which are dedicated to four priests. Cassian maintains that, unlike the first and second sets of conferences, they are perfectly suited to both the cenobitic and the anchoritic life, the distinction between which is discussed in the eighteenth conference. The preface concludes on a note that emphasizes the discretion that is so central to Cassian's view of monasticism: Those who read his work will, thanks to its question-and-answer format, be able to approach the abbas of *The Conferences* as if they were physically present to them, and they will learn from them the time-tried discipline of the monastic life rather than relying on their own insights.

CASSIAN'S PREFACE TO THE THIRD PART

When, thanks to the grace of Christ, ten conferences of the fathers had been published, which were put together as well as could be at the request of the most blessed Bishops Helladius and Leontius, I dedicated seven others to the blessed Bishop Honoratus, honorable in both name and dignity, and also to Eucherius, the holy servant of Christ. And now I think that the same number should be dedicated to you, O holy brothers Jovinianus, Minervus, Leontius, and Theodore, since the last of you established the holy and excellent discipline of the cenobia in the Gallic provinces, with the strictness of the ancient virtues, while the rest of you by your instruction not only inspired monks to long for a cenobitic profession in the first place but also to desire the sublimity of an anchoritic way of life. 2. For these conferences of the greatest fathers were so carefully composed and are so balanced in all respects that they are appropriate to both professions which, thanks to you, flourish among immense bands of brothers not only in regions of the West but even in the Islands. That is to say, not only those who still remain in praiseworthy subjection in their congregations but also those who not long ago left your cenobia and desire to pursue the discipline of the anchorites are quite fully instructed with regard to the nature of the locations and their own status. 3. In this respect your own previous laborious effort has contributed in this way in particular—that those who are already practiced in and occupied with these exercises may seize more easily upon the precepts and institutes of the elders. Receiving the very authors of the conferences into their cells, along with the books of the conferences, and as it were speaking with them by way of daily questions and answers, they will not seek out by their own devices the hard and almost unknown path in this region (which is dangerous even where well-worn roads and innumerable examples of those who have gone before are already not lacking), but will become accustomed instead to lay hold of the discipline of the anchoritic life through their precepts, which both an ancient tradition and the effort of a long experience have arranged for every contingency.

3 praef. 1 On Helladius cf. the note at 1 praef. 2.

On Leontius cf. the note ibid.

On Honoratus cf. the note at 2 praef. 1. Between the composition of the second preface and that of the third, however, he became a bishop.

On Eucherius cf. the note ibid.

Of Jovinianus, Minervus, and Leontius (who is different from the preceding Leontius, being styled "brother") nothing further is known than what the preface itself tells us–namely, that they encouraged monasticism in Gaul. Theodore, however, in addition to founding cenobia in Gaul, also succeeded the first Leontius as bishop of Fréjus in 432.

3 praef. 2 Flourish: *Florere.* Cf. the note at 1.1.

The regions of the West that are mentioned here are most likely Gaul, where the addressees of *The Conferences* came from.

According to Gazet in PL 49.1089, the islands referred to here are the Stoechadian Islands, for which cf. the note at 2 praef. 3.

3 praef. 3 On "long experience" contributing to spiritual knowledge cf. the note at 3.7.4.

EIGHTEENTH CONFERENCE
THE CONFERENCE OF ABBA PIAMUN: ON THE THREE KINDS OF MONKS

TRANSLATOR'S INTRODUCTION

The first conference of this final section of the work brings Cassian and Germanus to a new setting–the region near the town of Diolcos, which lay *between* two mouths of the Nile, the Sebennytic and the Phatnic (rather than *at* one of the mouths, as Cassian says in 18.1.1), on the shore of the Mediterranean in the province of Aegyptus Secunda. (On Diolcos cf. also *Inst.* 5.36.) Abba Piamun, who leads the conference, had already been mentioned in 17.24, and he appears also in *Hist. monach. in Aegypto* 25 and Sozomen, *Hist. eccl.* 6.29.

The discussion begins when the two friends tell Piamun that they have come from Syria in search of perfection. Upon hearing this the old man does not hesitate to take a swipe at previous monastic visitors from that region, who seem to have learned nothing from their sojourn in Egypt. Clearly implying the superiority of Egyptian to Syrian monasticism, as in the seventeenth conference, Piamun insists that Cassian and Germanus must give up everything that they had previously learned and be instructed anew by Egyptian teachers. They must practice discretion, humbly and unquestioningly submitting themselves to their elders, much along the lines already drawn in the second conference.

With this Piamun turns somewhat abruptly to the matter of the origin and life-style of the different sorts of monks. In a passage that recalls *Inst.* 2.5 (and that looks forward to *Conlat.* 21.30) he gives an idealized brief history of the rise of cenobitism, the communal monasticism which he claims is its oldest form. The account betrays what can only be called an elitist understanding on Cassian's part of cenobitism in particular and of monasticism in general. (On the motivations for and the consequences of this "myth" concerning the origins of monasticism cf. Adalbert de Vogüé, "Monachisme et Eglise dans la pensée de Cassien," in *Théologie de la vie monastique: Etudes sur la Tradition patristique* [Aubier, 1961], 213–240, esp. 219–240.) The whole Church, Piamun declares, was effectively cenobitic in apostolic times, and in the period of decline that succeeded that era only those who came to be known as monks maintained the apostolic tradition. With the appearance of Paul and Antony in the second half of the third century the anchorite profession—the second form of monasticism—was born. Anchorites, taking Elijah and Elisha and John the Baptist as their models, seek in the solitude of the desert a still higher perfection than that offered by communal life. In addition to these two legitimate kinds of monasticism Piamun mentions two others, which are as it were degenerate variations of the first two. The sarabaites live in small groups, to be sure, but pursue their own wills and practice neither discretion nor poverty. The fourth set of monks, to which no name is attached and which is added to the list almost in passing, begins by living in cenobia, but then its members go off by themselves. In the solitude their vices multiply apace since there is no one to correct them.

In a famous letter written four decades before the composition of *The Conferences,* Jerome too gives a list and description of the different kinds of monks with which he was familiar. He speaks of only three, however, but they correspond to Cassian's first three; the equivalents of the sarabaites he knows as *remnuoth.* (Cf. *Ep.* 22.34ff.) It is possible that Cassian was influenced directly by this letter; he seems to have known Jerome's *V. S. Pauli,* as 18.5.4f. suggests. But he need not have been thus influenced, and it may just as well be that he is merely repeating common knowledge. It is likely, on the other hand, that *Reg. Magistri* 1 and Benedict, *Reg.* 1, with their lists of the kinds of monks (cenobites, anchorites, sarabaites, and gyrovagues), borrowed from Cassian at least in part.

Having distinguished among the different groups of monks, Piamun is now requested to distinguish between a monastery and a cenobium. The former is simply a dwelling for one or several monks, whereas the latter implies a gathering of several monks who share a common life.

The remainder of the conference deals largely with the cultivation of humility and patience. The connection here with what had preceded is not abundantly clear. It lies perhaps in Piamun's words in the final chapter to the effect that virtue (in this case patience) resides within a person and does not depend on "the recesses of our cell or the remoteness of the desert or the companionship of holy persons" (18.16.1). Otherwise stated, the embracing of neither the cenobitic nor the anchoritic life will guarantee the monk virtue. The instruction concludes with several pages devoted to the control of envy, which Piamun claims to be particularly destructive.

The conference as a whole ends with Cassian's remark that, inspired by Piamun's words, he and Germanus were all the more "drawn away from the first training ground of the cenobium to the next step, that of the anchorite's life" (18.16.15). This expressed belief in the superiority of the anchoritic to the cenobitic life is in keeping with 18.6.1, where anchorites are said to be desirous of "higher progress and divine contemplation," as well as with much of the rest of *The Conferences*. But Cassian sows a certain amount of unintended confusion when in 18.5.4 he refers to cenobitism as "first not only in time but also in grace" *(monachorum genus, quod non solum tempore sed etiam gratia primum est)* and when in 18.11.1 he calls cenobites "the best kind of monks" *(optimo genere monachorum)*. This language gives the impression of contradicting the preeminence that is otherwise accorded to anchoritism. A glance at *Inst.* 5.36.1, however, is helpful in this regard. There Cassian begins by speaking of the cenobites as "the best order of monks, which is also the first" *(optimo ordine monachorum, qui etiam primus est)*, and then proceeds to say that the anchorites are "considered still more excellent" *(excellentior habetur, id est anachoretarum)*. It is clear, then, that Cassian can apply superlatives to the cenobitic life without denying even greater superlatives to the anchoritic life, and all in virtually the same breath. What is perhaps equally confusing, though, is the fact that Cassian chooses to give cenobitism an earlier origin than anchoritism. Would it not have made more sense, considering the esteem in which the author held anchoritism, for him to have found a way to make it the original form of monasticism, closer to the apostolic Church? The matter is a puzzling one. The solution offered by de Vogüé (namely, that the history of the successive institutions, first cenobitic and then anchoritic, parallels the history of the individual monk, who must pass through the cenobium before embracing the solitary life, art. cit. 221), is interesting, but it must remain in the realm of speculation. And, of course, it could also be that Cassian himself really believed that there was a direct link between the apostolic community and cenobitism, which he did not feel free to ignore even though he might have wished that it were otherwise.

This conference and the following one are often understood as being referred to in *Inst.* 5.4.3: "Although our religion has one end, there are nonetheless different professions by which to go to God, as will be more fully discussed in the conferences of the elders." If it is true that Conferences 18 and 19 are indicated in the passage from *The Institutes,* this would seem to militate against the suggestion advanced in the present commentary (cf. pp. 8, 397–98) that Cassian initially intended to complete *The Conferences* with the tenth one. There are three possible solutions that would, with varying degrees of convincingness, maintain in the face of this difficulty the defensibility of the view that Cassian's original intention had been to conclude *The Conferences* with the tenth, which is in any event highly plausible for several other reasons. These solutions are as follows: (1) Cassian is referring in *Inst.* 5.4.3 not to the particular discussion of the different kinds of monks in Conferences 18 and 19 but to the more general allusions to them throughout the first ten conferences. (2) He is referring in *Inst.* 5.4.3 to the discussion of the different callings and renunciations in *Conlat.* 3.3ff. (3) After having written Conferences 18 and 19, he modified the text of *Inst.* 5.4.3 so as to make mention of the subsequent discussion.

XVIII. The Conference of Abba Piamun: On the Three Kinds of Monks

Chapters

I.1. After seeing and speaking with those three old men, whose conferences we put together as well as we could at the urging of our holy brother Eucherius, when we desired with still greater ardor to seek out also the more distant parts of Egypt in which a larger and more perfect number of holy men were dwelling, we came to a town called Diolcos, located at one of the seven mouths of the River Nile. In this we were urged on not so much by the requirements of our journey as by a yearning for the holy men who were living there. 2. When, like the most avid of merchants, we had heard of many very famous cenobia there, founded by the early fathers, we at once as it were took ship in an uncertain quest, spurred on by the hope of greater gain. After floating around for a long while, we cast inquisitive eyes on the mountains that were everywhere and that were conspicuous for the loftiness of their virtue, and our searching gaze fell first upon Abba Piamun, the elder of all the anchorites living there and their priest, who was like a kind of very high lighthouse. 3. For, like that gospel city set on a hill,[1] he shone at once upon our faces. We believe that the mighty deeds and miracles of his, which were accomplished by him in our very sight while divine grace bore witness to his worthiness, should be passed over in silence lest we ignore the arrangement that we agreed upon and unduly lengthen this volume. For we have promised to write not of the miracles of God but of the institutes and works of the holy men that we are able to remember, so that we may offer to our readers only what is necessary for instruction in the perfect life and not a useless and vain object of wonderment without any correction for faults.

4. When, therefore, the blessed Piamun had fed us with appropriate hospitality, after having received us with great gladness, and he had found out that we were not from that region, he first inquired carefully where we were from and why we had sought out Egypt. On learning that we had come to him from a cenobium in Syria on account of a desire for perfection, he began as follows:

II.1. "My sons, whenever a person wishes to acquire skill in some art, he must give himself over with all his care and attentiveness to the study of the discipline that he wants to grasp and must observe the precepts and institutes of the most accomplished teachers in that area of work or knowledge; otherwise he longs in vain and with idle desire to achieve a resemblance to those persons whose care and effort he fails to imitate. 2. For we have known some people who have come to this place from your region in order to go around to the monasteries of the brothers merely for the sake of getting acquainted with them, but not in order to receive the rules and institutes for which they came here or, while sitting apart in their cells, to attempt to put into practice what they had seen or been told. Holding on to the behavior and concerns to which they were accustomed, they were thought to have changed provinces not for the sake of their own progress but out of a need to escape poverty, and many people reproach them for this. 3. Not only were they unable to acquire any instruction but they could not even stay longer in these parts, due to the obstinacy of their stubborn minds. For since they changed neither their way of fasting nor their manner of psalmody nor even the clothes that they wore, why should they be thought to have come to this region for anything else than just their supply of food?

III.1. "Therefore, if, as we believe, concern for God has drawn you to seek after our knowledge, you must completely renounce all the institutes that accompanied your first beginnings in the former place and follow with great humility whatever you see our elders do or teach. Nor should you be moved or diverted or held back from imitating them even if the reason or the cause for a particular thing or deed is not clear to you at the time, because the knowledge of everything is attained by those who think well and with simplicity about all matters and who strive to imitate faithfully rather than to discuss everything that they see being taught and done by the elders. 2. But whoever begins to learn by discussion will never enter into the reason for the truth, because the enemy will see him trusting in his own judgment rather than in that of the fathers and will easily drive him to the point where even things which are very beneficial and salutary will seem useless and harmful to him. The clever foe will so play upon his presumption that, stubbornly clinging to his own unreasonable understandings, he will persuade himself that only that is holy which he considers to be correct and righteous, guided by his erroneous obstinacy alone.

IV.1. "Therefore, the first thing that you must know is how and where the order and origin of our profession came about. For a person will be able to pursue the discipline of the desired art more effectively and be drawn to exercise it more ardently when he recognizes the dignity of its authors and founders.

2. "There are in Egypt three kinds of monks. Two of them are very good, while the third is lukewarm and utterly to be avoided. The first is that of the cenobites, who live together in a community and are governed by the judgment of one elder. The greatest number of monks dwelling throughout Egypt are of this kind. The second is that of the anchorites, who are first instructed in the cenobia and then, perfected in their practical way of life, choose the recesses of the desert. We too have chosen to be part of this profession. The third and blameworthy one is that of the sarabaites. We shall discuss each of these in order and at greater length.

3. "You must first know, then, as we have said, the founders of these three professions. In this way you will be able to arouse both a hatred for the profession which should be avoided and a desire for that which should be pursued, because each path inevitably draws the one who takes it to the end at which its author and discoverer arrived.

V.1. "The discipline of the cenobites took its rise at the time of the apostolic preaching. For such was the whole multitude of believers in Jerusalem, which is described thus in the Acts of the Apostles: 'The multitude of believers had one heart and one soul, and none of them said that what he possessed was his own, but all things were common to them.[2] They sold their possessions and their belongings and distributed them to all as each had need.'[3] And again: 'Nor was there anyone needy among them, for as many as owned fields or houses sold them and brought the price of what they sold and laid it at the feet of the apostles, and this was distributed to each just as each had need.'[4]

2. "Such, I say, was the whole Church then, whereas now it is difficult to find even a few like that in the cenobia. But, at the

death of the apostles, the multitude of believers began to grow lukewarm, especially those who came over to the faith of Christ from different foreign nations. Out of regard for their rudimentary faith and their inveterate paganism, the apostles asked nothing more of them than that they abstain 'from things sacrificed to idols, from fornication, from things strangled, and from blood.'[5] But this liberty, which was conceded to the pagans because of the weakness of their new faith, gradually began to spoil the perfection of the Church which was in Jerusalem, and, as the number of natives and of foreigners daily increased, the warmth of that new faith grew cold, and not only those who had come over to the faith of Christ but even those who were the leaders of the Church relaxed their strictness. 3. For some people, thinking that what they saw conceded to the pagans because of their weakness was lawful for them as well, thought that it would be no loss to themselves if they believed in and confessed Christ while keeping their belongings and property.

"Those in whom the apostolic fervor still existed, however, were mindful of that earlier perfection. Abandoning their towns and the company of those who believed that the negligence of a more careless life was lawful for both themselves and the Church of God, they began to live in rural and more secluded places and to practice privately and individually what they remembered had been taught by the apostles in a general way throughout the body of the Church. So it was that there flourished the discipline which we have said came from the disciples who removed themselves from contamination. 4. As time went on they gradually separated themselves from the crowds of believers by reason of the fact that they abstained from marriage, cut themselves off from the company of their parents and from the life of this world, and were called monks or μοναζοντες because of the strictness of their individual and solitary lives. Consequently they are called cenobites from their common fellowship, and their cells and dwelling places are called cenobia. This alone, then, was the most ancient kind of monks, which is first not only in time but also in grace, and which remained inviolable throughout the years, up until the era of Abba Paul and Abba Antony. We see that remnants of it endure even now in strict cenobia.

VI.1. "From this number of the perfect, from what I would call this most fruitful root of holy persons, the flowers and fruit of the anchorites sprouted forth afterward. We know of the existence of the leaders of this profession, whom we mentioned shortly before—namely, the holy Paul and Antony. They sought out the recesses of the desert not, indeed, because of faintheartedness or an unhealthy impatience but from a desire for higher progress and divine contemplation, although the former of them is said to have penetrated the desert out of need, in order to escape the snares of his relatives during a time of persecution.

2. "In this way, then, another kind of perfection came out of the discipline that we have spoken of. Its followers are deservedly called anchorites—that is, those who go apart—because they are not at all content with the victory of treading underfoot the hidden snares of the devil in the midst of men. They desire to engage the demons in an open struggle and in out-and-out combat, and they are not afraid to penetrate the vast recesses of the desert in imitation of John the Baptist, who spent his whole life in the desert, and of Elijah and Elisha and the others whom the Apostle recalls thus: 'They went about in sheepskin and in goatskin, in distress, afflicted, needy, the world unworthy of them, wandering in deserts and mountains and caves and caverns of the earth.'[6] 3. Of them the Lord also speaks figuratively to Job: 'Who has sent out the wild ass free and loosed his bonds? I have made his dwelling the desert, and his tents the salt waste. He laughs at the multitude of the city, and he does not hear the complaint of the overseer. He will consider the mountains of his pasturage, and he seeks after every green thing.'[7] In the psalms too: 'Let now those who have been redeemed by the Lord say, whom he redeemed from the hand of the enemy.'[8] And a little later: 'They wandered in the desert, in a waterless place. They did not find the path to a city to dwell in. They were hungry and thirsty; their soul fainted within them. And they cried to the Lord when they were afflicted, and he freed them from their distress.'[9] 4. Jeremiah also describes them as follows: 'Blessed is the one who has borne the yoke from his youth. He shall sit solitary and be still, because he has taken it upon himself.'[10] And they sing in disposition and in act the words

of the psalmist: 'I have become like a pelican in the desert. I watched, and I became like a sparrow alone on the roof.'[11]

VII.1. "And as the Christian religion was rejoicing in these two professions of the monks, although the latter class had also begun to deteriorate gradually, there appeared thereafter the worst kind of monks, who are faithless. Or rather that harmful plant took new life, which, when it was sprouting at the beginning of the Church under Ananias and Sapphira, was cut down by the severity of the apostle Peter.[12] Among the monks this has been considered detestable and abominable, and it has not been practiced by anyone ever since there was instilled into the consciousness of believers the fear of that most rigorous sentence by which the blessed apostle did not permit the aforesaid leaders of the new outrage to be healed by repentance or by any act of reparation but cut down the wicked shoot by a swift death.

2. "When this example, which was punished with apostolic rigor in Ananias and Sapphira, had gradually faded from the thoughts of some, due to long neglect and to the forgetfulness that comes with time, there emerged the kind known as sarabaites. They are rightly called sarabaites in the Egyptian language because they withdrew themselves from the communities of the cenobia and as individuals cared for their own needs. They came from the number of those whom we have already spoken about, who preferred to feign gospel perfection rather than really to lay hold of it, being incited by rivalry with and by the praises of those who prefer Christ's utter deprivation to all the wealth in the world.

3. "These, then, while faintheartedly affecting the highest virtue, have been compelled to come to this profession out of necessity, being eager to be accounted merely as bearing the name of monks without making any effort to imitate them. In no way do they long for the discipline of the cenobia. They do not submit to the judgment of the elders, nor are they formed in their traditions, and they do not learn to conquer their own wills; neither do they accept, as a result of some prescribed training, any rule of sound discretion. Instead, they only make a public renunciation–that is, in the sight of men–and either remain in their dwellings, bound to the same occupations, thanks to the privilege of this name, or build themselves cells and call them monasteries, living in them at

liberty under their own law and never obeying the gospel precepts.[13] They do this so that they might not be preoccupied with any concern for daily food or with any worries over domestic affairs. 4. But, beyond the shadow of a doubt, this is only achieved by those who have abandoned all their possessions in this world and who so subject themselves to the ones in charge of the cenobia that they do not say that they are their own masters. Those who, however, as we have said, leave the strictness of the cenobium and live in cells by twos and threes, not content to be governed by the care and judgment of an abba but rather being especially concerned to be loosed from the yoke of the elders and to be free to exercise their own wills, to go wherever they please and to wander about and act as it suits them, are even more taken up with daily matters day and night than those who live in the cenobia, although not with the same faith and chosen orientation. 5. They behave in this way not in order to place the fruit of their labor at the disposal of a superintendent but to acquire money to hoard.

"See what a difference there is between them. The ones think nothing of the morrow and offer God the most pleasing fruits of their toil, while the others draw out their faithless concern not only to the morrow but even over many years, believing that God is either a liar or ineffectual, either unable or unwilling to provide them with the sufficiency of daily food and clothing that he promised. The ones desire with utmost longing to possess ακτημοσυνη, which is the deprivation of all things and enduring poverty, while the others chase after an abundance of every resource. 6. The ones earnestly endeavor to go beyond the established measure in their daily work so that whatever exceeds the holy needs of the monastery may be given away, in accordance with the abba's judgment, to prisons or lodgings for travelers or hospitals or to the poor, while the others do this so that whatever is left over from their daily gormandizing may minister to prodigality or at least be hoarded in the interests of the vice of avarice. Finally, even granting that what is accumulated by these latter persons with an imperfect intention can be distributed better than we have said, they still do not approach the dignity of this virtue and perfection. 7. For the former ones, who bring in considerable revenue to their monastery and daily renounce it, remain in such humble subjection that they are stripped of their power over the things which they procure by their own effort, just as they are of that over themselves, and they constantly renew the fervor of their first renunciation by daily depriving themselves of the fruit of their toil. But these others slip daily down the precipice in their pride at giving something to the poor. The patience and strictness with which the former remain so devotedly in their profession, once they have taken it up, never fulfilling their own desires, crucifies them daily to this world and makes living martyrs of them, but the lukewarmness of the latter's will plunges them into hell.

8. "These two kinds of monks, nearly equal in numbers, rival one another in this province. But in the other provinces, which the requirements of the Catholic faith have obliged me to travel through, we know that this third kind, the sarabaites, abounds and exists almost by itself. For in the time of Lucius, who was a bishop of the Arian perfidy during the reign of Valens, as we were bringing some assistance to our brothers who had been sent from Egypt and the Thebaid to the mines of Pontus and Armenia on account of their perseverance in the Catholic faith, although we saw that the discipline of the cenobia was very rare and existed in only a few cities, we learned that the very name itself of the anchorites had not yet been heard among them.

VIII.1. "There is in fact a fourth kind as well, which we see has appeared recently among those who fancy themselves in the style and likeness of anchorites and who seem, when they are starting out, to long for the perfection of the cenobium with a sort of short-lived fervor. But all at once they grow lukewarm, contemning the curtailment of their earlier behavior and vices, not content with bearing the yoke of humility and patience any longer and disdaining to place themselves under the rule of the elders. They long for separate cells and want to live by themselves, so that they may be irritated by no one and may be considered patient, mild, and humble by men. This form of life—or rather lukewarmness—does not permit those whom it has once infected ever to attain to perfection. 2. For in this way their vices are not only not cut off but even grow worse, since they are challenged by no one. They are like some deadly internal venom: The more it is concealed, the more deeply the serpent works an incurable disease in the sick person. For out of respect for his secluded cell no one dares to reproach the solitary for his vices, which he prefers to be ignored rather than healed. Virtues, however, are begotten not by hiding one's vices but by fighting them."

IX. GERMANUS: "Is there any distinction between a cenobium and a monastery, or are they the same thing with two different names?"

X. PIAMUN: "Although some people are in the habit of speaking of monasteries instead of cenobia, without drawing a distinction, nonetheless the difference is that monastery is the name of a dwelling and means nothing more than a place—that is, a lodging—for monks, whereas cenobium indicates the character and discipline of the profession itself. The habitation of even one monk can be called a monastery, but something cannot be called a cenobium unless a united community with several inhabitants lives there. Indeed, even where groups of sarabaites live are said to be monasteries.

XI.1. "Therefore, since I see that you have learned the principles of this profession from the best kind of monks—that is, from the praiseworthy school of the cenobia—and that you are heading toward the highest reaches of anchorite discipline, toward the virtue of humility and patience which I do not doubt that you learned there, you should pursue this with a sincerely disposed heart, not feigning it, as some do, by a false humility of speech or an affected and unnecessary inclination to certain practices of the body.

2. "Abba Serapion once cleverly mocked this feigned humility. When someone came to him displaying the greatest abjection in dress and speech and the old man encouraged him, as was the custom, to say the prayer, the man did not accede to the request. He demeaned himself and said that he had been involved in such wicked behavior that he did not deserve to breathe the same air as everyone else; he even refused to sit on a mat but sat on the ground instead. 3. But when he refused still more definitively to have his feet washed, Abba Serapion, having finished the meal and having been given the opportunity by the customary conference, began to warn him kindly and gently not to wander about everywhere in fickle and frivolous fashion like a lazy vagrant, especially

since he was young and strong, but to sit in his cell in keeping with the rule of the elders and to prefer being supported by his own toil rather than by others' generosity. He said that the apostle Paul did not let this happen and that, in fact, although he should rightly have been provided for because he was laboring for the sake of the Gospel, nonetheless he preferred to work day and night in order to earn his daily bread with his own hands both for himself and for those who were ministering to him and could not work.[14] 4. At this the man was filled with such annoyance and chagrin that he was unable to conceal on his face the bitterness that he had conceived in his heart. The old man said to him: 'Up until now, my son, you have burdened yourself with the full weight of your misdeeds, not fearing to incur a notorious reputation by confessing such atrocious crimes. Why, I ask you now in reference to our simple little admonition, which contained no reproach at all but rather a disposition of edification and love, do I see you moved with such indignation that you are unable to hide it on your face or to disguise it by a calm appearance? Were you perhaps, in humiliating yourself, hoping for these words from our mouth: "The righteous man is his own accuser at the beginning of his speech"?'[15]

5. "Hence, a humility of heart must be maintained which is genuine and which does not come from an affected humbleness of body and speech but from a deep humbleness of mind. It will glow with the clearest indications of patience precisely when a person does not boast to others about crimes of his that are not to be believed but rather disregards what is insolently said against him by someone else and endures insults inflicted upon him with a gentle and placid spirit."

XII. GERMANUS: "We want to know how this tranquillity can be acquired and maintained so that, just as we draw the bars of our mouth and hold back the flow of our words when silence is demanded of us, we may likewise be able to keep a gentle heart, because sometimes even though the tongue is restrained one still loses one's state of peacefulness within. For this reason we are of the opinion that a person cannot hold on to the good of gentleness except by having a cell far away and a solitary dwelling."

XIII.1. PIAMUN: "True patience and tranquillity are not acquired or held onto without profound humility of heart. If they proceed from this source they will stand in need of neither the benefit of a cell nor the refuge of solitude. For whatever is sustained within by the virtue of humility, which is its begetter and guardian, does not require the protection of anything without. But if we are so provoked as to be angered by someone, it is certain that the foundations of humility have not been firmly established in us, and it is for that reason that our edifice is ruinously shaken by the onslaught of even an insignificant squall. For patience would not be praiseworthy or admirable if it maintained its intended tranquillity without having been assailed by any of the enemy's darts, but it is distinguished and glorious when it remains unmoved while storms of trial break upon it. 2. For it is strengthened at the very moment that it believes itself to be troubled and broken by adversity, and it is sharpened at the very moment that it thinks itself to be blunted. Everyone knows that patience takes its name from suffering and endurance, and therefore it is clear that no one can be called patient but the person who puts up with everything that is inflicted upon him without indignation. Therefore he is not undeservedly praised by Solomon: 'Better is the one who is patient than the one who is strong, and the one who restrains his anger than the one who captures a city.'[16] And again: 'A forbearing man is great in prudence, but a fainthearted man is foolish indeed.'[17]

3. "When, therefore, someone who has suffered mistreatment is inflamed with the fire of anger, it must not be believed that his bitterness at the abuse inflicted on him is the cause of his sin, but rather that it is the manifestation of a hidden weakness. This is in accordance with the parable of the Lord, the Savior, which he told about the two houses–one that was established on solid rock and the other on sand, upon the both of which there fell, he says, rainstorms and torrents and tempests. But the one that was established on solid rock experienced no damage from that violent onslaught, whereas the one that was built on the uncertain and shifting sands collapsed at once.[18] It appears to have caved in not, indeed, because it was struck by an outpouring of torrential rain but because it was foolishly built on sand.

4. "For the holy man does not differ from the sinner in that he too is not tried in like fashion but rather in that he is not con-

quered even by a great onslaught, while the other is overcome even by a slight trial. As we have said, the fortitude of a righteous man would not be praiseworthy if he were victorious without having been tried, when in fact there can be no place for victory without the adversity of a struggle. For 'blessed is the man who undergoes trial, because when he has been tested he will receive the crown of life, which God has promised to those who love him.'[19] 5. According to the apostle Paul too, strength is perfected not in leisure and pleasure but in weakness.[20] 'For, behold,' it says, 'I have made you today into a fortified city and an iron pillar and a brass wall over all the land, to the kings of Judah and to its princes and its priests and to all the people of the land. And they will fight against you and they shall not prevail, because I am with you, says the Lord, to deliver you.'[21]

XIV.1. "I want to give you at least two examples of this patience, then. One is of a certain religious woman, who pursued the virtue of patience with such eagerness that she not only did not escape attacks of trial but even brought moments of affliction upon herself to which she would not yield, although she was frequently provoked. Although she was living at Alexandria and came from a good family and was serving the Lord devoutly in the home that had been left her by her parents, she approached Bishop Athanasius of blessed memory and asked him to give her a widow to support, who was being looked after at the expense of the Church. 2. Let us express her request in her own words: 'Give me,' she said, 'one of the sisters to take care of.' The bishop, then, after having praised the woman's proposal because he had seen her so eager to perform a work of mercy, ordered a widow to be selected from among all of them, who would stand out from the others by reason of her good character, seriousness, and discipline. Thus her desire would not be outweighed by the sinfulness of the recipient of her graciousness, and she who sought gain in a poor woman would not be offended by her wicked behavior and suffer damage to her faith.

3. "When she was performing all sorts of services for her once she had been brought home, and she had experienced her virtuous modesty and gentleness and saw that she was being honored by her with thanks at every moment for her hospitable min-

istrations, she went back to the aforementioned bishop after a few days. 'I had asked,' she said, 'that you order me to be given someone to look after and to minister to with diligent attention.' Not yet understanding the woman's proposal and desire he thought that her petition had been overlooked through the carelessness of an official. When he inquired into the reasons for the delay, not without some mental irritation, and at once discovered that a widow more respectable than the others had been assigned to her, he secretly ordered that one who was worse than the others be given to her, who by reason of her anger, her quarrelsomeness, her winebibbing, and her talkativeness would exceed all the others in whom those vices held sway. 4. When this person was even more easily found and brought to her, and when she had begun to have her at home and was ministering to her with the same diligence that she had shown the first widow, and even more attentively, all that she received by way of thanks for such great services was that she was constantly loaded with scathing abuse and bothered with continual reproaches and complaints from her, as she opposed her and rebuked her with foul invective. For she had asked for her from the bishop not for her own relaxation but for her torment and disparagement, and so that she might go from rest to labor rather than from labor to rest. When, therefore, her unceasing contentiousness had reached the point where the insolent woman would not even refrain from raising her hand, the other doubled her ministrations with still more humble service, having learned to overcome the shrew not by resisting her but by subjecting herself more humbly, so that, after having been provoked by numerous indignities, she might calm the scold's rage with her soothing hospitality.

5. "When she had been fully confirmed as a result of these exercises and had attained to the virtue of perfect patience that she desired, she went to the aforesaid bishop to thank him both for the good judgment of his choice and for the benefit that she had gained from this training. For, in keeping with her desire, he had finally provided her with a most worthy teacher of patience. Thanks to her constant insults she was strengthened daily as if by the kind of oil that wrestlers use, and she attained to the highest patience of mind. 'At last,' she said, 'you have given me someone

to take care of, for the previous one was honoring me and looking after me with her ministrations.'

"Let it suffice to have said this about the feminine sex, so that by calling this to mind we may not only be edified but even be humbled—we who are unable to maintain our patience unless we have hidden in the recesses of our cells like wild animals.

XV.1. "Now let us offer another example, that of Abba Paphnutius. He persisted with such great zeal in the depths of the renowned and universally praised desert of Skete, where he is now a priest, that the other anchorites gave him the name of "the Buffalo," because out of what I might call an innate desire he always rejoiced in dwelling in the desert.

2. "Since he was so virtuous and graced in boyhood that even famous and highly placed men at that time admired his seriousness and unchanging firmness and, although he was young, nonetheless considered him equal to his elders because of his virtues and thought that he should enjoy their rank, the envy that once aroused the minds of his brothers against the patriarch Joseph[22] inflamed one of the brothers with a fire of consuming jealousy. Desiring to deform his beauty as it were by a blemish or stain, he concocted the following evil deed and seized an occasion when Paphnutius would be going to church on a Sunday and would be away from his cell. 3. Making his way in there in thievish fashion, he surreptitiously concealed one of his own books among the cords that the other used to weave from palm leaves and, untroubled about the deed that he had carried out, he went off to church, as if his conscience were clean and guileless. And when the whole solemnity had been celebrated in the usual way, he brought a complaint to the holy Isidore, who was priest in the same desert previous to Paphnutius, in the presence of all the brothers, and declared that his book had been stolen from his cell. 4. His complaint so unsettled the minds of all the brothers and of the priest in particular that they did not know what to think or what course to take, since everyone was struck with the greatest astonishment at such a crime, unheard of up until then. Indeed, no one could remember anything like it having been committed before that time in the desert, and it has never happened since. Thereupon the accuser, who had brought the charge, urged

that everyone be kept in the church and that some selected persons be sent to examine the cells of all the brothers one by one. When this had been enjoined on three elders by the priest, they went around to every cell and finally, in Paphnutius's cell, discovered the book concealed among the palm cords which they call *sirae,* just as the sneak had hidden it. 5. When the searchers brought the book at once to the church and produced it in front of everyone, Paphnutius, although untroubled in the sincerity of his own conscience, nonetheless gave himself over totally to reparation and humbly asked for a place of repentance, as if he were acknowledging the crime of theft. He did this out of regard for his sense of shame and modesty, lest if he tried to talk himself out of the stigma of thievery he be marked with that of lying as well, as no one would believe something different than what had been found out. And from the moment that he left the church, not so much cast down in mind as relying on the judgment of God, he prayed with a continual outpouring of tears, trebled his fasting, and lowered himself by the greatest humility of mind in the sight of men. 6. But when he had subjected himself in utter brokenness of flesh and spirit for nearly two weeks, to the degree that he would go out on Saturday and Sunday morning not to receive Holy Communion but to prostrate himself at the threshold of the church and humbly ask for pardon, the Witness and Judge of all things hidden no longer let him be ground down by himself and defamed by others. For what the discoverer of the crime, the wicked thief of his own property, the cunning destroyer of another's good reputation had done with no human witness, he disclosed through the devil, who had been the instigator of the crime itself. 7. For he was seized by a most dreadful demon and laid bare all the ins and outs of his hidden deed, and the very one who planned the accusations and deceptions was their betrayer. He was troubled by that unclean spirit so seriously and for such a long time that he could not be cleansed even by the prayers of the holy persons who were there, who were commanding the demons on the strength of their divine gifts. Not even the unique grace of the priest Isidore himself drove the cruel tormentor out of him, although such great power had been conferred on him by the Lord's generosity that any possessed person who was brought as far as his threshold would be healed at once. For Christ was reserving this glory for the young Paphnutius, so that the man might be purged exclusively by the prayers of him whom he had sought to deceive, and so that the envious foe, proclaiming his name, might receive pardon for his sin and an end to his present punishment by the prayers of the one whose good reputation he had believed he was capable of detracting from.

8. "In his adolescence, then, while still in his boyish years, he gave these indications of his future character, even then sketching the outline of a perfection that would be increased at a mature age. If, therefore, we wish to attain to the height of his virtues, such must be the first foundations that we lay.

XVI.1. "Two reasons have in fact drawn me to narrate this incident. The first is that, while reflecting on the steadfastness and constancy of this man, we may be less besieged by the snares of the enemy the more we lay hold of the disposition of peacefulness and patience. The next is that we may firmly hold that we cannot be safe from the tumult of trial and from the attacks of the devil if we place all the defense of our patience and all our confidence not in the strength of our inner man but in the recesses of our cell or the remoteness of the desert or the companionship of holy persons or the defense of something that is outside ourselves. 2. For unless he who said in the Gospel that 'the kingdom of God is within you'[23] has strengthened our mind with the power of his protection, we believe in vain that we can overcome the snares of the airy foe by the help of those with whom we live, or that we can keep them at a distance or resist them by a fortified shelter. Although none of these things were lacking to the holy Paphnutius, still the one who put him to the test was able to find a way to attack him, and the enclosure of walls and the solitude of the desert and the great worthiness of the holy persons in that community did not repel the wicked spirit. 3. But because the holy servant of God had fixed his heart's hope not on the things that are without but on the very Judge of all things hidden, he could never be shaken by the engines of such an assault. On the contrary, did not he whom envy had driven to such a crime also enjoy the benefit of the desert, the protection of a distant dwelling place, and the companionship of the blessed Isidore, abba and priest, and of other holy persons? And still, because a diabolical tempest found that he was on sand, it not only struck his house but even overthrew it.

"Let us not, then, look for our peace without, or think that another's patience can mitigate the vice of our own impatience. 4. For, just as the kingdom of God is within us, so also 'a person's enemies are those of his own household,'[24] because no one is more opposed to me than my own disposition, which truly is the most intimate part of my household. Therefore, if we are careful, we shall be unable to be troubled by internal enemies, for where those of our own household are not opposed to us, there also the kingdom of God is attained in tranquillity of mind.

"Let us investigate the matter more closely. I shall not be able to be troubled by anyone, however malicious he may be, if I do not fight against myself with a turbulent heart. But if I am hurt, it is not the fault of another's attack but of my own impatience. 5. For just as heavy and solid food is beneficial for a healthy person, so also it is dangerous for a sick one. It cannot hurt the one who takes it, however, unless the recipient's weakness confers on it a harmful power. Therefore, if ever a like trial should occur among the brothers, we should by no means swerve off the course of tranquillity and give access to the blasphemous disparagement of worldly persons.

"Nor should we be surprised that some wicked and detestable persons have been mingled in the number of holy men and lie concealed among them, because, as long as we are trampled upon and ground down on the threshing floor of this world, the chaff which will be assigned to an eternal fire will inevitably be mixed in with the grain of the elect.[25] 6. If we recall that Satan was one of the angels, Judas was one of the apostles, and Nicolaus, author of a most vicious heresy, was one of the chosen deacons,[26] we shall not be surprised that very wicked persons are found mingled in the company of the holy. For although some people assert that this Nicolaus was not the same one who was chosen by the apostles for the work of ministering, nevertheless they still cannot deny that he was from the number of the disciples who at that time were all clearly so perfect and of a sort that we can barely find a few of now in the cenobia.

7. "We are not giving you as an example, then, the ruin of the aforesaid brother who experienced such a disastrous downfall in that desert, or the terrible stain which he nonetheless did away with afterward by copious tears of repentance, but rather the case of the blessed Paphnutius. And let us not be destroyed by the overthrow of the former, whose feigned religiosity made the ancient vice of envy even worse, but let us pursue with all our strength the humility of the latter, which the peace of the desert did not suddenly beget for him, but which the desert perfected and refined once it had been acquired in the midst of human beings.

8. "It should certainly be known that the disease of envy is healed with greater difficulty than the other vices. I would almost say that he whom it has once infected with its pestilential poison has no cure. For this is the epidemic of which it is figuratively said by the prophet: 'Behold, I will send among you serpents, basilisks, against which there is no charm, and they shall bite you.'[27] Rightly, then, does the prophet compare the bites of envy to the poison of the deadly basilisk: By it the first author and contriver of all poisons perished and died. For he destroyed himself before he poured out his deadly venom on the man, being his own murderer before being his of whom he was envious. For 'by the envy of the devil death entered into the world. Those who are on his side, then, imitate him.'[28] 9. Just as he who was first infected with the plague of this evil received neither the healing of repentance nor any curative poultice, so also those who have let themselves be bitten by these same bites cut off all assistance from the holy charmer. For, since in fact they are not envious of their faults but rather are tormented by their prosperity, they blush to acknowledge the truth and they look outside themselves for foolish and absurd causes for their having been offended. The remedy for these, since they are utterly false, is in vain, inasmuch as the deadly poison that they do not wish to acknowledge lies hidden deep within them. 10. Concerning these people that most wise man has well expressed it: 'If a serpent bites without hissing, there is no abundance for the charmer.'[29] These are the silent bites for which alone the medicine of the wise provides no relief. For so incurable is this bane that it is worsened by flattery, puffed up by attentiveness, and irritated by favors, because, as the same

Solomon says, 'envy endures nothing.'[30] The more someone else makes progress in humble submission or virtuous patience or praiseworthy generosity, the more a person is driven by still greater urges of envy, because he desires nothing less than the downfall and death of the one whom he envies. 11. To such an extent could the envy of the eleven patriarchs not be softened by the submission of their innocent brother that Scripture says of them: 'His brothers envied him because his father loved him, and they were not able to say anything peaceable to him.'[31] Finally their envy, which could endure none of the graciousness of their dutiful and submissive sibling, sought his death and could hardly be satisfied with the crime of selling their brother.

"It is clear, then, that envy is more ruinous and more difficult to purge away than all the other vices, because it is inflamed by the very remedies by which the others are extinguished. For example, a person who laments a loss inflicted on him is cured by a generous recompense, and a person who is angered by having been subjected to mistreatment is placated by humble reparation. 12. What would you do in the case of a person who is offended by the very fact that he sees that you are humbler and kinder; whom neither avarice, which is pacified by money, nor hurtful mistreatment nor love of revenge, which is overcome by flattering attentions, arouse to wrath; but whom only the success of someone else's happiness irritates? Who is there, however, who, in order to satisfy someone envious of him, would wish to fall from his good fortune or suffer losses or be entangled in some disaster? Therefore, lest the basilisk destroy completely, with one bite of this great evil, whatever in us is alive and animated as it were by the vital quickening of the Holy Spirit, let us constantly implore the divine assistance, for which nothing is impossible. 13. For the other poisons of serpents—that is, carnal sins and vices, from which human frailty is as easily purged as it is quickly entangled in them—leave the marks of their wounds in the flesh. Although the earthly body swells up with them in ruinous fashion, nonetheless if some very skillful charmer, singing divine songs, applies an antidote or a remedy of saving words, the ruinous poison will not bring about the everlasting death of the soul. But the poison of envy, poured out as it were by the serpent basilisk, cuts off the very life of religion and faith before a wound is felt in the body. 14. For the blasphemer clearly raises himself up against God and not against a human being. He carps at nothing in his brother but his happiness, finding fault not with a human being's guilt but only with God's judgments.

"This, then, is 'the root of bitterness, springing up,'[32] which raises itself to the heights and tends to the abuse of the Creator himself, who bestows good things on human beings. Nor should it disturb anyone that God would threaten to send serpents, basilisks, to bite those by whose crimes he is offended. For although it is certain that God cannot be the author of envy, yet it is fitting and worthy of the divine judgment that, inasmuch as good gifts are bestowed on the humble and refused to the proud and reprobate, he should strike and consume with an envy that has been, so to speak, sent by him, those who, according to the Apostle, deserve to be given over 'to a reprobate mind.'[33] As it is written: 'They have provoked me to jealousy with those who are not gods, and I will make them jealous with those who are not a people.'"[34]

15. With this discussion the blessed Piamun inflamed more ardently our desire, whereby we had begun to be drawn away from the first training ground of the cenobium to the next step, that of the anchorite's life. For, thanks to his instruction in the first place, we took up the rudiments of solitary living, the knowledge of which we pursued more fully afterward in Skete.

Textual References

1. Cf. Mt 5:14.
2. Acts 4:32.
3. Acts 2:45.
4. Acts 4:34–35.
5. Acts 15:29.
6. Heb 11:37–38.
7. Jb 39:5–8 LXX.
8. Ps 107:2.
9. Ps 107:4–6.
10. Lam 3:27–28.
11. Ps 102:6–7.
12. Cf. Acts 5:1–11.
13. Cf. Mt 6:25.
14. Cf. 2 Thes 3:8; Acts 20:34.
15. Prv 18:17 LXX.
16. Prv 16:32 LXX.
17. Prv 14:29 LXX.
18. Cf. Mt 7:24–27.
19. Jas 1:12.
20. Cf. 2 Cor 12:9.
21. Jer 1:18–19.
22. Cf. Gn 37:11.
23. Lk 17:21.
24. Mt 10:36.
25. Cf. Mt 3:12.
26. Cf. Acts 6:5; Rv 2:15.
27. Jer 8:17.
28. Wis 2:24.
29. Sir 10:11 LXX.
30. Prv 27:4 LXX.
31. Gn 37:4 LXX.
32. Heb 12:15.
33. Rom 1:28.
34. Dt 32:21 LXX.

18.1.1 On Eucherius cf. the note at 2 praef. 1.

18.1.2 On the marine image here cf. the note at 1 praef. 3f.

Mountains are symbols of spiritual persons in Augustine, *Enarr. in Ps.* 39.6; cf. also ibid. 124.4ff.

18.1.3 On Cassian's refusal to speak of Piamun's miracles cf. pp. 533–34. The mere allusion, however, to the fact that Piamun accomplished much more than will be narrated of him is at least partly intended to attract the reader's attention. Cf. Athanasius, *V. S. Antonii,* prooem.; Sulpicius Severus, *V. S. Martini* 1.

18.2.1 The reference to acquiring a skill somewhat recalls 1.2 and 14.1.2f.

18.2.2ff. For other demeaning references to Syrian monasticism cf. the note at 3.22.4.

18.5 The theme of the decline from an original ideal (whether in the Church at large or in monastic life in particular) is a recurrent one in Cassian. Cf. 7.23, 19.5.2, 19.6.2, 21.30; *Inst.* 2.5. For its appearance elsewhere in monastic literature cf. Jerome, *V. Malchi* 1; *Apophthegmata patrum,* de abbate Elia 8; ibid., de abbate Poemene 166; *Verba seniorum* 10.105, 10.114, 17.19; Benedict, *Reg.* 18.25, 40.6; John Moschus, *Pratum spirituale* 54, 130, 162, 168. The notion of decadence can be found in the Bible, perhaps most notably in Gn 6:1ff., 1 Kgs 11ff., Is 1ff., and in Greek literature as early as Plato, *Rep.* 8.1ff.

18.5.4 Monks or μοναζοντες: *Monachi sive* μοναζοντες. For recent studies on the origin and use of the term *monachus,* which is merely a Latinization of the Greek μοναχος, cf. Antoine Guillaumont, "Monachisme et éthique judéo-chrétienne," in *Judéo-christianisme: Recherches historiques et théologiques offertes en hommage au Cardinal Jean Daniélou* (Paris, 1972), 199–218; Françoise-E. Morand, "Monachos, Moine: Histoire du terme grec jusqu'au 4e siècle," in *Freiburger Zeitschrift für Philosophie und Theologie* 20 (1973): 332–411; E. A.

Judge, "The Earliest Use of Monachos for 'Monk' (P. Coll. Youtie 77) and the Origins of Monasticism," in JAC 20 (1977): 72–89. The first article links the word in particular with μοναζοντες, with its resonances of celibacy and, more broadly, of living a unified life; the second suggests a previous gnostic use of the word that was eventually forgotten by the fourth century, when it was popularized especially by Athanasius; the third explains the word as designating a person with a particular social status, whatever the remote origins of *monachos* may have been. Μοναζοντες means "those who live apart," and Cassian, like *Itinerarium Egeriae* 24, identifies this term with *monachi,* which was quite reasonable by his time.

Coenobiota (cenobite) and *coenobium* (cenobium) are simply Latinizations of Greek words, which are to be understood as Cassian understands them.

The Paul mentioned here is the subject of Jerome's *V. S. Pauli,* who was at least partly an invention of the author; but he cannot be dismissed as utterly fictional. Cf. *Lexikon für Theologie und Kirche* 8 (1963): 214.

This Antony is the subject of Athanasius's *V. S. Antonii.*

18.6.1 The detail that Cassian records concerning Paul's flight out of need is also found in Jerome, *V. S. Pauli* 4f. Cf. likewise 3.4.4.ff.

18.6.2 *Anachoreta* (anchorite) is a Latinization of the Greek equivalent, to be understood in Cassian's sense. For a study of the pagan and early Christian use of αναχωρειν, the verb form, cf. André-Jean Festugière, *Personal Religion among the Greeks* (Berkeley/Los Angeles, 1954), 53–67. Festugière rejects the idea that the Christian use of the term is in any way, apart from pure chance, related to one of its Egyptian uses—namely, as indicating flight from taxation. For a further precision cf. Julien Leroy, "Les préfaces des écrits monastiques de Jean Cassien," in RAM 42 (1966): 179–180 and n. 94.

John the Baptist, like Elijah and Elisha (cf. 14.4.1 and the relevant note), is an occasionally cited model of the anchorite life. Cf. *V. prima gr. Pachomii* 2; *Apophthegmata patrum,* de abbate Ioanne Persa 4.

Heb 11:37–38 reappears in almost the same context in 21.4.2; here, though, it more explicitly refers to monks. For a similar application of these verses to monks cf. *Inst.* 1.7; *V. prima gr. Pachomii* 1; Cyril of Scythopolis, *V. S. Euthymii* 1.

18.7.2 Sarabaites: Cassian is the earliest source in Christian literature for the use of this word.

18.7.6 Monks' almsgiving, the result of their hard labors, is also mentioned in *Inst.* 10.22. Cf. Augustine, *De mor. cath. eccl.* 31.67.

18.7.7 That the monastic life is a form of martyrdom is a frequent theme in desert literature, starting with Athanasius, *V. S. Antonii* 47. Cf. Edward E. Malone, *The Monk and the Martyr: The Monk as the Successor of the Martyr* (SCA 12) (1950).

18.7.8 These two kinds of monks: Namely, cenobites and sarabaites.

Lucius was the Arian bishop of Alexandria from 373 to 378.

Arianism, named after an Alexandrian priest (cf. the note at 7.32.3), was a heretical doctrine that asserted the inferiority of the Son to the Father. It convulsed the Church in the eastern part of the Empire in particular for much of the fourth century.

Valens was emperor in the eastern half of the Empire from 364 to 378. He was an Arian sympathizer.

Assistance: *Diaconiam.* The word is taken to mean charitable assistance by way of almsgiving also in 21.1.2, 21.8.1, and 21.9.7. In its Greek original it appears as such in 2 Cor 9:1 and 12f. For precisions cf. Thomas Sternberg, "Der vermeintliche Ursprung der westlichen Diakonien in Ägypten und die Conlationes des Johannes Cassian," JAC 31 (1988): 173–209, esp.

208, where the author summarizes: Cassian "indicated with this word taken from the Greek...a very specific institution of Egyptian monasticism–a comprehensive stewardship of property that included care of the poor, such as he had come to know it during his stay in Egypt and which, in all its breadth of meaning, could not be paraphrased by any Latin word."

Pontus was a region adjoining the south-east shore of the Black Sea, largely located in present-day Turkey. Armenia was to the south and east of Pontus.

18.8.2 That the solitary is inaccessible to correction is one of the arguments made against the solitary life in Basil, *Reg. fus. tract.* 7.

18.10 The term "monastery" as applying to the dwelling of a single monk is used in 2.13.6 (?), 8.18.2, 11.4.1, 24.9.2; *Inst.* 10.6 (?); Athanasius, *V. S. Antonii* 39.

18.11.1 School: *Palaestra.* Although the word means school, it also has athletic connotations and can be translated as "wrestling-ground." Cf. the note at 7.20.

18.11.2 To say the prayer: *Ut orationem colligeret.* Reference seems to be made here to the prayer that was customarily said after each psalm at the synaxis. Cf. *Inst.* 2.7.3.

On the mat used for sitting cf. the note at 1.23.4. Jerome, *Ep.* 22.27, adverts to the spiritual pride that can lurk in choosing the lowest seat for oneself.

18.11.12 This Serapion is probably the abba around whom the fifth conference is built. Cf. p. 177.

18.13.1 On the idea, expressed here and in 18.13.4f., that it is better to be engaged in struggle than to be free of trials, cf. the note at 2.13.9f.

18.13.2 Patience takes its name from suffering and endurance: *A passionibus enim ac sustentatione patientiam dici.*

18.14 The story that is told here (which is repeated with a few variations in John Moschus, *Pratum spirituale* 206) is based on the fact, among others, that poor widows were supported by the Church, as was the case since apostolic times. Cf. 1 Tm 5:9–16. The difficulty in dealing with widows, hinted at by Cassian in 18.14.3, is plain in 1 Tm 5:13 and in Chrysostom, *De sacerd.* 3.12. The latter observes in particular that unwished-for poverty has an embittering quality that leads to recriminations and ingratitude. Cassian's comment in 18.14.4. that the widow in question "was very easily found" implies that her problematic personality was not at all unusual.

18.14.1 Athanasius was bishop of Alexandria from 328 to 373 and author of numerous tracts against the Arians as well as of the *V. S. Antonii.*

18.14.5 On the athletic imagery used here cf. the note at 7.20.

18.15 On the similarity and dissimilarity of the story narrated here vis-à-vis an apophthegm recorded by Paul Euergetinos, cf. Weber 87–88. There is a somewhat similar story in John Moschus, *Pratum spirituale* 116.

18.15.1 Paphnutius is the leader of the third conference, where he is also referred to as "the Buffalo."

18.15.2 Paphnutius's great maturity, despite his youth, is noted again in 18.15.8. Uncommon maturity in youth is a typical characteristic of sanctity. Cf. Athanasius, *V. S. Antonii* 1; Prudentius, *Peristeph.* 3.19ff.; Ambrose, *De virginibus* 1.2.5ff.; Sulpicius Severus, *V. S. Martini* 2.

Paphnutius's beauty, spoken of here, is of course spiritual. For a lengthy commentary on true beauty and its acquisition cf. Gregory of Nyssa, *De virg.* 11f.

18.15.3 It is uncertain whether this Isidore is to be identified with another priest of the same name who was involved in the rivalry between John Chrysostom and Theophilus of Alexandria. Cf. Palladius, *Dial.* 6; Socrates, *Hist. eccl.* 6.9; Sozomen, *Hist. eccl.* 8.2.

18.15.4 The emphasis on the utterly unheard-of nature of Paphnutius's "crime" is almost certainly intended as a kind of roundabout compliment with respect to the secure and well-ordered life of the desert.

On *sirae* cf. Gazet's commentary in PL 49.1116.

18.15.6 On going to church on Saturday and Sunday cf. the note at 3.1.1.

18.16.2 The airy foe: Cf. the note at 8.12.1.

18.16.6 Among ancient authors Irenaeus, *Adv. haer.* 1.23.3 and 3.11.1, identifies the Nicolaus of Acts 6:5 and the unnamed founder of the Nicolaitans of Rv 2:5. Clement of Alexandria, *Strom.* 2.20.118 and 3.4.25f. (cited ap. Eusebius, *Hist. eccl.* 3.29.2ff.), however, implies that there is no connection between the two.

NINETEENTH CONFERENCE
THE CONFERENCE OF ABBA JOHN: THE END OF THE CENOBITE AND OF THE HERMIT

TRANSLATOR'S INTRODUCTION

The nineteenth conference follows neatly on the eighteenth. The first of the two had begun to discuss the difference between the cenobitic and anchoritic professions, and the present one continues that discussion in a somewhat more systematic fashion. But it opens with the account of an incident that Cassian and Germanus witnessed while attending an anniversary service at a cenobium under the direction of a certain Abba Paul. The reason for the placement of this brief narrative, which offers the reader an example of astonishing patience, is somewhat unclear. Perhaps Cassian is resuming one of the major themes of the second half of the previous conference—namely, that of patience—or anticipating that same theme as it will appear toward the end of the present conference. In any event, the incident in question suggests to Cassian an unfavorable comparison with the examples of patience that he had seen in his own monastery in Syria.

Of the identity of the Abba John who speaks to the two friends in this conference we cannot be sure. There is a John, disciple of Paul, who figures in the *Apophthegmata patrum*. But, despite the fact that Cassian's John lived in Paul's cenobium and that the Pauls of both the *Apophthegmata* and *The Conferences* had a penchant for hitting people (the former strikes John a blow in order to humiliate him, just as the latter gives an unknown monk a resounding slap), it is likely that the John and Paul of the

Apophthegmata were solitaries and hence not the same as Cassian's two cenobites.

The dialogue begins when Cassian and Germanus question why John, who had lived as a solitary for twenty years, would have left that life for the cenobitic. John's immediate answer is to praise the anchoritic profession while briefly alluding to some of its dangers. After mentioning the ecstasies into which he would habitually fall when dwelling alone, which he does in order to leave his hearers in no doubt as to the grandeur of which the anchoritic life is capable, he proceeds to measure it against the cenobitic life. If the former is marked by the possibilities of rapture and ardent prayer, the latter is ideally characterized by an evangelical disregard for the morrow (cf. Mt 6:34) and by submission to the elders. On the negative side anchorites are tempted to pride, vainglory, and arrogance, and they run the risk of being preoccupied by food and possessions. More than that, they are besieged by visitors, and they must make visits in return. If the negative aspect of cenobitism is a certain diminution of that purity of heart whose importance was stressed at the very start of *The Conferences,* this is amply compensated, at least in John's opinion, by the observance of the gospel precept to give no thought to the morrow.

Since John is proficient in both the anchoritic and the cenobitic professions, Germanus is moved to ask him what their respective ends are. Perfection in both lives, John replies, is a rare thing. Then, in more direct response to the question, he states clearly: "The end of the cenobite is to put to death and to crucify all his desires and, in accordance with the gospel precept, to have no thought for the next day....But the perfection of the hermit is to have a mind bare of all earthly things and, as much as human frailty permits, to unite it thus with Christ" (19.8.3f.). Returning to a matter that he had raised a few moments previously, however, John observes that the most complete perfection lies in the practice of the virtues of both professions. With this he gives examples of solitaries whose hospitality was such that one would not know whether they were inclined more to the common or to the eremitical life.

John's remark that some solitaries cannot bear the interruptions of their brother monks or have even left the cenobitic life out of disgust for community causes Germanus to ask whether he and Cassian are ready for an eremitical existence, inasmuch as they left their cenobitic training rather abruptly. The old man's answer is not necessarily encouraging: Those who go into the desert with insufficient maturity will discover that their sinful tendencies may not show themselves exteriorly but that they still disturb their minds. Germanus acknowledges the truth of this and requests John's advice as to a remedy. The remedy, he is told, is to drive out a given vice by replacing it with the opposing virtue. This will mean both imagining difficult and unpleasant situations in which to exercise certain virtues and pursuing such practices as fasting and watching. The result will be the destruction of those vices that should have already been rooted out in the cenobium; anger, in particular, will yield to patience.

But, Germanus wants to know, can the spirit of fornication be handled in the same way? Is it right to imagine lustful situations in order to exercise one's chastity? John responds in the negative: The slightest lustful thought is dangerous and must not be pursued. Nonetheless those who are perfectly chaste may occasionally test their chastity by vivid imaginings. On this note, which recalls 15.10.3, the present conference concludes.

Although Cassian manifests an increasing sympathy for the cenobitic life in this conference and goes so far as to say that cenobitic virtues are necessary complements to anchoritic ones, the anchoritic life is still clearly the ideal and the next step after cenobitism. So true is this that the four monks who are offered in 19.9.1f. as examples of the successful combining of both cenobitic and anchoritic virtues are in fact themselves anchorites. John's own passage from solitude to community is an act of humility on his part and represents an option for what could be called the "safer" way. It is noteworthy, finally, that the definition of the end of the cenobite in 19.8.3, cited above, does not include any mention of the cenobite's community, however implicit, even though it is clear from later passages, especially 19.16.1f., that the community—"human society"—has no small role to play in a monk's development. There is, indeed, nothing essential to prevent the definition of the cenobite, as it stands, from forming part of the definition of the hermit.

XIX. The Conference of Abba John: The End of the Cenobite and of the Hermit

Chapters

I. On the cenobium of Abba Paul and the patience of a certain brother.
II. The humility of Abba John, and our question.
III. The reply of Abba John as to why he left the desert.
IV. On the virtue of the aforesaid old man, which he practiced in the anchorite life.
V. The benefits of the desert.
VI. The advantage of the cenobium.
VII. A question about the cenobium and about the fruit of the desert.
VIII. The reply to the question that was asked.
IX. On complete and true perfection.
X. On the imperfect who seek out the desert.
XI. A question about the remedy for those who have quickly abandoned the community of their cenobium.
XII. The reply: how the solitary can recognize his vices.
XIII. A question about how one who has entered the desert without having cleansed himself of his vices can be healed.
XIV. The reply, on their cure.
XV. A question as to whether chastity should be examined like the other passions.
XVI. The reply: By what proofs it can be recognized.

I.1. After a very few days we were drawn by the desire for further instruction, and we returned in great haste to the cenobium of Abba Paul. Although more than two hundred brothers were living there, nonetheless an immense throng of monks from other cenobia as well had come together for the sake of the rite which was taking place then, for the anniversary of the death of a former abba who had been in charge of this same cenobium was being observed. We have mentioned this gathering in order to indicate briefly a certain brother's patience, which because of its unwavering gentleness shone out before that entire congregation. 2. For although this work is concerned with something else—namely, with our citing the words of Abba John, who left the desert and with the most virtuous humility submitted himself to this cenobium—we still do not think it at all out of place if, as we believe, those who are eager for great virtue may be edified without much wordiness. As the multitude of monks, then, was sitting in a large open court in separate circles of twelve, and one of the brothers was a little late in bringing around the serving dish that he had received, the aforesaid Abba Paul, who was running about anxiously among the crowds of brothers who were waiting on table, saw this and gave him such a slap with his outstretched hand in the sight of all that the sound of his striking palm even echoed in the ears of those who had their backs turned or who were sitting at a distance. 3. But the young man was remarkable for his patience and received this with such a gentle mind that not only did no word fall from his mouth or the slightest murmur move silently on his lips, but even the very modesty and peaceableness of his mouth and his color were not in the least changed. This fact was noteworthy not only to us who had recently come from our monastery in Syria and had never seen the virtue of patience so clearly exemplified but also to all those who were not bereft of a corresponding zeal. As a result a valuable lesson was given even to the most advanced men, because even a paternal correction had not shaken his patience, nor had such a multitude of onlookers caused his face so much as to blush.

II.1. In this cenobium, then, we found an old man of great age named John, whose words as well as whose humility, in which he surpassed all the other holy ones, we thought should not be passed over in silence. We know that he was especially proficient in this perfection which, although it is the mother of all the virtues and the most solid foundation of the entire spiritual structure, is completely absent from our own institutes. 2. Hence it is no wonder that we cannot mount to the heights of these men—we who are barely content to endure the yoke of submission for two years and immediately flee to the arrogance of a harmful freedom, never mind being able to remain under the discipline of the cenobium until old age. Yet even for such a short while as that we seem to be subject to the governance of an elder not according to a strict rule but with an eye out for our own freedom of will.

3. When we had seen this old man in the cenobium of the aforesaid Abba Paul, then, we first wondered at the man's age and the grace with which he had been endowed. Then, with eyes cast down, we began to beseech him to deign to explain to us why he had left the freedom of the desert and that sublime profession, wherein a very celebrated reputation had given him precedence over others leading the same life, and chosen to place himself under the yoke of the cenobium. 4. He said that, being unequal to the anchorite discipline and unworthy of such heights of perfection, he had returned to the school for juniors in order to see if he could still carry out the institutes that were in keeping with the level of their profession. When our opposition, couched in petition, refused to accept this humble response, he finally began as follows:

III.1. "I not only do not reject and deny the anchorite discipline, which you are amazed to see that I have abandoned, but, on the contrary, I embrace and esteem it with utter veneration. I am glad that, after having lived thirty years in a cenobium, I passed another twenty in it. Thus I should never, like those who pursued it lukewarmly, be blamed for laziness. 2. But because the purity that I experienced there was occasionally soiled by a concern for carnal matters, it seemed more appropriate to return to the cenobium so that the readier perfection of an easier chosen orientation—the one that I took up—might be acquired and there might be less danger from the humility of a more sublime profession that had been presumed upon. For it is better to be found faithful in keeping little promises than careless in keeping great ones.

"Therefore, if I mention something rather proudly and perhaps even rather freely, I ask that you consider it to be motivated not by the vice of boastfulness but by a concern for your edification. And because I think that no part of the truth should be withheld from you who are so eagerly seeking it, you should reckon it to the account of love rather than of boastfulness. 3. For I am of the opinion that some instruction can be given you if I lay humility aside for a short while and tell you in direct fashion the whole truth about my chosen orientation. I am confident that I shall not get a reputation for vainglory with you because of the candor of my words, nor shall I bring upon my own conscience the crime of lying, as it were, for having suppressed the truth.

IV.1. "Whoever else may have delighted in the remoteness of the desert, may have forgotten human companionship and been able to say in the words of Jeremiah: 'You know that I have not desired the day of man,'[1] I confess that I too, thanks to the grace that the Lord bestowed, have pursued this or at least have made an effort to pursue it. I recall that, as a result of our Lord's kind gift, I was frequently seized by such an ecstasy that I forgot that I was clothed in the burden of bodily frailty, and my mind abruptly rejected all external contacts and was completely absent from every material concern, such that neither my eyes nor my ears exercised their proper function. My mind was so filled with divine meditation and spiritual theoria that I often did not know whether I had taken my evening meal, and the next day I would have no idea as to whether I had broken my fast the day before. 2. For this reason seven days' worth of food—that is, seven pairs of biscuits—was set aside in a *prochirium*, or handbasket, on Saturday, so that the meal which had been omitted would not escape my notice. In this way another problem with forgetfulness was eliminated, for when the course of a week was up the number of loaves that were consumed indicated that the solemn day had returned again, and the celebration of the sacred day and the solemn gathering of the solitaries could not escape my notice. But even if the ecstasy of mind that we have spoken about would perchance disturb this arrangement, still the schedule of daily work would indicate the number of days and prevent a mistake.

3. "Passing over in silence the other virtues of the desert, for our concern is not with their number and multitude but with the end of the desert and of the cenobium, I shall instead explain briefly why I chose to leave the former, which you also wanted to know, and I shall compress into a few words all the fruits of the solitary life that I have mentioned, showing that they are inferior to more sublime advantages on the other side.

V.1. "Time was when those who dwelled in the desert were rare and a greater freedom embraced us by reason of the more expansive vastness of the desert, when we lived in more remote and larger solitudes and were frequently seized by heavenly ecstasies, and such a multitude of visiting brothers rushing in upon us, with the obligation to be hospitable, did not weigh down our thoughts with the distractions of enormous concerns. It was then that I sought out with an insatiable desire and with all the ardor of my mind the utterly tranquil recesses of the desert and that way of life which must be compared to angelic blessedness. 2. But when, as I have said, a greater number of brothers began to long to dwell in that desert and, having cramped the freedom of the vast desert, not only caused the fire of divine contemplation to chill but even tied down my mind in many ways with the fetters of carnal matters, I chose to pursue the orientation of this discipline as best I could rather than grow sluggish in that profession, which is so sublime, by having to provide for the needs of the flesh. Thus, even though that freedom and those spiritual ecstasies might be denied me, nonetheless, once care for the next day had been completely cast aside, the carrying out of the gospel precept would comfort me,[2] and what I would lose in the heights of theoria would be made up for by an obedient submission. For it is a wretched thing for a person to profess the knowledge of some art or profession and not to achieve perfection in it.

VI.1. "Therefore I shall briefly explain how many advantages I enjoy now in this way of life. It is up to you to judge, after I have spoken my piece, whether the gains of the desert can be compensated for by these benefits. From this it will also be possible to see whether I chose to be constrained by the restrictions of the cenobium out of disgust for that solitary purity or out of desire for it.

"In this way of life, then, there is no providing for daily work, no distractions concerning buying or selling, no inescapable worries about the year's supply of food, no concern about the bodily matters that are involved in attending to the needs not only of ourselves but also of our many visitors, and finally none of the arrogance that comes from human praise, which is more unclean than anything else in the sight of God, and which sometimes brings to naught even the great labors of the desert.

2. "But, passing over the waves of spiritual pride and the dangers of a fatal vainglory that are found in the anchorite discipline, let us turn to the burden that affects everyone–that is, to the common concern of preparing food. This has thus far not only ignored the limits established by a former strictness that did not know the use of oil at all, but it has even begun to be dissatisfied with the relaxation of our own time, in keeping with which a sixth of a measure of oil and a modius of lentils are readied for the use of visitors and are sufficient for the needs of eating the whole year through. The upshot is that nowadays the requirements for food can barely be met by a double or triple amount. 3. To such an extent has this harmful relaxation increased among some persons that, when they mix vinegar and salt water, they do not add the single drop of oil which our predecessors, who followed the institutes of the desert with more of the virtue of abstinence, were accustomed to put in merely for the sake of avoiding vainglory. Rather, they break an Egyptian cheese for their enjoyment and pour more oil on it than is necessary, and so they make one pleasant flavor out of two foods that have distinctive tastes, each of which could serve very nicely to feed a monk at different times. 4. To such an extent, indeed, has this υλικη κτησιs–that is, the possession of material things–increased that anchorites have even begun to keep a blanket in their cells under the guise of hospitality and a welcoming spirit, which is something that I cannot speak of without shame.

"I am passing over those things with which the soul that is seized by and always intent upon spiritual theoria is more particularly hampered–namely, the visits of the brothers, the duties of welcoming them and bidding them farewell, the returning of visits and the interminable worry that comes from different conversations and occupations, the very expectation of which strains the mind even when these things no longer seem to be nuisances, since this constant and habitual distraction keeps it tense. 5. Thus the freedom of the anchorite, when it is tied down in this way, never at all mounts to that unspeakable joy of heart, and it loses the fruit of the hermit's profession. If this is denied to me now that I am in a community and surrounded by multitudes, at least I do not lack a peace of soul and a tranquillity of heart free from every preoccupation. Unless these things are also present to those who dwell in the desert, they will indeed endure the labors of the anchorite life, but they will be deprived of its fruit, which is only gathered by a mind that is peaceful and stable.

6. "Finally, even if I should suffer some loss of purity of heart while I am in the cenobium, I shall happily be compensated by the gospel precept alone, which certainly cannot be subordinated to any of the other fruits of the desert, so that I need have no thought for the next day. And, subject to an abba until death, I shall seem to a certain degree to imitate him of whom it is said: 'He humbled himself, having become obedient until death.'[3] And I shall deserve to say humbly in his own words: 'I have not come to do my own will but the will of him who sent me, the Father.'"[4]

VII. GERMANUS: "Since it is clear that you have not, like so many people, been merely a beginner in both professions but have scaled their very heights, we want to know what the end of the cenobite is and what the end of the hermit is. For there is no doubt that nobody can discuss this more confidently and more fully than the person who has pursued both perfections over a long period, with experience as his teacher. He can make known their value and end by a trustworthy teaching."

VIII.1. JOHN: "I would be able to say in unqualified fashion that one and the same person could not be perfect in both professions did not the example of a very few prevent me. Since it is a great thing to find someone who is accomplished in one of them, it is obvious that it is all the more difficult—and I would almost say impossible—for a person to be fully perfect in both. Yet if this happens sometimes, it cannot all at once be generalized about. 2. For a universal rule should not be made based upon a small minority—that is, with reference to a few people—but upon what is available to the many, and indeed to everyone. But the things that are attained to very rarely and by very few people, that go beyond the possibilities of ordinary virtue and that are conceded to be as it were above the condition of human weakness and above nature, should not be mentioned along with general precepts, and they should be put forward not as examples but as marvels. Hence I shall speak briefly of what you are asking about, as much as my mediocre intelligence permits.

3. "The end of the cenobite is to put to death and to crucify all his desires and, in accordance with the saving command of gospel perfection, to have no thought for the next day. It is very certain that this perfection cannot be arrived at by anyone but a cenobite. The prophet Isaiah describes this man and blesses and praises him as follows: 'If you turn away your foot from the sabbath, from doing your own will on my holy day, and if you glorify him while not following your own ways, and if your own will to speak a word is not found, then you shall delight over the Lord, and I will lift you up above the heights of the earth, and I will feed you with the inheritance of Jacob your father. For the mouth of the Lord has spoken.'[5]

4. "But the perfection of the hermit is to have a mind bare of all earthly things and, as much as human frailty permits, to unite it thus with Christ. The prophet Jeremiah describes this man and says: 'Blessed is the man who has borne the yoke from his youth. He shall sit solitary and be still, because he has taken it upon himself.'[6] The psalmist also: 'I have become like a pelican in the desert. I watched, and I became like a sparrow alone on the roof.'[7]

"Unless each of them arrives at the end, therefore, which we have said belongs to his own profession, in vain does the one pursue the discipline of the cenobium and the other that of the anchorite life, for neither has practiced the virtue of his own profession.

IX.1. "But this μερικη—that is, a perfection that is not integral and complete in all respects—is only a part of perfection. Perfection is rare, then, and is conceded to very few by God's gift. For a person is truly and not partially perfect when he endures both the bleakness of solitude in the desert and the weakness of his brothers in the cenobium with equal greatness of soul. Consequently it is difficult to find someone who is completely accomplished in both professions because the anchorite cannot wholly attain to ακτημοσυνη—that is, to the contempt and privation of material things—nor can the cenobite wholly attain to the purity of theoria.

"Nonetheless we know that Abba Moses and Abba Paphnutius and the two Macarii possessed both perfectly, 2. and thus they were perfect in both professions. They went off further than all the other dwellers of the desert and were nourished insatiably in the recesses of the desert. Never, as much as in them lay, did they seek human companionship. Yet they so put up with the throng of those who sought them out and with their weaknesses that, although an innumerable multitude of brothers came to see them for the sake of their own profit, they endured with a steady patience the almost constant annoyance of welcoming them, and they gave the impression of having taught and practiced nothing else their whole life through than the showing of kindness to visitors, such that no one was sure which profession of theirs they gave more of an effort to—that is, whether their greatness of soul was more wonderfully fit for eremetical purity or for the communal way of life.

X.1. "But some people become so savage due to the unbroken silence of the desert that they are utterly distraught at the society of human beings, and when they depart even a little from the habits of their reclusion because of the visit of some brothers they are shaken by a remarkable mental anguish and by manifest indications of faintheartedness. This is usually the case in particular with those who have not been instructed perfectly in the cenobia and have not purified themselves of their former vices, but have betaken themselves to the solitary life out of an immature desire. These people, always imperfect and weak in any event, are moved wherever the wind of disturbance blows. 2. Just as they are shaken with impatience at the society of the brothers or at an interruption from them, so also when they are living in the desert they cannot bear the vastness of that very silence that they have sought out, for in fact they do not even know the reason why the desert should be desired or sought out. Rather, they consider this alone to be virtuous and the height of their profession–that they reject the society of the brothers and flee from and detest the sight of human beings."

XI.1. GERMANUS: "What remedy, then, will be able to be of service to us or to others who have the same weakness and the same limitations–we who have barely been instructed in cenobitic discipline and, before having rid ourselves of all our vices, have begun to take up living in the desert? Or how shall we be able to acquire a constant and undistracted mind and an unchanging and firm patience–we who have given up the community of the cenobium at an inopportune moment and have abandoned as it were the school and training ground of this practice, in which our beginnings ought to have been fully developed and perfected? 2. How, then, now that we are living in solitude, shall we pursue the perfection of long-suffering and patience? Or how will our conscience, which searches into interior movements, understand the virtues that it has and those that are lacking to it, when we may be deceived in our judgment and believe that we possess a firmly tranquil mind, since we are not aroused by annoyances from people when we are removed from their society?"

XII.1. JOHN: "In truth, curative remedies cannot be lacking to those who look for healing from that most true Physician of souls. This is especially the case with respect to those who do not disregard their ill health out of despair or negligence, or hide their dangerous wounds, or reject the medication of repentance with an impudent mind, but, once having gotten sick through ignorance or error or necessity, have recourse with humble yet cautious mind to the heavenly Physician. Consequently we should know that, if we go off to the desert or to remote places with our vices not yet attended to, only their effects will be repressed, but the dispositions to them will not be extinguished.

2. "For there lies concealed within us–indeed, there creeps about within us–the unplucked root of all our sins, which we see is still alive in us from the following indications. For example, when we live in the desert and react to the arrival of the brothers or a very brief delay of theirs with an anxious and upset mind, then we know that the stuff of impatience is still very much alive in us. But when we are looking forward to the arrival of a brother

and he has perchance been delayed a short while out of some necessity, if even an unspoken mental anger blames him for his delay and if concern over our protracted waiting disturbs our mind, then an examination of our conscience will show that the vices of anger and annoyance manifestly remain in us. 3. Again, if a brother asks for a book to read or some other thing to use and either his request annoys us or our refusal puts him off, then there is no doubt that we are still held bound in the snares of avarice and the love of money. If either a sudden thought or a passage of Holy Scripture conjures up the memory of a woman for us and we feel ourselves somewhat titillated by it, then we should know that the ardor of fornication is not yet extinct in our members. And if our mind is even only very slightly tempted to be lifted up at the comparison of our own strictness and someone else's laxity, then it is certain that we have been corrupted by the foul plague of pride.

4. "When, therefore, we perceive the indications of these vices in our heart, we should recognize clearly that it is not the disposition to sin but its effect that is lacking in us. Indeed, if we sometimes get ourselves involved in a human way of life, these passions immediately emerge from the caverns of our thoughts and demonstrate that they were not born when first they erupted but rather that they appeared then precisely because they had lain hidden for a long time. Thus even the solitary, who strives not to show his purity to human beings but to manifest it inviolate before him from whom no secrets of the heart can be hidden, perceives from telltale indications whether the roots of each vice are implanted in him."

XIII.1. GERMANUS: "We have followed quite well and easily the proofs by which the indications of our weaknesses are made clear and also the method of discerning our illnesses–that is, how the vices that lie hidden in us can be perceived. For, as a result of our everyday experience and of the daily movement of our thoughts, we see that all of this is precisely as has been stated. What remains, then, is that just as the proofs and causes of our maladies have been shown us with the utmost clarity, so also the medicine for curing them be pointed out. For no one doubts that the person who first perceived the causes and origins of these evil diseases, with the awareness of the sick as his attestation, is in the best position to be able to discuss their remedy.

2. "And so the teaching of your blessedness has laid bare our secret wounds, with the result that now we dare to hope for some remedy, because such an open manifestation of the malady promises the hope of a remedy. Yet still, because, as you say, the first beginning of salvation is acquired in communities and people cannot be sound in the desert unless the medicine of the cenobia has first made them sound, we are caught again in a terrible desperation, lest perchance we who left the cenobium imperfect should never now be able to be perfect in the desert."

XIV.1. JOHN: "For those who are concerned about a cure for their maladies a salutary remedy cannot be lacking. Therefore, the remedies should be sought out in the same way as the indications of each vice are perceived. Just as we said that the vices of a human way of life are not lacking to solitaries, so neither do we deny that zeal for virtue and the means of health are available to all who are cut off from a human way of life.

2. "When, therefore, thanks to the indications that we cited previously, someone perceives that he is being troubled by the disturbances of impatience or anger, he should always exercise himself by applying their opposites. Placing before himself various kinds of misfortunes and setbacks, as if they had been brought on him by someone else, he should accustom his mind to submit with perfect humility to everything that wickedness can inflict, and, frequently imagining certain difficulties and intolerable situations, he should meditate constantly and with an utterly contrite heart on what great gentleness he should face these things with. Thus, with an eye to the sufferings of all the holy ones and of the Lord himself, and admitting that every dishonor and even punishment is less than he deserves, he will prepare himself to bear every sorrow.

3. "And occasionally he will be invited to gatherings of the brothers, which must happen, if only rarely, even to the strictest inhabitants of the desert. If he perceives then that his mind is silently disturbed even by some insignificant things, he should at once, like a kind of severe censor of his own hidden emotions, blame himself for those hard sorts of offenses, whereby he used to bring himself to perfect endurance by his daily meditations, and

reproaching and reprimanding himself he should say: Are you not the one, my good man, who presumed so very tenaciously that you could overcome every evil while you were exercising on the training ground of your solitude? Was it not you who recently believed that you were strong and unyielding enough in the face of every tempest, when you pictured for yourself not only the most bitter dishonors but even unbearable punishments? 4. How did that unvanquished patience of yours get upset as soon as the most trivial word was said? How has a light breeze shaken your house, which seemed to you to be built so massively on the most solid rock?[8] Where is what you used to cry out with foolish confidence, desiring war in the midst of peace: 'I am ready, and I am unshaken'?[9] And what you often said along with the prophet: 'Examine me, Lord, and try me; stir up my reins and my heart'?[10] And: 'Examine me, Lord, and know my heart. Question me, and know my paths, and see if there is in me a path of wickedness'?[11] How did the merest shadow of a foe terrify a huge engine of war? 5. Condemning himself, then, by reproaching himself with compunction of this sort, he should not let this unexpected turmoil go unavenged. Rather, chastising his flesh still more rigorously with the corrective of fasting and vigils and torturing his blameworthy fickleness with the constant punishment of abstinence, he should, now that he is dwelling in the desert, destroy with the fire of these practices what he ought to have completely burned away in the cenobitic way of life.

"This, in any event, is what must be consistently and firmly maintained in order to acquire a constant and unyielding patience—namely, that it is not permitted us, to whom the divine law forbids not only the revenge of wrongs but even their remembrance, to be moved to anger because of some unpleasantness or irritation. 6. For what more serious loss can occur to the soul than that it be deprived of the brightness of the true and eternal light through the sudden blindness of emotion and no longer contemplate him 'who is meek and humble of heart'?[12] What, I ask, is more awful and what more tragic than that a person should lose the ability to judge what is good and the rule and discipline of a careful discretion and, sane and sober, perpetrate things that even a drunkard and someone bereft of his senses could not pardonably commit?

7. "Whoever reflects on these unpleasantnesses and others like them, then, will easily endure and disdain not only all kinds of losses but also whatever mistreatment and punishments can be inflicted upon him by the most cruel persons. He will esteem nothing more of a loss than anger and nothing more precious than a peaceful mind and a heart that is always pure. On their account are to be spurned the advantages not only of carnal things but even of those that seem to be spiritual, if they cannot be acquired and perfected other than by disturbing this tranquillity."

XV. GERMANUS: "As the cure for other wounds–that is, for anger, sadness, and impatience–has been shown to be in the application of opposite things, so also we want to be taught what kind of remedy to apply against the spirit of fornication. That is, can the fire of lust be extinguished by imagining still greater irritants, as is true in other cases? For we believe that it is quite contrary to chastity not merely if our wanton impulses are increased but even if they pass fleetingly before the mind's eye."

XVI.1. JOHN: "Your penetrating question has anticipated the topic that we were going to discuss next, even if you had said nothing. Therefore I have no doubt that it will be effectively grasped by your intelligence, since your sharp insight has in fact gotten ahead of our instruction. For the obscurity of any topic is easily enlightened when the question anticipates its answer and precedes it where it must go.

"And so, human society not only indeed does not hinder the remedies for the vices that we have spoken of previously, but it even contributes a great deal. 2. For the more often their frequent impatience is revealed, the more other people bring upon those who have been overcome by it the enduring sorrow of compunction, and the more they contribute to a speedy recovery for those who are laboring under this. Hence even if we dwell in the desert, where the incitement to and the stuff of irritation cannot arise from human beings, nonetheless we must reflect on–even painfully–the provocations to these same things, so that a more prompt remedy may be given us as we struggle against them in the constant battle of our thoughts.

3. "But against the spirit of fornication the method is different, just as the cause is not the same. For as the body must be

deprived of the opportunity for wantonness and of its close relationship to the flesh, so also the mind must be utterly deprived of the recollection of these things. It is very dangerous to permit hearts that are still weak and sickly even the slightest memory of this passion, given that sometimes the urge of a harmful titillation excites them even while they are remembering some holy women or reading Holy Scripture. For this reason our elders are very wisely in the habit of passing over readings of this sort when they are in the presence of the younger men.

"For those, however, who are already perfect and accomplished in the disposition of chastity, there cannot lack tests by which they should be able to examine themselves and by which their perfect integrity of heart may be proved by the incorrupt judgment of their conscience. 4. For the man who is perfect, then, there will be a similar test even with regard to this passion, so that he who knows that he has completely pulled out the roots of this disease may, for the sake of examining his chastity, imagine something with a lascivious mind. But it is not at all proper for this examination, whereby a person reflects in his heart on intercourse with a woman and on some kind of tender and very soft caress, to be attempted by those who are still weak, as it will be more harmful than useful to them. 5. When, therefore, someone established in perfect virtue perceives in himself that no assent of the mind or movement of the flesh has occurred at the most seductive of the lascivious touches that he has imagined, he will have the most certain proof of his purity, such that by exercising himself for the sake of holding firmly onto this purity he will not only possess the good of chastity and incorruption in his mind but will also be horrified if some necessity brings him into bodily contact with a woman."

With this Abba John, having noticed that the meal at the ninth hour was ready, put an end to his conference.

TEXTUAL REFERENCES

1. Jer 17:16.
2. Cf. Mt 6:34.
3. Phil 2:8.
4. Jn 6:38.
5. Is 58:13–14.
6. Jer 3:27–28.
7. Ps 102:6–7.
8. Cf. Mt 7:24–25.
9. Ps 119:60.
10. Ps 26:2.
11. Ps 139:23–24.
12. Mt 11:29.

19.1 The Paul who is mentioned here cannot be placed exactly.

On the commemoration of the death of a former abba cf. the note at 2.5.5. This event is not referred to as a synaxis, and it is uncertain whether it may have included the eucharist.

19.1.2 The arrangement of the monks, who are sitting "in separate circles of twelve," suggests both a symbolic intent (the twelve apostles?) and a profound sense of order. With regard to the latter, one is reminded of the legislation in the Pachomian rule, which governed even some of the slightest details of a monk's activity.

19.1.3 The anonymous young monk's remarkable composure in an extraordinary circumstance represents the carrying out of a monastic ideal discussed in 6.9.3. Cf. the relevant note. A similar example of composure is found in *Inst.* 4.24.4.

19.1.3ff. For other demeaning references to Syrian monasticism cf. the note at 3.22.4.

19.3.1 I passed another twenty in it: Namely, in solitary life.

19.4.1f. On the description of ecstasy here cf. 3.7.3 (with the relevant note) and 9.31.

19.4.2 Seven days' worth of food...seven pairs of biscuits: Cf. 2.19.

On the term *prochirium* cf. Gazet's commentary in PL 49.1131.

It is evident here that the solitaries with whom John was associated assembled on Sunday ("the solemn day," "the sacred day") for the eucharist. It is possible, however, that they would have already begun to gather by Saturday evening. Cf. *Inst.* 2.18 (?); *Apophthegmata patrum,* de abbate Arsenio 30.

19.5.2 On the theme of decadence here and in 19.6.2f. cf. the note at 18.5.

19.6.2 On the sixth of a measure (*sextarius*) and the modius cf. *Oxford Latin Dictionary* (1982) s. vv.

19.6.2f. On the monastic diet in general cf. 8.1 and the relevant note, and on the use of oil in particular cf. 8.1.1.

19.7 On experience as an indispensable teacher of spiritual truths cf. the note at 3.7.4.

19.8.3 The end of the cenobite is...to crucify all his desires: The theme of crucifixion in a cenobitic context is emphasized in *Inst.* 4.34f.

19.9.1 Who this Moses might be is uncertain. He is quite possibly the abba around whom the first two conferences are built.

The Paphnutius who appears here may be the abba of the third conference, nicknamed "the Buffalo." Cf. p. 113.

The two Macarii are almost certainly Macarius of Egypt and Macarius of Alexandria. They are sometimes mentioned in tandem, as in Palladius, *Hist. laus.* 17.1. On distinguishing them from one another cf. Antoine Guillaumont, "Le problème des deux Macaire dans les *Apophthegmata Patrum,*" *Irénikon* 48 (1975): 41–59.

19.11.1 Training ground: *Palaestram.* Cf. also 19.14.3 and the note at 18.11.1.

19.11.2 Germanus's question about how one may pursue long-suffering and patience in solitude is paralleled by Basil's argument in favor of cenobitism and against the solitary life in *Reg. fus. tract.* 7.4.

19.12.1 On Christ as physician cf. the note at 2.13.7.

Effects...dispositions: *Effectus...affectus.* Cf. also 19.12.4.

19.12.2f. "Annoyance" and "annoys" are translations of *tristitiae* and *contristaverit,* usually rendered as "sadness" and "saddens." Cf. 16.6.2ff. and the relevant note.

19.14.2 The idea that the vices may be driven out by their contrary virtues, which also appears in *Inst.* 12.8.1, can be found in Evagrius, *De vitiis quae opposita sunt virtutibus* (PL 79.1139–1144); idem, *Schol. in Prov.* 157 (SC

340.254), 176 (ibid. 270), 181 (ibid. 274); Augustine, *De doct. christ.* 1.14.13.

19.16.3 The possibility of being titillated even while reading Scripture is mentioned by Origen in connection (understandably) with the Song of Songs, and he warns those who are still under the influence of their passions that they should not read it. Cf. *Comm. in Cant. Cant.*, prol. (GCS 33.62).

TWENTIETH CONFERENCE THE CONFERENCE OF ABBA PINUFIUS: ON THE END OF REPENTANCE AND ON THE MARK OF REPARATION

TRANSLATOR'S INTRODUCTION

Cassian begins the present conference, over which Abba Pinufius presides, with a story that he had already told of the abba in question in *Inst.* 4.30f. What is related here and in *The Institutes* is all that we know of this Pinufius. Indeed, it is possible that the account given of him in both places is modeled on a similar story told of Macarius of Alexandria in Palladius (*Hist. laus.* 18.12ff.; cf. Weber 96–97). In any event, there is a similarity between Abba John's abandonment of the solitary in favor of the cenobitic life, as recounted in 19.2.3ff., and Pinufius's own flights from a cenobium in which he was famous to ones in which he was unknown, and the similarity helps to establish a link between the twentieth conference and its predecessor. The motive that drives both men is humility, the desire to place themselves under others, which we may also speak of as part of that discretion which was discussed at such length in the second conference.

The dialogue itself begins with a further reference to *Inst.* 4—namely, to 4.32ff., which contains a long instruction given by Pinufius to a brother who was going to become a member of the cenobium. Pinufius's words there are in many respects a synthesis of cenobitic perfection, emphasizing death to self, humility, and patience; they are summarized neatly in *Inst.* 4.43. It is implied that the present interchange occurred very shortly after that instruction, for Cassian and Germanus are said to be grieved by their inability to attain to the degree of renunciation that was set forth in it. Germanus then asks Pinufius to speak to them "about the end of repentance *[fine paenitentiae]* and particularly about the mark of reparation *[satisfactionis indicio]* so that, sure of the forgiveness of our past sins, we too may be heartened to mount the heights of the aforementioned perfection" (20.3.2). Germanus's question, consequently, is not about perfect renunciation, which is to be understood here as one way of expressing the goal of monasticism, but rather about a preliminary step—namely, the assurance of forgiveness.

Pinufius replies by suggesting that perhaps Cassian's and Germanus's humility has hidden their own virtuousness from them. He then observes that they are not concerned with the character *(qualitas)* of repentance, which he seems to equate with its intercessory power and its dignity. From there, finally, he defines both repentance and the mark of reparation. Repentance means "that we should never again commit the sins for which we do penance and on account of which our conscience is pricked" (20.5.1). The mark of reparation, on the other hand, "is the fact that the disposition toward them has been driven from our hearts" (ibid.). In a word, "the stain of former vices should be believed to be pardoned us only when both the desires and the passions associated with present sensual pleasures have been expelled from our heart" (20.5.3).

To this Germanus raises the objection that compunction seems to depend on the recollection of our sinfulness, and he cites several passages of Scripture to support his view. Pinufius's response is in the form of a distinction: Such recollection is good when we are in the process of doing penance, but it disappears once we have been forgiven. It is not clear here, however, whether Pinufius intends the forgetfulness of sinfulness to be understood literally or metaphorically.

There follows a long chapter on the fruits of repentance *(paenitentiae fructus)*—namely, acts or dispositions that obtain the forgiveness of sins. The list of these fruits is classic, and a very similar one had been drawn up two centuries previously in Origen (*Hom. in Lev.* 2.4); in addition to martyrdom, it includes a loving disposition, almsgiving, tears, the confession of sins, self-imposed affliction, others' intercession, mercy and faith, the conversion of others, and the forgiveness of others. At least one of these methods of acquiring forgiveness is accessible to everyone.

Then Pinufius returns to the matter of the recollection of one's past sins. This must be done not only in a spirit of repentance but also with caution, for the remembrance of one's evil deeds could contaminate the mind and upset it. Consequently it is better to yearn for virtue and to look for the kingdom of God than to dwell on one's sins. As far as reparation is concerned, this cannot be attained without the complete extirpation of one's sinful tendencies. Yet all of this, Pinufius continues, has to do only with grave sins, since it is impossible to avoid the little offenses that we commit every day for any number of reasons. Finally, he remarks that it is not enough to avoid sin if one has not also acquired virtue "through purity of heart and the perfection of apostolic love" (20.12.4).

The conference closes with Pinufius's invitation to Cassian and Germanus to stay in his cenobium, but they declare that they are anxious to hasten on to Skete.

XX. The Conference of Abba Pinufius: On the End of Repentance and on the Mark of Reparation

Chapters

I. On the humility of Abba Pinufius and on his place of retreat.
II. On our coming to him.
III. A question about the end of repentance and about the mark of reparation.
IV. The reply, on the humility of our question.
V. On the method of repentance and on the proof of forgiveness.
VI. A question as to whether sins should be recalled for the sake of compunction of heart.
VII. The reply: For how long the memory of past acts should be retained.
VIII. On the different fruits of repentance.
IX. That forgetting one's sin is beneficial to the perfect.
X. That the memory of shameful deeds should be avoided.
XI. On the mark of reparation and on the pardon of past misdeeds.
XII. In what respect penance is a temporal matter and in what respect it can have no end.

I.1. As I start to speak of the precepts of the excellent and remarkable man, Abba Pinufius, on the end of repentance, it seems to me a loss of a significant part of the material if I pass over in silence here, lest I bore the reader, the praise of his humility that I compressed into a few words in the fourth book of *The Institutes,* which is entitled "How the Renunciants Should Be Instructed." This is especially so in view of the fact that many who are unaware of that little work may chance to read this one, and all the authority of the speaker's words will be lost if his virtuousness goes unmentioned.

2. When he was presiding as abba and priest over a large cenobium not very far from Panephysis (an Egyptian city, as was previously said), the whole province was making so much of him because of the glory of his virtues and his miracles that he seemed to himself to have already received the reward of his labors in the remuneration of human praise, and he feared in particular that the detestable vanity of popularity might deprive him of the fruit of an eternal reward. So he secretly fled his monastery and hastened to the remote retreat of the monks of Tabenna, where he chose not the solitude of the desert and the security of a life by himself—which even some who are imperfect pursue, often with proud presumption, not enduring the labor of obedience in the cenobia—but rather submission in a thronging cenobium. 3. And when he put on worldly clothing, lest he be noticed because of anything that he was wearing, and for many days lay weeping before the doors, as the custom is in that place, and embraced the knees of everyone after having experienced the protracted disdain of those who said, in order to test his desire, that he had been compelled by hunger in his old age and was not really seeking the holiness of that chosen orientation, he at last gained admission. There, having been assigned to help a certain young brother who was in charge of the garden, he not only carried out with marvelous holy humility everything that this same overseer would order and that the work imposed on him demanded, but

he also took care of certain necessary chores that were avoided by the others through disgust. This he did stealthily and at night, so that when morning broke the whole community was astonished and did not know who was performing such useful tasks.

But when he had thus spent nearly three years there, rejoicing in the longed-for labors of his burdensome submission, it happened that a certain brother who was known to him arrived from those parts of Egypt that he himself had left. 4. This person hesitated for a long time, because the meanness of his clothing and of his work prevented immediate recognition, but, after looking him over closely, he embraced his knees and thereupon astonished all the brothers. Then, uttering his name, which was well known among them on account of the report of his extraordinary holiness, he made them feel compunction for having assigned a man of such worth, and a priest, to such burdensome tasks. 5. But after he was led back to his own monastery—weeping copiously and imputing to diabolical envy what seemed to him a grave case of betrayal—in the honorable custody of his brothers, and had stayed there a short while, he once again grew dismayed at the attention that was being paid to his fame and his high position. So, stealthily taking passage on a boat, he went off to the province of Palestine in Syria. There he was accepted as a beginner and a novice in a house of the monastery where we were staying, and he was ordered by the abba to live in our cell. But his virtue and his worth could not remain hidden there for long, to be sure, for by a similar betrayal he was discovered and brought back to his own monastery with considerable honor and praise.

II.1. When, therefore, after a short while a desire for holy instruction had compelled us to come to Egypt ourselves, and we had sought out this man with great longing and desire, we were received with such graciousness and hospitality that he even honored us, as former sharers of the same cell, with lodging in his own cell, which he had built at the far end of his garden. 2. When, for the sake of a certain brother who was submitting to the rule of the monastery in the presence of all the brothers gathered in the assembly, he had set down the very difficult and lofty precepts that I laid out as briefly as I could in the fourth book of *The Institutes,* as we remarked, the heights of true renunciation seemed so ungraspable and so wondrous to us that in no way did we believe that our lowliness could attain to them. 3. Cast down in desperation, then, and showing by our very looks the profound bitterness of our thoughts, we hastened back to the blessed old man in a very anxious state. When he had at once asked the reason for such dejection, Abba GERMANUS groaned deeply and replied to him as follows:

III.1. "The words of a teaching unknown to us have opened up the arduous path of a most noble renunciation and have disclosed its terminus, which is established in the heavens, now that as it were the mist has been removed from our eyes, and the more magnificent and lofty it appears the more we are crushed by the burden of desperation. Measuring its immensity against the insignificance of our abilities and comparing the exceeding lowliness of our ignorance with the infinite height of the virtue that was shown us, we not only feel that our littleness cannot reach it but that it may even fall from where it is. 2. For we are oppressed with the weight of an exceeding desperation and are somehow slipping away from low places to still lower ones. Hence one thing alone can help to bring healing to our wounds–to learn something about the end of repentance and particularly about the mark of reparation so that, sure of the forgiveness of our past sins, we too may be heartened to mount the heights of the aforementioned perfection."

IV.1. PINUFIUS: "I am gladdened indeed by the very abundant fruits of your humility, which I even noticed with no small interest when I was living in that cell, and I greatly rejoice that you seize with such wonder upon what is prescribed by us, the least of all Christians, with perhaps a certain candor of speech, so that I would not be surprised if you accomplished them no sooner than we have uttered them. And although, as I remember, the importance of what was said hardly measures up to the laboriousness of your undertaking, you so hide the greatness of your virtue that you have no inkling of the things that you daily achieve. 2. But since it is most worthy of the highest praise when you assert that these institutes of holy persons are unknown to you, as if you were still untrained, we shall set forth as briefly as possible what you anxiously ask of us. For, apart from our capability and strength, we must be ready to carry out a command imposed by your long-standing friendship.

"Many people have said a great deal in both oral and written form about the intercessory power and dignity of repentance, showing how beneficial, virtuous, and graced it is. They go so far as to suggest, if such a thing can be said, that before a God offended by past misdeeds and demanding an exact punishment for such great crimes it places a kind of barrier and as it were stays the hand of the One who, so to speak, takes vengeance against his own will. 3. But I do not doubt that all these things are so well known to you, either through natural wisdom or through the constant study of Holy Scripture, that thanks to them your conversion's first planting has taken firm root. You are concerned, then, not about the character of repentance but about its end and about the mark of reparation, and you are inquiring very perceptively into what has been passed over by others.

V.1. "Hence, in order to respond to your request briefly and summarily, here is the full and perfect definition of repentance: that we should never again commit the sins for which we do penance and on account of which our conscience is pricked. But the mark of reparation and forgiveness is the fact that the disposition toward them has been driven from our hearts. 2. For a person should know that he is not absolved of his former sins as long as the image of the things that he did or of similar misdeeds dances before his eyes while he is giving himself over to reparation and groaning, or if their recollection—to say nothing of delight in them—infests the deepest recesses of his mind. The one who watches over himself closely for the sake of reparation, then, should realize that he has been forgiven his misdeeds and received pardon for his past offenses when he sees that his heart is not at all touched by the seductiveness and the images of these same vices. 3. Therefore the truest judge of repentance and the mark of forgiveness resides in our conscience, which reveals to us who are still living in the flesh the absolution of our sinfulness before the day of recognition and judgment and discloses the end of reparation and the grace of pardon.

"Let what has been said be expressed still more precisely: The stain of former vices should be believed to be pardoned us only when both the desires and the passions associated with present sensual pleasures have been expelled from our heart."

VI.1. GERMANUS: "And how can there be born in us such a holy and salutary compunction of humiliation as is thus spoken of in the person of the penitent: 'I have made known my sin, and I have not covered over my unrighteousness. I said: Against myself I will proclaim my unrighteousness to the Lord,'[1] so that we may also deserve to say effectively what follows: 'And you forgave the wickedness of my heart'?[2] And how can we, prostrate in prayer, move ourselves to tears of confession, by which we may deserve to attain the pardon of our sins, as it is written: 'Every night I will wash my bed; I will sprinkle my resting place with tears,'[3] if we drive from our hearts the memory of our sins, when on the contrary we are commanded to remember them tenaciously, as the Lord says: 'I will not keep a record of your iniquities. But you remember them'?[4] 2. Therefore I make every effort, not only when working but also when praying, to turn my mind to the recollection of my sins so that I may incline more effectively to true humility and contrition of heart and may dare to say with the prophet: 'See my humility and my toil, and forgive all my sins.'"[5]

VII.1. PINUFIUS: "Your question, as has already been said, was not about the character of repentance but about its end and about the mark of reparation. I think that I have responded adequately and consistently to this. What you said, moreover, about the remembering of sins is quite useful and necessary, but it is such for those who are still repenting, so that they might proclaim with constant brokenness of heart: 'I acknowledge my iniquity, and my sin is always before me.'[6] And also: 'I will reflect on my sin.'[7] As we repent, then, and are still bitten by the memory of our wrongdoing, the torrent of tears which has arisen from the confession of our sins will certainly put out the fire of our conscience.

2. "But when the recollection of these things has faded away in a person who is firmly established in this humility of heart and contrition of spirit and who is constantly toiling and groaning, and when the thorn of conscience has been pulled out of the inmost part of the soul by the grace of a merciful God, it is certain that that person has achieved the end of reparation, is worthy of being forgiven, and has been cleansed of the stain of the misdeeds

that he has committed. One does not attain to this forgetfulness in any other way, however, than by the obliteration of former vices and dispositions and by a perfect and integral purity of heart. There is no doubt that no one will arrive at this condition who, through laziness or contempt, has neglected to purge away his vices, but only the one who, through constant mournful groans and sighs, has destroyed every stain of previous uncleanness, and who by his virtuous mind and his deeds proclaims to the Lord: 3. 'I have made known my wrongdoing, and I have not covered over my unrighteousness.' And: 'My tears have been my bread by day and by night.'[8] As a result he will deserve to hear: 'Let your voice cease from lamentation and your eyes from tears, for there is a reward for your work, says the Lord.'[9] In similar fashion the voice of the Lord also says this to him: 'I have destroyed your iniquities like a cloud, and your sins like a mist.'[10] And again: 'I am the one who destroys your iniquities for my own sake, and I will not keep record of your sins.'[11] And so, having been freed 'from the cords of his sins,' by which 'everyone is bound,'[12] he will sing to the Lord with all thanksgiving: 'You have broken my chains. To you will I offer a sacrifice of praise.'[13]

VIII.1. "In addition to the common grace of baptism and to the most precious gift of martyrdom, which is obtained by the washing of blood, there are many fruits of repentance by which the expiation of sins is achieved. For eternal salvation is promised not only under the particular name of repentance, as when the blessed apostle Peter says: 'Repent and be converted, so that your sins may be wiped away,'[14] as well as John the Baptist and the Lord himself: 'Repent, for the kingdom of heaven is at hand.'[15] The burden of sin is also lifted by a loving disposition, for 'love covers a multitude of sins.'[16] 2. In similar fashion healing is furnished our wounds through the fruit of almsgiving, because 'just as water extinguishes a fire, so almsgiving extinguishes sin.'[17] Likewise, too, forgiveness of sins is obtained by the shedding of tears, for 'every night I will wash my bed; I will sprinkle my resting place with tears.' And then this is added to show that they have not been shed in vain: 'Depart from me, all you who work iniquity, for the Lord has heard the voice of my weeping.'[18] 3. Forgiveness is also bestowed through the confession of sins, for 'against myself I will proclaim my unrighteousness to the Lord, and you forgave the wickedness of my heart.' And again: 'Tell your iniquities first, that you may be justified.'[19] Pardon for crimes committed is acquired, too, by the affliction of heart and body, for it says: 'See my humility and my toil, and forgive all my sins.' This is especially true with regard to the correction of one's behavior: 'Remove,' it is said, 'the evil of your thoughts from my sight. Cease acting perversely and learn to do good. Seek after judgment, come to the help of the downtrodden, judge the orphan, defend the widow. And come, reason with me, says the Lord, and if your sins were like scarlet, they shall become as white as snow, and if they were as red as crimson, they shall be as clean as wool.'[20] 4. Sometimes pardon for sins is also won through the intercession of holy persons, for 'whoever knows that his brother is committing a sin that is not unto death asks, and he will give life to the one who is not sinning unto death.'[21] And again: 'Is anyone of you sick? Let him bring in the elders of the Church, and let them pray over him, anointing him with oil in the name of the Lord. And the prayer of faith will save the sick person, and the Lord will raise him up, and if he is in sins, they will be forgiven him.'[22] 5. The stain of vice is sometimes destroyed in virtue of mercy and faith, in accordance with the words: 'Sins are purged away by mercy and faith.'[23] And sometimes this occurs thanks to the conversion and salvation of those who are saved by our warnings and preaching: 'For the one who converts a sinner from the error of his ways will save his soul from death and cover over a multitude of sins.'[24] It is no less the case that pardon is gained for our wrongdoings by our own acts of pardon and forgiveness: 'For if you forgive people their sins, your heavenly Father will also forgive you your sins.'[25]

"You see, then, how many opportunities for mercy the clemency of the Savior has disclosed, so that no one who desires salvation should be broken by despair when he sees so many life-giving remedies at his disposal. 6. For if you complain that because of some weakness of the flesh you cannot wipe away your sins by the affliction of fasting, and you cannot say: 'My knees are weak from fasting, and my flesh is changed for oil, for I ate ashes for bread, and I mixed my drink with tears,'[26] then redeem them with almsgiving. If you do not have anything to bestow on the poor (although the burden of want and poverty excludes no one from this work, when in fact the widow's two small coins are preferred to the large gifts of the wealthy,[27] and the Lord promises that he will give a reward for a cup of cold water[28]), certainly you can be cleansed by correcting your behavior. 7. But if you cannot acquire the perfection of virtue by destroying all your vices, exercise a kindly concern for helping others to salvation. If, however, you bemoan your inadequacy for this ministry, you will be able to cover over your sins by a loving disposition. If in this too some frailty of mind has weakened you, at least beg submissively and humbly for healing for your wounds through the prayer and intercession of holy persons. Finally, who is there who cannot humbly say: 'I have made known my sin, and I have not covered over my unrighteousness,' so that by this profession he may also deserve to add: 'And you forgave the wickedness of my heart'? 8. But if shame restrains you and you blush to reveal such things to others, you should not cease to confess them in constant supplication to the One from whom they cannot be concealed, who is accustomed to healing without disclosing what is shameful and to forgiving sins without reproachfulness, and say to him: 'I acknowledge my iniquity, and my sin is always before me. Against you alone have I sinned, and I have done evil in your presence.'[29] In addition to this, the divine condescension has accorded us another very prompt and sure help that is still easier, and he has placed at our own disposal the very means of the remedy, so that based upon our own dispositions we may presume the forgiveness of our misdeeds when we say to him: 'Forgive us our trespasses as we forgive those who trespass against us.'[30]

9. "Whoever, therefore, desires to obtain the forgiveness of his sins should strive to use these methods. The obstinacy of a hardened heart should turn no one away from a salutary healing and from the source of so great a mercy, for even if we did all these things they would be ineffective for the expiation of our crimes unless the goodness and mercy of the Lord destroyed them. When he has seen the services of a devout effort rendered by us with a humble mind, he supplements these feeble and small efforts with his own measureless generosity, as he says: 'I am the

one who destroys your iniquities for my own sake, and I will not keep record of your sins.'

10. "Whoever, therefore, is intent upon the condition about which we have been speaking will acquire the grace of reparation by daily fasts and by mortification of heart and body, as it is written: 'There is no forgiveness without the shedding of blood.'[31] Rightly is this so, for 'flesh and blood cannot possess the kingdom of God.'[32] Therefore, whoever wants to prevent 'the sword of the Spirit, which is the word of God,'[33] from shedding this blood will without doubt be struck with the curse of which Jeremiah speaks. For, he says, 'cursed is the one who keeps his sword from blood.'[34] 11. This is the sword that salutarily pours out the harmful blood by which the stuff of sinfulness is animated; it cuts off and removes whatever it discovers in the members of our soul has hardened into carnality and earthiness; and those who have died to their vices it makes live to God and flourish with spiritual virtues. And so he will begin to weep no more over the memory of past sins but rather with the hope of future joys. Thinking not so much of past evils as of the good things that are to come, he will shed tears not from bitterness over his sins but from the delight of eternal joy. And, 'forgetting what is behind'—that is, the carnal vices—he will reach out 'to what is ahead'[35]—that is, to the spiritual gifts and virtues.

IX.1. "But you ought not at all to reflect intently upon the memory of past sins, as you said before. Indeed, if this comes upon you violently it should at once be thrust out. For this greatly withdraws the mind from the contemplation of purity, especially in the case of one who lives in the desert, involving it in the filth of this world and suffocating it in the stench of the vices. When you reconsider the things that you perpetrated out of ignorance or wantonness when you were following the prince of this world, although I grant you that no delight may be stealing in as you dwell on these thoughts, it is certainly inevitable that the merest contact with something putrid from the past will, with its foul stench, contaminate the mind and cut off the spiritual fragrance of the virtues—that is, the sweetness of their good odor.

2. "When, therefore, the memory of past vices upsets the mind, one must recoil from it just as an upright and serious man

flees if a shameless and impudent woman tries to speak with him or embrace him in public. Indeed, if he does not remove himself from contact with her at once and permits even the briefest delay for an immoral conversation, he will not avoid a notorious and blameworthy reputation in the judgment of all onlookers, even if he does not consent to shameful pleasure.

3. "When we have been led astray by a dangerous recollection into thoughts of this kind, then, we too should quickly give up reflecting on them and fulfill what is commanded by Solomon: 'Go forth,' he says, 'do not tarry in her place or set your eye on her.'[36] Otherwise the angels, seeing us taken up with impure and vile thoughts, will not be able to say to us as they pass by: 'The blessing of the Lord be upon you.'[37] 4. For it is impossible for the mind to linger upon good thoughts when the heart's principal concern is given over to vile and earthly considerations. The words of Solomon are true: 'When your eyes see a strange woman, then your mouth will speak wicked things, and you will lie as it were in the heart of the sea, and like a pilot in a great storm. But you will say: They strike me, but I did not grieve, and they mocked me, but I was unaware.'[38]

5. "Having abandoned, therefore, not only every vile thought but also every earthly one, the attention of our mind should always be raised to heavenly things, in accordance with the words of our Savior: 'Where I am,' he says, 'there also will my servant be.'[39] For it frequently happens that, when a person reflects with a commiserating spirit on his own falls or those of others, he himself is also struck by the pleasurable feeling of a very subtle dart, and what was begun under the guise of goodness concludes with a filthy and harmful ending, for 'there are paths that seem right in the sight of men, but they arrive finally at the depths of hell.'[40]

X. "Hence we must seek to rouse ourselves to this praiseworthy compunction by a yearning for virtue and a desire for the kingdom of heaven rather than by harmful recollections of vice, because anyone who chooses to stand over a sewer or to stir up its muck will inevitably be suffocated by its pestilential stench.

XI.1. "But we know, as we have often said, that we have made reparation for past sins precisely when these very movements and dispositions, in accordance with which we perpetrated regrettable acts, have been cut out of our hearts. Yet no one should believe himself capable of attaining to this who has not first cut away, with all the fervor of his spirit, the very causes and matter whereby he fell into those misdeeds. For example, if someone has fallen into fornication or adultery because of a dangerous familiarity with women, he should make every effort to avoid even looking at them. Or, if he has been inflamed by too much wine and by overeating, he should certainly discipline this gluttony for unlawful food with the utmost strictness. 2. Again, if he has been corrupted by a desire and love for money and commits perjury or theft or murder or blasphemy, he should cut off the stuff of avarice that seduced him into being deceived. If he is forced by the passion of pride into the vice of anger, he should pull out the root of this arrogance with the lofty virtue of humility. Thus, in order for each sin to be extinguished, the cause and the occasion by which or on account of which it was committed must be cut out at the very beginning. There is no doubt that by this healing remedy a person may attain to the forgetfulness of the sins that he has committed.

XII.1. "But this understanding of the aforementioned forgetfulness refers only to the grave sins that are also condemned by the Mosaic law, the dispositions to which are put aside and destroyed by a good way of life. So too their repentance has an end.

"But there will be no end of penance for those little offenses by which 'the righteous person falls seven times,' as it is written, 'and gets up again.'[41] 2. For we commit these frequently every day, unwillingly or willingly, whether through ignorance or forgetfulness or thought or word or surprise or necessity or weakness of the flesh or pollution during a dream. On account of these David asks the Lord in prayer for purification and forgiveness, saying: 'Who understands his sins? From my hidden ones cleanse me, and from those of others spare your servant.'[42] And the Apostle says: 'The good that I want, I do not do, but the evil that I do not want, this I do.'[43] And on their account he also cried out mournfully: 'Wretched man that I am! Who will free me from the body of this death?'[44] 3. For in these things we slip so easily, as if by a natural law, that they cannot be completely avoided, however cautiously and carefully they are guarded against. One of the disciples, the one 'whom Jesus loved,'[45] spoke about these in very few words when he said: 'If we say that we have no sin, we are deceiving ourselves and his word is not in us.'[46]

"Hence it will be of no great help to the person who desires to arrive at the height of perfection to have attained to the end of repentance–that is, abstaining from what is unlawful–if he does not also constantly and tirelessly reach out to those virtues by which one attains to the marks of reparation. 4. For it is not enough for someone to have abstained from the stinking filth of sins that disgust the Lord if he does not also possess, through purity of heart and the perfection of apostolic love, that good fragrance of virtuousness wherein the Lord takes delight."

Thus far did Abba Pinufius discuss the mark of reparation and the end of repentance. Although he beseeched us with anxious love to choose to stay in his cenobium, nonetheless when he could not keep us, drawn as we were by the reputation of the desert of Skete, he let us go.

Textual References

1. Ps 31:5–6a LXX.
2. Ps 31:6b LXX.
3. Ps 6:7 LXX.
4. Is 43:25–26a LXX.
5. Ps 25:18.
6. Ps 51:3.
7. Ps 38:18.
8. Ps 42:3.
9. Jer 31:16.
10. Is 44:22.
11. Is 43:25.
12. Prv 5:22 LXX.
13. Ps 116:16–17.
14. Acts 3:19.
15. Mt 3:2.
16. 1 Pt 4:8.
17. Sir 3:30.
18. Ps 6:9 LXX.
19. Is 43:26b LXX.
20. Is 1:16–18.
21. 1 Jn 5:16.
22. Jas 5:14–15.
23. Prv 15:27.
24. Jas 5:20.
25. Mt 6:14.
26. Pss 109:24; 102:9.
27. Cf. Lk 21:1–4.
28. Cf. Mt 10:42.
29. Ps 51:3–4.
30. Mt 6:12.
31. Heb 9:22.
32. 1 Cor 15:50.
33. Eph 6:17.
34. Jer 48:10.
35. Phil 3:13.
36. Prv 9:18 LXX.
37. Ps 129:8.
38. Prv 23:33–35 LXX.

39. Jn 12:26.
40. Prv 16:25 LXX.
41. Prv 24:16.
42. Ps 19:12–13.
43. Rom 7:19.
44. Rom 7:24.
45. Jn 13:23.
46. 1 Jn 1:8, 10.

20.1.2 On Panephysis cf. 7.26.2 and 11.3 with the relevant notes.

The parenthetical phrase that follows the mention of the town refers to the fact that its location in Egypt had already been spoken of in the passage in question from *The Institutes*–namely, *Inst.* 4.30.

Tabenna, which had been a deserted village, was located in Thebais Secunda in southern Egypt. It became the site of Pachomius's first cenobitic foundation around the year 320. Cf. *V. prima gr. Pachomii* 12ff. The cenobium there is described briefly in *Inst.* 4.1.

20.1.3 The way in which a candidate for the monastic life was treated in Tabenna, as depicted here, is also described in *Inst.* 4.3.1. Cf., however, Pachomius, *Praecepta* 49, where it is merely said that the candidate is to remain outside the door of the monastery for a few days and learn the Lord's Prayer and as many of the psalms as he can; there is no mention of mistreatment by design. The act of embracing another person's knees was, in antiquity, a typical gesture of seeking mercy and compassion. Cf. the citations listed in the *Oxford Latin Dictionary*, s.v. *genu* 1 c.

Pinufius's nighttime service recalls a passage in *Inst.* 4.19.1.

20.5.3 Truest judge of repentance: *Verissimus...examinator paenitentiae.* The judge in our conscience, spoken of also in 21.22.2, may be understood, according to the Latin, as either a person or a quality. If a person, it is almost certainly Christ, who is the judge par excellence. Cf. Ps.-Macarius, Coll. 3, *Hom.* 28.5.1 (SC 275.344). If a quality, it is the foundation of truth in a human being that can only be destroyed with difficulty. Cf. 2.11.3.

20.7 Contrast Cassian's view of the dangers attendant on remembering one's past sinfulness here and in 20.9f. with Augustine's words on the possibility of remembering one's sinfulness without bad effects in *Conf.*

2.7.15 and 10.14.21f. But the two positions are not necessarily contradictory: Cassian approaches the matter more practically, Augustine more metaphysically. For Cassian, here at least, remembering seems to be understood almost as the reenactment of a past event, and apart from a context of compunction such a reenactment could only be problematic.

20.8 For a longer and more nuanced treatment of the means to the forgiveness of sins cf. Augustine, *De civ. Dei* 21.18ff.; idem, *Enchir.* 19.70ff. The classic basic list of such means was comprised of prayer, fasting, and almsgiving. Cf. *2 Clem.* 16.4.

20.8.1 For other references to baptism cf. the note at 1.1.

Martyrdom is first mentioned as having the power to forgive sins in Tertullian, *De bapt.* 16.

20.8.3 The confession of sins spoken of here is not necessarily that which we understand today as sacramental. In fact the practice of sacramental or ecclesiastical confession, such as it existed in antiquity, is hardly referred to in desert literature. Even grave sins were confessed to an elder or to the brothers in assembly with the expectation of forgiveness—not perhaps because of any powers belonging to the persons confessed to but rather because of the humility of the one making the confession. Cf. Palladius, *Hist. laus.* 26.4. Sometimes a penance was imposed. Cf. *Verba seniorum* 5.34. And sometimes the sinner performed a penance that seemed in his own estimation to be proportionate to the sin committed. Cf. ibid. 5.26. This is not to suggest, though, that sacramental confession was utterly unknown in the desert; we just do not hear of it. Cf. Chadwick 79–80.

20.8.6 On the universal obligation to give alms, to which Cassian alludes here, cf. Ramsey, "Almsgiving" 235–238.

20.8.11 The harmful blood by which the stuff of sinfulness is animated: The expression seems to be based on the view that life is in the blood. Cf. Lv 17:11; Origen, *Dial. c. Heracl.* 10ff.

20.9.1 On the stench of sin and the fragrance of virtue here and in 20.10 and 20.12.4 cf. the notes at 1.1 and 2.11.5.

20.9.3 The passersby of Ps 129:8 are also referred to as angels in Hesychius of Jerusalem (Ps.-Athanasius), *De titulis psalm.* 129.13 (PG 27.1244). Cassian, however, is probably not interpreting the passersby as angels so much as putting the words of the psalms in their mouths.

20.12.1ff. On the unavoidable "little offenses" of which Cassian speaks here cf. the note at 11.9.5f.

TWENTY-FIRST CONFERENCE THE FIRST CONFERENCE OF ABBA THEONAS: ON THE RELAXATION AT PENTECOST

Translator's Introduction

The conference at hand opens in a manner similar to its predecessor—that is, with an unusually long and graphic account of a phase in the life of an elder whose teaching the conference will embody. Abba Theonas, in this case, is otherwise unknown. He is assuredly not the Theonas of *Hist. monach. in Aegypto* 6, for this source says nothing of his unusual conversion, which would certainly not have gone unmentioned there; there are, moreover, several other discrepancies.

The conversion in question, which is recounted in the first nine chapters, occurs when Theonas, at the time a young married property-holder, and others bring offerings of tithes and firstfruits to a certain Abba John, the almoner of the local monastery, for redistribution to the poor. John takes advantage of the presence of the group to give a talk, which occupies most of the conversion narrative. This discourse begins with words of praise for the spirit in which the offerings were made. Very soon after, however, John sets before his listeners a higher ideal than that represented by tithes and firstfruits; these were adequate for the fulfillment of the law, but the Gospel urges a far greater abnegation of self. The difference between the law and the Gospel lies in the fact that the law commands whereas the Gospel persuades, and John's point is that it is a nobler thing to be persuaded by the latter than to be commanded by the former. He concludes by declaring that it lies in his hearers' power to choose between the law and the Gospel. It is clear from John's words, although he never says so explicitly, that the gospel ideal which stands in such strong contrast to the mere observance of the law is identical with the monastic ideal, and it is with this understanding in mind that Theonas listens to the discourse. He is moved to return to his wife and to ask her if the two of them could live chastely together (and thus transcend the merely "lawful" aspect of marriage, as it appears in 21.1.1). When, after repeatedly beseeching her in this vein, she refuses his request, he finally abandons her and departs for a monastery.

The position that Theonas takes was proleptically condemned in Origen (*Frag. in 1 Cor.* 33 [*The Journal of Theological Studies* 9 (1908): 500]), where it is argued that in marriage the mutual love of the spouses is more important than the desire of one of them for a chastity that would seem to contravene the good of the other. As for Cassian, he insists that he deserves neither praise nor blame for what another person—Theonas—has done. But his disclaimer of intent to demean marriage is somewhat compromised by the fact that he has told the story at all and by his warning his reader "to refrain from censorious criticism, lest he believe himself fairer or holier than the divine judgment, by which even the wonders of apostolic miracles were conferred on this man" (21.10.3). One is reminded of similar disclaimers concerning the same topic in, for example, Ambrose (*De virginibus* 1.6.24) and Gregory of Nyssa (*De virg.* 7.1).

At length the dialogue itself begins. The two friends ask Theonas about the custom of not kneeling during the fifty days of Pentecost and of observing a modified schedule of fasting during that season. Theonas first makes a bow to the authority of the ancients. Then, addressing himself to the issue of fasting, he distinguishes between absolute goods and absolute evils on the one hand and those things that are, on the other hand, either good or bad depending on how they are used. Fasting is not an absolute good; if it were, then it would be wrong ever to eat. It is, instead, something indifferent, which is to be practiced for the sake of acquiring an absolute or essential good. The characteristics of an absolute good, however, are that "it is good by itself and not by reason of something else,...necessary for its own sake and not for the sake of something else,...unchangeable and always good,...its removal or cessation cannot but bring on the gravest evil,...[and that] similarly, the essential evil, which is its opposite, cannot ever become good" (21.16.1). This definition, so typical of Cassian in its precision, can in no way apply to fasting. With two allusions to the subordination of fasting to the acquisition of purity of heart in 21.16.2 and 21.17.1 we are once again in the atmosphere of the first conference, and especially of 1.7.

Referring to a remark that Theonas had made about Christ's having feasted with his disciples for forty days after his resurrection, until his ascension, Germanus asks the old man why the fast is modified for the whole fifty days of Pentecost rather than for only forty. Theonas replies by saying that at the end of seven weeks—that is, on the fiftieth day after Easter—the Holy Spirit came, and firstfruits, in the form of the conversion of five thousand men, were offered to the Lord in fulfillment of the Old Testament figure in Deuteronomy 16:9–10. Consequently the whole fifty days are to be celebrated with equal joy—namely, with no kneeling and with a mitigated fast.

It is worth noting here that these chapters of the conference depict the encounter of two different traditions concerning the observance of the period following the feast of Easter. Cassian and Germanus seem to be unaware of a fifty-day celebration, or at least they need to be instructed in its meaning, "because we had never seen [this tradition] observed with such care in the monasteries of Syria" (21.11). Theonas, however, knows of no other way of celebrating this period than that which has been described. Theonas's way, and that of Egypt in general at the time, was in fact the ancient one. (Cf. Robert Cabié, *La Pentecôte: L'évolution de la Cinquantaine pascale au cours des cinq premiers siècles* [Tournai, 1965], 73–75, 150–152.)

Having heard Theonas's explanation of Pentecost, Germanus objects that a break in the pattern of fasting, such as is proposed to be practiced in that season, could weaken the spirit's control over the body, especially among the young. The old man begins his response with some words on discretion and good judgment with respect to fasting in particular. In this context, then, he explains how the relaxation of the fast is to occur—

namely, by taking the same amount of food earlier than the usual time, around noon rather than at mid-afternoon.

Germanus's attention now turns to the number of days in Lent. Here as well there is a question of two traditions. Although the Latin for the season is "Quadragesima," meaning "forty," Germanus knows of a Lent lasting thirty-five or thirty-six days. Momentarily disregarding the problem of forty, Theonas replies by pointing out that in fact the period of fasting extends for exactly thirty-six and a half days, which constitutes a tenth or a tithe of the whole year, offered to God. On the other hand, first-fruits are a person's first thoughts, offered to God at the start of each day. Returning to the question of the number of days in Lent, Theonas remarks that the season is called Quadragesima because the original concept of tithing has been forgotten and because a forty-day period can easily be associated with many events in the Bible—for example, Moses', Elijah's, and Jesus' own fasts of forty days and the Israelites' forty years of wandering. The evolution of Lent in antiquity is a much disputed problem, for which cf. esp. C. Callewaert, "La durée et le charactère du Carême ancien dans l'Eglise latine," in idem, *Sacris Erudiri* (Steenbrugge, 1940), 449–506; DS 2.1.137–139.

But whatever the length of Lent, Theonas continues, the perfect are not burdened by any law: They offer their whole lives to the Lord, rather than a mere tithe, and they may relax their fasting whenever a need arises. The Lenten fast, indeed, was imposed only when the ardor of the earliest Christians had cooled. The perfect, who stand not under law but under grace, remain ardent, and thus they attain to that state where they are not dominated by sin. On hearing this, Germanus wonders how, despite Paul's words in Romans 6:14 about the sinlessness of the righteous, sin does in fact flourish in all the baptized. Theonas's answer consists in distinguishing between a life lived under grace and one lived under the law: The law does not destroy the seeds of sin, unlike grace, for it is impossible not to slip into what is unlawful when one clings to the law and keeps it as one's standard. The old man's answer is not completely satisfactory (although Germanus professes that he finds it acceptable); he implies that he is himself aware of this when he observes at both the beginning and the end of his answer (21.32.1 and 21.34.4) that only a very experienced person, such as he himself does not claim to be, can uncover the meaning of the Apostle's words. This lack of satisfaction stems at least in part from the fact that the teaching of the final chapter of the previous conference, on the universality of sin, is not somehow alluded to here.

Germanus's last question is on the relationship of fasting to chastity. He is puzzled as to why nocturnal emissions occur even after he has fasted. In response Theonas distinguishes between external and internal chastity and remarks that the latter is at issue in this case. But he defers a fuller response; that must wait until the following conference. And so the present conference, the longest of the twenty-four, comes to an end.

From the perspective of the conclusion the initial story of Theonas's conversion no longer appears as merely an informational and (perhaps) edifying account of the old man's discovery of monasticism. It also serves to introduce a number of the themes that are reprised in the remainder of the conference. The tithes and firstfruits that Theonas and the others offer and on which Abba John expatiates reappear later under the form of Lent and of morning thoughts worthy of the Lord. John's sharp distinction between law and grace becomes Theonas's own later on. And Theonas's divorce becomes an example (albeit flawed) of the freedom of the perfect vis-à-vis the law. Finally, and on another level, the passing on of the teaching on the law and the Gospel from John to Theonas to Cassian and Germanus—as well as the passing on of the teaching on the observance of Pentecost from "our forebears" and "fathers" (21.12.1) to Theonas and from him to the two friends—offers a model of the practice of discretion, as first spoken of in the second conference, in those who receive that teaching.

XXI. The First Conference of Abba Theonas: On the Relaxation at Pentecost

Chapters

I.1. Before we start to put down the words of the present conference, which we had with the very great man Abba Theonas, I think it necessary to give a brief account of the beginning of his conversion, because from this the worth and grace of the man will be more clearly apparent to the reader.

When he was still a very young man, then, he was married at his parents' insistence and command. Inasmuch as they were looking out for his chastity with religious concern and feared a dangerous fall at that difficult age, they believed that the passions of youth would be fended off by the lawful remedy of marriage. 2. When, therefore, he had spent five years with his spouse, he went to Abba John, who at that time had been chosen on account of his marvelous holiness to administer the distribution of alms. Not just anyone is promoted to this rank because of his own desire or ambition, but he whom the assembly of all the elders considers more excellent and more distinguished than the rest by reason of the prerogative of age and the witness of his faith and virtue. 3. It was to this blessed John that the aforesaid young man came, then, aflame with dutiful devotion and bearing religious gifts. He was with other property-holders who were eagerly offering tithes and firstfruits from what belonged to them to the aforementioned old man. When the old man saw these people thronging to him with their many donations, he wanted to repay their devotion, and, as the Apostle says, he began to sow spiritual gifts among them while reaping their carnal ones.[1] And so, he started to instruct them in these words:

II. "I am indeed delighted, my sons, at the kind generosity of your donations, and I gratefully accept the devotion that is part of this oblation, whose distribution has been entrusted to me. For it is out of faith that you are offering your firstfruits and tithes as a sacrifice well pleasing to the Lord, to be of service to the needs of the poor. That is, by offering these things you believe that your entire harvest and all your property, from which you have given this for the Lord's sake, will be abundantly blessed and that you yourselves will be heaped high with a vast abundance of every good thing even in this world, in keeping with his trustworthy command: 'Honor the Lord from your righteous labors, and give to him from the fruits of your righteousness, so that your barns may be full of an abundance of wheat and your winepresses may be overflowing with wine.'[2] Know that when you exercise this devout practice in faith you have fulfilled the righteousness of the old law, which those who were under it then transgressed, unavoidably incurring guilt, while even when they did fulfill it they were unable to attain to the summit of perfection.

III. "For, by the precept of the Lord, tithes were for the use of the Levites,[3] whereas oblations and firstfruits were consecrated to the priests.[4] The arrangement for firstfruits was that the fiftieth part of both harvest and animals was offered for the service of the Temple and the priests. Those who were rather lukewarm faithlessly diminished this measure, but those who were more religious even increased it, the former paying out the sixtieth part of their harvest and the latter the fortieth.

"For the righteous, upon whom no law has been imposed,[5] are proven to be not under the law in that they strive not only to fulfill the righteousness of the law but even to exceed it, and their devotion is greater than the law's command, because, while carrying out the precepts in their fullness, they add of their own free will to what is obligatory.

IV.1. "Thus we read that Abraham went beyond the precepts of the law that was to come when, after having conquered the four kings, he refused to touch anything at all of the spoil of the Sodomites, which was rightly owed to him as victor, even when the very king whose spoil he had brought back humbly offered it to him. Calling upon the divine name he proclaimed: 'I lift up my hand to the Most High Lord, who made heaven and earth, that I will not take anything from a piece of thread to a sandal strap of all that is yours.'[6]

2. "We know that David went beyond the precepts of the law when, despite Moses' command to pay back one's enemies in kind,[7] he not only did not do this but even embraced his persecutors in love, prayed devoutly to the Lord on their behalf, even wept mournfully for them, and revenged them when they were slain.[8]

"Likewise we see that Elijah and Jeremiah were not under the law either. When they could have guiltlessly enjoyed a lawful marriage they chose to remain virgins nonetheless.

"We read that Elisha and other holy men of the same chosen orientation exceeded the commands of Moses. Of them the Apostle says as follows: 'They went about in sheepskin and in goatskin, in distress, afflicted, needy, the world unworthy of them, wandering in deserts and mountains and caves and caverns of the earth.'[9]

3. "What shall I say of the sons of Jonadab, the son of Rechab? We read that they replied thus to the prophet Jeremiah when he offered them wine at the Lord's command: 'We do not drink wine because our father Jonadab, the son of Rechab, ordered us, saying: You and your sons shall not drink wine forever. And you shall not build a house or sow seed or plant vines and possess them, but you shall live in tents all your days.'[10] 4. Hence they also deserved to hear from this same prophet: 'Thus says the Lord of hosts, the God of Israel: There shall not lack a man from the stock of Jonadab, the son of Rechab, to stand in my sight forever.'[11]

"None of these were content to offer tithes of their possessions. Instead, disdaining property, they offered themselves and their own souls to God, for which no exchange can be made by a human being, as the Lord affirms in the Gospel: 'What will a person give in exchange for his own soul?'[12]

V.1. "For this reason we should know that we from whom the observance of the law is no longer demanded but for whom the gospel word daily sounds–'If you wish to be perfect, go, sell all that you have and give to the poor, and you will have treasure in heaven, and come, follow me'[13]–are, when we offer God tithes of what we own, in some way still held under the burden of the law and have not yet attained to the heights of the Gospel, which grants those who obey it not only advantages in the present life but even rewards in the one to come. 2. For the law promises those who practice it not the rewards of the heavenly kingdom but the consolations of this life when it says: 'The one who does these things shall live in them.'[14] But the Lord says to his disciples: 'Blessed are the poor in spirit, for theirs is the kingdom of heaven.'[15] And: 'Everyone who leaves house or brothers or sisters or father or mother or wife or children or field for the sake of my name shall receive a hundredfold and shall possess eternal life.'[16] Rightly so. For it is not as praiseworthy for us to abstain from unlawful things as it is to do so from lawful things, and not to use these latter out of reverence for him who permitted us their use because of our weakness.

3. "And so, if even those who faithfully offered the tithes of their produce and observed the ancient precepts of the Lord could not yet rise to the summit of the Gospel, you see very clearly how distant from it are they who do not do as much as this. For how can they who disdain to fulfill even the lighter precepts of the law share in the grace of the Gospel? The imperious words of the Lawgiver witness to how easy they are in that a curse is even pronounced on those who do not fulfill them: 'Cursed,' he says, 'is the one who does not keep to everything that is written in the book of the law, to do it.'[17] 4. Here, on account of the nobility and excellence of the commands, it is said: 'Let the one who can take it take it.'[18] There the forcefulness of the Lawgiver indicates the insignificance of the precepts: 'I call heaven and earth to witness today,' he says, 'that if you do not keep the commands of the Lord, your God, you shall perish from the face of the earth.'[19] Here the very magnificence of the sublime commands is indicated by the exhortatory rather than the imperative mode: 'If you wish to be perfect, go,' do this or that. There Moses places an unavoidable burden on those who reject it, while here Paul engages by persuasion alone those who are willing and eager for perfection.

5. "For what could not be grasped by everyone everywhere on account of its wonderful sublimity was not to be the subject of a general precept, nor was it to be demanded of everyone in what I might call canonical fashion. Instead, all are moved to grace by persuasion, so that those who are great may justifiably be crowned with the perfection of virtuousness, while those who are little and cannot fill up 'the measure of the stature of the fullness of Christ'[20] are nonetheless far from the dark curses of the law and will neither be given over to the scourge of present evils nor be struck with eternal punishment, even though they may seem to be hidden and overwhelmed by the brilliance as it were of greater stars.

6. "Christ, then, forces no one to the highest reaches of virtue by the obligation of a precept, but he moves by the power of a free will and inflames by salutary persuasion and by the desire for perfection. For where there is a precept, there is obligation, and consequently punishment as well. And those who observe the things to which they are constrained by the severity of an established law escape the punishment that it threatened them with, but they do not obtain recompense and rewards.

VI. "Thus, while the word of the Gospel lifts up the strong to what is noble and elevated, it does not permit the weak to sink to the depths. It does indeed bestow the fullness of blessedness on the perfect, but it imparts forgiveness to those who have been overcome by their frailty. For the law placed those who fulfilled its precepts in a kind of position between what each deserved, both cutting them off from the condemnation of sinners and distancing them from the glory of the perfect. How base and wretched this is you may notice even by comparing it with the condition of the present life, where it is held to be very deplorable if a person toils and labors merely to be considered not a criminal among honest people, without being at the same time either rich or honorable or glorious.

VII.1. "Hence it has been put in our power today to choose to live under either the grace of the Gospel or the terror of the law, for everyone is necessarily associated with one or the other in accordance with the quality of his behavior. Either the grace of Christ receives those who go beyond the law or else the law holds on to those who are weaker and as it were in debt to it and dependent upon it. Whoever transgresses the precepts of the law will never be able to attain to gospel perfection, even though he may boast in vain that he is a Christian and that he has been freed by the grace of the Lord. 2. For not only should the one who fails to fulfill what the law commands be believed to be still under the law, but also the one who is satisfied with observing no more than the law requires and who never brings forth fruit worthy of his calling and of the grace of Christ. There it is not said: 'You shall offer your tithes and firstfruits to the Lord, your God,'[21] but rather: 'Go, sell all that you have and give to the poor, and you will have treasure in heaven, and come, follow me.' There, because of the greatness of perfection, the disciple who asks for the briefest period of time to bury his father is not granted it,[22] and a duty of human charity is set aside in favor of the virtue of divine love."

VIII.1. When he heard these things the blessed Theonas was inflamed with an inextinguishable desire for gospel perfection. Now that the seed of the word had been planted in his fertile heart, he buried it as it were in the deep and cultivated furrows of his breast. He was especially humbled and moved by compunction because of the fact that the old man had said that he had not only not attained to gospel perfection but that he had barely even fulfilled the commands of the law itself. For although he was accustomed to paying out tithes of his harvest every year as an alms, he lamented that he had never heard of the arrangement regarding firstfruits. Yet, even if he had carried that out as well, he nonetheless humbly recognized that, in accordance with what the old man had said, he was far from gospel perfection.

2. And so he returned home downcast and touched by the kind of sorrow that works repentance unto a lasting salvation.[23] No longer hesitant about his own desire and determination, he turned all of his mind's concern and care to the salvation of his spouse, and by similar exhortations be began to incite in her the desire with which he himself had been inflamed and to urge upon her with tears day and night that they should serve God together in purity and chastity. He said that a conversion to a better life should never be delayed, because the vain hope of a youthful age would be no provision against the finality of a sudden death, which in fact had snatched off boys, youths, and young men as well as old men in its arbitrary choice.

IX.1. But although he persisted unremittingly in beseeching thus, his inflexible spouse would not give her consent to him, saying that she could never abstain from conjugal relations in the flower of her life, and that if she were abandoned by him and committed some sin it would have to be imputed to him instead for having broken the bonds of marriage.

Thereupon, after having set out at length the condition of human nature, which, because of its weakness and instability, it would be dangerous to entangle over an extended period in carnal desires and labors, he added that a person was not permitted to reject a good to which he had been taught that he must absolutely adhere, and that it was more dangerous to despise a known good than not to love an unknown one. Consequently, he was already ensnared in the guilt of sin if he preferred what was earthly and filthy to the goods that he had discovered, which were so excellent and so heavenly. 2. The greatness of perfection belonged to every age and to both sexes, and all the members of the Church were urged to scale the heights of lofty virtue by the Apostle, when he said: "Run in such a way as to obtain."[24] Nor should those who were ready and eager have to stand still because of the indolent and the lazy, when it was better for the slow to be spurred on by those who were running ahead than for those who were hastening to be held back by those who had stopped.

Consequently, he had determined and decided for himself to renounce secular life and to die to the world in order to be able to live to God. And if he was unable to have the blessing of joining Christ's company with his wife, he preferred to be saved even at the expense of one member and as it were to enter the kingdom of heaven crippled, rather than to be condemned with a sound body.[25] 3. He also added these words, and said: "If Moses permitted wives to be divorced because of hardness of heart,[26] why would Christ not allow this because of a desire for chastity? Indeed, not only the law but the Lord himself had commanded that, among other dispositions toward fathers and mothers and children, utter reverence was to be shown them. Yet, for his name's sake and out of a desire for perfection, he decreed that they should not only be merely despised but that they should even be hated, and to these he also joined the name of wife when he said: 'Everyone who leaves house or brothers or sisters or father or mother or wife or children for the sake of my name shall receive a hundredfold and shall possess eternal life.'" 4. To such an extent, then, did he permit nothing to be compared to the perfection which he preached that he even ordered the relationship with one's father and mother to be dissolved and to be despised for love of him, although, according to the Apostle, this involves the first commandment with a promise–namely: "Honor your father and mother, which is the first commandment with a promise, that it may go well with you and that you may be long-lived upon the earth."[27] Clearly, then, just as the word of the Gospel condemns those who break the bonds of marriage by the crime of adultery,[28] so also it promises hundredfold rewards to those who, on account of a love for Christ and a desire for chastity, have rejected the yoke of the flesh.

5. "Hence, if it is possible for you to accept this reasoning and to turn with me to that most desirable form of life, so that together we might serve the Lord and escape the punishment of Gehenna, I will not reject our married love. On the contrary, I will embrace it with still greater affection. For I recognize and venerate the helpmeet who was assigned to me by the Lord's decree, and I do not refuse to cling to her in Christ by an unbroken covenant of love. Nor will I separate from myself what the Lord has joined to me by the law of our primordial condition[29] as long as you yourself are what the Creator wanted you to be. 6. But if you want to be not my helpmeet but my seducer, and if you prefer to give your support not to me but to the adversary, and if you think that the sacrament of matrimony was given you so that you might defraud yourself of the salvation offered you and also keep me from being the Savior's disciple, then I will manfully lay hold of the words uttered by Abba John, or rather by Christ himself, to the effect that no carnal affection should be able to keep me from a spiritual good. For 'whoever does not hate father and mother and children and brothers and sisters and wife and fields, and his own soul besides, cannot be my disciple.'"[30]

7. When, therefore, despite these and other such words the woman's attitude was unbending, and she remained obstinate and unyielding, the blessed Theonas said: "If I am unable to keep you from death, neither shall you separate me from Christ. It is safer for me to be divorced from a human being than from God." And so, inspired by the grace of God, he at once took steps to carry out his decision, and he did not permit the ardor of his desire to grow cold on account of any delay. For he immediately stripped himself of all his worldly property and took flight to a monastery. There in a brief period he shone so brightly with holiness and humility that, when John of blessed memory left this world's light for the Lord, and the holy man Elijah—who was not inferior to his predecessor—

had also died, Theonas was the third to be chosen when everyone was polled, and he succeeded them in the distribution of alms.

X.1. But no one should think that we have made all of this up in order to encourage spouses to divorce. We not only do not condemn marriage but we even say in accordance with the words of the Apostle: "Marriage is honorable among all, and the marriage bed is undefiled."[31] We wanted to describe faithfully to the reader, however, the beginning of the conversion wherein this great man was dedicated to the Lord. 2. I ask the reader kindly first of all to find me blameless, whether he is pleased or displeased with this, and either to praise or to blame the actual doer of the deed. I myself have not offered my own viewpoint in this matter but have presented a factual history in simple narrative form, and it is right that, just as I do not claim for myself any praise from those who approve of this deed, neither should I feel the anger of those who disapprove of it. 3. Let each person, then, have his own opinion about this, as we have said. But I warn him to refrain from censorious criticism, lest he believe himself fairer or holier than the divine judgment, by which even the wonders of apostolic miracles were conferred on this man. I shall not even mention the opinion of numerous fathers, who manifestly did not only not blame his action but even lauded it to the extent that they preferred him to the most eminent and distinguished men in the choice for almsgiving. And I am sure that the judgment made by so many spiritual men, which had God as its author, was not erroneous, having been confirmed by such marvelous wonders, as has already been said.

XI. But it is now time for us to follow the plan of the promised discussion. It was during the days of Pentecost, then, that Abba Theonas visited us in our cell, and when evening prayers were over and we had been sitting for a short while on the ground we began to question him in considerable detail as to why they were so careful that no one ever kneel in prayer during all of Pentecost or presume to fast until the ninth hour, and we sought to understand this with so much the more diligence because we had never seen it observed with such care in the monasteries of Syria.

XII.1. Thereupon Abba THEONAS began to speak as follows: "It certainly behooves us, even when the reason for it has not been grasped, to yield to the authority of the fathers and to a custom of our forebears which has existed for so many years, up until our own day, and to maintain it, as it was passed on of old, by a constant and reverent observance.

2. "But since you want to know the causes and the reason for this, listen for a short while to what has been passed down by our elders about this custom. Before the authority of the divine Scriptures is produced, however, we should say a little, if you are willing, about the nature and character of fasting, so that the subsequent authority of Scripture may confirm what we have said.

3. "In Ecclesiastes the divine wisdom has indicated that there is an appropriate time for everything–that is, for all things, whether they be fortunate or be considered unfortunate and sad. As it says: 'There is a time for all things, and a time for everything under heaven: a time for bringing forth and a time for dying, a time for planting and a time for uprooting what was planted, a time for killing and a time for healing, a time for destroying and a time for building, a time for weeping and a time for laughing, a time for mourning and a time for dancing, a time for casting stones and a time for gathering stones, a time for embracing and a time to be far from embracing, a time for acquiring and a time for losing, a time for keeping and a time for throwing away, a time for breaking and a time for repairing, a time for being silent and a time for speaking, a time for loving and a time for hating, a time for war and a time for peace.'[32] And a little later it says that 'there is a time for everything and for every deed.'[33]

4. "It has therefore been determined that none of these things is a permanent good, except when it is carried out at the right time and in correct fashion. Thus, the very things that turn out well now, since they were done at the right time, are found to be disadvantageous and harmful if they are tried at an inopportune or inappropriate moment. The only exception to this is those things that are essentially and of themselves either good or bad and that can never be turned to their contraries, such as justice, prudence, fortitude, temperance, and the other virtues, and, on the other hand, the vices, which can never be understood differently. But if they can sometimes have different effects, so that they are found to be good or bad in accordance with the character of those who are exercising them, they are perceived not in absolute

terms relative to their nature but as sometimes advantageous and sometimes harmful in keeping with the disposition of the one exercising them and with the opportuneness of the moment.

XIII.1. "Hence we should now pursue the question about the practice of fasting, and see whether it too is a good in the same way that we have spoken of justice, prudence, fortitude, and temperance, which can never become their contraries, or whether it is something indifferent, which can be beneficial when it is sometimes done and cannot be condemned when it is sometimes left undone, and which never to have done is blameworthy and never to have left undone is praiseworthy.

2. "If we include fasting among those things that are understood as virtues, by placing abstinence from food among the essential goods, then eating will be utterly evil and sinful. For whatever is contrary to an essential good is certainly to be considered essentially evil. The authority of Holy Scripture does not permit us to say this, 3. because if we fast with such an understanding and attitude as to believe that we commit sin when we eat, then not only do we gain no fruit from our abstinence but, according to the Apostle, we even bring upon ourselves very grave guilt and the crime of sacrilege: 'They abstain from food that God created to be eaten with thanksgiving by the faithful and by those who know the truth. For every creature of God is good, and nothing is to be rejected that is received with thanksgiving.'[34] For 'whoever thinks that a thing is common, to him it is common.'[35] Therefore we read that no one is condemned merely for eating food, unless perchance something is joined or added to it afterward that would justify his condemnation.

XIV.1. "And so this appears quite clearly to be something indifferent from the fact that, just as it makes a person righteous when it is observed, so it does not condemn him when it is interrupted, unless perchance it is the transgression of a precept that is being punished, rather than eating. But there must be no time that is bereft of essential goods. It is not permitted anyone to be without them, because in their absence the neglectful person inevitably falls into wickedness. Nor, on the other hand, is any time to be given to an essential evil, because that which is always harmful can never, once it has been done, not be harmful or change into something praiseworthy.

2. "Therefore the things for which we see that conditions and times have been fixed and which sanctify when they are observed but do not do damage when they are omitted are obviously indifferent, such as marriage, farming, wealth, the solitude of the desert, vigils, the reading of and meditation on Holy Scripture, and fasting itself, which is how this discussion started. No divine precept and no authority in Holy Scripture has decreed that any of these are to be pursued so incessantly and maintained so constantly that not occupying oneself with them for a short while is wicked. 3. For whatever is decreed in the form of a command brings death with it if it is not carried out, whereas whatever is recommended rather than commanded is of benefit when done, but the not doing of it is not punishable. Consequently our forebears ordered us to do carefully all of these things, or at least some of them, in keeping with the situation, the place, the method, and the time, and to observe them thoughtfully, because if any of these is done properly it is useful and good, but if improperly it is harmful and dangerous.

"If someone wants to maintain an austere fast when a brother comes, in whom he should refresh Christ hospitably and embrace him with a most gracious welcome, would he not be committing a sin of inhospitality rather than gaining the praise and virtue of religious devotion? 4. Or if someone refuses to relax a rigorous abstinence when fleshly weakness and frailty demand that he recruit his strength by taking some food, should he not be considered the cruel murderer of his own body rather than the procurer of his salvation? Likewise, when a time of celebration permits the pleasant glow that comes from eating and a meal that is necessarily abundant, if someone wishes to hold to a rigid and unbroken fast, he will certainly be seen not as devout but as confused and irrational.

5. "But these things will also be found problematic by those who are on the watch for human praise because of their fasting, and who are acquiring a reputation for holiness because of their vain and showy pallor. The words of the Gospel declare that such people have received their reward in the present,[36] and the Lord

curses their fasting by the prophet. First he speaks in their person and reproaches himself: 'Why have we fasted and you have not noticed? Why have we humiliated our souls and you were unaware?'[37] Then at once he answers, giving the reasons why they do not deserve to be heard: 'Behold,' he says, 'in the days of your fasting your own will is found, and you make exactions of all your debtors. Behold, you fast for arguments and contention, and you strike wickedly with the fist. Do not fast as you have up until this day, that your cry may be heard on high. Is such the fast that I have chosen, for a person to afflict his soul for a day? To turn his head like a circle and to spread out sackcloth and ashes? Will you call that a fast and a day acceptable to the Lord?'[38] 6. Then he begins to teach how a faster's abstinence may become acceptable, and he says clearly that fasting by itself cannot have any value unless the following conditions are joined to it: 'Is not this the fast that I have chosen?' he says. 'Loose the bonds of wickedness, undo the oppressive bundles, let those who are broken go free, and smash every burden. Break your bread for the hungry and bring the needy and the wandering into your house. When you see someone naked, cover him and do not despise your own flesh. Then your light shall burst forth like the morning, and your health shall swiftly rise, and your righteousness shall go before your face, and the glory of the Lord shall gather you up. Then you shall call and the Lord shall hear you. You shall cry out and he shall say: Behold, here I am.'[39]

7. "You see, then, that fasting is by no means considered an essential good by the Lord, inasmuch as it does not become good and pleasing to God by itself but in conjunction with other works. On the other hand, by reason of accessory circumstances it might be considered not only vain but even hateful, as the Lord says: 'When they fast I will not hear their prayers.'[40]

XV.1. "For mercy, patience, and love, as well as the precepts of the aforementioned virtues, in which the good is an essential one, are not to be exercised on account of fasting, but rather fasting on account of them. An effort must be made to acquire by fasting those virtues which are truly good, and not to turn the exercise of the virtues toward the goal of fasting. The affliction of the flesh is beneficial and the medicine of hunger should be taken in order that thereby we might be able to attain to love. Therein lies the permanent good, which is stable and not subject to the vicissitudes of time. For the disciplines of medicine, goldsmithing, and the other skills that exist in this world are not pursued for the sake of the instruments that pertain to the work, but rather the tools are made for the sake of the skill. 2. As these are useful to experts, so they are useless to those who are not acquainted with the discipline of the skill. And as these are of great assistance to the former, who make good use of them to accomplish their work, so they can be of no assistance at all to the latter, who, ignorant of the reason why they were designed, are content just with possessing them, because they place the sum of their usefulness in merely having them and not in achieving a task.

"The essentially best thing, then, is that on account of which the indifferent things are done. This chief good itself, however, is not pursued for any reason other than its own goodness alone.

XVI.1. "This is distinguished from others, which we have spoken of as indifferent, in these ways: if it is good by itself and not by reason of something else; if it is necessary for its own sake and not for the sake of something else; if it is unchangeably and always good, constantly retaining its own character and never being able to become its opposite; if its removal or cessation cannot but bring on the gravest evil; if, similarly, the essential evil, which is its opposite, cannot ever become good.

2. "These defining elements, by which the character of the essential goods is distinguished, can never be applied to fasting. For it is neither good by itself nor necessary for its own sake, because it is properly exercised for the sake of acquiring purity of heart and body, so that the stings of the flesh might be dulled and a peaceful mind reconciled to its Creator. Nor is it unchangeably and always good, because we are not ordinarily hurt by its absence; indeed, sometimes when it is done inopportunely it ruins the soul. 3. Nor is that which seems opposed to it—that is, the naturally enjoyable taking of food—an essential evil. Unless intemperance or sensuality or some other vice accompanies it, it cannot be understood as evil, because 'it is not what enters the mouth that defiles a person, but the things that come out of the mouth that defile a person.'[41]

"And so, whoever derogates from an essential good and exercises it imperfectly and sinfully is pursuing it not for its own sake but on account of something else. For everything else is to be done for its sake, but it itself is to be sought after for itself alone.

XVII.1. "Consistently maintaining this understanding of the character of fasting, then, we should seek after it with all our strength, while yet knowing that it is only appropriate for us if it is practiced at the right time, with the right character and to the right extent, and not fixing all our hopes on it but making it possible for ourselves thereby to attain to purity of heart and apostolic love. From this it is clear, then, that fasting, for which not only special times have been assigned as to when it should be practiced or omitted but for which even a certain character and set measure have been determined, is not an essential good but something indifferent. 2. But the things that are, by an authoritative precept, either commanded as good or forbidden as harmful are never dependent on particular times, such that what has been prohibited may sometimes be done, while what has been ordered may sometimes be passed over. For no measure has been set for justice, patience, sobriety, purity, or love. Nor, on the other hand, has permission ever been freely given for injustice, impatience, wrath, impurity, or hatred.

XVIII.1. "Hence, now that we have said these things about the character of fasting, it seems that there must yet be added the authority of Holy Scripture, by which it may be more clearly proven that fasting neither should nor can be constantly maintained.

"According to the Gospel, the Pharisees as well as the disciples of John the Baptist used to fast, while the apostles, being the friends and companions of the heavenly bridegroom, were not yet keeping a fast. The disciples of John believed that they possessed all righteousness because of their fasting, since they were the followers of him who, as the outstanding preacher of repentance, offered a model to the whole people by his own example, to the extent that he not only renounced the various kinds of food that are furnished for human requirements but was even completely ignorant of common bread itself. Now, they complained to the Lord and said: 'Why do we and the Pharisees fast often, whereas your disciples do not fast?'[42] 2. In his reply to them the Lord clearly shows that fasting is not always appropriate, and that it is not necessary when some seasonal feast or some occasion for charity presents itself and brings with it the pleasure of a meal. 'Can,' he says, 'the children of the bridegroom mourn while the bridegroom is with them? But the days will come when the bridegroom will be taken away from them, and then they will fast.'[43] Although he said these words before the resurrection of his body, nonetheless they actually point to the time of Pentecost, during which, after his resurrection, the Lord feasted with his disciples over the course of forty days, and the joy of his daily presence did not permit them to fast."

XIX. GERMANUS: "Why, then, do we relax the rigor of abstinence in our meals for the whole of Pentecost, when in fact Christ only remained forty days with his disciples after the resurrection?"

XX.1. THEONAS: "Your question is not inappropriate, and it deserves an answer that is completely truthful. After the ascension of our Savior, which took place on the fortieth day of his resurrection, the apostles returned from Mount Olivet, where he showed himself when he was going to his Father, as a reading of the Acts of the Apostles also indicates, and they entered Jerusalem and are said to have waited for the coming of the Holy Spirit for ten days. When these were completed, on the fiftieth day they received him with rejoicing.[44] 2. Thus there was plainly realized the number of this festival, which we read was figuratively foreshadowed in the Old Testament too, when it was ordered that at the end of seven weeks the bread of firstfruits was to be offered to the Lord by the priests.[45] This, in very truth, is recognized as having been offered to the Lord by the preaching of the apostles, with which they are said to have exhorted the people on that day.[46] This was the true bread of the firstfruits, which was proffered at the beginning of the new teaching, when five thousand men were filled with the gift of its food, and which consecrated to the Lord a Christian people newly born from the Jews.

3. "Therefore, these ten days are to be celebrated with the previous forty with equal solemnity and joy. The tradition regarding their observance was transmitted to us by apostolic men and is to be kept in the same manner. Consequently on these days no gen-

uflection is made during prayer either, because bending the knee is as it were a sign of repentance and mourning. Hence on these days too we keep in every respect the same solemnity as on Sunday, on which our forebears taught that, out of reverence for the Lord's resurrection, neither fasting nor genuflecting was to be done."

XXI. GERMANUS: "Can this flesh, seduced by unaccustomed enjoyments over the course of such a lengthy festival, fail to produce a thorny growth even from a stock of vices that has been cut down? Or can the mind, burdened by taking rich food to which it is not used, fail to weaken its rigid control over its servant, the body, especially since our youthful age can quickly incite its subjected members to revolt if we take either our accustomed food somewhat too abundantly or unaccustomed food somewhat too freely?"

XXII.1. THEONAS: "If we weigh and examine everything that we do with a reasonable mind and always, out of the purity of our heart, take into consideration not others' judgments but our own conscience, it is certain that this interval of relaxation will be unable to damage a just strictness. But this will only be so if, as has been said, an unsullied mind weighs the proper measure of indulgence and abstinence on an accurate scale and chastises equally an excess on either side, distinguishing with true discretion whether the weight of pleasure is pressing down our spirit or a more austere abstinence is tipping it to the other side, that of the body, and either lowering or raising the part that it thinks is too light or too heavy.

2. "For our Lord wants nothing to be done for his worship and honor without the moderating force of judgment, because 'the king's honor loves judgment.'[47] Therefore, so that we might tip to neither side by an erring judgment, the most wise Solomon says by way of admonition: 'Honor God from your righteous labors, and give to him from the fruits of your righteousness.'[48] For there is in our conscience an incorrupt and true judge, who alone is never mistaken about the state of our purity, even though all others may be misled.

3. "Therefore the attention of a constantly circumspect heart ought to be maintained with every care and effort. Otherwise, if the judgment of our discretion is somehow misled,

we may either be inflamed with the yearning for an ill-considered abstinence or be seduced by the desire for too great a relaxation, and we may weigh the substance of our strength on an inaccurate scale. But we should place purity of soul on one side of the scale and bodily strength on the other and weigh both with true judgment of conscience, so that we may not, having been swayed by an overwhelming disposition toward one thing, tip the scale of fairness in favor of one side, whether to an undue strictness or to an excessive relaxation, and so that there may not be said to us because of an excess of either relaxation or strictness: 'If you offer rightly but do not divide rightly, have you not sinned?'[49]

4. "For the victims of fasting that we imprudently squeeze out of ourselves by violently wrenching our stomachs and that we believe we are offering rightly to the Lord are detested by him who 'loves mercy and judgment,'[50] when he says: 'I the Lord love judgment, but I hate robbery in a holocaust.'[51] The divine word also condemns as fraudulent workers those who offer the Lord their leavings and the smallest portion, while keeping for the pleasure of the flesh and for their own use the best parts of their oblations—that is, their duties and acts: 'Cursed is the one who does the works of the Lord fraudulently.'[52] 5. Not unjustly, then, does the Lord rebuke him who deceives himself by an inaccurate evaluation, when he says: 'Vain are the children of men. The children of men are liars on the balances, so that they may deceive.'[53] Therefore the blessed Apostle urges us to maintain the rule of discretion and not to be swayed to either side, seduced by excess, when he speaks of 'your rational service.'[54] The Lawgiver also forbids this in like fashion when he orders as follows: 'Let the balance be just and the weights equal, a just modius and an equal sextarius.'[55] Solomon too offers a similar opinion in this regard: 'The great and small weights and the double measures are both unclean before the Lord, and whoever uses them will be hindered in his plans.'[56]

6. "Furthermore, we must be careful not to have either unjust weights in our hearts or double measures in the storerooms of our conscience not only in the way that we have spoken of but also in the following way. That is, we must not burden those to whom we preach the word of the Lord with stricter and heavier

precepts than we ourselves are able to bear, while taking it upon ourselves to lighten with a greater and more indulgent relaxation the things that pertain to our rule of strictness. If we do this, what are we doing but weighing and measuring the revenue and fruit of the Lord's precepts with a double weight and measure? For if we weigh them out in one way for ourselves and in another for our brothers, we are rightly rebuked by the Lord for having deceptive balances and double measures, according to the words of Solomon, where it is said: 'A double weight is an abomination to the Lord, and a deceptive balance is not good in his sight.'[57]

7. "We also clearly incur the guilt of a deceptive weight and a double measure if, out of a desire for human praise, we show ourselves off as more strict in front of the brothers than we usually are when we are alone in our cells–namely, by cultivating an air, in the eyes of human beings rather than in God's, of greater abstinence and holiness. This sickness in particular we must not only avoid but even despise.

"But in the meantime we have digressed a little from the question that was asked, and we should return to it from where we left off.

XXIII.1. "The celebration of the aforesaid days is to be observed in such a way, then, that the relaxation which has been conceded helps rather than hinders the well-being of the body and the soul, because neither can the joy of any festival blunt the stings of the flesh nor can the cruel adversary be appeased out of reverence for these days. 2. Therefore, in order that on feastdays the customary and established solemnity might be maintained and the most salutary degree of privation not be exceeded, it suffices for us to let the indulgence of relaxation go this far: The food which would normally be taken at the ninth hour of the day should be taken a little earlier–that is, at the sixth hour–on account of the festal season. But this is only under the condition that the usual amount and quality of the food not be changed, lest the purity of body and integrity of mind that was sought in the abstinence of Lent be lost in the relaxation of Pentecost and it be of no value to us to have acquired by fasting what a heedless satiety soon forces us to let go of, especially since our enemy, with his well-known cunning, assaults the battlements of our purity particularly at the moment when he notices that its guard has been relaxed because of the celebration of some feast.

3. "Hence we should be very much on the watch to see that the vigor of our mind is never enfeebled by flattering seductions and that, as has already been said earlier, we do not, in the repose and calm of Pentecost, lose the chaste purity of Lent that we were pursuing with unceasing effort. Therefore neither a higher quality nor an extra amount of food must ever be permitted us, but even on the most festive days we should exercise moderation with respect to foods, the abstention from which protected the integrity of our purity on ordinary days. Otherwise the joy of the celebration may provoke in us a very dangerous combat of carnal impulses, and it may come to grief; it may snatch from us the nobler festival of the mind, which exults in the joy of incorruption and, after the brief vanity of carnal enjoyment, we may begin to mourn our lost purity of heart with a long and sad repentance. 4. We must be careful indeed, so that the warning of the prophetic exhortation will not be directed to us in vain: 'Celebrate your festivals, O Judah, and pay your vows.'[58] For if the occasional celebration of certain days does not interrupt a constant abstinence, we shall always enjoy spiritual feastdays, and thus, when we cease from servile activity, there shall be 'month upon month and sabbath upon sabbath.'"[59]

XXIV. GERMANUS: "Why is it that Lent is celebrated for six weeks, while in certain provinces it seems that what might be a greater religious zeal has added even a seventh week, although neither number results in forty days, once Sunday and Saturday have been subtracted? For there are only thirty-six days in these weeks."

XXV.1. THEONAS: "Although the devout simplicity of some people would not put up with a question on this topic, nonetheless, because you who are carefully delving into things that someone else would have asked about in an unworthy fashion are seeking to learn the whole truth about our practices and about this mystery, listen to the reason for it, which is utterly clear, so that you may the more readily see that our forebears handed down nothing that was unreasonable.

2. "The universal precept promulgated in the Mosaic law for all the people is: 'You shall offer your tithes and firstfruits to the

Lord, your God.' And so, since we are ordered to offer tithes of what we own and of our produce, all the more necessary is it that we offer tithes of our very lives, of our human activity and of our works, which is very obviously accomplished in the reckoning up of Lent. 3. For the tithe of the entire number of days which complete the turning year is thirty-six and a half days. Now if the Sundays and Saturdays are subtracted from seven weeks, there remain thirty-five days assigned for fasting. If the day of vigil is added, however, on which the fast is prolonged until cockcrow on Sunday morning, not only is the number of thirty-six days arrived at but, in regard to the tithe of the five days that seemed to be left out, nothing will be wanting to complete the whole sum if the period of night that was added be included in.

XXVI.1. "But what shall I say about firstfruits, which are certainly offered every day by all who serve Christ faithfully? For when they wake up out of sleep and arise with something like a renewed joy after their slumber and, before conceiving any thought in their heart or letting in a memory or care concerning business, they consecrate the source and beginning of their thoughts by divine holocausts, what are they doing in fact but presenting their firstfruits through the high priest Jesus Christ, for use in this life and in the form of a daily resurrection? 2. And those who are roused from sleep and likewise present God with the sacrifice of their jubilation, calling upon him with their tongue's first movement, celebrating his name and praises and opening the doors of their lips in order to sing hymns to him, are offering God the worship of their mouth. In like manner they also bring him the first libations of their hands and their steps when they get out of their beds and stand in prayer and, before they use their limbs for their own affairs, garner nothing beforehand for themselves from their service, but take their steps in his honor and stand still in praise of him. Thus they offer the firstfruits of all their movements, in the stretching out of their hands, in the bending of their knees, and in the prostration of their whole body.

3. "For what is sung in the psalm—'I anticipated the dawn, and I cried out,'[60] and: 'My eyes, to you, anticipated the break of day, so that I might meditate on your words,'[61] and: 'In the morning my prayer shall come before you'[62]—we cannot fulfill other-

wise than by trying to take nothing at all for our own use from any faculty of mind or body after we have been recalled from the repose of sleep, as it were (as we said previously) out of darkness and death, into this light. 4. For there is no morning which the prophet anticipated or which we should anticipate other than either ourselves—that is, our occupations and our mortal dispositions and concerns, without which we cannot exist—or the very subtle suggestions of the enemy, which he tries to insinuate in us by way of fantastic and foolish dreams while we are still at rest and sunk in sleep. He would preoccupy us with them and entangle us in them when we awake shortly thereafter, so that he himself may take the best of our firstfruits and be the first to garner them.

5. "Hence we must take every precaution if we still want to fulfill in deed the sense of the aforesaid verse, so that an insightful watchfulness may protect the first beginning of our morning thoughts, lest our jealous enemy filthy some of them due to his swift foresight and cause our firstfruits to be rejected by the Lord as cheap and common. If he is not anticipated by us with a vigilant and cautious mind, he will not cease to lie in wait, as he usually does in wicked fashion, nor will he stop anticipating us daily with his deceptions. 6. Therefore, if we wish to offer God pleasing and acceptable firstfruits from the harvest of our mind, we must expend no little concern to see that we preserve incorrupt and whole in every respect, like the Lord's sacrosanct holocausts, all the senses of our body, especially in the morning hours. Even many people in the world practice this kind of devotion very carefully. Rising before the light or at daybreak, they never engage in the business and activity of this world without first hastening to the church and striving to consecrate the firstfruits of all their actions and deeds in the divine presence.

XXVII.1. "Moreover, concerning what you said about Lent being celebrated in a different manner—that is, for six or seven weeks—in some provinces, one outlook and the same way of fasting are maintained in the different observances of the weeks. For those who think that Saturday should be a fast day too have set an observance of six weeks for themselves. They keep six fasts in a week, therefore, which comes to the same thirty-six days when repeated six times. Consequently, as we have said, there is one outlook and the same way of fasting, even though a discrepancy appears in the number of weeks.

XXVIII.1. "But when human negligence had completely forgotten the reasoning for this, this season, when the annual tithes are offered to God with thirty-six and a half days of fasting, as was said, took the name of Quadragesima. Perhaps it seemed that it should in fact be called by this title because Moses[63] and Elijah[64] and our Lord Jesus Christ himself[65] are said to have fasted for forty days. 2. To the mystery of this number there are not unjustifiably attached as well the forty years that Israel spent in the desert[66] and likewise the forty stops that it is described as having made in mystical fashion.[67] Or perhaps this tithing took the name of Quadragesima from the usages of the tax-collector's office. For this is what the public tax is popularly called, from which as large a portion of money is set aside for the king's good pleasure as is exacted from us by the King of all ages for the needs of our life in the legal tribute of Lent.

3. "Although, to be sure, it has nothing to do with the question that was posed, nonetheless I do not think that I should pass over the following, since the occasion has presented itself in the course of the discussion: Our elders used to testify very frequently that on those days the whole race of monks would be mightily assaulted according to the ancient custom of a hostile people, and would be cruelly harassed so that they would leave their settlements. The reason for this is that it bears a resemblance to what happened when the Egyptians of old used to oppress the children of Israel with terrible afflictions, and so now too the spiritual Egyptians try to break the true Israel—that is, the people of the monks—under heavy and rough labors, lest by means of the calm that is dear to God we abandon the land of Egypt and, for our salvation, cross over to the desert of virtuousness. Then Pharaoh would rage against us and say: 4. 'They are lazy, and therefore they are crying out and saying: Let us go and sacrifice to the Lord, our God. Let them be oppressed with labor, and be harassed in their work, and not be harassed with mere words.'[68] Their vanity, indeed, considered that the holy sacrifice of the Lord, which is offered only in the desert of a free heart, was the highest vanity, for 'religion is an abomination to the sinner.'[69]

XXIX.1. "The one who is righteous and perfect, then, is not inhibited by the law of Lent, nor is he satisfied with being subject to this modest rule. The leaders of the churches have in fact laid it down for those who are entangled the whole year through in worldly pleasures and business, so that they may be constrained by a kind of legal obligation and be compelled to give at least these days to the Lord and dedicate to the Lord a tithe of the days of their life, all of which they would have swallowed up as if they were edible.

2. "But the righteous, upon whom no law has been imposed, and who spend no small part—that is, a tithe—but the whole extent of their lives in spiritual works, because they are free of the legal tax of tithing, venture to relax their stational fasting without any scruple if a good and holy need presents itself and urges them. For it is not a paltry tithe that is being subtracted from by those who have offered their all to the Lord along with themselves. Certainly the person who offers nothing of his own will and is compelled by legal necessity, without recourse, to pay his tithes to God cannot do this without being seriously guilty of fraud. 3. Hence it is eminently clear that the one who is perfect cannot be a slave of the law, watching out for things that are forbidden and carrying out things that are commanded, and that the perfect are those who do not make use even of things permitted by the law. And thus, although it is said of the Mosaic law that 'the law brought nothing to perfection,'[70] we read that some holy persons in the Old Testament were perfect, because they went beyond the law's command and lived in gospel perfection, 'knowing that the law was not imposed on the righteous but on the unrighteous and the disobedient, on the wicked and on sinners, on criminals and on the defiled,'[71] and so forth.

XXX.1. "It should certainly be known that this observance of Lent did not exist at all as long as the perfection of the primitive Church remained unsullied. For those who practiced an unbroken fast throughout the course of the year were not bound by the tight confines of fast days; they were constrained neither by the obligation of this precept nor by a kind of legal sanction. 2. But a time came when the multitude of believers began daily to fall away from that apostolic fervor and to look out for their own wealth rather than distributing it for the use of all the faithful, according to the institutes of the apostles.[72] Not content with following the example of Ananias and Sapphira,[73] they concerned themselves privately with their own incomes, which they strove not merely to keep at the same level but even to increase. Then it pleased all the priests to summon the people who were fettered by worldly concerns and who were, as I might say, almost ignorant of abstinence and compunction, and to recall them to the holy task of fasting through a fixed schedule and to place them under the obligation as it were of legal tithes. This, indeed, could be useful for the weak, and it could not harm the perfect, who lived under the grace of the Gospel and exceeded the law by their willing devotion. Thus they would be able to attain to the blessedness of the apostolic words: 3. 'Sin shall not have dominion over you, for you are not under the law but under grace.'[74] For, truly, sin cannot exercise dominion in one who stands faithfully under the freedom of grace."

XXXI. GERMANUS: "Since these words of the Apostle, which promise security not only to monks but to all Christians in general, cannot be false, they seem exceedingly obscure to us. For inasmuch as he declares that all who believe in the Gospel are free from the yoke and dominion of sin and removed from it, how is it that the dominion of sin flourishes in nearly all the baptized, according to the words of the Lord, where it says: 'Everyone who commits sin is a slave of sin'?"[75]

XXXII.1. THEONAS: "Your inquiry once again raises an overarching question for us. Although I know that the answer to it can be neither given nor understood by the inexperienced, nonetheless, to the extent that I am able, I shall try to respond to it and to explain it briefly in words—if only your understanding would pursue what we say in deeds. For just as whatever is known not from teaching but from experience cannot be handed on by someone who is inexperienced, so likewise it cannot be mentally conceived of or grasped by someone who has not been grounded in a similar education and training. 2. Therefore I am of the opinion that we must first investigate carefully what the intention and will of the law is, and what the discipline and perfection of grace is, so that as a result we may be able to understand from these things the dominion of sin and how it can be expelled.

"And so, the law commands that marriage be pursued as a great good: 'Blessed is the one who has seed in Zion and a household in Jerusalem.'[76] And: 'Cursed is the barren who has not borne.'[77] 3. On the other hand, grace encourages us to an everlasting and incorrupt purity and the chastity of a blessed virginity when it says: 'Blessed are the barren and the breasts that have not given suck.'[78] And: 'Whoever does not hate father and mother and wife cannot be my disciple.'[79] And the words of the Apostle: 'It remains that those who have wives should be as those not having them.'[80]

"The law says: 'You shall not delay in offering your tithes and firstfruits.'[81] But grace says: 'If you wish to be perfect, go, sell all that you have and give to the poor.'

4. "The law does not forbid the retaliation of wrongs and revenge for injustices when it says: 'An eye for an eye, a tooth for a tooth.'[82] Grace wants our patience to be proven by a redoubling of the mistreatment and the blows that come upon us, and it commands us to be ready to endure double hurt when it says: 'Whoever strikes you on your right cheek, offer him the other. And to him who wants to contend with you at law and to take away your coat, give him your cloak as well.'[83] The former says that enemies must be hated, the latter decrees that they are to be loved to such an extent that we must even pray to God continually on their behalf.[84]

XXXIII.1. "Whoever, then, mounts to this summit of gospel perfection is, by reason of his great virtuousness, raised far above the whole of the law. Despising everything that Moses commanded as insignificant, he knows that he is solely under the grace of the Savior, by whose help he realizes that he has arrived at this most sublime condition. Sin, then, has no dominion over him, 'because the love of God that has been poured out in our hearts by the Holy Spirit, who has been given to us,'[85] excludes every disposition of any other kind. Nor can he desire forbidden things or disdain things that are commanded, since all his concentration and all his longing are constantly fixed upon the divine love, and to such a degree does he not take delight in base things that he does not even make use of those things that have been conceded him.

2. "In the law, however, in which the rights of spouses are observed, it is impossible for the stings of carnal desire not to flour-

ish, even though a roving lasciviousness is restrained and given over to only one woman. It is difficult for the fire, to which fuel is purposely added, to stay within defined limits such that it does not break free and set ablaze whatever it touches. Even if there is always something to block it, so that it is not permitted to flare up outside, it still burns while restrained, because the will itself is guilty and its familiarity with sexual intercourse quickly carries it away to the excesses of adultery. 3. But those whom the grace of the Savior has inflamed with a holy love of incorruption burn up all the thorns of carnal desires with the fire of the Lord's love, such that a dying ember of vice does not diminish the coolness of their integrity.

"By their use of what is lawful, therefore, the slaves of the law slip into what is unlawful, but those who partake of grace know nothing of what is unlawful, for they disdain what is lawful. Just as sin dwells in the lover of marriage, so also does it in one who is content to make an offering of merely his tithes and firstfruits. For when he delays or is neglectful, he will inevitably sin with regard to their quality or their quantity or their daily distribution. 4. For even if someone who is ordered to put his property unwearyingly at the service of the poor dispenses it with the greatest possible faith and devotion, it is still hard for him not to fall frequently into the traps of sin. But sin can have no dominion over those who have not spurned the Lord's counsel but give all their property to the poor, take up their cross, and follow the giver of grace.[86] For no faithless concern about obtaining food will sting someone who, by a pious generosity, dispenses his property and his money, which is already consecrated to Christ and as it were not his own. Nor will a mournful hesitation cut short the cheerfulness of his almsgiving, because all that he has once offered to God he dispenses as something no longer his, without thought of his own need and without fear of insufficient food, for he is convinced that once he has attained to the impoverishment that he desires he will be fed by God much more than a bird of the sky.[87] 5. On the other hand, however magnanimously he may disperse his property, the person who clings to his earthly goods and distributes the tithes of his harvest, his firstfruits, and a portion of his money because he is required to do so under pain of the old law can never completely escape from the dominion of sin (unless perchance by the grace of the Savior he gets rid of the very desire for possession along with his property), even though he may in large part put out the fire of his sins by the dew of almsgiving.[88]

6. "In the same way, whoever chooses to tear out an eye for an eye or a tooth for a tooth, in accordance with the precept of the law, or to hate his enemy cannot but be enslaved under the cruel domination of sin, because he is inevitably always aroused by the disturbance of wrath and anger when he decides to revenge mistreatment by meeting it with retaliation, and in that he is the slave of his bitter hatred for his enemies. But whoever lives in the light of gospel grace and overcomes evil not by resisting it but by putting up with it, not hesitating of his own will to offer his other cheek to the one who is striking his right; who gives his cloak as well to the one who wants to go to law against him for his coat; who loves his enemies and prays for those who slander him—this person has put off the yoke of sin and broken its fetters. 7. For he does not live under the law, which does not destroy the seeds of sin. (Hence the blessed Apostle justifiably says concerning it: 'There is a setting aside of the previous commandment on account of its weakness and uselessness, for the law brought nothing to perfection.'[89] And the Lord says through the prophet: 'I gave them precepts that were not good and ordinances in which they could not live.'[90]) Rather he lives under grace, which not only cuts off the branches of wickedness but completely tears up the very roots of an evil will.

XXXIV.1. "Whoever, therefore, strives to hold to the perfection of the gospel teaching lives under grace and is not oppressed by the dominion of sin, for to be under grace means to fulfill what is commanded by grace. But whoever does not wish to be subject to the fullness of gospel perfection should realize that, although he may seem to himself to be baptized and a monk, he is not under grace but is still bound by the fetters of the law and weighed down by the burden of sin. 2. For it is the intention of him who, by the grace of adoption, has accepted all who have received him not to destroy but to build upon, not to abolish but to fulfill the Mosaic prescriptions.[91] Some, who have no inkling of this and who are unaware of Christ's magnificent counsels and exhortations, feel so liberated by the security of a presumptuous freedom that they not only have nothing to do with the precepts of Christ because they are hard, but they also disdain as outdated the very things that the Mosaic law imposed on beginners and children, saying in their wicked freedom what the Apostle abhors: 'We have sinned because we are not under the law but under grace.'[92] 3. The one who is neither under grace, because he has never mounted to the summit of the Lord's teaching, nor under the law, because he has not accepted even the smallest commands of the law, is burdened by a double rule of sin and believes that he has received the grace of Christ solely in order that he may liberate himself from him by this wicked freedom. Thereby he falls into what the apostle Peter warns that we must not bring upon ourselves: 'Act as free persons,' he says, 'and not as those who have their freedom as a cover for wickedness.'[93] The blessed apostle Paul says too: 'You have been called to freedom, brothers'—that is, so that you may be released from the dominion of sin—'only do not use your freedom as an opportunity for the flesh'[94]—that is, do not believe that the abolition of the legal precepts is a permission to sin. 4. But this freedom is only where the Lord is, as Paul the apostle teaches when he says: 'The Lord is the Spirit, but where the Spirit of the Lord is, there is freedom.'[95]

"Therefore I do not know whether I can express and elucidate the meaning of the blessed Apostle as can those who are experienced. One thing I know very clearly—that it is revealed without anyone's explanation, in fact, to all those who have a perfect grasp of πρακτικη, or practical, discipline. For they do not labor to understand by discussion what they have learned by doing."

XXXV. GERMANUS: "You have shed considerable light on an extremely obscure matter, and one that is, in our opinion, incomprehensible to many. Hence we beseech you to contribute to our progress by explaining carefully why, even sometimes when we are fasting more intently and are worn out and weary, our body is provoked to attack us more vehemently. For frequently even on awaking from sleep, when we notice that we bear the stain of the vile fluid, we are so downcast in conscience that we dare not even rise dutifully for prayer itself."

XXXVI.1. THEONAS: "Your zealous desire to attain to the way of perfection, not merely for a while but fully and perfectly, urges us to pursue this discussion unwearyingly. For you are inquiring carefully not about external purity and outward circumcision but about that which is hidden, knowing that the fullness of perfection does not consist in this visible abstinence of the flesh, which can be possessed either out of necessity or out of hypocrisy even by the faithless, but in the willed and invisible purity of the heart, which the blessed Apostle preaches thus: 2. 'He is not a Jew who is so outwardly, nor is circumcision that which is outwardly on the flesh, but he is a Jew who is so inwardly, and circumcision is of the heart, in spirit and not in letter, the praise of which is not from men but from God,'[96] who alone searches out the secrets of hearts.

"Yet, because your desire cannot be fully satisfied, since the brief time that remains of the night is insufficient to go into this very abstruse matter, I think that it is appropriate to put it off for a while. 3. For these things should be put forth by us gradually and with a heart utterly free of clamoring thoughts, and that is also how they should be received in your minds. Just as it behooves them to be examined for the sake of our common purity, so they cannot be taught and handed on by someone who has not experienced the gift of integrity. For what is being sought may be inculcated not by arguments over empty words but by a faith within one's conscience and by the greater power of truth. 4. Therefore, the knowledge and teaching of this purification cannot be put forth except by one who has some experience of it, nor can it be communicated except to the most ardent and indeed anxious lover of truth itself, who wishes to attain to it not by learning vain and empty words but by pursuing it with all the strength of his mind—that is, not by a zeal for fruitless talkativeness but by a desire for inner purification."

Textual References

1. Cf. 1 Cor 9:11.
2. Prv 3:9–10 LXX.
3. Cf. Nm 18:26.
4. Cf. Nm 5:9–10.
5. Cf. 1 Tm 1:9a.
6. Gn 14:22–23.
7. Cf. Ex 21:23–25.
8. Cf. 1 Sm 24; 2 Sm 1.
9. Heb 11:37–38.
10. Jer 35:6–7.
11. Jer 35:19.
12. Mt 16:26.
13. Mt 19:21.
14. Lv 18:5.
15. Mt 5:3.
16. Mt 19:29.
17. Dt 27:26.
18. Mt 19:12.
19. Dt 4:26.
20. Eph 4:13.
21. Ex 22:28.
22. Cf. Mt 8:21–22.
23. Cf. 2 Cor 7:10.
24. 1 Cor 9:24.
25. Cf. Mt 5:30.
26. Cf. Mt 19:8.
27. Eph 6:2–3.
28. Cf. Mt 5:32.
29. Cf. Gn 2:18.
30. Lk 14:26.
31. Heb 13:4.
32. Eccl 3:1–8 LXX.
33. Eccl 3:17 LXX.
34. 1 Tm 4:3–4.
35. Rom 14:14.
36. Cf. Mt 6:16.
37. Is 58:3a.
38. Is 58:3b–5.

39. Is 58:6–9.
40. Jer 14:12.
41. Mt 15:11.
42. Mt 9:14.
43. Mt 9:15.
44. Cf. Acts 1:12–2:4.
45. Cf. Dt 16:9–10.
46. Cf. Acts 2:14–40.
47. Ps 99:4.
48. Prv 3:9 LXX.
49. Gn 4:7 LXX.
50. Ps 33:5.
51. Is 61:8.
52. Jer 48:10 LXX.
53. Ps 62:9.
54. Rom 12:1.
55. Lv 19:36.
56. Prv 20:10–11 LXX.
57. Prv 20:23 LXX.
58. Na 2:1.
59. Is 66:23.
60. Ps 119:147.
61. Ps 119:148.
62. Ps 88:13.
63. Cf. Ex 34:28.
64. Cf. 1 Kgs 19:8.
65. Cf. Mt 4:2.
66. Cf. Dt 29:4.
67. Cf. Nm 33:1–49.
68. Ex 5:8–9 LXX.
69. Sir 1:24 LXX.
70. Heb 7:19.
71. 1 Tm 1:9–10.
72. Cf. Acts 2:44–45, 4:32, 34–35.
73. Cf. Acts 5:1–2.
74. Rom 6:14.
75. Jn 8:34.
76. Is 31:9 LXX.

77. Jb 24:21?.
78. Lk 23:29.
79. Lk 14:26.
80. 1 Cor 7:29.
81. Ex 22:28.
82. Ex 21:24.
83. Mt 5:39–40.
84. Cf. Mt 5:44.
85. Rom 5:5.
86. Cf. Mt 16:24.
87. Cf. Mt 6:26.
88. Cf. Sir 3:30.
89. Heb 7:18–19.
90. Ez 20:25 LXX.
91. Cf. Mt 5:17.
92. Rom 6:15.
93. 1 Pt 2:16.
94. Gal 5:13.
95. 2 Cor 3:17.
96. Rom 2:28–29.

21.1.1 The lawful remedy of marriage: *Licito nuptiarum remedio.* The notion of marriage as a remedy for the passions of youth or for concupiscence appears clearly in Chrysostom, *De virg.* 9.1, 19.1; Augustine, *De bono coniug.* 3.3; idem, *De Gen. ad litt.* 9.7.12. Whereas Augustine perceives this remedy as but one aspect of marriage among others, Chrysostom comes close to seeing marriage exclusively from its perspective. Cassian's own view of marriage, especially given what is said in 21.9ff., seems nearer to Chrysostom's than to Augustine's. But note that in 21.14.2 he classifies marriage among things indifferent, and that these include practices with which he is in complete sympathy–namely, the solitary life, vigils, reading, meditation, and fasting.

21.1.2 Who this John is we cannot be certain.

Distribution of alms: *Diaconiae.* Cf. the note at 18.7.8. The task of distributing alms seems to have been considered a highly important one in the community: The distributor himself was chosen after a poll of the brothers, and it was customary to select one of the oldest and most distinguished among them. Cf. also 21.9.7, 21.10.3. There are basically two views in ancient monastic literature concerning the receiving of money or goods to be redistributed to the needy. One is represented by Cassian here and holds that the practice is an acceptable one. The second doubts whether a monk should have any dealings at all with money or goods, even if he is not keeping such things for himself. Cf. Ramsey, "Almsgiving," 236–237, n. 54.

21.1.3 On the offering of tithes and firstfruits cf. the note at 14.7.1.

21.3ff. The principle addressed in these chapters is succinctly presented in *Inst.* 3.2: "A voluntary service is more pleasing than functions which are carried out by canonical obligation."

21.4.2 Elijah in particular frequently appears as a symbol or a model of the virginal life. Cf. *Inst.* 1.1.2, 6.4.1; Ambrose, *De virginibus* 1.3.2; Jerome, *C. Iovinianum* 2.15; Chrysostom, *De virg.* 79; Sozomen, *Hist. eccl.* 3.14. Cf. also the note at 14.4.1.

On the use of Heb 11:37–38, cited here, cf. the note at 18.6.2.

21.7.1 Hence it has been put in our power today: These words suggest the optimistic attitude regarding the capabilities of human nature that is found particularly in the thirteenth conference.

21.8.1 On the notion of the heart as a garden, such as appears here, cf. the note at 1.22.2.

21.8.2 Theonas begs his wife to live with him in a nongenital union. On this theme cf. the note at 14.7.4.

21.9.2 Further identification of this Elijah is not possible.

21.9.6 But if you want to be...adversary: These words suggest a comparison of Theonas's wife with the Eve of Gn 3.

21.11 For other demeaning references to Syria cf. the note at 3.22.4.

21.12.4 Justice, prudence, fortitude, temperance: These four "cardinal" virtues, ultimately Platonic (cf. *Symposium* 196f.; *Leg.* 631), are also a heritage of Stoic thought. Cf. Johannes Stelzenberger, *Die Beziehungen der frühchristlichen Sittenlehre zur Ethik der Stoa* (Munich, 1933), 355–378. They also appear in Evagrius, *Gnost.* 44 (SC 356.172–174).

21.14.1ff. On the language of good, bad, and indifferent used here cf. the note at 3.9.1ff.

21.14.3 The willingness to break one's own fast for one's guests is encouraged in *Inst.* 5.24ff.

21.20.2 On the symbolism of seven weeks, "a week of weeks," cf. Cabié, 49–52.

21.20.3 The prohibition of kneeling during Pentecost, for the reason given here, appears already at the end of the second century in Tertullian, *De orat.* 23.

21.22.2 An incorrupt and true judge: *Incorruptus...ac verus iudex.* Cf. 20.5.3 and the relevant note.

21.23.2 Jerome, *Ep.* 22.35, also informs us that the monks of Egypt took their single meal at noonday rather than in the evening during Pentecost: "By doing this they both satisfy ecclesiastical tradition and avoid burdening their stomach with a double portion of food." This practice, largely maintained in *Reg. Magistri* 28.37ff. (except that supper was taken as well on Thursdays and Sundays of Pentecost), was completely dropped in Benedict, *Reg.* 41.1, where it is stated that there are to be both noon and evening meals.

21.26 Prayer immediately on arising, which is attested to in Hippolytus, *Trad. apost.* 41, is discussed at some length in Maximus of Turin, *Serm.* 73.2f. (CCSL 23.305–306).

21.26.2 Standing and stretching out one's hands in the form of a cross was the typical gesture of prayer in the early Church. Cf. Tertullian, *De orat.* 16f.; Origen, *De orat.* 31.2. Prostration as a gesture of prayer is mentioned in 23.16.1; Rv 5:8 and 14, 7:11, 11:16, 19:4; Tertullian, *De orat.* 23.

21.26.6 It is unlikely that the laypersons who are said to hasten to church early in the morning did so in order to participate in a eucharistic liturgy. Daily Mass—although not the daily reception of Holy Communion (cf. 7.30.2 and the relevant note)—seems to have been unknown in Egypt at this time. This is, rather, probably a reference to assisting at lauds/morning prayer or an early instance of what has come to be called "making a visit."

21.28.2 On tithing having taken the name of Quadragesima from tax-collecting practices cf. Gazet's commentary in PL 49.1203–1205.

21.28.3 The harassing of the Egyptian monks that Cassian reports here used to take place during Lent is an otherwise unknown occurrence. Isolated incidents of spontaneous antimonastic behavior are known, however. Cf. 12.13.3.

The expression "true Israel" is usually understood of the Church as a whole in early Christian literature. Cf. Marcel Simon, *Verus Israel: Etude sur les relations entre chrétiens et juifs dans l'Empire Romain (135–425)* (Paris, 1948), 100–124. The application of the term to the monks alone is an instance of a certain monastic elitism. For the application of a related expression to an individual monk cf. Eucherius, *De laude heremi* 44 *(tu nunc verior Israhel).*

21.29.2 On stational fasting cf. the note at 2.25.

21.30 On the theme of decline from an ancient ideal, as suggested in this chapter, cf. the note at 18.5.

21.31 For other references to baptism, mentioned here and in 21.34.1f., cf. the note at 1.1.

21.32.1 On the notion, expressed here and in 21.34.4 and 21.36.3f., that experience is the best teacher cf. the note at 3.7.4.

21.33.5 On almsgiving as having the power to forgive sins cf. 20.8.2.

21.34.4 On practical discipline cf. the fourteenth conference, passim.

21.35 Vile fluid: Namely, an emission of semen. Cf. 12.4.4, 12.7.6, 22.3ff.

21.36.3f. On the idea that the inexpert or impure cannot teach (or be taught) cf. the note at 14.14.1.

TWENTY-SECOND CONFERENCE THE SECOND CONFERENCE OF ABBA THEONAS: ON NOCTURNAL ILLUSIONS

Translator's Introduction

The discussion between Abba Theonas and the two friends, Cassian and Germanus, resumes seven days after the celebration of Pentecost, and it opens with Theonas's praise of the two young men for having been willing to wait so long after their first conference with him. The teacher of spiritual things, he observes moreover, profits from his own service of instruction. He then repeats the question that had been asked at the end of the previous conference—namely, as to why fasting does not always seem to guarantee freedom from the nocturnal emission of seed. To this there are three possible answers: Either a surfeit of food and drink has demanded this sort of release; or some kind of spiritual neglect has provoked it; or, finally, the devil himself has brought this about in order to humiliate a person who is otherwise progressing in purity, thus making him hesitate to receive Holy Communion. In this last case the devil often succeeds in frightening monks away from fasting, because they feel that it bears no fruit when they have had an emission. But fasting, Theonas insists, is necessary for purity; the conquest of gluttony has as its consequence that of other vices as well, inasmuch as all the vices are linked together.

Hereupon Germanus asks whether the fact of having experienced a nocturnal emission is sufficient reason to avoid receiving communion. The old man's answer is that if such an emission is the devil's doing and we bear no responsibility for it, then we should confidently approach the altar; but if we are responsible, on the other hand, then our reception of the sacrament would bring upon us the spiritual sickness and death that is spoken of in 1 Corinthians 11:30. With this Theonas gives an example of a certain brother who experienced an emission whenever he was preparing to receive communion. The elders to whom he brought his case determined, after investigating the various possibilities, that this was the devil's work, and they advised him to communicate. Once having communicated, he was freed from the attacks, which only proved that the devil did not want him to receive the sacrament.

It is possible for a person, Theonas continues, to control the number of emissions and, on being established in purity, to arrive at the state of the eunuchs spoken of in Isaiah 56:4–5, or the state of the virgins who, in Revelation 14:4, are said to follow the Lamb wherever he goes. But no one must ever think that, because of this purity, he is worthy to receive communion. Indeed, it would be impossible to attain to such a degree of holiness both because the eucharist is so majestic and so much a gift of divine condescension and because, as had already been noted in 20.12.1ff., no one can be utterly free of infrequent and lesser sins.

Germanus then asks how one who is sinful and hence not holy may be permitted to receive communion. Theonas's response is to distinguish between being holy or righteous and being immaculate. This distinction had already been made in Evagrius, *De iustis et perfectis* (trans. by Muyldermans, *Evagriana Syriaca* [Bibliothèque du Muséon 31], Louvain, 1952, 143–146). Whereas Evagrius, however, attributes a possible sinlessness to human beings (cf. ibid. 1: "The just do not commit adultery and are not subject to condemnation; the perfect have no concupiscence and are not subject to faults"), Cassian does not. Other human beings may be holy, he declares, but Christ alone is immaculate. Here begins a fairly long christological section that is reminiscent of 5.5f. in many respects. Theonas discusses several New Testament passages that raise the issue of Christ's relationship to sin—1 Peter 2:22a and Hebrews 4:15 (outright denials of any sinfulness on his part), Matthew 4:3ff. (the temptations in the desert), and particularly Romans 8:3 ("God sent his Son in the likeness of sinful flesh"). With regard to this last, the old man's position is that the term "likeness" applies to "sinful" and not to "flesh." In fact, "just as his flesh was never subject to sin, neither was his soul to ignorance" (22.11.3). The Gospels demonstrate, moreover, that what seemed to be sinful flesh in Christ was offset by actions that clearly manifested his divinity. Whoever, then, declares that he is sinless commits blasphemy by making himself equal to Christ.

After this excursus on the unique sinlessness of Christ, Theonas returns to the topic of the sinfulness of the holy or righteous person. He lists the seven ways of lapsing into sin that characterize such a person—namely, by anticipating something seriously sinful in one's thoughts, through ignorance, through forgetfulness, by a careless word, by momentary doubt, through vainglory and, finally, by reason of some demand of nature. As an example of a holy person who fell into sin without departing from righteousness he mentions Peter. The righteous do not fall irrevocably, the old man says, thanks to divine grace. He then refers to Paul and to his apparent admission of frailty in Romans 7:19ff. At this, however, Germanus demurs and wonders whether the Apostle, who seemed to have attained to the highest perfection, was speaking of himself or not rather of sinners in general. Theonas, realizing that his response will necessarily be lengthy, says that he must defer it until the following day, and so the discussion ends.

Although the present conference had started with the theme of the possibility of achieving a state in which nocturnal emissions could be eliminated, it rather quickly moves from there to a discussion of the reception of Holy Communion, the sinlessness of Christ, and, ultimately, the sinfulness of the rest of humankind. The exchange on nocturnal emissions, while important in itself and of no small interest to monks who could give only the most unsettling account to themselves of their biological mechanisms, in fact serves to set the stage for the much longer exchange on sinfulness that follows. By confronting his readers with a bodily phenomenon that inevitably reminds them of the shadowy powers at work within them that cannot be completely controlled, Cassian prepares them to be confronted some pages later with that general state of outright sinfulness which marks all of humanity apart from Christ. Indeed, the twenty-second conference as a whole is a prelude to the still longer discussion of the same topic of sinfulness that will be pursued in the twenty-third.

XXII. The Second Conference of Abba Theonas: On Nocturnal Illusions

Chapters

I.1. After nearly seven days the celebration of Pentecost was over. Just as the night began—that is, after the evening synaxis—we entered the cell of the holy Theonas, anxiously awaiting the promised discussion, and the alert old man, his face cheerful and kind, addressed us first with these words:

"I admired," he said, "how your very ardent zeal was able to put off for seven days the answer to the question that was asked, and how it was able to offer such a lengthy delay to its debtor, even when he did not ask for it. 2. Hence it is most just that, since your graciousness has willingly conceded me such a long hiatus, I myself not delay in repaying my debt. For it is a pleasant aspect of this usury that it produces greater profits when it is repayed, and that it not only enriches the receiver but also does not diminish the lender. The one who dispenses spiritual things in fact makes a double gain, because he profits greatly not only from his listener's progress but even from his own discourse, arousing in himself no small desire for perfection while he instructs his listener. 3. Hence your ardor is my progress and your anxiety is my compunction. For, indeed, my mind was dulled and I could not find in my heart what you were searching for until your ardor and expectation roused me from a kind of sleep to the recollection of spiritual things. Therefore let the question be brought up, if you wish, whose answer we chose to put off a short while ago because of insufficient time.

II. "Unless I am mistaken, your question had to do with why we are sometimes titillated by lighter stings of the flesh when we are enjoying some relaxation, while occasionally we are harassed by sharper impulses when we are abstaining strictly and our body is afflicted and worn out, with the result that, as your own avowal made clear, when we awake we discover that we have been wet by the emission of natural moisture.

III.1. "Our forebears have taught that there are three causes for this onslaught, which occurs at irregular and inopportune moments. It is either stored up due to a surfeit of food, or it flows forth due to a careless mind, or it is provoked by the snares of the mocking enemy.

"The first, then, is the vice of gluttony (that is, of overeating or gormandizing), which causes this excess of the vile moisture to be expelled. When it pollutes our purity during a time of strict abstinence, it is spilled out not because of present hunger, as you may think, but because of the excess of past satiety. 2. For what had been amassed within a person through the gluttony of overeating will inevitably be evacuated by some irritation, even when the body is unaware and has been weakened by much fasting. Therefore, by an evenhanded abstinence, we should not only keep from richer dishes but also be temperate regarding more common foods. Indeed, we should even beware of a satiety of bread and water, so that the purity of body which we have acquired may long remain in us and imitate in some respect our inviolate chastity of spirit. Yet it is necessary for us to recognize that there are occasionally some who, even without any effort of mind, because of either the equilibrium of their bodies or their mature age, are rarely soiled or indeed never polluted by the emission of this fluid. 3. But it is one thing to attain to peace by passive good fortune and another to be worthy of a triumph thanks to one's glorious virtues. The power of the latter, victorious over every vice, is worthy of admiration, while I would say that in the former case, where an ineluctable good offered protection despite one's own indolence, there is more that is worthy of pity than of praise.

4. "The second cause of this unclean emission arises when the mind is empty of spiritual pursuits and practices and is not instructed in the discipline of the inner man. Then it leads astray the person who is draped in laziness, in keeping with his habitual and continual torpor, or else it lusts after bits of impure thoughts, so indolently unconcerned about the most sublime purity of heart that it thinks that the whole of perfection and the height of purity consist exclusively in the asceticism of the outer man. Through the fault of his error and negligence it consequently happens that not only do numerous roving thoughts break into the hidden places of the mind in bold and impudent fashion, but also the seeds of all one's former passions remain there. 5. To whatever degree the body may be chastised by rigid fasting, as long as these lie con-

cealed in the depths of the mind they still disturb with their wanton fantasies the person who is sleeping. As a result of them the vile moisture is expelled before its customary time, by reason not of natural necessity but of wicked deception. Even if this cannot be completely arrested not so much by the flesh in its weakness as by the caution and strength of the mind, at least it can be reduced to a simple emission with the help of God's grace. Therefore the first thing to be done is to restrain our wandering thoughts, lest the mind grow accustomed to these diversions and, while dreaming, be drawn to still more horrible temptations of lasciviousness.

6. "The third cause arises when, through a well-ordered and careful practice of abstinence, we wish to acquire the perpetual purity of chastity by contrition of heart and body, but in his hatred the deceitful enemy assaults us in the following way while we are carefully looking out for the welfare of our flesh and our spirit: Striving to destroy the assurance of our conscience and to humiliate us by some kind of guilt, especially on those days when we want to be pleasing in the sight of God by reason of a greater wholesomeness, he pollutes us without any irritation of the flesh or consent of the mind, nor by the illusion of some fantasy, but by the simple emission of fluid, thus keeping us from Holy Communion. But in certain persons—beginners and those whose bodies have not yet been enfeebled by the lengthy chastisement of fasting—this illusion may be believed to come about at the devil's doing so that, when he sees that they are pursuing more intense fasts, he may overthrow all their attempts by this ruse. Thus, feeling not only that they have made no progress in bodily purity by their stricter fasting but that they have even fallen seriously behind, they are horrified by strict fasting, which is the teacher of incorruption and the mother of purity, as if it were an enemy.

7. "Hence we should realize that we must not be purified of a given vice merely because it preoccupies our thoughts with its own disturbances but because it is not content to hold sway alone without the company of others, and once a group of more cruel vices has been admitted they ravage the mind that is subject to them and hold it captive in manifold ways. Therefore gluttony is not to be overcome only on account of itself—namely, lest it ruin us by a burdensome surfeit—nor merely lest it inflame us with the fire of car-

nal desire, but also lest it enslave us to wrath and rage and sadness and every other passion. 8. For if food and drink are given us in too small a portion, or late, or in a careless way when we are under the dominion of gormandizing, the result is that we are also agitated by the urges of wrath. Again, we cannot enjoy delightful tastes without the plague of avarice, thanks to whose abundant means luxury takes pleasure in large expenses. But avarice, vainglory, and pride and the whole multitude of the vices are joined together as one, and thus each vice, even if it begins to flourish in us by itself, furnishes the possibility of growth to others."

IV. GERMANUS: "We believe that this subject has been raised by the design of God so that, thanks to the occasion provided by the present conference and moved by the very order of the discussion, we would dare to ask in confidence about things that we would never be able to learn, since embarrassment had checked our confidence in asking questions. If, then, at the time when it behooves us to approach the sacred mysteries, we see that we have been polluted by an illusion in a dream, should we presume to receive the sacred and saving food, or should we avoid it?"

V.1. THEONAS: "We should indeed strive with all the effort that we are capable of to maintain the purity of chastity unstained particularly at the moment when we wish to stand at the holy altar, and we should exercise the must cautious watchfulness lest the integrity of flesh that we had preserved up to that time be snatched away especially on the night that we are preparing ourselves for the communion of the saving banquet. 2. Yet if the most wicked enemy deceives the sentinels of our slumbering mind in order to remove the medicine of heavenly healing from us, and he does this in such a way that no guilty irritation occurs and there is no contamination resulting from an assent to pleasure, and if he just provokes a natural emission compelled by necessity, which only occurs at the onslaught of the devil and without any feeling of wantonness, all for the sake of hindering our sanctity, then we can and should confidently approach the grace of the saving food.

"But if this accumulation is emitted through our sinfulness, then we should accuse our conscience and stand in fear of the apostolic words: 'Whoever eats the bread and drinks the cup of the Lord unworthily is guilty of the body and blood of the Lord.

Let a person examine himself, and thus eat of that bread and drink of that cup. 3. For whoever eats the bread and drinks the cup of the Lord unworthily, without discerning the body, eats and drinks judgment upon himself.'[1] That is, whoever does not distinguish this heavenly food from common and ordinary food does not realize that it is not such as is permitted to be received by any but a pure mind and body. Then he says: 'That is why many of you are weak and sick, and many have fallen asleep.'[2] That is, he says that spiritual weakness and death are begotten principally from this kind of reception. For many who receive it unlawfully and abusively are weakened in faith and grow sick in mind by catching the diseases of the passions, and they fall asleep in the sleep of sinfulness, never rising from this mortal slumber through a concern for their salvation. 4. After this there follows: 'But if we judged ourselves, we would certainly not be judged.'[3] That is, if we judged ourselves unworthy of receiving the sacraments whenever we have been wounded by sin, we would indeed make an effort to be able to approach them worthily thanks to the correction of penance. Then we would not be chastised by the Lord for our unworthiness with the harsh scourges of sickness, so that we might experience compunction and have recourse to a remedy for our wounds. Otherwise, not having been considered worthy of the briefest punishment in the present age, we shall be condemned in the future one together with the sinners of this world.

5. "This is also taught in clear language in Leviticus: 'Everyone who is clean shall eat flesh, but whatever soul in which there is uncleanness eats of the flesh of the saving sacrifice, which is the Lord's, shall perish before the Lord.'[4] In Deuteronomy too the unclean person is mystically separated from the camp of the spiritual in similar fashion: 'If there is a man among you,' it says, 'who has been polluted at night in a dream, he shall leave the camp and shall not return until he has washed himself in water at eventide, and after sunset he shall come back to the camp.'[5]

VI.1. "But let us show more clearly that this impurity also occurs sometimes at the devil's doing. We know a brother who, although he possessed a constant purity of heart and body due to his great watchfulness and humility and was never tried by nocturnal deceptions, nevertheless used to be sullied in his sleep by an unclean emission whenever he would be preparing himself to receive the Lord's communion. After having held back from the sacred mysteries for a long time because of fear, he finally raised this problem with the elders, confident that, as a result of their healing counsel, he would obtain a remedy against these attacks and for his own suffering.

2. "But when the spiritual physicians in their learning were examining the first cause of this disease, which usually derives from taking a large quantity of food, they saw that this was not the case with the aforementioned brother, and it was clear to them that this illusion did not come from the vice of satiety, since the brother's well-known strictness and the unusual fact that this pollution occurred on feastdays did not permit them to think thus. Thereupon they transferred their examination to the second cause of this malady. They investigated whether perhaps, through the fault of the soul, his flesh, worn out by fasting, was being troubled by the impure illusions that even the strictest men are polluted with when, due to the vice of pride, they are somewhat inflated by their purity of body, believing that they have acquired the principal gift of God–that is, bodily chastity–by human strength. 3. They asked him, then, whether he believed that he was so capable of this virtue through his own effort that he had no need of divine help. And when he abominated this impious idea with the utmost horror and humbly affirmed that in fact he would not have been able to maintain his bodily purity on the other days unless he had been aided in every respect by divine grace, they immediately saw the hidden snares of the devil's doing and they lighted on the third cause. Assured that there was no guilt of either soul or body, they were of the opinion that he should confidently participate in the sacred banquet. Otherwise, if he held to his position inflexibly, he would be caught in the wicked enemy's clever trap and would not be able to partake of the body of Christ, and by this deception he would be deprived of the healing remedy of salvation. 4. That the whole affair was a trick of the devil's doing became evident when, soon after, the habitual illusions, such as had taken place in the past, ceased as a result of the protection of the Lord's body. Thus the enemy's deceit was made clear. Thus, too, the opinion of the elders was borne out and verified, which taught that frequently this most

unclean emission is induced not by a vice of flesh or soul but by the adversary's sly trickery.

"In order that the deceitful imagination of our dreams, which is the provoker of this unclean emission, may go forever unexperienced, or at least for a number of months (in accordance with what I might call our rather humble and common condition), in addition to having faith, with which it behooves us to hope constantly for the gift of purity as a special grace of God, we must refrain from a surfeit of food and drink. 5. A superfluity of these inevitably causes this kind of moisture to increase, and since, when it is accumulated, it must be expelled and released by the very law of nature, it is voided when there is an irritation or an illusion. But when there is no repletion in the matter of eating, the upshot is that these unclean emissions are generated more slowly. Thus an ejaculation, and so also an illusion, will disturb sleepers more infrequently and not so strongly, because an emission does not so much come from the imagination as the imagination comes from an excess of fluid.

6. "Hence, if we wish to be freed from these seductive illusions, we must strive with all our strength first so that, once the passion of fornication has been overcome, 'sin may not reign in our mortal body,' according to the blessed Apostle, 'to make us obey its desires';[6] secondly so that, once the alluring movement of the body has itself been utterly stilled and calmed, 'we may never yield our members to sin as tools of iniquity';[7] and thirdly so that, once our inner man has become completely and profoundly deadened to wanton titillation, 'we may yield ourselves to God as those who have come from death to life.'[8] Thus, taking these steps, we shall acquire an enduring peace in our body, and we shall also yield our members to God as tools of righteousness[9] and no longer as tools of wantonness. 7. Once we have been established in the purity of chastity, 'sin shall not have dominion.'[10] For we are not 'under the law'[11] which, in commending the lawful rights of marriage, also fosters and stores up deep within us the heat that helps to promote the practice of unlawful fornication, but we are 'under grace'[12] which, in introducing the incorruption of virginity, also arrests that harmless and simple bodily movement and likewise the pleasure of lawful sexual intercourse.

"And, once all the moisture of this most unclean emission has dried up in this way and we have become the honorable and praiseworthy eunuchs spoken of by Isaiah, we shall deserve to possess the blessedness that is promised them: 'The Lord says this to the eunuchs: Those who observe my sabbaths and choose what I wish and keep my covenant, to them I will give a place in my house and within my walls, and a name better than sons and daughters. I will give them an everlasting name, which shall not perish.'[13] 8. Who are these sons and daughters to which these eunuchs are so preferred that they are told that they are going to receive an even better place and name if not the holy ones who, in the Old Testament, maintained the bond of marriage and rightly attained to the adoption of children of God through their observance of the commandments? And what is the name that is promised them as something special in place of the most sublime reward if not our being told that we are going to be called by the name of Christ? Concerning this name the same prophet says elsewhere: 'He shall call his servants by another name. In it he who is blessed on earth shall be blessed by God. Amen. And he who swears on earth shall swear by God. Amen.'[14] And again he says: 'You shall be called by a new name, which the mouth of the Lord will name.'[15]

9. "These persons, because of their purity of heart and body, also enjoy the special and unique blessing of being able to sing constantly the canticle that none of the other holy ones can sing, but only those who follow the Lamb wherever he goes, 'for they are virgins and have not soiled themselves with women.'[16] If, then, we wish to attain to the most sublime glory of the virgins, we must cultivate incorruptibility of mind and spirit with all our strength. Otherwise we shall fall into the number of those foolish virgins[17] to whom virginity was not imputed because in fact the only thing that they did was to preserve themselves untouched by carnal intercourse, and on this account they were virgins. They are called fools because, when the oil of inner purity in their lamps ran out, the brightness and splendor of bodily virginity was extinguished. 10. For chastity must be promoted even in the outer man by the warmth and fuel of inner purity, and it must constantly be attended to in order that a lasting incorruption may be preserved. Therefore these foolish women, even though they were virgins,

did not deserve to enter the glorious bridal chamber of the bridegroom along with those who were wise and who preserved their spirit, soul, and body whole and without reproach on the day of our Lord Jesus Christ.[18] For the true and uncorrupted virgins of Christ, who are considered admirable and honorable eunuchs, are not those who fear fornication and to whom it is not permitted, and who repress impurity, but those who have overcome even the slightest titillation of the mind and the least incitements to wantonness. They have subdued what I might call the feelings of their flesh to such an extent that they are affected not only by no pleasure arising from any movement thereof but not even by the most insignificant titillation.

VII.1. "We should protect our heart with such a sentinel of humility as to maintain the following understanding with a constant and unwavering intention: We can never attain to the dignity of such a purification. Thus, although by the grace of God we may have accomplished everything that I have already spoken of, we must nonetheless believe that we are unworthy of communion in the sacred body. 2. The first reason for this is that this heavenly manna is so majestic that no one enveloped in this flesh of slime receives its nourishment of his own deserving but rather thanks to the gracious generosity of the Lord. The second is that no one can be so circumspect in this world's struggle as not to be struck by at least the darts of infrequent and lesser sins, because it is impossible not to sin either through ignorance or carelessness or surprise or thought or need or forgetfulness or in sleep. Even if someone has mounted to the splendid summit of virtue, so that he may pronounce the Apostle's words without boasting: 'For me it is a small matter that I be judged by you or by any human day. I do not even judge myself, for I am aware of nothing in myself,'[19] he should still realize that he cannot be without sin. 3. For not for no reason did the same teacher add: 'But in this I am not justified.'[20] That is, I shall not at once possess the true glory of righteousness if I believe that I am righteous, nor because my conscience does not prick me with a sense of guilt for sin am I therefore unstained by any filthy contagion. For there are many things that lie hidden in my conscience which are known and manifest to God, even though they may be unknown and obscure to me. Therefore he says in addition: 'The one who judges me is the Lord.'[21] That is, the true judgment in my case is made only by him from whom the secrets of hearts are not hidden."

VIII. GERMANUS: "It was said before that none but the holy should partake of the heavenly sacraments, and now you add that it is impossible for a person to be completely untouched by wrongdoing. If no one is free of wrong, then no one is holy. If no one is holy, it follows that the person in whom holiness is lacking cannot participate in the mysteries of Christ and should not hope in the kingdom of heaven, which the Lord promises to the holy alone."

IX.1. THEONAS: "That many are indeed holy and righteous we cannot deny, but there is a great difference between being holy and being immaculate. It is one thing for someone to be holy—that is, consecrated to divine worship. According to the witness of Scripture, this term is applied not only to human beings but even to places and to the vessels and basins of the Temple. 2. But it is another thing to be without sin. This belongs to the dignity of one man alone, our Lord Jesus Christ, of whom the Apostle declares as being remarkable and special: 'He did not sin.'[22] He assigned him rather insignificant and unworthy praise by these words, in the guise of something incomparable and divine, if we too are able to lead a life untainted by any sinfulness. Again, the Apostle says to the Hebrews: 'We do not have a high priest who is unable to sympathize with our weaknesses, but one who was tried in every respect as we are, without sin.'[23] 3. If, then, we in our earthly lowliness can share in something of that excellent and divine High Priest, so that we too may be tried without committing any sin, why did the Apostle regard as unique and singular in him a dignity that he so clearly did not see in any other human being? By this exception alone, therefore, is he distinguished from the rest of us: It is evident that we are not without sin and that he, although he was tried, is without sin. 4. For what human being, however strong and warlike, is nonetheless not frequently exposed to the enemy's slings? Who is enveloped as it were in impenetrable flesh, so that he may without danger mingle in the great dangers of battle? He alone who is 'beautiful beyond the sons of men'[24] and has taken on the condition of human death with all the frailty of the flesh has never been soiled by any contact with filth.

X.1. "He was tried as we are, first of all, by the vice of gluttony, when the clever serpent sought to mock him in his hunger with the desire for food, in the same way that he had previously seduced Adam, saying: 'If you are the Son of God, tell these stones to become loaves of bread.'[25] But he fell into no sin as a result of this trial, although he was certainly capable of the deed, and he rejected the food offered him by the author of deception, saying: 'Man does not live on bread alone but on every word that comes from the mouth of God.'[26]

2. "He was also tried by vainglory, as we are, when it was said to him: 'If you are the Son of God, cast yourself down.'[27] But he was not taken in by the devil's treacherous suggestion, and he refuted the vain seducer with an objection from Scripture: 'You shall not tempt,' he said, 'the Lord your God.'[28]

"He was also tried by the swelling of pride, as we are, when the devil promised him all the kingdoms of the world and their glory. But he laughed at and reproached the vanity of the one who tried him, saying to him: 'Begone, Satan! It is written: You shall adore the Lord your God, and him only shall you serve.'[29] 3. From these texts we are taught that we too must resist the fraudulent suggestions of the enemy by resorting to Scripture in similar fashion. He was tried again by pride, as we are, when the same trickster started to offer him, through men, the kingdom that he had previously rejected when it was offered by himself. But he laughed at the snares of the one who tried him, and he remained without sin: 'When Jesus realized that they were coming to seize him and make him king, he fled back to the mountain alone.'[30]

4. "He was tried, as we are, with blows of the whip, with slapping, when he was spewed with disgusting spittle, and when, finally, he bore the refined tortures of the cross. But he was never drawn by the insults, to say nothing of the tortures, to the least show of anger—he who on the cross mercifully cried out: 'Father, forgive them, for they do not know what they are doing.'[31]

XI.1. "But what would be the meaning of what the Apostle says—namely, that he came in the likeness of sinful flesh—if we too could have a flesh unpolluted by any stain of sin? For he says this of him who alone is without sin as if it were something unique: 'God sent his Son in the likeness of sinful flesh,'[32] because, in having taken up the true and complete substance of human flesh, he must be believed not to have taken up the sin which is in it but the likeness of sin. 2. For 'likeness' is to be referred not to the reality of the flesh, according to the understanding of certain wicked heretics, but to the image of sin. For there was in him, indeed, a real flesh, but it was without sin; that is, it was similar to the sinful. The one pertains to the reality of the human substance, whereas the other refers to vices and behavior.

3. "He had the likeness of sinful flesh when, as though he were ignorant and worried about food, he inquired: 'How many loaves do you have?'[33] But just as his flesh was never subject to sin, neither was his soul to ignorance. Immediately afterward the evangelist adds: 'But Jesus said this to try them, but he himself knew what he was going to do.'[34] He had a flesh similar to that which was sinful when, as though he were thirsty, he asked for a drink from the Samaritan woman. But he was not polluted by the stain of sin because, on the contrary, the woman was moved to ask for the living water that would never let her thirst but that would become in her a source of water springing up to eternal life.[35] 4. He had the reality of this flesh when he was sleeping in the boat. But, lest those in the boat with him be mistaken regarding a likeness of sin, 'he rose up and rebuked the winds and the sea, and a great calm ensued.'[36] He seemed to be subject to the lot of sin in common with everyone else when it was said of him: 'If this man were a prophet, he would certainly know who and what sort of woman touched his feet.'[37] But he did not have the reality of sin, because he at once refuted the Pharisee's blasphemous thought by forgiving the woman's sins. 5. He was thought to bear sinful flesh along with everyone else when, as though he were in danger of death and struck with terror by imminent suffering, he prayed: 'Father, if it be possible, let this cup pass from me.'[38] And: 'My soul is sorrowful even to death.'[39] But that sorrow knew nothing of the contagion of sin, because the Author of life could not fear death, for he said: 'No one takes my life from me, but I lay it down of myself. I have power to lay it down, and I have power to take it up again.'[40]

XII.1. "That man, therefore, who was born of a virgin, was separated by a great distance from all those who are begotten by the mingling of the sexes, for, although all of us bear not the likeness but the reality of sin in our flesh, he took on not the reality but the likeness of sin in assuming real flesh. 2. The Pharisees, to be sure, very clearly remembered that it was written of him that 'he did not sin, nor was deceit found in his mouth.'[41] Nonetheless they were so mistaken with regard to the likeness of sinful flesh that they said: 'Behold, a glutton and a winebibber, a friend of tax collectors and sinners.'[42] And to the blind man who had received his sight they said: 'Give the glory to God, for we know that this man is a sinner.'[43] And to Pilate: 'If this man were not a sinner, we would not have handed him over to you.'[44]

3. "Whoever dares to say that he is without sin, therefore, claims for himself, by a criminal and blasphemous pride, an equality in the thing that is unique and proper to him alone. For the implication is that he says that he has the likeness of sinful flesh and not the reality of sin.

XIII.1. "But Scripture clearly declares that righteous and holy men are not immune from guilt, when it says: 'The righteous person falls seven times and gets up again.'[45] For what else is falling but sinning? And yet, although he is said to fall seven times, he is nonetheless declared righteous, and the lapse into human frailty does not militate against his righteousness, because there is a big difference between a holy person's lapse and a sinner's.

2. "For it is one thing to commit a deadly sin and it is another to anticipate it in thought, which is not without sinfulness; or to offend by the error of ignorance or forgetfulness or by a heedless word glibly uttered; or, by the vice of faithlessness, to doubt something for a moment, due to an inner thought; or to be moved by the subtle titillation of vainglory; or to fall back for a short while from the heights of perfection, due to some demand of nature. These are the seven kinds of lapses and, even though a holy man occasionally falls because of them, he still does not cease to be righteous. Yet, although they seem insignificant and small, they still make it impossible for him to be sinless. For on their account he must do penance every day, truly ask for pardon, and unceasingly pray for his sins, saying: 'Forgive us our trespasses.'[46]

3. "In order to prove by very clear examples that some holy persons have gone astray but have nonetheless not departed from righteousness, take the case of Peter, the most blessed and distinguished of the apostles. What else should he be believed to have been than holy, particularly when he was told by the Lord: 'Blessed are you, Simon BarJona, because flesh and blood has not revealed this to you, but my Father who is in heaven. And to you I will give the keys of the kingdom of heaven, and whatever you bind on earth shall be bound in heaven, and whatever you loose on earth shall be loosed in heaven.'[47] 4. What could be loftier than the Lord's praise, what more sublime than this power and blessedness? And yet shortly afterward, when, ignorant of the mystery of the passion and unaware of its great benefit to the human race, he opposed it and said: 'Far be it from you, Lord; this shall not happen to you,'[48] he deserved to hear: 'Get behind me, Satan. You are a stumbling block to me because you do not know the things of God but those of men.'[49] When Justice itself reproaches him in these words, is he to be believed never to have fallen or not to have departed from holiness and righteousness? 5. Is it to be denied that he obviously suffered a collapse when, out of fear of being persecuted, he found himself forced to deny the Lord three times? But, by washing away the stain of this great crime immediately afterward by the most bitter tears of penance, he did not lose the dignity of his holiness and righteousness.[50]

"With regard to him, then, and to other holy persons like him we must understand what is sung by David: 'A person's steps are guided by the Lord, and he will take great pleasure in his path. When the righteous falls he shall not be disturbed, for the Lord holds him by the hand.'[51] 6. Who else can this be than the righteous, whose steps are guided by the Lord? And yet it is said of him: 'When he falls he shall not be broken.' What does 'when he falls' mean but a lapse into some sin? 'He shall not be broken,' it says. That means that he shall not be oppressed for a long time by an onslaught of sin, but, although he may seem broken for the moment, he shall nonetheless be raised up by a swift resurrection when he implores the divine assistance, and he shall not lose his enduring righteousness. Or, even if he loses it for a while due to the weakness of the flesh, he shall recover thanks to the support of the Lord's hand. 7. For the one who recognizes that he cannot be justified by the faithfulness of his own works and who believes that he will be freed from the bonds of sin by the Lord's grace alone cannot cease to be holy after a collapse, and he does not cease from crying out with the Apostle: 'Wretched man that I am! Who will free me from the body of this death? The grace of God, through Jesus Christ our Lord.'[52]

XIV.1. "The Apostle Paul knew that the immeasurable abyss of purity could not be penetrated by man because of the resistance of seething and emotional thoughts. And, like one who had already been cast about on the seas for a long time, he said: 'The good that I want I do not do, but the evil that I hate, this I do.'[53] And again: 'But if I do what I do not want, it is no longer I who do it but sin dwelling in me.'[54] And: 'I delight in the law of God according to the inner man, but I see another law in my members at war with the law in my mind and making me captive to the law of sin that is in my members.'[55] Having had an exhaustive view of both his own frailty and nature's, and terrified by the depths, so immeasurable and vast, he fled to the safe harbor of divine help. As if despairing of his vessel's burden of mortality and of its being weighed down by natural weakness, he begged for a protection against shipwreck from him to whom nothing is impossible,[56] and he cried out in pitiable lament: 'Wretched man that I am! Who will free me from the body of this death?' And at once, thanks to the kindness of God, he presumed on the liberation that he had despaired of, due to the weakness of nature, and he confidently added: 'The grace of God, through Jesus Christ our Lord.'"

XV.1. GERMANUS: "Many people declare that this passage from the Apostle must be understood in this way: They are certain that he spoke it not in his own person but in that of sinners—namely, of those who wish to abstain from bodily charms and pleasures but are trapped in their former vices and captivated by the delights of fleshly passions, and who cannot restrain themselves as long as they are oppressed by the deep-rooted habit of vice as by the domination of a savage tyrant, being unable to hope for the freedom of purity. 2. For how could what he says apply to the blessed Apostle, who certainly attained to the highest level of utter perfection: 'The good that I want I do not do, but the evil that I hate, this I do'? And what comes after it: 'But if I do what I do not want, it is no longer I who do it but sin dwelling in me'? And this too: 'I delight in the law of God according to the inner man, but I see another law in my members at war with the law in my mind and making me captive to the law of sin that is in my members'? 3. In what respect could this pertain to the person of the Apostle? For what good thing was there that he could not accomplish? And, on the contrary, what bad thing was there that he did not want to do and detested but that he did anyway, compelled unwillingly by nature? To what law of sin could the vessel of election,[57] in whom the Lord Christ used to speak,[58] be held captive? For when he had taken captive all disobedience and 'every height lifting itself up against God,'[59] he said of himself with confidence: 'I have fought the good fight, I have finished the race, I have kept the faith. Now a crown of righteousness has been set aside for me, which the Lord, the just Judge, will bestow on me on that day.'[60]

XVI.1. THEONAS: "You are trying to bring me back to the boundless sea of a very deep question just as I am entering the safe harbor of silence. But, having seized the opportunity offered by a secure berth, let us drop the anchor of silence for a while here, now that we have finished the voyage of this long conference, so that tomorrow, if no storm comes up, we may open the sails of our conversation to the sure breeze of a prosperous wind."

TEXTUAL REFERENCES

1. 1 Cor 11:27–29.
2. 1 Cor 11:30.
3. 1 Cor 11:31.
4. Lv 7:19–20 LXX.
5. Dt 23:11–12.
6. Rom 6:12.
7. Rom 6:13a.
8. Rom 6:13b.
9. Cf. Rom 6:13c.
10. Rom 6:14a.
11. Rom 6:14c.
12. Rom 6:14b.
13. Is 56:4–5.
14. Is 65:15–16.
15. Is 62:2.
16. Rv 14:4.
17. Cf. Mt 25:1–13.
18. Cf. 1 Thes 5:23.
19. 1 Cor 4:3–4a.
20. 1 Cor 4:4b.
21. 1 Cor 4:4c.
22. 1 Pt 2:22a.
23. Heb 4:15.
24. Ps 45:2.
25. Mt 4:3.
26. Mt 4:4.
27. Mt 4:6.
28. Mt 4:7.
29. Mt 4:10.
30. Jn 6:15.
31. Lk 23:34.
32. Rom 8:3.
33. Mk 6:38.
34. Jn 6:6.
35. Cf. Jn 4:7–15.
36. Mt 8:26.
37. Lk 7:39.
38. Mt 26:39.

39. Mt 26:38.
40. Jn 10:18.
41. 1 Pt 2:22.
42. Mt 11:19.
43. Jn 9:24.
44. Jn 18:30.
45. Prv 24:16.
46. Mt 6:12.
47. Mt 16:17, 19.
48. Mt 16:22.
49. Mt 16:23.
50. Cf. Mt 26:69–75.
51. Ps 37:23–24.
52. Rom 7:24–25a.
53. Rom 7:19.
54. Rom 7:20.
55. Rom 7:22–23.
56. Cf. Mt 19:26.
57. Cf. Acts 9:15.
58. Cf. 2 Cor 13:3.
59. 2 Cor 10:5.
60. 2 Tm 4:7–8.

22.1.1 On Theonas's cheerful and kind face cf. the note at 7.1.

22.1.2 That the passing on of spiritual things "not only enriches the receiver but also does not diminish the lender" is a commonplace. Cf. Seneca, *Ep. moral.* 6.4.

22.3.2 On limiting one's intake of food and water in order to control nocturnal emissions here and in 22.6.4f. cf. the note at 12.11.4f.

22.3.3 On the superiority of virtuous struggle to passive good fortune cf. the note at 2.13.9f.

22.3.5 The reference here to making the emission of seed "simple" (*simplicem qualitatem*) is somewhat unclear. (For the use of *simplex* elsewhere in this context cf. 4.15.1, 7.2.1, 12.7.3 [?], 12.12.3 [?], 22.6.7; *Inst.* 7.3.1 [which seems to refer to a spontaneous erection].) Is Cassian implying that there is a masturbatory element in emissions that are not "simple"? The passage in 22.3.6 about the devil polluting "us without any irritation of the flesh or consent of the mind, nor by the illusion of some fantasy, but by the simple emission of fluid" suggests that masturbation may be at issue. *Pruritus*, or "irritation" (qualified as "guilty" in 22.5.2), is probably to be understood as the act of masturbation itself. Cf. *Inst.* 6.22. For the use of "simple" in a sexual context, but as implying no emission at all, cf. *Inst.* 3.5.

22.3.7f. The notion of an interlinking of the vices recalls 5.10.

22.4f. Germanus's question implies that some would have denied access to communion to those who had had a nocturnal emission, however innocent. This is paralleled by the prohibition, voiced by some, of receiving communion by those who had engaged in marital sexual activity the night before. Cf. Origen, *Selecta in Ezech.* 7.2 (PG 13.793); idem, *Frag. in 1 Cor.* 34 (*The Journal of Theological Studies* 9 [1908]: 502).

22.5.1 Holy altar: *Venerandis...altaribus*. On the use of the plural in this way cf. Aegidius Forcellini, *Totius latinitatis lexicon* 1 (Prato 1858–1860) s.v. altaria; DACL 1.2.3157–3158.

22.5.2 On the medicinal imagery of the eucharist here and at 22.6.3 cf. the note at 7.30.2.

22.6.2 On pride being punished by a fall into some kind of impurity cf. the note at 4.15ff.

22.6.3 For other clear references to the utter necessity of grace, as also in 22.13.7, cf. the note at 2.1.3f.

22.6.7 The association of marriage with law and of virginity with grace recalls what is said in 21.32.3f.

22.7.2 On the "infrequent and lesser sins" spoken of here and in 22.13.1ff. cf. 20.12.1ff. and the relevant note.

22.9.1 On the use of the term "holy" in pagan and Christian antiquity cf. Hippolyte Delehaye, *Sanctus: Essai sur le culte des saints dans l'antiquité* (Subsidia Hagiographica 17) (Brussels, 1927), 1–59. For Cassian's understanding of the term here as applying "not only to human beings but even to places and to the vessels and basins of the Temple" cf. ibid. 24.

22.11f Cassian's understanding of Rom 8:3 ("God sent his Son in the likeness of sinful flesh") is classic in its insistence on applying "likeness" to "sinful" rather than to "flesh." Cf. Tertullian, *De carne Christi* 16.3; Chrysostom, *Serm. in Rom.* 13.5; Theodoret of Cyrus, *Interpretatio Ep. ad Rom.*, ad loc.; Cyril of Alexandria, *Quod unus sit Christus* 744e (SC 97.402). The "wicked heretics" of 22.11.2 must be Docetists of some kind.

22.11.3ff. The repeatedly expressed antithesis between Christ "in the likeness of sinful flesh" and Christ untouched by sin (and hence divine) finds a precedent in Gregory Nazianzen, *Or.* 29.19f. Cf. also Leo the Great, *Ep.* 28 (*Tom. ad Flav.*) 4.

22.11.4 On the marine image here and in 22.16 cf. the note at 1 praef. 3f.

TWENTY-THIRD CONFERENCE THE THIRD CONFERENCE OF ABBA THEONAS: ON SINLESSNESS

TRANSLATOR'S INTRODUCTION

The last of Abba Theonas's three conferences takes up where the previous one had left off–namely, with the question of Paul's words in Romans 7:19ff. ("The good that I want to do I do not do, but the evil that I hate, this I do") and to whom they apply. Germanus had been of the opinion that Paul said them not of himself but of sinners. In this he followed, consciously or not, the view expressed by Origen, who had wondered how the interior struggle spoken of in the passage in question could be reconciled "with the apostolic dignity, and particularly with Paul, in whom Christ both lives and speaks." Paul, therefore, in this view, made himself the mouthpiece for others, in keeping with what he said in 1 Corinthians 9:22: "To the weak I became weak, in order to gain the weak." (Cf. Origen, *Comm. in Ep. ad Rom.* 6.9 [PG 14.1085–1086]. It bears noting in this context that Germanus's opinion was formed in an age that was capable of what seems to us toady-like adulation of Paul. Cf. Athanasius, *Ep. fest.* 11.1; Chrysostom, *De laudibus Pauli,* passim.) But Theonas's response is that the words of Romans 7:19ff. apply to those who are perfect, including the Apostle himself, for they speak of wrongdoing accomplished unwillingly; sinners, on the other hand, clearly do not do wrong unwillingly. If what Paul says is subjected to a careful scrutiny, it becomes evident that, despite his possession of so many virtues, the one thing that he lacked but that he desired to have was uninterrupted contemplation. This is the good beside which all other goods pale in comparison, just as the goodness of God overshadows all earthly goodness. Indeed, in the light of the divine goodness all human goodness may be referred to as evil. "Thus, although the value of all the virtues...is good and precious in itself, it is nonetheless obscured upon comparison with the brilliance of theoria. For it greatly hinders and holds back holy persons from the contemplation of that sublime good if they are taken up with what are still earthly pursuits, even if they are good works" (23.4.4).

Uninterrupted contemplation, then, which is of course identifiable with the purity of heart that is the scopos or goal of the monk, was the desired attainment whose absence Paul lamented in himself. As holy as he was, his mind was necessarily occasionally withdrawn from heavenly realities by reason of his preoccupation with earthly activities, and this created in him the profound tension that he expressed in Philippians 1:22–24 and Romans 9:3–4. The inability to maintain a grasp on the divine vision, however, obviously characterizes not only Paul but all others as well who strive for this goal and who realize that they cannot escape distractions even in the midst of their most fervent prayer.

Holy persons, in fact, are most aware of their imperfections, whereas those more conversant in sinfulness have difficulty seeing their faults, even when they are grave. The former grieve over their distractedness, but the latter are unaware that their distractedness so much as incurs guilt. Sinners do not care about sinlessness. Holy persons, on the other hand, make immediate reparation for whatever may have dragged them down from spiritual thoughts. Yet, although they hate the world and all its allurements, it is impossible that they not succumb at least occasionally to distractions. They are like tightrope walkers, in the striking image that Theonas employs, who try to tread the narrowest possible path at a lofty height, in the knowledge that the slightest misstep will bring death. But it is not God who kills them when they fall from contemplation; it is rather they who destroy themselves.

Thus it is that holy persons are conscious of their failure to cling to contemplation; they lament over it and apply the words of Paul to themselves. It is they who experience within themselves the tension of "the law of the mind" struggling against the "law of their members." The origin of this tension, which arises from human carnality, is Adam's sin, by which the rest of humanity was sold under sin. Yet, despite the fact that they are all constrained by sin, "the daily grace of Christ absolves all of his holy ones from this law of sin and death, which they constantly and involuntarily come up against, when they beseech the Lord for the forgiveness of their sins" (23.13.3).

With this Germanus asks whether Paul's words should not apply to those who are struggling against sin, sometimes unsuccessfully, rather than to either the Apostle himself or to grave sinners. The question gives Theonas the occasion to distinguish between grave sins (or crimes), which can only be cleansed by an extended period of repentance, and less serious ones, which can be forgiven by "the daily grace of Christ." It is into these latter that holy persons fall, and it is of them, once again, that Paul is speaking. But there can be no doubt, either, that Paul is also speaking of himself. These less serious sins, however, are the distractions that preoccupy the mind and that Theonas does not hesitate to identify with Paul's "body of death."

Holy persons grieve over their sins, and the scriptural words that might seem to pertain to others in this respect pertain to them alone. Their own consciences accuse them, and the more they engage in the contemplation of the divine the more clearly they see their sinfulness. But this sinfulness of theirs must not keep them from the reception of Holy Communion. The criterion for participation in the sacrament is not one's worthiness, for one is never worthy, but rather the realization of the need of an antidote to sin.

And so the twenty-third conference, which is little else than a lengthy and somewhat repetitive commentary on Romans 7:19ff., comes to an end. In the course of this commentary Cassian interprets Paul in a way that the Apostle could hardly have foreseen. Paul's account of the struggle of the human being in the face of the law, such that he can never claim sinlessness for himself, has become for Cassian the equally unsuccessful struggle to remain free of the mental distractions that disturb the contemplative spirit. These distractions are then qualified as sinful, but there is some lack of clarity here. Are they sinful simply because they cannot compare with the supreme blessedness that contemplation bestows? This position is suggested in 23.4. Or are they sinful because in fact there is some intrinsic impurity in them? This, in turn, is suggested in 23.13.1, where Cassian apparently identifies the distractions in question with the "natural impulses" that prick us "even when we are on fire with the love of purity." In neither case, however, can these distractions be qualified as voluntary sins and thus as sinful in the usual sense of the term.

Very possibly there is a link between Cassian's insistence on the sinfulness of a lapse in contemplation with the view, typically Egyptian, that the original and hence archetypal sin was the rejection of divine contemplation. (Cf. Origen, *De princ.* 2.8.3; Athanasius, *C. gentes* 3f.; idem, *De incarn.* 4; Evagrius [cited in Antoine Guillaumont, *Les "Kephalaia gnostica" d'Evagre le Pontique et l'histoire de l'origénisme chez les Grecs et chez les Syriens* (Patristica Sorboniensia 5), Paris, 1962, 37–38].) For Cassian the fall from contemplation need not be the original and archetypal sin, but it is in any event the all-pervasive and inescapable sin. His whole teaching here represents a certain elaboration and explicitation of what appears in the first conference, especially in 1.8ff. In that conference he seems rather more open to the necessity of engaging in temporal affairs, and thus departing from the practice of ceaseless contemplation, than he is in the twenty-third. In this latter conference contemplation is reduced to its narrowest limits and is made to exclude all other activity of any kind.

Whatever the more remote background in Egyptian theology may have been in Cassian's thinking, one may well pose the question as to whether, faced with both the doctrine of universal sinfulness and the fact of monks who seemed to live completely sinless lives in the desert, he might not have seized upon the sinfulness of mental distractions as the sole solution to the apparent dilemma. How else to include among the mass of sinful humankind, for instance, a monk who could declare to those gathered at his deathbed that he had never done his own will (cf. *Apophthegmata patrum,* de abbate Cassiano 5) or another who could avow that he had never said an angry word (cf. ibid., de abbate Isidoro 2)!

XXIII. The Third Conference of Abba Theonas: On Sinlessness

Chapters

I. The discussion of Abba Theonas on what the Apostle says: "The good that I want I do not do."
II. That the Apostle accomplished many good things.
III. What the good actually was which the Apostle testified that he himself could not achieve.
IV. That human goodness and righteousness are not good if they are compared with the divine goodness and righteousness.
V. That no one can be constantly intent upon the highest good.
VI. That those who believe that they are without sin are like the dim-sighted.
VII. That those who declare that a human being can be without sin are moved by a twofold error in this respect.
VIII. That few people understand sinfulness.
IX. How carefully a monk ought to keep the recollection of God.
X. That those who aim for perfection are truly humble and realize that they are always in need of God's grace.
XI. An explanation of the phrase: "I delight in the law of God according to the inner man," and so forth.
XII. And of this: "We know that the law is spiritual," and so forth.
XIII. And of this: "I know that good does not dwell in me—that is, in my flesh."
XIV. An objection to the effect that the words "The good that I want I do not do," and so forth, apply neither to unbelievers nor to the holy.
XV. The reply to the objection that was offered.
XVI. What the body of sin is.
XVII. That all holy persons have truthfully confessed themselves unclean and sinners.
XVIII. That even the righteous and the holy are not without sin.
XIX. That even at the very time of prayer it is hardly possible to keep from sin.

XX. From whom the destruction of sin and the perfection of virtue should be learned.

XXI. That, although we know that we are not without sin, we should nonetheless not keep ourselves from the Lord's communion.

I.1. Once it was light again, then, we very insistently obliged the old man to search out the depths of the question involving the Apostle, and he spoke as follows:

"You seek to prove that the apostle Paul was speaking not in his own person but in that of sinners when he said: 'The good that I want I do not do, but the evil that I hate, this I do.'[1] And this: 'But if I do what I do not want, it is no longer I who do it but sin dwelling in me.'[2] And what comes next: 'I delight in the law of God according to the inner man, but I see another law in my members at war with the law in my mind and making me captive to the law of sin that is in my members.'[3] On the contrary, these texts clearly show that this cannot at all apply to the person of sinners, but that what has been said only touches those who are perfect and pertains solely to the chastity of those who have acquired the dignity of the apostles. 2. How can these words apply to the person of sinners: 'The good that I want I do not do, but the evil that I hate, this I do'? And these as well: 'But if I do what I do not want, it is no longer I who do it but sin dwelling in me'? For what wrongdoer contaminates himself unwillingly with adultery and fornication, lays traps involuntarily for his neighbor, or is compelled by inescapable necessity to oppress another person by false witness or to defraud him by theft, to covet another's goods or to shed his blood? 3. Much to the contrary, as it is written, 'the human race has been diligently intent upon evil from its youth.'[4] For to such an extent are all those who are aflame with the love of vice desirous of accomplishing what they want that they are even constantly on the lookout for an opportunity to commit a crime, and they even fear lest they be too slow to satisfy their wantonness. They boast of their infamy and of their abundant crimes and they look for a kind of praise for themselves out of their shame, according to the words of the Apostle, who reprimands them.[5] 4. The prophet Jeremiah also asserts that not only do they not unwillingly commit disgraceful crimes, at the cost of peace of mind and body, but that they even make such laborious efforts to attain their end that they are not brought back from a deadly appetite for wrongdoing even when arduous difficulties stand in their way. As he says: 'They have labored to act wickedly.'[6]

5. "And who would say that the following applies to sinners: 'And so, I myself with my mind serve the law of God, but with my flesh the law of sin'[7] when it is clear that they serve God with neither mind nor flesh? And how might those who sin with body and mind serve God, when the flesh receives its incitement to sinfulness from the heart, and the very Author of both natures declares that the source and origin of sin flows from it? As he says: 'From the heart proceed evil thoughts, adultery, fornication, theft, false witness,'[8] and so forth.

6. "Thus it is clearly shown that in no way can this be understood concerning the persons of sinners, who not only do not hate but even love what is evil. To such an extent do they not serve God in either mind or flesh that they sin in mind before doing so in flesh, and before they satisfy their bodily pleasure they anticipate it by sinning in mind and thought.

II.1. "It remains, then, for us to gauge the significance of these words from the deepest dispositions of the one who spoke them, and to examine what the blessed Apostle calls good and what he pronounces bad by comparison, not in accordance with the surface meaning of the words but with the same insight that he himself had, and to look for an understanding that is in keeping with the dignity and rank of the speaker. We shall be able to grasp the words that were uttered under the inspiration of God, consonant with his intention and desire, when we have considered not in word but in experience the condition and dignity of those by whom they were put forth and have arrived at the same disposition, in accordance with which all these meanings were without a doubt conceived and these words uttered.

2. "Hence we should carefully investigate what in particular was the good that the Apostle could not accomplish, although he wanted to. For we know of many goods which we cannot deny that the blessed Apostle and other men like him both had by nature and acquired by grace. For chastity is good, abstinence is praiseworthy, prudence is admirable, hospitality is generous, sobriety is careful, temperance is modest, mercy is gracious, jus-

tice is holy. There is no doubt that all of these were so full and perfect in the apostle Paul and in those like him that they taught religion more by the authority of their virtues than by that of their words. 3. What if they were always consumed by their constant care and watchful concern for all the churches? What a good of mercy it is, what perfection it is, to burn with those who are offended and to be weak with the weak![9] Inasmuch as the Apostle abounded in such great gifts, then, we cannot know what good it was whose perfection he lacked unless we have attained to the disposition with which he himself spoke. 4. And so we have said that, although all the virtues that he possessed were like splendid and precious jewels, yet, if they are compared to that excellent and remarkable pearl which the gospel merchant was seeking and which he wanted to acquire by selling all that he owned,[10] their value is so negligible and insignificant that he would sell them without hesitation, and the possession of this one good alone would enrich the seller of all those other goods.

III.1. "What, then, is the one thing that is so incomparably superior to those great and innumerable goods that all of them should be spurned and rejected and it alone possessed? Without a doubt it is that excellent part whose magnificence and enduring quality Mary chose when she relinquished the service of welcoming and hospitality, which is thus spoken of by the Lord: 'Martha, Martha, you are concerned and troubled about many things, but few things are necessary, or even one. Mary has chosen the good part, which shall not be taken away from her.'[11]

"The one thing, then, is theoria, or the contemplation of God, whose dignity is greater than all the dignity of righteousness and all the zeal for virtuousness. And all of that, which we said existed in the apostle Paul, is not only good and beneficial but even great and sublime. 2. But, for example, some alloy which was thought to be useful and beautiful is very commonplace in regard to silver; again, the value of silver disappears by comparison with gold; then, too, gold itself is contemptible when contrasted with jewels; and, however great a multitude even of splendid jewels there may be, they are overwhelmed by the fineness of a single pearl. Thus, all the dignity of holiness, which not only is good and beneficial for the present but also obtains the gift of eternity, will nonetheless be considered commonplace and as it were salable if it is compared with the dignity of divine contemplation.

"By way of confirming this comparison on the authority of Scripture, does not Scripture say universally of all the things that were created by God: 'Behold, everything that God made was very good'?[12] And again: 'All the things that God has made are good in their season'?[13] 3. The things that belong to the present, then, are not declared good in a merely minimal sense but are emphatically 'very good.' For, in fact, they are useful for us while we are living in this world, whether to sustain life or as medicine for the body or on account of some benefit unknown to us. Or else they are very good in that they let us 'see the invisible things of God, his eternal power and his divinity, from the creation of the world, through things that have been made graspable'[14]–that is, from the great and well-ordered construction and arrangement of the world–and let us contemplate them from the existence of everything that is in it. Yet all of these will be unable to maintain their title to goodness if they are compared to the future age, where no mutability in good things and no corruption of true blessedness is to be feared. 4. The blessedness of this world is described as follows: 'The light of the moon shall be as the light of the sun, and the light of the sun shall be sevenfold, as the light of seven days.'[15] The things that are great, then, and splendid and marvelous to behold will immediately seem empty if they are compared to the future promises in faith, as David says: 'They shall all grow old like a garment, and you shall change them like clothing, and they shall be changed. But you yourself are the same, and your years shall not fail.'[16] Therefore, since nothing is stable of itself, nothing immutable, nothing good but the Godhead alone, and every creature acquires the blessedness of eternity and immutability by arriving at it not through its own nature but through participation with the Creator and through his grace, they cannot maintain the dignity of goodness when compared with their Creator.

IV.1. "But let us bolster this argument with still clearer texts. We read that many things are declared good in the Gospel, and that there is a good tree and a good treasure and a good man and a good servant, since, as it says: 'A good tree cannot bear bad fruit.'[17] And: 'A good man brings good things out of the good treasure of his heart.'[18] And: 'Well done, good and faithful servant.'[19] Indeed, there is no doubt that all of these are good in themselves. Yet, if we look at the goodness of God, none of them will be declared good. As the Lord says: 'No one is good but God alone.'[20] 2. In comparison with him even the apostles themselves, who in virtue of their having been chosen exceeded the goodness of humankind in many ways, are said to be evil, as the Lord says to them: 'If you, although you are evil, know how to give good things to your children, how much more will your Father who is in heaven give good things to those who ask him.'[21] And just as our goodness becomes wickedness in the light of the heavenly goodness, so also our righteousness, when compared with the divine righteousness, is considered like the cloth of a menstruous woman, as the prophet Isaiah says: 'All of our righteous deeds are like the cloth of a menstruous woman.'[22]

3. "To make this still clearer, consider the life-giving precepts of the law itself, which are said to 'have been given by angels by the hand of a mediator,'[23] and about which the same Apostle says: 'So the law is holy indeed, and the commandment is holy and righteous and good.'[24] If they are compared to gospel perfection, they are declared not good by the divine oracle. For he says: 'I gave them precepts that were not good and laws in which they could not live.'[25] The Apostle also affirms that the glory of the law was so dimmed by the light of the new covenant that, in comparison with the brilliance of the Gospel, he would not call it glorious, when he says: 'What was glorified is not glorious on account of a surpassing glory.'[26]

4. "Scripture maintains a comparison on the opposite side, too, by also weighing the deserts of sinners and by justifying those who sin much less in comparison with the wicked, when it says: 'Sodom is justified more than you.'[27] And again: 'How did your sister Sodom sin?'[28] And: 'The rebellious Israel has justified her soul in comparison with the disobedient Judah.'[29]

"Thus, although the value of all the virtues that I spoke of previously is good and precious in itself, it is nonetheless obscured upon comparison with the brilliance of theoria. For it greatly hinders and holds back holy persons from the contemplation of that sublime good if they are taken up with what are still earthly pursuits, even if they are good works.

V.1. "For if someone 'snatches the poor from the hand of those stronger than he and the needy and the poor from those despoiling him,'[30] and if he 'breaks the jaws of the wicked and seizes their booty from between their teeth,'[31] how can he, in the midst of his act of intervention, gaze with tranquil mind upon the glory of the divine majesty? If someone distributes sustenance to the poor or with gracious hospitality receives crowds of visitors, how can he, at the very moment when he is being distracted and is anxious in mind over the needs of his brothers, reflect upon the vastness of heavenly blessedness? And when he is struck with the concerns and cares of the present life, how can he look with a heart raised above the contagions of earthly things upon the state of the world to come?

2. "Hence the blessed David desires this alone when he concludes that it is good for a person to cling constantly to God, as he says: 'It is good for me to cling to God, to place my hope in the Lord.'[32] Ecclesiastes also declares that this cannot be accomplished by any of the holy without difficulty, when he says: 'There is no one who is righteous upon the earth, who does what is good and does not sin.'[33]

3. "For what person who has been enchained by the fetters of this body, however high a place he may occupy among all the righteous and the holy, may ever be believed to possess this highest good in such a way that he never departs from divine contemplation and may be considered not to have been drawn away by earthly thoughts for even the shortest period of time from him who alone is good? Who has never been worried about food, clothing, or other fleshly matters; has never been concerned about welcoming brothers, changing his location, or building a cell; or has never longed for the support of human assistance or been troubled by his lack of resources, so as to incur the Lord's words of rebuke: 'Do not be anxious for your life, about what to eat, nor for your body, about what to put on'?[34]

4. "We confidently affirm that even the apostle Paul, who surpassed the exertions of all the holy in the number of his sufferings, was never able to accomplish this, as he himself witnesses to

his disciples in the Acts of the Apostles: 'You yourselves know that these hands have labored for my needs and for the needs of those who are with me.'[35] Or when he writes to the Thessalonians and testifies that he 'worked night and day in labor and weariness.'[36] Although great rewards were prepared for him on account of what he accomplished thereby, nonetheless his mind—as holy and lofty as it was—could not but sometimes be withdrawn from heavenly theoria by reason of attention to earthly work. 5. He realized that he was endowed with many practical gifts, but, on the other hand, when he considered in his heart the good of theoria and as it were weighed on one scale the progress made from so many labors and on another the delight of divine contemplation, and when over a long time he had adjusted the balance of his breast, so to speak, with the vast rewards of his labors pleasing him sometimes and the desire for oneness and indissoluble fellowship with Christ moving him to depart from the flesh at other times, he at last cried out and said in his anxiety: 'I do not know what to choose. I am compelled on two sides, having a desire to be dissolved and to be with Christ, for that is far better, while remaining in the flesh is more necessary for your sake.'[37] 6. Although, therefore, in many ways he preferred this excellent good even to all the fruits of his preaching, nonetheless he submitted himself out of love, without which no one deserves the Lord, and for the sake of those to whom, like a nursing mother, he was still giving milk from the breasts of the Gospel, and he did not refuse to be separated from Christ, which was an evil indeed for him but a necessity for others. For he was compelled to make this his preferred choice out of the abundance of his virtuous graciousness. In keeping with this he even wished, were it possible, to bring upon himself the ultimate evil of anathema for the sake of his brothers' salvation. 7. 'For I myself wished,' he says, 'to be anathema from Christ for the sake of my brothers, who are my kinsmen according to the flesh, who are Israelites.'[38] That is, I would wish to be delivered over not only to temporal but even to everlasting punishment, provided that it were possible for all people to enjoy fellowship with Christ. For I am certain that the salvation of all is more beneficial to Christ and to me than my own is. So that the Apostle, then, might be able to acquire this highest good—namely, enjoying the vision of God and clinging constantly to Christ—he desired to be rid of this body, which was weak and overwhelmed by the many burdens of its own frailty and which could not but keep him from fellowship with Christ.

"For it is impossible for the mind, which is distracted by so many cares and harassed by such different and irritating concerns, to enjoy the divine vision constantly. For what desire of holy persons, however persistent, or what chosen orientation, however lofty, can there be that the crafty deceiver does not sometimes mock at? 8. Who has gone so deeply into the desert and has so rejected the fellowship of all mortals that he is never deluded by vain thoughts and, because of the things that he sees and the earthly responsibilities that take his time, never falls from that contemplation of God which alone is truly good? Who can continually maintain such fervor of spirit that he does not sometimes, when seductive thoughts take his attention away from prayer itself, plunge from heavenly to earthly realities? Which one of us (to pass over other examples of wandering) does not, at the very moment when he is beseeching God and lifting his mind to the heights, drop into a kind of stupor, thereby involuntarily causing offense by the very act by which he was hoping for the forgiveness of his sins? 9. Who, I say, is so ready and watchful that his mind never strays from the meaning of the Scriptures while he is singing a psalm to God? Who serves God so well and is so close to him that he may rejoice to have carried out the Apostle's order, in which he commanded us to pray without ceasing,[39] for even a single day? Although all of these may seem insignificant and utterly removed from sin to some people who are ensnared in grosser vices, nonetheless a number of even minor things is very serious to those who know the good of perfection.

VI.1. "Let us imagine two persons going together into some great house that is filled with bundles, tools, and vessels: One of them is clear-sighted, with eyes undamaged and sharp, whereas a bleariness obstructs the other's vision. Would not the one who had difficulty in seeing everything and whose sight was blocked be sure that there was nothing there but the chests, beds, benches, tables, and other things that he ran across, not so much with seeing eyes as with feeling hands? Would not the one who, on the other hand, even looked for hidden things with his very clear vision declare that there were many quite small objects in that place, whose number could hardly be estimated, and that if they were ever collected in one heap they would equal in number the few things that the other had touched, and perhaps even surpass that?

2. "Thus those who are holy and who see as it were, whose highest pursuit is perfection, wisely notice in themselves even things that the darkened sight of our mind does not grasp, and they condemn them severely. So true is this that those who, as far as our own carelessness can see, have not blackened the snowy whiteness of their body with the slightest stain of sin seem to themselves to be sprinkled with many blotches even if the recollection of a psalm that must be said distracts the attention of the one praying during the time of prayer, to say nothing of an immoral and vain thought creeping over the threshold of the mind.

3. "For if, they say, we ask some noble personage not, let us say, for our life and our well-being but just for the loan of some money, and we focus all the attention of our body and mind upon him and hang with apprehensive expectation on his will, fearing lest perchance an awkward or inappropriate word avert the listener's mercy; or if we are in the forum or in the courts of earthly judges, and our adversary is standing opposite, and we find ourselves coughing or clearing our throat or laughing or yawning or falling asleep in the midst of the trial and the conflict, with what hatred will our ever-watchful enemy provoke the judge's severity against us, to our detriment! 4. How much more should the Judge's kindness be implored with intent and earnest prayer when, on account of the imminent danger of everlasting death, we are beseeching the one who knows all things hidden, particularly when the one who is both our clever deceiver and our accuser is standing by opposite! And rightly will a person be guilty not only of no insignificant sin but in fact of the very serious crime of impiousness if, while pouring forth his prayer to God, he suddenly goes after a vain and immoral thought and abandons his presence, as if he neither saw nor heard. 5. But those who cover the eyes of their heart with a thick veil of vice and who, in the words of the Savior, 'seeing do not see and hearing do not hear, nor do they understand,'[40] hardly perceive in the depths of their

heart even great and capital crimes, and they cannot with purified vision look upon barely perceptible thoughts, at those fleeting and hidden insinuations in themselves which prick the mind with their vague and subtle suggestiveness, or at the blind spots in their own souls. Rather, constantly roving about in the midst of shameless thoughts, they neither know how to grieve when they are distracted from the contemplation that is unique, nor have they the wherewithal to be sorry, for those who lay open their minds to any thoughts that want to enter have no set point which they can hold on to as a principle or upon which they can fix all their desires.

VII.1. "What certainly causes us to fall into this error is the fact that we are utterly ignorant of the virtue of sinlessness, or impeccability, and we think that it is impossible for us to incur any guilt whatsoever from these careless and fleeting digressions of thought. Rather, dulled by stupidity and struck as it were by a blindness of the eyes, capital crimes are the only things that we can see in ourselves, and we believe that only those are to be avoided which are severely condemned as well by the laws of the world. If we think that we are even slightly free of these, we are of the opinion that there is nothing sinful in us at all.

2. "So, cut off from the number of those who see, because we do not see the many specks of dirt that have accumulated within us, we are never pricked by a salutary compunction if the malady of sadness troubles our mind; nor are we sorry when we are struck by a suggestion of vainglory; nor do we weep over a prayer that was made somewhat lazily or lukewarmly; nor do we consider it blameworthy when something other than the prayer or the psalm itself occurs to us while we are singing the psalms or praying; nor are we aghast that the many things that are shameful to say and do in the presence of others we are not embarrassed to conceive in our heart at that very moment, knowing that it lies open to the divine gaze; nor do we cleanse with an abundant washing of tears the pollution of vile dreams; 3. nor do we mourn over the fact that in the midst of the kindness of almsgiving, when we are coming to the aid of our brothers in need or providing sustenance for the poor, a stingy hesitation beclouds the serenity of our joy; nor do we believe that we suffer any setback when we abandon the recollection of God and think about what is tempo-

ral and corrupt, such that the words of Solomon apply quite well to us: 'They strike me, but I did not grieve, and they mocked me, but I was unaware.'[41]

VIII.1. "On the other hand, when those who place the entire sum of their pleasure and joy and blessedness solely in the contemplation of divine and spiritual realities are involuntarily and briefly distracted from that, due to impetuous thoughts, they punish this with the punishment of immediate penance as if it were a kind of sacrilege in themselves. Mourning the fact that they have shown preference to that most insignificant creature, to which their mind's glance was turned, over their Creator, they accuse themselves—I would almost say—of the crime of irreligion. Although they return the eyes of their heart with the utmost swiftness to gazing upon the brilliance of the divine glory, yet they cannot bear even the briefest darkness of carnal thoughts, and they detest whatever withdraws the attention of their mind from the true light.

2. "When the blessed apostle John wished to fill everyone with this disposition, he said: 'Little children, do not love the world and the things that are in the world. If anyone loves the world, the love of God is not in him, for all that there is in the world is the desire of the flesh and the desire of the eyes and the pride of life, which is not of the Father but of the world. And the world and its desire perishes, but the one who does the will of God abides forever.'[42] Those who are holy, then, are disgusted at all that this world consists in. But it is impossible that they not be caught up in these things by wandering thoughts at least for a brief while. Up to our own day no one, apart from our Lord and Savior, has so stilled the natural vagaries of his mind and remained in the constant contemplation of God that he has never been snatched away from it and sinned for love of some earthly thing. As Scripture says: 'The stars themselves are not pure in his sight.'[43] And again: 'If he puts no trust in his holy ones and finds wickedness in his angels.'[44] Or, as a better translation has it: 'Behold, among his holy ones there is no one who is changeless, and the heavens are not pure in his sight.'

IX.1. "Rightly, then, would I say that holy persons, who keep firm hold of the recollection of God and are as it were carried along on their lofty way by lines stretched out on high, should be compared to funambulists, popularly called tightrope walkers, who put the whole of their safety and their life on a rope's very narrow track and who have no doubt that they will immediately suffer a most horrible death if their foot goes even slightly astray or takes any but the right direction. 2. If they do not hold to the narrow path with cautious and careful restraint as they go their way, making their airy progress through the void, thanks to their marvelous skill, the earth, which is as it were the natural mooring for everyone and the most solid and safe foundation for all, becomes for them a present and manifest danger—not because its nature is changed but because they fall precipitously upon it by the weight of their body. Similarly, the unwearying goodness of God and his unchangeable substance itself certainly hurt no one, but we ourselves bring death upon ourselves by falling from the heights to the depths, for this very fall means death for the one who falls. 3. For it is said: 'Woe to them, for they have departed from me. They shall be destroyed, for they have transgressed against me.'[45] And again: 'Woe to them when I depart from them.'[46] For 'your own wickedness shall reprove you, and your own turning away shall reproach you. Know and see how evil and bitter it is for you to have abandoned the Lord your God.'[47] For 'everyone is bound by the cords of his sins.'[48] To such people the Lord quite appropriately directs this rebuke: 'Behold,' he says, 'all you who light a fire and are surrounded by flames, walk in the light of your fire and in the flames that you have kindled.'[49] And again: 'Whoever kindles wickedness,' he says, 'shall perish by it.'[50]

X.1. "When, therefore, holy persons feel that they are daily burdened by the weight of earthly thoughts; that they are falling from loftiness of mind and are involuntarily, indeed even unwittingly, being brought under the law of sin and death; and, not to speak of other things, that they are being kept from the presence of God by those good and indeed righteous but nonetheless earthly works that I spoke of previously; then they certainly have reasons for which to make constant lamentation to the Lord; then they truly have reasons for which to be humbled and to be struck by compunction, not in words alone but in disposition, to declare themselves sinners and continually to ask pardon of the Lord's grace for all the things that they do every day because they are overcome by the weakness of the flesh, and unceasingly to pour out tears of true repentance. For they seem to themselves to be entangled until the very end of their lives in the same seething emotions over which they constantly sorrow and are troubled, and to be unable even to offer their very prayers without the anxiety occasioned by these thoughts. 2. Therefore, knowing by experience that they cannot attain their desired end by human strength because of the resistant burden of the flesh, and that they are unable to be joined to the chief and highest good in accordance with the desire of their heart, but that they are led captive away from its sight to worldly things, they fly to the grace of God, 'who justifies the wicked,'[51] and they cry out with the Apostle: 'Wretched man that I am! Who will free me from the body of this death? The grace of God, through our Lord Jesus Christ.'[52] For they feel that they are unable to accomplish the good that they wish, but that they are always incurring the evil that they do not want and that they hate—that is, shifting thoughts and cares about fleshly things.

XI.1. "To be sure, they delight 'in the law of God according to the inner man,' who transcends all visible things and who constantly seeks to be united to God alone, but they see 'another law in their members'—that is, inserted in the nature of the human condition—which 'is at war with the law of their mind' and which leads captive their understanding by the violent law of sin, forcing it to abandon the chief good and to submit to earthly thoughts. 2. Although these seem necessary and useful when they occur in connection with meeting some religious need, yet, in comparison with the good that delights the eyes of all the holy, they are in fact perceived by them as evil and as something to be fled from, because they are in some measure and for a brief while distracted by them from the joy of that perfect blessedness. For this is the law of sin, which the transgression of its author brought upon the human race by his wrongdoing, and against him was leveled the sentence of the most just Judge: 'Cursed is the earth in your labors. It shall bring forth thorns and thistles for you, and you shall eat your bread in the sweat of your brow.'[53]

3. "This, I say, is the law that has been placed in the members of every mortal, which wars against the law of our mind and keeps it from the divine vision. Now that the earth has been

cursed in our works, after the knowledge of good and evil, it begins to bring forth the thorns and thistles of thoughts, by whose nettles the natural seeds of virtue are choked, so that we are unable, apart from the sweat of our brow, to eat our bread 'which has come down from heaven'[54] and which 'strengthens the heart of man.'[55] The entire human race, therefore, is universally subject to this law, without any exception. For there is no one, however holy, who does not eat the aforementioned bread in the sweat of his brow and with a heart inclined toward anxiety. But there are many rich people, as we see, who eat ordinary bread without any sweat of their brow.

XII.1. "The blessed Apostle also declares that this law is spiritual when he says: 'We know that the law is spiritual, but I am carnal, sold under sin.'[56] For this law is spiritual which commands us to eat the true bread 'which has come down from heaven' in the sweat of our brow, but being sold under sin makes us carnal.

2. "Do I ask what and whose sin this is? It is certainly Adam's, by whose transgression and—as I might call it—damnable dealing and deceitful transaction we were sold. When he was seduced by the serpent's persuasiveness and by eating the unlawful food he delivered over all his offspring, now led astray, to the yoke of perpetual slavery. For it is customary between buyer and seller that the one who wishes to put himself in another's power receives a price from his buyer for the loss of his freedom and for his being delivered over to perpetual slavery. 3. We see very clearly that this is what happened between Adam and the serpent. Upon eating of the forbidden tree he received the price of his freedom from the serpent and, abandoning his natural freedom, he chose to surrender himself in perpetual slavery to him from whom he had obtained the deadly price of the forbidden fruit. Constrained from then on by this condition, he quite understandably subjected the whole line of his posterity to the same perpetual servitude in which he had become enslaved. For what else can a marriage between slaves beget than slaves?

"What, then? Did that sly and clever buyer usurp the right of ownership from the true and lawful owner? 4. By no means. For he did not inveigle away all of God's belongings by a single fraudulent trick, so that the true owner, who puts the buyer himself—

however fugitive and rebellious—under the yoke of slavery, would lose power over his property. But inasmuch as the Creator had bestowed freedom of choice on all rational creatures, he could not, against their will, recall to their inborn freedom those who by the sin of a gluttonous desire had sold themselves contrary to his command. For whatever is opposed to goodness and justice is repugnant to the Author of righteousness and piety. 5. For it would have been an evil thing if he had revoked the benefit of the freedom that he had bestowed, and it would have been unjust if he had by force oppressed and taken captive a free man and not permitted him to exercise the power of the freedom that he had received, since he was reserving his salvation for future ages, so that the fullness of the set time might be attained in the proper order. 6. It was necessary that his offspring remain in this hereditary condition until, having been freed of their primordial fetters, he restored them to their ancient state of freedom by the grace of their first Lord and at the price of his blood. He could have saved them then, but he did not wish to, because justice did not permit breaking the sanctions imposed by his own decree.

"Do you want to know the cause for your having been sold? Listen to your Redeemer himself declaring very openly by the prophet Isaiah: 'What is your mother's bill of divorce, by which I dismissed her? Or who is my creditor, to whom I sold you? Behold, you were sold in your wickedness, and for your crimes I dismissed your mother.'[57] 7. Do you also want to know clearly why he did not wish to redeem you by the strength of his own power when you were under the yoke of slavery? Listen to what he added to the previous words, with which he reproaches the same slaves of sin with the cause for their willful selling: 'Has my hand become short and small, so that I cannot redeem? Or is there in me no strength to save?'[58] But the same prophet shows what is always resistant to his most powerful mercy when he says: 'Behold, the hand of the Lord has not been shortened so that it cannot save, nor has his ear grown heavy so that it cannot hear. But your wickedness has created a division between you and your God, and your sins have concealed his face from you, so that he cannot hear.'[59]

XIII.1. "Since, then, that first curse of God made us fleshly and condemned us to thorns and thistles, and our father sold us by a wicked transaction, with the result that we cannot do the good that we want as long as we are torn from the recollection of the most high God and are compelled to have thoughts that are human and frail, we are frequently and involuntarily pricked by natural impulses, which we would wish to be utterly ignorant of, even when we are on fire with the love of purity. 2. 'We know that good does not dwell in our flesh'[60]—namely, the perpetual and constant tranquillity of this theoria and purity, which we have spoken of. But there has grown up in us a very bad and mournful separation, so that, although we wish to observe the law of God in our mind (that is, we wish never to shift our gaze from the divine brilliance), we are nonetheless enveloped in fleshly darkness and by a certain law of sin are forced to be torn from what we know is good. That is, we have fallen from loftiness of mind into the earthly cares and thoughts to which the law of sin—namely, the sentence of God, which the first wrongdoer received—not unjustifiably condemned us.

3. "Hence it is that the blessed Apostle, although he avows quite plainly that he and all the holy are constrained under the unavoidable obligation of this sin, nonetheless declares confidently that none of them are condemned on account of this, when he says: 'There is, therefore, no condemnation now for those who are in Christ Jesus. For the law of the spirit of life in Christ Jesus has freed me from the law of sin and death.'[61] That is, the daily grace of Christ absolves all of his holy ones from this law of sin and death, which they constantly and involuntarily come up against, when they beseech the Lord for the forgiveness of their sins.

4. "You see, then, that the blessed Apostle uttered these words in the person not of sinners but of those who are truly holy and perfect: 'The good that I want I do not do, but the evil that I hate, this I do.' And: 'I see another law in my members at war with the law in my mind and making me captive to the law of sin that is in my members.'"

XIV.1. GERMANUS: "We say that this can apply to the persons neither of those who are entangled in deadly crimes nor of the Apostle or those who have attained to his stature. We are of the opinion, rather, that this must properly be understood of those who have acquired the grace of God and a knowledge of the truth and who want to abstain from carnal vice, but who are dragged back by their former behavior, as by a law of nature that violently lords it over their members, to the ingrained desire of their passions. For the practice and frequency of wrongdoing becomes a kind of natural law which, implanted in humanly weak members, leads captive to vice the dispositions of the soul that is not yet fully instructed in zeal for virtue but is still, as I might say, of a naive and infantile chastity. Subjecting them to death by the ancient law, it places them under the yoke of a domineering sinfulness, and it does not permit them to attain to the good of purity that they love; instead it forces them to do the evil that they detest."

XV.1. THEONAS: "You have made considerable progress in your position. For now you yourselves have also begun to affirm that this cannot have reference to the person of those who are completely sinful, but that it rightly pertains to those who strive to abstain from carnal vices. Since you have distinguished these latter from the number of sinners, the upshot is that you should also gradually place them in the ranks of the faithful and the holy. For what kinds of sins do you say they can commit if, having gotten entangled in them after the grace of baptism, they can be freed again by the daily grace of Christ? Or of what body of death must the Apostle be believed to have said: 'Who will free me from the body of this death? The grace of God, through Jesus Christ our Lord'? 2. Is it not clear, as the truth obliged even you yourselves to confess, that there is nothing said here about those members of deadly crimes by which the wages of eternal death are gained—namely, murder, fornication, adultery, drunkenness, theft, and robbery—but rather about the aforesaid body to which the daily grace of Christ is applied? For whoever falls upon the body of death after having been baptized and known God should realize that he will not be cleansed by the daily grace of Christ—that is, by the easy forgiveness which our Lord is accustomed to grant to our misdeeds when he is beseeched at particular moments—but by the extended suffering of penance and by the woes of punishment. Or, because of these, he may even be given over in the future to the tortures of eternal fire, as the same Apostle declares thus: 'Do not be misled: No fornicators or idolaters or adulterers or effeminate persons or those who sleep with men or thieves or avaricious persons or drunkards or abusive talkers or robbers shall possess the kingdom of God.'[62] 3. Or what is the law that struggles in our members and that is at war with the law of our mind? When it submits us resisting and captive to the law of sin and death and makes us serve it in our flesh, does it not still permit us to observe the law of God in our mind? For I do not think that the law here refers to the disgrace of sin or can be understood in terms of the aforementioned crimes. If anyone perpetrates them he is not serving in his mind the law of God, which he must first abandon in his mind before he commits any of them in his flesh. For what does observing the law of sin mean other than carrying out the things commanded by sin? 4. What kind of sin is it, then, that when such holiness and perfection think that they are taken captive they still do not doubt that they will be freed by the grace of Christ? As it says: 'Wretched man that I am! Who will free me from the body of this death? The grace of God, through Jesus Christ our Lord.' What law, I say, will you affirm is in our members, which draws us away from the law of God and makes us captive to the law of sin, and which makes us wretched rather than wrongdoing, so that we are not given over to eternal punishment but instead long for the joy of blessedness, which has been interrupted, and with the Apostle declare him our helper who brings us back to it as we search for it: 'Wretched man that I am! Who will free me from the body of this death?' 5. For what does it mean to be taken captive by the law of sin if not to continue in the effects and work of sinfulness? Or what other chief good is there that the holy are unable to accomplish if not that in comparison with which, as we said before, nothing is good? To be sure, we know that there are many good things in this world, especially purity, abstinence, sobriety, humility, righteousness, mercy, temperance, and kindness. But none of these things can be equal to the highest good, and they can be pursued not only by apostles but even by the mediocre. If they are not done by them, then they are punished either by eternal torment or by the heavy toil of repentance, as was said previously, but they are not freed by the daily grace of Christ.

6. "It remains, then, that we may correctly say that these words of the Apostle apply only to the person of the holy. It is they who daily come up against this law, as we have said, not of

crime but of sin. Assured of the state of their salvation, they do not tumble into criminality but, as has often been said, fall from divine contemplation into the wretchedness of bodily thoughts and are frequently deprived of the good of that true blessedness. For if they felt that they were bound to daily crimes by this law in their members, they would certainly speak in terms not of a lack of happiness but of a lack of innocence, and the apostle Paul would not say: 'Wretched man that I am,' but rather: Unclean or criminal man that I am, and he would wish to be freed not from this body of death–that is, from the condition of mortality–but from the shameful deeds and crimes of this flesh. 7. But since he felt that he was held captive on account of his weak human condition–that is, led off to fleshly concerns and cares, which the law of sin and death brings about–he laments this law of sin, which he is involuntarily under, and he has recourse at once to Christ and is saved by the very present redemption of his grace. Therefore, whatever anxiety this law of sin, which by nature produces the thorns and thistles of mortal thoughts and cares, germinates even in the soil of the Apostle's heart is soon uprooted by the law of grace. 'For,' he says, 'the law of the spirit of life in Christ Jesus has freed you from the law of sin and death.'

XVI.1. "This, then, is the inescapable body of death, in which the perfect and those who have tasted 'how sweet the Lord is'[63] are dragged along, and they feel with the prophet 'how evil for himself and how bitter it is to depart from the Lord his God.'[64] This is the body of death which takes them from the heavenly vision and brings them down to earthly things, which makes them think of human shapes or words or business or empty actions while they are singing the psalms and lying prostrate in prayer. 2. This is the body of death on account of which those who seek to imitate the holiness of the angels and desire to cling constantly to the Lord are nonetheless unable to discover the perfection of this good, since the body of death stands in the way, and instead they do the evil that they do not want–that is, they are led off by their mind to things that have nothing to do with progress in virtue and perfection.

"Finally, so that the blessed Apostle might show clearly that he said this about the holy and the perfect and those like himself, he pointed to himself alone as it were and said immediately after:

'And so, I myself'—that is, I who declare these things reveal the secrets of my own conscience and not someone else's. 3. The Apostle is in the habit of using this manner of speaking when he wants to refer to himself in particular. For instance: 'I, Paul, myself beseech you by the mildness and modesty of Christ.'[65] And again: 'Except that I myself did not burden you.'[66] And again: 'But so be it that I myself did not burden you.'[67] And elsewhere: 'I, Paul, myself tell you: If you are circumcised, Christ will profit you nothing.'[68] And to the Romans: 'I myself wished to be anathema from Christ for the sake of my brothers.'[69] 4. There can be no doubt, then, that he says 'and so, I myself' quite expressly and emphatically, meaning me whom you know to be an apostle of Christ, whom you venerate with the utmost respect, whom you believe to be lofty and perfect and in whom Christ speaks. Although I observe the law of God in my mind, still I confess that I observe the law of sin in my flesh—that is, because of the preoccupations of the human condition I sometimes fall from heavenly to earthly things, and my mind in its sublimity slips into care for humble matters. At particular moments I feel myself so taken captive by the law of sin that, although I persist in an unshakable desire with regard to the law of God, I nonetheless feel unable in any respect to escape the force of this captivity unless I constantly take refuge in the grace of the Savior.

XVII.1. "Therefore all those who are holy are struck with compunction because of the weakness of their constitution, and with daily sighs they scrutinize their different thoughts and the hidden and secret places of their conscience, humbly crying out: 'Do not enter into judgment with your servant, for in your sight no one living shall be justified.'[70] And this: 'Who will boast of having a chaste heart? Or who will have confidence that he is pure of sin?'[71] And again: 'There is no one who is righteous upon the earth, who does what is good and does not sin.' And also this: 'Who understands his sins?'[72]

2. "They consider the righteousness of human beings so weak and imperfect and constantly in need of God's mercy that one of them, whose iniquities and sins God cleansed with the fiery coal of his word that was sent from his altar, said after having contemplated God in wondrous fashion and after having seen the

lofty seraphim and a revelation of the heavenly mysteries: 'Woe is me, for I am a man of unclean lips, and I dwell in the midst of a people with unclean lips.'[73] 3. In my estimation he would perhaps not even then have felt the uncleanness of his lips if he had not deserved to know the true and integral purity of perfection, thanks to his having contemplated God. Upon seeing him he immediately recognized an uncleanness that had hitherto been unknown to him. For when he says: 'Woe is me, for I am a man of unclean lips,' he shows by what follows—'and I dwell in the midst of a people with unclean lips'—that he was speaking of his own lips and not of the people's uncleanness.

4. "But even when he prays and confesses the impurity of all sinners, as it were, he includes in a general supplication not only the wicked but also the righteous, saying: 'Behold, you are angry, and we have sinned. We have always been in them, and we shall be saved. All of us have become as one who is impure, and all our righteous deeds are like the cloth of a menstruous woman.'[74] I wonder what could be clearer than these words, in which the prophet included not merely one but all our righteous deeds and, looking around at everything that is judged impure and horrible, chose to compare them to the cloth of a menstruous woman because he could find nothing in human life that was more filthy and impure. 5. In vain, then, does your penetrating and thorny objection—when you said shortly before that if no one is sinless then no one is holy, and that if no one is holy then no one will be saved—pose a problem for a most evident truth. For the difficulty in this question can be resolved from the text of the prophet, where he says: 'Behold, you are angry, and we have sinned.' That is, when you turned away from the pride and heedlessness of our hearts and deprived us of your help, the abyss of our sins immediately engulfed us. It was as if someone had said to the sun in all its splendor: Behold, you have set, and at once thick darkness has covered us over. 6. And yet, although he says that the holy have sinned, and not only that they have sinned but they have always remained in their sins, he does not utterly despair of salvation, but he adds: 'We have always been in them, and we shall be saved.'

"I shall compare these words—'Behold, you are angry, and we have sinned'—with those of the Apostle: 'Wretched man that I am!

Who will free me from the body of this death?' Again, what the prophet adds—'We have always been in them, and we shall be saved'—corresponds to the words of the Apostle that follow: 'The grace of God, through Jesus Christ our Lord.' 7. Likewise, what the same prophet also says—'Woe is me, for I am a man of unclean lips, and I dwell in the midst of a people with unclean lips'—also seems to smack of the aforementioned words: 'Wretched man that I am! Who will free me from the body of this death?' Similarly, what follows in the prophet—'Behold, one of the seraphim flew to me, and in his hand there was a coal (or a stone), which he had brought from the altar with a tongs. And he touched my mouth and said: Behold, I have touched your lips, and your iniquity shall be removed and your sinfulness shall be cleansed'[75]—is like what seems to be uttered by the mouth of Paul, when he says: 'The grace of God, through Jesus Christ our Lord.'

8. "You see, then, how all the holy truthfully confess themselves sinners not in the person of the people but in their own. Yet they are not at all hopeless about their salvation; rather, thanks to the grace and mercy of the Lord, they presume upon the complete justification that they despair of being able to attain due to the condition of their human frailty.

XVIII.1. "The Savior's instruction also teaches us that no one in this life, however holy, is clear of the debt of sin. When he was handing on to his disciples the formula for perfect prayer, he ordered the following to be included among those lofty and most sacred commands which were given only to the holy and the perfect, since they can have nothing to do with the wicked and the unbelieving: 'Forgive us our trespasses as we forgive those who trespass against us.'[76] 2. If, therefore, this prayer is true and is uttered by the holy, as we certainly ought to believe, who could be so insolent and presumptuous, so filled with the pride of diabolical madness, as to declare himself without sin and not only to believe that he is greater than the apostles but even as it were to accuse the Savior of ignorance or futility, because he either did not know that some people could be clear of debts or uselessly taught those who he knew did not need the medicine of this prayer? But if all the holy ones who observe the precepts of their King say explicitly every day 'Forgive us our trespasses,' and if they speak the truth, then truly no one is free of guilt. But if they are dissembling, then it is equally true that they are not without the sin of lying.

3. "Hence also the most wise Ecclesiastes, running through every human act and pursuit in his mind, declared without any exception: 'There is no one who is righteous upon the earth, who does what is good and does not sin.' That is, there has never been nor could there ever be on this earth someone so holy, so diligent, and so single-minded, someone so capable of clinging constantly to the true and unique good, that he would not be drawn away from it every day and feel that he had abandoned it. Yet although such a person cannot be declared inoffensive, it is nonetheless not denied that he is righteous.

XIX.1. "Whoever, then, ascribes sinlessness—that is, impeccability—to human nature must go against not empty words but the witness and proof of his own conscience, which is on our side, and he may declare that he is without sin only when he feels that he has not been snatched away from the highest good. For, indeed, whoever looks into his own conscience, to give but one example, and sees that he has attended even one synaxis without having been interrupted by any word or deed or thought may declare that he is sinless. So, since we confess that the flighty wandering of the human mind cannot be without all these idle and vain things, we must as a result truthfully confess that we cannot be without sin. 2. For, with whatever carefulness a person may strive to keep watch over his own heart, he will never safeguard it according to the desire of his spirit, given the resistant character of the flesh. The more the human mind makes greater progress and attains to a more sincere purity of contemplation, the more unclean it will see itself in the mirror of its purity, so to speak, because it is inevitably the case that, as the mind presses on to a loftier vision and, looking about itself, yearns for greater things than it is pursuing, it despises the state in which it is as ever more inferior and mean. 3. For a more sincere sight sees more things, a blameless life begets greater sorrow for itself when it acts reproachfully, and an improved behavior and an intense desire for virtue multiply groans and sighs. For no one can be satisfied with the level to which he has attained. The more a person is purified in mind, the filthier he sees himself and the more he finds reasons for humility rather than pride; and the more quickly he mounts to loftier things, the more he sees how much further there is to go.

4. "The privileged apostle, 'whom Jesus loved,'[77] drew forth these words from the Lord's heart, so to speak, as he lay on his breast: 'If we say that we have no sin, we are deceiving ourselves and the truth is not in us.'[78] And so if, in saying that we do not have sin, we do not have the truth—that is, Christ[79]—in us, what good do we do but prove by this very profession that we are, from among sinners, criminal and wicked?

XX. "Finally, if it is in our heart to investigate more carefully whether it is possible for a human being to possess sinlessness, from whom could we learn this more easily than from those who 'have crucified their flesh with its vices and lusts,'[80] and to whom the world has truly been crucified?[81] Although they have not only uprooted all of their vices but are even attempting to cut off the thought and the recollection of their sins, they nonetheless profess daily and faithfully that they cannot be free of the stain of sin for even a single hour.

XXI.1. "Yet we should not keep away from the Lord's communion because we know that we are sinners, but we should hasten to it all the more avidly for the sake of our soul's healing and our spirit's purification, yet with that humility of mind and faith that will cause us, while judging ourselves unworthy to receive such a grace, to seek it instead as medicine for our wounds. Otherwise communion may not be worthily received even once a year, as is the case with some who live in monasteries and who are so in awe of the dignity and holiness and worth of the heavenly sacraments that they think that no one should receive them but the holy and stainless, rather than that it is they that make us holy and pure by receiving them. 2. These people are guilty of a more arrogant presumption than they seem to themselves to avoid, because they judge themselves worthy of receiving them when they do receive them. But it is much more righteous for us to receive the sacred mysteries every Sunday as a remedy for our sickness, and to do so with that humility of heart by which we believe and confess that we can never approach them because of our own deserts, than to be puffed up with a foolish attitude of heart and to believe that we are worthy to participate in them even once a year.

3. "Hence, in order to be able to understand this and to maintain it fruitfully, let us intently beseech the mercy of the Lord to help us to accomplish this, which is not at all learned, as other human skills are, by a previous verbal explanation, but rather by previous action and experience. Likewise, unless it is frequently subjected to examination and elaborated in the conferences of spiritual men and carefully scrutinized through instruction and daily experience, it diminishes through neglect or perishes through heedless forgetfulness."

Textual References

1. Rom 7:19.
2. Rom 7:20.
3. Rom 7:22–23.
4. Gn 8:21 LXX.
5. Cf. Phil 3:19.
6. Jer 9:4.
7. Rom 7:25b.
8. Mt 15:19.
9. Cf. 2 Cor 11:28–29.
10. Cf. Mt 13:45–46.
11. Lk 10:41–42.
12. Gn 1:31 LXX.
13. Sir 39:16 LXX.
14. Rom 1:20.
15. Is 30:26.
16. Ps 102:26–27.
17. Mt 7:18.
18. Mt 12:35.
19. Mt 25:21.
20. Lk 18:19.
21. Mt 7:11.
22. Is 64:5.
23. Gal 3:19.
24. Rom 7:12.
25. Ez 20:25 LXX.
26. 2 Cor 3:10.
27. Ez 16:52.
28. Ez 16:49.
29. Jer 3:11.
30. Ps 35:10.
31. Jb 29:17 LXX.
32. Ps 73:28.
33. Eccl 7:21 LXX.
34. Mt 6:25.
35. Acts 20:34.
36. 2 Thes 3:8.
37. Phil 1:22–24.
38. Rom 9:3–4.

39. Cf. 1 Thes 5:17.
40. Mt 13:13.
41. Prv 23:35 LXX.
42. 1 Jn 2:15–17.
43. Jb 25:5.
44. Jb 15:15 LXX.
45. Hos 7:13.
46. Hos 9:12.
47. Jer 2:19.
48. Prv 5:22 LXX.
49. Is 50:11.
50. Prv 19:9 LXX.
51. Rom 4:5.
52. Rom 7:24–25a.
53. Gn 3:17–19.
54. Jn 6:33.
55. Ps 104:15.
56. Rom 7:14.
57. Is 50:1.
58. Is 50:2.
59. Is 59:1–2.
60. Rom 7:18a.
61. Rom 8:1–2.
62. 1 Cor 6:9–10.
63. Ps 34:8.
64. Jer 2:19b.
65. 2 Cor 10:1.
66. 2 Cor 12:13.
67. 2 Cor 12:16.
68. Gal 5:2.
69. Rom 9:3.
70. Ps 143:2.
71. Prv 20:9 LXX.
72. Ps 19:12.
73. Is 6:5.
74. Is 64:4–5.
75. Is 6:6–7.
76. Mt 6:12.

77. Jn 13:23.
78. 1 Jn 1:8.
79. Jn 14:6.
80. Gal 5:24.
81. Cf. Gal 6:14.

23.2.1 On the necessity of experience for grasping spiritual matters, here and in 23.21.3, cf. the note at 3.7.4.

23.2.2 On teaching by deeds as well as by words cf. the note at 11.2.2.

23.3.1 On the Mary and Martha imagery and on Cassian's understanding of "the good part" cf. 1.8 and the relevant note.

23.3.2 The ascending scale of valuable objects here, which terminates with a pearl, offers some indication of the great worth attached to pearls in antiquity and is in keeping with the parable of the pearl in Mt 13:45–46, mentioned in 23.2.4. Cf. Pliny, *Hist. nat.* 9.35.54.

23.3.4 On the divine immutability cf. also 6.14.3.

23.5.6 Milk from the breasts of the Gospel: This image is ultimately derived from Paul's words in 1 Cor 3:2. For more breast imagery cf. RAC 2.662–663.

23.5.7ff. For other references to mental distractions cf. the note at 1.5.4.

23.6.3 Coughing or clearing our throat or laughing or yawning or falling asleep: This passage, reminiscent of *Inst.* 2.10.1, provides a little glimpse into occasional monastic behavior at prayer. For a description of similar monastic behavior during a conference cf. *Inst.* 12.27.2f. Clement of Alexandria, *Paed.* 2.7.60, condemns just such behavior at mealtimes as unbefitting a Christian, and Ambrose, *De virginibus* 3.3.13, warns virgins not to engage in it during the eucharist.

23.8.2 "The better translation" is Jerome's. Cf. also *Inst.* 12.31.

23.9.1f. The use of tightrope walking as an image in a moral context is of Stoic origin. Cf. Epictetus, *Disc.* 3.12.2; Seneca, *De ira* 2.12.5. For its first and most extended use in Christian literature cf. Tertullian, *De pudicitia* 10, where, however, the image has a sarcastic tone. Cf. ACW 28.232–233, n.279.

23.11.3 But there are many rich people...: The purpose of this phrase is to indicate that the bread eaten in the sweat of one's brow is to be understood spiritually rather than literally.

23.12.4ff. The argument here, to the effect that God could not go back on his own word either by revoking human freedom or by breaking the sanctions that he had imposed, recalls a similar argument in Athanasius, *De incarn.* 6f.

23.15.1f. For other references to baptism cf. the note at 1.1.

23.15.2 The extended suffering of repentance and...the woes of punishment: This is almost certainly a reference to ecclesiastical penance, described in particular detail in Tertullian, *De paenitentia* 9.

23.15.7 The soil of the Apostle's heart: Cf. the note at 1.22.2.

23.16.1 On prostration in prayer cf. the note at 21.26.2.

23.21.1f. For the sake of our soul's healing...medicine for our wounds....Remedy for our sickness: Cf. the note at 7.30.2. Cassian refers here to the case of some monks who receive communion only once a year. Chrysostom speaks reproachfully of this custom to his Antiochene congregation in *Serm. in 1 Tim.* 5.3, and Ambrose mentions the same practice–followed by "Greeks in the East"–in *De sacr.* 5.25, when he encourages his own flock to receive communion on a daily basis.

23.21.2 This is the sole reference in *The Conferences* to the reception of communion on Sunday alone, as if that were the general practice.

TWENTY-FOURTH CONFERENCE THE CONFERENCE OF ABBA ABRAHAM: ON MORTIFICATION

Translator's Introduction

This final conference brings to the mystical number of twenty-four the conferences in Cassian's work, and a neat connection is drawn between the twenty-four elders of the Book of Revelation and those whose discourses Cassian has recorded, even though Cassian's elders only add up to fifteen. The last of these is Abba Abraham, who may be identical with one of the two of that name in the *Apophthegmata patrum,* the first of whom has a section allotted to him while the second appears as a disciple of Abba Sisoes. It is perhaps not coincidental that this Abraham, whoever he may be, has the same name as does that Old Testament patriarch who was commanded by God in Genesis 12:1: "Leave your country, your family and your father's house for the land I will show you," inasmuch as part of his task will be to reinculcate in his two charges the spirit that motivated that Abraham.

The discussion begins when the two friends tell the old man that they are moved to return to their homeland in order to be cared for by their relatives, and they express the hope that their presence might even help to effect their relatives' conversion. After a long silence and a deep groan, Abraham sets out with dispatch to lay bare the all too obvious self-deception implicit in this plan. He accuses Cassian and Germanus of slothfulness and tells them that the Egyptian monks would long since have taken advantage of their relatives' support and of other things that the world might have offered them had they not been dissuaded by the Gospel. Instead they chose to live in the harshest desert and, once there, to remain in their cells, concentrating on God and seeking to avoid distractions.

At this Germanus rejoins that, while remaining in one's cell is certainly a good rule to follow, it is unclear why one should keep a distance from one's relatives, particularly inasmuch as some Egyptian monks do not, without thereby hindering their advance toward perfection. Abraham answers by observing that different practices are useful for different persons, and that Egyptian customs might not carry over well into another context. Many Egyptian monks have the inner strength to live very near their relatives without being in the least troubled by them, and he cites the striking example of Abba Apollos. Cassian and Germanus, the old man implies, might not have the strength of character to resist their relatives' enervating attentions. Germanus admits that their relatives would never permit them to practice certain austerities. But would it not be desirable for their families to look after their food so that they themselves could read and pray without interruption? Here Abraham adduces the words of Antony to the effect that a life of toil is imposed upon the monk by scriptural precept. The demand that prayer not be separated from work, which is the burden of the eleventh and twelfth chapters, is a constant in monastic literature. (Cf. Athanasius, *V. S. Antonii* 3; Basil, *Reg. fus. tract.* 37; *Apophthegmata patrum*, de abbate Lucio; Augustine, *De opere monach.* 20.) Almost certainly the Messalian movement, which discarded work in favor of constant prayer, is being aimed at here by Cassian. (On Messalianism in general cf. DS 10.2.1074–1083, esp. 1081 on the problem of work and prayer; Columba Stewart, *"Working the Earth of the Heart": The Messalian Controversy in History, Texts, and Language to A.D. 431* [Oxford, 1991]; and on Cassian in particular cf. Alfons Kemmer, *Charisma maximum: Untersuchung zu Cassians Volkommenheitsideal und seiner Stellung zum Messalianismus* [Louvain, 1938].) Then, returning to the possibility raised by the two friends that they might be able to convert their relatives, Abraham declares that a quiet life in the desert is far safer than one in the world, however many converts one might gain.

Aware of their error, Germanus now asks the old man where such an idea might have come from and how it can be dealt with.

Abraham replies that all vice has a single source, although it shows itself in different ways, depending on what part of the soul it attacks—whether the reasonable, the irascible, or the concupiscible. In the case of Cassian and Germanus it is the reasonable part that suffers from presumption and vainglory, and it must be cured by humble discretion. The weaker parts of one's soul, in any event, are those that are first subjected to demonic onslaughts.

Germanus then voices a consideration that he says had made the possibility of leaving the desert look more attractive—namely, the fact that the occasional visits of the brothers interrupted the seclusion and fasting that they so desired. (The reader will view the consideration in question with a certain scepticism, and will wonder how the two friends would have prevented the visits of their relatives.) But Abraham says that such visits are signs of the holiness of the persons being visited and that, moreover, the devil tempts those who live in the desert to long for more distant places, for utopias where one may supposedly pursue one's religious practices with much less hindrance. In fact, however, the visits of the brothers have a salutary effect on both body and spirit: They serve as a necessary relaxation and refreshment.

Satisfied with this response, Germanus asks—apparently apropos of nothing in particular—for an explanation of Matthew 11:30: "My yoke is easy and my burden is light." The truth of these words of the Lord seems to be belied by other scriptural passages that promise suffering to the serious Christian. The key to understanding the passage, Abraham replies, is humility. The person who is humble and who submits his will to others will no longer experience as oppressive what would otherwise be qualified as a yoke or a burden. It is obstinacy, rather, and the insistence on pursuing one's own will that make the Christian life difficult and burdensome.

The final chapter of the conference deals with the hundredfold spoken of in Matthew 19:29 par., which can be understood in terms of the advantages that fall to those in monastic life. These advantages are not only the bonds among brothers, which are a hundred times more precious than those that exist among persons related by blood, but even the very number of the brothers, since they are that much more numerous than one's blood family. Thus the final moments of the conference return to the theme with which the discussion began, and here at last the reward for severing one's family ties is proposed. As far as the persecutions foretold in Mark 10:30 are concerned, these are the mortifications that the monks practice and the violence that they do to themselves. Abraham concludes his commentary on the hundredfold with the rather unexpected observation that it also refers to the honors that the rulers of this world shower on the monks.

The conference ends with some self-deprecating words of Cassian that touch on his ability to convey to others the fiery utterances of the abbas whose teachings he has attempted to record. And the last sentence, which is the last sentence of the work as a whole, recalls the sea voyage imagery of 1 praef. 3: The journey out upon the wide waters of speech, so dangerous to the monk, is finally over, and the safe harbor of silence lies near at hand.

XXIV. The Conference of Abba Abraham: On Mortification

Chapters

I. How we disclosed our secret thoughts to Abba Abraham.

II. How the old man made clear our errors.

III. On the characteristics of the places that should be sought out by anchorites.

IV. What kinds of work should be chosen by solitaries.

V. That an anxious heart is burdened rather than lightened by a wandering body.

VI. A comparison, concerning how a monk ought to keep watch over his thoughts.

VII. A question as to why the proximity of our relatives is thought to hinder us, whereas it does not hinder those who live in Egypt.

VIII. The reply, that not everything is appropriate for everyone.

IX. That those who can imitate the mortification of Abba Apollos do not need to fear the proximity of their relatives.

X. A question as to whether it is a hindrance to a monk if certain needs of his are taken care of by his relatives.

XI. The reply: What the holy Antony declared with respect to this.

XII. The benefit of work and the disadvantage of laziness.

XIII. A story about a barber's fee, composed in order to make the devil's illusions recognizable.

XIV. A question as to where the error of such thoughts creeps up on us from.

XV. The reply, on the threefold movement of the soul.

XVI. That the rational part of our soul has been corrupted.

XVII. That the weaker part of the soul is the first to succumb to diabolical temptations.

XVIII. A question as to whether we should be drawn back to our own country by a beneficial desire for greater silence.

XIX. The reply, on the devil's illusion in promising peace in the vast desert.

I.1. With this twenty-fourth conference of Abba Abraham, forged with the help of Christ, the teachings and precepts of all the elders come to an end. Once it is concluded, thanks to your prayers, and the number mystically corresponds to that of the twenty-four elders who in the holy Apocalypse are said to offer their crowns to the Lamb,[1] we believe that we shall be relieved of the debts of all our promises. If these twenty-four elders of ours have received crowns of glory because of the worthiness of their teaching, they will henceforth offer them with bowed heads to the Lamb who was slain for the salvation of the world. For he himself, for the honor of his name, deigned to give them an excellent understanding and us the words appropriate to such profundity. And the value of his gift must be referred to the Author of all good things; by the very fact that more is remitted by him more is owed to him.

2. And so, in an anxious confession, we laid before this Abraham the struggle of our thoughts, which prompt us with daily turmoil of soul to return to our own province and to see our relatives again. A great desire was occasioned in us by the fact that we remembered the aforementioned relatives of ours with such devotion and love that we imagined that they would never hinder our chosen orientation. We constantly thought over in our mind that we would receive much more from their solicitude and that we would be preoccupied by no worries about bodily things and not be distracted by looking for food if they concerned themselves joyfully with providing for absolutely all our needs. 3. Moreover, we also fed our souls with the hope of foolish joys, believing that we would gain very great fruit out of the conversion of the many persons who would be as it were guided to the way of salvation by our example and admonitions. In addition, there was painted before our eyes the setting of the ancestral property of our forebears and the pleasant and delightful nature of that region, and how graciously and agreeably it stretched out to the reaches of the wilderness, so that the recesses of the forests might not only gladden a monk but also provide sufficient supplies of food.

4. When we disclosed all of this, simply and in accordance with the faith of our conscience, to the aforesaid old man, and when we bore witness with abundant tears that we could no longer endure the force of the onslaught unless by the grace of God he came to our aid with a remedy, he kept silent for a long while and finally said with a deep groan:

II.1. "The weakness of your thoughts shows that you have not yet renounced your worldly desires or mortified your former yearnings. These errant desires of yours testify to the fecklessness of your heart. It is only in the flesh that you are enduring this pilgrimage and this absence from your relatives, which you should rather be taking up in your mind. For all of this would have already been buried and completely removed from your hearts if you had seized upon the reason for this renunciation and the principal motive of the solitary life that is ours. 2. Therefore I think that you are laboring under the malady of slothfulness, which is spoken of as follows in Proverbs: 'Every slothful person is full of desires.'[2] And again: 'Desires kill the lazy.'[3]

"For we ourselves would not be lacking the supplies of carnal goods that you spoke about if we believed that they were appropriate to our chosen orientation or if we judged that we could get as much fruit for ourselves from the delights of these pleasures as we obtain from the harshness of our location and from the brokenness of our body. Nor are we so bereft of the comfort of our relatives that we would lack people who would rejoice to sustain us out of their own pockets if we were not confronted by the words of the Savior, which cut off whatever pertains to the nourishment of this flesh and which say: 'Whoever does not abandon [or hate] father and mother and children and brothers cannot be my disciple.'[4] 3. But even if we were utterly bereft of our relatives' assistance, we would not lack the kind offices of the powers of this world, who would gratefully rejoice to attend to our needs with the most prompt generosity. Supported by their munificence, we would not be worried about obtaining food if the prophetic curse did not act on us as a strong deterrent. For it is said: 'Cursed is the man who places his hope in man.'[5] And: 'Do not trust in princes.'[6] Likewise, if we had located our cells at least on the banks of the River Nile we would have had water at our doorsteps and we would not have been obliged to carry it on our backs for four thousand paces, except that the blessed Apostle made us unwearying in putting up with this labor and constantly encouraged us with the words that he said: 'Everyone shall receive his reward in proportion to his labor.'[7] 4. Nor are we unaware that there are also several pleasant retreats in our area, in which a supply of fruit and the delightful and abundant gardens would meet our need for food with a minimum of bodily labor, except that we fear the reproach which would be made against us and which was directed to the rich man in the Gospel: 'You received your consolation in your life.'[8]

"But we despise all these things and disdain them along with each one of this world's pleasures, and we delight only in this harshness, preferring the redoubtable vastness of this desert to every luxury. Nor can we compare the wealth of any field, however fertile, to the bleakness of this sand, for we are pursuing not the temporal profits of this body but the eternal gains of the spirit. 5. For it is a very small matter for a monk to have made a renunciation only once–that is, to have despised present things at the beginning of his conversion–if he does not continue to renounce them every day. Up until the end of this life we must say with the prophet: 'You know that I have not desired the day of man.'[9] Hence also the Lord says in the Gospel: 'If anyone wants to come after me, he must deny himself and take up his cross every day and follow me.'[10]

III.1. "Therefore, the person who keeps constant watch over the purity of the inner man must seek out places that do not draw his mind to the distraction of cultivating them because of their abundant fertility and that do not make him leave the fixed and set location of his cell and force him to do work outside, thus scattering his thoughts at large, as it were, and, by all sorts of things, utterly diverting the aim of his mind and that most delicate focus on his goal. 2. These cannot be provided for or seen by anyone, however careful and watchful, who has not kept his body and mind constantly enclosed within the confines of four walls. Thus, attentive and unmoving, like a clever fisherman looking out for his food with apostolic skill, he may catch the swarms of thoughts swimming about in the calmest depths of his heart and, like someone gazing intently into the depths from a jutting promontory, may with wise discretion judge which fish he should draw to himself with his saving hook and which ones he should let go and reject because they are wicked and harmful.

IV.1. "If someone perseveres continually in this watchfulness, therefore, he will effectively bring to pass what is quite plainly expressed by the prophet Habakkuk: 'I will stand on my watch and go up upon a rock, and I will look out to see what he will say in me and what I should reply to him who reproaches me.'[11] The laboriousness and difficulty of this is very clearly proved by the experiences of those who dwell in the desert of Calamus or Porphyrion. 2. They are cut off, it is true, from all cities and human habitation by a longer stretch of wilderness than is the desert of Skete, since those who penetrate the vast and deserted wilderness barely arrive at their remote cells after seven or eight stops. Yet, because they have dedicated themselves to gardening there and are not bound to their cells, when they come to the harsh places where we live or to Skete, they are troubled with such tumultuous thoughts and with such anxiety of mind that, like beginners and those who have never even slightly acquired the discipline of the desert, they cannot bear the staying in their cells and the stillness of the silence, and they are at once driven from there and made to leave, as if they were tyros and novices. 3. For they have not learned how to calm the movements of the inner man and to resist the storms of their thoughts by a constant concern and a persevering attentiveness, since they are working outdoors every day and are running about in the airy void not only in the flesh but even in the mind, scattering their thoughts everywhere in the open with their bodily activity. Therefore they neither experience the capricious vanity of their soul nor can they control its unstable wanderings. Not putting up with contrition of spirit, they consider their own constant silence unbearable. Unwearying in their burdensome rural labors, they are overcome by calm and are worn out by their own lengthy stillness.

V.1. "There is nothing surprising in the fact that someone staying in a cell, whose thoughts are gathered together as if in a very narrow closet, should be suffocated with a multitude of preoccupations, which burst out of the confines of the dwelling along with the person and which run about everywhere like unbridled horses. When they get free of their stables for a while, so to speak, there is at once a kind of brief and sad solace. But when the body returns to its cell, the whole troop of thoughts goes back as if to its own home, and the very habit of ingrained license excites more serious urges. 2. When those, then, who cannot yet or do not yet know how to resist the onslaughts of their desires are troubled in their cells by attacks of acedia in their hearts more violent than usual, and if by relaxing the strictness of the law they concede themselves the freedom of going out often, they will bring a worse plague upon themselves by this remedy, as they think it is. It is the same with certain people who believe that they can quell the force of internal fevers with a drink of very cold water, when in fact it is clear that this stirs up the fire rather than settling it, since a far graver sickness follows the momentary relief.

VI.1. "For this reason a monk's whole attention should constantly be fixed on one thing, and the beginnings and the roundabout turns of all his thoughts should be strenuously called back to this very thing–that is, to the recollection of God. It is as if someone wanted to construct a barrel-vaulted ceiling: He would have to trace a circle from its precise center all the way around, and in accordance with this fixed pattern he would establish the perfect roundness required for the structure. 2. But if someone tried to do this without having gauged the midpoint, however great his skill or clever his guess, he would be unable to keep it perfectly round without making a mistake, nor could he perceive merely by a glance how he had detracted from the beauty of the roundness by his error. Instead, he must have constant recourse to the standard of truth, adjusting the inner and outer circumference of his work from its vantage point and finishing off the edifice, so large and lofty, in reference to this single spot.

3. "Likewise, unless our mind turns about the love of the Lord alone, as an unchanging and fixed center, through each one of our works and through each moment of our activity, and unless it either adapts or rejects the character of all our thoughts in accordance with what I might call the proven compass of love, a person will never build with proven skill the structure of the spiritual edifice whose architect is Paul,[12] nor will it possess the beauty

of that house which the blessed David wanted to present to the Lord in his heart, when he said: 'Lord, I have loved the beauty of your house and the place where your glory dwells.'[13] Rather, he will foolishly erect in his heart an ugly and unworthy house for the Holy Spirit, and one that will collapse time and again, and he will not boast of his hospitality to the blessed Guest, but he will be mournfully oppressed by the downfall of his construction."

VII.1. GERMANUS: "This kind of activity, which can be practiced within one's cell, is enjoined by an institute that is quite beneficial and necessary. For the appropriateness of this has often been taught us not only by the example of your blessedness, which is founded upon the imitation of the apostolic virtues, but also by the witness of our own experience. But it is not particularly clear why the proximity of our relatives, which you yourselves did not utterly reject, should be so avoided by us. For since we see that you have proceeded blamelessly along the whole path of perfection, and not only that you live in your own country but that some of you have not even removed yourselves very far from your villages, why do you think that what is not harmful for you is dangerous for us?"

VIII.1. ABRAHAM: "We sometimes see bad examples drawn from good things. For if someone presumes to do the same things but not with the same disposition and orientation or with unlike virtue, he easily falls into the snares of deception and death on account of those very things from which others acquire the fruits of eternal life. 2. That brave boy who was set against the most warlike giant in a contest of arms would certainly have experienced this if he had put on Saul's manly and heavy armor, with which a person of more robust age would have laid low whole troops of the enemy. This would undoubtedly have imperiled the boy, except that with wise discretion he chose the kind of weaponry that was appropriate for his youth and armed himself against the dreadful foe not with the breastplate and shield that he saw others outfitted with but with the projectiles that he himself was able to fight with.[14]

"Hence it behooves each one of us to gauge the measure of his strength carefully beforehand and to follow the discipline that is in keeping with his abilities because, although all things are beneficial, nonetheless not all things can be fitting for all people. 3. Although the anchorite life is good, we see that it is not appropriate for everyone: For many it is not only unfruitful but is even felt to be dangerous. Although we profess that the rule of the cenobites and concern for one's brothers is holy and praiseworthy, we do not therefore consider that everyone should pursue it. There is also very abundant fruit in hospitality, but it cannot be practiced by everyone without detriment to their patience.

"The institutes of your own region and of this one must hence first be weighed against each other, and then the strengths of the persons, figured out from their constant attention to either virtue or vice, must be balanced out together on a separate scale. 4. For it can happen that what ingrained habit has somehow made natural for some persons is difficult or impossible for another kind of person. It is like peoples that are separated from one another by a vast expanse of land and that bear the force of the cold or the heat of the sun without any bodily covering, while others who have no experience of the weather's harshness cannot put up with this at all, however strong they may be. 5. So you too, who with the greatest effort of mind and body are trying to struggle in this region against many of the characteristics of your own homeland, so to speak, must consider carefully whether you could endure what I would refer to as this nakedness in those regions that report has it are sluggish and constrained as it were with the chill of a great unbelief. For in our case the long-standing nature of our holy way of life has given a kind of natural strength to our chosen orientation. If you see that you are our equals in constancy and virtue, in similar fashion you need not flee the proximity of your relatives and your brothers.

IX.1. "But so that you may be able to get a correct estimate of how much strength you have on the true scale of strictness, I shall make brief mention to you of the deed of a certain old man named Apollos. Thus, if a careful examination of your heart indicates that you are not inferior to him in chosen orientation and virtue, you may without damage to your chosen orientation and without danger to your profession dwell in your homeland and near your relatives, certain that neither a yearning for proximity nor pleasure in the location would be able to overcome the strict humility that not only you desire but also the obligations of your journey wring from you in this province.

2. "When, therefore, his own brother came to the aforesaid old man in the middle of the night and begged him to leave his monastery for a short while in order to help him pull an ox out of the mud of a distant bog that he complained tearfully it had gotten stuck in, because he would never be able to get it out by himself, Abba Apollos said in response to his persistent pleading: 'Why did you not ask our younger brother, whom you passed over even though he was nearer than I?' And he, thinking that he had forgotten that his brother had died and been buried long ago and that he was somewhat weak in mind on account of too much abstinence and constant solitude, replied: 'How can I call from the grave someone who died fifteen years ago?' 3. Thereupon Abba Apollos said: 'Do you not know, then, that I also died to this world twenty years ago and that from the grave of this cell I can no longer offer you any help as far as the present life is concerned? And so little does Christ permit me to veer away even momentarily from attending to the mortification that I have seized upon, so as to drag out your ox, that he has not conceded me the slightest pause even to bury my father,[15] which is something that ought to have been done much more quickly, justly, and honestly.'

4. "Examine the recesses of your heart, then, and investigate carefully whether you would be able to maintain constantly such strictness of mind with respect to your relatives. Only when you feel like him in this mortification of mind will you know that the proximity of your relatives and brothers will not cause you any harm either—when, namely, you live near them but consider yourselves dead, such that you do not permit them to receive your attentions nor yourselves to be softened by their services."

X.1. GERMANUS: "In this regard you have clearly left nothing in doubt. For we are certain that we could by no means wear our present ragged clothing or go about barefoot every day in their proximity, and that there we would not procure what was necessary for eating with the same effort, while here we are obliged to carry even our very water on our backs every day from three miles away. Neither our sensibilities nor theirs would ever let us do these things in their presence. But what harm would it do to our chosen orientation if, thanks to their ministrations, we were completely freed of all concern about getting food and occupied ourselves entirely with reading and prayer? Thus, once this toil that distracts us now was removed, we would dwell more intently on spiritual pursuits alone."

XI.1. ABRAHAM: "Against this I shall offer you not my own words but those of the blessed Antony, with which he confuted the laziness of a certain brother who was languishing in the lukewarmness of which you speak, and which will also cut through the knot of your question. When this particular person whom I was speaking about came to the aforementioned old man and said that the anchorite discipline was not admirable, declaring that it was more virtuous for a person to pursue what was proper to perfection among other people rather than in the desert, the blessed Antony asked him where he lived. 2. And when he said that he lived near his relatives and boasted that, thanks to their assistance, he was free of all the care and worry of daily toil and was constantly intent exclusively upon reading and prayer, without any distraction of spirit, the blessed Antony said in return: 'Tell me, friend, whether you are saddened when misfortune or adversity befalls them and whether, in like fashion, you rejoice at their prosperity.' He confessed that he shared in both aspects. To which the old man said: 'You should know that in the world to come you will also be joined in the fate of those with whom you partook in this life of either gain or loss, or joy or sorrow.'

3. "Not content with these words, the blessed Antony entered upon a wider field of discussion, and he said: 'This way of life and this most lukewarm condition not only cause you the loss that I have spoken of, even though you yourself may not now feel it and may somehow say in keeping with the sentence from Proverbs: "They strike me, but I did not grieve, and they mocked me, but I was unaware."[16] And what is said in the prophet: "Strangers devoured his strength, and he himself did not know it."[17] 4. The reason for this is that they are constantly changing your mind every day to fit a variety of circumstances, and they are submerging it in earthly affairs. But in addition to this they are depriving you of the fruit of your hands and of the just reward of your labor. They do not permit you, when you are supported by

others' assistance, to prepare food every day for yourself with your own hands, in accordance with the rule of the blessed Apostle. When he was setting forth his final commands for the leaders of the church of the Ephesians he recalled that, although he was occupied with the sacred pursuit of preaching the Gospel, he not only provided for himself but even for those who were prevented from doing so because of their necessary obligations in respect to his ministry. As he said: "You yourselves know that these hands have labored for my needs and for the needs of those who are with me."[18] 5. But, in order to show that he did this as an example for our benefit, he said elsewhere: "We were not idle among you, nor did we eat anyone's bread for free, but we worked night and day in labor and weariness, lest we burden any of you. Not as if we did not have the right, but in order to make ourselves an example to you, so that you might imitate us."[19]

XII.1. "'And therefore, although our relatives' help would not be lacking to us either, nonetheless we prefer this deprivation to all their resources, and we have chosen to provide for the daily needs of our body by our own efforts rather than to be supported by the assured assistance of our relatives. We subordinate an idle meditation on Scripture and a fruitless attention to reading, which you were speaking of, to this most toilsome poverty. We would certainly pursue the former very willingly if the Apostle's authority had taught by example that it was more beneficial, or if the elders' institutes had laid it down in salutary fashion.

2. "'But you should know that you experience this disadvantage, too, no less than the one that we spoke of previously: Although you have a healthy and robust body, you are sustained by others' support, which rightly belongs only to the weak. For indeed the whole human race relies on the charitable compassion of others, with the sole exception of the race of monks which, in accordance with the Apostle's precept, lives by the daily toil of its hands. Hence it is certain that not only those who boast of being taken care of by their relatives' resources or by their friends' efforts or by the income from their own property but even the kings of this earth themselves are supported by charity. 3. The understanding of our forebears, who prescribed that whatever was set aside for the requirement of daily food which was not

made or produced by the labor of our hands should be given to charity, was in accord with the Apostle, who utterly forbade others' generous resources to the idle when he said: "Whoever does not work, let him not eat."'[20]

4. "The blessed Antony used these words against this particular person, and by examples rich in teaching he likewise instructed us to avoid the very harmful blandishments of our relatives and the charity of all who minister to our requirements for food, as well as a pleasant and gracious dwelling place. We should prefer sands rough with natural bitterness and regions wasted by floods of salt water, subject for that very reason to no human law or dominion, to all the wealth of this world. Thus, protected by the pathless desert, we shall not only escape communication with other human beings but, in addition, the quality of a rich soil will never move us to the distraction of some kind of farming, by which our mind might be drawn away from the principal concern of the heart and be too worn out for spiritual pursuits.

XIII.1. "Since you are confident that you could also save others, and you are anxious to see your homeland again in the hope of greater gain, listen to a story on this subject that was very charmingly and aptly conceived by Abba Macarius, which he himself offered as a remedy, in the form of a very apposite tale, to someone who was burning with similar desires.

"Once upon a time, he said, there was a very skilled barber in a certain city, who used to shave everyone for three denarii and who, on getting this small and meager fee for his work, used to furnish out of it what was necessary for his daily food, and when his body's needs were completely satisfied he used to put a hundred denarii in his wallet every day. 2. But when he had been saving up this profit over a long period, he heard that in a far-off city men would pay a solidus to be shaved. Upon discovering this he said: 'How long shall I content myself with this penury and with earning a fee of three denarii for my labor, when by going there and making a huge profit in solidi I could amass riches?' And so he at once took up the tools of his trade and, paying out in expenses everything that he had saved up there over a long period, he made his way with considerable effort to that most lucrative city. 3. On the day that he entered it he received from everyone the fee for his work that he had been informed of, and in the evening, seeing that he had earned many solidi, he went off happily to the market to buy what he needed for his supper. After he had purchased it at a high price in solidi and had spent everything that he had acquired on a small morsel of food, he took home not even a single denarius in profit. And when he saw his earnings being spent every day in this manner, so that he not only could keep nothing but was hardly even able to meet his needs for daily sustenance, he reconsidered in himself and said: 'I will return to my own city and ask for my small fee once more. After it satisfied all my bodily needs, there was a daily surplus which, when accumulated, would provide for my old age. 4. Although it seemed insignificant and paltry, nonetheless when it was constantly increased it came to no small amount. Indeed, that fee in coppers was more lucrative to me than the imaginary one in solidi, which has not only left no surplus to be saved up but has hardly even provided for the requirements of daily food.'

"Therefore it is better for us to go after, with unbroken constancy, the very small fruit of this desert, which no worldly concerns or earthly distractions or swelling vainglory or vanity can nibble away at, and no cares about daily needs can diminish, than to pursue greater profits which, even if they have been gotten by the very lucrative conversion of many, are nonetheless devoured by the demands of a worldly way of life and by the daily loss arising from distractions. For 'the little that the righteous has is better than the great wealth of sinners.'[21] 5. And according to the words of Solomon: 'A single handful with repose is better than two handfuls with toil and presumption of spirit.'[22] All those who are very weak are inevitably entangled in these illusions and losses. Even though their own salvation is in doubt and they still stand in need of others' teaching and instruction, they are prompted by diabolical illusions to convert and to govern others, and even if they have been able to acquire some gain and to make some conversions, they will lose whatever they got because of their impatience and their immoderate behavior. The prophet Haggai describes what will happen to them: 'The one who amasses riches puts them in a bag with holes.'[23] 6. For a person who, because of his undisciplined heart and daily distraction of mind, loses whatever he seemed to have acquired by the conversion of others truly puts his profits in a bag with holes. And so it is that, while believing themselves able to make greater profit by instructing others, they are deprived of their own betterment. For 'there are those who make themselves out as rich, although they have nothing, and there are those who humble themselves in the midst of great wealth.'[24] And: 'Better is the man who serves himself in obscurity than him who gains honor for himself and wants for bread.'"[25]

XIV. GERMANUS: "What you said by way of this story has pointed out quite clearly to us the errors of our illusions. Now we also want to recognize their causes and cures, and we likewise wish to learn where this deception came to us from. For there is no doubt that no one at all can recommend medicines for diseases except the person who has discovered the very origins of the illnesses."

XV.1. ABRAHAM: "There is a single source and wellspring for all the vices, but, according to the nature of the part or what I might refer to as the member which has been damaged in the soul, it is called by the names of different passions and pathologies. This is also demonstrably the case sometimes with bodily illnesses: Although they have one cause, they are nonetheless divided into different kinds of sickness in accordance with the nature of the members that have been affected. 2. For when a harmful humor seizes forcibly upon the body's citadel–that is, the head–it produces a headache; when it gets into the ears and eyes it becomes otalgia or ophthalmia; when it spreads to certain joints and to the extremities of the hands it is called arthritis and gout; but when it gets down to the feet its name is changed and it is called podagra. A harmful humor with one and the same origin is referred to by as many terms as there are parts of members that it has laid hold of.

3. "Similarly, passing from visible to invisible things, we should believe that a certain evil force inhabits the parts or what I might call the members of our soul. Since some very wise persons understand this last as having a threefold power, it must be that either the λογικον–that is, the reasonable–or the θυμικον–that is, the irascible–or the επιθυμητικον–that is, the concupiscible–will be damaged by some assault. When, therefore, a harmful passion

seizes forcibly upon someone in one of these dispositions, the name of the vice is also used for the pathology. 4. If the plague of vice infects the reasonable part, it will beget the vices of vainglory, arrogance, envy, pride, presumption, contention, and heresy. If it wounds the irascible disposition, it will bring forth rage, impatience, sadness, acedia, faintheartedness, and cruelty. If it corrupts the concupiscible portion, it will generate gluttony, fornication, avarice, covetousness, and harmful and earthly desires.

XVI. "Therefore, if you wish to know the source and origin of this vice, you should realize that the reasonable portion of your mind and soul, from which the vices of presumption and vainglory usually spring, has been corrupted. Hence you must cure what I might refer to as this first member of the soul with the judgment of correct discretion and the virtue of humility. For it has been hurt by your believing not only that you have already attained to the heights of perfection but even that you are able to teach others, and by your considering that you are adequate to and capable of instructing others. Your confession makes clear that you have been seized by this errant conceit because of swelling vainglory. You will be able to cut this off immediately without any difficulty if you are established, as I have said, in the humility of true discretion, if you learn with contrition of mind how toilsome and difficult it is for any one of us to save his soul, and if you acknowledge with the most heartfelt disposition that you are not only far removed from the presumption of teaching but also that you still need a teacher's help.

XVII.1. "Therefore, apply to this member or part of your soul, which we specifically said was wounded, the medicine of true humility. Because, as far as can be seen, it is weaker than the other powers of your soul, it will inevitably be the first to succumb to a diabolical assault. 2. As when certain illnesses occur that come about either through work that has been taken on or through unhealthful air, and, as is usually the case with respect to human bodies, those that are weaker are the first to give in and succumb in such instances, and, as when the disease rages in them more violently the healthy parts as well are injured by the same malady, it is likewise inevitably the case that, when the pestilential breath of vice as it were blows over us, the soul of each one of us is tried most severely by the passion in its feebler and weaker part, which does not so strongly resist the onslaughts of the powerful enemy. It runs the risk of being taken captive the more nonchalantly it leaves itself open to betrayal as a result of negligent custody.

3. "Balaam clearly realized that the people of God could be deceived in this way. He advised that wicked snares be laid for them in the area where he knew that the children of Israel were weak, and he had no doubt that they would immediately fall into the ruin of fornication if they were offered many women, because he knew that the concupiscible parts of their soul had been corrupted.[26] Similarly, then, the evil spirits greatly try each one of us by their sly wickedness, and they set snares in particular for those dispositions in which they sense that the soul is weak. Thus, for example, when they see that the rational parts of our soul have been damaged, they set about to deceive us in the way in which Scripture narrates that King Ahab was deceived by the Syrians, who said: 4. 'We know that the kings of Israel are merciful. So let us put sackcloth on our loins and ropes on our heads, and let us go out to the king of Israel and say to him: Your servant Benhadad says: I pray you, let my soul live.'[27] At this he was stirred not by genuine piety but by the empty praise of his mercy, and he said: 'If he still lives, he is my brother.'[28] Thus they deceive us as well in this way by error in the reasonable part, making us offend against God precisely where we believed that we were going to receive recompense and get a reward for our piety, and to us too it may be said with a similar rebuke: 5. 'Because you let escape from your hand a man who was worthy of death, your soul shall be for his soul, and your people for his people.'[29] Or when the unclean spirit said: 'I will go out and I will be a lying spirit in the mouth of all his prophets,'[30] he certainly spread snares of deception in the reasonable disposition, which he knew was open to his deadly traps. The same spirit had this in mind as well concerning our Lord when he tried him in the three dispositions of soul in which he knew that the whole human race was held captive. But, as clever as his traps were, he had no success. 6. For he attacked the concupiscible part of his mind when he said: 'Tell these stones to become loaves of bread';[31] the irascible part when he tried to provoke him to seek the power of the present age and the kingdoms of this world;[32] and

the rational part when he said: 'If you are the Son of God, cast yourself down.'[33] In this case his illusion was unsuccessful because, despite his conjecture, which he had arrived at by faulty guesswork, he discovered nothing in him that was harmed, and therefore no part of his soul gave in to the enemy's traps when it was tried. 'For behold,' he says, 'the prince of this world is coming, and he shall find nothing in me.'"[34]

XVIII. GERMANUS: "Among other kinds of illusions and errors of ours, which had inflamed us to yearn for our homeland by the vain promise of spiritual advantages, as your blessedness has seen with the sharp eyes of your mind, there is also this very important cause–namely, that the brothers sometimes throng to us, and we are utterly unable to keep to the constant seclusion and to the prolonged silence that we desire. Because of this the course and amount of our daily abstinence, which we want to maintain always unbroken for the sake of subduing our body, is inevitably interrupted upon the arrival of some of the brothers. We are confident that this would never happen in our own province, where it is impossible or at least highly unusual to find a man with this profession."

XIX.1. ABRAHAM: "It is an indication of an unreasonable and ill-considered strictness, or rather of the greatest lukewarmness, when a person is never visited by others. For whoever walks too slowly in the way that he has taken up and lives in the manner with which he was previously conversant is rightly approached by no one, and certainly not by those who are holy. But you, if you burn with genuine and perfect love of our Lord and follow God, who indeed is love,[35] with utter fervor of spirit, are certainly going to be thronged to by others in whatever inaccessible places you might flee to, and the more the warmth of divine love draws you closer to God, the more an increasing multitude of holy brothers will stream to you. 2. For, according to the words of the Lord, a city set on a hill cannot be hidden,[36] because, as the Lord says: 'I will glorify those who love me, but those who disdain me shall be abased.'[37]

"But you should know that this is the devil's most subtle ploy and his most hidden trap, into which he casts the wretched and heedless. That is to say, while promising them greater things he steals away the useful gain of their daily profit by persuading them to long for more impenetrable and vaster deserts and by depicting these in their hearts as being full of wonderful delights. He even invents unheard-of places, which exist nowhere at all, and treats them as if they were known and prepared and already within our grasp, and as if they could be possessed without any difficulty. 3. He also lies that the people of those regions are docile and are following the way of salvation. Thus, while promising more abundant fruits for the soul in those places, he fraudulently snatches away present gain. For when someone has been separated from the company of the elders by this empty hope and has been despoiled of everything that he had vainly pictured to himself in his heart, and when he arises as it were from out of the deepest slumber, he will find nothing of what he had been dreaming about while he was sleeping. 4. And so, once a person has been entrapped in the responsibilities of this life and in snares that he cannot escape from, the devil does not even let him hope for the things that he had previously promised himself. And once he is no longer tied down by the rare spiritual visits of the brothers, which he had formerly avoided, but by the daily incursions of worldly people, he will never permit him to return even to the moderate peace and discipline of the anchorite life.

XX.1. "Although the pleasant interval of relaxation and hospitality, which usually occurs upon the arrival of the brothers, may seem annoying and worth avoiding to you, nonetheless listen patiently for a while to how beneficial and salutary it is for both our body and our spirit. 2. It often happens even to the most experienced and to the perfect, to say nothing of novices and the weak, that, unless the intensity and the severity of their mind have been softened by some respite for the sake of change, they fall into lukewarmness of spirit or at least into serious bodily ill health. Therefore, when even frequent visits from the brothers interrupt them, the prudent and the perfect should not only bear them patiently but even embrace them gratefully. 3. First, they move us to desire ever more avidly the recesses of the desert, because, although they are somehow believed to impede our progress, they keep it unwearied and constant. If a person were not occasionally slowed down by some obstacle he would not be able to hold out until the end with untiring swiftness. Then, they indulge with the fruit of hospitality the feeble body's need for refreshment, conferring on us greater gain with this very pleasant respite than what it would have acquired by the fatigue of abstinence. In this regard I shall briefly recount a very apt story that has been circulating for a long time.

XXI.1. "It is said that the most blessed John, when he was softly stroking a partridge with his hands, suddenly saw a certain philosopher approaching him dressed like a hunter. He marveled that a man of such an estimable reputation would submit himself to pleasures so small and humble. 'Are you not,' he said, 'the John whose extraordinary and celebrated reputation drew me to you as well with the greatest desire to make your acquaintance? Why, then, are you occupied with such paltry pleasures?' 2. The blessed John said: 'What are you carrying in your hand?' And he said: 'A bow.' 'And why,' he asked, 'do you not always carry it about everywhere taut?' He replied to him: 'That is not supposed to be done. Constant bending would relax its tensile strength, and it would be weakened and ruined. Then, once the tension had been lost by excessive and continual bending, when I had to shoot heavier arrows at some animal, a stronger blow could not be struck.' 3. 'Nor,' said the blessed John, 'should this small and brief recreation of our mind offend you, young man. If by a certain relaxation it did not occasionally lighten and loosen its taut tension, it would not be able to harken to the power of the spirit when necessity demanded, since it would be weakened by its unrelenting exertion.'"

XXII. GERMANUS: "Since you have given us the remedies for every illusion, and since the diabolical snares that used to trouble us have been disclosed to us by your teaching and by the Lord's gift, we beseech you likewise to explain to us completely this phrase from the Gospel: 'My yoke is easy and my burden is light.'[38] For it seems quite contrary to the words of the prophet, which say: 'On account of the words of your lips I have kept to hard ways.'[39] Indeed, even the Apostle says: 'All who wish to live devoutly in Christ suffer persecution.'[40] Whatever is hard and has reference to persecution, however, can be neither light nor easy."

XXIII.1. ABRAHAM: "We shall demonstrate by the easy proof of experience itself that the words of our Lord and Savior are most true, if we set out on the path of perfection in lawful manner and in accordance with the will of Christ, mortifying all our desires and cutting off our harmful impulses, not only not permitting any of the substance of this world to remain in us, by which the enemy may find the power to ruin us and rip us apart whenever he chooses, but also realizing that we are not even our own masters. Thus we shall fulfill in truth what the Apostle says: 'I no longer live, but Christ lives in me.'[41]

2. "For what can be heavy or hard to the person who has taken up Christ's yoke with his whole mind, is established in true humility, reflects constantly upon the Lord's suffering, and rejoices in all the hardships that come upon him, saying: 'On this account I am content with weakness, reproaches, need, persecution, and distress for Christ's sake. For when I am weak, then I am strong'?[42] Will a person be tormented by the loss of some ordinary thing if he glories in utter deprivation and has willingly rejected all the pomps of this world, considering all its desires in general as dung so that he may gain Christ,[43] and if, through continual meditation on the gospel precept, he despises and rejects all concern over any losses? 'For what does it profit a person if he gains the whole world but suffers the loss of his soul? Or what shall a person give in exchange for his soul?'[44] 3. Will a person be saddened at being deprived of something if he knows that whatever can be taken away by others is not his own, and if he cries out with invincible courage: 'We have brought nothing into this world. It is certain that we can take nothing out of it'?[45] Will a person's fortitude be overcome by need and poverty if he knows how not to have a satchel on the road and money in his belt[46] but, with the Apostle, glories 'in much fasting, in hunger and thirst, in cold and in nakedness'?[47] 4. What toil or command of an elder, however difficult it may be, will be able to disturb the tranquil heart of the person who has no will of his own, who greets every order not only with patience but even with gratitude, and who, in keeping with the example of our Savior, seeks to do not his own but his Father's will, as he himself also says to his Father: 'Yet not as I will but as you do'?[48] What harm or what persecution will be terrifying, and indeed what torment cannot even be pleasant to the person who, with the apostles, rejoices in every suffering and wishes to be considered worthy to endure insults for the sake of Christ's name?[49]

XXIV.1. "But the fact that, on the other hand, the yoke of Christ seems neither light nor easy to us must rightly be ascribed to our obstinacy. Cast down by our lack of confidence and our unbelief, we fight with unbecoming perversity against the command, or rather the counsel, of him who says: 'If you wish to be perfect, go, sell [or get rid of] all your belongings, and come, follow me.'[50] That is to say, we hold on to our material and earthly possessions. 2. Since the devil binds and fetters our mind by these, what remains except that, when he wishes to keep us from spiritual joys and to sadden us by diminishing them and depriving us of them, he should conjure up clever deceptions so that, when the easiness of that yoke and the lightness of that burden have grown heavy upon us because of our wicked and depraved desires, he may constantly torment us with the scourge of worldly cares as we are caught up in the chains of the very wealth and prosperity that we had maintained for our comfort and consolation? Thus he wrenches from us the very thing by which we are torn apart. For 'everyone is bound by the cords of his sins.'[51] And they hear it said by the prophet: 'Behold, all you who light a fire and are surrounded by flames, walk in the light of your fire and in the flames that you have kindled.'[52] 3. For, as Solomon is witness, 'everyone shall be punished by that wherein he has sinned.'[53] The very pleasures that we enjoy are a torment to us, and the joys and delights of this flesh turn upon their author like torturers, because a person who has been supported by his former wealth and resources is certain to accept neither complete humility of heart nor full mortification with respect to harmful pleasures.

"But when virtue comes to our aid with its assistance, all the anguish of the present life and every loss that the enemy can inflict are borne not only very patiently but even very joyfully. When it is banished, on the other hand, pride, which is so wicked, takes root, so that we are wounded by the darts of a deadly impatience even as a result of the slightest insult, and this is said to us by the prophet Jeremiah: 4. 'What are you looking for now on the way to Egypt, to drink troubled water? And what are you looking for on the way to Assyria, to drink the water of the River? Your own wickedness shall reprove you, and your own turning away shall rebuke you. Know and see that your having abandoned the

Lord your God and that your having no fear of me is evil and bitter, says the Lord.'[54]

"Why, then, is the wonderful ease of the Lord's yoke felt to be bitter if not because the bitterness of our turning away has ruined it? Why does the pleasant lightness of the divine burden weigh so heavy if not because with insolent presumption we disdain what we used to be sustained by, all the more inasmuch as Scripture testifies to this very thing when it says: 'If they walked in straight paths, they would certainly have found the paths of righteousness smooth'?[55] 5. It is clearly we, I say, who make rough the straight and smooth paths of the Lord with the wicked and hard rocks of our desires, who very foolishly abandon the royal road paved with apostolic and prophetic stones and made level by the footsteps of all the holy ones and of the Lord himself, and who pursue byways and brambly roads. Blinded by the seductions of present pleasures, we crawl along the dark and obstructed trails, our feet lacerated by the thorns of vice and our wedding garment in tatters, and we are not only pierced by the sharp needles of thorny bushes but also brought low by the stings of the poisonous serpents and the scorpions that lie in wait there. For 'there are thistles and snares along wicked ways, but the one who fears the Lord will keep from them.'[56] 6. Of such the Lord also says elsewhere through the prophet: 'My people have forgotten. They sacrifice in vain, stumbling along on their own paths, in the ways of the world, walking on them on a way not trodden.'[57] For, in the words of Solomon, 'the ways of those who do nothing are strewn with thorns, but the ways of the strong are well trodden.'[58] Thus, having turned aside from the royal path, they are unable to get to that metropolis to which our journeying must ever and unswervingly be directed. Ecclesiastes also expressed this quite distinctly when he said: 'The toil of fools afflicts those who do not know how to go to the city'[59]—namely, to 'that heavenly Jerusalem, which is the mother of us all.'[60] 7. But whoever truly renounces this world, takes upon himself the yoke of Christ, learns from him and is instructed in the daily discipline of insults, because he is 'meek and humble of heart,'[61] will always remain unmoved in every trial, and 'everything will work together for the good'[62] for him. For, according to the prophet Obadiah, the words of God 'are good for the one who walks uprightly.'[63] And again: 'The ways of the Lord are right, and the upright shall walk in them, but transgressors shall fall in them.'[64]

XXV.1. "In the struggle with trials, then, the kindly grace of the Savior in our regard brings us greater rewards of praise than if he had removed from us all the strictures of combat. For it is more nobly and eminently virtuous to remain constantly unmoved when surrounded by persecution and affliction, to cling confidently and courageously to the protection of God, to triumph gloriously over impatience with the weapons of invincible virtue, so to speak, when humanly attacked, and in some way to acquire strength from weakness, because 'strength is perfected in weakness.'[65] 2. 'For, behold,' says the Lord, 'I have made you into an iron pillar and a brass wall over all the land, to the kings of Judah and to its princes and priests and to all the people of the land. And they will fight against you and they shall not prevail, because I am with you to deliver you, says the Lord.'[66]

"According to the unadulterated teaching of the Lord, then, the royal road is easy and smooth, although it may be felt as harsh and rough. 3. For when those who keep to it devoutly and faithfully take upon themselves the Lord's yoke and learn from him because he is 'meek and humble of heart,' they are already in a way putting down the burden of earthly passions and finding, with the Lord's help, not toil but rest for their souls. He himself has borne witness to this by the prophet Jeremiah: 'Stand on the ways and see. And, concerning the ancient paths, ask which is the right way, and walk in it, and you shall find refreshment for your souls.'[67] 4. To them it shall immediately happen that the 'crooked way becomes straight and the rough ways level.'[68] They shall taste and see 'that the Lord is sweet,'[69] and they shall hear Christ proclaiming in the Gospel: 'Come to me, all you who labor and are burdened, and I will give you rest.'[70] And once they have put down the loads of their vices they shall understand what follows: 'My yoke is easy and my burden is light.'

5. "The way of the Lord, then, gives repose if it is kept to in accordance with his law. But we make sorrow and torment for ourselves by our agitated distractions when we prefer to pursue, even at our peril and with great difficulty, the crooked and perverse

ways of this world. But when we make the Lord's yoke heavy and rough for ourselves in this manner, with blasphemous spirit we accuse as harsh and rough either the yoke itself or Christ who imposes it, in accordance with the words: 'A man's foolishness corrupts his ways, but he blames God in his heart.'[71] 6. And according to the prophet Haggai, when we say that 'the way of the Lord is not right,'[72] the Lord fittingly replies to us: 'Is my way not right? Is it not rather your ways that are crooked?'[73] And, in truth, if you want to compare the sweet-smelling flower of virginity and the most tender purity of chastity to the foul and rank wallows of wantonness, the peace and security of the monks to the dangers and distress in which the people of this world are entangled, and the repose of our poverty to the devouring sorrows and unsleeping anxieties of the rich, in which they are consumed–not without great danger to their lives–day and night, it will be most clearly apparent to you that Christ's yoke is very easy and his burden is very light.

XXVI.1. "Also, the recompense of reward may be understood correctly and most truly in the same way and without any harm to the faith. It was in this respect that the Lord promised a hundredfold to those who practice perfect renunciation in this life, when he said: 'Everyone who leaves house or brothers or sisters or father or mother or wife or children or fields on account of my name shall receive a hundredfold in the present age and shall possess eternal life.'[74] For many who have seized upon these words with an obtuse understanding are certain that these things are going to be bestowed upon the holy in carnal fashion during the millennium, although in fact they confess that that age, which they say will occur after the resurrection, cannot be equated with the present one. 2. It is much more credible, then, and much more obvious that the person who has spurned worldly dispositions and goods at the behest of Christ will even in this life receive love a hundred times more precious from his brothers and from those who are linked with him by spiritual bonds in his chosen orientation. For it is evident that what companionship joins together or blood relationship unites, between parents and children, brothers, spouses, and relatives, is quite brief and fragile. 3. Sometimes even good and filial children are cut off from the houses and property of their parents when they have grown up;

occasionally, too, even the marriage bond is broken for some good reason; and contentious division destroys the property of brothers. Monks alone enjoy a constant mutual union and possess all things in common, believing that everything that is theirs is their brothers' and that everything that is their brothers' is theirs. If, therefore, the grace of our love is compared to those dispositions by which carnal love maintains its unity, it is certainly a hundred times sweeter and nobler. In fact a hundred times greater delight is to be gotten from married abstinence, too, than that which is offered to two people in sexual intercourse. 4. Likewise, instead of the pleasure that a person has in possessing one field and house, he who has passed over into the adoption of the children of God[75] will enjoy a hundred times more all the riches that belong to the Eternal Father and that he will possess as his own, and in imitation of the true Son he will proclaim by disposition and by virtue: 'All that the Father has is mine.'[76] No longer occupied with the criminal concern of distraction and worry, but secure and happy, he will enter everywhere as it were into his property, and every day he will hear it said to him by the Apostle: 'All things are yours, whether the world or things present or things to come.'[77] And by Solomon: 'The faithful man has a whole world of riches.'[78]

5. "You have, then, the reward of the hundredfold expressed in its great value and in the incomparable difference of its nature. For if, in exchange for a particular weight of bronze or iron or some base metal, a person were to pay over the same weight, but in gold, it would even seem that not more than a hundredfold had been given. So, when spiritual gladness and the joy of a most precious love are weighed out in exchange for the contempt of pleasure and of earthly dispositions, even though the amount may be the same, still it is a hundred times greater and more splendid. 6. Let me make this clearer by going through it again. I once used to have a wife in the wanton 'passion of lust,'[79] but now I have her in the dignity of holiness and in the true love of Christ. The woman is the same, but the value of the love has grown a hundredfold. But if you weigh the constant mildness of patience against the disturbance of anger and rage, the calm of security against the anguish of worry and distraction, the fruit of

salutary sadness against the fruitless and criminal sadness of this world, and the abundance of spiritual joy against the emptiness of temporal joy, you will clearly see a hundredfold repayment in the transfer of these dispositions. 7. And if the values of the opposing virtues are compared to the brief and uncertain pleasure of some vice, the manifold joy will prove that the former are a hundred times better. The number one hundred is reckoned by going from the left hand to the right hand, and although the number of fingers seems to be the same in the calculation, nonetheless there is a large increase in the amount. For it will happen that we who seemed to be goatlike on the left hand shall attain to the status of sheep when we have gone over to the right hand.[80]

8. "Now let us pass on to the quantity of the things that Christ gives us in this world in exchange for the contempt of worldly goods, particularly as it is thus spoken of in the Gospel of Mark: 'There is no one who has left house or brothers or sisters or mother or children or fields for my sake and for the sake of the Gospel, who will not receive a hundredfold now in this time, houses and brothers and sisters and mothers and children and fields, with persecutions, and everlasting life in the world to come.'[81] 9. For whoever has despised the love of a father or a mother or a child for the sake of Christ's name and has gone over to the most sincere love of all, those who serve Christ will receive a hundred brothers and parents. That is, in place of one he will begin to have that many fathers and brothers, bound to him by a more fervent and excellent affection. Whoever has rejected one house for the sake of Christ's love will possess innumerable dwellings as his own in monasteries everywhere in the world, and they will be his own houses as if by right. Thus he will also be endowed with manifold property in houses and fields.

10. "For how will a person not receive a hundredfold and, if it is permitted to add something to our Lord's words, more than a hundredfold, if he relinquishes the unfaithful and forced service of ten or twenty servants to be supported by the voluntary attention of as many persons who are free and noble? If you have abandoned individual fathers and mothers and houses you have been able to see for yourselves that this is the case, thanks to your own experiences. Wherever in the world you may go, without any anx-

ious toil you gain innumerable fathers, mothers, and brothers, as well as houses, fields, and most faithful servants, who welcome you with great attentiveness, embrace you, nourish you, and venerate you, treating you as their masters. 11. But, I say, the holy ones who have first, with voluntary devotion, submitted themselves and all that is theirs to the service of the brotherhood are those who deservedly and faithfully enjoy these ministrations. For, according to the words of the Lord, they shall receive what they have themselves freely spent on others.[82] But if a person has not previously and in unfeigned humility offered these things to his companions, how will he let himself be open to receiving offerings from others to himself, when he knows that he is burdened rather than nourished by their attentions, inasmuch as he has chosen to accept the services of his brothers rather than to repay them? 12. Yet he will accept all of this not with nonchalant confidence or passive enjoyment but, in the words of the Lord, "with persecutions"—that is, with the tribulations of this world and with the greatest anguish of suffering, because, as that most wise man declares: 'One who is carefree and without sorrow shall be in need.'[83]

"For it is not the lazy, the negligent, the lax, the fastidious, or the weak who seize the kingdom of heaven, but the violent. Who, then, are these violent? They are the ones who exercise a noble violence not upon others but upon their own soul and who, by a praiseworthy pillage, snatch it away from every pleasure in present things. By the Lord's words they are declared excellent pillagers, and with plundering of this sort they gain violent entrance into the kingdom of heaven. 13. For, according to the words of the Lord, 'the kingdom of heaven suffers force, and the violent bear it away.'[84] These violent persons who forcibly prevent their own ruin are certainly praiseworthy. For, as it is written, 'a person in sorrow labors for himself and forcibly prevents his own ruin.'[85] Our ruin is delight in the present life and—by way of expressing it more clearly—the carrying out of our own desires and will. If a person removes these from his soul and mortifies them, he certainly prevents forcibly, in glorious and beneficial fashion, his own ruin, to the extent that he denies it its most pleasant desires, which the divine word frequently reproaches through the prophet when it says: 'In the days of your fasting your own will is found.'[86] And again: 'If you turn away your foot from the sabbath, from doing your own will on my holy day, and if you glorify him while not following your own ways, and if your will to speak a word is not found.'[87] 14. To this it immediately adds through the prophet what great blessedness is also promised: 'Then,' it says, 'you shall delight over the Lord, and I will lift you up above the heights of the earth, and I will feed you with the inheritance of Jacob your father. For the mouth of the Lord has spoken.'[88] For this reason our Lord and Savior, in order to provide us with a pattern for cutting off our own will, said: 'I have not come to do my own will but the will of him who sent me.'[89] And again: 'Not as I will but as you do.' Those who dwell in cenobia and are ruled by the command of an elder, who never follow their own judgment but whose will depends on the will of an abba, are the ones who exercise this virtue in particular.

15. "Finally, by way of concluding this discussion, I ask: Do not those who serve Christ faithfully most clearly receive grace a hundredfold also by being honored for his name's sake by the mightiest rulers? And, although they themselves do not look for human glory, do they not still become venerable to every judge and power even in the sufferings of their persecutions, when their insignificance could perhaps have been despicable even to the average person, on account of their obscure birth or their servile condition, if they had kept to a worldly way of life? 16. But, because of their soldiery for Christ, no one will dare raise a harsh word about the condition of their origin, and no one will dare object to the obscurity of their birth. On the contrary, by the very dishonor of the meanest of conditions, which usually embarrasses and shames other people, the servants of Christ are more gloriously ennobled. We can clearly see the truth of this in the case of Abba John, who lives in the desert that is near the town of Lycon. 17. Although born of an obscure family, he became so admired by nearly the whole human race on account of the name of Christ that the very lords of things present, who hold the government of this world and of the Empire and who are awesome even to all powers and kings, venerate him as their lord, seek out his oracles from far-off regions, and commit the welfare of their Empire,

their salvation, and the success of their wars to his prayers and good works."

18. In words of this sort the blessed Abraham discussed the origin of and the remedy for our illusion, and he as it were laid before our eyes which deceitful thoughts the devil was author of, inspiring us with a desire for true mortification, with which we believe that many may be inflamed, even though all of this has been recorded in unattractive language. For even if the feeble cinders of our utterance have concealed the fieriest thoughts of the greatest fathers, we nonetheless believe that the coldness of many who wish to give new life to their hidden thoughts may be warmed once the embers of our words have been removed. 19. But, O holy brothers, I have certainly not been so presumptuous in spirit as to send out to you this fire, which the Lord came to cast upon the earth and which he greatly desired to burn,[90] as if by the addition of this warmth I could enkindle the high ardor of your chosen orientation. This is, rather, for the purpose of increasing your authority among your sons, if the precepts of the greatest and most ancient fathers confirm what you yourselves teach by your living example, not by the dead sound of words.

It remains for the spiritual zephyr of your prayers to accompany me now, tossed about as I have been thus far by a most dangerous tempest, to the safe harbor of silence.

Textual References

1. Cf. Rv 4:4.
2. Prv 13:4 LXX.
3. Prv 21:25.
4. Lk 14:26.
5. Jer 17:5 LXX.
6. Ps 146:3.
7. 1 Cor 3:8.
8. Lk 16:25.
9. Jer 17:16.
10. Lk 9:23.
11. Hb 2:1 LXX.
12. Cf. 1 Cor 3:10.
13. Ps 26:8.
14. Cf. 1 Sm 17:38–40.
15. Cf. Mt 8:21–22.
16. Prv 23:35 LXX.
17. Hos 7:9.
18. Acts 20:34.
19. 2 Thes 3:7–9.
20. 2 Thes 3:10.
21. Ps 37:16.
22. Eccl 4:6 LXX.
23. Hg 1:6 LXX.
24. Prv 13:7 LXX.
25. Prv 12:9 LXX.
26. Cf. Nm 31:16; Rv 2:14.
27. 1 Kgs 20:31–32a.
28. 1 Kgs 20:32b.
29. 1 Kgs 20:42.
30. 1 Kgs 22:22.
31. Mt 4:3.
32. Cf. Mt 4:8–9.
33. Mt 4:6.
34. Jn 14:30.
35. Cf. 1 Jn 4:16.
36. Cf. Mt 5:14.
37. 1 Sm 2:30 LXX.
38. Mt 11:30.

39. Ps 17:4.
40. 2 Tm 3:12.
41. Gal 2:20.
42. 2 Cor 12:10.
43. Cf. Phil 3:8.
44. Mt 16:26.
45. 1 Tm 6:7.
46. Cf. Mt 10:9–10.
47. 2 Cor 11:27.
48. Mt 26:39.
49. Cf. Acts 5:41.
50. Mt 19:21.
51. Prv 5:22 LXX.
52. Is 50:11.
53. Wis 11:17 LXX.
54. Jer 2:18–19.
55. Prv 2:20 LXX.
56. Prv 22:5 LXX.
57. Jer 18:15.
58. Prv 15:19 LXX.
59. Eccl 10:15 LXX.
60. Gal 4:26.
61. Mt 11:29.
62. Rom 8:28.
63. Mi 2:7.
64. Hos 14:10.
65. 2 Cor 12:9.
66. Jer 1:18–19.
67. Jer 6:16.
68. Is 40:4.
69. Ps 34:8.
70. Mt 11:28.
71. Prv 19:3 LXX.
72. Ez 18:25a LXX.
73. Ez 18:25b LXX.
74. Mt 19:29.
75. Cf. Eph 1:5.
76. Jn 16:15.

77. 1 Cor 3:22.
78. Prv 17:6 LXX.
79. 1 Thes 4:5.
80. Cf. Mt 25:33.
81. Mk 10:29–30.
82. Cf. Mt 7:2.
83. Prv 14:23 LXX.
84. Mt 11:12.
85. Prv 16:26 LXX.
86. Is 58:3.
87. Is 58:13.
88. Is 58:14.
89. Jn 6:38.
90. Cf. Lk 12:49.

24.1.2ff. The temptation of the monk to be preoccupied with his family is mentioned in Athanasius, *V. S. Antonii* 3, 36. On breaking definitively one's links with one's family cf. Basil, *Reg. fus. tract.* 32. Cf. also 1 praef. 6 and 1.2.3.

24.1.3 This is the sole reference in Cassian's works to his family property, and it suggests a rather well-off background. For its value in possibly giving a precise location to Cassian's birthplace cf. Henri-Irénée Marrou, "La patrie de Jean Cassien," in *Patristique et humanisme: Mélanges* (Patristica Sorboniensia 9) (Paris, 1976), 345–361, esp. 346, 354–361.

24.1.4 On Abraham's groan cf. also 2.13.7 and the relevant note.

24.2.3 On carrying one's supply of water over a long distance, as mentioned here and in 24.10, cf. the note at 3.1.1.

24.3ff. On wandering thoughts cf. the note at 1.5.4.

24.3.2 This image of the monk as fisherman, observing his thoughts as if they were fish, may be unique. The unusual reference to "apostolic skill" *(apostolica arte),* and perhaps as well to the "saving hook" *(hamo...salutari),* suggests that the image may be at least partly inspired by Mt 4:19 par. This is one of two places in the present conference where thoughts are presented as living creatures; in 24.5.1 they are compared to horses.

24.4.1 On Calamus or Porphyrion cf. the note at 3.5.2.

24.5.1 The ungovernableness of unbridled horses is a theme that appears in Ps 32:9. In Clement of Alexandria, *Paed.* 3, Hymnus 1 (SC 158.192), Christ is spoken of as "the bridle of unbroken ponies." For a comparison of the human soul with a horse in monastic literature cf. Ps.-Macarius, Coll. 3, *Hom.* 8.3.4f. (SC 275.150–152). On the necessity of controlling the divergent tendencies of the soul, symbolized by horses, cf. Ambrose, *De*

Isaac vel anima 8.65. Vices are compared with unbridled horses in *Inst.* 8.18 and an avaricious monk with an unbridled horse ibid. 7.8. Cf. also Plato, *Phaedrus* 247b.

24.6.1 A barrel-vaulted ceiling: *Teretis absidiae cameram.*

24.7 On learning spiritual truths from experience, here and in 24.23.1, cf. the note at 3.7.4.

24.9.1ff. On this Apollos cf. the note at 2.13.5.

24.9.2 On the use of the term "monastery" for the dwelling of a single monk, as here, cf. 18.10 and the relevant note.

24.9.2f. The same story is told in an apophthegm recounted in PL 74.379. Cf. Weber 98–99. Cassian's position here is balanced by what he says in *Inst.* 5.38, to the effect that a monk may aid his family members (or at least his mother) if the need is dire.

24.11f. The Antony cited here is the subject of Athanasius's biography.

24.13.1 The exact identity of this Macarius is unknown. Cf. the note at 5.12.3.

24.13.1ff. On the value of the denarius cf. the note at 1.20.1, and on that of the solidus cf. the note at 9.5.5.

24.13.4 Coppers: *Nummorum.* In Cassian's time the nummus was officially valued at 7200 to one gold solidus. Cf. Pauly-Wissowa 17.2.1460.

24.15.3ff. Cassian's teaching on the threefold nature of the soul seems to be taken almost literally from Evagrius, *Prac.* 86. Cf. Weber 52. But the doctrine is ultimately Platonic (cf. Plato, *Rep.* 4.12ff.; Jerome, *Comm. in Hiez.* 1, ad 1:6–8), mediated by Middle Stoic psychology (cf. Colish 118).

24.18ff. On the ambiguity with which monks viewed guests, well expressed in this passage, and on hospitality in the desert in general, cf. Denys Gorce, "Die

Gastfreundlichkeit der altchristlichen Einsiedler und Mönche," JAC 15 (1972): 66–91.

24.19.1f. That the holy solitary is the object of throngs of visitors may be observed constantly in desert literature. *The Conferences* themselves, as well as Palladius's *Hist. laus.* and the *Hist. monach. in Aegypto* (to mention only the most notable works of their kind), are the result of just such visits. For perhaps the classic text on the subject cf. Athanasius, *V. S. Antonii* 14.

24.21 The story of blessed John and the partridge appears to be a conflation from two sources–*Acta Ioannis* 56* (ed. by Lipsius-Bonnet, 3.178–179), where a priest is said to be surprised to see the apostle John watching a partridge take a dust bath; and *Apophthegmata patrum*, de abbate Antonio 13, where a hunter is said to be shocked to see Antony enjoying himself with other monks, and Antony uses the image of the bow to explain to him the necessity of occasional relaxation. Cf. Weber 108–109; CCSA 1.153–156. The use of the image of the bow in such an instance seems well-worn. Cf. Phaedrus, *Fabulae* 3.14 (ed. by Brenot, Paris, 1923, 47). It appears much later in monastic literature in Bruno, *Ep. ad Radulphum Viridem* 5 (SC 88.68–70).

24.24.5f. On the "royal road" *(viam regiam)* here and in 24.25.2 and on the "royal path" *(itinere regio)* cf. the note at 4.12.5.

24.25.1 On the idea that it is better to struggle against temptation than not to be tempted cf. the note at 2.13.9f.

24.25.6 The sweet-smelling flower of virginity: On the fragrance of virtue cf. the note at 1.1.

The foul and rank wallows of wantonness: On the repugnant odor of vice cf. the note at 2.11.5.

The repose of our poverty...the unsleeping anxieties of the rich: That the poor sleep better, and are generally happier, than the rich is a commonplace in ancient literature. Cf. Lucan, *Pharsalia* 5.527ff.;

Chrysostom, *Serm. in Matth.* 53.6; Ambrose, *Exameron* 6.8.52; Augustine, *Enarr. in Ps.* 127.16.

24.26 Rousseau 212 claims that the realistic tone of this chapter shows that Cassian was less concerned with a theoretical triumph of poverty than with regulating it and placing it in a predetermined context. That the practice of poverty might lead to wealth and reputation, at least spiritually understood (although that cannot necessarily be taken for granted here), is the burden of Evagrius, *Gnost.* 38 (SC 356.160): "Do not be concerned about food or clothing, but remember Abener the Levite. After he welcomed the ark of the Lord he became rich, although he had been poor, and renowned, although he had been despised."

24.26.1 The "carnal" understanding of the millennium spoken of here refers to a materialistic interpretation of Rv 20:1–6 that was supported by Jewish speculations. Known as millenarianism or chiliasm, it flourished until the beginnings of the fifth century, at which point it declined in importance. Cf. James Hastings, ed., *Encyclopaedia of Religion and Ethics* 5.387–389; DTC 10.2.1760–1763. The millenarian interpretation of Mt 19:29 seems to have been well known. Cf. Jerome, *Comm. in Matth.* 3, ad loc.; Augustine, *De civ. Dei* 20.7.

24.26.3 On married abstinence here and in 24.26.6 cf. the note at 14.7.4.

24.26.5 For if, in exchange for a particular weight...: *Neque enim si pro aeris aut feri aut vilioris cuiusquam metalli certo pondere sed auri quispiam reddidisset, non etiam amplius restituisse quam centuplum videretur.* Gibson reads: "For if for a fixed weight of brass or iron or some still commoner metal, one had given in exchange the same weight only in gold, he would appear to have given much more than an hundredfold." Pichery's translation likewise has the gold being worth more than a hundred times the value of the brass (or bronze) or iron. The Latin suggests otherwise, however, despite the initial unbelievability of the passage. But the point is that, as the succeeding lines make clear, even the exchange of brass for gold does not, on its own terms, approach the exchange of earthly pleasures for spiritual joys.

24.26.7 On counting on one's fingers cf. RAC 7.915–920 (with illustrations) as well as Gazet's very comprehensive note in PL 49.1234–1236. The most important Christian text on the subject—namely, Jerome, *C. Iovinianum* 1.3—is mistakenly cited in Gazet as 1.1. Jerome also expatiates on digital computation in the context of marriage and abstinence, and it is possible that Cassian borrowed from him.

24.26.16 Soldiery for Christ: Cf. the note at 1.1.

24.26.16f. On John of Lycon cf. the note at 1.21.1. John's most exalted contact was with Theodosius the Great (d. 395), to whom he predicted (by courier) some military victories. Cf. *Hist. monach. in Aegypto* 1.1; Augustine, *De cura gerenda pro mortuis* 17.21; idem, *De civ. Dei* 5.26; Theodoret of Cyrus, *Hist. eccl.* 5.24.

24.26.18f. On Cassian's self-deprecating language here cf. the note at 1 praef. 3.

24.26.19 The "holy brothers" in question are Jovinianus, Minervus, Leontius, and Theodore, for whom cf. the note at 3 praef. 1.

On teaching by example and not merely by words cf. the note at 11.2.2.

On the marine imagery here cf. the note at 1 praef. 3f.

INDEX OF SCRIPTURAL CITATIONS AND ALLUSIONS

Ecclesiastes

Song of Songs

Acts of the Apostles

1 Corinthians

2 Corinthians

INDEX OF NONSCRIPTURAL CITATIONS AND ALLUSIONS

INDEX OF NONSCRIPTURAL PERSONS

INDEX OF PLACES